INERRANCY

INERRANCY

Edited by
Norman L. Geisler

Academie
Books Grand Rapids, Michigan
Zondervan Publishing House

INERRANCY
Copyright © 1980 by The Zondervan Corporation
Grand Rapids, Michigan

ACADEMIE BOOKS are printed by Zondervan
Publishing House, 1415 Lake Drive, S.E.,
Grand Rapids, Michigan 49506

Library of Congress Cataloging in Publication Data

Main entry under title:
    Inerrancy.
      1. Bible—Evidences, authority, etc.—Addresses,
essays, lectures.   I. Geisler, Norman L.
BS480.I42   220.I'3   79-23959

ISBN 0-310-39281-0

All scripture quotations, unless otherwise noted, are taken from the HOLY BIBLE: NEW INTERNATIONAL VERSION (North American Edition). Copyright © 1978 by The International Bible Society. Used by permission of Zondervan Bible Publishers.

Printed in the United States of America

85 86 87 88 89 90 91 / 15 14 13 12 11 10 9 8 7

In memory of
Dr. J. Barton Payne, whose inspiration, scholarship, and pioneer efforts helped evangelicals focus on the importance of the inerrant Word.

CONTENTS

PREFACE

The International Conference on Biblical Inerrancy (ICBI) called together in Chicago some three hundred scholars, pastors, and laymen in October 1978. The chapters of this book are the refined result of the fourteen scholarly papers presented at this conference. In connection with these presentations, the conferees formulated the nineteen-article "Chicago Statement" (see Appendix), which defines the biblical and historic position on the inerrancy of Scripture.

As the backgrounds of the varied conferees and authors of these chapters would indicate, there is a wide range of denominations and theological opinion represented—Anglican, Baptist, Free Church, Lutheran, Methodist, Presbyterian, and others—all united in the defense of the inerrancy of Holy Scripture. Perhaps no theological cause in modern times has brought together such divergent elements of the Christian community in such a spirit of unity as did this conference. The conference and this book is a clear indication that there is no true unity apart from unity in the truth, and there is no unity in the truth apart from God's Word, which is truth (John 17:17).

This volume is offered as a consensus of contemporary evangelical scholarship on the crucial importance of biblical inerrancy for the present and future vitality of the Christian church. Other volumes that serve to further evangelical awareness of this same issue have already appeared under ICBI sponsorship, such as *The Foundation of Biblical Authority* (James Boice, ed. [Zondervan]), *Does Inerrancy Matter?* (James Boice [ICBI publication]), *Can We Trust the Bible?* (Earl Radmacher, ed. [Tyndale]). Two more books are scheduled for the near future, *Biblical Errancy: An Analysis of Its Philosophical Roots* (Norman L. Geisler, ed. [Zondervan])and *Commentary on the Nineteen Articles of the Chicago Statement* (R. C. Sproul [Tyndale]). Other projects from the biblical, historical, and theological points of view are under way for the future.

It is the stated purpose of ICBI to define, defend, and apply the doctrine of biblical inerrancy as an essential element of the authority of Scripture and a necessary ingredient for the health of the church of Christ in an attempt to win the church back to this historic position. This volume is offered as a significant contribution in this crucial cause.

The executive council of the ICBI is composed of the following members: Gleason L. Archer, James M. Boice, Edmund P. Clowney, Norman L. Geisler, John H. Gerstner, Jay H. Grimstead, Harold W. Hoehner, Don E. Hoke, A. Wetherell Johnson, Kenneth S. Kantzer, James I. Packer, Robert D. Preus, Earl D. Radmacher, Francis A. Schaeffer, and R. C. Sproul. The national office has its headquarters in Oakland, California (P.O. Box 13261, ZIP 94661), and is under the direction of Karen Hoyt.

Norman L. Geisler

CHRIST'S VIEW OF SCRIPTURE

John W. Wenham

John W. Wenham is an ordained minister in the Church of England. He is a graduate of the University of Cambridge (M.A.) and the University of London (B.D.). His academic appointments have included those of Vice Principal of Tyndale Hall, Bristol, and Warden of Latimer House, Oxford. He has served as Chaplain in the Royal Air Force and as Vicar of St. Nicholas Church, Durham. His books include The Elements of New Testament Greek; Christ and the Bible; *and* The Goodness of God.

CHAPTER SUMMARY

Christ's view of Scripture stands out with great clarity for those who believe that the Gospels, whether inerrant or not, present a fairly reliable account of His teaching. We have a wealth of material coming from all four Gospels and from all the major strata of the Gospels. We have hundreds of quotations and allusions that appear spontaneously from a great variety of situations, and these are often the more telling for revealing Jesus' basic assumptions rather than His specific teachings. He consistently treats the historical narratives as straightforward records of fact, and the force of His teaching often depends on their literal truth. He uses the teaching of the Old Testament as a court of appeal in matters of controversy in both doctrine and ethics. That this was His own standpoint and not an *ad hominem* stance adopted by way of accommodation to His hearers is shown by His use of Scripture in countering the devil. That it was not the result of His human limitations is shown by His stress on Scripture after His resurrection. He treats the very words of Scripture, even "the smallest letter" and "the least stroke of a pen," as inspired. He recognizes that its books have human authors, but to Him the primary author of Scripture is God Himself. This attestation of detailed verbal truth, coupled with historical and doctrinal truth, necessitates a doctrine of inerrancy in historical as well as in doctrinal matters. The supposed abrogation of Scripture by Jesus (for example in the Sermon on the Mount), by which Jesus is alleged to have contradicted Himself, is based on a misunderstanding of the passages in question. To Christ the Old Testament was true, authoritative, inspired. To Him the God of the Old Testament was the living God, and the teaching of the Old Testament was the teaching of the living God. To Him, what Scripture said, God said.

CHRIST'S VIEW OF SCRIPTURE

THE HISTORICITY OF THE OLD TESTAMENT

In some circles it is necessary in the present theological climate to ask the question, Is it possible to gain solid knowledge of the teaching of Jesus? Was not this teaching so overlaid by the theologizing and pious storytelling of the early Christians as to be past recovery? The depth of contemporary skepticism was brought home to me recently while I was browsing through the books on New Testament theology in a theological college library. I could find abundant material on the theology of Paul, Matthew, Luke, Q, and the fourth Gospel, but when I looked for substantial treatment of the teaching of Jesus, there was almost nothing of recent vintage. Many biblical scholars today consider it impossible to know what Jesus really taught.

Broadly speaking, it is possible to take one of three positions with regard to the historicity of the Gospels: (1) The Gospels are reliable records of history, examined and approved by members of the apostolic body and received as such by the leaders of the churches they founded. This was the traditional, "catholic" position and remained the standard position of mainstream Christianity until the end of the nineteenth century. (2) The Gospels are a mixture of the historical and the unhistorical. This was the position of nineteenth-century liberalism, and it remains very influential to the present time. (3) The Gospels are so slanted

3

theologically and are so much the product of early Christian imagination that they should not be regarded as a source of information about Jesus but only about the early church.

I regard the skepticism of the last position as a *reductio ad absurdum*. Only a Jesus like the Jesus of the Gospels can explain the emergence of the church. Without such a Jesus, it is impossible to understand how the church came into being and how it succeeded in creating the sublime figure portrayed for us by the four evangelists. The modern growth of a nonhistorical view of the Gospels is akin to the growth of Gnostic views of the Gospels in the second century. Gnosticism gained great influence, especially among the intellectuals, but was decisively rejected by the early church as an innovation and as being contrary to the teaching of the apostles.

This issue may seem remote from the inerrancy debate among conservative evangelical Christians, but in fact it is quite relevant. Once the notion grasps the mind that the fourth Gospel or the synoptic Gospels (or for that matter the Pentateuch) were never *intended* to be taken as history, then even an evangelical Christian may feel driven to believe that the most truly *biblical* position is a radical one. After all, is he not being true to the original and intended meaning of Scripture in saying that the evangelists wrote theology and not history, and that the infancy narratives and the miracle stories and the "discrepant" resurrection accounts should not be taken literally?[1][*] It is thus possible to adopt the most extreme critical positions and yet claim to be utterly true to the Bible. We need, therefore, to be on our guard as to where uncritical acceptance of biblical criticism may lead us. It is important to continue to take the Scriptures as the primitive and historic church took them and understood them.[2]

The debate among evangelicals is more obviously concerned with positions 1 and 2 above. We have a wholehearted commitment to the incarnation of God the Son and a wholehearted commitment to the miracles in the Gospels, but some among us wonder if a sound historical method may not require us to sift a certain amount of unhistorical matter out of these narratives. Some assume that everything in the Gospels is true until proved false. Scholars who hold this position inevitably differ greatly in what they think constitutes proof. There is, happily, abundant evidence on which to determine our Lord's own view of the

---

[*]References to substantive notes are printed in boldface.

historicity of Old Testament persons and events. Even for those who consider many Gospel passages to be of doubtful authenticity, there is still much evidence. Indeed, it is probable that if we cannot know Jesus' teaching about this, we cannot know His teaching about anything.

We will not assume, at this stage of the argument, that all Gospel material is good history, less still that it is all inerrant. We will assume merely that it is good enough history to give us a clear view of Jesus' own attitude toward Scripture. A fully satisfying apologetic, however, should eventually explain the interrelations of the Gospels and establish a clear rationale for their similarities and differences. There is now a flux in New Testament scholarship concerning the synoptic problem, greater perhaps than at any time since the dawn of the critical era. Evangelical scholars surely should be in the forefront of this great rethinking. My own view is that present-day scholars, including many evangelicals, tend to date the Gospels far too late,[3] but I am not sanguine enough to consider it likely that we will quickly or easily convert the scholarly world to a different standpoint. However desirable such conversion might be as a long-term objective, it is not necessary, for our present argument, to take a particular view of the overall historicity of the Gospels.[4]

We will extract evidence for Jesus' view of the Old Testament from all four Gospels without discrimination. This is *not*, we reemphasize, to prejudge whether everything in the Gospels is accurate. We recognize that some scholars believe certain parts of the Gospels have less value than others as historical evidence. Except for total skepticism, we can at this stage of the argument allow for a great variety of critical conclusions. What one critic will allow and another refuse is usually heavily influenced either by subjective considerations or by the exigencies of a hypothesis for which there is no demonstrative evidence. To embark on a critical discussion of every disputed passage would likely prove to be both inconclusive and laborious. We ask only that the reader accept the historicity of the Gospel picture in general outline.

If this approach produces a consistent view of Christ, that evidence in itself should tend to confirm that the Gospels are presenting a figure of history and that the Jesus they depict is not, as radical critics maintain, the creation of diverse minds from diverse and scattered communities. The reader can, if he wishes, make subtractions according to his best critical judgment as he goes along. Even if such subtractions reached the point of reducing the Gospel picture of Christ to that of a ghost, the result would not disprove our conclusions but only make them uncertain through lack of evidence.

When we turn to the teachings of Jesus recorded in the Gospels, we find a wealth of relevant material in all four Gospels and in the four major strata of the synoptic Gospels (Mark; the material peculiar to Matthew; the material peculiar to Luke; and the material common to Matthew and Luke, usually called "Q"). We are not confined to a few key statements but have a host of quotations and allusions that appear in a great variety of situations. These accounts are often the more telling since they reveal Jesus' basic assumptions more than His specific teachings. We can hear Christ preaching to the multitudes and instructing disciples, refuting opponents and answering enquirers. We can hear Him in His private conflict with the tempter at the beginning of His ministry and in His final instructions prior to the Ascension. As we proceed, it will become clear that, throughout the Gospel material, Jesus' view of the Old Testament is unchanging. We will examine, in turn, His views of the truth of its history, the authority of its teaching, and the inspiration of its writing. As the evidence is assembled, it will lead us to a firm and objective conclusion. We will see that Christ held the Old Testament to be historically true, completely authoritative, and divinely inspired. To Him, the God of the Old Testament was the living God, and the teaching of the Old Testament was the teaching of the living God. To Him, what Scripture said, God said.[5]

Jesus consistently treats Old Testament historical narratives as straightforward records of fact. He refers to Abel (Luke 11:51), Noah (Matt. 24:37-39; Luke 17:26, 27), Abraham (John 8:56), the institution of circumcision (John 7:22; cf. Gen. 17:10-12; Lev. 12:3), Sodom and Gomorrah (Matt. 10:15; 11:23, 24; Luke 10:12), Lot (Luke 17:28-32), Isaac and Jacob (Matt. 8:11; Luke 13:28), manna (John 6:31, 49, 58), the snake in the desert (John 3:14), David eating the consecrated bread (Matt. 12:3, 4; Mark 2:25, 26; Luke 6:3, 4), David as a psalm writer (Matt. 22:43; Mark 12:36; Luke 20:42), Solomon (Matt. 6:29; 12:42; Luke 11:31; 12:27), Elijah (Luke 4:25, 26), Elisha (Luke 4:27), Jonah (Matt. 12:39-41; Luke 11:29, 30, 32), and

Zechariah (Luke 11:51). The last passage brings out Jesus' sense of the unity of history and His grasp of its wide sweep. His eye surveys the whole course of history from "the creation of the world" to "this generation." He repeatedly refers to Moses as the giver of the Law (Matt. 8:4; 19:8; Mark 1:44; 7:10; 10:5; 12:26; Luke 5:14; 20:37; John 5:46; 7:19). He frequently mentions the sufferings of the true prophets (Matt. 5:12; 13:57; 21:34-36; 23:29-37; Mark 6:4 [cf. Luke 4:24; John 4:44]; 12:2-5; Luke 6:23; 11:47-51; 13:34; 20:10-12) and comments on the popularity of the false prophets (Luke 6:26). He sets the stamp of His approval on such significant passages as Genesis 1 and 2 (Matt. 19:4, 5; Mark 10:6–8).

These quotations are taken by our Lord more or less at random from different parts of the Old Testament, and some periods of its history are covered more fully than others. Yet it is evident that He was familiar with most, if not all, of the Old Testament and that He treated all parts of it equally as history. Curiously enough, the narratives that are least acceptable to the "modern mind" are the very ones that He seemed most fond of choosing for illustrations.

It is, of course, arguable that our Lord's use of the Old Testament stories does not of necessity imply that He regarded them all as unimpeachable history. It is perfectly legitimate to use avowed legends and allegories to illustrate spiritual truth. The stories of Ulysses and the sirens or of Christian and Doubting Castle may quite properly be used as illustrations of a spiritual truth without implying belief in their historicity. But a careful review of the way in which our Lord used Old Testament narratives seems decisively to preclude His considering them anything but historical. While there is no evidence to suggest that Jesus understood any of the passages quoted above in any but a literal way, a literal meaning is not essential to the basic teaching of all of them. There would be no significant loss in meaning if the injunction "Offer the sacrifices that Moses commanded" (Mark 1:44; cf. Matt. 8:4; Luke 5:14) were to be read, "Offer the sacrifices that the law of Moses commands" or if instead of "Moses said, Honor your father . . ." (Mark 7:10) we were to read, "The law of Moses says, Honor your father. . . ." The reference to "Solomon in all his splendor" would be as graphic of a legendary figure as of a historical one. The teaching of monogamy as being God's plan from "the beginning of creation" perhaps does not necessitate a literal interpretation of chapters 1 and 2 of Genesis for its validity; but subsequent reference to the changed situation under Moses seems to require it (Mark 10:2ff.; cf. Matt. 19:3ff.). Seldom can a nonliteral meaning be applied without some loss of vividness and effectiveness.

A dozen other Old Testament stories might arguably be taken in a nonliteral sense.[6] As the matter is pursued, however, the impression gains in strength that our Lord understood these stories to be ordinary history and that His teaching should be taken straightforwardly. This impression is strongly reinforced when we come to a further collection of passages in which the historical truth of an account seems essential to its validity as an illustration.

It is difficult to deny that the words of T. T. Perowne on Matthew 12:41 apply to a number of Old Testament references in the Gospels. Jesus says, "The men of Nineveh will stand up at the judgment with this generation and condemn it; for they repented at the preaching of Jonah, and now one greater than Jonah is here." Perowne comments:

> Is it possible to understand a reference like this on the non-historic theory of the book of Jonah? The future Judge is speaking words of solemn warning to those who shall hereafter stand convicted at his bar. Intensely real he would make the scene in anticipation to them, as it was real, as if then present, to himself. And yet we are to suppose him to say that imaginary persons who at the imaginary preaching of an imaginary prophet repented in imagination, shall rise up in that day and condemn the actual impenitence of those his actual hearers.[7]

There is, of course, a nonliteral element here, as in all portrayals of the world to come. The rising up on the day of judgment will not, presumably, involve individual verbal accusations. The accusation will be in the resurrection itself. The resurrection to life of the penitent Ninevites is the witness against our Lord's impenitent hearers. It might not be impossible to consider this an illustration taken from a folk tale, yet it is difficult to avoid the conclusion that this and several other passages are deprived of force if their historical basis is removed. In all honesty, there seems no hint that our Lord intended anything of the sort. The conclusion is reinforced by the immediate juxtaposition of the visit of "the Queen of the South" as a strictly parallel illustration (Matt. 12:42). To regard the Book of Jonah as intentional parable or allegory or historical fiction may seem plausible, but we can hardly so regard the Book of Kings.

The statement "As it was in the days of Noah, so it will be at the coming of the Son of Man" (Matt. 24:37) is a similar example. The context is most solemn. Our Lord has introduced His statement with the emphatic assertion, "Heaven and earth will pass away, but my words will never pass away." Then, drawing a vivid picture of the everyday life of those who lived in the days before the flood, He says, "So it will be at the coming of the Son of Man." It is true that a popular preacher may play on the emotions of his hearers by painting graphic and moving scenes that are avowedly fictitious. If he should finish such an account with a dramatic "And the same will happen to you!" it might be very powerful. But an oratorical device to arouse the imagination adds nothing to the argument. Here our Lord is building up a solemn warning by appealing to the dreadful acts of God recorded in Holy Scripture, which both He and His hearers accept as divine authority.

To Capernaum He uttered a warning based on another terrible act of judgment. "If the miracles that were performed in you had been performed in Sodom, it would have remained to this day. But I tell you that it will be more tolerable for Sodom on the day of judgment than for you" (Matt. 11:23–24). Since Noah's flood and the destruction of Sodom are taken as historical in these passages, the same must apply to Luke 17:26–32, which ends with the warning "Remember Lot's wife!" Again, with encouragements and warnings about more immediate coming events, historical happenings of the past are used as a foundation for future expectations. Looking over the whole sweep of biblical history from the first book of the Hebrew canon to the last, He says that "this generation will be held responsible for the blood of all the prophets that has been shed since the beginning of the world, from the blood of Abel to the blood of Zechariah, who was killed between the altar and the sanctuary. Yes, I tell you, this generation will be held responsible for it all" (Luke 11:50–51). Old Testament history was to find its fearful consummation in the events of A.D. 70. And it was the divine aid given to the persecuted prophets in earlier times that was to be the consolation of persecuted disciples. "Rejoice and be glad, because great is your reward in heaven, for in the same way they persecuted the prophets who were before you" (Matt. 5:12).

When our Lord said, "Your father Abraham rejoiced at the thought of seeing my day . . . . Before Abraham was born, I am" (John 8:56–58), His hearers took up stones to throw at Him. But if Abraham and the messianic promise were not historical, Jesus' reference to them was meaningless. At Nazareth, "the people . . . were furious. . . . They . . . took him to the brow of the hill on which the town was built, in order to throw him down the cliff" (Luke 4:28–29). His offending remarks about Elijah and Elisha (Luke 4:25–27) had no validity unless the events referred to really happened.

THE AUTHORITY OF THE OLD TESTAMENT

Pharisees and Sadducees

Our Lord used the Old Testament as the court of appeal in matters of controversy. Both with Pharisee and Sadducee, He did not call into question their appeal to Scripture; rather He rebuked them for failure to study it profoundly enough. Even the seeming waste of time and effort by the Pharisees on detailed legal formulations based on their study of the Torah He commended rather than condemned. "You should have practiced the latter," He said. Their mistake was not that they applied the Law too rigorously, but that they left undone its more important matters (Matt. 23:23). Matthew gives two most remarkable instances of this teaching—so remarkable that it is unlikely the sayings were invented, particularly after Gentiles had gained full recognition in the church. The first passage precedes the "It was said to the people long ago . . . but I tell you . . ." section of the Sermon on the Mount:

> Do not think that I have come to abolish the Law or the Prophets; I have come not to abolish them but to fulfill them. I tell you the truth, until heaven and earth disappear, not the smallest letter, not the least stroke of a pen, will by any means disappear from the Law until everything is accomplished. Anyone who breaks one of the least of these commandments and teaches others to do the same will be called least in the kingdom of heaven, but whoever practices and teaches these commands will be called great in the kingdom of heaven. For I tell you that unless your righteousness surpasses that of the Pharisees and the teachers of the law, you will certainly not enter the kingdom of heaven. (Matt. 5:17–20)

Jesus taught His disciples the need for obedience to the Law, first and foremost in spirit, but also in letter.

The second passage is even more remarkable: "The teachers of the law and the Pharisees sit in Moses' seat. So you must obey them and do everything they tell you. But do not do what they do, for they do not practice what they preach" (Matt. 23:2, 3). To Jesus, certain teachings of the law could be valuable if linked with spiritual understanding. "Every teacher of the law who has been instructed about the kingdom of heaven is like the owner of a house who brings out of his storeroom new treasures as well as old" (Matt. 13:52). There is no hint of a belittling specific Old Testament teaching. Rightly understood, that teaching was the word and command of God. Willful, spiritual obtuseness and the displacement of Scripture by "traditions of men" were the twin evils that made the Word ineffective (Matt. 15:1–9; Mark 7:1–13). The Jews who did not believe, who would not come to Jesus for life and who did not have the love of God in them searched the Scriptures in vain (John 5:39–47). They had set their hope on Moses, but he proved to be their accuser. They did not really believe Moses; hence their unbelief regarding Jesus. "For," Jesus said, "he wrote about me. But since you do not believe what he wrote, how are you going to believe what I say?" (vv. 46–47). Faith, love, and a right attitude of will were the keys to an understanding of Moses and of Christ.

The Sadducees escaped no more lightly. Their supposed rationality was met by the fierce and scathing denunciation, "You are in error because you do not know the Scriptures or the power of God" (Matt. 22:29; cf. Mark 12:24). Jesus was not content with the Pharisees' knowledge of the letter of Scripture but was concerned that there should be genuine spiritual understanding. In speaking to the Sadducees, He makes it plain that such understanding does not come by study of Scripture enlightened only by human reason; it comes through knowledge of the Scriptures that has been illuminated by the power of God. He concludes His answer to the question of the future state of the much-married woman by further appeal to the Bible: "Have you not read what God said to you, 'I am the God of Abraham . . .'?" (Matt. 22:31, 32; cf. Mark 12:26; Luke 20:37).

The Right Use of Reason

Jesus condemns neither minuteness of study nor the exercise of reason. His condemnation comes when the wickedness of men so perverts their reason or their methods of study that they become blind to the inner principles of divine revelation. He himself knew how to stimulate reason and repeatedly encouraged His hearers to go beneath the externals of Scripture language and discover its underlying principles. This approach is seen clearly in His expositions on the commands "You shall not kill" and "You shall not commit adultery." It is also powerfully displayed in connection with His two citations of Hosea's statement, "I desire mercy, not sacrifice" (Hos. 6:6; Matt. 9:13; 12:7). In two quite different contexts, neither of which has any direct reference to ceremonial sacrifice (one relating to His practice of consorting with tax collectors and the other to Sabbath observance), He rebuked the Pharisees for failure to grasp the implication of Hosea's words. Jesus demands more thought, not less; but the thinking must be done in a humble and teachable spirit that is directed by God Himself. The need for divine instruction is brought out in John 6:45, where Jesus refers to the Old Testament as looking forward to greater God-given illumination. He quotes Isaiah 54:13, which says, "All your sons will be taught by the LORD." He required that study and thought be applied to the records, which were objectively given, but the study must be done under the subjective influence of Him who gave them.

A Guide to Ethics

We see the same principle in Jesus' use of the Old Testament as a guide in matters of ethics. The Old Testament provides objective moral standards and demands the obedience of our inmost heart. Jesus' answer to the young man who inquired about gaining eternal life was given in the form of a series of quotations from the Ten Commandments, together with the injunction from Leviticus, "Love your neighbor as yourself" (Matt. 19:18, 19; cf. Mark 10:19; Luke 18:20).

When the lawyer asked, "Which is the greatest commandment in the Law?" Jesus replied with two quotations from the Pentateuch: " 'Love the Lord your God with all your heart and with all your soul and with all your mind.' This is the first and greatest commandment. And the second is like it. 'Love your neighbor as yourself.' " To Him these two quotations sum up the teaching of the Old Testament. "All the Law and the Prophets," He said, "hang on these two commandments" (Matt. 22:37–40; cf. Mark 12:29–31).

Note carefully that, to our Lord, these two commandments

sum up, not the Gospel but the Old Testament. Many people think that these two commandments are the heart of the New Testament, forgetting that they are found in the law of Moses, dating back centuries before the time of Christ. According to our Lord, they are the heart of the Old Testament. To be more precise, they are the heart of the Old Testament law. There is no higher law than the Old Testament law as here expressed, and there never can be. The New Testament does not reveal a higher *law*; it reveals the gospel.

The demands of God's law had proved far beyond the reach of sinful men and had brought only condemnation. The gospel was good news of salvation to the helpless and the condemned. It is extraordinary what a hold the utterly unbiblical notion of the contrariety of the two testaments has obtained. We have had so much erroneous teaching for so many years that even intelligent people often believe that the testaments represent two irreconcilably opposed points of view, the Old Testament God being one of wrath and the New Testament God being one of love. Such a view would have been repudiated with horror by Jesus and by every New Testament writer. To them the God of the Old Testament and the God of the New Testament were the same. In both testaments He is a God of wrath and of love. The great difference between the Old and the New Testament is that in the former the gospel, though by no means invisible, is veiled, whereas in the latter it is clearly revealed. Thus, "all the Law and the Prophets hang on these two [Old Testament] commandments."

In passing, it is perhaps worthwhile to point out that here—as also in connection with the Golden Rule (Matt. 7:12), of which He says, "This is the law and the prophets"—Jesus set His seal on the sacred writings as a unitary whole.[8] Also the summary itself brings home forcibly the fact that within the Old Testament its elements are not all equally fundamental. Cases often arise where the law gives no specific ruling. Jesus makes it clear that in such cases guidance is to be found, not in multiplication of casuistic rules, but by appealing to fundamental principles of Scripture. In other words, He is simply saying once again that the mind of God is to be found by a spiritually minded approach to the Scriptures. They are the court of appeal, but their study must be prompted by love for God and man.

G. Vos describes Jesus' treatment of the law like this:

He once more made the voice of the law the voice of the living God, who is present in every commandment, so absolute in his demands, so personally interested in man's conduct, so all-observant, that the thought of yielding to him less than the whole inner life, the heart, the soul, the mind, the strength, can no longer be tolerated. Thus quickened by the spirit of God's personality, the law becomes in our Lord's hands a living organism, in which soul and body, spirit and letter, the greater and smaller commandments are to be distinguished, and which admits of being reduced to great comprehensive principles in whose light the weight and purport of all single precepts are to be intelligently appreciated.[9]

Accommodation to the Beliefs of His Hearers

Jesus' use of Scripture as a court of appeal in controversy is undoubted, but some scholars suggest the possibility that He simply met His contemporaries on their own ground, without committing Himself to the correctness of their premises. In other words, He made *ad hominem* arguments, aimed more at discrediting His opponents than laying foundations on which to build eternal truth. Indeed could we not go even further and suggest that (since His aim was the positive one of leading His contemporaries forward from their valuable, though imperfect, Old Testament conceptions of the character of God) He deliberately refrained from unsettling them by questioning their belief in the inspiration of their Scriptures? The gentler processes of time would gradually bring home to them the imperfect character of what they revered.

Plausible as this view may appear, it seems impossible to accept it as Christ's. He did not show Himself unduly sensitive about undermining current beliefs. He was not slow to denounce pharisaic traditionalism. In the Sermon on the Mount, for instance, He carefully distinguished between the divine law and later false deductions from it. On another occasion He commended the scribes and Pharisees for upholding the law of God, yet rebuked them for binding "heavy loads" on others (Matt. 23:2-4). He was not slow to repudiate nationalist conceptions of the Messiah. He was prepared to face the Cross for defying current misconceptions. Surely He would have explained clearly a mingling of divine truth and human error in Scripture had He thought such to exist. The notion that our Lord was fully aware that the view of Holy Scripture current in His day was erroneous, and that He deliberately accommodated His teaching to the beliefs of his hearers, will not square with the facts.[10] His use of the Old Testament seems altogether too insistent, positive, and absolute. He unequivocally maintained that "the Scripture cannot be broken" (John 10:35); "Not the smallest letter, not the least stroke of a pen, will by any means disappear from the Law . . ." (Matt. 5:18); "It is easier for heaven and earth to disappear than for the least stroke of a pen to drop out of the Law" (Luke 16:17). In fearful earnestness He says to the Pharisees, "Isaiah was right when he prophesied about you hypocrites, as it is written; "These people honor me with their lips, but their hearts are far from me. They worship me in vain; their teachings are but rules taught by men. . . . You have a fine way of setting aside the commands of God in order to observe your own traditions! . . . Thus you nullify the word of God" (Mark 7:6–13). It was no mere debating point that made Him say to the Sadducees, "You are in error because you do not know the Scriptures or the power of God" (Matt. 22:29). When speaking of the irreversible separation of the after-world, He put into the mouth of Abraham these words: "They have Moses and the Prophets; let them listen to them. . . . If they do not listen to Moses and the prophets, they will not be convinced even if someone rises from the dead" (Luke 16:29–31). As we have already seen, when He quoted Old Testament references to the fearful judgments of God, He did so to bring home the seriousness of contemporary issues.

The Temptation

The suggestion that Jesus' use of the Old Testament was of an *ad hominem* nature breaks down most obviously in the accounts of His temptation. He introduces each of His three answers by the decisive formula "It is written" (Matt. 4:4ff.; Luke 4:4ff.). Are we to believe that the opponent here concerned would not have strongly challenged an argument based on a false premise? There is a grand and solid objectivity about the perfect tense, γέγραπται (*gegraptai*, "It stands written"). "Here," Jesus was saying, "is the permanent, unchangeable witness of the eternal God, committed to writing for our instruction." Such it appears to have been to Jesus' inmost soul, quite apart from any convenience to Him in controversy. In the hour of utmost crisis and at the moment of death, words of Scripture came to his lips: "My

God, my God why have you forsaken me?" (Ps. 22:1; Matt.
27:46; Mark 15:34); "Into your hands I commit my spirit" (Ps.
31:5; Luke 23:46).

Postresurrection Teaching

Any lingering doubts we might have as to the fundamental
importance of the Old Testament to Jesus are dispelled by a
consideration of His postresurrection teaching. Between His
resurrection and ascension Jesus transcended human limitations
much more obviously than before. Then, if at any time during
His earthly ministry, we must believe that He had access to the
mind of God. During the postresurrection period He gave His
final instructions to the leaders of the embryo church and emphasized again, for their rapidly developing understanding, the
fundamentals on which the church was to be built. It would
appear from Luke's account that the main purpose of this
teaching was exposition of the Old Testament. Tracing through
"all the Scriptures," "beginning with Moses and all the Prophets," He showed from each of the three sections of the Hebrew
Scriptures—the Law, the Prophets, and the Writings—how
their basic messages pointed to and were fulfilled in Him (Luke
24:25–47).

At first it seems puzzling that Luke should speak of these
expositions only in general terms, whereas a detailed account of
our Lord's teaching would be so interesting and informative. But
is it not probable that Luke has preserved the main ingredients
of this teaching, not in his Gospel but in Acts? In the earliest
years of the church its members were almost all Jews and its
message was presented almost entirely to Jews. The chief preoccupation of these believers, consequently, was to demonstrate
that the Old Testament found its true fulfillment in Jesus. The
outline of their apologetic would have been derived from the
example of their risen Master.[11] Thus the general apostolic use
of Scripture, particularly as recorded in the early chapters of Acts,
must be regarded as an important witness to our Lord's own
teaching. The teaching of the apostles underlines that of Christ.

The Inspiration of the Old Testament

Our Lord not only believed the truth of Old Testament history
and used the Scriptures as final authority in matters of faith and
conduct, He also regarded the writings themselves as inspired.

To him, Moses, the prophets, David, and the other Scripture writers were given their messages by the Spirit of God. There is no trace of the modern idea that the men were inspired but not their writings. If anything one might infer the reverse. The Old Testament makes no attempt to gloss over the sins of its saints. The greatest of them, such as Moses and David, are convicted of grievous sins, and our Lord made no attempt to whitewash their characters. But their writings were regarded quite differently.

The writings are authoritative, not because of the human author, but because God is regarded as the ultimate author. The human authors are real authors; there is no idea of mechanical dictation. Nonetheless, God's Spirit spoke through them, and it is the divine authorship that gives their writing unique importance. Our Lord often prefaced a quotation of Scripture with such words as "Moses said" (Mark 7:10): "Isaiah was right when he prophesied" (Mark 7:6; cf. Matt. 13:14), or "David himself, speaking by the Holy Spirit" (Mark 12:36). He referred to the abomination of desolation, "spoken of through the prophet Daniel" (Matt. 24:15). But, as is clear from the context, the injunctions "Honor your father and mother" and "Anyone who curses his father or mother must be put to death" did not, for Jesus, derive their authority from the fact that Moses uttered them, but from God Himself. Without the original "God said" or "The Lord said to Moses," the expression "Moses said" would have had little force. The words of Isaiah and Daniel likewise have authority because these men are prophets, the essence of prophecy being that the prophet speaks God's words, or, more vividly, that God speaks *through* the prophet. David (who, incidentally, is called a prophet in the first Christian address delivered after the ascension, Acts 2:30) is expressly said by our Lord to have spoken "by the Holy Spirit" (Matt. 22:43).

James Barr, in an interesting passage, takes fundamentalists to task for using the authority of Jesus to decide questions of biblical criticism. They seem to think, he says, "that Jesus is placing all his personal and spiritual authority in support of the thesis that there was a historical Jonah who was factually within the whale"; "that Jesus is personally guaranteeing that the Psalm was historically written by the original David"; and that "the historical Jesus is staking his whole authority and credibility as a teacher upon the assertion that the passage referred to was actually spoken by a historical Daniel." He continues:

Its distortion of the proper proportions of the Christian faith is
extreme . . . [it is] a simple literary function-mistake. The entirety
of utterances ascribed to Jesus is treated as 'teaching'; and no
adequate distinction is drawn between that which Jesus seeks to
teach . . . and any or all of the elements which are found in his
utterance.

In illustration he quotes John Huxtable, who says that if an
absent-minded professor tells the wrong time for the arrival of a
train, one does not regard him as a liar or any less reputable as a
scholar. One does not "suppose that being a great authority on
Homer makes him a reliable substitute for a timetable. . . . Jesus
Christ came into the world to be its Saviour, not an authority on
biblical criticism."[12]

Barr is right in thus stressing the importance of keeping the
Christian faith in proper proportion. Jesus Himself distinguished
between the "greatest" commandment and the "least" of commandments, though He urged obedience to both. There are
similarly greater and lesser utterances made by the Holy Spirit.
It is an exaggeration to talk about Jesus "staking his whole
authority and credibility" on an incidental historical reference,
but it is nonetheless a natural assumption that *God's* words
should be regarded as entirely true in small matters as well as
great. God is not like an absent-minded professor. It was part of
the Lord's saviorhood that He spoke words of life and truth that
were to be implicitly trusted and obeyed if His followers were to
build on rock. We must be wary of dogmatism in pushing the
words of Jesus beyond their natural sense, but we are right to
take His guidance in holding the Old Testament to be accurate
in historical minutiae as well as in great theological truths.

Fulfillment of Prophecy

Jesus' references to the necessity for fulfillment of Scripture
prophecies are numerous. It is not always easy to discern the
principles of interpretation that governed His understanding of
prophecy, prophecies being sometimes interpreted literally and
sometimes typologically. But these exegetical problems serve
only to throw into stronger relief the implied God-givenness of
the whole body of prophetic writings that by divine necessity
must be fulfilled.[13] The fact that correspondence between prophecy and fulfillment is by no means always obvious on the surface
makes the conviction that these ancient writings contain the

foreshadowing of later events the more remarkable. Our Lord not only saw fulfillment of prophecy in events that had already taken place, but He possessed a sense of divine predestination in the events that were ahead. These things had to come to pass in order that the Scriptures might be fulfilled.

Here are the more important references to His teaching about fulfillment of prophecy: "Today this scripture is fulfilled in your hearing" (Luke 4:21). "This is the one about whom it is written. "I will send my messenger ahead of you . . ." (Matt. 11:10; cf. Luke 7:27). "Elijah does come first, and restores all things. Why then is it written that the Son of Man must suffer much and be rejected? But I tell you, Elijah has come, and they have done to him everything they wished, just as it is written about him" (Mark 9:12, 13). "We are going up to Jerusalem, and everything that is written by the prophets about the Son of Man will be fulfilled. He will be handed over to the Gentiles. . . . they will . . . flog him and kill him. On the third day he will rise again" (Luke 18:31–33). "This is the time of punishment in fulfillment of all that has been written" (Luke 21:22). "The Son of Man will go just as it is written about him . . ." (Matt. 26:24; Mark 14:21). "It is written: 'And he was numbered with the transgressors'; and I tell you that this must be fulfilled in me. Yes, what is written about me is reaching its fulfillment" (Luke 22:37). "This very night you will all fall away on account of me, for it is written, 'I will strike the shepherd . . .' " (Matt. 26:31; cf. Mark 14:27; Zech. 13:7). "Do you think I cannot call on my Father, and he will at once put at my disposal more than twelve legions of angels? But how then would the Scriptures be fulfilled, that say it must happen in this way? . . . But this has all taken place that the writings of the prophets might be fulfilled" (Matt. 26:53–56; cf. Mark 14:49). " 'How foolish you are, and how slow of heart to believe all that the prophets have spoken! Did not the Christ have to suffer these things and then enter his glory?' And beginning with Moses and all the Prophets, he explained to them what was said in all the Scriptures concerning himself" (Luke 24:25–27). " 'This is what I told you while I was still with you. Everything must be fulfilled that is written about me in the Law of Moses, the Prophets and the Psalms.' Then he opened their minds so that they could understand the Scriptures. He told them, 'This is what is written: The Christ will suffer and rise from the dead on the third day, and repentance and forgiveness

of sins will be preached in his name to all nations, beginning at
Jerusalem' " (Luke 24:44–47). "The Scriptures . . . testify about
me. . . . If you believed Moses, you would believe me, for he
wrote about me. But since you do not believe what he wrote, how
are you going to believe what I say?" (John 5:39–47). "I am not
referring to you all; I know those I have chosen. But this is to
fulfill the Scripture: 'He who shares my bread has lifted up his
heel against me' " (John 13:18; Ps. 41:9). "This is to fulfill what
is written in their Law: 'They hated me without reason' " (John
15:25; Ps. 35:19). "None has been lost except the one doomed to
destruction so that Scripture would be fulfilled" (John 17:12).
Our Lord's acceptance of the divine character of the prophetic
Scriptures was clear, full, and emphatic.

Scripture and Verbal Inspiration

The witness of Jesus to the verbal inspiration of Scripture
demands special attention, because, wittingly or unwittingly,
verbal inspiration is continually being contradicted by Christian
writers. Some maintain that the very notion of verbal inspiration
is obviously outmoded. Many hold that, in a formal sense, there
is no difference between the inspiration of the Bible and that of
other great literature. A reliable doctrine of verbal inspiration
plainly needs careful statement, but that some sort of verbal
inspiration was believed and taught by Christ is clear. It is to the
writings, rather than to the writers, that He ascribes basic authority. Writings are made up of words; therefore, written inspiration must necessarily involve some form of word inspiration.

In any balanced statement of the doctrine of biblical inspiration it is most important to remember that our Lord acknowledged the real authorship of the human writers. It is also important, however, to note that His references to human authorship
are quite secondary. Often He is content to speak simply of
"scripture," God being the obviously implied author. Here are
some such references: "Today this scripture has been fulfilled in
your hearing . . ." (Luke 4:21). "Have you never read in the
scriptures: 'The very stone which the builders rejected . . .'?"
(Matt. 21:42; cf. Mark 12:10; Luke 20:17; Ps. 118:22). "How
then should the scriptures be fulfilled, that it must be so?" (Matt.
26:54). "The scriptures . . . bear witness to me" (John 5:39).
"He who believes in me, as the scripture has said . . ." (John
7:38). The Scriptures collectively state, and each individual

Scripture passage states, the teaching of God. Scripture was Scripture to Christ because it has God as its primary author—in a way that no other writing has.

For Jesus to say, as He does in so many places, "Have you not read . . .?" is equivalent to His saying, "Do you not know that God has said . . .?" (cf. Matt. 12:3; 19:4; 21:16; 22:31; Mark 2:25; 12:10, 26; Luke 6:3). Divine authority is clearly implied in the expression γέγραπται (*gegraptai*, "it is written"), already mentioned in connection with the temptations, but used often at other times (Matt. 11:10; 21:13; 26:24, 31; Mark 9:12, 13; 11:17; 14:21, 27; Luke 7:27; 19:46). The inspiration and authority implied by these various phrases is applied not only to oracular, prophetic utterances but to all parts of Scripture without discrimination—to history, to laws, to psalms, to prophesies.

Interchangeability of "Scripture" and "God"

There is a remarkable interchangeability of the terms *God* and *scripture* in certain New Testament passages. We find that "scripture" is sometimes used where one might expect "God," and "God" is used where one might expect "scripture."[14] Romans 9:17 reads, "The scripture says to Pharaoh: 'I raised you up for this very purpose, that I might display my power in you.' " The meaning, of course, is, "In the scripture narrative, God says to Pharaoh. . . ." Similarly, in Galatians 3:8 we read, "The scripture foresaw that God would justify the Gentiles by faith, and announced the gospel in advance to Abraham." Jesus, in one instance, uses the same figure of speech, though in reverse. An Old Testament quotation, which in its context is not a statement by God, is cited as having God as its author. Jesus declared, "The Creator said, 'For this reason a man will leave his father and mother' " (Matt. 19:4–5). The quotation is from Genesis 2:24, where the statement is not attributed directly to God but is simply a comment introduced in the course of the narrative by the writer of Genesis. The expected form of Jesus' citation, therefore, would be, "Scripture says, 'For this reason. . . .' " Yet God is so completely regarded as the author of Scripture that in these contexts "God" and "scripture" are interchangeable. What Scripture says is the Word of God. God is its author. Though Jesus never exalted Scripture for its own sake, He never allowed a wedge to be driven between Scripture itself and its message. To our Lord the Old Testament was true as history; it was of divine authority, and its very words were inspired by God Himself.

Infallibility and Inerrancy

In recent years there has been a serious attempt to distinguish between infallibility and inerrancy and to attribute to Jesus a belief in the first but not the second. Infallibility is taken to mean that Scripture is factually true and authoritative in all matters "crucially relevant to Christian faith and practice," but not in peripheral matters.[15] The trouble is that such a distinction is nowhere to be found in Jesus' own teaching and seems to be precluded by His testimony both to the unqualified historical accuracy and the inspiration of the Old Testament. The jots and tittles, whether in matters of doctrine or ethics or history or prophecy, come from God. Our Lord received the Old Testament—the books of Moses, Isaiah, Daniel, Jonah, and the rest—in the way the Jewish church of His day received it, as inspired in its whole and in its parts. The attempt to discriminate between the crucial and the peripheral appears to be a product of the nineteenth and twentieth centuries.

ALLUSIONS TO THE OLD TESTAMENT

We have now covered the ground sufficiently to give a clear idea of our Lord's view of Scripture, but citation of numerous outstanding references does not of itself convey the full weight of the evidence. To these must be added the many allusions that come out in the course of His teaching. The Sermon on the Mount, for instance, has few explicit quotations; but it is so replete with Old Testament language and ideas that it is impossible to say what may have been conscious allusion and what was not. In many passages there is simply no way to distinguish between Jesus' conscious allusion to the Old Testament and His normal, habitual use of Old Testament words and thought forms. The Holy Scriptures penetrated the warp and woof of Christ's mind. It would take too long to examine the vast number of references in His teachings one by one. Further evidence is not required to prove the case already adequately established, but it is perhaps worthwhile to mention a few of Jesus' more interesting allusions to the Old Testament.

Three are peculiar to Mark. "As soon as the grain is ripe, he puts the sickle to it, because the harvest has come" (Mark 4:29) recalls Joel 3:13; "Do you have eyes but fail to see, and ears but fail to hear?" (Mark 8:18) is from Jeremiah 5:21; and "Their worm does not die, and the fire is not quenched" (Mark 9:48) is from Isaiah 66:24. In the Sermon on the Mount, the phrases "the meek . . . will inherit the earth" and "the pure in heart" are not original to Jesus but come from the Old Testament (Pss. 37:11; 73:1). "Away from me, you evildoers!" (Matt. 7:23; cf. Luke 13:27) is from Psalm 6:8. "Children will rebel against their parents . . ." (Matt. 10:21, 35; Mark 13:12; cf. Luke 12:53) is from Micah 7:6. In one of Jesus' rare items of ecclesiastical legislation (Matt. 18:15–20), He invokes Deuteronomy 19:15, "that every matter may be established by the testimony of two or three witnesses." The parable of the wicked husbandmen (Matt. 21:33–41; Mark 12:1–9; Luke 20:9–16) recalls Isaiah 5. The Mount of Olives discourse (Matt. 24; Mark 13; Luke 21) is full of Old Testament language. "They will dash you to the ground, you and the children within" (Luke 19:44) echoes that fiercest of imprecatory psalms, Psalm 137.

The total impression that these and many other allusions in the Gospels give is that the mind of Christ was saturated with the Old Testament. As He spoke, there flowed out perfectly naturally a complete range of uses varying from direct quotation to unconscious reflections of Old Testament phraseology. There is no trace of artificial quotation of Scripture as a matter of pious habit. Jesus' mind was so steeped in both the words and principles of Scripture that quotation and allusion came to His lips naturally and appositely in all sorts of circumstances.

Supposed Abrogations of the Old Testament

But is there not another side to this question? Didn't Jesus sometimes qualify or even abrogate some of the Old Testament teachings? Did He not on occasion treat the Scriptures in a much freer way than this essay would suggest—in a way that revealed a quietly critical element? J. K. S. Reid, for instance, says, "There is a class of sayings (or actions) in which he improves upon what is written in the Scripture he knew, and another where he endorses what is there."[16] B. H. Branscomb says, "He flatly rejected a portion of it by appealing to another portion."[17]

There are seven main examples from our Lord's teaching that are used to illustrate the thesis that He criticized, and so by implication repudiated, parts of the Old Testament.

The Sabbath

Jesus said, "The Son of Man is Lord even of the Sabbath" (Mark 2:28; cf. Matt. 12:8; Luke 6:5). This example hardly seems to merit comment, because it so obviously cannot seriously be used to illustrate a low view of the Old Testament. The Pharisees had objected to the disciples' picking and eating some grain on the Sabbath. Quite the reverse of making an appeal apart from Scripture, the Lord answered them by appealing to Bible history, reminding them of what David had done. He repudiated the petty "traditions of the elders" in favor of sane and spiritually minded attention to the Old Testament. The passage is significant, not for its lowered view of Scripture, but for the height of our Lord's claims implied in it. God gave the Sabbath law, and Jesus claimed to possess God's authority to define limitations of that law.

Sacrifice

Jesus' twofold citation of Hosea 6:6, "I desire mercy, not sacrifice" (Matt. 9:13; 12:7), has been used as an example of His critical approach to the Old Testament in setting aside important elements of Jewish ceremony. It is very doubtful, however, that either Hosea's original words or the Lord's quotation of them contained or conveyed to those who heard them any idea of a literal abrogation of sacrifice. Certainly the Gospel contexts suggest nothing of the kind, and such thoughts do not appear to have been seriously entertained by the apostles until some years after the ascension. At least they did not take their Master seriously or literally enough to abandon sacrificial worship in Jerusalem.

The biblical writers were by no means as literal as we today normally are, and yet we would hardly misunderstand an impassioned clergyman who said, "I am concerned about your spiritual devotion, not your money." We would not expect to see church collections suddenly disappear! But even if we take Jesus' quotation of Hosea 6:6 literally, we have still proved nothing at all. No Christian today, not even a Seventh Day Adventist, believes that the Mosaic sacrificial system is now binding. Yet orthodox Christians have always held that the Mosaic injunctions were given by God, though many of them were temporary, being effective only until they were fulfilled in Christ. For the Son of God to abrogate a law of God is in no way a denial that it was first enacted by God.

Cleansing All Foods

In Mark 7:18, 19 we read, " 'Don't you see that nothing that enters a man from the outside can make him "unclean"? For it doesn't go into his heart but into his stomach, and then out of his body.' (In saying this, Jesus declared all foods 'clean.')" This passage has been used to show Christ's supposed abrogation, during His earthly ministry, of the distinction between clean and unclean animals. Perhaps the apostle Peter, after his vision of the great sheet let down from heaven (Acts 10:9–16), saw in this statement of Jesus an implicit abrogation that predated the one in his vision. In any case, neither Jesus nor Peter denied, implicitly or explicitly, the divine origin of the law that was now repealed. Indeed, the context of Jesus' declaration points precisely the other way. Mark 7:1–13, which immediately precedes, is a devastating attack on those who leave the commandments of God and hold to the traditions of men.

"But I Tell You . . ."

Of primary importance is the well-known section of the Sermon on the Mount in which our Lord's teachings are contrasted with what "was said to the people of long ago" (Matt. 5:17–48). Christ used the language of loftiest authority. "It was said . . ., but I tell you. . . ." This formula is often construed by superficial readers as a repudiation of the "barbarous" ethic of the Old Testament and a replacement of it by a contrary Christian ethic. It is suggested that Christ declared the teaching of the Old Testament to be fundamentally wrong and put a new and true doctrine in its place. Even if this were a correct interpretation, it would indicate a remarkable claim of authority by Jesus. He made, if possible, an even higher claim, however. He deliberately set the Old Testament on the highest pinnacle of authority and then proceeded to set Himself above it. He introduced these teachings by saying,

> Do not think that I have come to abolish the Law or the Prophets; I have not come to abolish them but to fulfill them. I tell you the truth, until heaven and earth disappear, not the smallest letter, not the least stroke of a pen, will by any means disappear from the Law until everything is accomplished. Anyone who breaks one of the least of these commandments and teaches others to do the same will be called least in the kingdom of heaven, but whoever practices and teaches these commands will be called great in the kingdom of heaven (Matt. 5:17–19).

It has been common practice in some scholastic circles, to posit two sources of authority reflected in Sermon on the Mount: the first (as seen in the passage just quoted) accepts a strict rabbinical doctrine of Scripture; the second (as seen in the phrase "but I say to you") overthrows it. There is an intrinsic absurdity in combining two contradictory sources in this way. Also, as D. Daube has shown, the sequence of *principle* ("Do not think that I have come to abolish") and *cases* ("you have heard") is very common in Rabbinic literature. To "fulfill" or "uphold" (*qiyyem*) the law, is "to show that the text is in agreement with your teaching." The test of any teaching was in giving full effect to, upholding every word of the law.[18] So it was that, after His opening comments concerning the blessedness of discipleship, the first truth that Jesus drives home is that of the authority of the Old Testament. Likewise, the sermon virtually ends with "this is the law and the prophets" (Matt. 7:12). Its final word is an earnest appeal to beware of false prophets and to build on Jesus' words.

Jesus did not negate the Old Testament commands; rather, He showed their full scope and stripped them of prevalent misinterpretations. Evidently it was not clear to His disciples that He intended to abrogate even the Levitical sacrifices and all the paraphernalia of temple worship. It was left to Paul to bring into clear light the implications of this teaching in the light of Jesus' sacrificial death and resurrection. It is certainly not in the Sermon on the Mount that we find abrogation of the Old Testament. Christ did not say, "The Old Testament says, 'You shall not murder'; but I say, 'You may commit murder.'" To the contrary, He was explaining that God does not restrict His commandments to the mere letter of the law, but that He disapproves even of the hating spirit that leads to murder and of lustful intentions, which in God's sight are equivalent to adultery.

Divorce

Since Jesus' teaching on divorce (Matt. 5:31, 32; cf. 19:3ff.; Mark 10:2ff.; Luke 16:18) is often regarded as an instance of His giving an Old Testament passage something less than divine authority, it may be worthwhile to make a short digression to clear up a common confusion.

Deuteronomy gives strict instructions that a wife, formally

divorced and remarried, may on no account return to her former
husband:

> If a man marries a woman who becomes displeasing to him be-
> cause he finds something indecent about her, and he writes her a
> certificate of divorce, gives it to her and sends her from his house,
> and if after she leaves his house she becomes the wife of another
> man, and her second husband dislikes her and writes her a
> certificate of divorce, gives it to her and sends her from his house,
> or if he dies, then her first husband, who divorced her, is not
> allowed to marry her again after she had been defiled. That
> would be detestable in the eyes of the LORD (Deut. 24:1–4).

Here is one of the statutes and ordinances that the LORD commanded the people to follow (Deut. 26:16), and there is no good
ground for thinking that in attributing this injunction to Moses
(Mark 10:3–5) Jesus and His questioners meant to deny that it
came from God. The question related to what deductions might
be drawn from it. It was then currently interpreted as giving
divine approval for divorce. It is certainly not a command to
divorce; it is not properly even permission to divorce, since the
divine pattern of Genesis 2:24, in which a man is "united to his
wife, and they . . . become one flesh," had never been modified.
It is rather a disapproving recognition of the fact of divorce, with
regulations to mitigate its worst evils. The form is, "If . . . and if
. . . , then . . . ." The law gave civil permission, but not moral
sanction, for divorce.

There are two possible legitimate interpretations of Jesus'
teaching on this matter, and neither of them denies the divine
origin of the Mosaic teaching. One possibility is that the allow-
ance of divorce was for spiritually immature Israel and that the
revocation was a new standard for the spiritually more mature
church. That is, there were two different laws for two different
sets of circumstances, and both laws were given by God. The
other possibility is that the allowing of divorce was a specific *law*
on Israel's statute book, designed to meet the practical needs of a
very imperfect people; whereas the teaching concerning the in-
dissolubility of marriage was an *ideal* for mankind in general and
for Christians in particular. This distinction between law and
ideal is a simple one, yet it is very fundamental and is often
overlooked. No wise lawgiver, least of all the all-wise Lawgiver,
would frame a law on the principle that hate is equivalent to
murder, or lust to adultery. Law can deal only with overt acts,

not with secret thoughts. A wise law and a wise ideal, though emanating from the same person, must of necessity be quite different. The ideal will, in a sense, be far higher than the law. It is this confusion between law and ideal or, in other words, between civil law and moral law that leads the superficial reader to regard the Sermon on the Mount as a repudiation of the Old Testament. In fact, it is explicitly stated to be a *fulfillment* of the Law and the Prophets. The same principle is clear in Mark 10:2–12. In quoting both Genesis 1:27, "God 'made them male and female,' " and 2:24, "For this reason a man will leave his father and mother and be united to his wife, and the two will become one flesh," Jesus interpreted Scripture by Scripture. It is *on the authority of Scripture itself* that He denied the validity of the traditional interpretation of Deuteronomy 24:1, which gave approval to divorce.

"Eye for Eye"

Even Jesus' repudiation (Matt. 5:38–42) of the "eye for eye" principle of the Old Testament cannot fairly be said to be a repudiation of what, in its context, the Old Testament basically taught. In Exodus 21:24; Leviticus 24:20; and Deuteronomy 19:21, laws are given for the administration of public justice. Private revenge and family feuds were to be replaced by strictly fair and impartial public administration of justice.[19] In our Lord's day this excellent, if stern, principle of judicial retribution was used as an excuse for the very thing it was instituted to abolish, namely personal revenge. Christ gives no hint that He wished to see magistrates relax their important function of upholding the majesty of the law and the sanctity of justice. He did, however, discourage His disciples from appealing to a form of justice for the merely selfish purpose of gaining their own rights. Similarly, in the story of the woman caught in adultery (John 8:1–11), Jesus does not indicate what would be proper treatment in a legally constituted court. He says in effect, "I am not here now as Judge [cf. John 3:17]. I am here to call people to repentance while there is time. I call this woman, *and all her accusers,* to repentance."

"Hate Your Enemy"

Jesus' final contrast of principles also repudiated a current misinterpretation of the Old Testament. The Old Testament gives the command "Love your neighbor," which had long been interpreted as involving the corollary, "Hate your enemy" (Matt. 5:43). In making this addition, which is not a quotation from the Old Testament, the popular teaching had given the command a meaning not even implied in the context. Leviticus 19:18 was intended to embrace every member of the Israelite community, and the rest of the verse makes it clear that an Israelite was not to seek vengeance or harbor grudges against any of his compatriots. Leviticus 19:34 applies the same principle to the resident alien: "The alien living with you must be treated as one of your native-born. Love him as yourself." "Love your neighbor" in the Levitical rule already implied "Love your enemies."

It is true that the Old Testament in some sense expects the godly man to hate the enemies of God and the enemies of the people of God (cf. Deut. 20:16–18; 23:6; 25:17–19; Pss. 109; 139:21–24). So in some sense does the New Testament. The disciple must be prepared to "hate his father and mother, his wife and children" (Luke 14:26). The Son of man himself will one day utter the words, "Depart from me, you who are cursed, into the eternal fire" (Matt. 25:41). He underlined and completely identified Himself with the Old Testament judgments of God against sinners and with those judgments foretold as yet to come. At the same time He forgave His enemies and loved them even to the point of dying on the cross. The fact that He forbade James and John to follow the example of Elijah in calling down fire from heaven to consume His opponents does not deny His recognition of divine judgment (Luke 9:51–56; 2 Kings 1:10, 12).

CONCLUSION

It has been said with truth that the attempt to evade the evidence for our Lord's teaching the God-givenness of Scripture is as futile as a mathematician's attempt to prove that it is theoretically possible to dodge an avalanche.[20] He may satisfy himself that the trajectory of each boulder is calculable and that an agile man could step out of the way of any one of them. Critical ingenuity may satisfy itself that it can, one by one, find ways of disposing of many of Jesus' statements about the Old Testament. But these statements cannot reasonably be considered independently. They form together a great avalanche of cumulative evidence that cannot honestly be evaded. Furthermore, the consistency of the results obtained by taking the Gospel evidence as it stands is itself a vindication of this approach. The items of evidence support one another, suggesting that they derive from one consistent mind, not from a miscellany of dubious church traditions.[21]

Many profess that they would be willing to accept Jesus' teaching about the Bible, if only they could know for certain what that teaching was. But, they say, the accumulated errors of translation, of oral tradition, and of scribal transmission leave them quite uncertain as to what He actually taught. Taking refuge behind this belief, they do not grapple with the Gospel evidence and feel free to build their theology with a view of Scripture different from that which ordinary historical investigation shows to have been believed and taught by Christ. But however much one may nibble at details of the Gospel record on critical grounds, the overall picture can be distorted only by wholesale rejection of practically all of the evidence. This is a length to which few critics, however radical, are prepared to go. The evidence is abundantly clear:

To Christ the Old Testament was true, authoritative, inspired.

To Him the God of the Old Testament was the one living God, and the teaching of the Old Testament was the teaching of this living God.

To Him what Scripture said, God said.

POSTSCRIPT

Jesus' view of the Old Testament is of the greatest importance to any Christian who regards Him as Master and who seeks to follow His teaching. To many, however, the foregoing arguments may seem to raise as many questions as they answer.

It would go beyond my brief discussion to deal with further questions. But I should like to add a note, expressing in the strongest terms, my belief that it is in the area of secondary questions that perplexed Christians are in the greatest need of help at the present time. I thought it might be helpful to mention some questions that are dealt with in my previously published works that may not be covered in other chapters of this symposium.

For example, most scholars would agree substantially with my analysis of Jesus' views of Scripture, but many of them (including many who regard themselves as committed Christians) would not feel bound to make His views their own. And this for a simple reason. "You have merely shown," they would say, "that Jesus was a devout first-century Jew—and that's not a very original or revolutionary conclusion! If He were truly man, He could hardly have believed anything else. As a real man, He must have shared the ignorance and errors of His own day, and some of these errors can be seen in the Gospels. Was He not wrong, for example, about the time of His Second Coming, about the authorship of Psalm 110, about Abiathar being high priest when David ate the bread of the Presence, and about the identity of Zechariah the son of Barachiah?"

Another question concerns the way the New Testament often quotes the Old Testament. Frequently a quotation is inexact and, according to some interpreters, even misleading (e.g., "Out of Egypt I called my son" [Matt. 2:15; cf. Hosea 11:1]; "seed," not "seeds" [Gal. 3:16; cf. Gen. 12:7]). Do such citations show that the New Testament writers had a less respectful view of the Old Testament than the one proposed in this chapter? And what about the matters of typology and the favorable references to noncanonical literature?

Another obvious question is: What about the accuracy and authority of the New Testament itself? Obviously no argument concerning Jesus' view of the Old Testament can be transferred to the New Testament directly, since none of the latter existed during His lifetime. An authoritative Old Testament without an authoritative New Testament can hardly be satisfying to a Christian.

Still further questions are: How are we to regard the Apocrypha? What about Luther's strictures on the Epistle of James? What is the significance of an inerrant original, if we do not possess it and if it has been corrupted in transmission? These and other questions are discussed in my book *Christ and the Bible* (cf. note 4).

Another area of difficulty concerns the morality of the Bible. If we accept Jesus' high view of the Old Testament, what are we to make of such things as the imprecatory psalms and God's command to the Israelites to exterminate their enemies? What of the horrors of the divine judgments. These and related questions are discussed in my book *The Goodness of God* (InterVarsity Press, 1974).

ADDITIONAL NOTE
Radical Criticism of the Gospels

It must be rare for a convert from a non-Christian religion to declare his faith in Christ if he has not first come to believe the Gospels or the basic gospel story to be substantially true. Conversion is normally the end of a process of growing belief that the Gospel story is true and that Jesus was all that He claimed to be. For those brought up in a Christian culture, however, the matter is often not so simple. A second-hand Christian belief subjected to criticism may become progressively less sure, while never reaching the point of being explicitly abandoned. Beliefs are often not abandoned outright but radically reinterpreted. Faith in Christ is still affirmed, while reliable knowledge of the Jesus of history is disclaimed. Such is the position of many New Testament critics today as the result of their study of source, form, and redaction criticism. The Gospels, they believe, tell us much about the faith of the early church, but give little factual information about Jesus. It is our belief that this position has been arrived at by adopting a naturalistic approach to the Gospels. It is outside the scope of this book to deal with this question, but a few remarks may be in order.

H. E. W. Turner has distinguished two basic approaches to the Gospels: the historical and the interpretative.[22] The former holds that the Gospels were intended to be, and in fact are, historical records; the latter maintains that they were essentially well-meaning propaganda, written to foster a particular view of Jesus. The former assumes that the records are true unless good reason can be shown to the contrary; the latter assumes the opposite. The view that Bultmann and his school hold in regard to the Gospel record has been summarized as follows:

> (1) If it [a given account] reflects the faith of the church after the resurrection, it must be regarded as a creation of the church, rather than an authentic saying of Jesus. (2) If there is a parallel saying attributed to a Rabbi, it must be held as a Jewish tradition which has erroneously been attributed to Jesus. But if it is neither—if it is clearly distinct both from the faith of the church and from Judaism—then it may be safely accepted as authentic.[23]

This would mean, of course, that any appeal to Scripture by Jesus is at once suspect. This approach produces an improbable view both of Jesus and of the early church. Jesus becomes an

eccentric who took almost nothing from His environment. The
church becomes inexplicable, since it took almost nothing from
its Master. Rather, it so altered what it received from and about
Him that its teachings are in sharp contrast to the few genuine
sayings of His that it preserved.

Such an approach is possible only on the suppositions of a long
interval between the uttering of Christ's words and their being
committed to writing and of a general lack of interest in preserving His words accurately. The widely accepted notion that
the church was almost entirely dependent on oral tradition for
forty or more years is itself highly questionable. The idea that it
had little concern to preserve accurate accounts of the words and
deeds of Jesus is even more improbable. In Judaism oral material was learned verbatim and passed on verbatim, as "holy
tradition." There is nothing to suggest that Christians learned
vast amounts of tradition mechanically but there is much to
suggest that salient material was memorized and carefully
handed on. Much of the teaching of Jesus is in easily memorized
form. Throughout the New Testament special respect is shown
for the sayings of Jesus. For instance, in 1 Corinthians 7:8, 10,
12, 25, 40, Paul declares his own words to be authoritative, yet
puts the words of the Lord on a special plane.

> Where Paul has no saying of Jesus to quote, he does not presume
> to invent one. While quotations of the words of Jesus in the
> epistles are not common, we have no evidence of the attribution
> to Jesus in the epistles of sayings invented to meet contemporary
> needs, nor do we find in the sayings attributed to Jesus in the
> gospels material culled from Pauline or other known Christian
> writings. The words of Jesus were treated as *sui generis*.[24]

The New Testament writers faithfully protected and transmitted
the words of their Lord.

To one who has been captured in heart and mind by the Jesus
of the Gospels, there appears to be a host of reasons for believing
in the authenticity of the records. To regard the great mass of
Gospel teaching as the creation of the Christian community
seems to posit a marvelous effect without a plausible cause. Here
is what may fairly be claimed as the greatest literature of all
time, yet supposedly created by the imaginations of an undistin-
guished community! It seems far easier and more reasonable to
suppose that the Jesus of the Gospels created the community

than that the community created the Jesus of the Gospels.

Many features in the Gospels have an appearance of primitiveness and originality. Included are teachings that are liable to offend or perplex; the term "Son of man" (though hardly used in the early church) is a favorite title; the theme of the kingdom of God has far greater prominence in the Gospels than in the rest of the New Testament; Aramaisms abound. The Gospels contain no material on such burning issues in the apostolic church as circumcision or charismatic gifts. Little is said about baptism, the Gentile mission, food laws, and relations between church and state. What little material there is on these matters relates uniquely to the period of Jesus' ministry and not to the form in which these issues confronted the church thirty years later. The question of Sabbath observance and of Corban apparently were not live issues at a later period.

It seems hard to conceive that a religious movement so close to the life and death of its founder would not be interested in His words and deeds. In his Gospel prologue Luke claims to be giving accurate information. To one who believes in the authenticity of the Gospels the person of Jesus has depth and breadth and balance and richness. He is real. He is known. What He said and what He did are of vital importance.

For one who does not see Him so, there is no invincible argument. It may be, on the contrary, that for such a person it is the scientific approach that seems invincible in the twentieth century. If, therefore, science "demands" a skeptical approach to miracles, then only a skeptical approach to the Gospels, and to the Christ of the Gospels, will do. We may wonder what ground is left for faith in Christ and whether belief in the incarnation by one who holds this view must not be something quite different from that of historic Christianity. Such an antimiraculous, supposedly scientific approach is itself based on the unproved and unprovable dogma that nature behaves with invariable uniformity—a notion that is both unbiblical and unprovable and which we reject. To believe that God has both revealed Himself in Christ and has given us a true portrait of Christ in the Gospels is, even on the purely human level, no more contrary to reason than is skepticism. In fact, if such revelation is indeed true and God-given, it is infinitely more reasonable than skepticism. By studying it and believing it, we are able to think God's thoughts after Him.

For Further Reading

The question of miracles is helpfully discussed by C. S. Lewis in *Miracles* (New York: Macmillan, 1963). The key miracle is, of course, the Resurrection. If this event took place, there is no difficulty in accounting for the other miracles. In *The Evidence for the Resurrection* (Downers Grove, Ill.: InterVarsity, n.d.) J. N. D. Anderson treats the subject concisely and clearly. D. P. Fuller's *Easter Faith and History* (Grand Rapids: Eerdmans, 1968) discusses related critical and theological questions. I hope to deal with the harmony of the resurrection narratives (together with the dating and interrelation of the four Gospels) in a later volume.

On a more popular level, the following are useful in studying the authenticity of the Gospels:

Bruce, F. F. *The New Testament Documents: Are They Reliable?* 5th ed. London: Inter-Varsity, 1960.

Green, E. M. B. *Runaway World.* London: Inter-Varsity, 1968. See chapter 1.

Phillips, J. B. *Ring of Truth.* Wheaton: Shaw, 1977.

Among the more scholarly books, written from a variety of standpoints, the following contain valuable material:

Baird, J. A. *The Justice of God in the Teaching of Jesus.* London: SCM, 1963. See chapter 1, "The Question of the Historical Jesus."

Borchert, O. *The Original Jesus.* London: Lutterworth, 1933. The author argues the difficulty of believing that first-century thought could have invented the Jesus of the Gospels.

Bruce, F. F. *New Testament History.* New York: Doubleday, 1972. This book is the standard conservative history.

France, R. T. *Jesus and the Old Testament.* London: Tyndale, 1971.

Guthrie, Donald. *New Testament Introduction,* rev. ed. Downers Grove, Ill.: InterVarsity, 1971. This book is the standard conservative introduction.

Hanson, A. T., ed. *Vindications.* London: SCM, 1966. Most of the contributors to this volume are form critics who do not share the skeptical attitude toward Gospel history held by many followers of this school.

Jeremias, Joachim. *New Testament Theology,* vol. 1. London: SCM, 1971 library repr. ed. New York: Scribner. See chapter 1, "How Reliable Is the Tradition of the Sayings of Jesus?"

Leon-Dufour, Xavier. *The Gospels and the Jesus of History.* New York: Doubleday, n.d.

Morris, Leon. *Studies in the Fourth Gospel.* Grand Rapids, Eerdmans, 1969.

Moule, Charles F. D. *The Birth of the New Testament,* 2nd ed. Naperville, Ill.: Allenson, 1966.

Redlich, E. B. *Form Criticism: Its Value and Limitations.* London: Duckworth, 1939. This is a useful critique of the formative period of *Formgeschichte.*

THE APOSTLES' VIEW
OF SCRIPTURE

Edwin A. Blum

Edwin A. Blum is Associate Professor of Historical Theology, Dallas Theological Seminary, Dallas, Texas. He is a graduate of Dallas Theological Seminary (Th.M. and Th.D.) and the University of Basel (D.Theol.). He has done graduate study at Rice University. Dr. Blum has been an instructor, Dallas Bible College, and instructor and Assistant Professor in New Testament Literature and Exegesis and Assistant Professor of Systematic Theology, Dallas Theological Seminary. He is a teaching elder at Trinity Fellowship, Dallas, and the director of the Theological Students' Fellowship (TSF/IV).

CHAPTER SUMMARY

The New Testament writers wrote because of their connection with and commitment to Jesus Christ. They shared the same high view of Scripture that their Master held. The Old Testament was for them *the authority* in religious matters because God had spoken it by His Spirit through human writers. The New Testament writers also reveal that their own writings are the commands of the Lord and equal in authority to the Old Testament revelation. This authority is not human authority but the Spirit of Christ giving the commands of Christ to His people.

THE APOSTLES' VIEW
OF SCRIPTURE

I N SEEKING to understand the Bible, it is basic to listen to what the Bible says about itself. Its own self-testimony should be the source of the crucial doctrine of Scripture. What do the documents themselves say? How did the human authors of the New Testament view the Old Testament? How did they view their own writings? Were they aware of other New Testament writers? If so, how did they view their writings? Since Christ's view of the Bible is explored in chapter 1, I will not deal with that subject except to note the connection between Christ's view and that of His apostles.[1]

THE CONNECTION TO CHRIST

Jesus Christ is the central theme of the New Testament and the foundation of its existence as writings. The men who wrote did so because of their connection with Jesus Christ. Without Him, they would not have written what they did nor would they have written in the manner they did.[2] The material they record of Jesus' view of Scripture is written because of their personal faith in Jesus and because of His instruction of His disciples. The Gospel writers portray Him as the great Teacher, in addition to their main portrayal of Him as the Savior. As the true Teacher, He teaches the way of God in truth (Matt. 22:16). In particular, He is the Teacher of the Word of God. He is the only one who fully understands its force and is able to expound its significance (cf. Matt.

4:4-10; 5:17-44; 7:28-29).[3] The views of Jesus on the Old Testament are also the views of the Gospel writers. These men depict Jesus and His views with obvious approval, and an examination of their own use of Scripture reveals the same reverence and submission to its authority as He showed. In particular, the following six passages may be cited: Matthew 5:17-19; 22:23-32; Luke 17:16-17; 18:31; 24:25, 44; John 10:33-36.[4] These passages not only show us Christ's belief that the Old Testament prophecies would be fulfilled to the most minute point, but they also provide evidence for the views of the Gospel writers themselves.[5]

All the New Testament writers are connected to Jesus in relation to His authority. Jesus in His ministry revealed Himself as having authority in His own words (Matt. 7:29; Mark 1:22, 27; Luke 4:32). The authority of His words was demonstrated in the sign deeds that He did (Mark 2:10; Luke 4:36). The mighty power or authority of the Father was given to the exalted Son in His resurrection. He could say, "All authority in heaven and on earth has been given to me" (Matt. 28:18). Because of this authority, He could and did delegate authority to His apostles (Matt. 28:19-20; John 20:21-23). These apostles form the human foundation of the church (Matt. 16:18-19; Gal. 2:9; Eph. 2:20). As part of their endowment, Jesus gave the promise of the Holy Spirit, who would guide and lead them into all truth (John 14:26; 15:26, 27; 16:13-15). The truth that the Spirit of truth taught them was about Jesus—truth that before His death, burial, and resurrection the disciples were unable to comprehend. But afterward the Holy Spirit enabled them to understand and to believe these events and their significance (cf. John 2:22). As the apostles were commissioned to preach the message of Jesus' death and resurrection, they were also instructed and enabled by the Holy Spirit to teach these truths to the church. Understanding the authoritative teaching ministry given the writers of Scripture in the enablement of the Holy Spirit of truth is a fundamental consideration in estimating the value and trustworthiness of their individual statements.

THE NEW TESTAMENT WRITERS' VIEW
OF THE OLD TESTAMENT

Quotations and Allusions to the Old Testament

In reading the New Testament, one is struck by the great number of quotations and allusions to the Old Testament.

Nicole estimates 295 quotations, with many more allusions—at least 10 percent of the New Testament text being Old Testament material.[6] D. Hay counts 239 quotations that use an introductory formula, 1,600 citations of the the Old Testament, and many more allusions to it.[7]

Old Testament material is used in a variety of ways. For example, it may be reproduced to support or to illustrate an argument, to serve as a point of departure in a discussion, or to act as a proof text. Constant throughout all New Testament books is the view that the Old Testament is authoritative. It is common among writers in the present day to cite an authority when it is needed. This procedure was followed by the ancient writers as well. For example, the Gospel of John contains fifteen direct quotations. Four are found in chapter 12, which concerns Jesus' entry into Jerusalem and His explanation of Jewish spiritual blindness. Another four citations are in chapter 19, which relates to Jesus' death. The remainder of the quotes are also at significant places. The author cites the Old Testament as authority—to establish his point, to explain an event or saying, or to demonstrate a fulfillment of prophecy.

In chapters 9, 10, and 11 of Romans, Paul illustrates the use of the Old Testament by a New Testament writer. In his letters he cites the Old Testament 93 times (1/3 of the total Old Testament citations, with introductory formulas, in the New); yet twenty-six of his quotes occur in these three chapters of Romans. Doubtless his reasons for quotation were manifold, but one of his main reasons was to give explanation and clarification of the difficult-to-understand problem of the Jewish people not recognizing and accepting Jesus as Messiah. The "hard" teachings of God's sovereign mercy and punishment are also buttressed by Old Testament Scripture (Rom. 9:12, 13, 15, 17).

To the apostles, the Old Testament Scripture was clearly their supreme authority! It is an absolute, not a relative, authority. They do not attempt to correct it, nor do they seek to put one Old Testament book or saying against another.[8] They assume it speaks with a unified voice. They plainly recognize that the books were written by human authors, but even more explicitly they maintain that *God* speaks in and through these writings (Acts 4:25; 28:25; Rom. 9:27, 29). The author of the book of Hebrews has a distinctive style of quotations in that he mentions the human authors of the Old Testament writings in only two places (9:20; 12:21). In all other cases, it is God the Father, Christ, or the Holy Spirit who speaks (see 1:5-13; 2:12-13; 3:7-11).

In light of the current controversy on inerrancy within evangelicalism, we would do well to pay close attention to the emphasis of the author of the Book of Hebrews. After two centuries of historical-critical study, many biblical scholars have focused their attention on "Paul's view" or "John's view" or "first Isaiah's view," to the near exclusion of what *God* is saying. Without lapsing into a docetic view of the human and divine authors, the modern evangelical should recognize that what the human author says, God says *in* and *through* him (see 1 Cor. 14:37; Gal. 3:8; Heb. 3:7; 4:7).[9] It is significant that men spoke and wrote, but far more significant that *God speaks*. That the author of *Hebrews* recognized this truth is clearly reflected in his use of Old Testament quotations.

The Introductory Formulas

The New Testament writers use various introductory formulas that help to understand their view of the Old Testament. One of the most common is the Greek expression *gegraptai*, "it is written." Shrenk discusses the use of *grapho* in its various forms and expressions and finds a similarity in both the Greek and Israelite employment. In both spheres, it is used as a legal expression for that which is authoritatively binding. "What is quoted as *gegraptai* is normative because it is guaranteed by the binding power of Yahweh, the King and Lawgiver."[10] Warfield's article on "It says:" "Scripture says:" "God says:" though old, is still valuable for its collection of material on authoritative citation.[11] To the New Testament writers, according to the constant interchange of the introductory formulas, Scripture speaking is God speaking (see Acts 13:34; Rom. 9:13, 15, 17).

The introductory formulas do not ignore the human authors of Scripture. Paul uses such expressions as: "He says also in Hosea" (Rom. 9:25); "Isaiah cries out" (Rom. 9:27); "As Isaiah foretold" (Rom. 9:29); "Moses says" (Rom. 10:19); and "Isaiah is very bold and says" (Rom. 10:20). Obviously Paul's view of inspiration gives full place to the human personalities. Yet, the words they write are God's words, given by the prophetic spirit (cf. 1 Cor. 2:12-14; 14:37).[12]

The Oracles of God

The expression *ta logia*, "the oracles," is often used by New Testament writers to describe the Old Testament. Paul, in speaking of the Jewish advantages over the Gentiles, says, "First of all, they have been entrusted with the very words of God" (Rom. 3:2). What does he mean by "very words"? In classical Greek the term was used to denote a declaration given by a god. In the Greek Old Testament (Septuagint) it is used in a variety of ways: to categorize an individual divine statement, to refer to God's commandments, or to speak of the Word of God in a general way (see Deut. 33:9; Ps. 119 [LXX, 118]; Isa. 28:13).[13] Romans 3:2 is best understood as referring to the whole Old Testament rather than to particulars of it. The expression would then mean that the *whole Old Testament is God's speech* in written form. The oracle may be given through a spokesman, but the ultimate product is "Thus says the Lord."

The other New Testament uses of the word are: (1) in Acts 7:38 concerning Moses, "He received living words to pass on to us"; (2) in 1 Peter 4:11, "If anyone speaks, he should do it as one speaking the very words of God"; and (3) in Hebrews 5:12, "You need someone to teach you the elementary truths of God's word all over again." Of these three texts, the Acts reference is next in significance to Romans 3:2 and stresses the divine origin of Moses' legislation.

The Scriptures

The writers of the New Testament constantly refer to the Old Testament writings as *graphē*, "Scripture." The term is used, in the singular or the plural, about fifty times in the New Testament. Originally the Greek word meant anything written or published, secular or sacred. In the New Testament it is used exclusively of the sacred writings, or Holy Scripture.[14] This use comes from Judaism, which possessed its Law (*Torah*), Prophets (*Nebiim*) and (other) writings (*Ketubim*).[15] The writers of the New Testament books (Jews in the main) can be expected to have held the positions of their contemporaries in regard to the Scriptures. Paul, for example, calls the Old Testament "Holy Scriptures" (Rom. 1:2). Schrenk characterizes the Judaistic view in these words:

> According to the later Jewish view, Scripture has sacred, authoritative, and normative significance. It is of permanent and

unassailable validity. As the dictate of God, it is given by His Spirit. This view referred originally to the Pentateuch [Law] but was then transferred to the Prophets and Writings. The implication of the doctrine of inspiration is that the revealed truth of God *characterizes every word* (italics mine).[16]

(The word *dictate* is here used in the sense of "will" or "commands.")

Old Testament passages such as the following show God's penetration into the personalities of the human authors of Scripture:

> The Spirit of the LORD spoke through me;
>   his word was on my tongue (2 Sam. 23:2).

> But the LORD said to me, "Do not say, 'I am only a child.' You must go to everyone I send you to and say whatever I command you. . . . Then the LORD reached out his hand and touched my mouth and said to me, "Now, I have put my words in your mouth" (Jer. 1:7-9).

> You will be my spokesman (Jer. 15:19; cf. 20:7-9).

> So Jeremiah called Baruch son of Neriah, and while Jeremiah dictated all the words the LORD had spoken to him, Baruch wrote them on a scroll (Jer. 36:4).

Consideration of the term *Scripture* and of the work of the Spirit of God in its production leads to examination of the three classical New Testament texts on the inspiration of the Old Testament.

2 Timothy 3:13–17

> Evil men and imposters will go from bad to worse, deceiving and being deceived. But as for you, continue in what you have learned and have become convinced of, because you know those from whom you learned it, and how from infancy you have known the holy Scriptures, which are able to make you wise for salvation through faith in Christ Jesus. All Scripture is God-breathed and is useful for teaching, rebuking, correcting and training in righteousness, so that the man of God may be thoroughly equipped for every good work (2 Tim. 3:13–17).

Paul, in the last letter he wrote, was writing to his young disciple, Timothy. He sought to prepare him and the growing infant church for the difficult days ahead. He himself had been persecuted, as would be all those who sought to live godly lives in the midst of an age of increasing wickedness. In the midst of conflict, it is natural to be anxious and perhaps irresolute. Paul wanted Timothy and, through him, the church to be strong and steadfast, not pulling back in the face of opposition against the truth. The church and its leaders must continue in their proclamation and teaching ministry with confidence and conviction. Timothy was to have confidence for two reasons. First, in contrast to the deception of the false teachers, Timothy knew the proven character of those from whom he had learned—his mother, his grandmother, and Paul. Second, his confidence was based on the foundation of the "sacred writings" (*hiera grammata*), in which he had been instructed since childhood.

These sacred writings are what we know as the Old Testament books and are so valuable because they have the ability to give the "wisdom that leads to salvation through faith which is in Christ Jesus." Scripture is not rightly used or understood unless through it one comes to faith in Jesus as the Messiah and personal Savior. In contrast to ungodly men, who may learn a great amount but never come to the knowledge of the truth (2 Tim. 3:1–9), the believer comes to know truth by scriptural instruction. In another passage, Paul speaks of "the truth that is in Jesus" (Eph. 4:21). It is Paul's conviction, of course, that Scripture speaks of the Messiah and that Jesus is the Messiah. "For what I received I passed on to you as of first importance: that Christ [Messiah] died for our sins according to the Scriptures, that he was buried, that he was raised on the third day according to the Scriptures . . ." (1 Cor. 15:3–4). In 2 Timothy 3:14–17, Paul expresses his firm purpose to help Timothy persevere (*mene*). Paul's reminder of the profitability and purpose of Scripture is his main emphasis, as is clearly seen by his use of "for" (*pros*) five times in vv. 16–17 and the use of "so that" (*hina*) in v. 17.

The crucial words in v. 16 are πᾶσα γραφὴ θεόπνευστος καὶ ὠφελιμος (*pasa graphē theopneustos kai ōphelimos*), translated, "All Scripture is God-breathed and is useful. . . ." The marginal note in NASB mentions the possible rendering of "Every Scripture inspired by God is also . . . ." By comparing various English translations, even the reader without a knowledge of Greek can quickly see the exegetical problems and possibilities. Conservative translations and commentators tend to favor "all Scripture" rather than "every Scripture." First, because the syntax of *pas* "all, every" with an anarthrous noun (a noun without an article) presents special problems. C. F. D. Moule, in his study of Greek idioms, comments that in 2

Timothy 3:16 πᾶσα γραφὴ θεόπνευστος "is most unlikely to mean *every inspired Scripture,* and much more probably means *the whole of Scripture* [is] inspired."[17] Second, the context favors the idea that Paul is thinking of the Old Testament in its entirety. Third, the translation "every Scripture" is ambiguous and has sometimes been taken to mean "Every *inspired* Scripture [is profitable]," suggesting that there may be other "Scripture" or parts of Scripture that are not inspired or profitable. Based on the Greek text alone—without consideration of the context, the usage of *graphē* in the New Testament, or the Jewish ideas of inspiration—such an interpretation is possible. But if one takes these other important factors into consideration, the rendering of "All Scripture" is preferable.

Other technical matters of translation are controverted in regard to this key text. In the NASB (All Scripture is inspired by God and profitable") the adding of the word *is* (not in the Greek text) and the translation of "and" for the Greek *kai* are sometimes disputed. The translation of "and" for *kai* is normal, but the less common rendering of "also" would almost be required if the copula *is* is inserted in a different place—as, for example, "Every inspired Scripture *is also* useful." The omission of the word for "is" is a common feature of Greek grammar.[18] The placing of "is" before "inspired and profitable" is justified because both words are adjectives and it seems natural to take them in parallel form as predicative. The structure of the sentence in Greek is the same as that of 1 Timothy 4:4, which is usually translated with both adjectives as predicative.[19]

Another item to be considered in this first key passage is the meaning of the adjective *theopneustos,* "inspired by God." Kelly holds that the literal meaning is "breathed into by God."[20] Lexicographers normally, however, translate "inspired by God."[21] In a fifty-page article on the meaning of this term, B. B. Warfield in 1900 concluded:

> From all points of approach alike we appear to be conducted to the conclusion that it is primarily expressive of the origination of Scripture, not of its nature and much less of its effects. What is θεόπνευστος is "God-breathed," produced by the creative breath of the Almighty. And Scripture is called θεόπνευστος in order to designate it as "God-breathed," the project of Divine inspiration, the creation of that Spirit who is in all spheres of the Divine activity the executive of the Godhead. The traditional translation of the word by the Latin *inspiratus a Deo* is no doubt

also discredited, if we are to take it at the foot of the letter. It does not express a breathing *into* the Scriptures by God. But the ordinary conception attached to it, whether among the Fathers or the Dogmaticians, is in general vindicated. What it affirms is that the Scriptures owe their origin to an activity of God the Holy Ghost and are in the highest and truest sense His creation. It is on this foundation of Divine origin that all the high attributes of Scripture are built.[22]

Warfield, therefore, stressed that the meaning of the term is "God-breathed" rather than "inspired" or "breathed into" by God. Many modern writers and lexicographers seem to ignore his work or give no evidence of knowing about it.[23]

The profitability of Scripture is due to its origin, which is "God-breathed." That is, profitable.

Another matter may be considered in relation to this passage. What were the Jewish or Hellenistic teachings of inspiration at this time? Paul Billerback, in his *Kommentar zum Neuen Testament aus Talmud und Midrasch*, has a section on the Jewish understandings of the concept.[24] The Law was often considered to be preexistent. It was taught to Moses, dictated to him, or even written directly by God Himself. The Prophets and Writings were also considered of divine origination by the early writers of Judaism. Three theories were offered. The oldest and dominant view was that God supplied the content of the books to the authors by inspiration. Another early view held that the contents were revealed to Moses at Sinai and transmitted by tradition. A later view maintained that God gave the contents of the Prophets and Writings to the preexistent souls of their authors at Mt. Sinai.

E. Schweizer says of the 2 Timothy 3:16 passage, "The usage is Hellenistic, hence Hellenistic inspiration manticism lies behind it → 345,4 ff."[25] In the Hellenistic world, Apollo was thought to fill a woman with his divine breath and so possess her. A variety of effects accompanied the possession, including Bacchantic frenzy, ecstatic speech and, at Delphi, prophecy.[26] But the New Testament does not use the distinctive language of the world of mythological enthusiasm.[27]

Several points should be noted. Whether one accepts a Hellenistic or a Judaistic background to the concept of "inspiration" in 2 Timothy 3:16, both stress God as the originator of the utterances or written material. From the New Testament viewpoint, Helleistic manticism would appear to be closer to demon posses-

sion than to the working of the Holy Spirit. In the biblical cases
of demon possession, the human personality seems often to be
overpowered and completely suppressed (see Matt. 15:22; Mark
5:3–7; Luke 9:39–42). The major Rabbinic conceptions, with
their stress on dictation, also do not seem to do justice to the
involvement of the human authors. In contrast, the New Testament conception of "inspiration" stresses divine origination but
at the same time clearly involves the human personality (see
Rom. 10:20; 1 Cor. 2:13; 14:37; 2 Peter 1:20–21).

2 Peter 1:19–21

A study of 2 Peter 1:20–21 may help in the understanding of
the biblical writers' view of the origin of the Old Testament
Scripture.

> And we have the word of the prophets made more certain, and
> you will do well to pay attention to it, as to a lamp shining in a
> dark place, until the day dawns and the morning star rises in your
> hearts. Above all, you must understand that no prophecy of
> Scripture came about by the prophet's own interpretation. For
> prophecy never had its origin in the will of man, but men spoke
> from God as they were carried along by the Holy Spirit (2 Peter
> 1:19–21).

Peter, in his second letter, writes to remind Christians of the
basic truths of Christianity, so they will be firmly established in
the truth even after his death (1:12–15).[28] The apostolic message
about the glory of Jesus is not mythical; it is based on eyewitness
testimony of the apostles themselves (1:16–18). The heavenly
testimony that God gave to His Son at the Transfiguration
confirmed the message of prophecy (1:17–19). In view of the
christological fulfillment and the Father's confirmation of the
Old Testament Scriptures, Christians are to study and pay
careful attention to the Word of God. It will provide light in the
midst of murky darkness for the Christian until the return of
Christ, who will bring the bright daylight of God's day and
transform the heart (1:19). Most translators and commentators
interpret verse 20 as a warning against the misuse of Scripture
through faulty interpretation. The correct interpretation is the
one intended by the Holy Spirit, since He is the originator of the
prophecies.[29] The verse makes good sense if translated, "Recognize this truth to be of the utmost importance—that no prophecy
of Scripture arises from private untying. . . ."[30] The critical word

is *epilyseos* and the basic idea of both the noun and the related verb in classical Greek is to "release from" or "loose" or "untie." The derived meanings shade into "solving difficulties" or "giving explanations" or even into the idea of origination.

Whichever view is taken of verse 20, the thought of verse 21 is not seriously affected. But if the *origination*, rather than the *interpretation*, of Scripture is the subject of verse 20, verse 21 becomes a conclusion to the argument of the paragraph. The *gar*, "for," explains the origin of the prophetic word to which the Christian is to pay careful attention. Christians can have confidence because the human writers of Scripture were not like the false prophets who merely spoke their own ideas and who, in the Old Testament, were often condemned.

> This is what the LORD Almighty says: "Do not listen to what the prophets are prophesying to you; they fill you with false hopes. They speak visions from their own minds, not from the mouth of the LORD" (Jer. 16:23).
>
> This is what the Sovereign LORD says: Woe to the foolish prophets who follow their own spirit and have seen nothing! (Ezek. 13:3).

Peter affirms that "prophecy never had its origin in the will of man, but men spoke from God as they were carried along by the Holy Spirit" (2 Peter 1:21). This text remarkably clarifies the cooperation of the dual authors of Scripture. Green explains the key figure of speech in this passage.

> He [Peter] uses a fascinating maritime metaphor in verse 21 (cf. Acts xxvii. 15, 17, where the same word, *pheromene*, is used of a ship carried along by the wind). The prophets raised their sails, so to speak (they were obedient and receptive), and the Holy Spirit filled them and carried their craft along in the direction He wished. Men spoke: God spoke.[31]

Peter's teaching on inspiration may be taken as common to all the New Testament writers. Extrabiblical sources confirm the common belief among the Jews concerning the production of the Scriptures. To the testimonies cited in Strack-Billerbeck (n. 24), the testimony of the Qumran writings (e.g., 1 QS 8:16; 6 QD 2:12) and those of Philo and Josephus may be added. An interesting passage occurs in Josephus's work, *Against Apion* (1. 37, 38), in which he affirms that the Jewish prophets obtained knowledge of their history:

... through the inspiration which they owed to God, and committing to writing a clear account of the events of their own time just as they occurred—it follows, I say, that we do not possess myriads of inconsistent books, conflicting with each other. Our books, those which are justly accredited, are but two and twenty, and contain the record of all time.[32]

In the light of the current controversy over inerrancy, in which some affirm errors in the inspired text, the words of Josephus show that the idea of an inspired-errant Bible is not new. Modern attempts to synthesize the biblical concept of inspiration with the historical-critical method are but contemporary reflections of the same view. For example, Herman Ridderbos claims," We see occasionally that one evangelist purposely introduces changes into what another has written, sometimes, apparently, in order to correct him."[33] In spite of his generally conservative position, his guarded language, and his desire to avoid an "abstract theological concept of the inspiration and authority of the Scriptures," Ridderbos falls into an unbiblical view of inspiration. He proposes a "conservative historical-critical view."[34]

Galatians 3:16

An instructive example of the New Testament writers' view of the Old Testament is Paul's use of the word *seed* in Galatians 3:16—"The promises were spoken to Abraham and to his seed. The Scripture does not say 'and to seeds,' meaning many people, but 'and to your seed,' meaning one person, who is Christ." Other examples of the New Testament writers' belief in the accuracy of the Old Testament, down to the most minute detail, could be cited (e.g., Matt. 21:2–5 and John 19:23–24, which speak of fulfillment even to the point of including the original Hebrew parallelism). Paul's argument in Galatians 3:16 is classic, for it sees significance in the use of a singular rather than a plural noun. Many have objected to Paul's understanding as fanciful or as being merely a traditional rabbinic view without merit. Yet the whole argument of Galatians 3 is based on this one linguistic point. In it Paul argues that "faith hearers," not "law doers" are Abraham's true descendants. The Judaizers were teaching that to participate in the Abrahamic blessings, the Galatian Christians would have to keep the Law. Paul counters with the argument that if people subsequent to the giving of the

Law become Abraham's seed by doing the law, then there are *two kinds of seed*: "faith-hearer seed" and "law-doer seed." Paul notes that the Old Testament does not speak of "seeds" but "seed." He sees great significance in the grammatical form. It may be noted that the use of a collective singular stresses the idea of one *kind* of seed rather than one numerical seed, for Christ is *the* seed and Christians are also seed (v. 29).

THE NEW TESTAMENT WRITERS' VIEW OF THEIR OWN WRITINGS

The New Testament writers' viewed their authority as coming from God. Paul, in particular, calls himself an apostle, a herald, a witness, and an ambassador (Rom. 1:1, 5; Gal. 1:8, 9; 1 Thess. 2:13; 1 Tim. 2:7).[35] He declared that the letters he wrote were to be read in the churches and obeyed (Col. 4:16; 2 Thess. 3:14). This public reading followed the practice of the synagogue, in which the Old Testament writings were read (Luke 4:16–17; Acts 13:15). The new prophetic word is now also to be read and obeyed (Rev. 1:3).

Within Paul's letters, one finds many indications of his conviction that what he is communicating is authoritative. First Corinthians 2:13 reads, "This is what we speak, not in words taught us by human wisdom but in words taught by the Spirit, expressing spiritual truths in spiritual words." The sentence probably does not refer directly to Paul's writing ministry but rather to his preaching and teaching. His primary point is that the Spirit teaches him, so that what he teaches is not his own human wisdom but divine. First Corinthians 7:12 reads, "To the rest I say this (I, not the Lord). . . ." Contrary to some interpretations, Paul is not here disclaiming inspiration or authority for what he says, but rather he is distinguishing the word of command that the Lord Jesus gave during the days of His stay on earth (v. 10) from that which Paul now gives as a command to the people of God in a new situation with the spread of the gospel.[36] In support of this interpretation it should be noted that Paul's command (*diatasso*, "I order" or "command") is to all the churches (1 Cor. 7:17).

In the same letter he writes, "If anyone thinks he is a prophet or spiritually gifted, let him acknowledge that what I am writing to you is the Lord's command" (1 Cor. 14:37). Paul's writing to the church of Corinth is linked with the Lord's command. To ask

the question, which then troubled the church): "Are there errors
in the Scripture (Old Testament) or in the New Testament letters?" and to wonder, "How would Paul have answered?" is
interesting. Could Paul have conceived of a command of the
Lord with error in it? Could he have said, "Christ is speaking
through me" (2 Cor. 13:3) and thought of that speaking as erroneous or imperfect? Certainly Christ, "in whom are hidden all
the treasures of wisdom and knowledge" (Col. 2:3) and who is
truth Himself (John 14:6) could not err.

Other New Testament writers give similar witness. Luke, for
example, in the prologue to his Gospel (1:1–4), mentions his care
in writing so that the reader's faith may be built on unshakable
historical fact. John also affirms that the things about which he
writes actually took place and were, in fact, done in the presence
of witnesses (John 20:30) and that his own eyewitness testimony
about Jesus is true (John 19:35). In addition, there is the promised Holy Spirit, who would remind, teach, and guide the apostles regarding all truth (John 14:26; 15:26; 16:13).[37] Peter states
that apostolic witness is not based on error or myth but on
eyewitness experience (2 Peter 1:16). John in the Book of Revelation states that what he writes is the word of God, to which or
from which not one word should be added or deleted, under
penalty of a curse (1:1, 2, 11; 22:18–19). Believers are to read the
book and obey it (1:3).

In 1 Timothy 5:18 Paul writes, "For the Scripture says 'Do not
muzzle the ox while it is treading out the grain,' and 'The worker
deserves his wages.'" The first quotation comes from Deuteronomy 25:4 and the second from Luke 10:7. The most normal
inference is that Paul considers both Deuteronomy and Luke to
be Scripture.

In conclusion, the words of Peter are profitable to remember:

> So then, dear friends, since you are looking forward to this, make
> every effort to be found spotless, blameless and at peace with him.
> Bear in mind that our Lord's patience means salvation, just as
> our dear brother Paul also wrote you with the wisdom that God
> gave him. He writes the same way in all his letters, speaking in
> them of these matters. His letters contain some things that are
> hard to understand, which ignorant and unstable people distort,
> as they do the other Scriptures, to their own destruction.
> Therefore, dear friends, since you already know this, be on
> your guard to that you may not be carried away by the error of
> lawless men and fall from your secure position. But grow in the

grace and knowledge of our Lord and Savior Jesus Christ. To him
be glory both now and forever! Amen (2 Peter 3:14–18).

Peter warns of false teachers and their erroneous understanding
of Scripture. He calls *Paul's writings* "Scriptures" (on the same
level as the Old Testament), which some do not understand and
which many distort. This warning to the church should cause us
to listen carefully to Scripture to see what the Spirit is saying
through it. May the church faithfully hold to the view of Scripture that Christ and His apostles held. Only in so doing can we
be truly biblical in our theology.

ALLEGED ERRORS
AND DISCREPANCIES
IN THE ORIGINAL MANUSCRIPTS
OF THE BIBLE

Gleason L. Archer

Gleason L. Archer is Professor of Old Testament, Trinity Evangelical Divinity School, Deerfield, Illinois. He holds degrees from Harvard College (B.A. and A.M.), Princeton Theological Seminary (B.D.), Suffolk University Law School (LL.B.), and Harvard Graduate School (Ph.D.). Dr Archer has authored In the Shadow of the Cross; *a translation of* Jerome's Commentary on Daniel; *two commentaries,* The Epistle to the Hebrews *and* The Epistle to the Romans; *and* Survey of Old Testament Introduction. *Before coming to Trinity in 1965, he served as student pastor of two churches in New Jersey; Assistant Pastor of Park Street Church, Boston, Massachusetts; and Professor of Biblical Languages and Acting Dean at Fuller Theological Seminary, Pasadena, California. He has served as president of the New England Association of Christian Schools and is a member of the Council of ICBI.*

CHAPTER SUMMARY

This chapter discusses certain difficulties in Scripture—difficulties that are referred to by some as "errors"—and demonstrates why these do not pose serious problems. Specifically this paper addresses the difficulties raised by two authors: William LaSor in *Theology, News and Notes* and Dewey Beegle in *Scripture, Tradition and Infallibility*. Some of the difficulties La Sor is concerned with are the discrepancies in numbers between Chronicles and Samuel/Kings, the differences in the resurrection narratives, the dating of the Exodus, and Peter's denial of Christ. Beegle lists only one area that concerns La Sor, but poses several others that he feels are damaging to the doctrine of the inerrancy of Scripture—such as the length of the reign of King Pekah of Israel, the age of Terah when Abraham left Haran, the burial place of Jacob, the length of Israel's sojourn in Egypt, and how many times the cock crowed after Peter's denial of Christ. This paper shows how all of these alleged errors and difficulties have reasonable explanations.

ALLEGED ERRORS
AND DISCREPANCIES
IN THE ORIGINAL MANUSCRIPTS
OF THE BIBLE

I N A 1976 publication of Fuller Seminary an article appears by William LaSor entitled, "Life under Tension—Fuller Theological Seminary and 'The Battle for the Bible.' "[1] In this memoir concerning the first seventeen years of Fuller Seminary's history, LaSor makes a plea for a concept of biblical authority that preserves the theological errorlessness of Scripture without vouching for its freedom from factual mistake in matters of history or physical science. He states firmly: "I believe that the Bible is without error, but I refuse to let someone else define what that means in such a way that I have to go to ridiculous extremes to defend my faith." In other words LaSor prefers a defense for the Christian faith that does not require support of the trustworthiness of Scripture in areas where its veracity can be factually tested. He regards the alleged inaccuracies of the biblical text in regard to names, numbers, genealogies, and episodical details as being of minor importance and hardly worth arguing about. He even suggests that Christ would regard dispute about such details as inconsequential, in the same class with tithing mint, dill, and cummin. He makes this query: "I wonder what he [Jesus] thinks of our internecine battle over the lesser matters of Scripture."

To my mind it is clear what Christ thinks about the importance of the total trustworthiness of Scripture. In His acceptance of the historicity of Jonah's adventure with the great fish (Matt. 12:40), of the destruction of almost all mankind by a flood in the days of Noah (Matt. 24:38–39), of the miraculous feeding of the Israelite host during the Exodus wanderings (John 6:49), and of such precise details as the three and one-half years of Elijah's famine (Luke 4:25), the Lord Jesus made it clear that, regardless of the skepticism of unbelieving critics, these events took place in history just as the Old Testament records them. It is safe to say that in no recorded utterance of Jesus and in no written or spoken statement of His apostles is there any suggestion of scientific or historical inaccuracy in any Old Testament record. Whatever the Hebrew Scriptures affirmed—whether in regard to theology, history, or science—was assumed to be trustworthy and accurate at every level and in every detail, according to the intention of the original author. To the naturalistic skepticism of the Sadduccees, who denied the resurrection of the dead, Jesus yielded no ground. He showed from God's recorded affirmation to Moses at the burning bush (Exod. 6:3) that Abraham, Isaac, and Jacob were alive and well four centuries after their deaths. Christ and the apostles firmly believed that all mankind were descended from a historical Adam and Eve (Matt. 19:4–5; Rom. 5:12–19; 1 Tim. 2:13–14), exactly as recorded in Genesis 1—3.

Since these and other such facts are rejected by modern scientists who are not committed to the Christian position, and likewise by nonevangelical Bible scholars and theologians, the issue seems to be drawn at this very point, which has nevertheless been downgraded even by some evangelicals to the status of a minor detail, not worthy of "internecine strife" among professing Christians. To Jesus Himself matters of technical accuracy were of real importance, and He showed Himself unswayed by considerations of "scientific probability" or historical likelihood, which bulk so large in the eyes of those today who reject the inerrancy of Scripture.

It would have been strange if Christ had restricted His beliefs and teachings to the bounds of historical or scientific probability, since nothing in the universe could have been so improbable as God's becoming man through the virgin birth. Compared to the unlikelihood of the Incarnation, other objections regarding probability fade into insignificance. Yet it is because of this "near impossibility"—that He who died for us on the cross was both Man and God, in two distinct natures and yet in one person—that fallen mankind has hope of salvation and eternal life. We must therefore conclude that *any* event or fact related in Scripture—whether it pertains to doctrine, science, or history—is to be accepted by the Christian as totally reliable and trustworthy, no matter what modern scientists or philosophers may think of it.

God's written revelation came in inerrant form, free from discrepancies or contradictions, and this inerrancy contributes to its achieving its saving purpose. If there were genuine mistakes of any sort in the original manuscripts, it would mean, obviously, that the Bible contains error along with truth. As such it would become subject to human judgment, just like any other religious document. The validity of such judgment, of course, depends upon the judge's own knowledge and wisdom. If he rejects the truth of the scriptural record simply because it seems to him to be unlikely or improbable, then he is in danger of eternal loss. The charge of scriptural self-contradiction or factual error is to be taken quite seriously; it cannot be brushed off as a matter of minor consequence. At stake is the credibility and reliability of the Bible as authentic revelation from God.

In a court of law, particularly in a criminal case, the trustworthiness of a witness is of prime importance. The cross-examining attorney will make every effort to prove that the witness cannot be believed, that he is not a truthful person. The attorney may put various kinds of questions to the witness in an endeavor to trip him up in a discrepancy, thus showing the jury that in one statement or the other the witness must be lying or confused. Even though the discrepancy may pertain to a matter not directly germane to the case, the jury's confidence in the witness's general credibility is necessarily shaken, and they may reasonably reject his testimony relating to other, more important matters.

It is in this way that antisupernaturalists and rationalists attack the Bible's overall trustworthiness, by attempting to show that Scripture contains various discrepancies and contradictions and demonstrable errors in matters of history and science. If they are honest and careful, they are as justified in this procedure as is the lawyer cross-examining a witness. For this reason there is no such thing as an inconsequential scriptural error. If any part of the Bible can be proved to be in error, then any other part of it—including the doctrinal, theological parts—may also be in error. We are referring here, of course, to the original manuscripts in Hebrew, Aramaic, and Greek; we make no such claim concerning later copies of those manuscripts.

After these preliminary observations, I would like to discuss the nine specific examples cited by LaSor that cause him to question the infallibility or the factual trustworthiness of Scripture in matters of history and science. None of these alleged problems have been unnoticed or unanswered by Bible scholars of former generations. Since, however, they have been raised anew in the current debate, it seems appropriate to deal with them once again.

1. Numerical Discrepancies in Historical Books

In 2 Samuel 10:18 we read that in his defeat of a Syrian commander named Shobak, David slew seven *hundred* men of their chariotry. But in the parallel account in 1 Chronicles 19:18, he slew the men of seven *thousand* chariots. Here we have a discrepancy in the Masoretic Text that involves what amounts to a decimal point. Yet there is nothing to prove that this discrepancy existed in the original manuscripts of Samuel and Chronicles. Errors of this kind are found in various passages of the Old Testament, most probably because of the difficulty of making out numerals when copying from a worn-out or smudged *Vorlage* (the earlier manuscript that the scribe reproduces). It is very easy to leave off or inadvertently add a "zero" when copying down a number in round figures. The ancient systems of numerical notation were susceptible to this kind of mistake, for they too used decimal notations that were as easily confused as Arabic or Roman numerals. LaSor implies that it is generally in Chronicles that the higher number occurs (he suggests seven or eight examples),[2] but it should be noted that there are also quite a few instances of discrepancy in the other direction. In 2 Samuel 10:18, for example, the figure of forty thousand is given for the Syrian *cavalry,* whereas the Chronicles parallel lists the forty thousand as *infantrymen*—the latter being more credible. In this case, the exaggeration is on the side of Samuel rather than Chronicles. The same is true of 2 Chronicles 36:9, which gives the age of Jehoiachin at his accession as eight, whereas in 2 Kings 24:8 the age given is eighteen. Again, in 1 Kings 4:26 Solomon is said to have built forty thousand stalls for his warhorses, but in 2 Chronicles 9:25 the figure is four thousand.

A different type of discrepancy appears in 1 Chronicles 11:11, which states that in a single engagement the Hebrew champion Jashobeam slew three hundred of the foe; 2 Samuel 23:8 makes the figure eight hundred. In 1 Samuel 6:19 the figure of fifty thousand and seventy as the number of Beth-shemesh men slain by the Lord for their sacrilege seems surprisingly high; however, this may be another example of garbling decimals in the process of textual transmission (the account is omitted in Chronicles, so we have no comparison). There appear to be eighteen numerical discrepancies between Chronicles and Samuel/Kings; of these, fully a third have higher figures in Samuel/Kings than in Chronicles.[3] In light of these facts, the charge that the author of Chronicles exaggerated numerals in order to enhance the glory of ancient Israel (or for some other reason) seems ill-founded. (Although he does not mention it, LaSor is doubtless familiar with this theory set forth by Henry Preserved Smith in the 1890s).

2. GENEALOGIES OF CHRIST

The second major discrepancy LaSor mentions pertains to the genealogies of Christ as given in Matthew 1 and in Luke 3. It is true that from the reign of David onward lists of ancestors differ. More links are given in Luke than in Matthew. But it was understood by the church fathers that Matthew refers to the line of Joseph, the legal father of Jesus, whereas Luke gives the lineage of Mary, His mother.[4] There seems to be no valid reason for rejecting this explanation.

3. THE LOCATION OF JOSEPH'S GRAVE

In Acts 7:16 Stephen states that the bones of Joseph were laid in the tomb that *Abraham* had bought from the sons of Hamor in Shechem (there is good textual evidence for the variant, "the sons of Shechem"). But in Joshua 24:32 the remains of Joseph are said to have been laid in a plot of ground that *Jacob* had bought from the sons of Hamor, the father of Shechem. Does this not amount to a contradiction? Not necessarily. There is a parallel case in regard to the well of Beersheba, which Abraham dug. For the payment of seven lambs he bought from King Abimelech of Gerar the rights to the land in which the well was dug (Gen. 21:22–31). Nevertheless, because of the nomadic habits of Abraham and his family, it later became necessary for his son Isaac, after his father's death, to confirm his ownership by a sacrificial, covenant-sealing ceremony with Abimelech, possibly a son named after the father who had dealt with Abraham (Gen. 26:26–33). Apparently the original Abrahamic well had been stopped up by hostile tribesmen or had caved in from natural causes. At any rate, Isaac found it expedient to reestablish his right to a well that had belonged to Abraham. This being the case, there seems to be little difficulty in assuming that Jacob encountered a similar problem in claiming his ancestral rights to the burial field near Shechem. During his extensive sojourn there he had occasion to buy again the plot on which he pitched his tent (Gen. 33:18–20). Though there is no explicit mention of Abraham's purchase of this land in the Genesis account, Stephen, no doubt, was aware of it through oral tradition and saw fit to mention it. It is significant that Shechem was the region where Abraham erected his first altar after migrating to the Holy Land from Haran (Gen. 12:6–7).

4. The Number of Angels at Jesus' Tomb

In regard to the number of angels that appeared by the tomb of Jesus on Easter morning, LaSor points out that Matthew (28:5) mentions only one—as does Mark (16:5), who refers to him as a "young man" dressed in a white robe. But Luke (24:4) specifies two angels, and so does John (20:12), who says that Mary Magdalene saw them both. According to LaSor, these differing accounts add up to a discrepancy or contradiction. This is not necessarily the case. Several other instances occur in the Gospels where one account mentions two men, whereas corresponding accounts refer only to one. For example, in Matthew 8:28 we are told that *two* demoniacs came to meet Jesus when he landed near Gadara; Mark 5:2 and Luke 8:27, however, refer to but *one*. Apparently the more aggressive and articulate of the pair was the one named Legion; the other man, then, would have played no particular role in the conversation with Christ. The same could be true of Jesus' encounter with Bartimaeus outside Jericho. Matthew 20:30 indicates that *two* blind men petitioned Jesus for their sight; Mark 10:46 and Luke 18:35 mention only *one*. Again, the one specifically named was probably the more vocal of the two. Similarly, in the case of the angels mentioned above, only Luke records that two appeared to the three women at their first approach to the empty tomb. John (20:11) adds that Mary Magdalene came back to the tomb a second time, after

Peter and John had been there. It was then that Mary saw and talked to both angels as they sat by the tomb. Matthew indicates that the same angel caused the earthquake, rolled back the stone door, frightened away the guards, and spoke to the three women at their first approach. A careful comparison of the four accounts shows that two angels were involved, although the miracle-working angel was probably the more prominent of the two. There is no demonstrable discrepancy.

5. Other Numerical Discrepancies

LaSor's fifth example, or category of examples, has already been dealt with under item 1 above, relating to the number of chariots in 1 Chronicles 19:18 and the alleged tendency of the Chronicler to give numbers higher than the corresponding numbers in Samuel or Kings. So we come to his sixth problem.

6. The Source of the Potter's-Field Reference

LaSor notes that Matthew 27:9 attributes to Jeremiah a quotation from Zechariah 11:13. But this again is not too difficult a matter to clear up. Matthew 27:9 quotes partly from Zechariah: ". . . the handsome price at which they priced me! So I took the thirty pieces of silver and threw them into the house of the LORD to the potter" (11:13). But Matthew goes on to specify the *field* of the potter. Zechariah makes no mention of a field, which is the main point of the quotation, in the light of the preceding context relating to the purchase of a burial plot for paupers (Matt. 27:6–9). Only in Jeremiah do we find mention of the potter's field near Jerusalem (Jer. 19:2, 11). Jeremiah also mentions the purchase of a certain field for a specified number of shekels (Jer. 32:9). We therefore have a conflate of Zechariah and Jeremiah, rather than a quote from Zechariah alone. In such cases, where more than one Old Testament author is quoted, the general practice of New Testament writers was to refer only to the one who was the more famous. Compare Mark 1:2–3, where a conflate quotation is taken from Malachi 3:1 and Isaiah 40:3. Only Isaiah is referred to by name. The procedure is the same as with Matthew 27:9.

7. Dating of the Exodus

First Kings 6:1 states that the Exodus took place 480 years before the commencement of Solomon's temple. This comes out

to about 1446 B.C. Yet the Book of Exodus (1:11) refers to the city
of Raamses as the scene of the slave labor of the Israelites, implying that the Exodus must have taken place after 1300, if that
city was named after Rameses the Great. LaSor seems to imply
that the 1446 date is supported by 1 Kings 6:1 alone; yet this is
by no means true. In Judges 11:26 Jephthah is quoted as saying
to the Ammonite invaders who challenged the rights of Israel to
the territory just to the north of Moab: "For three hundred years
Israel occupied Heshbon, Aroer, the surrounding settlements
and all the towns along the Arnon. Why didn't you retake them
during that time?" Since Jephthah lived well before the time of
King Saul, he must have made this statement to the Ammonites
around 1100. If Israel had then possessed the land for 300 years,
the conquest of Canaan must have taken place by 1400. Add 40
years of wandering in the wilderness, and the date of the Exodus
comes out to near 1440. Again, Paul states in Acts 13:19–20 that
God gave the Israelites the land of Canaan for a possession until
the time of Samuel, for a period of 450 years. Therefore the
interval between the Exodus and the end of Samuel's career was
about 450 years. David's reign in Jerusalem began about 1000;
adding 450 years brings the date very near to 1446.

The reference (Exod. 1:11) to the city of Raamses is not strong
evidence for the proposed 1290 date for the Exodus. Obviously, if
the Exodus took place in 1290, and Moses was 80 years of age at
that time, and if the work on the city of Raamses took place before
Moses' birth, then there is no conceivable way in which there
could have been a city of Raamses, named after Rameses the
Great, in 1370—long before Rameses was born! The name
Ramose (in Egyptian, close in spelling to "Raamses") occurs as
the name of a nobleman in the reign of Amenhotep the Third,[5]
and there is good reason to believe—as Dr. William Albright
suggests—that the name was already current in the Hyksos
period, before Moses' birth in 1526.

The early chapters of Exodus indicate that extensive construction was under way at that time within commuting distance of
Goshen. Yet LaSor is under the impression that no building was
going on in the Delta region (where Goshen was located) during
the time of Thutmose III, who lived (1482-1447) prior to the
earlier dating (ca. 1440) of the Exodus. A careful examination of
the archaeological data, however, demonstrates that Thutmose
III maintained a palace in the Delta, in which his son,

Amenhotep II, was born, and from which the young prince used to ride out to the pyramids of Gizeh for target practice with his bow. Thutmose boasted in his obelisks of being "Lord of Heliopolis." He erected those obelisks in front of temples that he had built there (Heliopolis was located in the lower Delta, near the site of the modern city of Cairo). Other archaeological factors make the Rameses II date an impossibility, and the Thutmose III–Amenhotep II period the only reasonable option for the date of the Exodus.[6] What LaSor has brought up in this connection presents no embarrassment to biblical historical inerrancy.

8. Laver Measurements

The next example is first suggested by LaSor and then withdrawn, as constituting a very minor problem or no problem at all. It has to do with the measurements of the bronze "sea" of holy water in the court of Solomon's temple. First Kings 7:23 states that the diameter of this enormous laver was 10 cubits, and its circumference 30 cubits. If it was indeed a perfect circle, the circumference must have been slightly larger, since the relationship of circumference to diameter is 3.14159. But LaSor rightly recognizes that this is no serious problem, whether the 30 cubits is intended to be an approximate number, rounded off from the more precise 31.4 cubits, or whether it represents the ratio of the radius to the 6 chords that would have measured the *inside* circumference.[7]

9. The Number of Peter's Denials

LaSor criticizes Harold Lindsell's handling of the problem of Peter's three denials of Christ in the garden of the high priest.[8] Lindsell seems to rely principally on the work of Johnston M. Cheney, who concluded that there were no fewer than six denials by Peter as he fended off the accusations of the servants of Annas and Caiaphas. I, too, find this suggested solution unsatisfactory. The Gospels refer only to three denials, and Christ required Peter to reaffirm his love for Him three times in that memorable interview by the Sea of Galilee recorded in John 21. But a questionable interpretation of the data does not constitute error in the original manuscripts of the four Gospels.

As we compare the four Gospels, which supplement one another and together give us a fuller, composite picture stage by stage, we come to the following results: (1) On the eve of Peter's failure Jesus warned him, "Before the rooster crows twice (only Mark 14:30 adds "twice"), you will three times deny that you know me" (Mark omits "know"). There is no contradiction in the four accounts, though Mark alone adds one detail and omits another. (2) Peter was admitted to the outer court of the high priest after John had spoken to the doorkeeper, who may have been male (although *thyrōros* can be either gender). He then sat down in the court (Matt. 26:69) near a fire (Luke 22:56), and the girl who was doorkeeper on the inner side began to look intently at Peter and finally blurted out, "You, too, were with Jesus, the Galilean." (John adds:) "You aren't one of his disciples, are you?" To this Peter replied, "I am not!" (18:17). (3) Peter then wandered off into the porch of the building itself, but he continued to draw attention. Another servant girl said to the bystanders, "This fellow was with Jesus of Nazareth" (Matt. 26:71). She had probably picked up the idea from the female inner doorkeeper, and confirmed to the bystanders: "This fellow is one of them" (Mark 14:69). At this, one of the male bystanders leveled the accusation directly at Peter, saying, "You also are one of them" (Luke 22:58). Peter had by this time joined a group standing about a fire (a different fire from the one in the outer court, mentioned earlier), and so they, too, chimed in with the question, "Surely you are not another of his disciples, are you?" Peter answered, "I am not" (John 18:25). (4) Somewhat later, perhaps an hour after that second denial (Luke 22:59), a man who was a relative of Malchus (the soldier whom Peter had wounded at Gethsemane) spotted him and shouted, "Didn't I see you with him in the olive grove?" (John 18:26). Luke adds, "Certainly this fellow was with him, for he is a Galilean" (22:59). The other bystanders then took up the accusation, saying, "Surely you are one of them, for you are a Galilean" (Mark 14:70). "Surely you are . . ., for your accent gives you away" (Matt. 26:73). At this Peter began to panic and started cursing and swearing. "I don't even know who you're talking about!" (Matt. 26:74; Mark 14:71; Luke 22:60). (5) As soon as he had uttered these words, Peter noticed a rooster was crowing. He recalled with shame that Jesus had warned him the night before (after his boast of faithfulness unto death): "Before the rooster crows twice, you yourself will disown me three times!" It is not clear whether the rooster had crowed only once or whether it was twice by the time Peter noticed him. If it was only once, the triple denial obviously took place before the second crowing. We may thus piece together the various details in the four accounts and not come out with any genuine discrepancies or contradictions.

10. PHENOMENOLOGICAL LANGUAGE

LaSor's final objection is likewise leveled at Lindsell's reasoning, rather than at a discrepancy in the Scripture itself. He refers to Lindsell's comment that the Bible speaks in "phenomenological language"—which LaSor accepts as true. But he challenges Lindsell's statement that the ancients were not teaching that the sun revolves around the earth when they used phenomenological language. He suggests that they really did believe that the sun did the orbiting rather than the earth. He then adds, "At this point it seems to me that Lindsell is himself placing something above Scripture, namely modern scientific knowledge and theory."[9]

It appears that LaSor has left out of consideration the dual authorship of Scripture as he voices this criticism. I am at a loss to know why he does this, because I feel sure (on the basis of sixteen years of fellowship with him on the Fuller faculty) that he does believe God is the ultimate Author of the Bible, even though He employed human prophets and apostles to write down what He revealed to them. If we believe that God is the creator of all the phenomena of creation and the controller of all the laws of physics, then it must follow that there is no contradiction or discrepancy between the operations of nature and the revelations of Holy Scripture. How fully and completely the ancient human authors of the Bible understood such matters as the rotation of the earth and its yearly revolution around the sun can only be conjectured. Under the influence of God the Holy Spirit, Moses may have understood a good deal more than LaSor gives him credit for. But what Moses or the prophets or psalmists understood by the words they wrote down under inspiration is quite secondary to the question of what God Himself meant by those words.

From this standpoint it is quite proper to speak of the language of Scripture as being phenomenological. But even today everyone uses the geocentric terms "sunrise" and "sunset" without incurring the accusation of putting modern science above the authority of Scripture! If God is the author of the data of science and the author of the revelation of Holy Scripture, there can be no question of putting true science "above" the Bible. It is simply a question of our using the increasing knowledge of physics or astronomy or biology or geology—whatever the science may be—to understand more perfectly what the Divine Author meant by the terms He caused the human authors to use when matters of this sort were being discussed. God does not and cannot contradict Himself!

Dewey M. Beegle has done a similar study in his book *Scripture, Tradition and Infallibility*. In chapter 8 "Inerrancy and the Phenomena of Scripture"[10] he discusses eleven passages he considers damaging to the doctrine of scriptural inerrancy. Only one of these, the Acts 7:16 passage, was brought up by LaSor. We will deal with the others in the somewhat random order in which he presents them.

1. Jude's Reference to Enoch

Jude 14 reads, "Enoch, the seventh from Adam, prophesied. . . ." The problem here is that Jude has not drawn from the Old Testament, but apparently from the pseudepigraphical Book of Enoch (1:9). First Enoch 93:3 quotes Enoch as saying, "I was born the seventh in the first week, while judgment and righteousness still endured." Beegle infers therefore, that Jude thought that the Book of Enoch derived from the antediluvian patriarch himself, rather than from a writer in the later intertestamental period. Beegle then poses the question: "Is it possible that Abraham, Isaac, and Jacob and the Israelites knew of this oral tradition and yet failed to mention it? Hardly. It is equally difficult to show that God preserved the material by an oral tradition distinct from Abraham and the people of promise."[11]

In reply, let it be said that the detailed dialogue between Adam and Eve and the serpent in Eden and the comments of Yahweh Himself were without any question preserved by oral tradition for thousands of years before they were ever reduced to writing. Whether we date Adam around 10,000 B.C. or a few millennia later, there was a far greater time interval between Adam and Moses than between Enoch and Jude! Nor can Enoch's prophecy be said to be any less preserved by the "people of promise" than were the remarks of Adam, Eve, or Cain, which were finally written down by Moses in the late fifteenth century B.C.

There is absolutely no reason why pseudepigraphical works, such as the apocryphal books, may not have included some facts and reports that were historically accurate. Furthermore, it is certain that Abraham, Isaac, and Jacob knew far more about the deeds and words of their forebears, even from the time before the Deluge, than has been recorded for us in Genesis. For the most part, no more has been recorded for us concerning the words of Abraham, Isaac, and Jacob than what essentially relates to the pivotal experiences of their careers. The same is true of many other biblical figures, such as Elijah and Elisha in the books of 1 Kings and 2 Kings. It would be wrong to suppose that they prophesied nothing but what appears in that record.

2. JUDE'S REFERENCE TO MICHAEL AND SATAN

Jude 9 speaks of the archangel Michael contending with Satan over the body of Moses after Moses' death. Beegle remarks, "Joshua and the prophets never refer to any such struggle, so there is no biblical reason, aside from Jude's allusion, for believing in the actuality of the story." The underlying assumption seems to be that Jude had no other valid source of information but the Hebrew text of the Old Testament. In other words, although his writing was inspired, he enjoyed no advantage over twentieth-century Bible students in regard to knowledge of Moses' time. Furthermore, Beegle apparently feels that actions or statements referred to in Holy Scripture must appear more than once in the Bible in order to be trusted. This line of reasoning seems all the more strange from one who seems to accept John 3:16 as authentic and trustworthy, even though it occurs only once in the Bible. Beegle appears to apply his criteria very selectively, as it suits his basic purpose to prove the Bible contains error.

3. LENGTH OF PEKAH'S REIGN

Beegle condemns as mistaken the figures given in 2 Kings for the reign of King Pekah of Israel, who is said to have begun to reign "in the fifty-second year of Azariah" and to have reigned in Samaria for twenty years (15:27). Since Pekah did not begin to reign in Samaria until the death of Pekahiah, son of Menahem, in 739, a twenty-year reign would end up at 720—a year or two after the northern kingdom of Israel had been carried into captivity by the Assyrians. And, of course, the 720 date leaves no room for the nine-year rule of Hoshea, who lost his throne in 723 or 722.

Beegle shows familiarity with the solution worked out by Thiele, namely, that Pekah may well have laid claim to the throne of Israel at the same time Shallum or Menahem seized power in Samaria.[12] Pekah's domain may have been restricted to Gilead until he made some kind of deal with Pekahiah and secured an appointment in the army, which gave him access to the king. He then invaded the king's quarters with fifty loyal Gileadite henchmen and murdered him, installing himself as the rightful and legitimate king in Samaria (2 Kings 15:25). Beegle, however, insists that verse 27 makes the biblical author clearly in error, since this verse ends with the statement, "Pekah . . . became king of Israel in Samaria, and he reigned twenty years." Beegle makes this interesting comment: "The scribe who composed 2 Kings 15:32 was working up his synchronisms . . . about 125 to 150 years after the fall of Samaria."[13] (It should be noted that in assigning the composition of 2 Kings to the 570s B.C., Beegle fails to explain the eight instances of the phrase "to this day," which occur throughout the book, with the clear implication that the southern kingdom of Judah was still in power prior to the fall of Jerusalem in 587.) Beegle continues, "This slip may appear a bit foolish, but the scribe in Judah knew nothing of B.C. or A.D. and of the specific numbers we are using as dates." This comment leaves no doubt whatsoever as to Beegle's concept of the authors of the Bible—they had no guidance or control whatsoever from God the Holy Spirit, so far as avoiding error was concerned. They could make such obvious mistakes as to make them appear ridiculous in the eyes of modern historians. We are left to wonder why such bunglers were allowed to write the books of the Bible!

We are not, however, compelled to interpret 2 Kings 15:27 in exactly the way Beegle does. From the standpoint of the official government position at the time of Pekah's death, Pekah had been the only legitimate king of Israel during the entire twenty years, from 752 to 732. The reigns of Menahem and his son Pekahiah, from 752 to 740, were usurpations. Although Pekah was confined to Gilead for the first twelve years, he even then claimed the throne of Israel and regarded Samaria as his rightful capital, from which he had been unjustly excluded. Just as David is said in 1 Kings 2:11 to have reigned over Israel forty years, even though during the first seven years his authority was limited to the tribes of Judah and Simeon only, so Pekah's official reign was reckoned as twenty years in Samaria.

It was only natural for the contestant who ended up victorious in the dynastic struggle to claim the legitimacy of his throne for the entire period, from his first coronation in Gilead. This was quite in keeping with ancient practice. King Thutmose III of the Egyptian 18th Dynasty officially acceded to his father's throne in 1501 B.C., or a few years later. However, he was a mere infant at the time, and so his stepmother, Hatshepsut, became Queen Regent during his minority. But in the course of her regency she promoted herself to the authority and title of Pharaoh in her own right and even set up statues of herself adorned with a royal beard on her chin! About 1482 she was put out of the way—whether by assassination or by illness we do not know. It was not until this time that Thutmose's actual reign began, enduring until 1447. He was effectively in power for only thirty-five years, yet his official reign was reckoned as beginning in 1501, making a total of forty-eight or forty-nine years.[14]

4. DATING OF SENNACHERIB'S INVASION

Beegle rightly points out that there is a discrepancy between 2 Kings 18:1 ("In the third year of Hoshea . . . Hezekiah son of Ahaz king of Judah began to reign") and verse 13 of the same chapter. "In the fourteenth year of King Hezekiah's reign, Sennacherib king of Assyria attacked all the fortified cities of Judah and captured them." The third year of Hoshea was no later than 728. Apparently Hezekiah was installed as viceroy at that time (a frequent custom in Judah), and his father Ahaz lived on until 725, when Hezekiah became sole king. The fourteenth year of Hezekiah's reign therefore would be either 714 or 711, depending on which *terminus a quo* is chosen. But Sennacherib did not come to the throne in Nineveh until 705, and according to his own annals, the invasion of Judah took place in 701. Therefore it must have been in the twenty-fourth year of Hezekiah's reign rather than the fourteenth.

How are we to account for this discrepancy? Obviously a scribal error was made in the transmission of the decade numeral. If the *Vorlage* (earlier model copied from) had a blurred horizontal stroke, the numeral "20" preceding the "4" would have looked like a "10" (as numerical notations in the Elephantine Papyri clearly show). Or, if the number was spelled out, the error could have been caused by the mistaking of a *mem* for a *he* (the only difference in the Hebrew for "fourteen" and for "twenty-four," according to the spelling that prevailed in Isaiah's time). It is for this reason that E. J. Young in his Commentary on Isaiah (vol. ii. pp. 540–42) concludes that this is the most likely explanation for the mistaken reading in 2 Kings 18:13.

It should be noted that all other datings in 2 Kings are compatible with a 728 date of accession for Hezekiah (rather than the impossible 715 advocated by Thiele and some other conservative scholars). That is to say, 2 Kings 15:30; 16:1–2; 17:1; and 18:1 all support 728 in the clearest possible fashion. The textual correction (in 18:13) from "fourteen" to "twenty-four" is all that is needed to harmonize all the accounts. Here again no convincing case can be made for a mistake in the original manuscript.

5. THE TIME SPAN OF GENESIS 5 GENEALOGIES

Beegle belabors the point that the formula followed by the Hebrew authors (**A** became the father of **B** at such-and-such an age, lived such-and-such a number of years afterward until he died) compels us to conclude that this chapter teaches that the human race began at a very recent point in time—between 4004 of Ussher and the 3760 of Jewish tradition.[15] He argues—with some justice, perhaps—that it was not until the development of geological science and geochronology that evangelicals began to revise their interpretation of Genesis 5 to allow for gaps in the genealogical chain. He then raises the challenge: "But how did this relate to the intent of the author?" The clear assumption here is that Genesis 5 was authored by a naive, unscientific human author who did not know any better. But if 2 Peter 1:21 is not mistaken in its affirmation that the Old Testament authors were holy men borne along by the Holy Spirit as they wrote, then we must reckon with the intent of the divine Author as well as of the human author in regard to Genesis 5.

We have clear evidence from Luke 3:36 that there was at least one gap in the similar genealogy found in Genesis 10:24—Cainan the son of Arphaxad. Genesis 10:24 states that Arphaxad was the "father" of Shelah. Compare also Matthew 1:8, which states that Joram "begot" Uzziah—although from 2 Kings we know that Jehoram was the great-great-grandfather of Uzziah. Careful study of the actual usages of the Hebrew and Greek terms for "father" and "beget" reveals that they often signified nothing more definite than direct line of ancestry. Perfectly clear in the Gospel record is the fact that Jesus was addressed by suppliants as "Son of David," though He was born over 960 years after David died. 1 Chronicles 7:13 similarly lists Bilhah's grandsons as being her "sons."

It is highly significant that neither Genesis 5 nor Genesis 10 mentions any specific time period that totals up the entire span from Adam to Noah or from Noah to Abraham. Such specified periods, however, are found in connection with the date of the commencement of Solomon's temple (i.e., 480 years after the Exodus under Moses) and in connection with the length of the Hebrew sojourn in Egypt (430 years, according to Exod. 12:40). Likewise the interval between the founding of the northern kingdom in 931 B.C. and its dissolution in 721 is stated as 390 years (Ezek. 4:5). No such totals are given, however, in the pre-Abrahamic genealogies of Genesis.

6. THE AGE OF TERAH WHEN ABRAHAM LEFT HARAN

According to Genesis 11:26, maintains Beegle, Terah was 70 years old when Abraham left Haran (a highly debatable inference, as we shall see), and died there at the age of 205 (Gen. 11:32). But Genesis 12:4 specifies that Abraham was 75 when he migrated to Shechem, in the land of Canaan. On what grounds, then, could Stephen claim that Abraham did not leave Haran until after his father died (Acts 7:4)? This would mean that Abraham was 130, instead of 75, when he made the move to Canaan. We can assume that Terah lived on for a good 60 years after Abraham left him. Was not Stephen clearly in error, therefore, even though he was inspired by the Holy Spirit in his utterance (Acts 6:10; 7:55)? On the more careful examination of the evidence we feel certain that it is Beegle, not the inspired Stephen, who is in error.

The fallacy of the above reasoning is found in the initial premise. Genesis 11:26 does not specifically say that Abraham was born to Terah when Terah was 70. It says that Terah was 70 when he had his first son: "After Terah had lived 70 years, he became the father of Abram, Nahor and Haran." It is altogether unlikely that these three were triplets. Scripture records two or three cases of twins but never mentions triplets. We have to look for further evidence before we can conclude that Abram was the

child who made Terah a father at the age of 70. To be sure, he is
mentioned before his two brothers, but that may well have been
because he was by far the most prominent and important of the
three. It is significant that Haran was the first to die (Gen.
11:28); normally the older die before the younger. We are not
very well informed about Nahor. He is not said to have accompanied Terah and Abram when they migrated from Ur to
Haran, though his descendants, Laban and Rebekah, were living
in the general region of Haran at the time of Isaac's
marriage—by which time Nahor had certainly passed away. It
would normally be expected, then, that Abraham died last because he was the youngest of the three brothers. If that was the
case, there is no special difficulty in supposing that he was born
to Terah when the latter was 130 years of age. This may seem to
us like a remarkably advanced age for paternity, but it should
not be forgotten that Abraham was not bereaved of Sarah until
he was 137. He then took Keturah as wife and had six sons by
her. He did not die until he was 175 (Gen. 25:7). Thus the case
against Stephen's accuracy in Acts 7:4 collapses.

7. JACOB'S BURIAL PLACE

We have already discussed, in connection with LaSor's third
item, the possibility of Abraham's original purchase of the plot of
land near Shechem—a plot that, some 180 years later, Jacob
had to pay for again. We have shown, in the case of the two
Beersheba purchases, that there was good precedent for this
practice. Beegle's objection centers mainly on the question of
where the body of Jacob was finally interred. He interprets Acts
7:16 as affirming that Jacob was buried in Shechem, whereas
Genesis 50:13 (cf. 23:19) clearly states that Jacob was buried in
Hebron. But Beegle seriously misinterprets the Greek text of
Acts 7:16. It is rendered by the NASB as follows: "And from
there [i.e., from Egypt; the words "from there" are supplied in
italics, not being in the Greek] they were removed to Shechem,
and laid in the tomb which Abraham had purchased for a sum of
money from the sons of Hamor in Shechem." The previous verse
specifies the antecedent of "they," namely Jacob and "our
fathers"—that is to say, Jacob and his twelve sons, the pro-
genitors of the twelve tribes of Israel.

The verb *metetithēsan* ("they were removed") is highly
significant, because it implies that the embalmed bodies of the

persons involved had first been temporarily interred in Egypt. Only later, after the conquest of Canaan around 1400 B.C., were they *transferred* to permanent tombs in Shechem. Therefore *metetithēsan* must be construed as referring to the coffins of the twelve sons, not to the coffin of Jacob. It was perfectly clear from Genesis 50:13 that the body of Jacob, which was never buried in Egypt, was, immediately after his death, taken up to Canaan and interred in the tomb of Sarah and Abraham at Hebron. Without question, Stephen, who includes so much of the Genesis narrative in his speech in Acts 7, was well aware of this. He did not state, as Beegle supposes he did, that *Jacob* was transferred from Egypt to a burial place in Palestine. *Metetithēsan* is plural and therefore demands a plural antecedent, namely the twelve sons of Jacob.

In his zeal to find error, Beegle seems to have overlooked an elementary rule of exegesis. Beyond any question the body of Joseph was at first interred in Egypt, and from there he and his eleven brothers were transferred, as Stephen correctly informs us, to Shechem. Joshua 24:32 states, "And Joseph's bones, which the Israelites had brought up from Egypt, were buried at Shechem in the tract of land that Jacob bought for a hundred pieces of silver from the sons of Hamor, the father of Shechem. This became the inheritance of Joseph's decendants." This verse does not explicitly tell us where the rest of Jacob's sons were finally interred, but it is fair to assume that most, if not all, of them were likewise buried in Shechem. Here again, the effort to convict Stephen of inaccuracy is a failure.

8. LENGTH OF ISRAELITE SOJOURN IN EGYPT

In Galatians 3:17 Paul says: "The law, introduced 430 years later [i.e., after God's promise to Abraham and his descendants] does not set aside the covenant previously established by God and thus do away with the promise." He is making the point here that the legal code revealed and entrusted by the Lord to Moses was never intended to annul the covenant promises made to Abraham and to his seed—and to all the nations of the earth who would be blessed through Abraham's race. The item that draws Beegle's attention is the time span of 430 years.

The Septuagint Greek translation of Exodus 12:40 implies that the 430 years included the entire sojourn of Abraham and his descendants both in Canaan and in Egypt, down to the time of

Moses. But the Masoretic Hebrew text indicates that the 430 years was the length of the Egyptian sojourn only. Beegle rightly concludes that the Hebrew reading is the more reliable, for the increase from seventy or seventy-five souls (the number of people in Jacob's family when they went to Egypt) to a great host of over 2 million by Moses' time is far more credible with a span of 430 years than with 215 (the 430 years *minus* the time of the Canaan sojourn). Yet Beegle goes on to suggest that Paul, who so frequently quoted from the Septuagint in his references to the Old Testament, relied upon its inferior reading in this case. In other words, the interval between God's first promise to Abraham and the giving of the Law at Mt. Sinai under Moses was a mere 430 years, rather than the more probable 645 years (the 430 years *plus* the Canaan sojourn). Therefore, he says, Paul was guilty of an error in chronology by relying on a mistaken reading in the Septuagint. Beegle then adds this illuminating comment: "Evidently it seemed good to the Holy Spirit to let Paul use the traditional 430 years, without informing him that he was technically wrong and should be using 645 years, as found in the Hebrew"![16] Here, then, we find a Holy Spirit who did not superintend the accuracy of the Scripture even when it was first committed to writing. Here we have a God who is not overly concerned about truth!

This line of thinking leads inevitably to relegating the Bible to the same class as pagan religious literature. Without question, heathen scriptures also contain much that is true, along with all the error that infects them. If God Himself is not concerned with *total* truth—including the area of history—then the Bible must be submitted to the scrutiny and judgment of man in order to determine what portions of it are valid and what are invalid. No longer does God's Word sit in judgment on man; man sits in judgment on God's Word. We cannot rely on God to speak the truth, or at least always to have guided the human authors of Scripture into truth. There is no great difference between this position and the skepticism of Robert Ingersoll, who used arguments of this very sort to try to prove the Bible was not the Word of God.

Beegle, however, has wrongly interpreted the thrust of Paul's remark. Paul is not telling us the time interval between the action of Genesis 12 and that of Exodus 20, the first giving of the Law. As we examine the Old Testament record, we find that in

Genesis 46:3–4 Yahweh renewed His covenant promises to the aged Jacob, as he was about to go down to live in Egypt. The promises made to Abraham, Isaac, and Jacob were all essentially the same—as Moses makes abundantly clear by his repeated references in Deuteronomy to the promises that Yahweh "swore to Abraham, Isaac, and Jacob." Plainly, these promises were viewed by Moses as a single package or complex. The period prior to the migration to Egypt was the period of promise. Then ensued the Egyptian sojourn for 430 years, followed by the Exodus under Moses and the giving of the Law at Mt. Sinai.

Paul is saying that the detailed legal system given to the Israelites as a constitution for their theocracy (being 430 years later than the time of the three patriarchs to whom the promises came) was never intended to annul or supersede those promises. He simply mentions the well-known interval of the Egyptian sojourn as separating the period of covenant promise and the period of Mosaic legislation. As such, Paul's comment was perfectly historical and accurate. There is no need for the destructive conclusions drawn by Beegle and others.

9. THE NUMBER OF ROOSTER CROWS AT THE TIME OF PETER'S DENIAL

Unlike LaSor, Beegle does not bring up the question of reconciling the synoptic accounts of Peter's triple denial of Christ in the Court of Caiaphas, except in one detail. In Matthew 26:34 Jesus is quoted as telling Peter that before the rooster would crow (presumably once) the next morning, Peter would deny he even knew Him. After the third denial Peter recalled this prediction and realized to his shame that he had fulfilled it (Matt. 26:74–75). Luke 22:34, 60–61 has essentially the same wording. It is only in Mark 14:30 that Jesus says, "Before the rooster crows twice you yourself will disown me three times"—the second cock-crowing being correspondingly emphasized in verse 72. There is a seeming discrepancy between the implied "once" and the "twice." Beegle comments, in a somewhat patronizing fashion: "But what essential difference is there if the other Gospel writers, Matthew and Luke, follow the general tradition of the rooster's crowing just once? All three Gospels contain the historical features necessary to convey the truth of the matter."

There is no discrepancy here at all. Various witnesses to an incident remember the details somewhat differently from one

another. Eyewitness accounts of the same episode often vary in
what they summarize or generalize and in what they give in
detail. As mentioned earlier, one Gospel writer recalls that there
were actually two wild men from Gadara who encountered
Jesus; another evangelist mentions but one, since this one was
the spokesman. One Gospel mentions Bartimaeus alone (Mark
10:46) as begging Christ for the gift of sight when He visited
Jericho; Matthew 20:30 recalls that there were actually two blind
men, though Bartimaeus acted as spokesman. In relation to
Christ's Palm Sunday entrance into Jerusalem, Mark 11:2 mentions only the donkey colt, on which Jesus sat. In Matthew 21:2
the detail is added that the colt was tied up next to its mother—
and we learn there were *two* donkeys involved.

Such variations are a common phenomenon in the Gospels
(and are seen frequently in the parallel passages of Kings and
Chronicles). Mark recalls (perhaps reflecting the way Peter related his account of the episode—if indeed Mark was his under-
study in Rome, as tradition holds) that Jesus actually said, "Before the rooster crows twice. . . ." Matthew and Luke do not
mention "twice," and simply say, "Before the rooster crows.
. . ." Obviously, if the rooster crowed twice, he first crowed once.
The verb *phonēsai* ("crows") does not specify whether the bird is
going to sound forth once, twice, or three times before Peter
perjures himself the third time. The New Testament uses the
term *alektrophonia* ("cockcrowing") to indicate the break of day
(Mark 13:35). Were you to have asked a native at that time what
exactly that term meant, he would have answered, "That is the
hour when roosters crow and herald the sunrise." We can only
establish that Mark is more specific than Matthew or Luke at
this point, not that there is a contradiction.

10. PAUL'S QUOTING ELIPHAZ

Beegle points out that Paul's quotation, "He catches the wise in
their craftiness" (1 Cor. 3:19), is taken from Job 5:13, a statement by Eliphaz in his first speech to Job. He then remarks:
"Traditionally speaking, Eliphaz has never been considered
. . . inspired. Job, so it is claimed, was the inspired one. . . .
Apparently Paul did not care who said it, nor whether he was
inspired. The statement was true as far as he was concerned, and
so he used it in his argument."[17] Beegle concludes that this
amounts to an inspired, infallible *account* of error.

It is hard to see why Beegle bothers to mention the matter at all, as if it were a problem for inerrancy. No evangelical scholar I know of, ancient or modern, has claimed that the Bible quotes as valid only the statements of inspired saints or that all statements by these saints are valid. Some of the reproaches that Job directed against God were less than inspired, and for these he was rightly rebuked, both by Elihu (Job 34:1–9) and by Yahweh Himself (Job 38:1–2; 40:2). On the other hand, many of the sentiments expressed by the three counselors were doctrinally correct. Job himself declares, "I could say such things as those," and he reiterates many of the sentiments they express concerning the wisdom, power, and grandeur of God.

It should also be remembered, in regard to this general point, that God used even so wicked an unbeliever as the high priest Caiaphas to express prophetic truth. In John 11:50 he is quoted as saying, "It is better for you that one man die for the people than that the whole nation perish." John then comments, "He did not say this on his own, but as high priest that year, he prophesied that Jesus would die for the Jewish nation." *A fortiori*, Paul's quotation from Eliphaz in 1 Corinthians 3:19 poses no problem whatever for biblical inerrancy.

11. THE LEADING OF DAVID TO MAKE THE CENSUS

In 1 Chronicles 21:1 we read: "Satan rose up against Israel and incited David to take a census of Israel." Second Samuel 24:1 reads: "Again the anger of the LORD burned against Israel, and he incited David against them, saying, 'Go and count Israel and Judah.' " The chronicler assigns to Satan the responsibility for leading David to take the census; the author of Samuel attributes the leading to God. Beegle suggests that the chronicler felt no hesitancy in revising the text of his source when he differed from its interpretation—". . . apparently on the understanding that his understanding was more accurate. It is obvious that he simply did not believe that God incited David to take a census in order to express his anger against Israel."[18] Beegle notes that the traditional harmonization of the accounts maintains that Samuel speaks of the *permissive* will of God. But he speculates that, had the two authors met together, they would have engaged in vigorous debate over the subject. He ends with the comment: "Although it is difficult to prove an error, it is evident that partial truth is involved in the interpretations.

There are numerous biblical examples of theological interpretations of one generation being revised slightly or even rejected by
another." Unfortunately he gives no examples of these "numerous" other examples. Had he done so, they would very likely
prove as ill-founded as this one.

David's census taking illustrates a recurring problem in God's
dealings with a stubbornly unbelieving and disobedient people.
The Bible tells us that God may permit a believer who is out of
fellowship with Him to take an action that is unwise or displeas-
ing to God, in order that after he reaps the bitter fruit of this
misdeed, he will undergo appropriate disciplinary judgment and
thereby be brought back, chastened in spirit, to closer fellowship
with the Lord. Such certainly was the case with Jonah, who tried
to escape God's call by taking ship for Tarshish. The Lord used
the storm and the great fish to turn him around and get him back
on the path of obedience. Other passages speak of divine judicial
hardening inflicted because of earlier rejection of the truth and
will of God. Romans 1:21–22 says of mankind in its decline into
idolatry and immorality: "For although they knew God, they
neither glorified him as God nor gave thanks to him, but their
thinking became futile and their foolish hearts were darkened.
Although they claimed to be wise, they became fools." In verses
24–25 we then read: "Therefore God gave them over in the sinful
desires of their hearts to sexual impurity for the degrading of
their bodies with one another. They exchanged the truth of God
for a lie." We also know that it is the special interest of Satan to
encourage and intensify every impulse of man to disobedience of
God. He or his cohorts are always on hand to help us sin. A
classic passage on this interplay between the permission of God
and the malignity of Satan is 2 Thessalonians 2:8–12. We are
told that, in the last days before the second coming of Christ, the
"lawless one" will be revealed, whose coming "will be in accordance with the work of Satan." We then read: "For this reason
God [will send] them a powerful delusion so that they will believe the lie and so that all will be condemned who have not
believed the truth but have delighted in wickedness."

In the latter part of David's reign, both the king and the
nation began to be confident in their increasing numbers and
material resources to such an extent that they needed disciplinary judgment to bring them back to proper dependence on
God. The Lord therefore permitted Satan to encourage David to

undertake the census, at the completion of which He sent a severe plague on the nation to seriously deplete its ranks. Viewed from this perspective, 1 Chronicles 21 and 2 Samuel 24 are not contradictory. Both accounts are true, for both God and Satan influenced David.

We have weighed all of Beegle's arguments and found them falling far short of his announced purpose of proving the Bible guilty of mistakes even in the autographa. It is outside the purpose of this present discussion to deal with the larger philosophical issue he raises in his book. Suffice it to say that his attempt to establish objective authority for the Bible, while deeming it guilty of error, is a total and complete failure. A Bible containing mistakes in its original manuscripts is a combination of truth and error and is therefore in the same class as the religious scriptures composed by pagan authors as expressions of their own search after God. As such, it must be subjected to the judicial processes of human reason, and in the effort to sift out the valid from the false, any human judge—whoever he may be—is necessarily influenced by subjective factors. All he can be sure of is his own opinion—and even that may change from year to year. At best he comes up with conjectures and guesswork, which he may try to dignify with the label of sanctified intuition or something of the sort. But he has no truly reliable, objective basis for knowledge of the one true God or of His will for our salvation or way of living. Whether Beegle is willing to face it or not, his epistemology is fatally defective, and he has no firmer grasp of spiritual truth than his own "inerrant" judgment may extend. To many of us there is far greater prospect of reliability and security in the inerrancy of the Word of God itself than in the judgments of it by finite, sinful man.

Our final comment is this: Beegle speaks out vigorously against the principle that if a single genuine error is found in Scripture, it proves that error may be found in any other part of Scripture. He insists that any number of errors may be found in the Bible and that it still may be the Word of God. Yet the Bible itself teaches us that "God is not a man, that He should lie." Beegle may see no difficulty in the proposition that God may inspire, or at least tolerate, falsehood in some parts of His holy record. But clear and honest thinking can only view this approach as vitiated by the law of noncontradiction. We may as well protest that a single sin demonstrable against the Lord Jesus

Christ does not necessarily disprove His sinlessness, or that a single false prediction given by God does not impair His promise-keeping integrity.

Luther said, "When the Scripture speaks, God speaks." Like the great Reformer, we put our entire confidence in the accuracy and veracity of God's written Word, even as did Jesus of Nazareth in all of His references to the Hebrew Scriptures of the Old Testament.

HIGHER CRITICISM AND BIBLICAL INERRANCY

J. Barton Payne

J. Barton Payne is the late Professor of Old Testament at Covenant Theological Seminary, St. Louis, Missouri. He was a graduate of the University of California, (B.A.); San Francisco Theological Seminary, (B.D.); Princeton Theological Seminary, (M.A. in Semitic languages and in biblical literature, Ph.D. in Old Testament). He served as a Presbyterian pastor, Chairman of the Department of Graduate Old Testament at Bob Jones University, Professor of Old Testament at Wheaton College Graduate School of Theology, Professor of Old Testament at Trinity Evangelical Divinity School, lecturer and excavation supervisor at the Near East School of Archaeological and Biblical Studies, Jordan, and Director of the Wheaton Summer Institute of Biblical Studies, Israel. His writings include An Outline of Hebrew History; Hebrew Vocabularies; The Imminent Appearing of Christ; Theology of the Older Testament; New Perspectives on the Old Testament; Encyclopedia of Biblical Prophecy; Biblical Prophecy for Today; *and* The Prophecy Map of World History. *He has also served on translation committees for* The New American Standard Bible *and the* New International Version. *Dr. Payne was a member of the Evangelical Theological Society, for which he served as president and national secretary, and was a member of the Council of ICBI.*

CHAPTER SUMMARY

Higher criticism is the art of seeing literature exactly as it is and of estimating it accordingly. It becomes negative criticism, often described as "the historical-critical method," when it assumes the right to pass rationalistic judgment on Scripture's own claims about its composition and historicity. Such a method necessarily presupposes that the Bible's claims are not inerrant. It thus disqualifies itself as truly scientific criticism, since it refuses to view the object being analyzed according to its proper (divine) character. Examples are provided, both of valid and of invalid criticism, together with an evaluation of present-day attempts by negative critics to infiltrate evangelicalism with views that subordinate the authority of Christ and of Scripture to the judgments of men.

4 *J. Barton Payne*

HIGHER CRITICISM
AND BIBLICAL INERRANCY

$\mathbb{A}$T THE HEART of today's trend among some conservative Christians to give up belief in the full, inerrant authority of Scripture lies negative higher criticism.[1] Christ's followers need the Bible, and they know it; they do not want to lose its infallible word. But certain former evangelicals have decided that, though it means opposing Jesus' own teachings about the validity of Scripture, they *must* accept negative higher criticism. It is as simple as that.

DEFINITION

Are you a higher critic? Am I? It all depends. It depends on who is asking the question and how it is asked. Under the proper circumstances evangelicals will reply, "Yes, of course I am"; under others, they will bristle at the very suggestion—while, it is hoped, preserving love toward the questioner.

Just what is "higher criticism," and, in particular, "negative higher criticism"? Its three word elements may be considered in reverse order.

Criticism

Stemming from the Greek root *krinō*, "to cut," and thus "to judge," the term *criticism* derives specifically from the adjectival form, *kritikos*, which means "fit for judging," and thus critical, in

85

the sense of being "decisive." An illness has reached its "critical" stage at the point where its outcome is being determined.

Criticism relates to literature in a special way. The *Oxford English Dictionary* presents this definition: "The art of estimating the qualities and character of literary artistic work." The goal of criticism is to see a writing exactly as it is and to estimate it accordingly. It is not captious faultfinding, and truly great art has nothing to fear from the critic. Honest criticism will only enhance its inherent value.

Higher Criticism

In order to see a given writing exactly as it is, investigators are involved first of all in "the search for the original wording of the text," which is the discipline of lower criticism—now often designated as textual criticism.[2] Its primary concern is with manuscripts and textual transmission; its goal is to recover, as far as possible, the original wording of the biblical writings. It is preliminary, and fundamental to all further investigation—hence its designation as "lower" (in the sense of foundational). Its sequel, then, is the discipline of higher criticism, which investigates the source of the original texts. Higher criticism asks about the circumstances of composition, including such matters as date, place, authorship, unity, purpose, literal style, and the influence the different books may have had. It also considers how their inspiration came to be recognized and how all the books were gathered together (canon formation). When a person asks, "Who wrote the Epistle to the Hebrews?" he is a higher critic!

Inquiry characterizes both of these divisions of criticism. Whether lower or higher, they employ a common method, that of asking questions. As Harry Boer puts it: "Both were conceived in, and have issued from, the same womb. This womb is the rational human mind."[3] In his historical survey of the theological shift that has occurred at Fuller Seminary, William LaSor allies himself with the essence of higher criticism when he says: "Many of the tensions of the early days of the Seminary developed because some of us were willing to explore the implications of modern scholarship, whereas others tended to retreat to the defense of nineteenth-century viewpoints."[4] Did LaSor's interest in modern scholarship go no further than to "explore" it? Did his opponents who defended traditional biblical orthodoxy even "tend" to retreat from this kind of exploration? The publications of Gleason Archer (a former Fuller faculty member), for example, hardly exemplify reticence toward interaction with the implications of liberal higher criticism. But LaSor's sympathies generally correspond to our basic definition of criticism, that it is "the science of inquiry." The real question, then, concerns the kind of inquiry it is.

Negative Higher Criticism

In his defining of terms, Boer grants that the above-cited quotation from the *Oxford Dictionary* is actually its second definition for *criticism* and that the first is this: "The action of passing judgment upon the qualities or merits of anything, especially the passing of an unfavorable judgment . . . censure."[5] Boer is vehement in his repudiation of this negative aspect; he calls it, "wholly erroneous . . . not in any sense the meaning of the term 'biblical criticism.' " Yet historically, biblical criticism has become the domain of liberalism. As James M. Robinson points out in *The New Hermeneutic,* "Liberalism and conservatism tended to divide criticism and hermeneutics between them. This in part explains why hermeneutics[6] as a discipline has survived in conservative circles even down to the present."[7] It also explains why "higher critic" has often come to mean simply "skeptic."

A phrase now often used, especially in liberal circles, in place of "higher criticism" is "the historical-critical method." In theory, this too, is a good term. Evangelicals are as much committed to *history* as are their opponents, in fact, they should be more fully committed to it (cf. 1 Cor. 15:14). As already discussed, evangelicals are also committed to *criticism* (in the sense of seeking to see Scripture exactly as it is). But the phrase *historical-critical method* has become so identified with rationalistic skepticism (see Soulen's quote on page 93 and related note) that it would seem no longer to be salvageable for use by Bible believers.

In theory, higher criticism need not be negative. Its avowed goal is objective description. Criticism becomes warped—that is, it "goes wrong" and fails to see a worthy object for what it really is—only when coupled with presuppositions that turn it into dishonest, unobjective criticism. The question, of course, then arises, What constitutes a warping presupposition? Liberalism and evangelicalism come up with diametrically opposed answers, and these in turn determine their respective judgments of Scripture.

Liberalism demands freedom. George Ladd, returning from a sabbatical on the Continent, declared that he did not like what he had seen. He put it this way: "German theology is . . . an adventure of inquiring minds which refuse to be in bondage to the traditions of the past. . . . It insists that only when the scholar approaches the Scripture free from all presuppositions can he really understand the Bible as an historical book."[8] Such an approach forbids one to come to the Word knowing in advance that it is true. Kasemann says bluntly, "Scripture to which one surrenders . . . uncritically, leads . . . to indistinguishability between faith and superstition."[9] The purpose, therefore, of Boer's book *Above the Battle? The Bible and Its Critics* is to pronounce a resounding "No!" to the question, Is Scripture above the battle? The Bible is not and, he says, must not be kept exempt from attack. Liberalism insists that no other approach can be tolerated. As H. H. Rowley once explained:

> There were conservative writers who stood outside the general body of critical scholars and who rejected most of their conclusions, but they did not seriously affect the position. For while many of them had considerable learning, they made little secret of the fact that they were employing their learning to defend positions which were dogmatically reached. Their work had little influence, therefore, amongst scientific scholars who were concerned only with the evidence, and the conclusions to which it might naturally lead.[10]

Yet—and this is a fact that has to be noted—Rowley's exclusivistic stress on freedom is itself a presupposition. Thus, when the crisis at Concordia Seminary was approaching in the fall of 1973 and the denominational president, J. A. O. Preus, offered the liberal element under John Tietjen a compromise solution—by which twenty conservative professors would be hired at the seminary—it became a matter of principle that "the proposal was received with disdain."[11] Liberalism simply cannot be liberal with those who threaten its methodology and its own presuppositions through "biased" criticism, that is, criticism that assumes biblical inerrancy.

Rowley's explanation also bears witness to the fact that "most of the conclusions" produced by his school of criticism are negative and end up being rejected by conservatives. Furthermore, in its very theory, the presupposition of critical freedom has to assume "in advance" an *un*favorable judgment against Scripture. Norman Gottwald does not hesitate to go on record in this regard. He says, "The only presupposition common to all Old Testament critics is the necessity of questioning tradition, examining a religious literature as we would examine any other writings in order to determine authorship, date, sources, and historical background. This at once sounds the death knell for verbal inspiration." He recognizes that the Old Testament claims verbal inspiration for itself; but, he replies, "value judgments are inescapable. We all come to the Old Testament with some ultimate perspective, even if it is to deny the ultimacy of the Hebrew claim."[12]

Conservatism, on the other hand, demands commitment. The Protestant E. J. Young follows the example of Catholic Wilhelm Moeller in citing Exodus 3:5 in the preface to his Old Testament *Introduction:* "Put off thy shoes from off thy feet, for the place whereon thou standest is holy ground."[13] After looking into the positions both of Young and of Gottwald, Samuel Schultz concludes:

> Basic among all these questions is the presupposition of the critics regarding the trustworthiness of the Bible. This is the watershed that ultimately divides them into two camps. One group regards the Bible at face value—reliable, trustworthy, and inerrant. The other group may presuppose various other positions except the recognition that the Bible is reliable throughout. . . . [Instead, it is] treated on the purely human level.[14]

His objection to Gottwald's liberalism is that "for the latter [the liberal] the value judgment of the critic is imposed on Scripture, while for the former [the evangelical] the Scripture is accepted as the standard to which all value judgments are subjected."[15] Schultz's position is that the only way to criticize Scripture—the only way really to see it as it is in history—is to refrain from imposing negative human judgments on it. This position obviously demands commitment. At the very least it means that the Bible text should be considered innocent until proven guilty. Legitimate, honest criticism takes the text on its own terms first, before attempting (if it ever has the right to do so) to impose modern categories on it. It also means, incidentally, that the evangelical often finds himself in a bind semantically. The moment he opens his mouth in complaint against some aspect of modern biblical criticism, someone always seems to jump to his feet in defense of criticism, as such. The Bible

believer must then stop and explain that he is all for honest
inquiry and that what he is against is *negative* higher criticism
(see the opening sentence of this chapter).

LIMITS

Which presupposition, then, is proper—that of freedom,
which produces negative higher criticism, or that of commitment, accompanied by criticism that affirms Scripture? The
question becomes one of limits—of deciding just how far the
critic can or should go. May he carry his task beyond that of
objective description into one of sifting textual ideas so as to
establish or modify their truth? The liberal says yes. Without the
right to sift, and to reject what seems unworthy, he says, the
critic cannot be true to himself, and criticism is a farce. The
evangelical says no. By claiming the right to sift, he declares, the
critic cannot be true to the divinely inerrant nature of the biblical
literature that is under scrutiny, and criticism is misapplied. If,
therefore, a proper decision is to be reached, the limits that are at
issue must be accurately defined.

The Nature of the Limits

When Rowley contends for his freedom, as a biblical scholar,
to follow wherever the evidence "might naturally lead," and
when Gottwald decries anyone's imposing different limits (on his
treatment of religious literature) from the way he would "examine any other writings," both men thereby limit Scripture to a
naturalistic category. Gerhard Maier observes, "the concept that
the Bible must be treated like any other book has plunged theology into an endless chain of perplexities and inner contradictions."[16] The reason goes back to the kind of limits the former
two scholars impose. As George Ladd says, in following up his
description of the adventurous Germans who were seeking to
understand the Bible as a historical book:

> They interpret the Bible from within the presuppositions of the
> contemporary scientific world view. Such a world view *assumes*
> that all historical events are capable of being explained by other
> known historical events. In other words, what we call the super-
> natural is not the immediate activity of the living God; for it
> belongs to the area of legend and myth and not to the area of
> historical reality.[17]

Which will we choose: to limit the Bible, and thus also the

Christian faith, along with God Himself, or to limit the critic? Although Peter Stuhlmacher bitterly opposes the "anticritical" stance of his former protegé, Maier, he concedes the truth of the latter's insistence that negative criticism damages theology. He acknowledges that, "a historical criticism of the biblical tradition which is *unchecked* can allow irreconcilable fronts to emerge between scientific insight on the one hand and vital Christian faith on the other" (italics mine).[18]

The pattern that exists between "checks" and today's higher criticism can be laid out by means of the following charts. Their goal, if we assume a proposition that "X did Y," is to plot the legitimacy of both affirmative and negative evaluations of this proposition, in a variety of literary contexts.

1. In a *noninspired* book:

EVALUATION of "X did Y"	LEGITIMACY
(possible responses that one can give to this proposition)	(whether such a response can be made by a reasonable person)
I know it IS true	A man CAN say this
I know it is NOT true	He CAN say this, too

(Liberalism takes this approach toward the Bible.)

2. In a *supposedly inspired* book, which would contain both natural and supernatural matter:

EVALUATION	LEGITIMACY	
	natural matter	*and supernatural*
I know it IS true	He CAN say this	He CANNOT tell
I know it IS NOT true	He CAN say this	He CANNOT tell

(As an example of a natural matter in a supposedly inspired book, let us say that X = Joseph Smith and Y = his translating of a Roman-period Egyptian funerary text on Osiris, which he converts into words of Abraham about Isaac. With our present knowledge of Egyptian literature, anyone can judge this assertion, that "X did Y," and say it either is true or is not.[19] But neither the liberal nor the evangelical is in a position, in himself, to make judgments if the category is supernatural. Let us say further that X = an angel called Moroni and Y = his speaking to Mr. Smith. Who am I to say whether there really was an X that did or did not do Y? Only another supernatural source can guide me; and He may! So when a liberal claims he CAN judge the supernatural, he actually brings it down to his own natural level and thus denies in advance, its reality. Criticism has "gone wrong" by adopting a presupposition that opposes the potential character of the object being judged.)

3. In *Scripture*, with its content, both natural and supernatural:

EVALUATION	LEGITIMACY	
	natural	*and supernatural*
I know it IS true	He CAN say this	He CAN say this, too (because another supernatural source, Christ, validates Scripture)
I know it IS NOT true	He CANNOT say this	He CANNOT say this (because Christ has said Scripture cannot be broken, John 10:35)[20]

(Further, the evangelical says he CANNOT negatively judge even the natural elements in Scripture. Let us say, for example, that X = Matthew and Y = his quoting (27:9–10) words from Zechariah 11:12–13 [with possible allusions to Jer. 18:2 and 19:2], ascribing them to Jeremiah the prophet.[21] When the believer says he CANNOT deny this, he does so on the basis of a presupposition. As a starting point he holds that the claims of the book itself to be words of God are to be accepted as a working hypothesis and ultimately, that all Scripture is inerrant [see Christ's statement in John 10:35 again]. This presupposition does not destroy legitimate criticism. For, rather than eliminating or even claiming to have answered the few seeming discrepancies that do occur,[22] the evangelical simply transfers these to the supernaturalistic column. He places them where man is not to judge for himself, and where God [who is the only One in a position to know] denies him the privilege of saying, "It's not true," because God tells him that Scripture is inerrant.)

For every critic—the liberal just as much as the evangelical—establishing limits is a matter of faith, either in one's own, internal competence or in another's (Christ's) external authority.

The Scientific Approach

Without the least hesitancy, Rowley equates the practice of negative higher criticism with what is done "amongst scientific scholars." By *scientific* he means, as pointed out by Ladd, being faithful to the contemporary world view that explains all events on the basis of other known events. Stuhlmacher classifies this "rationalistic notion of history and reality" as an outworking of "the principle of analogy. . . . All historical experiences which resist rationalism [as it observes analogous incidents] are subject to skepticism."[23] His classification is a legitimate one, being accepted, for example, in R. N. Soulen's current *Handbook of Biblical Criticism,* which explains:

> The term Historical Critical Method refers to that principle of historical reasoning . . . that reality is uniform and universal, that it is accessible to human reason and investigation, that all events historical and natural occurring within it are in principle comparable by analogy, and that man's contemporary experience of reality can provide the objective criteria by which what could or could not have happened in the past is to be determined.[24]

But is criticism of Scripture that is based on analogy truly scientific? Gerhard Maier immediately raises philosophical objections: "How can the *pure* historian without further ado reject something just because it happens only once? What can be experienced and what has analogies can certainly not be declared synonymous."[25] E. J. Young goes further and raises the following theological objection against

> the so-called "scientific" method, which assumes that man can approach the facts of the universe, including the Bible, with a neutral mind, and pronounce a just judgment upon them. It is time that we cease to call such a method scientific. It is not scientific, for it does not take into consideration all the facts, and the basic fact it overlooks is that of God and His relation to the world which He has created.[26]

On these same grounds Maier has entitled his most recent study *The End of the Historical-Critical Method;* and he concludes, "Because this method is not suited to the subject, in fact even opposes its obvious tendency, we must reject it."[27]

In place of the "analogy" method, N. H. Ridderbos refers to some of the oldest portions of Scripture and proposes: "In order to come to a proper historical understanding of the events of Moses' time, we must take reckoning of the personal intervention of Yahweh, of which the sources bear witness, and work out a scholarly historical method that takes account of this intervention."[28]

What then constitutes a truly scientific approach? If biblical revelation cannot be placed in the analogist's test tube for repeatable experimentation, so to make "natural" evaluations—as in certain fields of the physical sciences—what course should one follow? It would appear that proper biblical criticism can be conducted only on the basis of the testimony of competent witnesses—as is the procedure in any other historical discipline. We cannot infer from analogous events today what must have transpired centuries ago. In respect to religious phenomena, Soulen goes so far as to conclude: "If in fact every event in history is in some sense unique, of what value is the principle of analogy?"[29] Accepting, then, the principle of "testimony of competent witnesses," we find that God Himself, through Christ (John 1:18), becomes the only authority who can really tell us about His own writing.

This principle, moreover, admits of no compromise. There are those today—ranging from certain of the more thoroughgoing critics, such as Stuhlmacher or Boer, down to some more neoevangelical opponents of biblical inerrancy, such as Maier[30] or Davis—who appeal for a genuine openness to transcendence and who repudiate the use of the historical-critical method when it binds itself totally to antisupernaturalistic philosophical presuppositions (such as underlie Bultmann's demythologizing of the New Testament),[31] but who still employ negative higher criticism to reject those lesser aspects of Scripture that they happen to find objectionable, either historically or theologically (such as Joshua's religiously based destruction of the Canaanites).[32]

While Stuhlmacher therefore pleads for a "hermeneutics of consent"—by which he means an openness to hearing the Word of God—he is in fact only calling for historical criticism's being willing to engage in "critical dialogue with the tradition" of Scripture.[33] Human rationalism still sits in judgment over the results. The principle of the analogy of modern secular thought retains at least partial control, and methodologically it might as well be total! A truly open-minded scientist, on the contrary, must be willing to operate entirely within whatever methods are appropriate to the object of his criticism; otherwise his conclusions will inevitably go wrong.

The alternative method, which is both self-consistent and also scientifically congruous to its subject matter, has been forthrightly defined by Maier: "The correlation or counterpart to revelation is not critique but obedience."[34] This principle is what made James Orr's inductive attempt to construct a doctrine of inspiration on the basis of his own evaluation of the observable phenomena of Scripture, with all its various difficulties, basically illegitimate. It is what made B. B. Warfield's approach of deductively deriving biblical inerrancy from the revealed teaching of Christ and His apostles sound.[35] Evangelicals, in other words, do not support Warfield as one who is immune to criticism (as those who resist inerrancy sometimes insinuate) but simply as one whose methodology is consistent with the object of his investigation.

It is important at this juncture to distinguish rationalism from rationality. While evangelicals reject the former, they do not minimize the latter, namely, the God-given significance and place of human intelligence. They do not wish to inhibit those areas of thought pertinent to man's Spirit-directed exercise of his intellectual responsibility. We are responsible for examining the historical (especially the resurrection) data that lead to acceptance of Jesus Christ (1 Cor. 15:1–11). We are responsible for seeking an exact understanding of what our Lord taught, specifically concerning Scripture (Luke 24:45). Lastly, we are responsible for interpreting with diligence all the truths of Scripture (2 Tim. 2:15). But evangelicals deny the right of anyone to contradict what God says He has said. In doing this, he in effect, establishes a criterion above God Himself, which amounts to nothing less than idolatry.[36]

What, then, was the teaching of Christ and His apostles? Simply that what Scripture says, God says. Scripture therefore cannot be broken; it cannot be made subject to negative criticism.

Standards

Having established, philosophically, that the truly scientific approach to biblical criticism is the way of obedience—indeed, of total obedience—to the witness of Jesus Christ, the evangelical is still obligated to formulate, hermeneutically, definite standards for marking off the limits between critical procedures that are legitimate and those that are not.[37] At the outset, as an extension of the descriptive task of biblical introduction, it may be assumed that for a given portion of Scripture any theory about the circumstances of literary origin is acceptable if it adequately incorporates the biblical data and proceeds to develop its conclusions from them. Stuhlmacher thus appears to have some basis for opposing Maier's strictures against form criticism, except for permitting its analysis of canonical hymns and parables.[38] After all, the form-critical study of Deuteronomy as a 1400 B.C. Hittite type of suzerainty testament has done much both for the understanding of the book and for its authentication to this very period.[39] But once theory moves away from description into evaluation and begins to adopt a negative stance toward the data that it is supposed to be explaining—by seeking to sift out the erroneous from the valid, the false from the true, and the superstitious from the divine—at that moment it has gone beyond its tether and placed itself in opposition to the standards of Jesus. It has decided, in essence, that the Bible is not divine. This is not to say that the liberal may not believe, in a measure, in revelation in the sense of divine "speaking." But he does not believe in inspiration, as this is theologically understood, as divine writing. The Bible, skeptics insist, is at best a human book about God, and, as such, may be criticized like other human books. The evangelical, too, believes that the Bible is a human book, but that it is also, and more fundamentally, a divine book and is to be so treated. The two approaches therefore end up poles apart.

As we come to Scripture, accepting it as the Book authored by God, to be understood in ways that He directs, we find that His teachings touch on the following two categories: (1) biblical statements about its own composition and (2) the historicity of the biblical content.

Biblical statements about its own composition. Who wrote the book of Job? I don't know! In light of his other wisdom writings, a case can be made for Solomon, but neither the words of Christ nor the words of Scripture in general contain statements that bear on this aspect of higher criticism.[40] The evangelical scholar is left to his own resources. The same holds true for the subject of textual transmission, a division of lower criticism. As Maier puts it, there is only one course: "The comparison of variants must be carried out critically, that is, with reasonable and intelligent standards."[41] Advocates of negative criticism have claimed that this "lets the cat out of the bag." Barth's more left-wing colleague, the neoorthodox theologian Emil Brunner, argued, "Once textual criticism had been accepted it was soon discovered that the text might need to face a far more searching criticism, [involving] . . . inconsistencies or contradictions in the Bible."[42] Boer's chief argument supporting freedom for higher criticism is its inseparability from lower criticism: "The two . . . are so interrelated . . . that it is impossible to use the one properly without acknowledging the legitimacy and necessity of the other." He asks, "IF the consistent use of lower criticism is . . . praiseworthy and even necessary, why is the consistent [i.e., negative] use of higher criticism regarded with suspicion and antipathy?"[43]

The answer, of course, lies in the need to conform to the Bible's own statements about itself. Maier says, "Textual criticism does not infer [imply?] criticism *of* the text but refers to critically *finding* the text." Stated concretely, when we ask whether one should follow MSS A, B, C, and D in omitting the "Amen" at the end of Matthew (28:20, stating the Great Commission) or MSS E, F, G, and H in adding it, we are simply engaging in the legitimate endeavor to recover, as closely as possible, the text of Matthew's autograph. Neither he nor any of the other apostles included within their inspired statements directives (predictions!) about which manuscripts should be copied four centuries or so later. We are free to engage in such criticism as best we can.

If, however, we follow redaction criticism concerning the Great Commission's formula for baptism ("in the name of the Father and the Son and the Holy Spirit," (28:19) and conclude "that at some point the tradition of Matthew expanded an original monadic formula . . . to make Jesus' teachings meaningful to their own *Sitz im Leben* rather than to present them unedited,"[44] we indulge in illegitimate negative higher criticism, especially if we raise questions against the reliability of Matthew's autograph. The apostle specifies in his inspired statements that Jesus spoke this baptismal formula (28:18) and gives the circumstances of its verbal composition: It was uttered in Galilee,

on a mountain, to the eleven disciples who had witnessed Jesus'
resurrection (28:17). We are therefore committed to the validity
of God's inerrant Word.

This example from the first Gospel raises a crucial issue that
seems to be emerging among conservative scholars today. Some
interpreters consider themselves advocates of inerrancy, but are
willing, nevertheless, to grant the existence of erroneous statements in Scripture about the circumstances of the origin of a
given passage. The errors are due to the literary genre, or form
(namely, the Gospels) in which the statements occur. Since the
Bible contains such literary figures as hyperbole and parable,
both of which are fictional, could it not be, they argue, that the
Gospels form a particular type of Christian literary genre, in
which a redactor, in the interests of his theological message,
reshapes the historical tradition he has received?[45] The message
is thus said to prevail over historical accuracy, with no attempt
to deceive being intended by the author/redactor. In other
words, the question is simply one of exegesis and hermeneutics,
not of errancy.

While such a reconstruction is theoretically possible, it would
seem to be highly inappropriate for at least the narrative portions of the Gospels. An author who intends to use a fictional
form should make this fact, as well as his reason for using such a
form, clear to his readers. The four Gospels, however, contain no
clues that they are fictional in the sense claimed by those using
the methods of current redaction criticism. They assert just the
opposite (Luke 1:1–4), and for 1900 years readers have been
impressed by their form as one that intends and assumes historicity.

Two areas of biblical introduction are especially involved regarding this standard of upholding Scripture's statements about
its own composition: its claims of authorship and its claims of
integrity. A significant question relating to the former appears in
the concession made by a critical expositor of a previous generation. In asserting that the latter part of the Book of Isaiah was
not authored by that prophet, George Adam Smith observed
that if Christ had made use of Isaiah's name in His citations
from chapters 40–66, "as, for instance, is the case of David's
name in the quotation made from Psalm 110, then those who
deny the unity of the Book of Isaiah would be face to face with a
very serious problem indeed."[46] Departing for a moment from

our discussion of the Isaianic problem, we should observe that for those who are committed to Christ and to what the Bible says about its own composition, denial of the Davidic authorship of the 110th Psalm ceases to be a viable option, even as a theoretical possibility.

Concerning the integrity of the biblical books, we refer to Samuel Sandmel's denial of the authenticity of the conclusion to the Book of Amos. He says,

> It has come to be accepted among free biblical scholars . . . that the section is an addition. . . . Of course, religious conservatives reject entirely any supposition that there are such additions . . . on the premise that the initial words of a biblical book, in this case, "The words of Amos," are a complete guarantee of its authenticity.[47]

Yet what other premise could one entertain about the intention of the complier of this book in its final form? And here we must remember the status of the compiler (presumably Amos himself), who, in any event, was the ultimate instrument through whom God's Holy Spirit worked in inspiring this biblical writing. Sandmel's "of course" testifies to his awareness of this consideration, but he simply is not committed to the truth of what he recognizes to be Scripture's own claim.

The historicity of the biblical content. A closely related standard, which sets further limits to the degree to which the critic is left free to exercise his own rational resources, is this: No theory of literary origins may be considered legitimate that calls into question the historicity of the biblical content it is seeking to explain. The following three examples apply to successive portions of the Book of Genesis, analyzed in increasing detail; they also concern three different subcategories found within present-day higher criticism: form, tradition-history, and literary. All three illustrate how critical methods that are supposed to provide students with clearer insights into the nature of the biblical literature conclude by creating historical discrepancies where the biblical text itself suggests none.

1. Genesis 1–11 is a record of the origin and early history of the world, preliminary to the accounts of the patriarchs. *Form criticism* seeks to discern various blocks of material that, often having existed as oral traditions, may underlie this record. Gene Tucker's handbook distinguishes one such *form* as "saga," which he defines in this way: "Saga frequently reports things which are

incredible, while history reports the credible. Saga may speak of the direct intervention of God in the affairs of men, but when history speaks of God it is only as the ultimate cause of everything." He concludes, "Genesis is for the most part a collection of sagas."[48] By assigning the first book of Moses to this form category, he automatically downgrades the historicity of its content. (One may even wonder if he might not already have entertained certain presuppositions about the nature of history before he defined his forms!) He acknowledges that

> the results of such analysis often are taken to be entirely negative, and in certain cases they are, in the sense that the historical reliability of some material has been called into question. But such an analysis can lead to a positive reassessment. [In] saga . . . primitive peoples ask questions about the world and produce answers which, though incorrect, are interesting.[49]

2. Genesis 28 is the record of a theophany granted to the patriarch Jacob at Bethel. *Tradition-history* seeks to trace out how various elements or forms were brought together to produce the present narrative. Walter Rast explains, "Tradition historians propose that these episodes . . . reflect localized cult legends"; and he proposes that the pillar "may have had a prehistory of Canaanite worship" and the heavenly ladder "was probably a ziggurat." Yet "at some point the tradition of the Bethel theophany has interpreted it as . . . underscoring God's special care for the patriarch. . . . But even this is not the end . . . the latest meaning of the tradition becomes part of a pledge which embraces the descendants of the patriarch as well."[50] What Scripture says about the Bethel incident is almost totally divorced from what may "really" have happened.

3. Genesis 37:28, in its present Hebrew text, is a record of Joseph and his brothers: "So when the Midianite merchants came by, his brothers pulled Joseph up out of the cistern and sold him for twenty shekels of silver to the Ishmaelites, who took him to Egypt." *Literary criticism* seeks to recreate certain written sources that supposedly underlie the present text. Long ago S. R. Driver applied Wellhausen's documentary hypothesis (a form of literary criticism) to this passage. Unwilling to grant that the Midianites could be included under Ishmaelites (cf. Judg. 8:24), he divided up verse 28 and assigned the first part—"There passed by Midianites . . . and they lifted Joseph up out of the pit"(ASV)—to an assumed "E" document, separate from the "J"

matter that precedes and follows it. By so dividing the verse, however, he *created* discrepancies. First is that of positing two different groups, corresponding to the two sources, to whom Joseph would have been sold. Also, by removing the brothers from this part of E's record, the "they" is made to "refer to the Midianite merchants passing by, who drew up Joseph from the pit without his brothers' knowledge."[51] What then really happened? Was Joseph lifted up and sold by his brothers, or was he lifted up and kidnapped by the merchants? Who can say— except that, as the result of this process of literary dissection, the historicity of one part (and perhaps both parts) of the verse has been denied. Higher criticism ends up rejecting the truth of the biblical content it is supposed to clarify.

True criticism should, on the contrary, serve as a tool that assists readers of Scripture to gain deeper appreciation for the historicity of its contents. Thus when apparent discrepancies arise—for example, between parallel statements in the synoptic Gospels—critical principles such as the following may be invoked. (1) Discrepancies between quotations should not be considered contradictions when each may be a fair translation (in Greek) of an original statement in another language (as Aramaic). (2) Variations in statement are not contradictions when they arise either from recording different parts of some common event or from assigning different emphases or degrees of importance to the same part. (3) Incidents are not to be identified with each other simply because of similarities of circumstance or description.[52]

EXAMPLES

The following section approaches five questions that are most discussed today within Old Testament and New Testament criticism. Its purpose is not to present a comprehensive treatment, but rather to apply the standards that have been proposed (see "Standards," pp. 95ff.) and to suggest limits within which a truly scientific critic, who respects the nature of his divinely inspired subject matter (see "The Scientific Approach," pp. 93ff.), may freely exercise rational judgment.

1. *Mosaic authorship of the Pentateuch*

Basic to all Old Testament study is Pentateuchal criticism. Of special concern is the Mosaicity of these "five books of Moses."

Scripture suggests three ways in which the concept may be understood. (1) If by *Mosaicity* we mean those portions that were inscripturated, written down, by the hand of Moses himself, such a concept would embrace the following sections:

Passage:	*Wellhausen's "document"*	*Biblical Claim of Mosaicity:*
Exod. 17:8–13	E	Exod. 17:14
Exod. 20:22—23:33	E	Exod. 24:4
Exod. 34:10–26	J	Exod. 34:27
Lev. 18:5	H (in P)	Rom. 10:5
Num. 33:3–49	P	Num. 33:2
Deut. 5–30	D	Deut. 31:9
Deut. 32:1–42	D	Deut. 31:22

These sections amount to fewer than 32 chapters out of the total of 187; for the remaining five-sixths of the Pentateuch, scholars who are committed to the truthfulness of the record are not bound to hypotheses of Mosaic inscripturation. Yet this tabulation demonstrates that Moses wrote sections that appear in all of Wellhausen's various "documents," each of which is supposed to have had its own author (or authors) and distinctive style. The very fact that the New Testament states that Moses wrote down Leviticus 18:5, even though this truth is not indicated in the text of the Pentateuch, suggests that Moses may have authored considerably more than Scripture specifically indicates.

(2) The term *Mosaicity* may refer to those parts composed by Moses—whether actually written down by him or not—such as the address in Deuteronomy 1:6—4:40 or the song in 33:2–29. Assuming the inspiration and accuracy of those who finally compiled the books of Scripture, we realize that this category is, for all practical purposes, equivalent to the first.[53] Still, it means that the rest of the words, which Scripture does not specifically assign to Moses, need not be attributed to him. These include such difficult passages as the observation that Moses was the most humble man on earth (Num. 12:3) or the description of his death (Deut. 34).

(3) Later Scripture teaches a generally Mosaic character that marks the Pentateuch as a whole. Jesus equated the Old Testament with "Moses and the Prophets" (Luke 16:29; cf. 24:44 or Mark 12:26), and the Chronicler speaks of "the book of the law

of the Lord given by Moses [literally, *by the hand of* Moses]"
(2 Chron. 34:14). The Pentateuch, therefore, including Genesis
(which makes no internal claim about its authorship), must be
seen, in a very real sense, as constituting "the five books of
Moses"—datable to his time and produced under his direction,
perhaps with the aid of the seventy elders (see Num. 11:16–17,
24–25) or of Joshua (see Josh. 27:18–20).

The critical theory of a small Mosaic "core" of writings,
supplemented over the centuries by various redactors, is
specifically refuted by Pentateuchal laws forbidding just such
additions (Deut. 4:2; 12:32). Old Testament scholars are thus
free to speculate about pre-Mosaic "forms" or documents to
their hearts' content, provided they do not thereby bring into
question the historical claims of the biblical contents—as
through proposals of disharmonious double recordings or of contradictory strata (so that "J," for example, teaches a 40-day
flood and "P" one of 150 days). Most exegetes, however, seem to
lose their interest in higher criticism when confronted by these
divinely imposed limits. Yet our Lord Himself insisted that
Moses wrote about Him and added, "But since you do not believe what he wrote, how are you going to believe what I say?"
(John 5:46–47).

2. *Authorship of Isaiah 40–66*

One of the so-called "assured results of modern criticism" is
the denial that Isaiah wrote chapters 40–66 of the book that
bears his name. Without going into the internal arguments,
about which a great deal could be said both pro and con,[54]
suffice it at this point to summarize the external (New Testament) argument. The recorded words of Jesus remain silent as
far as assigning the material of these chapters to Isaiah is concerned; but His apostles clearly assign it to the eighth-century
prophet. Have we then a limit imposed on critical speculation at
this point? An evangelical such as Clark Pinnock says no. He
writes:

> Spokesmen such as Schaeffer and Lindsell tend to confuse the
> high view of Scripture with their own interpretations of it . . .
> [e.g., making] a good deal out of the fact that the NT is accus-
> tomed to citing the whole book of Isaiah under the prophet's
> name, thus settling definitively the question of its authorship. . . .
> They apparently have assumed the right to foreclose on the

exegetical options available as if they could somehow dictate to all other evangelicals, including those trained in biblical studies, the interpretation they must accept. Enough of that![55]

In regard to passages where the Book of Isaiah is simply generally cited under the prophet's name, as in Mark 1:2, and perhaps in 7:6, evangelicals must meticulously avoid imposing personal interpretations on others. But in a passage such as John 12:41, where both parts of Isaiah are cited and the apostle testifies, "Isaiah said this because he saw Jesus' glory and spoke about him,"[56] is denial of Isaiah's personal authorship to be considered "interpretation," or is it a violation of the apostolic meaning?[57] The issue is clear: he who is open-minded about accepting the disunity of Isaiah's prophecy is already close-minded against accepting the inerrant authority of John's Gospel, and therefore of Scripture as a whole.

3. Authenticity of Daniel's predictions

A third area of Old Testament criticism where current differences between the free (negative) and the committed (positive) approaches to the subject become most apparent is that of Daniel's predictions. Representing the former approach, R. H. Pfeiffer was candid in expressing himself about both of the standards that have been proposed above for establishing the limits appropriate to biblical criticism. Concerning historicity of content, he asserted flatly: "Such miracles as the revelation to Daniel of the details of Nebuchadnezzar's dream and their meaning (2:19), the divine deliverance of . . . Daniel from the lions (6:22–24), and a hand without a body writing a message on a wall (5:5), lie outside the realm of historical facts." Concerning the book's own statements about its sixth-century, exilic composition, he adds, "The historical background of Daniel, as was discovered immediately after its publication, is not that of the sixth but the second century. . . . In dating an apocalypse such as Daniel, the period in which the seer is said to have received the revelations is entirely irrelevant."[58]

Pfeiffer, with almost all of today's negative critics, relegates the book's author to legend and its predictions to the time of the Maccabean revolt, specifically 165 B.C. Yet Christ's words in Matthew 24:15 ("When you see . . . the abomination that causes desolation, spoken of through the prophet Daniel . . .") testify to His belief not only in the historicity of the seer but also in a fulfillment of his predictions that was still future in A.D. 30.[59] To this day I can recall my shock when I mentioned these facts to a critically minded friend and he replied, "I know more about Daniel than Jesus did." It dramatizes how the lines are to be drawn concerning appropriate biblical criticism.

If one were to select similarly crucial areas in New Testament studies, he would probably turn to the matter of the historicity of all the accounts in John's Gospel, with its preincarnate divine Logos, or even to that of the synoptic stories, with their Son of man Christology. Harry Boer, for example, comments: "All that we know of . . . the words of Jesus in which he expressed his teaching we know through *reports* of the four evangelists . . . the same kind of human medium through which the rest of the Bible comes to us" (italics his). Boer eventually salvages enough facts to conclude that "Jesus again and again accommodated himself to existing beliefs which we no longer accept."[60] For the purpose, however, of illustrating legitimate boundaries to higher criticism, reference to the authorships of the following two books may prove to be particularly instructive.

4. *Authorship of Ephesians*

Ephesians has suffered more consistent criticism than any other Epistle in the Pauline corpus, except for the Pastorals. Not all of the criticism, however, has necessarily been negative. The question, To whom was it written? is a matter belonging to lower criticism. Most MSS (including A, D, and G) insert within 1:1 the qualifier "in Ephesus"; but the earliest and best MSS (including ℵ , B, and P"46") omit these two words. That is to say, Paul's inspired autograph, as well as we can reconstruct it, was silent at this point. Critics are thus free to consider Ephesians as an encyclical letter, perhaps (if it happened to be directed, among other churches, to the group at Laodicea) as the letter referred to in Colossians 4:16.[61]

The question, however, By whom was it written? belongs to higher criticism. All the MSS give the author as Paul (1:1; 3:1; cf. the apostle's personal references in 3:2–8). There is thus no question among critics about what the inspired autograph said, only about whether or not it is true. Many scholars today, through the application of rationalistic induction to the style and content of Ephesians, have judged it to be spurious and have assigned it a date near the close of the first century, a generation after the apostle's death[62]—a conclusion obviously impossible for those committed to Scripture's divine trustworthiness.

5. *Authorship of 2 Peter*

The single "most assured" denial made by modern New Testament criticism concerns the apostolic authorship of 2 Peter. Even such moderate critics as B. M. Metzger relegate this Epistle to the second century, "long after Peter's lifetime."[63] Here again, however, we are not able to go into the pros and cons of the argument. Suffice it to note that this book does not simply claim to be the words of "Peter, . . . apostle of Jesus Christ" (1:1) and allude to the writer's personal experiences with Jesus (1:12–14). It explicitly bases the authority of its teaching on the reality of its author's having been one of the three human eyewitnesses to Christ's transfiguration (1:16–18). One's choice between Petrine authenticity and pseudepigraphic fraud rests once again on the limits that are recognized as legitimate for criticism of the inerrant Word of God.

EVALUATION

In light of the relationship between higher criticism and biblical inerrancy, as this has been outlined above, Christians will ask, "How should we then live?" (Ezek. 33:10 KJV). Four particular factors, moreover, seem to demand the practical attention of those who would live in conformity to Jesus Christ.

Tension

Evangelicals need to be aware first of all of the intransigence of negative higher criticism and the seriousness of its conflict with biblical orthodoxy. The problem is not about to go away. Gerhard Maier may argue "till the cows come home," alleging, as he does the end of the historical-critical method. He may show how those who reject part of the Bible on higher critical grounds are unable to agree on a stopping place, so as to preserve some "canon in the canon" and how instead, as in the words of H. Braun, "man, who began critically to analyze revelation and to discover for himself what is normative, found at the end of the road: himself."[64] But his evidence and his logic falls on deaf ears (cf. 2 Cor. 4:4). Stuhlmacher retorts, on behalf of the critical consensus: "No contemporary theologian can forego the results

. . . of this biblical criticism. . . . Any scientific alternative to the historical-critical method is out of the question."[65]

Evangelicals not infrequently seek encouragement from current "Reversals of Old Testament Criticism,"[66] and call attention to the modern shift in Homeric criticism toward acceptance of Homeric authorship.[67] One might note, for example, a recent reversal in the critical position concerning the order of Ezra and Nehemiah. Where once only conservative interpreters, such as J. S. Wright, maintained the traditional order, this view has regained the support of a number of important scholars within the last decade, including Morton Smith, F.M. Cross, H. Tadmor, Y. Aharoni, M. Avi-Yonah, and B. Mazar.[68] Yet the mood and basic positions of negative higher criticism as a whole remain unchanged. Johannes Botterweck has inaugurated his massive project, the *Theological Dictionary of the Old Testament*, with this justifying explanation: "The form-critical and traditio-historical methods have been refined to such a point that one can expect rather certain results."[69] The articles in the dictionary indicate an almost total commitment to this belief.

Where revisions in the critical stance have occurred, the shift has seldom moved all the way back to full acceptance of the scriptural text. Antievangelicals such as James Barr have been quick to censure conservatives for their inconsistency in adopting the new stance themselves.[70] And when an important archaeological discovery, such as D. J. Wiseman's Nebuchadnezzar Chronicle, has completely overthrown a particular theory of negative criticism, its disciples nonetheless exhibit phenomenal ability to maintain their skepticism, even when having to furnish new reasons for their "faith."[71]

Scholarly conformity often extends even to the details of the higher critical system. As R. K. Harrison once remarked:

> Driver's work established the "standard of orthodoxy" in Old Testament liberal circles. While minor variations were permitted, an individual's academic respectability depended to a large extent upon the closeness with which he adhered to the pattern set forth by Driver. Thus there sprang up a curious liberal-conservatism which is still in evidence today in British scholarship.[72]

But whether in detail or in essence, the commitment demanded by positive (evangelical) higher criticism simply cannot coexist with the freedom, and skepticism, demanded by negative (liberal) higher criticism. The tension is irresolvable.

Temptation

Evangelicals, furthermore, must be aware of the resultant, perennial temptations confronting their theologians the moment they undertake—as stated by LaSor at the outset of this study—"to explore the implications of modern scholarship."[73] Boer, for example, grants that conservative denominations such as the Christian Reformed Church, of which he is a member, "have traditionally adhered to the view that the Bible as God's word cannot contain inconsistencies of any kind. . . .The words infallibility and inerrancy are usually applied to Scripture." He then declares, "The evangelical scholar cannot ignore this. But he also has his [internal] academic conscience and the general [external] theological community to live with."[74] By his allusion to the theological "community," Boer underlines the pressure toward conformity that Harrison mentions in his reference to British scholars.

Evangelical graduate students have sometimes sold their souls for a Ph.D. degree. Those who survive this hurdle find that when they have secured a professorship, their participation in research and in scholarly meetings subjects them to even more persistent temptations. Confronted by the ridicule, direct or indirect, of academic leaders like James Barr, who insist that "where the fundamentalist takes revelation to be identical with the propositions of the biblical text . . . he is in direct contradiction with modern science; and his position can be maintained only on the ground of simple credulity, defying everything that is thought and known. . . ."[75] Is it any wonder that younger scholars, especially, should develop second thoughts about inerrancy?

We should remember that what "is thought and known" by the unbelieving academic world is based on an uninhibited criticism that renders *itself* unscientific by perverting rationality into rationalism. It refuses to view its biblical subject within a supernaturalistic framework, which alone is appropriate to its divine nature.[76]

Boer's allusion to the internal "academic conscience" pinpoints what probably constitutes the most basic danger of all: personal pride. Soulen's *Handbook* defines biblical criticism as "that approach to the study of Scripture which consciously searches for and applies the canons of reason to its investigation."[77] S. T. David frankly admits: "It is true that no Christian who believes that the Bible errs can hold that the Bible *alone* is his authority for faith and practice. He must hold to some other authority or criterion as well. That authority, I am not embarrassed to say, is his own mind, his own ability to reason." Here, in fact, is the supreme appeal of negative higher criticism. As Davis bluntly sums it up, "I am the final judge of what I will believe or not believe."[78]

The scholar, whose work is constantly one of critical evaluation, faces the peculiar attraction of the built-in "occupational hazard" of pride. It is not without reason that time after time Christian organizations have found their educational institutions to be the initiators and leaders in apostasy from Scripture and the most resistant to the biblical demand of "casting down every high thing that exalteth itself against the knowledge of God, and bringing into captivity every thought to the obedience of Christ" (2 Cor. 10:5). As long as seminary professorships are filled by human beings, the church must be forever reminding itself that eternal vigilance is the price, not of liberty (= pride), but of Christian commitment (= humility—a quality that our race has ever found to be in such short supply!).

Results

Yet a most sobering antidote to the temptation of assuming critical autonomy is to look at its results, to consider the dilemmas that have been created by today's lapse into negative higher criticism. It is a heresy that affects our attitudes toward life, toward revelation, and toward Jesus Christ Himself. Biblical theologians like Otto Baab, who rejoiced that "the breakdown of medieval authoritarianism permitted the mind of the individual biblical scholar to examine freely and critically the documents which were the foundation of his faith," and who conceded that "an educated churchman finds it impossible to follow the ultra-conservatives, to whom the unquestioned Bible is the very word of life," must face the uncertainties and the vacuum in life that result. Baab continues:

> Modern man's dilemma is created by this failure to find a source of authority possessing ultimate validity and capable of giving him lasting peace in his personal and collective life . . . [and] for the creation of this dilemma . . . the biblical scholar of the modern school must accept a large measure of responsibility.[79]

Concerning God's revelation, the problem with which negative critics must wrestle is the inconsistency of their views with the very faith they claim to follow. S. T. Davis, for example, is honest enough to admit that "there is never any tendency in the New Testament to deny, question, or criticize the Old Testament." Instead, he finds an attitude not only of faith in general truths but also of commitment to specific facts: "The historicity of events and figures described in the Old Testament is taken for granted." He proceeds to list such "unlikely happenings" as the stories of Adam and Eve, Cain and Abel, the Flood, Lot's wife, Jonah and the great fish, and so on.[80] It is not at all easy to demonstrate consistent and practical devotion to a "revelation" with which you are in disagreement.

Most serious of all, the historicity of the events just listed is not simply the teaching of the New Testament, it is the teaching of Jesus Christ directly. Harry Boer expresses a concern that "appeal to the authority of Jesus is sometimes made to deprive higher critical study of the Bible of its legitimate place."[81] But, as his theological ancestor Abraham Kuyper put it, "If Christ attributed absolute authority to the Old Covenant . . . then the matter is settled for everyone who worships Him."[82] It seems to boil down to this: either human criticism gains the place of honor or Jesus does. Some critics are forthright enough to document their hesitancies toward the latter. Boer speaks of Jesus' accommodating Himself to popular beiiefs that He knew were wrong.[83] Davis seems to represent a more widely held view and speaks of Jesus' ignorance: "Perhaps he shared with the people of his day certain false beliefs."[84] Was His "ignorance" limited just to *certain* such beliefs? Sigmund Mowinckel says flatly, "He shared our imperfect insight into all matters pertaining to the world of sense. . . . He knew neither more nor less than most people of his class in Galilee concerning history . . . geography, or the history of biblical literature."[85]

Where, then, do such views leave the worship of Jesus? J. I. Packer's dictum seems valid: "Any view that subjects the written word of God to the opinions and pronouncements of men involves unbelief and disloyalty toward Christ."[86]

Strategy

Confronted by today's anti-Christian higher criticism and by its pervasive dominance within the academic community— including educational institutions, learned societies, and scholarly publications—evangelicals must be aware of what can, and what cannot, be achieved. In regard to liberalism and its disciples, who lead the negative critical movement, the battle must be fought in the area of preunderstanding. In the words of R. K. Harrison, "It seems abundantly clear that all future scholarship must adopt a more critical attitude toward its theoretical presuppositions."[87] Parts I and II of Gerhard Maier's *End of the Historical-Critical Method* serve as noteworthy examples of essentially philosophical refutation of the assumption of rationalistic autonomy. Such refutation must precede any positive presentation of what Maier styles the historical-biblical method—more often called the grammatico-historical method.

Put more concretely, until a scholar becomes willing to accept the lordship of Jesus Christ over his life and thought, it is futile to try to argue him out of Wellhausen's literary analysis of the Pentateuch, which, to the naturalistic mind set, is the only viable option. We may occasionally twist the lion's tail by showing, for example, how Daniel's third empire has the fourfold character of Greece (7:6; 8:22) and not the twofold character of Persia (7:5; 8:3, 20), with which liberalism identifies it. We should labor under no illusions, however, that such facts will perhaps persuade a negative critic to give up his Maccabean (antisupernaturalistic) understanding of Daniel in favor of a Roman (supernaturalistic) one.

For evangelicals the words that the Old Testament scholar N. H. Ridderbos spoke twenty years ago still bear repeating:

> Two dangers especially are present. The first is that it [evangelicalism] may fall short in its regard for the authority of God's Word [the very point stressed in the second evaluation, "Temptation," pp. 108ff. above]. But another danger is that orthodox Old Testament scholarship exists in too great a degree on the reaction against Old Testament criticism. Even though the critic often presents analysis of the books of the Bible in an unacceptable manner, this does not necessarily mean that every analysis thereof must be rejected. How can evangelicals keep from overreacting?[88]

Our strategy must, first of all, involve awareness. Both advanced students and lay people need to be fully informed about the nature and potentialities of higher criticism. We must then be prepared either for guarded acceptance or for categorical rejection of a given position, depending on circumstances. As indicated above (see "Standards," pp. 95ff.), thorough biblical criticism is not only permissible but desirable and, indeed, necessary, provided it studiously refrains from violating the Bible's statements about its own composition and from rejecting its factual reliability. Provisos of this sort are, of course, anathema to the proponents of uninhibited criticism, for they equate such restrictiveness with "the exclusion of any serious critical study of the Bible." Boer complains, "The historical evangelical view of Scripture takes no serious account of the findings of higher criticism except insofar as these are compatible with its basic presuppositions."[89] How right he is! If Romans 5:12–14 says that through one man, Adam, "sin entered the world, . . . and death through sin," then so long as evangelicals remain committed to apostolic authority, they cannot be "openminded" to critical theories that suggest the contrary. It is high time that believers behave more consistently in their rejection of negative criticism. Enough of those book reviews that seek to have it both ways, acknowledging the inerrancy of Scripture and yet courting academic prestige by extolling each new treatment of the myth of Adam's sin as more "stimulating," more "intriguing," and more of a "scholarly feast" than the last!

A final element that is becoming more and more crucial within evangelical strategy concerns equivocation. The battle for the Bible, as Harold Lindsell reminds us, is no longer limited to a conflict between the advocates of negative higher criticism "out there" in institutionalized liberalism and the advocates of biblical inerrancy "in here" among professing evangelicals. Those who sign annual teaching contracts or Evangelical Theological Society membership statements affirming the inerrancy of the scriptural autographs are among those subject to the insidious temptations of the rationalistic critical method. Harry Boer therefore puts his finger on "the evangelical scholar . . . [who] resolves the conflict by bowing verbally in both directions." If Boer detests such ambiguity as "conducive neither to theological clarity nor to theological integrity,"[90] how much more should those evangelicals who have a higher view of Scripture rise to the defense of their Christian heritage.

One must be careful, of course, to distinguish between a person who is simply uninformed or improperly taught or who has temporary doubts or unresolved questions and one who is a convinced and crusading critic. But if an advocate of negative higher criticism raises his head in a pulpit, classroom, publishing

)

house, or board chamber in which the committed Christian has a God-given voice or vote, the latter must speak out boldly and vigorously against any effort to make the Scriptures anything less than the inerrant Word of God.

It may be that some former evangelical has come to feel that he has to accept the dictates of today's criticism. That is a tragedy. It is an error from which we must protect the people of God for whom we happen to be responsible. It is a challenge for us to pray for the erring one and with tears, with words, and with love to seek to woo him back to a view of the Scriptures that is compatible with the God of truth, who inspired their writing.

LEGITIMATE HERMENEUTICS

Walter C. Kaiser, Jr.

Walter C. Kaiser, Jr., is Professor of Semitic Languages and Old Testament at Trinity Evangelical Divinity School, Deerfield, Illinois. He is a graduate of Wheaton College (B.A.), Wheaton Graduate School, (B.D.), Brandeis University (M.A. and Ph.D. in Mediterranean studies). Dr. Kaiser is the author of four books, including The Old Testament in Contemporary Preaching *and* Toward an Old Testament Theology. *He is also a contributor to* Moody Monthly, Journal of the Evangelical Theological Society, *and* Evangelical Quarterly. *He has taught at Wheaton College, frequently spoken to university groups, and ministered widely in the Evangelical Free Church of America. Dr. Kaiser is a member of the Society of Biblical Literature and the textbook committee of Moody Press. He is a board member of the Near East Archaeological Society and has served as national president of the Evangelical Theological Society.*

CHAPTER SUMMARY

Only by maintaining the important distinction between meaning (that *single* idea represented by the text *as meant by the human author* who received God's revelation) and significance (which represents a relationship that exists between that single meaning and the reader, a situation, or an idea) can Scripture be delivered from the hands of its enemies and its friends. The current crises in the doctrine of Scripture is directly linked to poor procedures and methods of handling Scripture. Three principles of general hermeneutics are balanced off with three especially troublesome issues for twentieth-century believers from the area of special hermeneutics—the implications of relating the single meaning of the text for those who live and read that text in different times and cultures. Five current bypasses used by some interpreters to escape this key distinction between meaning and significance are also examined and found wanting.

5 *Walter C. Kaiser, Jr.*

LEGITIMATE HERMENEUTICS

M UCH OF THE current debate over the Scriptures among believing Christians is, at its core, a result of failure on the part of evangelicals to come to terms with the issue of hermeneutics. Because we who are living in this century have been occupied with many other battles, usually not of our choosing, one issue that should have claimed our attention was neglected. Consequently, while many evangelicals may find a large amount of agreement on the doctrines of revelation, inspiration, and even canonicity, something close to a Babel of voices is heard on methods of interpreting the Scriptures.

Evangelicals are now being pressed on several sides, however, to attend to this missing part of theological curriculum. The hermeneutical debate outside our circles has grown so prolific and vigorous that at times it threatens to be, for some, the only issue. Yet the discussion may be "not less serious than that of the Reformation" itself.[1] Indeed, we believe something comparable to a hermeneutical reformation is needed in our day.

As one of the contributions that arose outside evangelical circles, the new hermeneutic of some existentialist theologians focused on the problem of transcending the historical particularity and the antique address of Scripture by stressing the words "now" and "today" and the need to recapitulate scriptural stories in the believer's present existence.[2] Meanwhile two other

117

offerings arose as a partial rebuke to the sterility[3] of the liberal historical-critical approach: new criticism[4] and canon criticism.[5] In both approaches the focus of attention was on the text itself rather than on the alleged literary sources and the reigning historical situation. As a redress to the previous imbalances and sterility of historical-critical exegesis, these solutions would have the interpreter now concentrate on repeated phrases, patterns, larger sense units, and the canon as a whole rather than on individual words, tenses, and literary sources. The literature and varieties of positions thus grew bulkier by the day, as more and more solutions were set forth.[6]

But what of evangelicals? The time was long past for our entry into this field once again. Already we were faced with problems arising from an accelerated culture, not to mention our own needs and the challenges of numerous novel hermeneutical systems. Where was one to begin?

In our judgment, we must first return to the basics and then make a frontal assault on the most difficult questions of interpretation faced today.

GENERAL HERMENEUTICS

No definition of interpretation could be more fundamental than this: *To interpret we must in every case reproduce the sense the Scriptural writer intended for his own words.* The first step in the interpretive process is to link only those ideas with the author's language that he connected with them. The second step is to express these ideas understandably.

Yet at no point has modern society, including many evangelicals, resisted hermeneutical rules more strenuously than at the point of this definition. In our post-Kantian relativism, most interpreters have concluded, as E. D. Hirsch correctly analyzes,[7] that "all 'knowledge' is relative"[8] and a return to the author's own meanings is considered both unnecessary and wrong. Instead, meaning has often become a personal, subjective, and changing thing. "What speaks to me," "what turns me on," "what I get out of a text" are the significant concerns, not what an author intended by his use of words.

But in our view, such "cognitive atheists"[9] subvert the goal of objective knowledge and threaten the very possibility of learning. All knowledge is reduced to the horizon of one's own prejudices and personal predilections. This is true whether it is done for "spiritual" or for philosophical reasons, both approaches usurp the author's revelatory stance and insert one's own authority for his. The only way our generation will be delivered from this kind of outrageous interpretive solipsism will be to adopt the earlier distinction of E. D. Hirsch between meaning and significance:

> *Meaning* is that which is represented by a text; it is what the author meant by his use of a particular sign sequence; it is what the signs represent. *Significance* on the other hand, names a relationship between that meaning and a person, or a conception or a situation.[10]

Only by maintaining these definitions and distinctions will Scripture be delivered from the hands of its enemies—and its friends. All our own notions of truth and principle must be set aside in favor of those the sacred writers taught if we are to be valid interpreters. In fact, the basic teaching of all of sacred theology is inseparably connected with the results of our hermeneutics; for what is that theology except what Scripture teaches? And the way to ascertain what Scripture teaches is to apply the rules and principles of interpretation. Therefore it is imperative that these rules be properly grounded and that their application be skillfully and faithfully applied. If the foundation itself is conjecture, imagination, or error, what more can be hoped for what is built on it?

The Bible Is to Be Interpreted by the Same Rules as Other Books

Now it may be laid down as a first rule that the Bible is to be interpreted in the same manner and with the same principles as all other books. Of course, we mean by this the manner they were interpreted before the literary revolution that came in 1946, which autocratically announced the autonomy of a work, that is, its freedom from its author, and which reversal E. D. Hirsch sought to rectify in his *Validity in Interpretation.*

But some will object that the Bible is not a common or profane book. It deals with supernatural things; therefore it ought to be treated separately from other books. While it is a fact that it is a unique revelation containing supernatural things that no human may aspire to know on his own, yet the above conclusion, often drawn from this agreed-on fact, is not necessary. After all, it is a *revelation* to us that God deliberately designed to communicate to human beings what they themselves could not or would not know unless they received it from Him. To deny this is to say that God gave a revelation in which nothing is revealed or that the disclosure of God is also a concealment! It reverses the meaning of words and of reality itself.

More recently, another objection has been voiced. To insist that Scripture is to be read like any other book, some maintain, cuts at the heart of understanding Scripture's unique status and how it continues to function as a norm in a religious community. The rules must be loose enough to allow altogether new "meanings" to be attached to the ancient words if they are to function for people removed from the original audience by several thousand years.[11] But this is to confuse the very distinction Hirsch makes between *meaning* and *significance*. Past particularity must not be transcended by substituting present significance as the new meaning of the text, for then the chasm between the "then" and "now" of the text is jumped too facilely and at terrible cost. One must sacrifice all objectivism and divine authority. The price is too high.

The point remains. God has deliberately decided to accommodate mankind by disclosing Himself in our language and according to the mode to which we are accustomed in other literary productions. While the content is vastly different, the medium of language is identical.

The Principles of Interpretation Are as Native and Universal to Man as Is Speech Itself [12]

A second rule is that man's basic ability to interpret is not derived from some science, technical skill, or exotic course open only to the more gifted intellects of a society. The general principles of interpreting are not learned, invented, or discovered by people. They are part and parcel of the nature of man as a being made in the image of God. Given the gift of communication and speech itself, man already began to practice the principles of hermeneutics. The art has been in use from the moment God spoke to Adam in the Garden, and from the time Adam addressed Eve, until the present. In human conversation, the speaker is always the author; the person spoken to is always the interpreter. Correct understanding must always begin with the meanings the speaker attaches to his own words.

It is agreed that proper interpretation is more than a native art. The science of hermeneutics collects these observed rules as already practiced by native speakers and arranges them in an orderly way for the purpose of study and reflection. But such a science does not alter the fact that the rules were in operation before they were codified and examined. The situation here is exactly as it is with grammars and dictionaries; they do not prescribe what a language must do; they only describe how its best speakers and writers use it. So it is with hermeneutics.

But all this sounds too facile to match the experience of many who have wrestled with the Greek, Hebrew, and Aramaic of the original text of Scripture. How can the art of interpretation be of such a common-sense variety when it seems to be so dependent on great learning and dedicated study, placing the interpreter, as it does, back into the government, climate, society, and religious conditions of biblical times? How can we accurately hear the prophets and apostles without possessing a good command of Hebrew and Greek? Is not the object of language study to place the interpreter as closely as possible to the times and thought of the sacred writers? But does not such study then contradict our second rule stated above?

On the contrary, this study is only preparatory, an antecedent for the task of hermeneutics, which still must follow. Never can any or all of this learning and study be substituted for actual interpretation or by itself constitute the science of hermeneutics. If birth and providence had so favored us that we were part of the culture and language when one or another of the prophets or apostles spoke, we could dispense with all background and language study. We would understand these areas as immediately as we now understand speakers and writers in our own day, basically without the aid of encyclopedias, grammars, dictionaries, and geographies. It is only the passing of time that has rendered these additional steps necessary for those who must not only declare what is transparently clear on the surface of Scripture with regard to our salvation (the perspicuity of Scripture; see pp. 128ff.) but must also teach the full counsel of God.

True, scholars have occasionally in the science of general hermeneutics laid down rules that depart from the principles known to us by virtue of the image of God and the gift of communication. Fortunately, however, their recognition has been short-lived, and more reliable leaders have arisen to call for a return to rules that do not violate what God-given *nature* has taught, *art* has practiced, and *science* has collected and arranged in systems.

A good deal of learning is sometimes necessary to understand words that we do not ordinarily know from daily experience. We must study those words until they become as much a part of us as our native vocabulary. But the principles for interpreting these foreign Hebrew and Greek words is not different from interpreting those of our normal conversations.

It would be wrong, of course, to argue that everyone is automatically and totally successful in the *practice* of hermeneutical art just because it is an integral part of the gift of communication. Surely there are conversations and books that are difficult for some persons to understand, because the words and general subject are not "part of the person" as yet. Here again learning is necessary. Yet the basic rules remain the same, whether the language is Isaiah's Hebrew, Virgil's Latin, Paul's Greek, or Shakespeare's English.

My Personal Reception and Application of an Author's Words Is a Distinct and Secondary Act From the Need First to Understand His Words

The "significance" of a literary work indicates a *relationship* between the "meaning" intended by the author in his use of a certain sequence of words and some person, idea, or situation—as Hirsch so aptly contests in the definition already given. It is wrong, therefore, to confuse meaning and significance.

But some will contend that it is God who speaks in the Bible and not men; the men who wrote the Scriptures were the mere receptacles of what God wanted to say through them. Revelation, in this view, perhaps concealed as much from the authors as it made known to them. Therefore the normal rules of interpretation do not apply.

The answer to this charge is easy. What God spoke, He spoke in human, not heavenly, language! Moreover, He spoke through the vocabularies, idioms, circumstances, and personalities of each of the chosen writers. Try translating each of the writers of Scripture, and this difference will be immediately apparent. You will wear out a lexicon looking up new Hebrew words in Job and Hosea, but you will read Genesis and Haggai with delightful speed and ease. The Greek grammar of the Book of Hebrews slows down even experienced translators to a snail's pace, but John's Gospel poses few grammatical problems. No, the superiority of the Scriptures over other books does not come in the *manner* we interpret it but in its *matter* and grand source.

Still, it will be argued that "the man without the Spirit does not accept the things that come from the Spirit of God . . . and he cannot understand them, because they are spiritually discerned" (1 Cor. 2:14). Surely, it is contended, the Bible calls for a different set of rules. A person must be spiritually enlightened before he can understand Scripture.

The case is overstated, however. It is not as if there were two logics and two hermeneutics in the world, one natural and the other spiritual. Paul's point (in 1 Cor. 2:14) has to do with the personal application and significance of the understood and basic meaning of his words. It is also true, of course, that a person must be in a sympathetic state of mind and in a proper mental condition to begin to understand subjects toward which he is not naturally inclined—whether those subjects are astrophysics, mathematics, poetry, or the Bible. Consequently, Paul's word cannot be used to claim that people without the Spirit do not understand any part of the Bible until they become spiritual. Such a claim plainly contradicts both our own experience and the teachings of Scripture that man will also be judged for rejecting that which Scripture itself declares should be abundantly clear to them, because they refuse to receive it. A professor at the university I attended gave one of the best explanations of Romans 1–6 I have ever heard, but when he was asked by a skeptical student if he "believed that stuff," he scoffed and mockingly replied: "Who said anything about personally believing it? I just said that's what Paul said, and you better remember that's what he said!" He understood Romans well enough to teach it, but he didn't "buy" it. He did not accept it, because he refused to see any relationship between the text and himself. We believe it is the special work of the Holy Spirit to convict people so that they see that relationship and believe and act accordingly. But it does not contradict the fact that God means for His revelation to be understood.

One more attempt is made to break this third rule of general hermeneutics. It suggests that the prophets confessed that they themselves sometimes did not understand the words they wrote. Why then should we attempt to return to the human author's meanings when they confessed their own ignorance (e.g., 1 Peter 1:10–12)?

I have examined this problem and the text of 1 Peter 1:10–12 in two other works.[13] I strongly affirm that the prophets claimed ignorance only on the matter of *time*. They decisively affirm that they knew five rather precise components of salvation. They knew they were writing about: (1) the Messiah, (2) His sufferings, (3) His glorified state yet to come, (4) the precedence of His suffering to His glory, and (5) the application of the salvation they announced in pre-Christian days as being not only to themselves but also to those in the Christian era! Scholars err badly when they translate the Greek phrase *eis tina ē poion kairon* ("what [time] or what manner of time") as if it meant "what [person]!" The Revised Standard Version, the New American Standard Bible, the Modern Language Bible, and the New English Bible (footnote) are definitely incorrect here. It is a grammatical impossibility! The passage teaches that these men were most aware of what they were writing.

The same arguments can be raised against the attempt to use Daniel 12:6–8 to prove that Daniel had no idea what he was predicting there,[14] using Caiaphas's prediction that "one man must die for the nation" (John 11:49–52) to prove that men can make unconscious predictions,[15] and extreme interpretations of Peter's claim that "no prophecy of Scripture is of any private loosing" (2 Peter 1:10–21).[16]

Some will cite the promises of our Lord that the Holy Spirit will "teach *you* all things" (John 14:26), "take from what is mine and make it known to *you*" (John 16:15), and "will guide *you* into all truth" (John 16:13).[17] These verses, however, were spoken only to the Lord's disciples and they specifically constitute the promise regarding the New Testament canon. If some should complain that this so severely restricts the "you" of this text that other instructions, such as the Great Commission, would thereby be similarly restricted, I reply, as did William Carey to his generation (who preferred to leave the work of discipling all nations to the first disciples of Jesus), by saying that the divine intention in Matthew 28 is a universal "you." The text continues, "And surely I will be with you always, [i.e., *all* believers] to the very end of the age." Where such extension is made, we must make it also. But where a command or promise is restricted to others (as in John 14:25–26; 15:2–27; 16:12–15), we must not expropriate it and arrogantly declare that, by a miracle of the Spirit's special revelation of the meaning of biblical passages, we are spared the difficult work of exegesis and interpretation!

ALLEGED EXCEPTIONS TO GENERAL HERMENEUTICAL PRINCIPLES

Some five principal by-passes have been used by various interpreters of Scripture to escape the three basic rules and the key distinction between meaning and significance already set forth in this chapter. They are: (1) allegorical interpretation, (2) overdependence on the principle of the "perspicuity of Scripture," (3) improper use of the principle of "progressive revelation," (4) unfair appropriation of the alleged freedom with which the New Testament writers cite the Old Testament, and (5) appeal to the implied presence of a dual sense in the messianic predictions of the Old Testament. Each of these claims must be examined, especially with a view to determining if divine revelation does indeed give some "hints" that qualify as a restriction of interpretation to the single intention of the author. Unfortunately, many hope that such procedures will protect their Bibles from errors and allow them to claim the doctrine of inerrancy with good conscience, while others are left only with what they call the mere letter of the text.[18]

Allegorical Interpretation

This method of explaining Scripture adopts as its ruling idea the principle that certain words have another meaning besides their natural one. Those who hold this view say either (1) that many passages of Scripture have, in addition to the literal (grammatical-historical) sense, a hidden (deeper, higher, spiritual) sense or (2) that Scripture has, besides the simple literal meaning, another deeper sense *under* the literal one, a *hypomoia*. Both views produce the same results, except that the second is a little more sophisticated in its approach.

The source for this pattern of thinking is not Scripture. It is built mostly on a so-called doctrine of correspondences, in which there is said to be a correspondence between the earthly or natural world and the heavenly or spiritual realm. The former produces correct and perfect analogies of the latter. This concept, of course, is clearly seen in ancient Platonic thought, where things of the visible world are only shadows of invisible and higher images. The Greeks adopted the view out of expediency and desperation as a tactic to conceal, excuse, and even venerate the mythological exploits of their gods and men, which were no longer accepted as literal. Likewise some Jewish philosophers, theosophists, and Pharisees found the method useful for deriving their own opinions and patterns of thinking from texts that otherwise would have resisted the boldest hermeneutical assaults.

No less vulnerable is much present-day evangelical preaching and teaching, which is often superficial and frothy, because of failure to spend enough time with the text and to patiently hear what it is saying first–rather than out of any overt embarrassment about the literal claims of an allegedly defunct Scripture. This method of sermonizing opens up an easy path—particularly for quick, adroit, fanciful, but lazy minds who, under pretense of truth and righteousness, teach *what* they will from *where* they will in Scripture. Fortunately for the church, little immediate harm is done in most cases (other than teaching poor methodology and starving God's people from the full counsel of God). Most evangelical practitioners of this method merely "gather wool" from various passages and then import the ideas into unnatural biblical contexts.

However, there is a serious wing of conservative interpreters who claim that the dual meaning of Scripture can in principle be argued from the fact that there is a dual set of authors for every text: *viz,* God and the writer. Still others allege that Scripture itself recommends this method by giving us two examples of "mild allegory"[19] in Galatians 4:19–26[20] and 1 Corinthians 9:8–10.

The first argument for dual authorship we have already dealt with in the first part of this chapter and we have examined at length 1 Corinthians 9:8–10 elsewhere.[21] But Galatians 4:22–26 appears at first blush to support the case. Two rejoinders may be made: (1) in Galatians 4:20, Paul confesses that he is somewhat hesitant as to just how he should address the Galatians but that he will now explain his point to them in their own way (*allaxai tēn phōnēn mou*),[22] using the Genesis story of Sarah and Hagar as an illustration to suit better their rabbinical tastes. (2) As Ellicott observed, Galatians 4:24 warns that Paul merely borrowed the Old Testament account as an illustration; he was not exegeting it. He clearly says, "*all which class of things*" (*hatina*) viewed in the most general way "*may be put into an allegory*" (*estin allēgoroumena*).[23] Paul supplies no comfort, either in this text or in 1 Corinthians 9:8–10, for an allegorical practice.

Surprisingly enough, what some interpreters label as the spiritual, deeper, or higher sense is often nothing more than the real and proper sense that the writer intended. For example, when Paul, in 1 Corinthians 10, mentions that Christ led the Israelites in the desert and gave them food and water, he is only pointing out that Christ was the angel of God in whom God had placed His name (Exod. 23:20–21; cf. 17:6). In fact even the theophoric name *Rock* of 1 Corinthians 10 is Mosaic (Deut. 32:4, 15, 18; 32:31). Our problem often is that we do not know the Old Testament well enough to recognize it in the New.

Another problem is that the word *literal* too frequently is automatically linked with features of the text that deal solely with the physical and the material. This practice is unjustifiable. No meaning of a text is complete until the interpreter has heard the *total single* intention of the author, who stood in the presence of God. Thus the command "Thou shalt not murder" does not simply forbid the overt act itself but also forbids every thought and emotion that may lead to murder. It likewise encourages every positive act whereby one seeks to promote and enhance the lives of one's fellow beings, as seen in subsequent examples given in the "Covenant Code" of Exodus 21–23. These are not double or triple senses of the literal meaning but together give the full sense included in the author's *single* meaning. This truth can be demonstrated from the antecedent revelations of God against which background new words are given. The portion of Scripture available to writers at a given time acted as an informing theology.

We conclude, therefore, that the so-called "literal" interpretation must include the same *depth* of meaning as the writer himself included. The interpretation is controlled by the words the writer uses, by the range of meaning he gives to those words as judged by his usage elsewhere, by the total context of his thought, and by the preceding revealed theology in existence when he wrote and to which he explicitly refers or clearly alludes by his use of phrases, concepts, or terms that were then generally known and accepted.

Another species of allegorical argument views the Old Testament as containing the New Testament "under a *veil*." This argument is treated below under "The Precedent of New Testament Quotations of the Old Testament" (pp. 133ff.) and "The Alleged Dual Sense of Messianic Prophecies" (pp. 135ff.). For the present, we conclude that the allegorical method cannot be established as a legitimate means for interpreting Scripture.

While Scripture itself sometimes uses allegory (e.g., Prov. 5:15–19), such uses are clearly marked by the writer's intention and not the interpreter's wish, however sincere. Only in these instances may the interpreter employ the rules for interpreting allegory.

The Principle of the Perspicuity of Scripture

The principle of perspicuity means simply that the Bible is sufficiently clear in and of itself for believers to understand it. As J. Stafford Wright has stated, the principle implies three things: (1) "Scripture is clear enough for the simplest person to live by it," (2) "Scripture is deep enough to form an inexhaustible mine for readers of the highest intellectual capacity," and (3) the perspicuity of the Scriptures resides in the fact that God "intend[ed] all Scripture to be revelation of Himself to man."[24] Thus, just as the natural order is sufficiently simple for the ordinary person to live in it without being aware of all that the physical and natural scientist knows, so the spiritual order is sufficiently clear. The comparison is more than accidental.

But this principle may be overextended if it is used as an excuse against further investigation and strenuous study by believers who were not contemporaries of the prophets and apostles who first spoke the Word of God. Scripture, in any faithful translation, is sufficiently perspicuous (clear) to show us our sinfulness, the basic facts of the gospel, what we must do if we are to be part of the family of God, and how to live for Christ. This does not mean, however, that in seeing (and even understanding) these truths we have exhausted the teaching of Scripture. Neither does it imply that the solution to every difficult question in Scripture or life is simple, much less simplistic. It only affirms that, despite the difficulties we find in Scripture, there is more than enough that is plainly taught to keep all believers well nourished.[25]

A story attributed to Dwight L. Moody related that he was once accosted by a woman who asked in a complaining tone, "Mr. Moody, what shall I do about the hard things I can't understand in the Bible?" He replied, "Madam, have you ever eaten chicken?" Somewhat upset by this *non sequitur*, she hesitantly replied, "Ye-es." "What did you do with the bones?" interrupted Moody. "I put them on the side of my plate," she responded. "Then put the difficult verses there also," advised

Moody; "there's more than enough food to digest in the rest that you *can* understand." This is the principle of perspicuity.

Two related problems, however, must be raised: (1) How can the principle of perspicuity be squared with the wide divergence of scriptural interpretations in Christendom, even among equally committed believers? and (2) Why should so much emphasis be placed on advanced training of teachers, preachers, and other interpreters in Christ's church when all believers have an anointing from the Holy Spirit, by which they know the truth (1 John 2:20)? In both of these instances, if perspicuity is pressed beyond what is intended in its proper definition, it becomes a magic wand that gives the interpreter not just sufficient and adequate answers for salvation and living but a kind of total knowledge of Scripture.

To answer the first question more specifically, we must point out that the amount of agreement in Christendom is really large and impressive—and it exists precisely in those areas and in those church councils where patient listening to large blocks of biblical texts has been uppermost. When, however, tradition or certain patterns of thinking were required as prior commitments to the hearing of the Word of God itself, the Word became bound. It was forced to serve these systems, traditions, and hermeneutics. More subtle differences between believers may be caused by overemphasis of certain truths or parts of Scripture. God may certainly raise up a person or group to emphasize a neglected truth. But once this truth is generally recognized, continued special emphasis tends to produce imbalance. What was formerly underemphasized is now overemphasized. Sometimes lack of candor prevents us from distinguishing truths from those that are primarily descriptive and are especially cherished for personal and historical reasons.

The second question is more serious. First John 2: 20 was not meant to deny the need for explaining some texts. If it did, then this very letter of John would violate its own teaching. The teaching of 1 John about the anointing of the Holy Spirit is similar to that of 1 Corinthians 2 about the spiritual person's reception of the Word. Ideally, a believer should not need to be urged by teachers to make personal application of clear scriptural teachings or be urged to see their wider and fuller significance. But application and comprehension should not be confused with interpretation. Furthermore, is it not true that the more removed a reader is from the original languages and from the times in which the biblical authors wrote, the greater will be his need for specially trained teachers and various other kinds of assistance?

We need to recall the system of checks and balances used by the Reformers to grapple with the very problem we face here. They argued for the priesthood of believers (for it was taught in Scripture and embodied the truth of the perspicuity of Scripture), but they also insisted that the final court of appeal was the original languages in which Scripture was written. It was the prophets and apostles, not we, who stood in the counsel of God and received His precise Word. Our generation must reflect the same balance or we will suffer for our recklessness.

The Principle of Progressive Revelation

One of the chief areas of concern for interpreters of Scripture is that of the progressiveness of revelation, especially as it bears on certain moral issues. Unfortunately, despite the popularity of the term, not all are agreed on exactly what is meant by progressive revelation.

C. H. Dodd devoted a key chapter in his book *The Authority of the Bible*[26] to showing that Jesus Christ was "the climax to a whole complex process which we have traced in the Bible," and since this process was "of the highest spiritual worth, . . . we must recognize it in the fullest sense as a revelation of God."[27] For liberal Protestants, the phrase "progressive revelation" is important for three reasons: (1) From a critical standpoint, the idea tends to downgrade, and label as late or unauthentic, those elements scholars are most skeptical about, while it elevates the "highest" truths of Scripture. Thus, liberal scholars have a standard by which to correct or negate the "baser elements" of Scripture. (2) Similarly, from an apologetic standpoint the term gives a rationale by which one can excuse and justify the more "primitive" morality of the Bible by means of later revelation that allegedly corrects it. (3) From a theological standpoint, progressive revelation often becomes a slogan for the arbitrary and inconsistent process of selecting a favored few teachings out of the total history of biblical revelation and drawing the doctrines of the Bible from these.[28]

Yet, when all is said and done, the implied and explicit claims in the liberal's use of the phrase do not answer our problem.

Certainly everyone agrees that a revelation that has been mediated throughout an expanse of history must necessarily have been progressive in some sense. But this then raises the key question: How much accommodation of the *message* was involved? Even if we are convinced, as we should be, that the revelation of God was, from the very inception of the Old Testament, of the loftiest type, a serious difficulty still remains. What about those teachings or records that appear to involve God Himself in a practice that later revelation decries? Abraham is commanded by God to sacrifice his son Isaac; Deborah, a prophetess, pronounces Jael blessed when she literally nails Sisera down; Moses' teaching includes provisions for slavery and divorce; Joshua is commanded to totally wipe out all Canaanites; and David, "the sweet psalmist of Israel," invokes curses on his enemies and prays for their destruction.[29] The problems are well known. The answers are not!

It is not enough, nor is it an adequate response, to note that a good deal of the morality described in that earlier age fell under the judgment of God. It is a fact that Jesus did not regard the Mosaic law on divorce as superseding the earlier statements in Genesis but declared that it was given because of the hardness of men's hearts. It is also true that, though polygamy and unchastity are plainly described, they are only that—descriptions of the sins of mankind.[30]

Neither is it proper to accept the critical solution, with its outright denial of the revelation of God, that limits these so-called mistaken notions to the human writers, who speculated according to the best light they possessed. Nor can we allegorize all problem passages and attempt to overlook their plain statements. There are enough problems without adding to them.

A whole treatise on the ethics of the Old Testament would be necessary to deal adequately with the issues raised here (and this we will do in another work, the Lord willing), but for now let it be suggested that the best response still is given in the 1929 Princeton lectures on ethics given by William Brenton Greene, Jr.[31]

Nevertheless, we will deal with the issues presented by the progress of revelation insofar as they bear on the subject of scriptural interpretation. It seems in order to make the following observations:

1. Whenever the charge is leveled that *God* is depicted in the Old Testament as vengeful, hateful, partial to a few favor-

ites, and even vindictive, let the interpreter beware. He must strive all the more to understand both the words used and the concepts appealed to by the biblical writer. For example, the common depiction of Yahweh as a vengeful and wrathful God is relieved by a fair understanding of the meaning and use of the Hebrew *naqam*. When George Mendenhall studied this term, he concluded that "if we analyze the actual word uses that have supported the ideas of blood vengeance held by many modern scholars, the results are simply incompatible both with the ideas of primitive tribal organization and the concept of God that have long been considered to be self-evident."[32] According to Mendenhall's studies, God's vengeance is no more than the exercise of responsible sovereignty. So it is with the wrath and hate of God. Abraham Heschel devotes a large segment of his book *The Prophets* to the problem of divine wrath and concludes that it is a problem for us because of the associations we now have with the word *anger* or *wrath* and not because of the meanings of the biblical writers.[33]

2. The interpreter must distinguish what the Bible teaches and approves from what it merely reports or records. The lies of Shiphrah, Puah, and Rahab are just that: lies. Nevertheless, the women themselves are approved on other grounds—for heroic acts of faith. We must be aware that approval of *one* act or characteristic is not an endorsement of a biblical individual in *all* that he does or is. Abraham and David are guilty of great lapses of faith, yet they are nonetheless used, and even especially commended, by God.

3. The Scriptures' own assessment of a thing must be preferred to our own offhand impressions. Thievery is not approved in the Israelites's massive "borrowing" from the Egyptians. The word *ša'al* means they "asked" for jewels and precious ornaments from the Egyptians. God then gave His people favor in their oppressors' eyes. Likewise believers must not try to plead the case for the condemned Canaanites and Amalekites (Gen. 9:25–27; Exod. 17:14–16) without first understanding how long the righteous patience of God has endured the sinful outrages and continuation of their eponymous hero's own sexual perversions (Gen. 9:22) and their barbaric form of attack on the sick, elderly, and defenseless. Here again the solution is not

in evolutionary arrangement of revelation and morality but in letting the text itself speak clearly and fully.

4. The prayers of imprecation in the Old Testament (and New Testament!—2 Tim. 4:14; Gal. 5:12; Rev. 6:10) must be understood as couched in an inbred hatred for sin and wickedness wherever it occurs. They should also be interpreted in the light of the writer's earnest wish that all attacks on the kingdom of God receive such public and stinging rebuke that they will not impede God's imminent triumph over all evil. And again, hardly a single curse in one of the sixty-five verses of imprecation in the whole Psalter cannot be found elsewhere in the Bible as a declarative sentence or a simple statement of fact as to what the fate of the cause and persons of wickedness will be![34]

Progressive revelation, rightly understood, does not open the door to the idea that inferior revelations were a prelude to more satisfactory and less embarrassing later revelations. This concept of progress and accommodation derives from philosophic ideas imported from our culture. As James Orr concludes (in a better part of his essay):

> Revelation can be held responsible only for *the new element which it introduces*. . . . Revelation . . . implants a truth, constitutes a relation, establishes a principle, which may have a whole rich content implicit in it, but it cannot convey to the recipient from the first a full, all-around apprehension of everything that principle involves (italics his).[35]

Surely, in every case the total subject to which a revelation belongs is greater by far than any single revelation that contributes to that subject!

The Precedent of New Testament Quotations of the Old Testament

A widespread school of thought today emphasizes the point that New Testament authors were often extremely free in their use of Old Testament texts. This school generally follows the thought that leading rabbinical practice in New Testament times allowed pesher, midrashic, or multiple senses in interpreting biblical passages. Some modern evangelical scholars affirm, on shaky hermeneutical grounds, that the rather free New Testament quotation of the Old Testament sets for us a precedent that allows for a "fuller sense" (the Catholic contribution of *sensus plenior*) of the Old Testament text than what the original Old

Testament human authors intended or understood. Some, knowing what a Pandora's box this opens up for hermeneutics, have tried to insist that this privilege be restricted to the New Testament writers alone, since they had a "revelatory stance."[36] The problem, however, is that many who hold the "fuller sense" point of view often do not heed this qualification and argue that what was good enough for the apostles will certainly also produce good results for them as teachers and preachers of the Word. The issue must be faced.

To be fair, we must limit our discussion solely to those passages where the New Testament writers were in debate with the Jews or where they invoked the authority of the Old Testament. If in these passages we claim some fuller or secondary sense as an authoritative interpretation of the text, it becomes clear that our wish is parent to the thought. This hermeneutical principle must then be acknowledged to be a priori, as it is in Richard Longenecker's masterful presentation:

> The Jewish roots of Christianity make it *a priori* likely that the exegetical procedures of the New Testament would resemble to some extent those of then [sic] contemporary Judaism. This has long been established with regard to the hermeneutics of Paul and the Talmud, and it is becoming increasingly evident with respect to the Qumran texts as well.[36]

It must follow, then, as Donald Hagner states, that "the true value of the arguments from the *sensus plenior* of the Old Testament is for those who are already in the household of faith."[38] Then the real problem emerges. Of what use would that "value" be to the new, struggling New Testament faith that was trying to establish its credibility, appeal, and direct continuity with the ancient predictions given through the Jews? "In-house" words were the last thing needed. As long ago as 1885, Frederic Gardiner announced:

> In all quotations which are used argumentatively, or to establish any fact or doctrine, it is obviously necessary that the passage in question should be fairly cited according to its real intent and meaning in order that the argument drawn from it may be valid. There has been much rash criticism of some of these passages, and the assertion has been unthinkingly made that the apostles, and especially St. Paul, brought up in rabbinical schools of thought, quoted the Scriptures after a rabbinical and inconsequential fashion. A patient and careful examination of the passages themselves will remove such misapprehensions.[39]

A full examination of every relevant passage cannot be attempted here, though we have elsewhere demonstrated solutions to some of these passages.[40] We can, however, list some errors that should be avoided in this area. They include: (1) using the New Testament as a proving ground to identify possible predictions in earlier texts (2) using the New Testament to set the meaning that an Old Testament text may have (3) allowing New Testament argumentative quotation of the Old Testament to reinterpret or to supersede the original meaning and sense of the Old Testament writer and (4) separating the doctrinal sense of a New Testament argumentative use of the Old Testament from the doctrinal sense of the Old Testament writer and thereby breaking continuity in the progress of God's revelation.

One of the chief confusions in this area results from the argument by analogy and, on top of that, the use of subsequent revelation as an exegetical tool to unlock God's Word to earlier generations. While we acknowledge that the analogy of faith has its place in the summary and conclusion of the exegetical procedure, it is totally out of place methodologically when used as a type of "divining rod" to unlock previous revelations. Words, clauses, and sentences must first be understood as the writer's own usage indicates before theological comparisons are added.

We certainly recognize that a passage may have a fuller *significance* than what was realized by the writer. We also wholeheartedly agree that the *subject* to which the Old Testament prophets made individual contributions was wider by miles than what they ever dreamed of. But the whole revelation of God as revelation hangs in jeopardy if we, an apostle, or an angel from heaven try to add to, delete, rearrange, or reassign the sense or meaning that a prophet himself received. In so doing, the friends of Scripture imperil the Scriptures as much as do her enemies. We beg the church to take another look at this area as well.

The Alleged Dual Sense of Messianic Prophecies

Closely related to the preceding topic is the question of the predictions of the Messiah in the Old Testament and their fulfillment in the New. The issue is the same as we have seen above. Milton S. Terry states it best when he affirms that "the moment we admit the principle that portions of Scripture contain an occult or double sense, we introduce an element of uncertainty in the Sacred Volume, and unsettle all scientific interpretation."[41]

In this situation, not as in some of the ones already examined, I suspect that the problem is one of terminology, definition, and adequate explanation that fits all the biblical data. The trouble begins when terms such as "double fulfillment" and "double reference" are used synonymously with "double sense" or "double meaning" and interpreters begin talking about an early versus a later meaning. Specific terms used in regard to this practice include "gap prophecy," "foreshortening of prophetic perspective," "generic prophecy," "corporate solidarity," and several others. Not all of these terms are bad but they are often undefined and present the possibility for misunderstanding and misuse.

Earlier expositors tended to separate the *literal* sense in the immediate context of the prophecy and a secondary *mystical* sense in its New Testament fulfillment.[42] Our response to this practice is the same as that given above regarding the New Testament argumentative use of the Old Testament. Other expositors have included additional distinctions that need not concern us here. All who take this general approach focus on several specific issues: Scripture did address the generation living at the time of the original prophecy but it also speaks of a distant fulfillment; indeed it often includes several intermediate fulfillments, which line up with the climactic conclusion. In this lies the issue for hermeneutics.

Let us be clear about the biblical facts. When Scripture predicts a victorious "seed" for Eve and repeats that word to each of the patriarchs and each Davidite before the prophecy is fulfilled in Christ, that is a single idea with a single meaning and single sense, which also has multiple fulfillments. Moreover, that "seed" is deliberately given as a collective or corporate term. The divinely authorized meaning, as communicated by the Old Testament writers, is that believers were to share in an identity with the coming "Seed," who would be their representative. Accordingly, when Paul insisted that the "seed" in Genesis was singular and not plural (Gal. 3:16) and added that if we belong to Christ then we too are part of Abraham's "seed" (Gal. 3:29), he was neither pulling a rabbinical trick of exegesis nor giving a "fuller sense" to the text than Moses had intended in Genesis 12:3. That was the original scope of the word *seed* and also was the single intent of the Old Testament writer, even though the fulfillments were multiple and lasted over many generations. Similar single meanings with multiple fulfillments relate to other biblical terms: "firstborn," "my son" (Exod. 4:22), "servant of the Lord" (thirty-two times in Isaiah, beginning in 42:1), "your Holy One" (e.g., Ps. 16:10), and many others.

In regard to the examples given thus far, the "law of double reference" errs only when it slips in the idea of double *meaning* or when it implies that there were *only* two foci involved: the moment of the predicted word and the moment of its fulfillment in the New Testament. Nevertheless, we believe Christ's church would be better served if some other term, such as Willis J. Beecher's *generic prophecy*, were adopted. He defines a generic prophecy as

> one which regards an event as occurring in a series of parts, separated by intervals, and expresses itself in language that may apply indifferently to the nearest part, or to the remoter parts, or to the whole—in other words, a prediction which, in applying to the whole of a complex event also applies to . . . its parts.[43]

Beecher sounded an important note when he stressed that interpreters should study the historical *means* (as recorded in Scripture) that God uses to fulfill His purposes as well as the predictive word itself and its climactic fulfillment.[44] The whole complex had a single meaning in the intention of prophet. Therefore it would be wrong to speak of a literal sense of the ancient historic word, which was contemporaneous with its announcement, and of a deeper, mystical, or double sense that became clear when the "prediction" (?) was fulfilled. Patient and careful examination of every Old Testament prediction that we are aware of will bear out this claim.

The teaching of the *nearness* of the day of the Lord may serve as a good example. Five prophets, who spanned about four centuries, each proclaimed the day of the Lord was "near," was "at hand," and had been fulfilled at least in part—the locust plague of Joel, the destruction of Jerusalem in 586 in Isaiah and Zephaniah (Obad. 15; Joel 1:15; 2:1; Isa. 13:6; Zeph. 1:7, 14; Ezek. 30:3). They also spoke of fulfillment yet to come, when our Lord returns a second time (Joel 3:14; Zech. 14:1; cf. 2 Peter 3:10). Thus the Day of the Lord is a generic, collective term wherein the prophet saw the near event, some of the intervening events, and the final climactic fulfillment all in a single literal sense. The case is absolutely no different whether the text is James's use of Amos 9:11 at the Jerusalem council (Acts 15:16), Isaiah's prediction of a virgin conceiving and bearing a son (Isaiah 7:14), Matthew's appeal (2:15) to Hosea 11:1 ("Out of Egypt I called my son"), or Peter's appeal to Psalm 16:8–11 on the Day of Pentecost—in which, incidentially, Peter affirmed under inspiration that David, "seeing what was ahead, . . . spoke of the resurrection of the Christ" as well as of the final triumphant enthronement of his own seed when he wrote that Psalm (Acts 2:29–31). That should settle the argument for evangelicals!

SPECIAL HERMENEUTICS

If the key hermeneutical question is, as we have argued thus far, "What was the biblical author's meaning when he wrote a particular text?" then we must address ourselves to another question, which has also become troublesome for twentieth century believers: "What are the implications of that single meaning for those who live and read that text in a different time and culture?"

One of the most distinguishing features of God's revelation is its historical element. Does not Hebrews 1:1–2 clearly declare the same? "In the past God spoke to our forefathers through the prophets at many times and in various ways, but in these last days he has spoken to us by his Son." This raises another question for contemporary men and women: "To what extent is the relevance of the Bible limited or conditioned by the history, culture, customs, and modes of expression of the era in which the text was written?" In fact, would there not be an equation of inverse proportionality here: the more suited the text was for the original listeners and readers the less apparent and relevant its message is for subsequent readers like ourselves?

Nonevangelicals in particular have repeatedly argued that the cultures of the writers of Scripture so conditioned and bound the Word of God that it often reflects no more than the ancient views of life, history, culture, customs, religion, and the world that were current in those days. But most of this modern attitude can be attributed to a predisposed denial of revelation and supernaturalism, or to personal dislike for many of the concepts of Scripture. Accordingly, Rudolph Bultmann's program for "demythologizing" the Bible is more accurately a program for dividing Scripture into a dualism of a this-world view and an upper-world view—with the upper-world view being firmly rejected. This is no reliable solution. It is solving the issue by determining our own philosophical grid and imposing it over Scripture. The real hermeneutical work is still to be done. The author's abiding and transcultural message must be identified along with his so-called dated information. Indeed, the biblical Word did come to specific people in a specific setting during a specific time and with specific idioms. Why then should these very characteristics of revelation, which were so helpful to the people in their first reception of the message, now be used as an argument against its trustworthiness by a later generation—a generation that boasts of a knowledge superior to that of the ancients?

What are the primary areas of tension that have been generated concerning historical particularities of the text? They are (1) divine commands that are directed to special persons or isolated situations, (2) practices or customs that may merely reflect the cultural norm of the day but that nevertheless cause consternation for subsequent readers who are puzzled over the problem of whether these descriptions are really prescriptions and are still normative, and (3) use of language dealing with factual matters outside the spiritual and moral realms, such as allusions to biology, geography, and cosmology.

The most disputed section of Scripture is, of course, Genesis 1—11. Can a consistent, legitimate hermeneutic piece together the puzzles found here? Can it sustain the view of inerrancy that affirms that the *extent* of divine activity in revelation and inspiration included provision for the writer's ability both (1) to *adequately select* and (2) to *accurately use* words in such a way that they would in every instance reflect God's estimate, evaluation, interpretation, and point of view for mortal beings? That position will receive strenuous examination in the areas now before us.

Direct Divine Commands to Specific Individuals in Specific Situations

Frequently Scripture addresses individuals with commands such as, "Take off your sandals, for the place where you are standing is holy ground" (Exod. 3:5); "Put out into deep water and let down the nets for a catch" (Luke 5:4); "Untie [the donkey and her colt] and bring them to me" (Matt. 21:2–3), or "Do not take a purse or bag or sandals; and do not greet anyone on the road" (Luke 10:4). These, obviously are commands directed to no one other than those to whom they were originally given. It must be readily acknowledged that our Lord addressed a significant number of commands and promises to His twelve disciples that do not apply (except perhaps coincidentally) to any others—as His calling certain of them to leave their occupations and follow Him.

There is much in Scripture that involves the local and the temporary, but such things should not raise a barrier between ourselves and the text, much less between us and the mind of God. The best statement on this problem came from Patrick Fairbairn in 1869:

> The principle is . . . that the *particular* features in revelation, derived from its historical accompaniments, were meant to be, not to the prejudice or the subversion, but rather for the sake of its *general* interest and application. They but served to give more point to its meaning, and render more secure its presentation in the world [much as illustrations serve to clarify the truth of sermons!]. So that, instead of saying, . . . I find therein a word of God to such a person, or at such a period in the past, therefore not strictly for me; I should rather, according to the method of Scripture, say, here, at such a time to such a party, was a revelation in the mind and will of Him who is Lord of heaven and earth, made to persons of like nature and calling with myself—made indeed *to* them, but only that it might *through* them be conveyed and certified to others; and coming as it does to me, a component part of the Word, which reveals the character of the Most High.[45]

Thus what was special in person, time, or place in the letters to the churches, the Gospels, the psalmists, the prophets, or the Law, possesses special *significance* for later generations, even if the *meaning* is not directed to them. The call to remember detailed individual items relating to previous times is heard constantly from biblical writers themselves. A striking illustration is Hosea's (12:4) finding special significance for his generation, though removed by a millennium, in the Jacob-Esau birth struggle (Gen. 25:26) and in Jacob's contest with the angel of God (Gen. 32:24ff.). Hosea declared, "[Jacob] met Him at Bethel and there He spoke with *us*" (Hos. 12:4 NASB). Some modern translators are so surprised by this pronoun that they arbitrarily emend it to "him," but the tactic is rebuked by numerous other biblical examples.[46] The first person plural pronoun is also used in Hebrews 6:18, in declaring that God gave a promise (Gen. 12, 15, 17) and an oath (Gen. 22) to Abraham so that "we" might have a strong consolation! Similarly, in 1 Corinthians 9:8–10 Paul affirms that the Mosaic instruction prohibiting the muzzling of oxen when they are threshing was also addressed to the Corinthians, for it was spoken especially (*pantos*) for "our" sakes! There was no hermeneutical trickery in this type of teaching, as we have argued in detail elsewhere,[47] but it was another affirmation of the principle that past particularity (sometimes called the doctrine of *particularisms*) is no obstruction to present significance. The distinction between *meaning* and *significance*, however, must be rigidly followed. There can be little doubt, according to both biblical example and declaration, that, while not all Scripture is addressed directly to us personally, all Scripture is given for our instruction.

Customs, Cultures, and Biblical Norms

Our concern for the abiding message of the Bible must not run roughshod over the cultural vehicles in which it was originally conveyed. Neither must the cultural vehicle become an excuse for considering certain truths of God to be ancient but now defunct advice. The presence of a multiplicity of historical cultural details—involving politics, economics, society, foods, clothing, institutions, and so forth—must be accounted for in a valid and legitimate hermeneutic. But how?[48]

It would appear that we are presented with the following options when handling the real cultural items in Scripture:

1. One hermeneutical procedure dictates that we retain, in some cases, both the theology taught (i.e., the principle affirmed or contextually implied) and the cultural-historical expression of that principle. For example, some would claim that 1 Corinthians 11:2–5 argues that the principle of divinely authorized lines of responsibility within the Godhead and the husband-wife relationship should be reflected in a certain coiffure for women when they pray or prophesy in public meetings.[49] Yet the matter of hair style was not intended by Scripture to be the abiding emphasis of this passage; the basic exhortation is that proper demeanor be evidenced by women who are prominently in the public eye. But the debate must be denied by the meaning of the text, not by our wishes or reactions. In 1 Corinthians 11:16 Paul affirms that neither he nor the churches of God have any such rule regarding women's coiffure (compare the Greek text to many translations).

2. In some cases, only the theology of a passage (i.e., the principle) is observed, but the behavioral expression is replaced with one that is more recent but equally meaningful. Thus the injunction to "greet the brethren with a holy kiss" will usually be best observed in the West by a hearty handshake. The scriptural precedent for such cultural replacements is seen in the New Testament use of the ceremonial and civil aspects of the moral law of God. Often the principle that undergirded these laws remains, while the illustration or sanction (i.e., the penalty) of it, or both, change because the culture has changed. Thus Paul urged that the mother and son guilty of incest be excommunicated (1 Cor. 5) rather than stoned to death as the Old Testament required (Lev. 20:11; cf. 18:7). Behind both the Old Testament and the New Testament rules against incest stand the holy character of God and the sanctity of marriage. Hence the principle also stands, though the means for enforcing it have changed.

Let it again be noted, however, that regardless of the position an interpreter assumes, if he desires to teach with the authority of Scripture, he needs to observe the clues that the writer has left in the text in order to validate the option chosen. No interpreter may, with the mere wave of the hand, consign recognized principles of God's Word to a mere cultural level in the text or vice versa.

The following list of guidelines should aid us in the job of arriving at the single meaning of the author in those places he includes cultural-historical elements.

1. In every case, the *reason* for the cultural command, custom, or historical practice must first be sought in the context. If the *reason* for a questioned practice or custom has its basis in God's unchanging nature, then the practice is of permanent relevance for all believers in all times. Genesis 9:6 commands that all who shed man's blood shall suffer capital punishment "for in the image of God has God made man." Consequently, because men are still in the image of God, they continue to have such worth, value, and esteem in God's eyes that the state owes the life of the murderer to *God*—not to the grieving family of the victim as a revenge nor to society as a warning to potential criminals!

2. The cultural *form* of a command may be modified even though the principle of that form remains unchanged for all subsequent readers. The principle of humility, for example,

abides, though the form of washing one another's feet (John 13:12–16; cf. Mark 10:42–45) has changed, due to changes in culture, geography, types of roads, and footwear. James urged believers to be nonpartial. The teaching is still valid, though we have never compelled the poor to sit on the floor in our church services.

3. When *practices* that are identified as integral parts of pagan culture and yet also concern God's moral nature are forbidden in the Old or New Testament, they are forbidden in our culture as well. In this category may be placed the strong biblical condemnation of beastiality, homosexuality, transvestment, and public nudity. Each of these offends one aspect or another of God's moral nature, His attributes, His image in us, or His provision and plan for sexuality, the family, and marriage.

4. A practice or cultural command is permanent when it is grounded in the nature of God or in the ordinances of creation. The issues, therefore, of divorce and remarriage, obedience to parents, and the legitimate respect owed to human government are unchanged and nonnegotiable. Thus the command, "What God has joined together, let man not separate" (Matt. 19:6) is still valid, in accordance with God's directive in creation.

Interestingly enough, the moral responsibility for deciding whether or not a believer should pay his taxes or give tolls to a government that he has come to believe is in opposition to accepted moral law, is lifted from his shoulders. Romans 13:7 puts these taxes in the same category as debts paid for services rendered by men who are in service professions. We pay plumbers, electricians, or others for their services to us, but do not thereby aid and abet any false beliefs or immoral practices they may be guilty of.

5. The last guideline I will mention is the biblical precedent for saying that circumstances sometimes alter the application of those laws of God that rest not on His nature (i.e., the moral law of God) but on His will for particular men and women in particular contexts. An example of such a change in the application of God's command can be seen in that given to Aaron and his sons. They alone were to eat of the sacred "bread of the Presence" (Lev. 24:8–9; cf. Exod. 25:30); yet our Lord not only approved of Ahimelech's offering that untouchable food to hungry David and his famished men (1 Sam. 21:1–6), but He used this example to reinforce His own practice of performing

emergency deeds of mercy on the Sabbath (Matt. 12:1-5; Mark 2:23-25; Luke 6:1-4). What appears, at first blush, to allow no exception, actually has a condition of *ceteris paribus* ("other things being equal") understood.[50]

There is an absolute loyalty in Scripture to the principles founded in the nature of God or in the ordinances of creation; yet there is flexibility in applying other commands, such as those regarding sanitary laws, dietary laws (see Mark 7:19 and Acts 10:15, where all foods are declared clean), and ceremonial regulations. Because the brazen altar was too small for the occasion, Solomon used the middle of the temple court to sacrifice the numerous animals during the dedication ceremony (1 Kings 8:64; cf. 2 Chron. 4:1). The principle of worship was identical with that prescribed, though the means of observing it was changed for this occasion. A similar instance is Hezekiah's observance of Passover in the second month rather than the first, since there was not sufficient time for the people to prepare after first learning of it (2 Chron. 30:2-4).

The Alleged Inadequate Language of Scripture in Factual Matters

Under the heavy pressure of the prestigious scholarship of the late nineteenth and the twentieth centuries, one view of this issue has become all but unanimous: Genesis 1—11 is primeval history, reflecting its ancient Near Eastern origins (mainly Babylonian). Furthermore, it is alleged, wherever Scripture becomes involved in such factual matters as cosmology, natural history, the sciences, historiography, botany, astronomy, or a dozen other such subjects, chances are that it reflects the level of cultural and intellectual achievement of that day and its statements, therefore, cannot be squared with reality. Among various exponents the wording may vary but the criticism usually reaches the same conclusion: Scripture may not be trusted in these details no matter how much we may trust it and even depend on it with our lives in regard to spiritual matters. In fact, goes the argument, it is unfair to ask Scripture to serve this subordinate function.

How may legitimate hermeneutics be employed to decide such problems? After all, has not this essay stressed the fact that meaning must terminate on that which the author himself intended? How then could the author possibly be expected to have spoken beyond his time and learning? Does not progressive revelation correct such past excesses (or primitiveness)?

But such questions exhibit an inadequate view of the type of revelation these writers claimed. To have stood in the counsel of God, as these men insist they did, and to have come up deficient in any area, does not square with their claim. And while *meaning* is restricted to the writer's own meanings, these meanings were received from God. One may not force a wedge between God and the writer—unless he cares nothing for the writer's own claims. Likewise, the suggested "help" from progressive revelation is also deficient, for the reasons stated previously.

The problems faced here may be best resolved by noting the following set of guidelines for interpreting scriptural language that points to facts outside the spiritual realm:

1. Determine the literary form to which the section under examination belongs. What textual (or contextual) clues does the writer offer that will aid us in deciding to what literary genre his statements belong? When the literary type is found, we may proceed with an interpretation according to the rules of that literary type.

As an example, let us compare the organization of Genesis 1—11 with that of Genesis 12—50. The writer used the rubric "These are the generations [i.e., histories] of . . ." (KJV) ten times throughout the book, six times in the first eleven chapters and four times in the remainder of the book. Since the historical nature of the patriarchal narratives of Genesis 12—50 is usually conceded to be "substantially accurate" even by many non-evangelical scholars, we believe it is fair to argue that the writer wanted to indicate that the prepatriarchal material is of similar nature.

2. Examine individual words and phrases to see if they have Near Eastern or classical backgrounds and then determine the type of similarity and the use made of them in Scripture.

For example, Psalm 74:13–14 declares that God crushed the heads of Leviathan, and Isaiah 27:1 speaks of the day when God will "punish . . . Leviathan the coiling serpent" and "slay the monster of the sea." It is a fairly easy task to show the parallels of these passages with the Ugaritic text 67:I:1–3 and the Anat text III:38–39. However, to insist that the biblical writers adopted Canaanite mythology as well as terminology is to go beyond the facts. These same writers clearly scorned pagan idols and myths. In these comparisons, therefore, we see borrowed imagery but not borrowed mythology.[51] The conclusion of Father John

McKenzie is correct: "In no sense can it be said that the Hebrews incorporated mythopoeic thought . . . into their own religious conceptions; they did, however, assimilate mythopoeic imagery and language."[52] Thus the mention of Leviathan and
other names in common with mythology was merely poetic garb
that offered no more than convenient similes and metaphors for
the theological claims of the writers. It should be noted that often
facile comparisons produce totally negative results, as in regard
to the alleged connection between the Babylonian goddess
Tiamat and the Hebrew *tehom*, "deep" (Gen. 1:2).[53] It turns out
that there is no connection between the two. Likewise the case
for a biblical triple-decked universe, patterned after pagan models, is also falsely constructed, since the Hebrew text gives no
credence to a hard dome complete with windows to serve as the
sky or to a flat earth or to literal pillars to support this earth.
Every step of the construction is faulty and without biblical support, as we and others have argued elsewhere.[54]

3. Note all figures of speech and determine the part they play
in the total statement of the author. This exegetical step is as
exacting and as subject to hermeneutical controls as any other. A
figure of speech must be named, the definition given, the case for
its presence in the verse noted and the function and meaning of
the figure in its broader context explained.

E. W. Bullinger lists approximately 150 different examples of
figurative language in Genesis 1—11 alone![55] But if one argues
that the mere presence of figures of speech consigns the whole
section to myth, parable, or apocalyptic-type literature, the response is clear: It does not. Genesis 1—11, for example, is prose,
and narrative prose at that. Its description of sequential acts
with a special form of the Hebrew verb, its use of the Hebrew
direct object sign, its use of the so-called relative pronoun, its
stress on definitions and sequence make it more than evident
that this section is not poetic. Similar arguments can be pressed
in regard to every other disputed text. While Scripture often uses
phenomenological language (even as we now do in weather reports and daily conversation) to communicate factual data, this
in no way commits the human author or God to distorted science
any more than do our references to the sun's "rising" and to the
four "corners" of the earth.

4. Whenever Scripture touches on factual matters, note the
way the author uses the data. Too frequently the interpreter

either prematurely dismisses such matters (e.g., it is often wrongly stated that Genesis 1 tells us *who* created the universe but not *how* it was done—an obvious slighting of the phrase repeated ten times, "and God said") or overenthusiastically embraces what is *described* as being part of what is also being *prescribed* by God—as in adopting on the basis of Genesis 30, a view of human or environmental prenatal influence on birthmarks, when, in fact, the birthmarks mentioned here were due to God's blessing, as Jacob himself later grudgingly concedes.

In conclusion, I affirm, with all the forcefulness I can muster, that our generation needs a whole new hermeneutical reformation. The current crisis regarding the doctrine of Scripture is directly linked to poor procedures and methods of handling Scripture. This crisis has shown little regard for traditional ecclesiastical or theological categories, for it has spread like the plague among liberal and evangelical scholars alike. As a partial corrective for this astonishing situation, I urge that talk *about* the Bible be modified to this extent: that evangelicals in particular get equally busy identifying the *meaning* of the text itself—the meaning the original writer of Scripture intended—before we go on to name the relationships between that meaning and ourselves, our country, our day, and our conception of things; that is, before we consider the *significance* of the text for us.

When liberalism excused itself from this demand, it turned its back on the revelation of God. If evangelicalism continues to dabble in the text as we have been doing for several decades, substituting Bible surveys and "what do you get out of it" types of pooled-ignorance sessions for the hard work of exegesis, we will also pay the supreme price—there will be no answer from God (Micah 3:7). It is possible that a strong confessional stand on Scripture and its inerrancy could remain orthodox, even long after the practice and method of interpreting Scripture had turned neoorthodox or liberal. Is this not a good enough reason to issue a call for legitimate hermeneutics?

THE INERRANCY
OF THE AUTOGRAPHA

Greg L. Bahnsen

Greg L. Bahnsen *is engaged full time in scholarship and writing. Until recently he served as Assistant Professor of Apologetics, Reformed Theological Seminary, Jackson, Mississippi. He is a graduate of Westmont College (B.A.), Westminster Theological Seminary (M.Div. and Th.M.), and the University of Southern California (Ph.D. in Philosophy). He is an ordained minister in the Orthodox Presbyterian Church. He has served as Youth Pastor, First Presbyterian Church, Manhattan Beach, California; Assistant Pastor, Calvary United Presbyterian Church, Wyncote, Pennsylvania; and Pastor, Trinity Chapel, Eagle Rock, California. Among his publications are* Theonomy in Christian Ethics; Homosexuality: A Biblical View; *and* A Biblical Introduction to Apologetics. *His articles include "Autographs, Amanuenses, and Restricted Inspiration" in* Evangelical Quarterly; *"Socrates or Christ: The Reformation of Christian Apologetics" and "Pragmatism, Prejudice, and Presuppositionalism" in* Foundations of Christian Scholarship; *"Inductivism, Inerrancy, and Presuppositionalism" in* Journal of the Evangelical Theological Society; *and other articles, letters, and reviews in the* Westminster Theological Journal, Journal of Christian Reconstruction, Presbyterian Guardian, Banner of Truth, Cambridge Fish, *and* Chalcedon Reports. *Dr. Bahnsen is a member of the* Evangelical Theological Society, Evangelical Philosophical Society, *and the Advisory Board of ICBI. He has been the recipient of numerous Fellowships.*

CHAPTER SUMMARY

While the Bible teaches its own inerrancy, the inscripturation and copying of God's Word require us to identify the specific and proper object of inerrancy as the text of the original autographa. This time-honored, common-sense view of evangelicals has been criticized and ridiculed since the days of the modernist controversy over Scripture. Nevertheless, according to the attitude of the biblical writers, who could and did distinguish copies from the autographa, copies of the Bible could serve the purposes of revelation and function with authority only because they were assumed to be tethered to the autographic text and its criteriological authority. The evangelical doctrine pertains to the autographic text, not the autographic codex, and maintains that present copies and translations are inerrant to the extent that they accurately reflect the biblical originals; thus the inspiration and inerrancy of present Bibles is not an all-or-nothing matter. Evangelicals maintain the doctrine of original inerrancy, not as an apologetic artifice, but on sound theological grounds: (1) the inspiration of copyists and the perfect transmission of Scripture have not been promised by God and (2) the extraordinary quality of God's revealed Word must be guarded against arbitrary alteration. The importance of original inerrancy is not that God cannot accomplish His purpose except through a completely errorless text, but that without it we cannot consistently confess the veracity of God, be fully assured of the scriptural promise of salvation, or maintain the epistemological authority and theological axiom of *sola Scriptura* (for errors in the original, unlike those in transmission, would not be correctable in principle). We can be assured that we possess the Word of God in our present Bibles because of God's providence; He does not allow His aims in revealing Himself to be frustrated. Indeed, the results of textual criticism confirm that we possess a biblical text that is substantially identical with the autographa. Finally, contrary to recent criticisms, the doctrine of original inerrancy (or inspiration) is not unprovable, is not undermined by the use of amanuenses by the biblical writers, and is not contravened by the New Testament use of the Septuagint as "Scripture." Therefore, the evangelical restriction of inerrancy to the original autographa is warranted, important, and defensible; further, it does not jeopardize the adequacy and authority of our present Bibles. Accordingly, the doctrine of original inerrancy can be commended to all believers who are sensitive to the authority of the Bible as the very Word of God and who wish to propagate it as such today.

THE INERRANCY
OF THE AUTOGRAPHA

IN ADDRESSING THE household and friends of Cornelius, Peter rehearsed how the anointed, or messianic, ministry of Jesus of Nazareth eventuated in His death and resurrection (Acts 10:36–40). After the Resurrection, Christ appeared to chosen witnesses, whom He charged to preach to the people and to testify that He was ordained of God as the eschatological Judge of mankind (vv. 41–42). According to Christ Himself, all the prophets bore witness to Him, that through His name all who believe on Him should receive remission of sins (v. 43). Here we see the heart of the gospel proclamation rehearsed and the vital commission given to have it publicized abroad for the eternal well-being of men. It should be obvious that the proclamation of this message in correct form was crucial if its hearers were to escape the wrath to come and enjoy genuine remission of their sins through Christ. A different or perverted gospel was, accordingly, nothing short of anathema; the life-giving good news could not have come from man but had to have originated in the revelation of Jesus Christ (Gal. 1:6–12).

Thus Peter informs us that the preaching of the gospel (of which the Spirit of Christ testified in the Old Testament) by the New Testament apostles was performed by means of the Holy Spirit sent forth from heaven (1 Peter 1:10–12). As with all genuine prophecy, this gospel proclamation did not come by the

will of men, but men spoke from God, being carried along by the
Holy Spirit (2 Peter 1:21). In accord with the promise of Christ,
this Spirit sent from heaven to inspire the preaching of the gospel
guided the apostles into *all truth* (John 16:13). As the Spirit of
truth He would not generate error in the life-giving good news of
Christ as publicized by the apostles; their message was made
inerrant. Furthermore, the apostles spoke *words* taught by the
Spirit of God (1 Cor. 2:12–13), and the Spirit speaking in them
directed both *what* was said and *how* it was said (cf. Matt.
10:19–20). Therefore, according to Scripture's own witness, the
verbal form and content of the apostolic publication of the gospel
message should be deemed wholly true and without error.

Throughout its record the Bible presupposes its own authority. For instance, the Old Testament is often cited in the New
Testament with such formulas as "God says" or "the Holy Spirit
says" (as in Acts 1:16; 3:24–25; 2 Cor. 6:16). What Scripture
says is identified with what God says (e.g., Gal. 3:8; Rom. 9:16).
For that reason all theological arguments are settled decisively
by the inherent authority signified in the formula "it stands
written" (literal translation). The same authority attaches to the
writings of the apostles (1 Cor. 15:1–2; 2 Thess. 2:15; 3:14), since
these writings are placed on a par with the Old Testament Scriptures (2 Peter 3:15–16; Rev. 1:3). Apostolic Scripture often has
the common formula "it stands written" applied to it (e.g., John
20:31). Therefore the Old and New Testaments are presented in
the Bible itself as the authoritative, written, Word of God.

Because of their divine origin the Scriptures are entirely
trustworthy and sure (cf. 1 Tim. 1:15; 3:1; 4:9; 2 Tim. 2:11; Titus
3:8; Heb. 2:3; 2 Peter 1:19), so that by means of them we are able
to discern between what is true and what is false (cf. 1 Thess.
5:21; 1 John 4:1). The Scriptures are the standard of trustworthiness (Luke 1:1–4) and will never fail us or bring us embarrassment (Isa. 28:16; John 19:35; 20:31; Rom. 9:33; 1 Peter 2:6;
1 John 1:1–3). Their accuracy extends to every minute detail,
as our Lord said—to every "jot" and "tittle" (Matt. 5:18)—in
such a way that the indestructible endurance of any minor part is
coextensive with that of the whole (cf. Isa. 40:8; Matt. 24:35; 1
Peter 1:24–25). Every single word of the Bible is, by its own
witness to itself, infallibly true. God's own declaration is: "I, the
LORD, speak the truth; I declare what is right" (Isa. 45:19).
Accordingly, the psalmist can say, "The sum of thy word is

truth" (Ps. 119:160),* and the wisdom literature can counsel us, "Every word of God is tried [proven, true, flawless]" (Prov. 30:5). If our doctrinal outlook is informed by the Word of God, then, we must confess that Scripture is entirely truthful, or inerrant. The unchallengeable testimony of Jesus was, "Thy word is truth" (John 17:17).

The Westminster Confession of Faith has good warrant for calling "all the books of the Old and New Testament" in their entirety "Holy Scripture or the Word of God written" (I.2), "all which are given by inspiration of God," who is "the author thereof," being Himself "truth itself" (I.4). These books of the Old and New Testaments, therefore, are in their entirety "of infallible truth and divine authority" (I.5), so that "a Christian believeth to be true whatsoever is revealed in the Word, for the authority of God himself speaking therein" (XIV.2). According to this grand confession of the church, no error can be attributed to the Bible at any place. After all, if God sets forth false assertions in minor areas where our research can check His accuracy (such as in historical or geographical details), how do we know that He does not also err in major concerns like theology?[1] If we cannot believe the Lord's Word when He speaks of earthly things, how can we believe Him when He tells us of heavenly things? (cf. John 3:12).

In this vein Archibald Alexander wrote, "And could it be shown that the evangelists had fallen into palpable mistakes in facts of minor importance, it would be impossible to demonstrate that they wrote anything by inspiration."[2] Likewise Charles Hodge declared that the Bible was "free from all error whether of doctrine, fact or precept"; inspiration, according to him, was "not confined to moral and religious truths, but extends to the statements of facts, whether scientific, historical, or geographical."[3] Alexander, Hodge, and B. B. Warfield all firmly maintained that the Bible is "absolutely errorless" in any of the subjects it touches on in teaching—whether statements about history, natural history, ethnology, archaeology, geography, natural science, physical or historical fact, psychological or philosophical principle, or spiritual doctrine and duty.[4] This doctrine of scriptural inerrancy, whether presented in the pages of the Bible itself, in church confessions, or by stalwart theolo-

---

*In this chapter, Scripture quotations are from the American Standard Version, unless otherwise indicated.

gians, is never an academic curiosity or aside; it goes to the very
heart of the trustworthiness and truth of the life-giving message
of the gospel found in God's written Word. If the Bible is not
wholly true, then our assurance of salvation has no dependable
and divine warrant; it rests rather on the minimal and fallible
authority of men. Warfield saw this clearly:

> The present controversy concerns something much more vital
> than the bare "inerrancy" of the Scriptures, whether in the copies
> or in the "autographs." It concerns the trustworthiness of the
> Bible in its express declarations, and in the fundamental concep-
> tions of its writers as to the course of the history of God's dealings
> with his people. It concerns, in a word, the authority of the Bibli-
> cal representations concerning the nature of revealed religion,
> and the mode and course of its revelation. The issue raised is
> whether we are to look upon the Bible as containing a divinely
> guaranteed and wholly trustworthy account of God's redemptive
> revelation, and the course of his gracious dealings with his people;
> or as merely a mass of more or less trustworthy materials, out of
> which we are to sift the facts in order to put together a trustwor-
> thy account of God's redemptive revelation and the course of his
> dealings with his people.[5]

The church, following God's Word, confesses the entire inerrancy of Scripture as a crucial and inalienable aspect of the
authority of God's revelation, by which we come to a genuine
knowledge of Christ and the assured enjoyment of eternal life (cf.
2 Tim. 3:15–16).

INSCRIPTURATION AND DISTINCTION

For the sake of preserving the apostolic testimony and extending the fellowship of the church around the "word of life"
(1 John 1:1–4), the proclamation and teaching of the apostles
has been reduced to written form. Such inscripturation of God's
revelation was required if the church was to teach it until the end
of the age (Matt. 28:18–20). Van Til points out that inscripturation of God's word gives it the greatest possible permanence of
form, being less liable to perversion than oral tradition would
be.[6]

> The great attribute of the written word is *objectivity*. The oral
> word too has its measure of objectivity, but it cannot match either
> the flexibility or the durability of the written word. Memory is
> imperfect. The desire to change or pervert is ever present.[7]

The drawback to having revelation in oral form (or tradition) is that it is much more subject to various kinds of corrupting influences that stem from man's imperfect abilities and sinful nature (e.g., lapses of memory and intentional distortion). To curb these forces, taught Kuyper, God cast His word into written form—thereby achieving greater durability, fixity, purity, and catholicity.[8] A written document is capable of universal distribution through repeated copying, and yet it can be preserved in various kinds of depositories from generation to generation. As such it can function both as a fixed standard by which to test all doctrines of men and as a pure guide to the way of life.

Yet this admirable feature of inscripturation itself generates a difficulty for the doctrine of scriptural inerrancy—a difficulty that we must now face. A written word may have great advantages over oral tradition but it is not immune from what Kuyper called "the vicissitudes of time." The spreading of God's Word by textual transmission and translation opens up the door to variance betwen the original form of the written word and secondary forms (copies and translations). This variance requires a refinement of the doctrine of biblical inerrancy, for now we must ask what constitutes the proper object of this inerrancy that we attribute to Scripture. Does inerrancy (or infallibility, inspiration) pertain to the original writings (autographa), to copies of them (and perhaps translations), or to both?

To be sure, in answering such a question some have gone to unscholarly excess in the interest of protecting the divine authority of Scripture. Certain superstitious stories led Philo to postulate inspiration of the Septuagint translation of the Old Testament. Some Roman Catholics, following the declaration of Pope Sixtus V that the Vulgate was the authentic Scripture, attributed inspiration to this translation. Some Protestants have argued for the inspired infallibility of the vowel points in the Hebrew Old Testament (e.g., the Buxtorfs and John Owen; the Formula Consensus Helvetica more cautiously spoke of the inspiration of "at least the power of the points"). The errorless transmission and preservation of the original text of Scripture has been taught by men such as Hollaz, Quenstedt, and Turretin, who failed to recognize the significance of textual variants in the copies of Scripture that have existed throughout the history of the church.[9]

Notwithstanding such positions, the view that has persisted

throughout the centuries and is common among evangelicals
today is that the inerrancy (or infallibility, inspiration) of the
Scriptures pertains only to the text of the original autographa. In
a letter to Jerome (Letter 82), Augustine said about anything he
found in the biblical books that seemed contrary to the truth: "I
decide that either the text is corrupt, or the translator did not
follow what was really said, or that I failed to understand it."
Here the distinction between the autographa and copies of Scripture is clear, as is also the restriction of inerrancy to the former.
Likewise, in his conviction that the original was free from error,
Calvin showed concern about textual corruption; see his commentaries at Hebrews 9:1 and James 4:7.[10] Luther labored diligently as a translator and exegete to recover the original reading
of the scriptural text.[11] Richard Baxter said, "No error or contradiction is in it [Scripture], but what is in some copies, by
failure of preservers, transcribers, printers, and translators."
Warfield quotes this statement and goes on to allude to the work
of other men such as John Lightfoot, Ussher and Walton, and
Rutherford, illustrating how the question of restricting inspiration to the autographa was a burning question in the age of the
Westminster Assembly.[12] He also expounded the Westminster
Confession of Faith I.8 as teaching that immediate inspiration
applies only to the autographa of Scripture, not to the copies,
that the original text has been providentially kept pure in the
transmitted texts (but not, as Smith and Beegle contended, in
every or in any one copy),[13] and that present translations were
adequate for the needs of God's people in every age.[14]

For themselves, A. A. Hodge and B. B. Warfield asserted:

> Nevertheless the historical faith of the church has always been,
> that all the affirmations of Scripture of all kinds . . . are without
> error, when the *ipsissima verba* of the original autographs are as-
> certained and interpreted in their natural and intended sense. . . .
> No "error" can be asserted, therefore, which cannot be proved to
> have been aboriginal in the text.[15]

Edwin Palmer cites Kuyper and Bavinck to the same effect
and he quotes Dijk as saying that the authority of the Bible
"pertains always and only to the original (and not to the translation) and to the pure text that is to be found in the autographa."[16] Others who can be readily quoted as distinguishing
between the autographa and copies of Scripture and as restricting inerrancy (or infallibility, inspiration) to the autographa in-

clude J. Gresham Machen, W. H. Griffith Thomas, James M. Gray, Lewis Sperry Chafer, Loraine Boettner, Edward J. Young, R. Surburg, J. I. Packer, John R. W. Stott, Carl F. H. Henry, et al.[17] What Henry says is representative:

> Inerrancy pertains only to the oral or written proclamation of the originally inspired prophets and apostles. Not only was their communication of the Word of God efficacious in teaching the truth of revelation, but their transmission of that Word was error-free. Inerrancy does not extend to copies, translations or versions, however.

It is evident that H. P. Smith and C. A. Briggs were quite mistaken when they alleged that the assertion of an original inerrancy for Scripture was a new doctrine generated by "modern scholastics."[18] Warfield's response was, as usual, appropriate:

> This is a rather serious arraignment of the common sense of the whole series of preceding generations. What! Are we to believe that no man until our wonderful nineteenth century, ever had acumen enough to detect a printer's error or to realize the liability of hand-copied manuscripts to occasional corruption? Are we really to believe that the happy possessors of "the Wicked Bible" held "thou shalt commit adultery" to be as divinely "inerrant" as the genuine text of the seventh commandment—on the ground that the "inerrancy of the original autographs of the Holy Scriptures" must not be asserted "as distinguished from the Holy Scriptures which we now possess"? . . . Of course, every man of common sense from the beginning of the world has recognized the difference between the genuine text and the errors of transmission, and has attached his confidence to the former in rejection of the latter.[19]

The time-honored and common-sense perspective among Christian believers who have considered the inescapable question raised by the inscripturation of God's word (viz., do inspiration, infallibility, and/or inerrancy pertain to the autographa, to copies of it, or to both?) has been that inerrancy is restricted to the original, autographical text of Scripture.

Nevertheless, this basic evangelical doctrine of Scripture has come under severe ridicule and criticism from many quarters in recent years, thus calling us to a defense of it. H. P. Smith charged that the doctrine of original inerrancy is speculative and is concerned with a text that no longer exists and cannot con-

ceivably ever be recovered[20] David Hubbard reiterates that the
standard evangelical view contends for the inerrancy, not of any
present texts, but of the original autographs to which no generation of the church has ever had access.[21] Accordingly, the approach to scriptural inerrancy that restricts it to the autographa
is held to be trivial and without value, as charged by C. A. Briggs
nearly a century ago: "We will never be able to attain the sacred
writings as they gladdened the eyes of those who first saw them,
and rejoiced the hearts of those who first heard them. If the
external words of the original were inspired, it does not profit us.
We are cut off from them forever."[22] The distinction between
inspired or infallible autographa and uninspired or fallible copies
was characterized by Brunner as useless, idolatrous, and untenable in the light of textual criticism.[23] The distinction is irrelevant or of no practical value, he believes, since the praiseworthy
quality (be it inspiration, infallibility, or inerrancy) applies to no
extant text. It is absurd because it is impossible to define the
character of a text that has disappeared. The originals are unimportant since we cannot completely restore them, and obviously
God does not think that it is necessary for us to have them.
Moreover, we can still receive spiritual blessing from errant
copies, so we could as well receive such a blessing from errant
originals. It turns out, so the argument goes, that restriction of
inerrancy to the autographa is simply an intellectually dishonest
escape from embarrassment or an apologetical "cop-out." Such
a line of reasoning is often encountered,[24] and a large dose of
sarcasm is often mixed with it.

> Their [the assailants of the trustworthiness of the Scriptures] con-
> tention has ever been twofold: that God never gave an errorless
> Bible, and if he did, that errorless Bible is no longer in the posses-
> sion of men. The air has been thick with satirical references to
> autographic copies which no man has ever seen, which are
> hopelessly lost, which can never be recovered. And the defenders
> of the trustworthiness of Scripture have been sarcastically asked
> what the use is of contending so strenuously for the plenary inspi-
> ration of autographs which have thus forever passed away.[25]

Great mirth has been evoked in this vein over the so-called
"lost Princeton Bible." Lester DeKoster has gone to the limit of
his reach in pressing sarcasm into service against those who
restrict inerrancy to the autographa: nobody can use those lost
autographa; the Bible on our table is not the inerrant and infalli-

ble word of God, and so today the church has no inerrant Bible by which to live, and preaching is thereby made impossible because it would be founded on the uninspired word of man.[26] It now appears that the doctrine of biblical inerrancy, which at first appeared so clearly in accord with the Scripture's own witness, is threatened with a necessary qualification or restriction that vitiates the significance and importance of the doctrine. What can we say in response?

In the following sections we will explore the *biblical attitude* toward autographa and copies, which should be the starting point of all genuinely Christian theological commitments. From that platform we go on to *explain* the evangelical restriction of inerrancy to the autographa, indicating that our evaluation of copies and translations is not an all-or-nothing affair. The *rationale* for the evangelical restriction is then reviewed, followed by various indications of the *importance* of this doctrine regarding Scripture. Different aspects of the *assurance* that we can have with respect to possessing God's Word today will subsequently be broached. Finally, we will conclude with an examination of some explicit *critiques* of the evangelical restriction of inerrancy (or infallibility, inspiration) to the scriptural autographa. We will conclude that the doctrine of original inerrancy is both warranted and defensible, and is a doctrine to be commended to all believers who are sensitive to the authority of the Bible as the very Word of God.

THE BIBLICAL ATTITUDE

Scripture has scattered indications of interest in or recognition of copies and translations of God's Word in distinction from the autographical manuscripts. We can also draw useful inferences from various passages that tell us something of the scriptural attitude toward the then-extant copies and subsequent translations. What we primarily learn is that these nonautographical manuscripts were deemed adequate to perform the purposes for which God originally gave the Scriptures. What King Solomon possessed was obviously a copy of the original Mosaic law (cf. Deut. 17:18), and yet it was considered to contain, truly and genuinely, "the charge of Jehovah . . . according to that which was written in the law of Moses" (1 Kings 2:3).[27] The book of Proverbs pauses at one point to draw clear attention to the fact that "these are more proverbs of Solomon, copied by the men of Hezekiah king of Judah" (Prov. 25:1) The copies are themselves held to be canonical and divinely authoritative. The law of God that was in the hand of Ezra was obviously a copy, but nevertheless it functioned as the authority in his ministry (Ezra 7:14). When Ezra read from this law to the people, so that divine guidance might be given for their lives, he apparently read to them by way of translation, so they could understand the sense in the Aramaic to which they had become accustomed in exile: "And they read in the book, in the law of God, distinctly [with interpretation]; and they gave the sense, so that they understood the reading" (Neh. 8:8).[28] In all of these examples the secondary text does the work of God's written Word and shares its original authority in a practical sense.

The New Testament also evidences an interest in secondary copies of God's written Word. Paul was most concerned that he be brought the "books, especially the parchments" (2 Tim. 4:13). In the practice of collecting New Testament Epistles for the various churches (cf. Col. 4:16), encouragement would naturally be given to copying the original manuscripts. There is every reason, given the examples of Jesus and the apostles, to assume that these copies were held to be profitable for teaching and for instruction in righteousness (cf. 2 Tim. 3:16b). When New Testament writers appeal to the authority of the Old Testament, they used the texts and versions that were at hand, just as we do today.[29] Jesus preached from the existing scrolls and treated them as "Scripture" (Luke 4:16–21). The apostles used the Scriptures that were in hand for arguing (Acts 17:2) and demonstrating points (Acts 18:28). Their hearers checked the apostolic proclamation by searching the Old Testament Scriptures that they then possessed (Acts 17:11). Because their opponents shared a belief in the functional authority of the available manuscripts of the Scriptures, Jesus and the apostles confronted them on the common ground of the extant copies, without fretting about the autographa themselves.[30] This is illustrated in the present imperative given to search the Scriptures as testifying of Christ (John 5:39) and in the rhetorical and leading questions: "Have you not read . . . ?" and "What is written in the Law? How do you read it?" (e.g., in Matt. 12:3, 5; 21:16, 42; Luke 10:26). It may very well be true that the "holy Scriptures" that Timothy had known from his childhood were not only copies of the Scripture, but the Septuagint translation, at that.[31] Still they could make him "wise unto salvation."

These illustrations show that the *message* conveyed by the words of the autographa, and not the physical page on which we find printing, is the strict object of inspiration. Therefore, because that message was reliably reflected in the copies or translations available to the biblical writers, they could be used in an authoritative and practical manner. Contrary to the extreme and unfounded inferences drawn by Beegle,[32] the exhortation and challenges based on the copies of Scripture pertain to the conveyed *message* and tell us nothing about the extant texts per se. Much less do they demonstrate that the biblical authors made no distinction between the original text and its copies. Otherwise the unique and unalterable authority of the biblical message would not be guarded so strenuously by these same authors.

Because Christ raised no doubts about the adequacy of the Scriptures as His contemporaries knew them, we can safely assume that the first-century text of the Old Testament was a wholly adequate representation of the divine word originally given. Jesus regarded the extant copies of His day as so approximate to the originals in their message that He appealed to those copies as authoritative.[33] The respect that Jesus and His apostles held for the extant Old Testament text is, at base, an expression of their confidence in God's providential preservation of the copies and translations as substantially identical with the inspired originals. It is thus fallacious to argue that inerrancy was not restricted by them to the autographa and to say that their teaching about inspiration had reference to the imperfect copies in their possession.[34]

The fact is that, although present copies and translations had a practical authority and adequacy for the purposes of divine revelation, the Bible evidences a pervasive concern to *tether current copies to the autographical text*. There is, as one would expect, no explicit biblical teaching regarding the autographa and copies of them, but the point being made is still abundantly illustrated in the course of Scripture's teaching and statements. We therefore have an answer to the question of Pinnock, Is the restriction of inerrancy to the autographa strictly scriptural? and have a rebuttal to the allegation of Chapman that it is not biblical to restrict inspiration to the autographa.[35] According to Beegle, there is no explicit teaching in the New Testament that distinguishes between autographa and copies; the original writings are not set apart in a special position, for the authors of Scripture deemed the extant errant manuscripts inspired.[36] Our examination of the scriptural passages pertinent to this issue will undermine such claims as these.

We can begin our survey in the Old Testament, where we soon discover that:

> Most of the references to inspiration that are found in the Old Testament concern the Semitic autographs. The majority relate to the biblical writers' own compositions, which they identify, not as products of divine dictation, but as the equivalent of God's own words: e.g., David, "The Spirit of Jehovah spake by me" (II Samuel 23:2); Isaiah, "Seek ye out . . . (this) book of Jehovah, and read" (Isaiah 34:16); Jeremiah, "(God's) words . . . even all that is written in this book" (Jeremiah 25:13, cf. 30:2, 36:2), or perhaps even Solomon in Ecclesiastes 12:11.
>
> Others concern writings that were still fresh enough to imply the original manuscripts either as present, e.g., Joshua's referring to Moses' writings as "the book of the law of God" (Joshua 24:26), or as immediately accessible, e.g., Joel's quoting the contemporary (?) prophecy of Obadiah 17, "as Jehovah hath said" (Joel 2:32).[37]

The assumption throughout Scripture is that we are obliged to follow the original text of God's written Word. Present copies function authoritatively because they are viewed as reflecting the autographa correctly. This foundational perspective comes to the surface from time to time. For instance, Israel was required to do what God "commanded their fathers by Moses" (Judg. 3:4). This reference implicitly points to the original message, which came from the author himself. Isaiah was explicitly told to write, and his book was to be a witness forever (Isa. 8:1; 30:8); the autographical text was the permanent standard for the future. Daniel "understood by the books" (which we can assume to have been copies), but these very books indicate that the God-given words were "the word of Jehovah [which] came to Jeremiah" (Dan. 9:2). The perfect aspect indicates completed action with respect to the coming of the word of God to Jeremiah specifically.

Likewise the New Testament assumes that correct teaching can be found in copies of Scripture then in existence because they trace back to the autographical text. Matthew 1:22 quotes Isaiah

7:14 as "spoken by the Lord through the prophet" (cf. 2:15).
Jesus taught that we are to live by "every word that proceedeth
out of the mouth of God" (Matt. 4:4), thus tethering the authority of the Scriptures in hand to the original utterance given by
divine inspiration. What people read as "Scripture" in the books
of Moses was thought of as "spoken unto them by God" (Matt.
22:29–32; Mark 12:24–26). The inspired David himself spoke to
them in the copy of the Book of Psalms that they possessed
(Matt. 22:43; Mark 12:36; Luke 20:42), just as when one reads
the copy of Scripture he will see that which was spoken by Daniel
the prophet himself (Matt. 24:15; Mark 13:14). In each case the
autographical text is assumed to be present in the extant copy
that is consulted. When Christ asked, "Have you not read . . . [in
extant copies, no doubt]?" (Matt. 19:4; cf. v. 7), He was actually
seeking what Moses himself commanded the Jews (Mark
10:3). The Mosaic words that He quoted from Genesis 2:24 were
viewed by Him as fully equivalent to what "God said" as the
original author of Scripture (Matt. 19:4–5). Those who possess
existing scrolls "have Moses and the prophets" themselves, who,
accordingly, should be heard as such (Luke 16:29).

The actual distance between the autographa and the copies
can be for present purposes ignored, because the original text is
thought to appear in these copies. After all, it is the things written by the prophets themselves that bind us (Luke 18:31). In
expounding the extant Scriptures Christ actually expounded
what the prophets had spoken and He could therefore condemn
those who were slow to believe what the prophets themselves had
spoken (Luke 24:25–27). In the Scriptures as they were then
written, Christ's followers could find what is fulfilled by Him,
namely, all things "which were written" in all the Old Testament
(Luke 24:44–46, author's translation). The "writings" that were
then in hand, and that indicted their hearers, were assumed to be
identical with what Moses wrote (John 5:45–47), and the law
that was cited as relevant to a current controversy was understood to be given by Moses (John 7:19; cf. v. 23).

John 10:34–36 is particularly instructive. Jesus said, "Is it not
written in your law . . . ?" thereby indicating their own manuscript copies of the Old Testament. He then quotes Psalm 82:6,
resting the thrust of His argument on one word in that text. The
premise of His argument is that God "called them 'gods,' unto
whom the word of God came." That is, God called the judges

"gods" who were contemporary with Asaph, the psalm writer, and they were the ones to whom the word of God came. It is thus Asaph's original that is equated with the word of God. Jesus was able to accept, and work on the foundation of, the Jews' belief in the authority of "their law" (copies) because He deemed these to reflect the original accurately. The "Scripture" to which He appealed in this controversy is intimately connected with what was actually said to those "to whom the word of God came." The inscripturated word of God that originally came to the Israelites is now found written in their present-day law books. Here we find quite an explicit indication that the authority of present copies is traced to the autographa lying behind them.

The importance of the autographa for the New Testament Scriptures is already hinted at in Jesus' promise that the Holy Spirit would take His original words and bring them to the remembrance of the apostles for the sake of their writings (John 14:25–26). When the apostles cited the Old Testament in their preaching and writing, it was with the assumption that they were propounding the initially composed Scripture. Accordingly, Peter described "this Scripture" (i.e., Ps. 69:25) as that "which the Holy Spirit spake before by the mouth of David" (Acts 1:16; cf. 4:25). The earlier autograph, given beforehand by the Holy Spirit, is the primary referent of his preaching from present copies of the Psalm. Similarly Paul cited Isaiah 6:9–10, saying, "Well spake the Holy Spirit through Isaiah the prophet unto your fathers . . ." (Acts 28:25; cf. Rom. 3:2), and he proceeded on the understanding that his quotation was true to the original deliverance given many years previously. The citation of Jeremiah 31 in Hebrews 10 is viewed as a rendition of what the Holy Spirit originally said through the prophet (Hebrews 10:15). Indeed, the comfort that could be gained from the then-present copies of the Scriptures was tethered to "whatsoever things were written aforetime," the original text written in former days (Romans 15:4). In a similar way, that for which Paul claimed inspiration was his autographical text—"The things which I write unto you . . . are the commandment of the Lord" (1 Cor. 14:37; cf. 2:13).

Over and over again we are confronted with the obvious fact that the biblical writers made use of existing copies, with the significant assumption that their authority was tied to the original text of which the copies are a reliable reflection. It is especially important to note this fact with respect to two key verses that teach the inspiration of Scripture. In 2 Timothy 3:16 Paul stresses that all the Scriptures were God-breathed, placing obvious emphasis on their *origin*, and thus on their autographic form. The reason why the sacred writings known to Timothy (perhaps the Septuagint) could make him wise unto salvation is found in the fact that they were rooted in the original, divinely given Scripture—those writings that were the direct result of inspiration and that Paul here associated with Scripture's original form as coming from God. Likewise, in 2 Peter 1:19–21 we are told that "we have the prophetic word" (presumably in copies) and must heed it and treat it as authoritative. Why is this so? Because men spoke from God, being "carried along" by the Holy Spirit. The sufficiency and function of the extant biblical manuscripts is not divorced from, but rather explained in terms of, the original manuscripts, which were divine products.

We have noted a long list of illustrations that point to the fact that the adequacy of existing copies of the Bible was countenanced in terms of the autographical texts that are presumed to stand behind such copies.

The importance and criteriological authority of the autographical texts of Scripture are brought out in four specific Old Testament situations. Each shows us that the inspiration, infallibility, and inerrancy of the Bible must be found in the autographical text, which is normative for God's people and for identifying anything that would lay claim to the title of "God's Word."

The first known case of the need for textual restoration is related in Exodus 32 and 34. The first tablets of the law were written by God Himself (Exod. 32:15–16) but were subsequently destroyed by Moses in his anger (v. 19). God provided for the rewriting of the words of the original tablets (Exod. 34:1, 27–28), and Scripture makes the point that these second tablets were written "according to the first writing" (Deut. 10:2, 4). Here is a significant model for all later copying of the biblical autographs; they should reproduce the words that were on the first tablet or page in order to preserve the full divine authority of the message they convey.

So also, in Jeremiah 36:1–32 it is said that the prophet dictated the word of God to Baruch, who wrote it in a scroll. When this scroll, with its unfavorable message, was read to King

Jehoiakim, he cut it into pieces and burned it. The word of God then came to Jeremiah, instructing him to make a new copy of the Scripture, and we see quite plainly that the standard for the copy was the original text: "Take another scroll and write on it all the words that were on the first scroll" (v. 28). As common sense tells us, a reliable copy ought to reproduce the original text accurately.

The paradigmatic or criteriological nature of the autographic text of Scripture is also taught in Deuteronomy 17:18. Although the Mosaic autograph was placed by the Levites next to the ark of the covenant (Deut. 31:24–26), a copy of this law was to be written by the king in a book, "out of that which is before the priests and the Levites." The copy would offer authoritative guidance only as it correctly reflected the original. Without studied concern for a copy that accurately transmitted the autograph, the king could not be sure of himself in refraining from turning aside to the right or to the left from God's commandment (Deut. 17:19–20). Copies of Scripture, then, were not to deviate in the slightest from the original text.

The fourth key Old Testament situation that manifests the esteem and deference the Jews gave to the autographic text is recorded in 2 Kings 22 and 2 Chronicles 34, which relate the recovery of the temple copy of the Book of the Law during the reign of Josiah. The existence of the Book of the Law was previously known; it had been placed by the side of the ark of the covenant and used for public reading from time to time (Deut. 31:12, 24–26; 2 Chron. 35:3). However, though there were likely private copies of the Law in the hands of some priests and prophets,[38] the official, autographical copy had been lost from sight. Chronicles indicates that Josiah had already begun to follow the law in a hazy fashion, probably according to a traditional knowledge of it (34:3–7). Subsequently the temple began to be repaired, during which time the Book of the Law was found by Hilkiah, the high priest. Josiah's desire to repair the temple already demonstrated his disposition to foster the worship of Jehovah, and Hilkiah's discovery generated great excitement. In time Josiah became quite concerned about the words of "this book that is found" (2 Kings 22:13). Apparently it brought to his attention material (most likely the curse-threats of the covenant: 2 Kings 22:11, 13, 16, 18–19; cf. Deut. 28; Lev. 26) that was not found in the other available copies or traditions of the law.

What is relevant for our concern here is that this recovered Book of the Law, which corrected and supplemented Josiah's theological outlook, was, I believe, the original, officially preserved Mosaic autograph.[39] What was found was not simply "a book" (a copy of some generally known volume) but "*the* book of the law"—a manuscript somehow different from others (2 Kings 22:8). In particular, it was the book of the law "by the hand of Moses" (2 Chron. 34:14, literal translation). While the evidence is not fully decisive and the recovered book was not necessarily the autograph, the weight of evidence favors this interpretation; there is little obvious counterevidence.

This Old Testament incident magnifies the value, corrective function, and normative authority of the autographic text of Scripture over all copies or traditional understanding of what God had said. The sufficiency of a copy is proportionate to its accurate reflection of the original. Deviation from the autograph jeopardizes the profit of a copy for doctrinal instruction and for direction in righteous living.

The biblical writers clearly knew how to distinguish, then, between autographa and copies and they perceived the significance of the difference. Josiah's recovery of the autographic Scripture was a momentous occasion, not merely the addition of one more copy, among many manuscripts, to an undifferentiated repository of Bibles!

There are yet other ways in which Scripture teaches or illustrates the explicitly recognized or assumed normativity of the autographa for subsequent copies. First, the Bible warns us throughout against altering the text of God's Word. According to God's command, it is not to be added to or diminished (Deut. 4:2; 12:32). Proverbs counsels, "Add thou not unto his words, lest he reprove thee, and thou be found a liar" (30:6); honesty requires that one stick to the originally given message of God without supplementing it with new features. Otherwise the permanent norm of judgment could hardly be expressed in these words: "To the law and to the testimony! If they speak not according to *this word,* surely there is no morning for them" (Isa. 8:20).

The New Testament Scriptures evidence the same jealousy for the unaltered purity of the original text, as seen in the well-known warning of the book of Revelation (22:18–19). The normativity of the autographic message is the presupposition underlying the conflict with tradition pursued by Christ and the apostles (e.g., Matt. 15:6; Col. 2:8). As evidenced in Matthew 5:21ff., tradition conveyed the Old Testament text to some extent, but it was not to be allowed to *obscure* the authentic Word of God (Mark 7:1–13). Accordingly, we see Christ condemning Pharisaical teaching when it altered the text of the Old Testament Scriptures—e.g., with respect to hatred (Matt. 5:43) and with respect to divorce (Matt. 19:7). In the same vein with Old Testament warnings, Paul instructs Christians not to tamper with the Word of God (2 Cor. 4:2). The New Testament lays great stress on not accepting teachings that run counter to the apostolic message (e.g., Rom. 16:17; Gal. 1:8; 1 John 4:1–6). We find, even as we would expect, strong warning against departing from what is said in the apostolic text (2 Thess. 3:14, where the norm is "the word by this epistle"). Believers are to be on guard against what purports to be Scripture but is not. Do not be troubled, Paul says, by "an epistle as though from us" (2 Thess. 2:2). Paul usually wrote his own authentic letters by means of an amanuensis (e.g., Rom. 16:22)—an arrangement that created ripe conditions for forgery. However Paul's custom was to add his own authenticating signature to his letters, as he notes in 2 Thessalonians 3:17: "The salutation of me Paul with mine own hand, which is the token in every epistle: so I write" (cf. 1 Cor. 16:21; Gal. 6:11; Col. 4:18).[40] Significantly Paul makes this statement in the same Epistle in which he warns against spurious apostolic epistles. Here Paul draws attention to the quite literal "autograph" as authenticating the message that is to be believed and obeyed by Christ's people!

Criteriological textual authority, we conclude, is uniformly presented in Scripture as being the original, autographic texts of the biblical books. Copies are to be evaluated and heeded in the light of the autographa, which ought to be reflected in them. Their authority derives from the original text, whose own authority derives from God Himself.

We may now summarize the attitude that the Bible itself displays to the autographa and copies in this fashion. The authority and usefulness of extant copies and translations of the Scriptures is apparent throughout the Bible. They are adequate for bringing people to a knowledge of saving truth and for directing their lives. Yet it is also evident that the use of scriptural authority derived from copies has underlying it the implicit understanding, and often explicit qualification, that these extant copies are authoritative in that, and to the extent that, they reproduce the original, autographic text.

Biblical writers understood the distinction between the original and a copy and they manifest a commitment to the criteriological authority of the original. These two features—the adequacy of extant copies and the crucial and primal authority of the autographa—are rather nicely combined in the standard formula used in the New Testament for citing Scripture to clinch an argument: "it stands written." This form (the perfect tense) appears at least seventy-three times in the Gospels alone. It signifies that something has been established, accomplished, or completed and that it continues to be so or to have enduring effect. "It stands written" expresses the truth that what has been written in the original Scripture remains so written in the present copies. Conversely, that to which the writer appeals in the present copies of Scripture as normative is so because it is taken to be the enduring witness of the autographic text. New Testament arguments based on a phrase (as in Acts 15:13–17), a word (as in John 10:35), or even the difference between the singular and plural form of a word (as in Gal. 3:16) in the Old Testament would be completely emptied of genuine force if two things were not true: (1) that phrase, word, or form must appear in the present copies of the Old Testament, or else the argument falls to the ground with the intended opponent because it is spurious to begin with (i.e., there is no evidence to which appeal can be made against him), and (2) that phrase, word, or form must be assumed to have been present in the original text of the passage cited, or else the argument loses its authoritative foundation in the Word of God (i.e., such an element of the text would have no more authority than the word of any mere human at best and would be an embarrassing scribal error at worst). If the New Testament authors are not appealing through their extant copies to the original text, their arguments are futile.

We see, then, that the Bible demonstrates two points. First, the permanent need of God's people for the substantial reliability of the extant biblical text is satisfied. We *can* believe our copies of Scripture and be saved without having the autographic codex, for the Bible itself indicates that copies can faithfully reflect the original text and therefore function authoritatively. Second, the paramount features and qualities of Scripture—such as inspiration, infallibility, and inerrancy—are uniformly identified with God's own original word as found in the autographic text, which alone can be identified and esteemed as God's own word to man.[41]

A brief postscript to this section can be added regarding the use of the Septuagint in the New Testament and the problem of New Testament quotations of the Old Testament that appear to deviate from the original. Neither one of these practices undermines our previous conclusions. The Septuagint was used to facilitate the communication of the New Testament message. It was the popular version of the day. This fact, however, does not confer inspiration on it (a view held by men such as Philo and Augustine). Even Beegle admits that if the New Testament writers considered the Septuagint inspired, it was so "in a secondary or derivative sense."[42] As Jerome maintained in his dispute with Augustine over this matter, only the Hebrew text was strictly inspired. The authors of the New Testament, we must assume, used the Septuagint only to the extent that this translation did not deviate essentially from the Hebrew text. Just as people can write in their own vocabularies without introducing falsehoods and can quote questionable sources without incorporating erroneous portions from them,[43] so also the New Testament writers could use the vocabulary and text of the Septuagint without falling into error. Being carried along by the Holy Spirit in their work (cf. 2 Peter 1:21) they were shielded from such error, for that Spirit is the "Spirit of truth" (John 16:13). Textual diversity was recognized by the New Testament writers, but it was not a source of perplexity, since they were directed by the Spirit. They could select the reading that best carried the divine meaning,[44] often quoting the Septuagint as the Word of God and yet sometimes even correcting the Septuagint rendition!

A greater difficulty is found in the fact that the Septuagint is sometimes quoted in a way that initially appears to be contrary to the Hebrew text and as hardly permissible.[45] This relates to the problem posed by many critics, that the way in which the New Testament sometimes quotes the Old Testament seems to show little concern for accurate rendering of the original.[46] Fitzmyer says, "To modern critical scholarship their [the New Testament writers'] way of reading the Old Testament often appears quite arbitrary in that it disregards the sense and the content of the original."[47]

This is not the place to launch into a full discussion of the well-known, difficult passages related to this issue, some of which call for further study in the light of the broader attitude that Scripture itself teaches toward the issues of inerrancy and the original text. As always, the biblical phenomena must be considered in terms of the basic and background testimony of Scripture about itself—that is, in the light of Scripture's own given presuppositions. Suffice to say here that an artificial standard of precision that would have been foreign to the culture and literary habits of the day in which Scripture was penned need not be imposed on the Bible in the name of inerrancy or of fidelity to the autographa. Methods of quotation were not as precise in that age as they are today, and there is no reason why New Testament citations had to be verbally exact. The issue is whether the meaning of the autographic text is or is not assumed to lie behind the extant texts and translations used by the New Testament writers. I have given grounds above for adopting this as the assumption of the biblical witness. In focusing on a particular (sometimes narrow, sometimes general) point or insight, New Testament quotation of the the Old Testament need only embody an accuracy that suits the writer's purpose. Preachers today are not being unfaithful to Scripture when they mix passing allusion with strict quotation from the Bible, when they rearrange biblical phrases, or when they paraphrase contextual matters in getting to their specific target statement, phrase, or word. Their scriptural point can be communicated in a way that is true to the sense without being a pristine rendition of the specific text.

Therefore, the New Testament use of the Septuagint or of inexact renditions of the Old Testament does not belie the commitment of the involved writers to the criteriological authority of the autographa. The practice does, however, underline their unanxious acceptance of texts or versions that were not strictly autographic as being adequate for the practical purposes at hand in their teaching. These were adequate precisely because they could be assumed to portray the true *sense* of the original.

EXPLANATION AND RATIONALE FOR THE RESTRICTION

Given the previously explored biblical attitude toward the autographa and copies of them, we can proceed to explain the sense in which evangelicals correspondingly restrict inerrancy to the scriptural autographa and offer reasons for that restriction.

There is circulating at present a rather serious misunderstanding of the evangelical restriction of inerrancy (or inspiration, infallibility) to the autographic text and of the implications of that restriction. DeKoster claims that there are only two options: either the Bible on our pulpits is the inspired Word of God, *or* it is the uninspired word of man. Because inspiration and inerrancy are restricted to the autographa (which are lost, and therefore not found on our pulpits), then our Bibles, it is argued, must be the uninspired words of man and not the vitally needed word of God.[48] Others have misconstrued an epistemological argument for biblical inerrancy as holding that, if the Bible contains even one mistake, it cannot be believed true at any point; we cannot then rely on any part of it, and God cannot use it to communicate authoritatively to us.[49] From this mistaken starting point the critics go on to say that the evangelical restriction of inerrancy to the autographa means that, because of errors in all present versions, our Bibles today cannot be trusted at all, cannot communicate God's word to us, and cannot be the inspired Word of God. If our present Bibles, with their errors, are not inspired, then we are left with nothing (since the autographa are lost).

Such a dilemma rests on numerous fallacies and misunderstandings. In the first place, it confuses autographic *text* (the words) with autographic *codex* (the physical document). Loss of the latter does not automatically entail loss of the former. Certain manuscripts may have decayed or been lost, but the words of these manuscripts are still with us in good copies. Second, evangelicals do not, by their commitment to inerrancy, have to commit the logical fallacy of saying that if one point in a book is mistaken, then all points in it are likewise mistaken. Third, the predicate "inerrant" (or "inspired") is not one that can be applied only in an all-or-nothing fashion. We create a false dilemma in saying that a book either is totally inspired or totally uninspired (just as it is fallacious to think a book must be either completely true or completely false). Many predicates (e.g., "bald," "warm," "fast") apply in degrees. "Inerrant" and "inspired" can be counted among them. A book may be unerring for the most part and yet be slightly flawed. It can have inspired material to some measure and uninspired material to some measure. For example, an anthology of sacred texts from world religions would be inspired to the degree that it includes selections from the Bible. This is not to say that inerrancy or inspiration as qualities admit of degrees, as though some passages of the Bible could be "more inspired" than others, or some statement with a given sense in Scripture could be a mixture of truth and error. Rather, the objects (viz., certain books) of these predicates have elements or parts to which the predicates completely apply and elements or parts to which the predicates do not apply. That baldness can be applied in degrees means that certain objects (e.g., heads) may have hairy areas and nonhairy areas, not that there is some quality that itself is a cross between hair and nonhair.

It needs to be reiterated quite unambiguously that evangelical restriction of inerrancy to the autographa (1) is a restriction to the autographic *text*, thereby guarding the uniqueness of God's verbal message[50] and (2) does *not* imply that present Bibles, because they are not fully inerrant, fail to be the Word of God. The evangelical view does not mean that the inerrancy, or inspiration, of present Bibles is an all-or-nothing matter. My Old Cambridge edition of a Shakespearean play may contain mistaken or disputed words in comparison with the original text of Shakespeare, but that does not lead me to the extreme conclusion that the volume on my desk is not a work of Shakespeare. It *is* Shakespearean—to the degree that it reflects the author's own work, which (because of the generally accepted high degree of correlation) is a qualification that need not be explicitly and often stated. So also my American Standard Version of the Bible contains mistaken or disputed words with respect to the autographic text of Scripture, but it is still the very Word of God, inspired and inerrant—to the degree that it reflects the original work of God, which (because of the objective, universally accepted, and outstanding degree of correlation in the light of textual criticism) is a qualification that is very seldom in need of being stated.[51] As virtually anybody would understand, a copy counts as the words of a work only to the extent that it has not altered the very words of the author of that work.[52]

Therefore, let us clearly explain the implication of the evangelical view of inerrancy's restriction to the autographa. Francis Patton put it this way: "Just so far as our present Scripture text corresponds with the original documents is it inspired. . . . Have we a correct text? If we have not, then just in proportion to its incorrectness are we without the word of

God."[53] Many contemporary evangelicals have made the same kind of statement. Pinnock writes, "Our Bibles are the Word of God to the extent that they reflect the Scripture as originally given,"[54] and "a good copy of an original work can function like the original itself, to the extent to which it corresponds to the original and is in accord with it."[55] In the same way translations, as observed by Henry, "may be said to be infallible only to the extent that they faithfully represent the copies available to us."[56] Palmer accordingly answers DeKoster's false dilemma about having or not having the inerrant and inspired Word of God on his desk by pointing out that copies and translations are inspired, infallible, and inerrant to the extent that they have faithfully reproduced the original text. To the extent that they add to, subtract from, or distort the original, they are not the inspired Word of God.[57]

Is there any good reason for this point of view? What rationale can be offered by evangelicals for restricting inerrancy (inspiration, infallibility) to the biblical autographa? Critics have often assumed that inerrancy is restricted to the autographa for apologetical reasons and they have condemned this restriction as desperate weaseling and an "apologetical artifice" (to use Brunner's words), an intellectually dishonest cop-out arising from embarrassment.[58] Rogers attacks the evangelical restriction of inerrancy to the autographa as an attempt to secure an "unassailable apologetic stance" (which, Pinnock observes, would produce a position that is unfalsifiable yet meaningless).[59] Such abuse is misplaced. Evangelicals appeal to the missing autographa in a limited and specific fashion, where independent evidence (quite apart from apologetical embarrassment) supports the suggestion of transcriptional error.[60] Inerrancy critic Stephen Davis recognizes that restriction of inerrancy to the autographa is seldom a ridiculous apologetical maneuver on the part of evangelicals, because textual criticism has, for the most part, firmly established the biblical text.[61] Since that which the apologist defends is the teaching of the autographic *text* (apart from the presence or absence of the autographical manuscripts), he can hardly be charged with tactical retreat if he holds, with Warfield, that "the autographic text of the New Testament is distinctly within reach of criticism in so immensely the greater part of the volume, that we cannot despair of restoring to ourselves and the Church of God, His book, word for word, as He gave it by inspiration to men."[62] The restriction of inerrancy to the autographa does not leave the evangelical with only a chimera to defend. Moreover, evangelicals such as Warfield are not so deluded as to think that recovery of the autographic text would (though impossible with absolute perfection) rid them of all biblical difficulties for which to give an answer.

> That some of the difficulties and apparent discrepancies in current texts disappear on the restoration of the true text of Scripture is undoubtedly true. That all the difficulties and apparent discrepancies in current texts of Scripture are matters of textual corruption, and not, rather, often of historical or other ignorance on our part, no sane man ever asserted.[63]

Explaining evangelical restriction of inerrancy to the autographa by the supposed motivation to have an easy apologetical escape from difficulties can be safely dismissed. It simply is not so.

If evangelical rationale is not apologetical, then what is it? It is quite simply theological. God has not promised in His Word that the Scriptures would receive perfect transmission, and thus we have no ground to claim it a priori. Moreover, the inspired Word of God in the Scriptures has a uniqueness that must be guarded from distortion. Consequently we cannot be theologically blind to the significance of transmissional errors, nor can we theologically assume the absence of such errors. We are therefore theologically required to restrict inspiration, infallibility, and inerrancy to the autographa.

There is nothing absurd about holding that an infallible text has been fallibly transmitted, and the fact that a document is a copy of Holy Writ does not entail that it is wholly right. Although we can agree with Beegle that there is no inherent reason why God could not have preserved from defects the scribes who copied the Bible, he is certainly mistaken to think we should assume that copies of Scripture were the result of inspiration unless the Bible explicitly teaches us that they were not.[64] The fact is that inspiration is an extraordinary gift or predicate, which cannot be assumed to apply to just anybody. If one wishes to maintain that the scribes of the Bible were inspired in their work and automatically infallible in their results, then the burden of theological proof lies on him. As things stand in Scripture, however, inspiration refers to the original words produced under the Holy Spirit and not to the production of scribal copies.[65] Again contrary to Beegle, the fact that the original Scripture had its origin in God does not mean that the copies, as textual copies, also have their origin in God, but that the *message* they embody traces ultimately back in some measure to God's given revelation.[66] E. J. Young's reasoning is more cogent:

> If the Scripture is "God-breathed," it naturally follows that only the original is "God-breathed." If holy men of God spoke from God as they were borne by the Holy Spirit, then only what they spoke under the Spirit's bearing is inspired. It would certainly be unwarrantable to maintain that copies of what they spoke were also inspired, since these copies were not made as men were borne of the Spirit. They were therefore not "God-breathed" as was the original.[67]

It should now appear clear that restriction of inerrancy to the autographa is based on the unwillingness of evangelicals to contend for the precise infallibility or inerrancy of the transmitted text,[68] for Scripture nowhere gives us ground to maintain that its transmission and translation would be kept without error by God.[69] There is no scriptural warrant for holding that God will perform the perpetual miracle of preserving His written Word from all errors in its being transcribed from one copy to another.[70] Since the Bible does not claim that every copier, translator, typesetter, and printer will share the infallibility of the original document, Christians should not make such a claim either. The doctrine is not supported by Scripture, and Protestants are committed to the methodological principle of *sola Scriptura*. Here then is the basic rationale for restricting inerrancy to the original, prophetically and apostolically certified document of God's Word: there is biblical evidence for the inerrancy of the autographa, but not for the inerrancy of the copies; the distinction and restriction are therefore theologically warranted and necessary.[71]

> Everybody knows that no book was ever printed, much less hand-copied, into which some errors did not intrude in the process; and as we do not hold the author responsible for these in an ordinary book, neither ought we to hold God responsible for them in this extraordinary book which we call the Bible.[72]

This quote from Warfield indicates the common-sense nature of restricting the evaluative qualities of a literary work to its autographic text. Common sense tells us that the identity of a literary text is determined by its original autograph ("the first completed, personal or approved transcription of a unique word-group composed by its author").[73] When a slight mistake or distortion creeps into a copy of a literary work, it thereby creates a somewhat different literary text, with some degree of originality. Choosing to ignore minor changes, we can continue to label the original and the slightly distorted copy in similar fashion, but that does not mean we can afford to be indifferent to an accurate text.

> What modern author would view with equanimity an edition of one of his plays that substituted several hundred words scattered here and there from the corruptions of typists, compositors, and proof-readers? . . . One can no more permit "just a little corruption" to pass unheeded in the transmission of our literary heritage than "just a little sin" was possible in Eden.[74]

The actual value of an author's literary production cannot be safely estimated if one is not sure whether the text before him represents the author's work or the "originality" of a scribe. Say you are evaluating what you take to be Shakespeare's *Hamlet*, and you come across the phrase "solid flesh" in the famous line "O! that this too too solid flesh would melt" (Act I, Scene 2). On the basis of this reading you might well give a more or less favorable evaluation of this work supposedly by Shakespeare; but if you did, you would not only be embarrassed, you would actually be unfair to Shakespeare. Shakespeare wrote "sallied [i.e., sullied] flesh," despite the widespread replication of the "solid flesh" reading.[75] Shakespeare has Hamlet reflect on the fact that his natural or inherited honor has been soiled by the taint of his mother's dishonorable blood, as the original reading indicates, thereby making quite a difference to the sense of the line. The merit or demerit of the "solid flesh" reading belongs to some copyist or editor, not to the author. Common sense keeps us from attributing secondary alterations in the text and their value (or lack of it) to the author, for he is responsible only for the autographic text of his literary work.

This principle is equally true of God's Word. What we say about it by way of evaluation should be restricted to what God actually originated in the text and should not include the "originality" of intermediate scribes. As Warfield notes, "It is *the Bible* that we declare to be 'of infallible truth'—the Bible that God gave us, not the corruptions and slips which scribes and printers have given us."[76] Absolute truth can be attributed to God's Word but not to the words that are the results of errors by scribes and printers.

The identity of the Bible, or the Scriptures, then, must certainly be determined by the autographic text, and the evaluative predicate of "inerrancy" can be legitimately applied only to *that text* (regardless of how many manuscripts contain it).[77] Where we cannot be certain that a manuscript reflects that autographic text, we must refrain from judgment and reserve the evaluation for the original.[78] This is especially true with respect to God's word in the Scriptures, because they are uniquely the communication of God to man in human language. They have the extraordinary status of not being merely human in quality (cf. Gal. 1:12; 1 Thess. 2:13). The isolation of these writings as specially inspired is the very basis of the church's distinction between canonical and noncanonical compositions. Only what God Himself has said constitutes the standard for verifying Christian truth-claims as theologically authoritative.[79] And for this reason the textual readings that result from scribal mistakes cannot be elevated to divinely authoritative status simply because the transferred title of "Holy Scripture" is placed over them. What constitutes God's own Word is not thus elastic and changing but, rather, unique and standardized.

Even evangelicals who deny inerrancy must surely be sensitive to this rationale, for they too will want to protect the unique quality of God's inspired and infallible (although errant) Word. If they did not, they would be committed to the superstitious and absurd consequence that anything that is placed between the covers of a book formally labeled "The Bible" is God's inspired Word. Successive copying errors could conceivably destroy the message of God completely; would it then still qualify as "inspired"? Obviously not.

Evangelicals who believe the Scripture is not inerrant can offer no reason for thinking that copying mistakes must always be restricted to matters of history and science, while being absolutely precluded from texts touching on matters of faith and practice (the alleged exclusive domain of "infallibility" according to many theorists). The infamous "Wicked Bible" of 1631 rendered the seventh commandment as "Thou shalt commit adultery" (omitting the crucial word *not*), and for this scandalous misprint the printers were severely fined by the archbishop. Can any evangelical seriously hold that this reading is inspired and infallible? If not, then *all* evangelicals are committed in some sense to *restrict their bibliology to the autographa*. Even errancy evangelicals speak of the *unique* quality of God's written and inspired Word,[80] admitting that although salvation and instruction can come through a less than perfect translation, "it is the word of God only to the degree that it reflects and reproduces the original text."[81] Those who, like Davis, say that "these manuscripts [the autographs] play no particular role in my understanding of the Bible. I believe that presently existing Bibles are infallible works that constitute the word of God for all who read them"[82] are simply being shortsighted or naive. Restriction to the autographic text is a common-sense move made at some point by all evangelicals, for all want to guard the extraordinary quality of God's written Word.

The Importance of the Restriction

We have now rehearsed the biblical understanding of the relation of the autographa to copies and the significance of each. We have explained the sense in which evangelicals restrict inerrancy to the autographa and the implication this has for current copies, and we have established the theological rationale for that restriction. But the question quickly arises as to whether this is not, after all, just a trivial discussion, since the autographa are beyond our reach. Piepkorn declares, "Since the original documents are inaccessible and apparently irrecoverable, the ascription of inerrancy to these documents is in the last analysis *practically* irrelevant."[83] Evans rhetorically asks, how does it affect the value of today's errant record that the error was not there originally?[84]

The direct response to this perspective is that restricting inerrancy to the autographa *enables us to consistently confess the truthfulness of God*—and that is quite important indeed! Inability to do so would be quite theologically damaging. Only with an inerrant autograph can we avoid attributing error to the God of truth. An error in the original would be attributable to God Himself, because He, in the pages of Scripture, takes responsibility for the very words of the biblical authors. Errors in copies, however, are the sole responsibility of the scribes involved, in which case God's veracity is not impugned.

> Some years ago a "liberal" theologian . . . remarked that it was a matter of small consequence whether a pair of trousers were originally perfect if they were now rent. To which the valiant and witty David James Burrell replied that it might be a matter of

small consequence to the wearer of the trousers, but the tailor who made them would prefer to have it understood that they did not leave his shop that way. And then he added that, if the Most High must train among knights of the shears He might at least be regarded as the best of the guild, and One who drops no stitches and sends out no imperfect work.[85]

If the Scriptures, like the works of Homer and others, came to us merely by God's general providence in history, then errors in the original might make little difference to us, but inspiration is another thing altogether. "Amazing indeed is the cavalier manner in which modern theologians relegate this doctrine of an inerrant original Scripture to the limbo of the unimportant,"[86] exclaimed Young, for the veracity of God[87] and the perfection of the Godhead[88] are involved in that doctrinal outlook.

> He, of course, tells us that His Word is pure. If there are mistakes in that Word, however, we know better; it is not pure. . . . He declares that His law is the truth. His law contains the truth, let us grant Him that, but we know that it contains error. If the autographa of Scripture are marred by flecks of mistake, God simply has not told us the truth concerning His Word. To assume that He could breathe forth a Word that contained mistakes is to say, in effect, that God Himself can make mistakes.[89]

And the minute that we say that, we have in principle lost our ultimate foundation of theological knowledge. Our personal assurance of salvation, as objectively grounded in the Scriptures, is swept away—for God's well-meant promises of such might still be in error.

The fact that we cannot now see the inerrant autographa does not destroy the importance of the claim that they existed as such. As Van Til remarks, when one is crossing a river that has swollen to the point of placing the surface of the bridge under a few inches of water, he might not be able to see the bridge but he is very glad nonetheless that it is there![90] He would not think for a moment that this unseen bridge is without any significance and try to cross the river arbitrarily at just any other point. In looking at my present Bible I cannot see the autographa exactly, but I am most glad that inerrant originals undergird my walk and constitute a bridge that can bring me back to God. I would not arbitrarily try to be reunited with Him by just any other course. The value of my present Bible derives, in the long run, from its dependence on the errorless original, as is illustrated by R. Laird Harris:

Reflection will show that the doctrine of verbal inspiration is worthwhile even though the originals have perished. An illustration may be helpful. Suppose we wish to measure the length of a certain pencil. With a tape measure we measure it at 6½ inches. A more carefully made office ruler indicates 6 9/16 inches. Checking it with an engineer's scale, we find it to be slightly more than 6.58 inches. Careful measurement with a steel scale under laboratory conditions reveals it to be 6.577 inches. Not satisfied still, we send the pencil to Washington, where master gauges indicate a length of 6.5774 inches. The master guages themselves are checked against the standard United States yard marked on a platinum bar preserved in Washington. Now, suppose that we should read in the newspapers that a clever criminal had run off with the platinum bar and melted it down for the precious metal. As a matter of fact, this once happened to Britain's standard yard! What difference would this make to us? Very little. None of us has ever seen the platinum bar. Many of us perhaps never realized it existed. Yet we blithely use tape measures, rulers, scales, and similar measuring devices. These approximate measures derive their value from their being dependent on more accurate gauges. But even the approximate has tremendous value—if it has had a true standard behind it.[91]

We conclude that even though we can be blessed without an errorless text and can formulate the great doctrines of the faith, the inerrant autographa are not thereby rendered unimportant, and the claim that God did not have to give the scriptural originals inerrantly is specious.[92] God can work through our errant copies to bring us to saving faith, but that does not diminish the qualitative difference between the perfect original and imperfect copy—just as an imperfect map may bring us to our destination, but it is nevertheless qualitatively different from a strictly accurate map (e.g., in fine details).

There is tremendous importance in confessing the doctrine, and in drawing the distinction implicit in it, that inerrancy is restricted to the scriptural autographa. We can admit, with Davis, that God did not keep the copyists from error and that nevertheless the church has grown and survived with an errant text,[93] but to infer from these facts that an inerrant autograph was not vital to God or necessary for us would be to commit the fallacy of hasty generalization. The importance of original inerrancy is that it enables us to confess consistently the truthfulness of God Himself. We thereby can avoid saying that the one who calls Himself "the Truth" made errors and was false in His statements.

However some may still ask, "If God took the trouble and deemed it crucial to secure the entire accuracy of the original text of Scripture, why did He not take greater care to preserve the copies errorless? Why did He allow it to be corrupted in transmission?[94] Numerous evangelicals have suggested that God has done so in order to prevent His people from falling into idolatry with respect to the errorless manuscripts.[95] In so saying, however, they make the same mistake made by many critics of original inerrancy in regard to other points—namely, of confusing the autographic text with the autographic codex. The original manuscripts might well have perished, thereby preventing an idolatry of them, but the main question is why the *text* of the autographa has not been inerrantly preserved.[96] Perhaps a more convincing answer would be that the need for textual criticism, due to an errant text of Scripture, would have the effect of drawing attention away from trivial details of the text (by which, e.g., it could be used as a magic amulet or cabbala) and toward its conveyed message.[97] In the long run, however, we simply have to turn away from such questions, which presume to have an a priori idea of what to expect from God, and confess, "Why God was not pleased to preserve the text of the original copies of the Bible, we do not know."[98] "The secret things belong unto Jehovah our God, but the things that are revealed belong unto us" (Deut. 29:29). And God has not chosen to share with us His motivation for allowing the text of the autographa to become slightly corrupted in particular copies of the Scripture. Possession of an answer as to why God permitted this is surely not a necessary condition to holding to the restriction of inerrancy to the autographa, if the position is maintained on independently sufficient grounds.

Some evangelicals have written as though two very different kinds of restriction on the inerrancy of Scripture are equally damaging to the doctrine and are virtually on a par. Errancy evangelicals restrict the utter trustworthiness of Scripture to revelational matters that make us "wise unto salvation," whereas inerrancy evangelicals restrict inerrancy to the autographic text. Since it is thought that these two kinds of restriction have the same practical effect, errancy evangelicals sometimes maintain that opposition from inerrancy evangelicals to their viewpoint is trivial. After all, it is alleged, the epistemological status of the two views is the same, since errors in our present copies of

Scripture must be recognized, thereby jeopardizing the unchallengeable authority of these manuscripts. Careful attention to the issue, however, will show that the importance of original inerrancy is not undermined by such reasoning. If the *original* manuscripts of Scripture were errant, then we could not possibly know the *extent* of error in them. The range of possible faults is virtually unbounded, for who can say at what point an errant God stops making mistakes?[99] Who could presume to know how to set God's "mistakes" in order? (Compare Romans 3:4; 9:20; 11:34; 1 Corinthians 2:16.) On the other hand, errors in *transmission* are, *in principle, correctable* by textual criticism. Wenham has grasped the point here:

> It has been said that, since there is no need for a guaranteed inerrancy now, there is no reason to suppose that inerrancy was ever given. But the distinction between the Scripture as it was originally given and the Scripture as it is now is not mere pedantry. We must hold, on the one hand, to the absolute truth of direct divine utterance. God does not approximately speak the truth. Human expositions of what God has said, on the other hand, do approximate to truth, and one can speak meaningfully of different degrees of approximation. If the term 'essential infallibility' is applied to a divine utterance, it has no precise meaning. It is like a medicine that is known to be adulterated, but adulterated to an unknown degree. When, however, 'essential infallibility' is referred to Scriptures once inerrant but now slightly corrupt, the meaning can, within limits, be precise. We know to a close approximation the nature of the tiny textual adulterations. The bottle is, as it were, plainly labelled: "This mixture is guaranteed to contain less than 0.01% of impurities." And our Lord himself (in the case of the Old Testament) has set us an example by taking his own medicine. A man's last will and testament is not invalidated by superficial scribal errors; no more are the divine testaments in the Bible.[100]

An inerrancy restricted to matters of faith and practice (assuming for the moment that these can be separated from historical and scientific details of God's Word) is not after all on the same epistemological footing with an inerrancy extending to everything taught in God's Word but restricted to the autographic text.

It is impossible to maintain the theological principle of *sola Scriptura* on the basis of limited inerrancy, for an errant authority—being in need of correction by some outside source—cannot serve as the only source and judge of Christian theology.[101] The philosophical basis for certainty, Christ speaking inerrantly in the identifiable historical revelation of God's written Word, is in principle preserved by the doctrine of original inerrancy but is vitiated by a doctrine of limited inerrancy whereby God can speak mistakenly about some issues. The former view provides a starting point and final authority for finding truth and overcoming philosophical skepticism, whereas the latter leaves us in no better epistemological position or provides no more assured, final theological authority than is conceivably provided in pagan literature.[102] From a theological standpoint, why should we diligently seek the autographic text if the unerring word from God would not thereby be secured? "If error had permeated the original prophetic-apostolic verbalization of the revelation, no essential connection would exist between the recovery of any preferred text and the authentic meaning of God's revelation."[103]

By way of summary, the doctrine of original inerrancy permits doubts only about the *identification* of the text—doubts that can be allayed by textual critical methods. In this case God's Word remains innocent of error until proven guilty; that is, what I find written in my present Bible is assumed to be true unless someone has good reason to doubt the integrity of the text *qua* text. The doctrine of limited inerrancy, however, which asserts aboriginal textual errors in historical or scientific matters, elicits corrosive doubt about the *truth of God's Word,* such that its statements cannot be fully trusted until verified or cleared of error by some final, outside authority. To put matters another way, the difference between those who maintain original inerrancy and those who hold to limited inerrancy is indicated in the divergent outcomes of textual criticism for the two. When the proper text has been identified by someone holding to original inerrancy, he has an *incontestable truth.* However, someone holding to limited inerrancy who identifies the original text has simply found something that is only *possibly* true (and thus possibly false).[104]

We have seen, then, that the doctrine of restricting inerrancy to the biblical autographa is far from trivial or irrelevant. It has tremendous importance, not because inerrancy is necessary for God to use, and the reader to profit from a copy of Scripture but in order to maintain the veracity of God and the unchallengeable epistemological authority of our theological commitments.

THE ASSURANCE OF POSSESSING GOD'S WORD

Throughout the previous discussion we have insisted on and defended the restriction of inerrancy to the autographic text of the Bible. The question might now arise as to whether we actually can be sure of possessing the genuine Word of God in our present copies and translations of the Bible. After all, the inspiration and inerrancy of Scripture is reserved for the original text and applies to the current text only to the extent that it reflects the original. How can we know that our extant copies are substantially correct transcriptions of the autographa? The answer here is twofold: we know it from the providence of God and from the results of textual science.

If we do not assume that God has spoken clearly and given us an adequate means of learning what He has actually said, then the entire story of the Bible and its portrayal of the plan of God for man's salvation makes no sense whatever. As James Orr observed, because the preservation of the text of Scripture is part of the transmission of the knowledge of God, it is reasonable to expect that God will provide for it lest the aims of His revealing Himself to men be frustrated.[105] The providence of God superintends matters so that copies of Scripture do not become so corrupt as to become unintelligible for God's original purposes in giving it or so corrupt as to create a major falsification of His message's text.[106] Scripture itself promises that God's Word will abide forever (Isa. 40:8; Matt. 5:18; 24:35; Luke 16:17; 1 Peter 1:24–25), and by His providential control God secures the fulfillment of such a promise.

John Skilton gives a helpful response to our current question:

> We will grant that God's care and providence, singular though they have been, have not preserved for us any of the original manuscripts either of the Old Testament or of the New Testament. We will furthermore grant that God did not keep from error those who copied the Scriptures during the long period in which the sacred text was transmitted in copies written by hand. But we must maintain that the God who gave the Scriptures, who works all things after the counsel of his will, has exercised a remarkable care over his Word, has preserved it in all ages in a state of essential purity, and has enabled it to accomplish the purpose for which he gave it. It is inconceivable that the sovereign God who was pleased to give his Word as a vital and necessary instrument in the salvation of his people would permit his Word to become completely marred in its transmission and

unable to accomplish its ordained end. Rather, as surely as that he is God, we would expect to find him exercising a singular care in the preservation of his written revelation.[107]

Faith in the consistency of God—His faithfulness to His own intention to make men wise unto salvation—guarantees the inference that He never permits Scripture to become so corrupted that it can no longer fulfill that end adequately. We can conclude theologically that, for all practical purposes, the text of Scripture is always sufficiently accurate not to lead us astray.[108] If we presuppose a sovereign God, observes Van Til, it is no longer a matter for great worry that the transmission of Scripture is not altogether accurate; God's providence provides for the essential accuracy of the Bible's copying.[109]

We maintain, therefore, that the Bible which we have in our hands is fully adequate to bring us to Christ, to instruct us in His doctrine, and to guide us in righteous living. It is obvious that God has done His work in and through the church for centuries, despite the presence of minor flaws in the extant copies of the Scripture. Consequently it is clear that the necessity of restricting inerrancy to the autographa is not of the necessity-for-effectiveness kind. "It does not follow . . . that only an errorless text can be of devotional benefit to Christians, nor do those who believe in the inerrancy of Scripture maintain such a position."[110] The copies we now possess are known to be accurate and sufficient in all matters except minor details.[111] As the Westminster Confession of Faith goes on to say, having restricted immediate inspiration to the original text of Scripture, the ordinary vernacular Bibles in use among Christians are adequate for all of the purposes of the religious life and hope (I.8). We can usually ignore the distinction between the autographa and copies, being bold about the Word of God; yet when we engage in detailed study of Scripture, we must reckon with the distinction and remain teachable as to a more precise text.

The adequacy of our present copies and translations does not, of course, dismiss the need for textual criticism. "The truth and power of Scripture are not annulled by the presence of a degree of textual corruption. This fact, however, does not give grounds for complacency. An imperfect text should be replaced by a superior one."[112] After all, "if holy men spoke from God, as the Christian faith claims, then it is the account of their words that will concern us, and not a series of glosses interpolated by a medieval scribe."[113] Out of respect for God and the uniqueness of His Word, the church, as part of its stewardship of the Bible, seeks to do its best to correct the extant copies of Scripture so as to preserve the full impact of what was originally given and to be faithful in specific issues of faith and practice.[114]

People have, as we said earlier, asked, Of what use is an inerrant original if it is totally lost from recovery? "This is the problem of textual criticism," says Harris.[115] It is not possible in the short space afforded here to rehearse the principles, history, and results of textual criticism.[116] However, the outstanding quality of our existing biblical texts is well known. The original text has been transmitted to us in practically every detail, so that Frederick Kenyon could say:

> The Christian can take the whole Bible in his hand and say without fear or hesitation that he holds in it the true Word of God, handed down without essential loss from generation to generation, throughout the centuries.[117]

Textual criticism of the copies of the Scripture we possess has brought immensely comforting results to the church of Christ. Vos concludes that "we possess the text of the Bible today in a form which is substantially identical with the autographs."[118] Warfield's words also bear repeating here:

> On the other hand, if we compare the present state of the New Testament text with that of any other ancient writing, we must render the opposite verdict, and declare it to be marvellously correct. Such has been the care with which the New Testament has been copied,—a care which has doubtless grown out of true reverence for its holy words,—such has been the providence of God in preserving for His Church in each and every age a competently exact text of the Scriptures, that not only is the New Testament unrivalled among ancient writings in the purity of its text as actually transmitted and kept in use, but also in the abundance of testimony which has come down to us for castigating its comparatively infrequent blemishes. The divergence of its current text from the autograph may shock a modern printer of modern books; its wonderful approximation to its autograph is the undisguised envy of every modern reader of ancient books.
>
> The great mass of the New Testament, in other words, has been transmitted to us with no, or next to no, variation; and even in the most corrupt form in which it has ever appeared, to use the oft-quoted words of Richard Bentley, "the real text of the sacred writers is competently exact; ... nor is one article of faith or

moral precept either perverted or lost . . . choose as awkwardly as you will, choose the worst by design, out of the whole lump of readings." If, then, we undertake the textual criticism of the New Testament under a sense of duty, we may bring it to a conclusion under the inspiration of hope. The autographic text of the New Testament is distinctly within the reach of criticism in so immensely the greater part of the volume, that we cannot despair of restoring to ourselves and the Church of God, His Book, word for word, as He gave it by inspiration to men.[119]

Elsewhere Warfield said that those who ridicule the "lost autographs" often speak as though the Bible as given by God is lost beyond recovery and that men are now limited to texts so hopelessly corrupted that it is impossible to say what was in the autographic text. Over against this absurd and extreme view Warfield maintained that "we have the autographic text" among our copies in circulation and the restoration of the original is not impossible.[120]

The defenders of the trustworthiness of the Scriptures have constantly asserted, together, that God gave the Bible as the errorless record of his will to men, and that he has, in his superabounding grace, preserved it for them to this hour—yea, and will preserve it for them to the end of time. . . . Not only *was* the inspired Word, as it came from God, without error, but . . . it remains so. . . . It is as truly heresy to affirm that the inerrant Bible has been lost to men as it is to declare that there never was an inerrant Bible.[121]

The charge that God did not apparently deem the preservation of the original text important is pointless because, far from being hopelessly corrupt, our copies virtually supply us with the autographic text.[122] All the ridicule that is heaped on evangelicals about the "lost autographa" is simply vain, for we do not regard their text as lost at all! As Harris says,

To all intents and purposes we have the autographs, and thus when we say we believe in verbal inspiration of the autographs, we are not talking of something imaginary and far off but of the texts written by those inspired men and preserved for us so carefully by faithful believers of a long past age.[123]

The doctrine of original inerrancy, then, does not deprive believers today of the Word of God in an adequate form for all the purposes of God's revelation to His people. Presupposing the providence of God in the preservation of the biblical text, and noting the outstanding results of the textual criticism of the

Scriptures, we can have full assurance that we possess the Word of God necessary for our salvation and Christian walk. As a criticism of this evangelical doctrine, suggestions that the autographic text has been forever lost are groundless and futile. The Bibles in our hands are trustworthy renditions of God's original message, adequate for all intents and purposes as copies and conveyors of God's authoritative Word.

Concluding Criticisms

Before ending our discussion, we will examine three different remaining types of direct attacks on the doctrine of restricting inerrancy to the autographic text. The first alleges that the doctrine is unprovable, the second that it cannot be consistently maintained along with other evangelical doctrines and truths about the Bible, and the third that it is simply untrue to the teaching of Scripture itself.

First, there are those who would attempt to make much of the unprovable character of original inerrancy because the autographa are now gone. Since the original biblical manuscripts are not available for inspection, it is thought that taking them to have been without error is groundless speculation. After all, nobody today has actually seen these allegedly inerrant autographa. This criticism, however, misunderstands the nature and source of the doctrine of original inerrancy. It is not a doctrine derived from empirical investigation of certain written texts; it is a theological commitment rooted in the teaching of the Word of God itself. The nature of God (who is truth Himself) and the nature of the biblical books (as the very words of God) require that we view the original manuscripts, produced under the superintendence of the Holy Spirit of truth, as wholly true and without error. To the charge that the errorless autographa have not been seen we can reply that neither have errant autographa ever been seen; the view that the biblical originals contained errors is just as much divorced from direct empirical proof as the opposite view.[124] The basic question remains biblically oriented and answered. What is the nature of Scripture as it came from the very mouth of God? Evangelicals do not believe that their answer to that question is unprovable, but rather that it is fully demonstrated from the Word of God itself.

A second direct criticism of the restriction of inspiration (and thereby inerrancy) to the autographa comes from George Mavrodes,[125] who challenges evangelicals to be guided by the principle of *sola Scriptura* and to explicate a definition of "autograph" that applies to all of the biblical books and does not deny the use of uninspired amanuenses in the production of those autographic manuscripts[126] (thus discounting the notion of a literally handwritten copy by the author).[127] Moreover, the view must not arbitrarily restrict inspiration to the manuscripts produced by such amanuenses.

I have responded to this challenge in the same journal,[128] arguing that inspiration is not arbitrarily, but rather practically, restricted to the autographic text because we cannot be sure—without the actual autographa to use for comparison—that copies that are prone to error (since God has not promised inerrant copying of His Word) will be strictly accurate. In saying this I understood an autograph to be the first completed, personal, or approved transcription of a unique word-group composed by its author. In that sense we can see that every biblical book had an autograph, and we can accommodate the fact that amanuenses were used in their production, without attributing inspiration to the amanuenses. The fact that the *finished product* is designated "God-breathed" (2 Tim. 3:16) guarantees inerrant copying by the amanuensis without placing him in the same category as the author, who was moved by the Holy Spirit (cf. 2 Peter 1:21). Accordingly, the restriction of inspiration to the autographic text can be maintained consistently, along with important theological principles (such as *sola Scriptura*) and with obvious facts about the Bible (such as the use of amanuenses in its production).[129]

In response to my article, Sidney Chapman took another tack in criticizing the restriction of inspiration to the autographa.[130] He ends up contending for the implausible thesis that the Septuagint was inspired, arguing simply that, since "all Scripture is inspired" (2 Tim. 3:16) and Paul treated a virtual quote from the Septuagint as "Scripture" (in Rom. 4:3), therefore the Septuagint is inspired.[131] Chapman, however, falls into various logical fallacies in his argument. First, there is an obvious equivocation on the word *Scripture* as it is found in the two different texts cited. In Romans 4:3 Paul is simply interested in the sense or meaning of the scriptural teaching in the Old Testament at Genesis 15:6. This teaching can be conveyed by any accurate copy or translation, and, in view of his audience, Paul readily used the available

Septuagint version. In 2 Timothy 3:16, however, Paul is reflecting on the specific Scripture as it originated from God, and thus on the autographa alone (or identical texts in subsequent manuscripts).[132] Thus the Septuagintal reading can be called "Scripture" in virtue of its expressing the sense of the original, whereas the autographa is strictly and literally "Scripture" in and of itself. The fact that I can casually call my American Standard Version the "Scripture" (because I assume its essential accuracy in conveying the original) can hardly be grounds for concluding that I do not distinguish between this English translation and the Hebrew-Greek original, or that I do not differentiate between the autographa and its copies.

Second, Chapman needs to take account of the fact that Paul does not directly state that the Septuagint or any part of it is in fact "Scripture." He does not even mention the Septuagint as such. Moreover, Paul does not illustrate or imply that the Septuagint is "Scripture" in the same sense as 2 Timothy 3:16, for his reading is not strictly identical with the Septuagintal word-group or text.

Third, even if the Septuagint reading at this point were "Scripture" in the full sense (and not simply *scriptural*), one could confer the same status on *all* of the Septuagint texts only by the fallacy of composition or hasty generalization. Therefore, we must conclude that Romans 4:3 does not teach or illustrate the inspiration of the Septuagint as a version. Chapman has not presented a successful counterexample to the thesis that inspiration is restricted to the autographic text of Scripture.

Chapman's second line of argument against the restriction of inspiration to the autographa states that this restriction would also have to restrict the *profitableness* of Scripture (cf. 2 Tim. 3:16) to the autographa, in which case our present translations would not benefit us for doctrine and instruction in righteousness. However, this line of thought does not take account of the facts that (1) a present-day translation can be scriptural in its thrust as long as it conveys the original sense of God's Word; (2) because the predicates "profitable" and "inspired" are not mutually implicatory, a present translation can be profitable because it conveys God's Word and still not be an inspired text as such; and (3) the inspired and/or profitable quality of a copy or translation of the Scriptures can be applied by degrees (as was explained earlier in this chapter). Therefore, the fact that inspiration or inerrancy is restricted to the autographa need not deprive our present copies and translations of genuine profit to us in our Christian experience.

By way of summary, the present study has maintained that, while the Bible teaches its own inerrancy, the inscripturation and copying of God's Word requires us to identify the specific and proper object of inerrancy as the text of the original autographa. This time-honored, common-sense view of evangelicals has been criticized and ridiculed since the days of the modernist controversy over Scripture. Nevertheless, according to the attitude of the biblical writers, who could and did distinguish copies from the autographa, copies of the Bible serve the purposes of revelation and function with authority only because they are assumed to be tethered to the autographic text and its criteriological authority. The evangelical doctrine pertains to the autographic text, not the autographic codex, and maintains that present copies and translations are inerrant to the extent that they accurately reflect the biblical originals; thus the inspiration and inerrancy of present Bibles is not an all-or-nothing matter. Evangelicals maintain the doctrine of original inerrancy, not as an apologetical artifice, but on the theological grounds that: (1) the inspiration of copyists and the perfect transmission of Scripture have not been promised by God, and (2) the extraordinary quality of God's revealed Word must be guarded against arbitrary alteration. The importance of original inerrancy is not that God cannot accomplish His purpose except through a completely errorless text, but that without it we cannot consistently confess His veracity, be fully assured of the scriptural promise of salvation, or maintain the epistemological authority and theological axiom of *sola Scriptura* (since errors in the original, unlike those in transmission, would not be correctable in principle). We can be assured that we possess the Word of God in our present Bible because of God's providence; He does not allow His aims in revealing Himself to be frustrated. Indeed, the results of textual criticism confirm that we possess a biblical text that is substantially identical with the autographa.

Finally, contrary to recent criticisms, the doctrine of original inerrancy (or inspiration) is not unprovable, is not undermined by the use of amanuenses by the biblical writers, and is not contravened by the New Testament use of the Septuagint as "Scripture." Therefore, the evangelical restriction of inerrancy to the original autographa is warranted, important, and defensible. Further, it does not jeopardize the adequacy and authority of our present Bibles. Accordingly the doctrine of original inerrancy can be commended to all believers who are sensitive to the authority of the Bible as the very Word of God and who wish to propagate it as such today.

THE ADEQUACY
OF HUMAN LANGUAGE

James I. Packer

James I. Packer is Professor of Systematic Theology, Regent College, Vancouver, British Columbia. He was educated at Oxford University, where he took degrees in classics, philosophy, and theology and secured his doctorate in 1954 for research on the Puritan Richard Baxter. Following two years of service on the staff of a church in Birmingham, he was Senior Tutor of Tyndale Hall, an Anglican Seminary, 1955–61; Warden of Latimer House, a study center in Oxford, 1961–70; and Principal of Tyndale Hall, 1970–71. Following the 1972 merger of Tyndale Hall with two other colleges to become Trinity College, he assumed the position of Associate Principal of this institution until 1979. Dr. Packer is the author of "Fundamentalism" and the Word of God; Evangelism and the Sovereignty of God; God Has Spoken; Knowing God; I Want to Be a Christian, *two chapters (*"Sola Scriptura *in History and Today" and* "Calvin's View of Scripture"*) in* God's Inerrant Word, *edited by J. W. Montgomery, and a chapter (*"Encountering Present-Day Views of Scripture" *in* The Foundation of Biblical Authority, *edited by J. M. Boice.*

CHAPTER SUMMARY

Present-day skepticism about the capacity of human language to convey truth about God springs from at least four sources: (1) our sense of the inadequacy of language to communicate even between human beings; (2) positivistic skepticism as to whether words ever refer to, or make statements about, transcendent realities; (3) the assumption in much modern Protestant hermeneutics that the content of the communication between God and man that takes place through the Scriptures is nonverbal and noninformative; (4) the influence of Eastern ideas of what constitutes a "religious" state of mind, in which one is open to the divine.

The biblical writers purport to reveal truths about God, and in semantic terms the concepts of *analogy, model, image,* and *parable,* as characterizations of the Bible's theological language, show how this could be a true claim on their part. Biblical language will in that case be vindicated as adequate, not indeed for exhaustive knowledge of God, such as He has of Himself, but for authoritative guidance in living. This is exactly what the doctrine of verbal inspiration affirms because inspiration, biblically conceived, means that God has condescended to identify with what His messengers said and wrote: to identify so completely that their words and message are also equally His—therefore, not only their witness to Him, but also His own witness to Himself. The theological concept of inerrancy, which must be seen as belonging to the larger doctrine of God's communicative action, has its significance, in part at least, as a pointer to the completeness of this identification, for what is truly God's testimony must truly be true.

The question as to whether Bible language is adequate to give us knowledge of God by description and hence by acquaintance is parallel with the question as to whether the words, works, and personal impact of the biblical Christ, who is the Christ of history, are adequate for that purpose. Indeed, the two questions reduce to one, for Christ is the focal theme of Scripture, and Christ and the Bible attest to each other. Both share the same quality of historical particularity as means of God's self-revelation, and both embody the same divine humility in saving self-disclosure that Paul calls "weakness" and "foolishness" (1 Cor. 1:25). And where acknowledgment of Scripture as adequate verbal communication from God is lacking, acknowledgment of the biblical Christ as adequately bringing us to God is likely to be lacking, too.

THE ADEQUACY
OF HUMAN LANGUAGE

CAN HUMAN LANGUAGE, specifically the language of the Bible, be divine language also—God's own verbal utterance, whereby He gives us factual information about Himself? Can words of men really be words of God, conveying to us the Word—that is, the message—of God? Historically, the Christian answer has been yes. The common inclination among today's professed believers to say no appears, to say the least, to be an eccentricity. When we ask the reason for this shift, which seems something of an aberration, we find a clear case of failure to think straight. It is worth showing this failure in some detail as we begin.

God's Word Spoken, Written, and Understood

1. Four preliminary and foundational points should be clearly stated. If, as the New Testament writers and the Nicene Creed say, the Holy Spirit "spoke . . . through the prophets,"[1] and if the Galilean rabbi Jesus, the teacher who, though more than a prophet, was not less than a prophet (cf. Luke 13:33), was God incarnate, so that His teaching (given Him by His Father,[2] but at the same time set forth in His own authority)[3] was in the most direct and obvious sense teaching, speech, witness, and instruction from God, then the question whether God uses human language to tell man things is, in principle, settled. He does. The

phenomena of prophecy and incarnation prove this decisively.

2. The concept of biblical inspiration is essentially identical with that of prophetic inspiration. No new difficulty arises in acknowledging the former if one acknowledges the latter, for no new element is involved. God's statement to Jeremiah, "I have to put my words in your mouth" (1:9), gives the theological paradigm of what is involved: God causes His message to enter into a man's mind, by psychological processes that are in part opaque to us, so that the man may then faithfully relay the message to others. It is evident that inspiration could, and did, take different psychological forms from one writer to another, and for the same writer at different times. The *dualistic* inspiration of prophets and seers produced in them a sustained awareness of the distinction between their own thoughts and the visions and specific messages that God gave them. This is psychologically different from the state of mind resulting from the *didactic* inspiration of the biblical historians, wisdom teachers, and New Testament apostles. For them the effect of inspiration was that after observation, research, reflection, and prayer they knew just what they should say in God's name, as witnesses and interpreters of His work. Also, it is psychologically different from the *lyric* inspiration of the poets, who write the Psalms and the Song of Songs in responsive celebration of what they had come to know of God's goodness in creation, providence, and redemption. Subjectively, as all versifiers and hymn writers know, the experience of a poem "coming on" (cf. Pss. 39:3; 45:1), of its gradually taking form in consciousness, differs both from the way in which an oracle is received and from the way didactic certainty is given. But—and this is the point to note—in the Bible writers' view, which almost all the church shared from apostolic days until quite recently, the theological reality of inspiration is the same in each case. God so controlled the process of communication to and through His servants that, in the last analysis, He is the source and speaker not merely of biblical prophecy but also of biblical history, wisdom, and doctrine, and also of the poems, whose giant-size delineations of adoration and devotion set worshipers of every age a standard for what their own praise and prayer should be.

It makes no difference to inspiration (how could it?) whether its product is oral or written. When in the past evangelical theologians defined God's work of inspiration as the producing of

God-breathed Scriptures, they were not denying that God inspired words uttered orally as well. Indeed, in the case of prophets and apostles, the biblical way to put the point is to urge that the words in which these men wrote or dictated are *no less* God-given than the words in which they shared orally with individuals and congregations, for the spoken word came first.

Jeremiah's oracles, when written, were still "the words of the LORD" (Jer. 36:6, 8, 11) as well as being "the words of Jeremiah" (vs. 10). Paul, having claimed to speak (*laleō*) what the Spirit had revealed "in words taught by the Spirit" (1 Cor. 2:13), tells his readers that they should "acknowledge that what I am *writing* to you" (the immediate reference is to his set of directions about worship and the silence of women) is a command of the Lord (1 Cor. 14:37). He does not mean that he is quoting what Jesus said on earth (as in 7:10ff.), but that he, as an apostle, is actually speaking (here as elsewhere) in Jesus' name and under the power of inspiration.

Whether spoken viva voce or written, and whether dualistic or didactic or lyric in its psychological mode, inspiration—that divine combination of prompting and control that secures precise communication of God's mind by God's messenger—remains theologically the same thing. Of Scripture in particular we must say that, while it is the product of powerful religious experiences and has most inspiring effects, to call it *inspired* is directly to affirm neither of these things. In 2 Timothy 3:16, "inspired" represents the Greek adjective *theopneustos*, a word that means not, as the lexicons of Cremer and Bauer have said (and Barth after them),[4] "breathing out God" but, as Warfield proved long ago,[5] "breathed out by God." All Scripture, therefore, is a product of His creative power, and so is an authentic disclosure of His mind and presentation of His message.

3. It is clear (1) that our Lord and the apostles saw both their Bible (our Old Testament) and their own teaching as divinely authoritative for faith and life; (2) that they saw their own teaching as complementary and subordinate to that of their Bible, and indeed as expository of it; and (3) that they believed that both their Bible and their own teaching gave factual information about God. Thus they bequeathed to the church, in effect, the idea of the two Testaments, Old and New together, as constituting a *canon*, that is, a rule of belief and behavior, for all of God's people at all times. The idea of Scripture as a canon in

this sense is made explicit by the dominical and apostolic attitude to the Old Testament. Indeed, Paul's statement in 2 Timothy 3:16, "All Scripture is God-breathed and is [therefore] useful for teaching, rebuking, correcting, and training in righteousness," is an analysis of the meaning of canonicity in precise terms.[6]

The witness of our Lord to the canonical status of His Bible is especially striking. In the Gospels we find Him affirming the divine authority of teaching given in both the indicative and the imperative moods in many Old Testament passages. For example, in Matthew 19:4-5 He quotes Genesis 2:24 as the word of the Creator (because, presumably, it is a scriptural statement, for in context it is not a direct utterance of God) and deduces from it the impropriety of divorce. Moreover, we find Jesus declaring, categorically and comprehensively, that His ministry would be entirely misunderstood were it thought that He came to cancel or set aside the Law and the Prophets (i.e., the Old Testament). On the contrary, He had come to fulfill both. And clearly, for Him to let the Law and the Prophets shape His life and teaching (this is what "fulfill" implies) was an acknowledgment of their authority over Him. How complete that acknowledgment was appears from the temptation story, where Jesus three times embraces the God-prescribed counter to Satan's suggestions, and from the passion story, where we see Him going up to Jerusalem to die, because this scriptural prediction of Messiah's destiny had to be fulfilled.[7] That Jesus, being God in person, taught with divine authority and that His teaching constitutes a rule for His disciples is a Christian commonplace (cf. Matt. 7:21-29; 28:19, et al.); only by following Jesus' teaching can one be His disciple. Part of His teaching was that our Old Testament was canonical for Him and is to be so for His followers. A good deal of His teaching derived factual information about God from it. What sort of disciples are we if we decline to receive this basic strand of our Master's teaching?

Of the New Testament canon it need only be said that (1) apostolic witness to Christ, being Spirit-inspired, was always meant to function, in conjunction with the Old Testament, as a rule of faith;[8] (2) the only problem, therefore, at any stage was to identify the documents in which genuine apostolic instruction was given, either directly by apostles themselves or by their immediate and accredited associates (cf. 2 Thess. 2:2); (3) we have no good reason to question the twenty-seven books that the early church identified as apostolic in the required sense—for their external credentials are impressive, their doctrine is homogeneous,[9] and Christians of all generations have found in them that unique, transforming light and power that are the hallmarks of divinity on the biblical canon as a whole, evidencing it to be God's Word and thereby setting it apart from all other writings that the world has seen.

4. It is true that biblical revelation takes the form of an interpretive record of God's will, works, and ways as these were disclosed in a series of episodes in which He dealt with men of the ancient Near East. It is also true that the universally valid truths this record gives us as applied to particular Near Eastern folk of the far-off past, up to the first century A.D., need to be reapplied today. But since these universal truths are intrinsically clear and rational, such reapplication is always a practical possibility. The essential and continuing task of biblical interpretation is to reapply biblical principles to ourselves, having discerned through historical exegesis what the human author meant his contemporaries to gather from what he said and having distinguished between principle and application within his message. Historical exegesis is only the preliminary part of interpretation; application is its essence. Exegesis without application should not be called *interpretation* at all. The fear sometimes felt, that because of the distance between the cultures and outlooks of the biblical period and our own, these ancient Near Eastern documents cannot communicate God's mind and will for our lives in our own day, is groundless. God is rational and unchanging, and all men in every generation, being made in God's image, are capable of being addressed by Him. Within every culture in every age it is possible, through overhearing God's words of instruction to men of long ago, to hear God speaking to ourselves, as the Holy Spirit causes these words of long ago to be reapplied in our own minds and consciences. The proof that this is possible is that it actually happens. No proof can be more compelling that that!

PRESENT-DAY DOUBTS ABOUT LANGUAGE

It is clear, however, that some today find difficulty with the line of thought I have set out because their minds are already possessed by deep-rooted uncertainties about the power of human language to convey information (as distinct from evoking attitudes) in the realm of what philosophers might call the supersensible or transcendent and Christians would call the divine. Until these doubts are exorcised, the straightforward belief that in the Bible God tells us things will seem naive and hazardous. The temptation will be to follow the example of liberal and radical Protestant thinkers from Schleiermacher to Bultmann, Tillich, and their latter-day disciples and to turn the flank of the above exposition by agreeing that it states the Bible's own view. The Bible is treated as a collection of culturally conditioned myths, which for us can function only as symbols of nonverbal pressure that God exerts on the human spirit by evoking experiences of mystical, emotional, and ethical insight. So we need to take the measure of this fashionable skepticism about religious language—in particular, about biblical language. It appears to draw its strength from four features of today's skeptical culture.

The first source of skepticism is *a widespread sense of the inadequacy of all language as a means of personal communication*. This attitude, which finds vivid expression in poets like Stein, in novelists like Kafka, and in playwrights like Beckett, appears to be a symptom of a pervasive failure of nerve from which Western culture has conspicuously suffered in this century. Whereas writers from Shakespeare, Donne, and Milton to Hopkins, Housman, and Hardy celebrated and explored the resourcefulness of language as a means of communication at all levels, their successors show themselves burdened and oppressed at the isolation of each individual and the inadequacy of anyone's words to make known to others what is really going on in his innermost life. Ludwig Wittgenstein was very much a modern man when he declared that what can be said can be said clearly, that what we cannot say clearly we had best not try to say at all, and that the existential questions that matter most to us (*unsere Lebensprobleme*) are inexpressible.[10] T. S. Eliot was voicing what many today feel when he wrote in *Four Quartets* (Burnt Norton V) that in personal communication

> Words strain,
> Crash and sometimes break under the burden,
> Under the tension, slip, slide, perish,
> Decay with imprecision, will not stay in place,
> Will not stay still.

Moods do not always express either great insight or strong logic, but they are potent things while they last, and undoubtedly the modern mood is one of deep skepticism as to whether words can ever articulate the realities of personal existence and convey to others what is in the depth of one's own heart. And if this is true (so it is felt) among us who share a common human nature, surely it is much more true when God, who is so different from us, is the communicator. He can, no doubt, give us flashes of insight and illumination about ourselves, but precise information about His own will and purpose, His own thoughts and outlook?—surely not. Our post-Christian monotheistic paganism, which disbelieves the Incarnation and stresses God's remoteness, serves merely to reinforce this mood, and unless and until true faith in Christ revives in Western culture, belief that God, in Scripture, specifically tells us things about Himself is likely to go on being thought crude, unsophisticated, and naive.

The second source of skepticism is *widespread doubt as to whether language can convey transcendent realities at all.* At the presuppositional level, this doubt runs through much of the intensive study of language in which philosophers (mostly empiricists) and exponents of linguistics (a new academic discipline, developed mainly as a department of sociology) have been engaged for over half a century. While it is clear that the doubt was brought to this study rather than derived from it, it has so shaped professional procedures and techniques that, to casual observers, linguistic philosophy and semantic theory, with their stress on defining things by pointing to them, seem to confirm the doubt. Logically, of course, this is nonsense, just as the idea that naturalistic natural science can confirm its own uniformitarian presuppositions is nonsense. There is no denying, however, that it is, at present, potent nonsense.

The fountainheads of linguistic philosophy were Ludwig Wittgenstein's *Tractatus Logico–Philosophicus* (1922) and Alfred J. Ayer's *Language, Truth and Logic* (1935). Wittgenstein's book was deeply skeptical, and Ayer's reflected the positivist views of Rudolf Carnap's "Vienna Circle," whose members held that all facts are public and observable and therefore the ideal universal language is that of physics. Wittgenstein moved on to acknowledge a multiplicity of universes of discourse ("language-games"), and Ayer's tract went down in history as logical positivism's last manifesto as well as its first. Yet interest in the logic of language, "syntactics" as it is sometimes called, remains, and with it the convention, basic in both books just mentioned, of treating as eccentric any view that holds that language can connote, denote, and give information about anything that transcends the world of the senses. The study of semantics, that is, of the way language works as a means of expression and communication, stems from Ferdinand de Saussure's sociologically oriented pioneer work, *A Course in General Linguistics* (English translation, 1960, French original, 1915), and has tended to operate throughout its history in terms of a similar convention. The convention is arbitrary enough, but while it exists among the learned it cannot but create a climate of opinion in its own favor among those who, as students, seek to benefit from the professionals' expertise. Students naturally soak up what their teachers take for granted.

The third source of skepticism is *the widespread unwillingness of Christian teachers to allow that in and through the teaching of Scripture God is informing us about Himself.* Since liberalism took hold a century and a half ago, Protestant theologians, while remaining sure that Scripture mediates conscious, life-giving contact with God, have for the most part been equally sure that Scripture is not His Word in the sense expressed by Augustine's "what thy Scripture says, thou dost say." Kant, whose deism controlled his philosophy in a rather obvious way, had denied both the possibility and the need of verbal revelation from God, and liberal theologians took their cue from him. From the start, their thought was that Scripture is a product of religious and moral insight, which triggers similar insight in those who are capable of it. The actual theology of the Bible writers, however, is no more than culture-bound human witness to these awarenesses of God, awarenesses that in any case were essentially ineffable, as are all religious experiences. Schleiermacher, with his belief that the essence of all religion is an intuition (feeling) of dependence on God and that Christianity is distinctive only because in it this feeling was and is mediated through the impact of the historical figure of Jesus, is the archetypal liberal teacher and was in fact the fountainhead of this whole development. Ritschl is usually thought of as a liberal patriarch because he denied verbal revelation and miracles and was deeply agnostic about God, but his hostility to mysticism was uncharacteristic of the movement generally.

In this century, neoorthodoxy has stressed that through the Bible God's Word comes to us but has declined to conceive of that Word as simply Bible teaching applied to our situation. On the right wing, Barth viewed the Word as a breaking forth of something that Scripture "intends" and that the church needs to hear, rather than as a systematic and integrated application to us of what Scripture actually says. At the center, Brunner spent much time urging that, since God's revelation of Himself is personal, it cannot be in any sense propositional—a curious false antithesis that makes God's method of self-disclosure analogous to the nonverbal communication of Harpo Marx. On the left wing, Bultmann insisted that our life-transforming encounter with the Word of God yields no factual information whatever, and that the nature of true faith is to trust God, knowing that, in the strict sense, one knows nothing about Him at all. The practitioners of the *new hermeneutic* follow Bultmann in exploring the nature of "language-events" that alter our self-understanding without bringing us any direct understanding of God.

When leaders of theology thus decline to treat any of the statements of our thousand-plus-page, million-and-a-half-word Bible as information from God to us and trumpet abroad that there can be no such thing as God-given information and that it is an intellectual mistake to look for any, it is no wonder if folk lose faith in the capacity of biblical speech to tell us facts about our Maker. Were we all clearheadedly logical, we should see ourselves as called by this situation to choose between such modern theologians as those just mentioned and such older ones as Moses and the prophets, Jesus Christ, Peter, Paul, John, and the author of Hebrews. Seeing the issue that way we might resolve that, on this point at least, we should ditch the moderns. But because many people are muddleheadedly conventional, it is not always realized that this is the choice that faces us; nor, even when it is realized, is the right decision always made.

The fourth source of skepticism is *the widespread influence of Eastern religious ideas, all stressing that God is inexpressible by man.* Thus, for example, Lao-tse begins his treatise by saying: "The *tao* [way] that can be trodden is not the enduring and unchanging *tao*. The name that can be named is not the enduring and unchanging name." "In Lao-tse and in eastern mysticism generally," comments John Macquarrie, "the thought seems to be . . . of a primal undifferentiated Being, which we cannot even name

without giving it a determinate character, and so making it some
particular thing."[11] In Eastern thinking, as in the neoplatonism
that circled like smog around early Christianity, the ultimate
being does not have a determined character, in fact is not a
particular being at all. Christians believe that God made man in
His own image, so that He and man might talk together and,
furthermore, that Jesus is God incarnate, come to us to show us
what God eternally is; so the above-mentioned transcendentalist
hang-up does not touch us. Eastern faiths, however, lacking
these biblical truths and leaning as they do to either pantheistic
or deistic conceptions (e.g., Hinduism in the former case, Islam
in the latter) can hardly avoid it. To Westerners, for whom
Christianity is old hat and Eastern religion is a novelty, and who,
like the Athenians, are always going for new things, the thought
of God as wholly remote from the categories of human language
may seem, like Tennyson's white-clothed arm that grasped Ex-
calibur, "mystic, wonderful." Christians, however, will see the
idea as an embracing of darkness instead of light. But the Eastern notion of God as wholly inconceivable and inexpressible
certainly infects many minds today and reinforces the common
skeptical reaction when Christians claim that God has used
human language—Hebrew, Aramaic, and Greek, to be precise—to give us specific information about Himself.

OUR LANGUAGE-USING GOD

Such skepticism, however, is as far from the world of biblical
religion as it is from the historic faith of the church. As we have
already seen, Christianity from the start has been based on the
biblical conviction that in and through words spoken to and by
prophets and apostles, and supremely by Jesus Christ, the Word
made flesh, as well as by the voice heard from heaven (Mark
1:11; 9:7; John 12:28ff.; 2 Peter 1:17ff.), God has spoken, *in the
precise sense of using language to tell men things*. To assume, with the
liberals, that the biblical vocabulary of divine speech is metaphorical, in the sense of signifying nonverbal communication, or
is simply the spontaneous discernment by sensitive souls of spiritual values, is incorrect.

We may take the very explicit witness of the letter to the
Hebrews as proof. The writer opens with the great "In time past
God *spoke* to our forefathers at many times and in various ways,
but in these last days he has *spoken* to us by his Son" (Heb.

1:1–2). The phrase "various ways" recalls the visions, dreams, theophanies, angelic messages, and other forms of direct locution whereby God revealed His mind to His Old Testament messengers. It also indicates the occasional and fragmentary nature of the revelations themselves, at least when seen in the light of the final and definitive self-disclosure that God gave through His incarnate Son, Jesus Christ. But when the writer says that God *spoke* by His Son, what he has in mind is precisely verbal communication, just as when he says that God *spoke* through the prophets. His argument continues with the inference that, because of the Son's supreme dignity, we must pay all the greater attention to the message of the great salvation that He declared and that His first hearers, the apostles, relayed in their spoken testimony (Heb. 2:1–3). The author proceeds to make, or at least to buttress, every positive theological point in his whole exposition, up to the final chapter of the letter, by exposition and application of Old Testament passages—which he cites as what the Father or the Son or the Holy Spirit says to Christian believers (see 1:5–13; 5:5ff.; 8:3–12; 10:30, 37ff.; 12:26; 13:5 for the Father as speaker; 2:11–13; 10:5–9 for Christ as speaker; and 3:7–11; 9:8; 10:15–17 for the Holy Spirit as speaker).

We cannot here go into the fascinating question of the principles by which the writer of Hebrews interprets the meaning of these passages. Our present concern is simply with his conviction that the words of his Bible (our Old Testament), along with the words of Christ and the apostles, express both what God *said* on the public stage of the space-time continuum that we call world history and also what He *says now*, in personal application to all to whom the message comes and in a way that is decisive for their eternal destiny. This is the characteristic biblical conviction, found not only in Hebrews but wherever in Scripture the words of the Law, or the Prophets, or the apostles, or the Lord Jesus Christ are mentioned. It is this conviction that we must now examine.

As we have already seen, it is a conviction about *authority*, that is, about God's way of exerting His rightful claim to direct His rational human creatures into acknowledgment of His truth and obedience to His will. As such, it is a conviction both about the reality of communication from God to us, whereby He tells us what otherwise we could not have known, and about God's gracious plan to make us sinners His friends—which is the end to which the knowledge He gives us is meant to lead. Formally, the conviction is made up of these three strands: (1) God's word of direct self-disclosure to individuals in history—to Noah, Abraham, Moses, Jonah, Elijah, Jeremiah, Peter, Paul and others—were directly authoritative for their own belief and behavior. God having spoken to them, they were bound to believe what He had told them, knowing it to be true (because He is a God of truth), and bound also to do all that God had told them to do. (2) The same direct divine authority attached to all that God prompted His chosen spokesmen—prophets, wisdom writers, poets, apostles, and Jesus Christ Himself—to declare orally to others in His name. Their authority was not just that of deep human religious insight, deep though their religious insight was. Primarily and fundamentally, their authority was that of the God whose truth they were relaying in the verbal form to which He Himself had led them. Paul declares that "we [apostles] have . . . received . . . the Spirit who is from God, that we may understand what God has freely given us. This is what we speak . . . in words taught by the Spirit" (1 Cor. 2:12–13). Verbal inspiration, as here defined, conferred direct divine authority on the words that God's messengers spoke, authority that required their hearers to receive what they heard as from God Himself. (3) The same divine authority belongs to what they wrote, in the books that now constitute our canonical Scriptures.

As our God-inspired canon, the rule for faith and life, Holy Scripture may properly be called *law* (understanding that word in the sense of the Hebrew *torah*, which signifies the kind of authoritative instruction a father gives to his children). But this statement must not be taken to imply that all Scripture has the uniform linguistic quality of civil statutes or lawyers' textbooks, or that it all consists of simple factual assertions (propositions), with appended commands of a single logical type. The uses of language in the Bible are at least as varied as one would find in any sixty-six other books, and it is important to do justice to their complexity.

In ordinary communication, language appears to have five main functions at least. First, it may be *informative*, conveying factual data of one sort or another that the persons addressed are assumed not to know. Second, it may be *imperative*, communicating commands and calling for action. Third, it may be *illuminative*, using various devices to stir our imaginations into empathetic activity and so deepen our insight into, and understanding of, facts that at the conceptual level we know already. Thus poems about nature—sunny days, snow, rain, flowers, trees, and so on—are offered, not as versified meteorology or botany, but as transmitting the poet's vision of the significance of these familiar things. The analogies, metaphors, and parables with which we pepper our own prose are meant to be illuminative in a similar way. Fourth, language may be *performative*, actually bringing about states of affairs by announcing them to be the case. By saying, "I declare this road open," the mayor actually opens the new highway. By writing "His name is John" Zacharias actually settled what his son should be called (Luke 1:63). Fifth, language may be *celebratory*, focusing on a shared apprehension of things in a way that confirms that it is shared and so binds together more closely those who share it. Much ritual and ceremonial language, many speeches in many contexts, and all such utterances as "Isn't this lovely?" or "Look at that!" or even "Wow!" come in this category. Now, God's instruction given to sinful men as we find it set before us in Holy Scripture involves all five of these uses of language.

Informative language is basic, for every book of Scripture, in its own way, is didactic—making affirmations, implicit if not explicit, about God. This is true even of Esther, which celebrates God's providence, though the book does not mention His name, and also of the Song, which is a love duet celebrating in parable form the mutual devotion and affection of the Lord and His people. He who, in face of this, is still resolved to deny that revelation is informative—that is, to use the word that has been fashionable since the forties, "propositional"—ought logically, therefore, to deny outright that Holy Scripture is in any sense revelation. This view, being a departure from dominical and apostolic teaching, has no claim to be taken seriously. What believing Christians should hold, rather, is this: every assertion that the Bible, soundly exegeted, proves to be making, whether about matters of natural and historical fact within the created order or about the Creator's own plans and actions, should be received as information given and taught by God as part of the total presentation, interpretation, and celebration of redemption that Scripture essentially is.

Imperative language is equally basic. The Mosaic law, the wisdom literature, the moral teaching of the prophets, of Christ, and of the apostles, and abundant other particular narratives set forth God's commands: "You shall . . . you shall not . . ." (Exod. 20:3–17); "Do not . . ." (Matt. 5:34, 36, 39, 42; 6:3, 7ff., 16, 19, 25, 31, 34; 7:6, 35; et al.); "Go and do likewise" (Luke 10:37); "Watch" (Mark 13:33–37); and so on. This point needs no further illustration.

Illuminative language appears when such literary devices as analogy, allegory, imagery, or parable are used by God's spokesmen to help us grasp imaginatively and existentially, sometimes through traumatic self-judgment, the deep significance for them of events in their lives, and in particular how these events bear on their relationship with God. New facts are not here being communicated, but listeners are nudged into seeing old facts in a new light. Examples are Jotham's parable of the trees, spoken to the men of Shechem (Judg. 9:7ff.); Nathan's parable of the ewe lamb, directed to David (2 Sam. 12:1ff.); Ezekiel's allegories of the two eagles and the two sisters (Ezek. 17; 23); and Jesus' parables, whereby He sought to startle His popular-minded, prejudiced, uncommitted audience into grasping the revolutionary realities of His gospel of the kingdom. Jesus' parables "work" by vividly invoking everyday realities, sometimes with a built-in surprise (as in the stories of the laborers in the vineyard, of the great supper, and of the Pharisee and the publican) and sometimes not (as in the stories of the sower, the mustard seed, and the lost sheep). They always challenge the hearer to face with all seriousness God's ways in relation to him personally and to examine his own response to God in the matter of the kingdom. In other words (to use once more the language of an earlier generation), these parables have less to do with teaching doctrine than with applying doctrine already taught. They are an imaginative device for making folk see the personal bearing of what conceptually they knew before.

Performative language appears also, as when God, having told Abraham that He will make His covenant with him, proceeds to say, "This is my covenant with you" (Gen. 17:2–4). The use of these words causes the state of affairs spoken of to exist.

Celebratory language is found in the Psalms, Exodus 15, and similar passages, where known facts of God's work in His people's history are turned into themes of gratitude and praise.

Another important issue should be discussed before going on to the next section. When biblical inspiration is said to be *plenary* (as opposed to partial) and *verbal* (as opposed to the idea that God gives only inklings and insights, without determining in what words they should be expressed), this does not imply a Koranic view of inspiration, whereby translations of the original are precisely *not* the Holy Book. As Reformation theology used to say, it is the sense of Scripture that is Scripture, and all translations are in truth the Bible, at least to the extent that they are accurate. Nor does this view imply, as it is persistently thought to do, that because biblical words are God's words we may lawfully seek or find in Scripture meanings unrelated to what the human writers were conveying to those whom they were immediately addressing. The Bible is as fully human as it is divine, and the way to get into the present mind of God the Holy Spirit is by getting into the expressed mind of His human agents—the biblical authors, God's penmen—and by making appropriate application to ourselves of what they say. Allegorizing, and everything like it, is illegitimate. The point that *plenary* and *verbal* make is that the biblical words themselves (in Hebrew, Aramaic, or Greek) are to be seen as God-given. Men were not left to articulate information about, and interpretations of, God's ways with men apart from His superintending providence. On the contrary, the Lord who gave the Word also gave the words. It was not just the writers' thinking but "all Scripture," the written product, that is inspired by God (2 Tim. 3:16; cf. 2 Peter 1:21).

It is critically important, therefore, that, so far as possible, we make certain that we know what the God-given words are. Words, after all, are the vehicles and guardians of meaning; if we lose the words, we shall have lost the sense too. So the science of textual ("lower") criticism becomes a matter of key significance. When, for instance, the Basis of Faith of the British Inter-Varsity Fellowship (now the Universities' and Colleges' Christian Fellowship) ascribes inspiration and authority to Holy Scripture *as originally given*, the point of this phrase is not, as is sometimes thought, to give unrestricted license for suspecting textual corruption whenever an apparent discrepancy between passages arises. Its point is simply to make clear that mistranslations and demonstrable copyists' slips are not to be revered as God's truth but are rather to be detected and amended.

It has often been said, and rightly, that not one word in a thousand in the Greek text of the New Testament is open to serious doubt, and that there is no place at all in either Testament where uncertainty about the text raises a question of doctrinal substance. Also, it is often said, and surely rightly again, that no honest translation of the Bible has ever been so bad that God's life-giving message could not reach men through it. Nonetheless, human mistakes in translation and transmission can only obscure the divine word, and therefore we ought to try to weed them out, just as proofreaders ought to try to weed out all misprints, even if what is printed would be intelligible and generally reliable with the misprints there.

However, in thus stressing the importance of the particular words that the human authors, and through them God the Spirit, gave us, we must not forget that the semantic units (i.e., units of meaning) in the Bible, as in all other literature, include sentences, paragraphs, chapters, and ultimately whole books. It is always wrong to think of interpreting any document by combining all the possible meanings of each individual word as the dictionaries define it. It is doubly wrong when, in interpreting Scripture, we assume that each word that we think is theologically significant will always have the same acreage of meaning, and when we then define that meaning by reference to the way the word is used elsewhere in Scripture. The monumental mistake of Luther, in taking for granted that James meant by "justify," "works," and "faith" exactly what Paul meant by these words (and on this basis wishing to see James dropped from the canon because James 2:14–26 seemed to contradict Romans and Galatians) stands as a warning for all time against the danger of this false method. The ambiguous and easily misused dictum that the Bible should be read like any other book is true at least in this sense, that the ordinary rules of semantics must be recognized as applying to it, and any interpretative technique that violates them must be ruled out.[12] Docetic interpretations of Scripture (those that query the reality of its apparent humanness) are as objectionable as are docetic understandings—misunderstandings, rather—of the personal, human experiences of the incarnate Lord.

THE PROBLEM OF THEOLOGICAL LANGUAGE

We should now take notice that the position spelled out in the foregoing paragraphs—a position learned, as we believe, from the Bible itself—solves in principle two of the knottiest problems in current philosophy of religion; namely, how theological lan-

guage can have any definite meaning and how in particular it
can be a means of revelation, in the sense of communicating true
information about God.

During the past half-century, linguistic philosophers have frequently tried to show, on various logical grounds, that language
cannot possibly carry knowledge about God. Answers to them
have been given, with some success, in terms of the philosophers'
own assumption that our language is an evolutionary development, for which reference to physical sense-experience is, if
not exclusive, at least primary. Ian Ramsey has shown how,
by attaching well-chosen "qualifiers" to verbal "models"
("heavenly" to "Father," for instance), we can so "stretch" language as to direct men's minds to a transcendent object of reference and thereby, under God, precipitate a "disclosure" to them
of its reality.[13] John Macquarrie has analyzed theological language ("God-talk" as he calls it) as stemming from reflection on
existentially significant encounters with Holy Being.[14] Austin
Farrer has displayed biblical language as "working" in the manner of poetic imagery.[15] Eric Mascall, among others, has labored
to give new life to the classical doctrine on which Thomist
natural theology rests, namely, that God, being One whom we
resemble in some ways though not in others, can be known
metaphysically through the construction of analogies.[16] Basil
Mitchell, Ian Crombie, and others have exhibited biblical and
ecclesiastical phraseology as a combining and balancing of parables.[17] Frederick Ferré, having worked his way conscientiously
through various forms of skepticism and agnosticism concerning
the objective reference point of theological language, ends his
argument by affirming that if, as is claimed, the personal linguistic "models" of Christian theism unify and make sense of our
experience as a whole, that will decisively vindicate the claim
that they are both meaningful and true to reality.[18]

As *ad hominem* responses to the skeptics, starting from the
ground that skepticism occupies with regard to human language,
these expositions have merit. But their authors fail to query the
skeptical assumption that the systems of arbitrary signs, vocal
and visual, that we call language are "from below," i.e., are an
evolutionary development in which the signification of physical
entities is basic to everything else. This omission leaves their job
half-done, so that their apologia is only at half-strength.

Lack of both space and competence make it impossible to

explore here the many problems that arise concerning the origin and development of human language. But the main point is this: The opening chapters of Genesis—one *obiter dictum* (incidental comment) from which was quoted, we saw, by our Lord as the Creator's own word (Matt. 19:4ff., citing Gen. 2:24)—teach us that human beings were created in God's image (1:26ff.) and proceed on the basis that both a sense of God and a language in which to converse with Him were given to men as ingredients in, or perhaps preconditions of, the divine image from the start. By depicting God as the first language user (1:3, 6 et al.), Genesis shows us that human thought and speech have their counterparts and archetypes in Him. By telling us of Adam, Eve, and their descendants listening and responding to God, Genesis shows us that references to the Creator do not "stretch" ordinary language in an unnatural way; rather, such "stretching" is actually language's primary use. What is unnatural is the "shrinking" of language reflected in the supposition that it can talk easily and naturally only of physical objects. By making us aware that, from the start, God has used language to tell men things and so to teach them what to think about Him and how to talk to Him, Genesis both vindicates the language of theology and worship as meaningful and real and establishes God's own utterances as the standard of truth to which our theological notions must always conform.

Thus the biblical position that God's speaking and God's image in man imply a human capacity to grasp and respond to His verbal address shows up the arbitrariness, and indeed provincialism, of the post-Christian, positivistic theory of language on which the skepticism of linguistic philosophers rests. The final proof that human language can speak intelligibly of God is that God has actually spoken intelligibly about Himself in it. This intelligibility flows from the so-called anthropomorphism (manlikeness) of His account of Himself. But such anthropomorphism is primarily a witness to the essential theomorphism (Godlikeness) of man. The fact that God's self-disclosure is couched linguistically in the same personal terms in which we talk about ourselves and is therefore intelligible to us does not mean that God must have misrepresented Himself in what He has said. What it means, rather, is that in our personhood and in our capacity to give and receive verbal communication, we are less unlike God than perhaps we thought.

The conviction of latter-day Western philosophers is that the supposed difficulty of believing that human theological language can actually refer to God and express factual truth ("true truth," as Francis Schaeffer calls it) about Him springs from two sources. First, it is assumed that God (if real) must so differ from us that we can never be sure that any of our statements or concepts really fit Him. Second, He must be assumed to be silent, not helping us see what to say about Him by saying things to us about Himself. In these two convictions we meet the baleful legacy of Kant, as theologized in the liberal tradition from Schleiermacher on. It was Kant, with his lethal combination of a priori deism and a posteriori agnosticism (for this was the ultimate epistemological issue of his critical philosophy), who put abroad the ideas that no serious philosopher could believe in a God who speaks and that religion should be shaped by reflection "within the bounds of pure reason." While God might be a necessary postulate, He cannot strictly be *known* in any sense, by any means, at any time, any more than can be the *Ding-an-sich* (thing-in-itself) in the natural order. Kant hereby bequeathed to us the now chronic misunderstanding of God's transcendence and incomprehensibility as implying that, in His personal existence, He is both remote and unintelligible.

Some of the greatest of the moderns have been infected by this misunderstanding. "To Barth," wrote John Frame, "God's transcendence implies that he *cannot* be clearly revealed to men, clearly represented by human words and concepts." That is because Barth's thinking ran on good Kantian lines. But, notes Frame, "Scripture itself never deduces from God's transcendence the inadequacy and fallibility of all verbal revelation. Quite the contrary: in Scripture, verbal revelation is to be obeyed without question, *because* of the divine transcendence. . . . God's lordship, transcendence, demands unconditional belief in and obedience to the words of revelation; it *never* relativizes or softens the authority of these words." Is this an idolizing of human words, as Barth, blinkered by his Kantianism, would urge? No, says Frame, for the words of Scripture are no less the Word of God than they are the word of man, and divine authority is intrinsic to their message.[19] This is the proper correction of the Kantian mistake. Anglo-Saxon philosophers, no less than continental theologians, would do well to take note. Since God, though really transcendent, really says what Scripture says, and since man, being really theomorphic, as God's image bearer, really does apprehend what God in Scripture says, philosophical skepticism about the capacity of language to carry truth about the true God must be dismissed as an unhappy and indeed rather ludicrous mistake.

THE CONDESCENSION OF GOD

Paul calls the divine ordaining and encompassing of the cross of Jesus Christ the *foolishness* and *weakness* of God (1 Cor. 1:25). He is being ironical, of course, for he knows Christ to be God's wisdom and power (1 Cor. 1:25). He is insisting that the word of the cross only *appears* as folly to those who have not understood it. He is also making a positive theological point as well, namely, that the death of God's Son on Calvary shows how completely God, in love to mankind, was willing to hide His glory and become vulnerable to shame and dishonor. Now God in love calls men to embrace and boast of this foolish-seeming, weak-looking, disreputable event of the Cross as the means of their salvation. It is a challenge to sinful pride of both mind and heart.

Similarly (and this is our next point) God in love calls us to humble ourselves by bowing to Holy Scripture, which also has an appearance of foolishness and weakness when judged by some human standards, yet is truly His Word and the means of our knowing Him as Savior. God first humbled Himself for our salvation in the Incarnation and on the cross and now He humbles Himself for our knowledge of salvation by addressing us in and through the often humanly unimpressive words of the Bible. We are here confronted by that quality in God of which C. S. Lewis wrote: "The same divine humility which decreed that God should become a baby at a peasant woman's breast, and later an arrested field preacher in the hands of the Roman police, decreed also that he should be preached [and, we may add, written about] in a vulgar, prosaic and unliterary language."[20] For this quality in God whereby He lovingly identifies with what is beneath Him—the quality of which the Incarnation is the paradigm, though all His gracious dealings with men show it—the classical name is *condescension* (Greek, *synkatabasis*) and the etymological significance is "coming-down-to-be-with."

Calvin, who was perhaps overconscious of the literary limitations of some parts of the Bible, spoke emphatically of God's condescension in deigning, out of love, to talk to us in earthy and homespun language "with a contemptible meanness of words" (*sub contemptibili verborum humilitate*).[21] In this, as Calvin saw it, God's first aim is not so much to keep us humble, though that comes into it, as to help us understand. His simple mode of speech to us, in and through the words of the largely unsophisticated writers whom He used as His human penmen, is in itself a gesture of love. "God . . . condescends [*se demittit*] to our immaturity [*ruditatem*]. . . . When God prattles to us [*balbutit*] in Scripture in a clumsy, homely style [*crasse et plebeio stylo*], let us know that this is done on account of the love he bears us."[22] One sign of love to a child is adapting to the child's language when talking to him, and so, says Calvin, God in His love to us adapts to our childishness in spiritual things. Far from causing obscurity, therefore, God's "baby talk" (what Calvin calls his prattling) dispels it, making everything plainer to us than it could be otherwise.

Surely Calvin is right. The genuine human weaknesses and limitations that Scripture sometimes exhibits—from Paul's forgetfulness (1 Cor. 1:16) and coarseness (Gal. 5:12) to the bad Greek of Revelation and the wild, pain-wrenched rhetoric of Job—do in fact contribute to the communication that Scripture (i.e., God in and through Scripture) effects. That communication comprises not simply doctrinal truths but demonstrations of how divine grace works in the lives, not of paragons and plaster saints, but in those of all sorts of earthy, flesh-and-blood human beings. Just as God chose "undignified" mortals (even sinners like you and me!) to save, so He was ready to become "undignified" in both incarnation and inspiration in order to bring about our salvation. The condescension of God in becoming a baby Jew, in being executed on a Roman gibbet, and in proclaiming His goodness and His gospel to us via the down-to-earth, unliterary, often rustic words of the sixty-six canonical books, is one and the same and spells the same reality throughout—love to the uttermost.

But God's humility offends man's pride, and hence both incarnation and inspiration are rejected by some as incredible. It is instructive to note the parallel here. The pagan philosopher Celsus (ca. A.D. 150) led the van in ridiculing the Incarnation. How could God the Son, the supposedly infinite, eternal, and unchangeable Creator become man—let alone become a Jew!—and make Himself known within the limitations of human finitude? Surely the idea is absurd! Scripturally instructed Christians are content to reply that it *must* be possible, since God has actually done it. The incarnation is a wise and glorious mystery, despite its attendent weakness and shame, and from it comes salvation. At the end of the eighteenth century the deist philosopher Kant, as we have seen, turned away in comparable contempt from belief in inspiration, and thus pioneered a stance that has become typical of Western intellectual culture ever since. How could the infinite, transcendent, and incomprehensible Creator reveal Himself in the words of folk from the primitive Near East thousands of years ago? This, too, seems absurd! Again the Christian will reply, as in regard to the incarnation, that it *must* be possible, since God has done it. In fact He still reveals Himself by so applying to us what He said to others in the past that we come to know with certainty what He says to us in the present. This also is a wise and glorious mystery, and from it flows saving knowledge. In both cases, the correct reply to criticism is found in confession of God's salvation: how it was wrought in the first case, and how it is grasped and enjoyed in the second. In neither case, however, does the correct answer remove the offense that the criticism expresses.

God's condescension, we now see, is one aspect of His saving grace, whereby both in the Son's incarnation and in the Bible's inspiration He brought about a full union and identity of divine with human, our salvation being His goal. Such condescension gloriously displays His self-humbling, self-giving love. Any suggestion, therefore, that the unity of divine and human, whether in Jesus or in Scripture, is less than complete will reduce our apprehension of this love, and thus in reality dishonor it. When patristic writers urged that the Christ of the Gospels suffered impassibly (i.e., without feeling all the pain that we should have felt) or when they said that He suffered in His human nature apart from the divine (and wrought miracles in His divine nature apart from the human), they meant to honor Him by highlighting His deity. Actually, however, they took away His honor by questioning whether His condescension in becoming man was all that it seemed to be—whether, that is, Jesus was one fully divine-human person living a fully divine-human life throughout, or whether He was less than this. So, too, if it is urged that the parts of Scripture we think worthy of God are inspired and that the parts we think unworthy are not, the glory of His condescension (in so inspiring human witness to Him that it becomes His own witness to Himself) is at once blurred. Biblical passages that are mundane and raw in matter or manner or both are not any less inspired on that account, just as the baby talk of a genius like Einstein chatting to young children is not any less his speech because it is baby talk. What needs to be said here is that, just as all of Jesus' words, works, and experiences were words, works, and experiences of God the Son, so all the words of Scripture testifying to the God of grace—words of praise, prayer, narrative, celebration, teaching, and so on—are words of God testifying by these means to Himself. Only in light of this truth can the full glory of divine condescension, in inspiration as in incarnation, be grasped.

So now it appears that the confession of biblical *infallibility* and *inerrancy* (which words I treat as substantially synonymous) is important, not simply as undergirding Scripture's function as our divine authority for faith and practice, the whole teaching of which we receive as from the Lord, but also as showing the measure and extent of God's gracious condescension in bringing us to know Him savingly. For inerrancy and infallibility are entailed by inspiration; and inspiration, like incarnation, is a fruit of divine condescension. From this standpoint, biblical inerrancy is part of the doctrine of grace, and God's action in giving us a totally trustworthy Bible is a marvellous benefit. We may sense a certain lack of credibility in folk who question inerrancy while still claiming to be grateful for the Bible despite their uncertainty as to how much of it they can trust. Certainly, however, those who know they have received—as it were from their Savior's own hand—a Bible they can trust absolutely, as imparting to them the mind and knowledge and will of their God, will thank Him for this His second unspeakable gift with joy that knows no bounds.

THE ADEQUACY OF BIBLICAL LANGUAGE

It is asked whether biblical language is adequate to communicate knowledge about God. In the foregoing pages we have tried to spell out the principles that entitle us to affirm that it is. The key fact, as we saw, is the theomorphism of created man, whom God made a language user, able to receive God's linguistic communication and to respond in kind. But it is important, in saying this, not to appear to claim too much. If we ask what knowledge about God biblical language communicates, the answer is, not exhaustive knowledge of Himself and of all things in relation to Him—the knowledge that is distinctively His—but only knowledge of those matters that He sees to be adequate (i.e., sufficient) for our life of faith and obedience. "The secret things belong to the LORD our God, but the things revealed belong to us and to our children forever, that we may follow all the words of this law" (Deut. 29:29). This, in concrete terms, is the adequacy of biblical language: it suffices, not indeed to make us omniscient in any area, but as "a lamp to [our] feet and a light for [our] path" in discipleship (Ps. 119:105).

Those who doubt biblical inerrancy certainly claim too little with regard to the certainties that Bible readers may have, but it will not right the boat for those who affirm inerrancy to claim too much. All of us may need a warning here. What we know is that, as Jesus Christ is adequate to bring us to God, so Holy Scripture is adequate to bring us to Jesus Christ. Where acknowledgment of Scripture as adequate verbal communication from God is lacking, adequate acknowledgment of Jesus Christ is likely to be lacking too. If we can make plain to the church and to the world that our concern in contending for biblical inerrancy is in the first instance soteriological, obediential, doxological, and devotional—not rationalistic, but religious—we shall do well; if not, we shall do much less well. Failure here would be tragic! May it not be.

APPENDIX

NOTES ON SOME TECHNICAL QUESTIONS ABOUT BIBLICAL AND CHRISTIAN LANGUAGE

If the argument in this chapter was right, the apt model for understanding how God communicates with us is our own verbal communication with each other, by oral and written discourse, and we should approach the Bible in the light of the following principles:

1. God made us in His own image (i.e., among other things, reasoners and language users) so that He could address us through the medium of language, the means by which we address each other, and so draw us into a genuinely personal response to Himself, in which we in turn use language to address Him, the language of prayer and praise. The supreme demonstration of this is the preaching and teaching ministry of Jesus Christ, the Son of God incarnate.

2. Scripture, which in its character as human witness to God records many direct verbal communications from God to particular men, is through similar inspiration, equally and indeed primarily God's own witness to Himself. Imagine your boss handing to you, one of his employees, a policy memorandum written by some of his personal staff and assuring you as he does so that it exactly expresses his mind. This situation is parallel to that in which a Christian comes by God's providence to possess a Bible. The employee no doubt has some general idea of the boss's goals and strategy before he reads the memo, inasmuch as he belongs to the firm, but by studying the memo he comes to know the boss's mind with a precision not otherwise attainable. So it is with members of the Christian church as they study their Bibles.

3. The men who wrote the biblical books had in view a readership contemporary with themselves and wrote to be understood by that readership. So our task in biblical interpretation is twofold: first, to fix the historical meaning of each book (what it was saying to its first intended readers) and second, to apply to ourselves the truths about God and man that the original message embodies. We go to school with Abraham, Moses, David, Job, Jeremiah, Paul, the Israelites in the wilderness and before and after the exile, and the churches at Corinth, Colossae, Laodicea, and other places. We watch God dealing with these folk, overhearing what He said to them and seeing what He did to and for them. Hence, in the manner of observers in the classroom, we learn by inference His mind and will concerning us. Through the understanding God gives us of His ways with, and His will for, these biblical characters He draws near to call, correct, and challenge us today. Through the Spirit's agency, Jesus Christ, who is the same yesterday, today, and forever (Heb. 13:8), steps out of the Gospel stories to confront us with the same issues of faith, obedience, repentance, righteousness, and discipleship with which He confronted men when He was on earth. This is biblical interpretation: seeing first what the text *meant* and then what it *means*—that is, how what it says touches our lives.

4. While commentaries supply historical meanings, only the Holy Spirit can enable our sin-darkened minds to discern how biblical teaching applies to us. Prayerful dependence on the Spirit's help is therefore necessary if our attempts at interpreta-

tion are ever to succeed. Historical exegesis becomes interpretation only when the application is truly made.

5. Since all Scripture is God preaching in and through the preaching of His servants (for every biblical book is edificatory in intention and therefore homiletical in thrust), it is through being preached, and being heard and read as preaching, that it is most fully understood.

On the basis of these principles, more or less clearly focused and kept in view, the international, multiracial, multicultural community called the church, consisting of educated and uneducated, clever and less clever folk together, has sought to learn of God and hear His voice speaking in and through His Word. The solid testimony of the centuries is that precisely this has happened.

Against the background of these centuries of world-wide Christian experience one would not expect to find the assertion that it is impossible to talk significantly about God or to treat any biblical or ecclesiastical utterances that purport to refer to Him as fact-stating. This, however, as we have indicated, is exactly what certain teachers of philosophy in Western universities during the past half-century have claimed. They do not deny that such utterances may express and communicate the speaker's emotional or volitional attitudes (see, for instance, R. G. Braithwaite's analysis of religious assertions as expressing commitment to a behavior policy—in the case of Christian assertions, commitment to an agapeistic way of life).[23] What they deny is that these utterances can state public facts about God, that is, inform us of things concerning Him that are true irrespective of what any particular person thinks, feels, or intends.

What are their reasons for taking this position? The essential claim that all these teachers make in some form is that statements about God cannot fulfill the conditions of significant fact-stating speech. These conditions, it is urged, are (1) *specifiability*—you must be able to show that you are talking about something real and to show how that something is to be identified and distinguished from all other realities, and (2) *verifiability* or, at least, *falsifiability*—you must be able to show what would confirm the statement as true, or at least what would count against it. These conditions, it is urged, God-talk can never meet.[24]

Let us look at these two points in order.

1. It is argued that God is not *specifiable*; that is, when one speaks of Him there is no way of telling what one is talking about. There are two questions here: whether the word *God* connotes a specific being, distinguishable in thought from all other beings, and whether, if so, such a being exists, as distinct from being an insubstantial fantasy. The following responses suggest themselves.

First, the word *God* on Christian lips refers to the Creator-Redeemer whose actions and character are described in canonical Scripture.

Second, there are two sorts of realities that, at least *prima facie*, point to the real existence of a Creator-Redeemer corresponding to this description. For one thing, there are historical facts that seem inexplicable on any other hypothesis, notably the existence and character of the Christian church and the existence and contents of the Holy Scriptures. For another thing, there are the facts of religious experience, whereby countless human lives have been changed morally in such a way that facets of Christlikeness now appear in them that previously seemed out of their reach.

Two things may have given color to the idea that God is not specifiable. The first is the unwillingness of much Protestant theology in this century to treat biblical statements about God as revealed descriptions rather than high-minded guesses. The second is the observed defects of the classical Thomist doctrine of analogy, which was supposed to enable us to specify God in fundamental ways on the basis of natural theology alone, without appeal to the Bible (an intrinsically invalid method for fallen minds, some Protestants would think).

A word about these defects may be in order. Analogy was thought of as a kind and degree of likeness or correspondence of creature and Creator to each other. Two sorts of analogy were posited: the analogy of *attribution*, whereby formal qualities in man were held to correspond to qualities in God that ontologically were their creative cause, and the analogy of *proportionality*, whereby it was affirmed that God and man shared common qualities in a way appropriate to their distinct natures (as in the quality of existence: necessary and underived in God, contingent and derived in man). But neither of these modes of analogy, when pursued in the classical Thomist manner, on the basis of a cosmological "proof" of His reality alone (apart from reference to God's self-presentation in Scripture), yields determinate positive knowledge of what God is. The analogy of attribution requires us to ascribe to God all conceivable predicates, at least virtually, and thus proves to be saying only that God *somehow* causes everything that we are. The analogy of proportionality likewise fails to tell us how the characteristic predicated of both God and man is differentiated in the former from what it is in the latter. The classical doctrine of analogy does indeed seem to leave God unspecified and unspecifiable.[25]

There is, however, another use for the word *analogy* altogether, namely, as a description of the way in which the Bible—and Christian theological and liturgical speech, following the Bible—uses of God such predicates as "father," "loving," "wise," and "just," which are normally used of human beings who are finite. They are said to be used in reference to God not *univocally* (i.e., in exactly the same sense as that in which they are used of man) nor *equivocally* (i.e., in an entirely different sense) but *analogically*. *Analogically* here means "univocally up to a certain point." Only *some* of the implications of the normal use of these predicates, therefore, carry over.

To the question, How much of the original (human) meaning of each word remains when it is applied to God, Basil Mitchell replies by giving the following rule:

> A word should be presumed to carry with it as many of the original entailments as the new context allows, and this is determined by their compatibility with the other descriptions which there is reason to believe also apply to God. That God is incorporeal dictates that "father" does not mean "physical progenitor," but the word continues to bear the connotation of tender protective care. Similarly God's "wisdom" is qualified by the totality of other descriptions which are applicable to him; it does not, for example, have to be learned, since he is omniscient and eternal.[26]

This rule seems correct and valuable as a guide both for apprehending what God tells us of Himself through the biblical writers, and for learning to shape our own speech in a way that reproduces the substance of the biblical witness.

2. It is also argued, as noted above, that statements about God are neither *verifiable* nor *falsifiable*, and that this renders them vacuous. The fact that you do not know (so it is urged) what would tend to confirm or disprove such statements shows that they can have no determinate meaning, even to the one who

makes them. (There is a strong element of putting the Christian on the spot in all expositions of this point known to me, hence my *ad hominem* way of putting it here.) To this general thesis a five-point reply may be made:

(1) If, as is often the case in discussions of this point, very general statements about God (e.g., "God loves men") are considered in isolation, it can be made to look very hard to determine what they mean when a Christian asserts them. Because they are being considered out of context, their implications have to be laboriously beaten out as the discussion proceeds, and the impression is easily given that rigorous logical analysis hounds the Christians from pillar to post. At the start, therefore, it should be said that any assertions about God that Christians make are part of a coherent system of thought learned at each point from the testimony of the Bible (which is itself demonstrably coherent in its teaching), and the meaning of these assertions is finally fixed by the system as a whole.

(2) If it be said, in the manner of early logical positivism, that the meaning of an empirical statement (as distinct from an analytic statement, which is true by definition) is the method of its verification, or that it depends on knowing what would have to be done to verify the statement, the sufficient answer is that this verification principle, which is itself offered as an empirical statement, cannot itself be empirically verified. The positivist position self-destructs as being, by its own standards, meaningless.[27]

(3) A great deal that Christians, echoing Scripture, affirm about God has to do with future experiences of weal or woe, stretching ultimately beyond this life, which He will bring about. In the nature of the case such assertions (which at this point are like our own promises) can be verified only by future events fulfilling them. But the conceivability of this eschatological verification shows that they are entirely meaningful, in the strictest verificationist terms.

(4) If it be said, as later logical empiricists allow, that the question of meaning depends on what the statement in question is held to presuppose and to imply and that the question of its truth, once its meaning is determined, is a matter of evidence, then it will not be hard to say either what the various assertions of which Christian belief is made up mean or what states of affairs would in principle tend to verify or falsify them. If, for

instance, there were reason to think that Jesus never existed or, if He did, that He never rose from the dead, this would effectively falsify the Christian claim. But in fact there is no reason to think this and every reason to think the opposite.

(5) If it be allowed, as it should be, that verification can take the form of trustworthy assurance as well as of actual or possible experiences or observations, then it may properly be said that the testimony of our truth-telling God in Holy Scripture is itself the most cogent verification of what we believe.

The burden of these all-too-brief notes is to show that the logical grounds sometimes alleged for discounting Christian and biblical language about God as not being fact-stating are not cogent. The details of the philosophical doctrines that underlie this skepticism have not been exposed at all. Suffice it to have shown that, so far as criticism of Christian discourse is concerned, the skeptics have not established their points.

THE HUMAN AUTHORSHIP OF INSPIRED SCRIPTURE

Gordon R. Lewis

Gordon R. Lewis is Professor of Systematic Theology, Conservative Baptist Theological Seminary, Denver, Colorado. He is a graduate of Gordon College (A.B.), Faith Theological Seminary (M.Div.), and Syracuse University (M.A. and Ph.D.). He has served as pastor of People's Baptist Church, Hamilton Park, Delaware; Professor of Apologetics and Philosophy, Baptist Bible Seminary; and Visiting Professor of Theology, Union Biblical Seminary, Yeotmal, India. Dr. Lewis' books include Confronting the Cults; Decide for Yourself: A Theological Workbook; What Everyone Should Know About Transcendental Meditation; Judge for Yourself: A Workbook on Contemporary Challenges to Christian Faith; *and* Testing Christianity's Truth-Claims: Approaches to Apologetics. *Dr. Lewis is a member of the Evangelical Theological Society, the Advisory Board of ICBI, the American Philosophical Association, the American Academy of Religion, and the Evangelical Philosophical Society, which he has served as president.*

CHAPTER SUMMARY

Attention to the humanness of the Bible's writers has led some to deny its inerrancy, alleging that Scripture is time-bound and merely of functional value. In contrast, this study proposes that the Bible's teaching is truly divine and truly human without error, just as Jesus Christ was truly divine and truly human without sin. The inerrancy of finite, fallen human authors must be understood in the context of orthodox doctrines of God, creation, providence, and miracles. The human writers were not autonomous, but lived and moved and had their being in the all-wise Lord of all. Created with a capacity for self-transcendence in the image of God, they could receive changeless truths by revelation. Providentially prepared by God in their unique personalities, they also had characteristics common to all other human beings in all times and cultures. Their teaching originated, however, not with their own wills, but God's and came to them through a variety of means. In all the human writing processes, they were supernaturally overshadowed by the Holy Spirit, not in a way analogous to mechanical or unworthy human relationships, but as one loving person effectually influences another. What stands written, therefore, in human language is not merely human but also divine. What the human sentences teach, God teaches. The Bible's affirmations conform to the mind of God and to the reality God created. Although time-related, they are not time-bound. They are objectively true for all people of all times and cultures, whether received or not. The reason the Bible can function effectively to bring people to Christ is that its teachings are inerrant.

THE HUMAN AUTHORSHIP
OF INSPIRED SCRIPTURE

T HIS CHAPTER ADDRESSES itself to the humanness of writers of Scripture, an aspect often neglected or minimized in evangelical works.

The first section surveys the contributions of influential recent theologians who have found the humanness of the writers inconsistent with inerrancy.

Having acknowledged the force of their arguments for the relativism of biblical teaching, I will, in the second section of this paper, seek to outline directions in which one may go in accounting for the humanness of the biblical authors and at the same time affirming the inerrancy of their teaching. Because of the complexity of the subject, this chapter must be considered merely a preliminary draft of a major book or books needed on this issue, with all of its ramifications.

Many fine scholars in recent times suggest that defenders of an orthodox view of inspiration have failed to do justice to the Bible's humanity. In *Biblical Authority,* after a survey of liberal, new reformation, and conservative evangelical perspectives, Clark Pinnock concludes, "The prime theological issue which became evident in our survey of options on biblical authority is the need to maintain with equal force both the humanity and divinity of the word of Scripture."[1]

Conservative evangelicals, Pinnock indicates, have bordered

on the docetic heresy. "Although Protestant orthodoxy confesses both the divine and the human element in the Bible, as it also does in Christology, it has been happier affirming its divine authority than admitting its human characteristics." The position will remain unbalanced, Pinnock insists, "until full justice is done to the human traits as well."[2] One has to agree, after considerable research, that not as much attention has been devoted to the human as to the divine side of Scripture by conservative scholars. This may be explained because of the need to defend its divine side and because of the complexities that consideration of the humanity involves. Nevertheless, neglect of the human aspect in comparison with the divine can hardly be denied.

At the same time we miss, in Pinnock's recent plea, a crucial distinction he made in 1971 (in his *Biblical Revelation*) between the human and the sinful, or erroneous. He spoke strongly against "the puerile maxim: 'To err is human—Scripture is human—therefore Scripture errs.' For error is no more required of the Bible's humanity than sin is of Christ's." Pinnock then proposed a better maxim: "To err is human—ergo, God gave the Scripture by inspiration—so that it does not err."[3]

Clearly sin is not part of the human essence as created, as shared by Jesus Christ, or as it will be in its glorified state. There can be no a priori verdict, therefore, that because human writers contributed to the Scriptures, it is errant. We must examine both hypotheses to see which best accounts for the data. First we will survey the views of those who support the hypothesis that the humanness of the Bible makes inerrancy untenable and subsequently the hypothesis that the true humanity of the biblical writers is consistent with inerrancy.

The Author's Humanness as Inconsistent With Inerrancy

For many years now Karl Barth, Emil Brunner, Reinhold Niebuhr, Richard Niebuhr, and Paul Tillich have stimulated a chorus of writers who insist that the Bible was written by frail, fallible human beings whose errant witness nevertheless occasions encounters with God or union with the "ground of being." Although a review of the arguments of these men would be helpful, space limits us to more recent publications. To help see and feel the problem, we will look briefly at the Reformed writer Harry Boer and three Roman Catholics: Charles Davis, Leslie

Dewart, and Hans Kung. Because of its extensive treatment of the human side of the Bible, G. C. Berkouwer's *Holy Scripture* is given more thorough consideration.

Harry Boer

A passionate call to devote more attention to the human side of Scripture has come from Harry Boer's *Above the Battle? The Bible and Its Critics*. The Reformed missionary teacher asks, "Does the Word of God written sustain the same relationship to other literature as the personal Word made flesh sustains to our humanity?" Again, "Has the Word of God entrusted to prophets and apostles become human literature in the same sense in which the eternal Logos became a human being?" Boer replies, "The answer to these questions, at least from the Reformed segment of the church, has been a definite Yes."[4] He adds that the Bible "is a collection of writings which *as literary entities* have been produced by men in the same way in which any other book has been written."[5] There can be little question as to what is meant when he says, "I wish now to emphasize that the books of the Bible as a collection of religious writings are as human as *Pilgrim's Progress, Paradise Lost,* or Spurgeon's *Sermons.*"[6] He concludes that, whatever divine inspiration may mean, the Bible "lies before us in the form of a thoroughly human product."[7]

An illicit analogy appears, however, in Boer's parallel between the humanity of the Bible and the humanity of Christ. Although Christ was fully human, Boer does not affirm that He was sinful. Nevertheless, Boer berates those who hold a docetic view of the Bible and he stresses its humanity, attempting to support his case for its alleged errors of logic and fact.[8] If true humanness on the part of the scriptural authors implies errancy, then, to have a valid analogy to Christ, he must also argue that true humanness implies Christ's sinfulness. The more characteristic Reformed analogy is between the humanness of Christ without sin to the humanness of the Bible without error.

Charles Davis

According to Charles Davis, the humanness of any writer implies the relativity of his writing. Truth can exist only in changing human minds and, although some degree of objectivity can be attained, it is "always related to the knowing subject, so that all human truth is involved in the developing human intelligence." Hence all concepts share "in the imperfections, progress, and frequent tentativeness of all human thinking."[9]

Obviously drawing on Reinhold Niebuhr, Davis emphasizes the human capacity for self-transcendence. People move from one standpoint to the next, from one historical perspective to another and so never arrive at the truth. At best they only attain *their* truth. Illustrating his point, Davis writes:

> As a knowing subject man is like a person who cannot obtain a complete aerial view of a region, but has to move from hill to hill gradually to build up his mental picture of the lie of the land, except that with the knowledge in general the hills to be climbed are without number.[10]

The doctrinal content of the Christian faith, including the Roman Catholic traditions and papal bulls, are given in historical process and from particular standpoints. None of these can be regarded as absolutes and, therefore, as "unalterable concepts and immutable propositions existing outside history" or as giving a "God's-eye view."[11]

Relentlessly, Davis pursues the implications of the relativity of human thought. "It is impossible therefore, to isolate an absolute, unchanging core of Christian belief. To try to do so is an illusory project, because it is in effect an attempt to remove Christian belief from history."[12] Not even the gospel is exempt from relativism.

> Granted that a central message can be distinguished from secondary elements, the formulation of that message is always culturally conditioned and from a particular standpoint. Each age will ask new questions about its meaning and seek to formulate it afresh. There is no pure essence of Christian belief, abstracted from historically conditioned teaching.[13]

How does Davis view the actual statements of Scripture?

> What is true of Christian traditions generally is true of the Bible. The Bible is a unique and indispensable witness to God's revelation, which culminated in Christ. It is not, however, free from the limitations of its cultural context, or rather contexts, nor is it entirely without error. The limitations and errors do not destroy the unity and continuity of its teaching nor the fact that it embodies the absolute truth of God's Word. At the same time, it is a human and historical document, subject as such to inevitable imperfections and limitations. While it will remain the perennial centre of the Christian tradition and never be rendered obsolete,

both in itself and in its interpretation, it must be regarded as existing within the historical process. It cannot be isolated from history as an unhistorical absolute.[14]

Notice what is at stake in Davis's view. The humanness of Scripture necessitates the historical relativism of all its teaching. Consequently, Davis has no changeless kerygma, or gospel message. The Bible is not revelation; the Bible is a fallible human witness to revelation.

Leslie Dewart

For Leslie Dewart, the relativism of all human knowledge involves a revision of thinking about the nature of truth. Truth cannot be considered the conformity of an assertion to reality. He finds the assumption that one can know anything about reality to be contrary to logic and observation. To know anything in itself, as it really is, assumes that "we can conceive and understand knowledge from the outside, as if we could witness from a third 'higher' point of view the union of two lower things, object and subject."[15]

Given Dewart's antisupernatural assumption at this point, there *is,* of course, no higher point of view. A partial degree of self-transcendence will not achieve an eternal perspective. However, on supernaturalist views of special revelation and inspiration the human writers do receive an outside view, which includes both the knower and the object known. The Scriptures originate with God.

The concepts in which Christian beliefs are cast, Dewart thinks, are "true," not in virtue of their representative adequacy, but in virtue of their efficacious adequacy as generative forms of the truth of religious experiences.[16] A concept is true, he explains, "if it causes . . . a true human experience. Adequacy is viewed, not as conformity, but adjustment, usefulness, expediency, proficiency, sufficiency, and adaptation for the 'believer.' "[17]

The debatable assumption here is that you can have efficacious adequacy without having truths about reality as it is. Yet how can it be that the Spirit's work of inspiration is no longer efficacious to help the biblical writers tell it like it is, yet one's interpretation of his experience becomes efficacious?

Dewart has another argument against the inerrancy of the gospel:

This might be put more graphically in an epigram: we can search for the essence of Christianity behind its cultural manifestations only as long as we assume either that we can become conscious of God's self-revelation without God's use of any language (modernism), or else that God's mother tongues are Hebrew and Greek.[18]

I make a few brief comments in response at this point. We need not look for the essential truth of Christianity behind the Scripture, for it is conveyed in its teaching. God, who could have given His revelation in any language and any culture, freely chose to present it in Hebrew and Greek with their respective cultures. These languages are not God's "mother tongues," as if God were in any sense limited to them. But He created man in His image with linguistic ability to think His thoughts after Him.

Hans Kung

Another recent Catholic writer who has stressed the relativity of the human factor in Scripture shows that this relativity requires a new concept of faith and revelation. Hans Kung's massive work, *On Being a Christian*, asserts that the Bible

> is unequivocally man's word: collected, written down, given varied emphasis, sentence by sentence by quite definite individuals and developed in different ways. Hence it is not without shortcomings and mistakes, concealment and confusion, limitations and errors.[19]

Through their errors the biblical writers "are witnesses of faith and speak of the real ground and content of faith." He claims their witness is "frequently in halting speech and with utterly inadequate terminology."[20] He says flatly that the Scriptures are not divine revelation.[21] Furthermore, they do not present historical or scientific truth. The biblical meaning of truth, Kung thinks, designates

> the fidelity, constancy, trustworthiness of God himself who stands by his word and promises. There is not a single text in Scripture asserting its freedom from error. But every text in its wider or narrower context attests this unswerving fidelity of God to man, preventing God from ever becoming a liar.[22]

Kung does not limit his view to the results of inspiration but also speaks of its nonmiraculous mode. He rejects the notion of a supernatural work of the Spirit limited to a particular act of writing, preferring to speak of the writers, as of other New Testament believers, as Spirit-pervaded and Spirit-filled in their whole prehistory. I may observe that there is no need to make a choice between providential preparation and supernatural inspiration at the time of writing. Both have been maintained.

The Bible is inspired, Kung believes, basically because it is inspiring. Acknowledging his indebtedness to Karl Barth, Kung holds that man's word in the Bible becomes God's word for anyone who submits trustfully and in faith to its testimony and so to the God revealed in it and to Jesus Christ.[23] How can one submit trustfully to erroneous testimony? In spite of all the critical problems, "in all the words he grasps the Word, in the different gospels the one Gospel." A reader of Scripture must allow himself to be inspired by the Spirit and "the question whether and how the Bible itself is inspired word is far less important— even for the text of 2 Timothy mentioned above (3:16–17)—than the question of how man himself allows himself to be inspired by its word."[24] So the important thing is man's allowing the Spirit to work, not the inspiration of the original writers of the Bible.

To sum up, Boer, Davis, Dewart, and Kung have pointed out some of the implications of recognizing the humanity of biblical writers. All reject biblical inerrancy. Boer thinks the critical problems are insuperable. Davis eliminates any core of doctrines or kerygma from the essence of Christianity. Dewart is left with no way of knowing reality as it is, whether it is the reality of God or of the world; therefore truth is not tested by conformity with reality but by its functional values to oneself. Kung denies that the Bible is divine revelation and considers it to be simply a fallible human witness to something totally other than any human concept can designate.

Boer tries to maintain an infallibility without inerrancy, but it is difficult to distinguish this infallibility from mere functional value, as in the other views. Davis, Dewart, and Kung maintain that, once you accept the relativism of all human concepts and words, there is no exception for biblical assertions regarding Christ or salvation in the gospel.

G. C. Berkouwer

Unquestionably, one of the most thorough treatments of the humanity of Scripture comes from the pen of G. C. Berkouwer. His major volume entitled *Holy Scripture* presents a vigorous call to attend more perceptively to the Bible's humanity, with all that that implies.

Early in his book Berkouwer notes that "the church's tendency to minimize the human aspect of Scripture must be clearly recognized."[25] The human character of Scripture "is not an accidental or peripheral condition of the Word of God but something that legitimately deserves our full attention."[26] Although the church's confessions had never denied this human element, it was the rise of historical criticism that focused attention on it. Fundamentalism, in its defensiveness, "does not fully realize the significance of Holy Scripture as a prophetic-apostolic, and consequently human testimony."[27] At stake is nothing other than God's way with and in Scripture. However, "fundamentalism has hardly come to grips with the problem of whether attention for the human character of Holy Scripture might be of great importance for its correct understanding."[28] By an a priori acceptance of Scriptural inerrancy, fundamentalists preclude all dangers and ignore its human aspects.[29] No a priori theory, Berkouwer insists, can be the basis of certainty.[30]

Even though Berkouwer rejects the analogy between Christ and the Scriptures at some other points, he sees a similarity to docetism in Christology in the minimizing of the human aspect of Scripture in order to emphasize fully its divine character. The mere recognition of a human element is no guarantee, he observes, that justice is done to it.[31]

No affirmation of *propositional revelation* appears in Berkouwer's treatment of Scripture. Instead, he warns of an artificial view of revelation that is threatened by a study of the human side of Scripture.[32] "God's revelation must not be seen as a timeless and supra-historical event, but as a manifestation in history."[33] In view of the human, historical, and critical factors, Berkouwer cannot accept the interpretations of the creeds which affirm that

> Holy Scripture is the Word of God in such a manner that Scripture's divinity was thought to be found in its inner substantial form and had become an essential predicate of Holy Scripture as an inspired book that was elevated to the level of a source of supernatural truths.[34]

For Berkouwer the teachings of Scripture are not the supernaturally revealed Word of God nor the object of the Spirit's inspiration. Such "rationalization" introduces illegitimate foreign elements to the mystery of the Spirit.[35] To affirm that the

Bible teaches specially revealed truths obscures its relation to the testimony of the Spirit and gives the concept of revelation more and more formal traits. He is against such externalization, literalism, and abstracting from the testimony, which, he maintains, make revelation come in mere word and letters.[36] Scripture is part of a complex organic process of revelation[37] and he refuses to speculate on the mode of revelation,[38] though surely there was no special language of revelation.[39]

How then does Berkouwer understand inspiration? It is a factor in the organic process, not a supernatural or miraculous phenomenon.[40] In the words of men, active and not passive men, God breathes to accomplish an instrumental purpose, a witness to Christ. "Scripture is the Word of God because the Holy Spirit witnesses in it of Christ."[41] This witness must never be allowed to fade into a formal concept of inspiration, but this does not mean that it is not related to the words. Warnings are frequent that we must not approach the subject of inspiration with arguments concerning form and cause.[42] Students of Scripture must avoid a problems approach and must simply accept the mystery of the Spirit's witness.[43]

The doctrine of inspiration in Berkouwer tends to become primarily a doctrine of illumination. Although he says that 2 Timothy 3:16–17 points to the mystery of the words of man being filled with truth and trustworthiness and to an essential relationship between the breath of the Spirit and the *graphē*, "nevertheless, one hears in this passage that the written Scripture cannot be understood in a correct way without the breath of the Spirit."[44] As related to salvation, Paul's God-breathed words have a primarily functional character.[45] Throughout Scripture, man comes to the fore so that there is a very close connection between God's speaking and the human words.[46] But no one can ignore God's speaking via the humanness of the prophetic words. "One might speak here of 'identification' not as a mixture of the divine and the human, but in the sense of this 'sending,' this employing whereby the Word of God indeed comes to us just as it is upon the tongue of the prophets."[47]

What the Bible teaches is *time-bound* and *relative*. As time-bound, it reflects the localities and situations of the periods in which it was written. The Bible comes to us not only through changing circumstances but also in ideas and concepts determined by the time of writing.[48] "One must take note of the

cultural context and intent of the words within that period precisely *in order* to hear the Word of God."[49] This relativism, Berkouwer claims, does not lead to historicization. It does not adopt
the conclusion of the absolute relativity of all that is historical,
because that is "a conclusion which would exclude the mystery
of the God-breathed Scripture."[50] One wonders why arriving at
the same conclusion a posteriori would not face the same criticism. Berkouwer does not seek to distinguish within Scripture
between the word of God and the word of men; it is all the word
of men.

Ambiguously, Berkouwer says Scripture is time-related and
has universal *authority*.[51] I say ambiguously because the writings
are time-related, yet it is the Spirit's witness, and not the writings, that has universal authority. Commenting on Paul's statement concerning ministers, "we have this treasure in earthen
vessels," Berkouwer explains: "The earthen vessel does not
stand in the way of God's voice precisely because the power of
God is manifested in it and not because man in his own power
has this treasure at his disposal."[52] Alleging that his view represents that of the Reformers, Berkouwer says that they emphasized that the message of salvation really came through the
Scriptures. This implied an accessibility that was not in terms of
a theoretical construction.[53] One of Berkouwer's favorite passages (2 Tim. 2:9) assures him that, although the writings of the
Bible are time-bound, the Word of God is not bound. So "there
is every reason to remember the power of God's Word for all
times, and the blessing of the Word that is not fettered."[54] Berkouwer believes that he exalts the sovereignty of God by having
Him reveal Himself through statements by men who were simply
children of their limited times.

Although Berkouwer dismisses the concept of *inerrancy*, he
claims to retain belief in the Bible's *infallibility*. He rejects inerrancy because he thinks it does not recognize the time-bound
localities, the special circumstances, and the limited conceptions
of the writers.[55] Furthermore, he thinks the view involves a serious
formalization of the concept of error. Incorrectness is put on the
same level as sin and deception. Berkouwer is apparently unaware
that there are more than two ways to look at the Bible—his
approach, which develops a view of reliability in agreement with
the Bible's purpose (singular), and an a priori presuppositionalism, which imposes a technical concept of reliability on

Scripture. He ignores at least five of the six different epistemological routes used in defense of the Bible's inerrancy that I have
expounded elsewhere.[56] By the Bible's infallibility Berkouwer
means that the Spirit has not failed and will not fail in this mystery
of God-breathed Scripture and that in our interaction with Scripture by faith we will not be put to shame but be confirmed.[57]

Reinhold Niebuhr built an impregnable wall of relativism, so
that no one could ever know *the* truth but only *one's own* truth. He
made an exception, however, for one thought beyond all
thought—a Christian dialectic, or paradox of grace. But he did
such an effective job of showing that no finite, fallen person could
have final truth, that it is difficult to take him seriously when he
claims finality for Christianity. Similarly, Paul Tillich affirmed
the relativism of every theological statement except the assertion
that God is being itself. It is difficult to maintain such an absolute (!) relativism.

Like both Niebuhr and Tillich, Berkouwer makes an *exception*
to his consignment of every human affirmation to time-bound
relativity. In his consideration of Christ's resurrection, he finds
the differences of wording totally different from falsification,
which projects a wrong and misleading image.[58] Although the
biblical writers had "freedom in composing and expressing the
mystery of Christ,"[59] clearly their aim was not to mislead and
to deceive or to relate history in a manner "eternalizing or
abstract."[60] Here the apostle's language informs us that the
reality of salvation does not take flight from reality. Why must
we assent mentally to these assertions of fact? Because "everything is at stake," just as all preaching and faith are in vain if
Christ has not been raised (1 Cor. 15:14, 17). The testimony of
preaching would be false, since it would not be backed by the
truth (1 Cor. 15:15). Berkouwer here affirms cognitive truth
about historical reality when he says, "The idea is sharply condemned throughout the New Testament that the message of
salvation could be a creation or a projection of men, a fabrication
of the human spirit."[61] These assertions convey reliable statements of fact concerning what happened in reality. Here biblical
language is not merely functional but informative; faith involves
knowledge, with assent to the resurrection. "The limit of all
subjectivity and all variety in the portrayal of the mystery of
Christ is the reliability of that which is passed on, which was
seen, heard, and understood."[62]

Christ's resurrection is no Bultmannian myth. "The difference between eternity and time does not mean that a saving event can no longer be discussed in terms of an act of God *in time*."[63] Quoting Barth against Bultmann, Berkouwer writes, "The conviction stands, so Barth concludes: 'We must still accept the resurrection of Jesus, and His subsequent appearances to His disciples, as genuine history in its own particular time.' "[64] Furthermore, "Thielicke said that the ancient world view 'left open the door for the idea of transcendence.' Therefore it is precisely fitting 'to express the otherness of God and His intervention in salvation history.' "[65] Apparently, then, the difference between eternity and time is not so great that we cannot affirm truth in time-bound human language concerning God's action in time and in both objective and sacred history, even beyond the first century. In affirming Christ's resurrection, the Bible asserts a truth about history that is good for all time, and is in fact God's Word written. It does more than point to Christ in these passages, and its statements are not regarded as neutral or abstract.

In spite of his many qualifications, for Berkouwer the assertions about the Resurrection are no mere projection. It did occur in reality, and apparently his statements to this effect are not meant to be abstract or merely formal. Since the fully-human witnesses inspired by the Spirit are not allowed to fabricate matters at this point, there is no theological reason why the Spirit could not have kept them from error on anything of which they wrote. If in the central matters of the faith the truth attested is not merely relative to the knower and his times but true (inerrant) for all people in all times, there is no a priori reason why, on matters less directly related to salvation, what they affirm may not represent the way it is in reality, in itself.

Since Berkouwer's view is given extensive evaluation in chapter 14, I will forego further criticism here. It will suffice to note that his view is both inadequate and unorthodox in terms of the view developed below.

The Author's Humanness as Consistent With Inerrancy

In view of the multiple questions raised by those who hold that the humanness of Scripture implies its conceptual relativism, the presentation of an alternative position ought not be oversimplified. Richard J. Coleman, in a remarkably objective analysis of the issues between those he calls liberals and those he calls evangelicals, presents a significant challenge to both. To the defenders of inerrancy he writes:

> It is not enough for the evangelical to raise the importance of the conceptual side of revelation and faith; he must demonstrate ability to weld together objective doctrines about God and the contemporary experience of contingency and autonomy, faith in the Scriptural Word, and confidence in man's rational power to understand God.[66]

The second aspect of Coleman's challenge must also remain in our minds as we seek to expound a view of conceptual truth as essential to Christianity, revelation, inspiration, and witness of the Spirit and faith.

> In the future evangelicals must also give more attention to the inescapable question of relativity. The books and articles which have dealt with the subject from an evangelical viewpoint have been of little value. There is the understandable fear that to tackle this problem is to open Pandora's box, but nevertheless each year the crack becomes a little bigger. Recognition must be given to the hidden motivation to defend one's position by appealing to absolutes in a time of rapid change and loss of authority. The evangelical has been able to maintain an authoritative concept of revelation and Scripture only by being insensitive to the issue of historical relativity.[67]

Coleman's challenge to evangelicals calls for a work too extensive for this present scope, but I will try to outline at least some lines of approach.

The Human Authors Were Not Autonomous, but Under God

The writers of Scripture did not function in a vacuum. They lived and moved and had their being in God, as all people do (Acts 17:28). Many of them expressed their sense of God's presence, God's call, God's holiness, God's protection, and God's compelling them to speak and write His Word. They sensed their dependence on God and their obligation to know, love, and serve Him. It is important to focus more fully on some of the aspects of their God-consciousness.

The God of the biblical authors, although actively involved with them, was self-existent, eternal, and unchanging. The writers were dependent; God was independent. God existed before the mountains were born or people lived on earth (Ps. 90:1–2). He had life in Himself and was far from the abstract, static Being of the Greek philosophers (John 5:26). He was a living Spirit who actively created and sustained the world and who entered into gracious covenant relationships with particular people. His being could be known in part. It was not that men could reason their way to God but that He disclosed Himself to them as the Almighty and the I AM. His being was logically prior to His actions, His character to His functions. Words and actions disclosed not only the hearts of men but also the heart of God (Matt. 12:33–35).

As the disparate elements of the biblical authors' teaching about God are examined, it becomes clear that within the one eternal being are the three personal distinctions—Father, Son, and Spirit.[68] The Sabellians sought to reduce these distinctions to mere relational distinctions of the one God at different times and places. But the attempt to dismiss the ontological realities of persons who could intercede with each other in holy love failed. Those who would dismiss all ontological knowledge of God as He is in Himself surely know that they are thereby dismissing not just the "fundamentalist" view of revelation and inspiration but the orthodox view of trinitarianism. In another place I have argued that views of revelation as act or analysis or revelatory encounters, and even fallible propositional content, cannot support the biblical authors' progressively revealed teaching about God.[69] With the departure of conceptual revelation and inerrancy go many other classic truths of Christianity.

The God in whom the biblical authors lived and moved and had their being was a God whose "commands are true" (Ps. 119:151). This truth was not like the abstract forms in Plato's world of ideas. The Logos of all things was with God and indeed was God (John 1:1–3). The designs of things were in the mind of the intelligent and powerful Creator. In His omniscience He knows all that ever has been, is, or will be, and He knows what is for His glory and the good of mankind. There can be no question as to whether His ideas conform to reality as it is and ought to be (John 14:6).

The biblical writers knew that God's unlimited knowledge transcended their limited knowledge, "as the heavens are higher than the earth" (Isa. 55:8–9). This does not mean that God's knowledge was totally incommunicable to their minds in meaningful concepts. When Isaiah wrote that God's ways are not our ways, he countered the expectations of the wicked, as the context and parallel passages show: "Let the wicked forsake his way and the evil man his thoughts" (Isa. 55:7; cf. Pss. 36:5; 89:2; 103:11; Ezek. 18:29). According to Gustave Oehler's *Theology of the Old Testament*, the prophets "knew that the Spirit by which they were inspired was not the natural spirit of their nation; that their predictions were not the expression of popular expectations."[70]

In its context, then, the statement "my thoughts are not your thoughts" does not support the anticonceptualism of Barth, Berkouwer, and others. On the contrary, the emphasis of the passage is on the problem of the will following the everlasting covenant made with David (Isa. 55:3), which was made in meaningful assertions through a human language at a particular time and a particular place. As the history of the covenant people tragically reveals, knowledge of conceptual truth does not compel assent to it as Berkouwer imagines, and as Berkouwer himself exemplifies. The conceptual inerrancy of the covenants, promises, and judgments is not a sufficient condition for them. Important as it is, it needs the assurance of infallibility, the assurance that the word going forth from God's mouth "will not return to me empty, but will accomplish what I desire, and achieve the purpose for which I sent it" (Isa. 55:10–11). No rejection of inerrant content is necessary in order to have the values of infallibility of purpose. Each needs the other.

When the biblical writers affirmed that God was true and faithful, they referred not only to the reliability of His instruction, but also to the fidelity of His character. They exclaimed, "Great is your faithfulness" (Lam. 3:23). God's integrity means that He cannot be tempted by evil nor tempt anyone else to it (James 1:13). He is not a man that He should lie (Num. 23:19). He cannot deny Himself (Titus 1:2). It is immutably true that God cannot lie (Heb. 6:17–18). These are several things that even holy omnipotence itself cannot do.

Because God is true and faithful, it was unthinkable to the biblical authors that He could breathe out (inspire) any error through them. They rejoiced in the faithfulness of His words (Jer. 23:28), His commandments (Ps. 119:86), and His testimonies (Ps. 119:138). In their human tongues they declared His "faithful sayings" (2 Tim. 2:11, 13; Titus 3:8). In the language of a particular time and place the incarnate God, Jesus Christ, spoke words that remain faithful and true (Rev. 1:5; 3:14; 19:11).

In His faithfulness God is sovereign and free. His freedom is not to deny Himself, contradict Himself, or misrepresent the reality He sustains. He always acts in accord with His nature. His freedom is that of self-determination, not of arbitrary whim. The God of incomparable integrity can no more originate error than He can originate temptation or moral evil. Ascribing logical or factual errors to God's revelation does not magnify but demeans His faithfulness, His integrity, His fidelity.

If the biblical authors' God was changeless in character and purposes, how could He relate to time and change? The divine mind, which created man's mind in His image, has capacities similar to those by which man transcends the present instant of which he is conscious—namely, in memory and expectation. The fact that God knows all temporal things simultaneously does not rule out the significant and real succession of events. Augustine illustrated this from the repetition of a memorized Psalm:

> I am about to repeat a psalm that I know. Before I begin, my attention is extended to the whole; but when I have begun, as much of it as becomes past by my saying it is extended in my memory on account of what I have repeated, and my expectation, on account of what I am about to repeat; yet my consideration is present with me, through which that which was future may be carried over so that it may become past.[71]

In some such way God knows the entire sweep of history simultaneously and yet carries out His activities of creation and providence successively in accord with His changeless plans. God's eternity is not like that of the philosophers whose God negates time or renders it illusory. And the absolutes knowable to God and man are not limited to universal forms of immutable nature. There may be absolutes, as Bromiley suggests, for particulars.[72] According to His eternal plans for time, God created a particular couple, chose a particular nation, sent His prophets to particular people at particular times, and finally sent His Son into history as a particular human being in a particular culture. God is certainly not time-bound, although He is active in time.

However one explains it in detail, if the relation between time and eternity allows for the incarnation of Christ at a particular time and place, it also allows for the inscripturation of the gospel in a particular language and culture. The gospel asserts certain facts: Jesus was the Christ; He died; He was buried; He arose. The gospel also asserts the meaning of those facts. Jesus died "for our sins" (1 Cor. 15:3–4). Such assertions about events in the realm of the relative can be inerrantly or changelessly true, for what they assert conforms to the eternal plan of God for these particular events in time. The meaning "for our sins" is not time-bound in the sense that it was no more than an accepted opinion of some people during that phase in the world's development. The assertion is true for all human beings of all times, places, and situations.

Two implications may be drawn. On the one hand, if one's view of eternity and time allows for the inerrancy or absoluteness of the gospel in human concepts and language, it allows for the inerrancy of everything the Bible teaches. One may defend a limited inerrancy for the gospel and deny it elsewhere on other grounds. But having a view of eternity and time that permits faithful sayings concerning Jesus of Nazareth, one cannot say that the time relatedness of other information rules out the possibility of its inerrancy.

On the other hand, if one's view of eternity and time does not allow for any inerrant information, even regarding the gospel of Christ, then sooner or later he will see that his view of eternity and time also rules out an incarnation at a specific time and place. The depth of concern many have for inerrancy is not merely for the integrity of the Scriptures themselves, it is also for the reliability of the gospel message and for the integrity of Jesus' claims for Himself as the Savior of the world. While I appreciate Berkouwer's central emphasis on redemption, I fear he has undermined the foundation for the universal validity of the redemptive gospel he seeks to emphasize.

The Human Authors Have Characteristics Common to All People as Created in God's Image

Conceptual relativists may have become so preoccupied with the differences of people involved in history at different times that they have failed to consider the similarities. A scholarly approach must provide a responsible account of both similarities and differences. Because all human beings of all times and places have been created in God's image they have many common characteristics.

Man was created to fellowship with God and participate in His purposes in history. By creation man had a capacity for knowing God and for sharing God's moral concerns, as the Holy and righteous One. Writing with respect to naturalistic evolutionists, Carl Henry says:

> Humanistic anthropologists are prone to view man as a developing animal, and to regard all his basic dispositions as mere distillations of evolutionary experience. In deference to the theory of cultural relativity, they deny that any common principles or practices can be discerned in the history of humanity.[73]

Henry then observes that

> Christianity has never denied the vast range of moral relativity in fallen history. But it explains those perverse notions of the good and the failure of those who truly know the good to do it (Rom. 7:19–23) by a principle far superior to ethical relativism—man's moral revolt against his holy Creator. Christianity, moreover, specifically rejects the notion that man's nature as man bears no structures other than those derived from evolutionary development. The forms of logic and morality are not derived from experience; rather they are what make human experience possible. As the Psalmist puts it, the horse and the mule "have no understanding" (Ps. 32:9 KJV); it is patently obvious that animals have no religious propensities while on the other hand human history is replete with rational, moral, and religious concerns.[74]

In addition to capacities for moral discernment, man has a capacity for self-transcendence. Like God, a human being can have in his mind, as Augustine said, a memory of the past, consideration of the present, and expectation of the future. To the extent that these capacities are used, a person is not time-bound like an object. The biblical authors were not limited to knowledge of their own culture. Moses had been trained in the wisdom of the Egyptians. Other writers showed acquaintance with the nations surrounding Israel. Paul knew the philosophies of the Stoics and the Epicureans. The writers of Scripture knew different cultures and were able to transcend their own, freely rejecting and criticizing unjust influences. These writers were hardly conditioned in a behavioristic or almost helpless sense. They freely adopted and endorsed some factors and freely rejected others.

Furthermore, because he was created in God's image, man could develop ability to think and communicate in linguistic symbols. Eugene Nida, a linguistic expert on cultural differences, has found that effective communication is possible among the diverse linguistic cultures of the world for three reasons:

(1) the processes of human reasoning are essentially the same, irrespective of cultural diversity; (2) all people have a common range of experience, and (3) all peoples possess the capacity for at least some adjustment of the symbolic "grids" of others.[75]

Only by ignoring these fundamental data of experience can relativists argue that a revelation in a particular language such as Hebrew or Greek would be unintelligible to those of other languages. Crosscultural communication may be time-consuming and difficult, but it is regularly done at the United Nations. At least the offensiveness of choosing a particular language for biblical revelation should be lessened if one realizes that Greek and Hebrew participate in the common ranges of reason and experience of all other linguistic cultures.

The Scriptures indicate that a noetic aspect is part of the divine image in man. On this basis Paul exhorts, "Do not lie to each other, since you have . . . put on the new self, which is being renewed in *knowledge* in the image of its Creator" (Col. 3:9–10). The divinelike capacity for knowledge means we should not bear false witness against each other, misrepresent the facts, or contradict ourselves. It is also given so that we may think God's thoughts after Him. The same context adds, "Let the word of Christ dwell in you richly as you teach and admonish one another . . ." (Col. 3:16). Here "word" does not mean person, but information, as is predominantly the case in Old and New Testament usage. By reason of the intellectual ability given by God, we communicate with God as well as with others. We can love Him with mind as well as heart, worship in spirit and in truth, and pray not only with the spirit but also with the understanding (Matt. 22:37; John 4:24; 1 Cor. 14:15).

It is unfortunate that Berkouwer, like Barth, omits the import of conceptual knowledge in the image of God. In Berkouwer's entire work *Man: The Image of God* there are but three allusions to Colossians 3:10 and none of them expounds the significance of the word *knowledge*.[76] Much of the difficulty Barth had with identifying the words of inspired man with the Word of God resulted from his failure to see that man's mind was made like God's and that man can therefore know truth. Barth, by his own admission, began with an extreme view of divine transcendence.

> What expressions we used ... above all the famous "wholly other" breaking in upon us "perpendicularly from above" the not less famous "infinite qualitative distinction" between God and man, the vacuum, the mathematical point, and the tangent in which alone they must meet.[77]

Barth then confessed:

> We viewed this "wholly other" in isolation, abstracted and absolutized, and set it over against man, this miserable wretch—not to say boxed his ears with it—in such fashion that it continually showed greater similarity to the deity of the God of the philosophers than to the deity of the God of Abraham, Isaac, and Jacob.[78]

Barth came to see that God broke through to man in Christ's person, but he could never identify the words of the inspired men with God's Word, for God speaks only in Christ. In revelation, Barth said, we are concerned with the singular Word, spoken directly by God Himself, Christ.

> But in the Bible we are invariably concerned with human attempts to repeat and reproduce in human thoughts and expressions, this Word of God in definite human situations. . . . In the one case *Deux dixit*, in the other *Paulus dixit*. These are two different things.[79]

The Bible remained for Barth a merely fallible pointer to revelation. It is difficult to see that Berkouwer significantly differs from Barth's doctrine of revelation in Christ alone. Although Berkouwer holds to a general revelation, it is totally obscured to the unbelieving.[80] In Berkouwer's doctrine of special revelation, there is no objective scriptural content that is identified with the Word of God. The Bible remains merely a time-bound human witness to Christ.

By reason of man's creation in God's image intellectually, categories of human thought (logic principles) and categories of human speech (grammatical principles) need not be assumed to be totally other than God's. God made man to commune with Him in mind as well as in spirit. Furthermore, God made man to rule the world and the world to be ruled by man, so that there is no reason to manufacture an unbiblical total difference between the categories of human thought and reality in the world. A basis for knowledge of things as they are in themselves under God is laid in the doctrine of creation of the world and, in particular, of man in God's image. Because of man's fallenness, however, naive realism is often misled by superstition, fascination with the mysterious, etc. So therefore a critical realism requiring adequate criteria of verification is called for, as in the thought of Edward John Carnell.[81]

The Human Authors' Unique Perspectives Were Prepared by Divine Providence

Though they shared some basic principles common to all human beings, each of the biblical writers had his own unique combination of distinctives. Each was conditioned by factors distinctive of his time and place. Each had a distinctive heredity and environment. Each had a distinctive type and level of education or training. Although they all lived basically within a Judeo-Christian cultural environment over some fifteen centuries, they had quite different experiences within that basic culture and with other surrounding cultures. Each had distinctive interests and emphases—evident, for example, in the distinctive approaches of the four Gospels to Christ's life, death, and resurrection. Each had a distinctive vocabulary and writing style. Each reflects a distinctive cluster of natural and spiritual gifts. We can minimize the differences no more than the similarities.

Many immediately conclude that the many variables in the perspectives of the biblical authors necessitate the relativism of their teaching. Does not the limitedness of their perspectives, influenced by countless variables, keep them from writing absolute truth? If they actively participated in the research and writing, did they not necessarily distort God's truth? To grasp the answer, one must reckon with the all-inclusiveness of God's providence.

It is sometimes said, "If you want to train a person, you should begin with his grandparents!" When a college student arrives at seminary, it is too late for professors to shape his heredity and early training. However, in God's eternal plans, He could guide in all such particular factors. The writing of Scripture was no last-minute emergency operation in which God had to use whatever He could find to work with. He who knew all things from the beginning graciously planned to communicate through the oral and written work of the prophets and the apostles. Jeremiah was set apart from before his birth (Jer. 1:5), as was Paul (Gal. 1:15).

The Scriptures indicate that God's providential guidance relates to all things; it applies *a fortiori* to His activities of revelation and inspiration, which are so indispensable to His total redemptive program. Unlike a human editor of the writings of a number of different men, God did not have to wait helplessly to see what would come in. He could do far more than issue guidelines for the production. God, as an editor *par excellence*, could providentially bring into being the types of individuals, styles, and emphases He wanted. And that, if the doctrine of providence has not been lost, is what He did.

The awareness of conditioning factors in the lives of the biblical authors is not new. And B. B. Warfield was not insensitive to them. In his day the objection ran:

> As light that passes through the colored glass of a cathedral window, is light from heaven, but it is stained by the tints of the glass through which it passes, so any word of God which is passed through the mind and soul of a man must come out discolored by the personality through which it is given, and just to that degree ceases to be the pure word of God.

In answer to that basic issue, Warfield wrote:

> But what if this personality has itself been formed by God into precisely the personality it is, for the express purpose of communicating to the word given through it just the coloring which it gives it? What if the colors of the stained glass window have been designed by the architect for the express purpose of giving to the light that floods the cathedral precisely the tone and quality it receives from them? What if the word of God that comes to His people is framed by God into the word of God it is, precisely by means of the qualities of the men formed by Him for the purpose, through which it is given? When we think of God the Lord giving by His Spirit a body of authoritative Scriptures to His people, we must remember that He is the God of providence and of grace as well as of revelation and inspiration, and that He holds all the lines of preparation as fully under His direction as He does the specific operation which we call technically, in the narrow sense, by the name of "inspiration."[82]

The distinctive humanness of each biblical writer is no embarrassment to God, any more than the distinctively human qualities of Jesus are. And just as God could disclose Himself truly in Jesus Christ, so He could disclose His thoughts truly in the teaching of His providentially prepared spokesmen. Uniqueness is as much in the absolute plans of God as sameness. The particulars of the world and of biblical origins are no more illlusory than are the universal norms of morality and logical thought.

How did God prepare these writers? They received all the benefits of His common and special grace. God provided their food and drink and all the necessities of life; preserved them from evil; restrained those who would have destroyed them; gave them natural gifts; guided and governed all the innumerable factors in their individual lives, families, school, and social and political environments. In addition, God graciously called them to Himself, justified them by faith, gave them spiritual gifts, set them apart to their respective works as prophetic or apostolic men. He edified them through the means of the collective people of God in the Old and New Testament settings, their respective times and in their varied situations. In all of these and undoubtedly in other ways, God prepared unique individuals for writing His Word.

The Human Authors' Teachings Originated With God

The Holy Spirit directed not only in the personalities of the writers but also in the conceptual frameworks in which they thought and wrote. Although the Bible witnesses of experiences with Christ, its language is not merely evocative. It is informative. Implied in the "witness" and explicit in the doctrinal and practical teaching sections is the conceptual instruction about what is and what ought to be. A conceptual revelation is only unthinkable if one denies the noetic element in the image of God and affirms an infinite qualitative distinction between God's mind and man's. Then God's unlimited truth must be accommodated to the writers' limited conceptual and linguistic capacities. By appealing to accommodation, some have regarded the teaching of Scripture to be the frail and fallible word of man alone and not the Word of God. Accommodation to human "witness" rather than conceptual assertion of truth about reality does not escape the cognitive problems. Witnesses may be true witnesses or false witnesses. Their efforts may point in the direction intended or not, and they may point in the true direction adequately or inadequately.

To say that the Bible is God's revelation is to say that what the Bible teaches and attests was breathed out by God (2 Tim. 3:16) and had no mere human origination (2 Peter 1:20–21; 1 Thess.

2:13). These passages rule out a view that the Bible is a book that originated with man and is simply used by the Spirit to achieve redemptive ends, in spite of its human weaknesses. The Bible's teaching is from above as God guided the thinking of the authors by all the available providential means and in addition gave special information about His inner purpose of salvation by grace through faith based on the atonement and about all the revealed implications of His purposes with His people.

The divine origin and human adaptation of God's Word to man's thought can best be illustrated, again, in the Incarnation. The unlimited Son enjoying all the benefits of the Father's immediate presence chose to leave those privileges behind and to limit the use of His powers while existing as a human being. Though limited, He was without sin. Similarly, the Bible is limited, though without error. Large as it is, it does not contain all of God's infinite knowledge. Partial knowledge is, nevertheless, still knowledge.

Within the human frame of reference and the limitations of human language, Christ emphasized the relationship between content and power. To a Jewish audience He said, "If you hold to my teaching, you are really my disciples. Then you will know the truth, and the truth will set you free" (John 8:31–32). The freedom was experienced because of the teaching. Jesus could say, "The words I have spoken to you are spirit and they are life. Yet there are some of you who do not believe" (John 6:63–64). To receive eternal life by knowing God and Christ (John 17:3) is to know Christ's words, which came from the Father. "I gave them the words you gave me and they accepted them. They knew with certainty that I came from you, and they believed that you sent me" (John 17:8). Belief in the assertion that Jesus is from above is necessary if one is to trust in Him. In prayer Jesus continued to show the importance of truth: "Sanctify them by the truth; your word is truth" (John 17:17). The object of faith is indeed the person of Christ, but so too are the doctrine that He is God's Son and the words He taught.

The adaptation of Christ to a human body did not involve sin, and the adaptation of Christ's teachings to human concepts did not involve error. Berkouwer recognizes this when he notes that Jesus chose not to be consciously aware of the time of His second coming, but Berkouwer is "not the least prepared to speak of an error by Christ."[83] If Jesus' use of language and limitation of content for a particular time and place do not imply error, these human limitations in general do not constitute evidence against the Bible's inerrancy throughout.

Inscripturated truth, like incarnated truth, adapts itself to historical circumstances in an evident progressive revelation. If the revelation did not adapt itself to cultural levels, it would be unhistorical and anachronistic. The later revelation, however, does not destroy the earlier but carries it through to completion (Matt. 5:17–18). The validity of the new element that divine revelation introduces, however, is not determined by the situation. As J. Spykman explains, "Adapting itself to the existing level and addressing itself to its needs, it shapes man's understanding, rather than being shaped by it. . . . It is not exhaustive. It is nevertheless adequate and free of accommodational misrepresentation."[84]

One can adapt the teaching of Scripture to children without misrepresenting the teaching of Scripture to them. One can use parables to illustrate the kingdom of heaven, as Jesus did, without teaching error about the kingdom of heaven. One can use anthropomorphisms in speaking about God as spirit without teaching that God has flesh and bones. Again, one can teach about the origin of the world and nature in ordinary language of the appearance to the human eye without technical instruments and yet not teach error about the way it looks through a telescope. Jesus did not accommodate Himself to the errors of His day, though He adapted Himself to the level of understanding of His hearers. The prophets adapted the teaching of their message to the people of their times but did not teach the errors of pagan religions surrounding them in the process. Adaptation? Yes. Error? No.

Considerable attention was devoted to the cosmic and anthropic aspects of revelation in Bernard Ramm's *Special Revelation and the Word of God.* As the incomprehensible God reveals Himself to concrete specific men at particular times in the world, Ramm insists, "there is no loss of truth because revelation has this cosmic mediated form."[85] Conceptual truth, even of unique, once-for-all events, is always and everywhere true. If "Caesar crossed the Rubicon" was ever true, it remains as true today as it was the day the event occurred. Divine revelation originates with God and God uses the conceptual, historical framework of men to convey His propositional, conceptual truth.

Conceptual truth is not the brittle, inflexible thing often imagined. In Scripture it infrequently appears in the form "S is P." God is spirit (John 4:24). God is holy (1 Peter 1:15). God is love (1 John 4:8). "I am the way and the truth and the life" (John 14:6). Even this form conveys rich and living significance. Propositional content more often lies buried in literary, historical, and poetic forms; "nevertheless, out of the process of mining and smelting, the knowledge of God may be cast in discursive form."[86] Conceptual thought can designate visible objects, mental states, time sequences, changeless principles, volitional purposes, emotional feelings, and loving personal relationships.

Often propositional content receives unfortunate portrayals as being inconsistent with personal relationships. Against that specious disjunction, Bernard Ramm argues:

> What does it mean to disclose a Person? Certainly two people who are deaf, blind, and mute can hardly have any real encounter with each other apart from touch. Real encounter in life between persons is always within the context of mutual knowledge. This mutual knowledge is not opposed to the encounter, but it is its indispensable instrument.[87]

The Human Authors' Research and Writing Were Done Under Supernatural Supervision

Often it is said that the doctrine of inspiration asserts something about the reliability or usefulness of the end product (the Bible) but little of the process by which the Holy Spirit worked with the writers. Even those who say this, however, later assert something about the process. Increasingly they are saying that it was not an extraordinary supernatural activity of the Holy Spirit, but an ordinary, providential ministry common to all believers, such as His teaching and filling.

> If today the misleading term "inspiration" is to be used at all, it must certainly now be understood in the sense of that later theory of inspiration which conceives the activity of the divine Spirit as a miracle limited to certain particular acts of writing on the part of an apostle or biblical author.[88]

Kung has missed prior providential preparation of the biblical writer and, as if he is innovating a point, adds, "Not only the recording, but the whole pre-history and post-history of the writing, the whole process of acceptance in faith and transmission of the message, all these have something to do with the divine Spirit." The usual activity of the Spirit does not rule out the need for special, miraculous operations, however properly understood. Kung goes on to say, "This process can be described as Spirit-pervaded and Spirit-filled."[89] Kung proceeds to deny that the Scriptures are divine revelation and considers them merely human testimonies to revelatory experiences. Scripture, however, *seems* supernatural when a sinner reads the Bible with all of its human shortcomings and mistakes, concealment, limitations, and errors, and "in a wholly unmechanical way turns the documents themselves into Spirit-filled and Spirit-pervaded testimonies."[90]

Berkouwer similarly rejects a supernatural activity of the Spirit in inspiration of the biblical writers. "God's Word has not come to us as a stupendous miracle that shies away from every link with the human order thus to be truly divine. Rather, when God speaks, human voices ring in our ears."[91] (God's miracles often use human and natural means in an extraordinary way, one might remind himself here.) "It would be a mistake to formulate a supernaturalistic and mechanical theory of inspiration merely. . . ."[92] No one, of course, proposes a mechanical theory. Surely the extraordinary activity of God need not all be dismissed as mechanical. Berkouwer sees a trend giving "growing attention to the 'horizontality' of the genuinely human, to man's initiative and activity" explained in part by "a growing aversion to so-called supernaturalism which naively implied incidental and fragmentary 'supernatural' acts of God in 'nature.' "[93]

We need not see the supernatural work of God's Spirit as isolated, but as an essential part of the dramatic program for counteracting the power of evil. The majority of miracles in Scripture occurred during times of crisis. Clusters of miracles happened as Moses led the people out of Egyptian slavery, as Elijah and Elisha opposed the prophets of Baal, as Christ ministered and atoned for sin, and as apostles planted the church.[94] Scriptural revelation and inspiration occurred in this same historical context for similar purposes of preserving and enhancing God's redemptive program.

Neither need we see the supernatural work of God's Spirit in a mechanical way eliminating the humanness of the writers. Some miracles were done without the use of any temporal factors, as was the healing of the centurion's servant at a distance by Christ's word (Matt. 8:5–13). Others, like the healing of the blind man, occurred through the use of unusual means; mud and saliva were put on the man's eyes and he was commanded to wash in the pool of Siloam (John 9:6–7). The supernatural aspect of inspiration is not dictation apart from human means but the extraordinary use of human means such as research (Luke 1:1–4), memory (of events in Christ's life), and judgment (1 Cor. 7:25), so that what was written conformed to God's mind on the subject and did not teach error of fact, doctrine, or judgment.

In the miraculous conception of Christ a fully human woman was used in an extraordinary way, so that the child born of her could be called the Holy One, the Son of God (Luke 1:35). Similarly the miracle of the conception of Holy Scripture did not bypass human authors and their words but brought forth from them the Word of God.

All believers are indwelt, taught, and filled with the Spirit; only the writers of Scripture are said to have been inspired by the Spirit. The writers had the ministries of the Spirit common to all the people of God, but in addition they had the special supervision of the Spirit as prophetic and apostolic spokesmen in their work of composing and writing books of the Bible. The unique authority enjoyed by the prophets and the apostles among their peers was not common to all the people who experienced justification by faith. Our doctrine of inspiration should reflect something of that unique delegated, veracious, and special inspired authority.

As we think of the Spirit, the third person of the Trinity working with the persons who wrote Scripture, we must avoid not only mechanical analogies but also what I have called the "single-cause fallacy." Some imagine that if God does something then human beings do nothing in relation to it; or if they do something, then God does not. Many occurrences have multiple causes. In the salvation of souls there are often many factors on the human level in addition to the divine gift of new life. In inspiration we have not merely either a divine cause or a human cause but a divine-human concursive operation.

If we must have a model, I suggest one from management—getting things done through people. It involves at least four steps: planning, leading, organizing, and controlling. God is the wise and skilled manager who had the Bible written through prophets and apostles. He planned for them from before the foundation of the world, led in the development of their personalities and styles through His providential operations in the world, and organized their distinctive contributions to produce a book that could make a believer thoroughly equipped for every good work. He controlled the entire process of research, recall, and writing so that each writer conveyed the truth He wanted taught. In His work of providence God can prevent evil from occurring and *a fortiori* in His work of inspiration He can prevent errors of fact, thought, or judgment from corrupting His inscripturated Word. God is far more effective than the most effective human manager who accomplishes his objectives through people.

To change the analogy and put it more in the realm of loving human relationships, a good pastor achieves certain foreknown objectives through his people without reducing them to robots. A good parent can guide children to certain desirable goals without destroying their wills. And a good teacher can lead a class to fulfill certain purposes in a course without simply dictating answers. If human parents, pastors, and teachers can get things done through people without mechanical dictation and control, how much more can the all-wise God!

Charles Hodge has well said:

> If God without interfering with a man's free agency can make it infallibly certain that he will repent and believe (and that seems to be what even non-Calvinists are now saying they mean by the witness of the Spirit in the Scriptures), He can render it certain that he will not err in his teaching. It is in vain to profess to hold the common doctrine of theism, and yet assert that God cannot control rational creatures without turning them into machines.[95]

The Scriptures themselves explicitly acknowledge the activity of men under the Spirit's control. "David himself, speaking by the Holy Spirit, declared. . . ." (Mark 12:36). Peter said, "Brothers, the Scripture had to be fulfilled which the Holy Spirit spoke long ago through the mouth of David" (Acts 1:16). According to Paul, "The Holy Spirit spoke the truth to your forefathers when he said through Isaiah the prophet. . . ." (Acts 28:25). Luke was fully free to investigate previous attempts to write accounts of Jesus' deeds (Luke 1:1–4). Yet superintending all of this research was the Spirit, who kept Luke from including anything false about the life and teaching of the Lord and who guided him in including the things God wanted written. This view recognizes the fact that Paul may have had to speak on issues concerning which he had no direct quotation from the Savior but holds that, as Paul made his judgments, he did so under the control of divine inspiration (1 Cor. 7:25). Consequently his judgments are "the Lord's command" (1 Cor. 14:37).

How did the Holy Spirit do this? How does one person influence another? Why do some have a more effective impact on people than others? Undoubtedly many factors are involved, and the Scriptures provide little in the way of answers to questions of how. How God guides providentially, how He answers prayer, or how the Spirit regenerates we are not told in detail. We should not be surprised, then, that we are not told more about how the Holy Spirit inspired His providentially prepared spokesmen to write what He wanted written.

However, we do know several things about the process: (1) We know that the Holy Spirit so specially controlled the human authors' judgment that what they wrote is God's judgment. (2) We know that, apart from supernatural control, finite and fallen men could not have expressed such authoritative pronouncements. They would have been presumptuous prophets, claiming to speak for God a word that came merely from their own hearts. People were severely punished for just such presumption throughout Old Testament history. (3) We know that the Scriptures did not originate by the will of man but by God's breathing them out (2 Tim. 3:16; 2 Peter 1:20, 21). (4) We know that the divine spokesmen were "carried along by the Holy Spirit" (2 Peter 1:21). (5) We know that the Spirit's supervision applied to the written Word that would be available after the human writer was gone and that all of the previously written Old Testament and New Testament was viewed as the word of the prophets and other authors telling of the power and the coming of the Lord Jesus (2 Peter 1:16, 19–21) (6) We know that the Spirit's inspiration had the writing of Scripture, not subsequent readers of Scripture, as its object. Inspiration cannot be reduced to illumination. (7) We know that not all Scripture was given by dictation.

Since dictation is so frequently alleged to be connected with inerrancy, it deserves a further word. Like most persistent views, it contains an element of truth. In a few instances a biblical author heard an audible voice conveying God's message. When Moses "entered the Tent of Meeting to speak with the Lord, he heard the voice speaking to him from between the two cherubim above the atonement cover on the ark of the Testimony" (Num. 7:89; cf. Exod. 4:12; 19:3–6; Lev. 1:1; 1 Sam. 3:4–14, 21; Isa. 6:8–9; Rev. 14:13). In some instances God may have spoken inaudibly to men, just as He hears our inaudible speaking to Him (cf. 1 Sam. 1:13). More often, however, there seems to have been concursive inspiration, in which the prophet or apostle actively wrote and the Holy Spirit moved along with the speaking and writing in such a manner that the thing spoken or written was also the Word of God. Ramm defends these three forms of divine speaking: audible voice, inaudible voice, and concursive inspiration.[96] There is not sufficient evidence to support audible dictation of every passage. Indeed the theory of total dictation does not fit facts such as those of the differences of style, vocabulary, and personal emphasis.

If, apart from inspiration, brainstorming and serendipity sessions can stimulate creative thinking among people, how much more could the Holy Spirit have suggested ideas to people and motivated them to write freely and yet fulfill His ultimate purpose. Augustine spoke of the ineffable power operating within to stimulate ideas in the consciousness. His view of "spiritual suggestion" comes out in his exposition of the text, "the devil had already prompted Judas Iscariot, son of Simon, to betray Jesus" (John 13:2).

> Such a putting (into the heart) is a spiritual suggestion and entereth not by the ear, but through the thoughts; and thereby not in a way that is corporeal, but spiritual. For what we call spiritual is not always to be understood in a commendatory way. . . . For it is from a spiritual being the spiritual things get their name. But how such things are done, as that devilish suggestions should be introduced, and so mingle with human thoughts that man accounts them his own, how can he know? Nor can we doubt that good suggestions are likewise made by a good spirit in the same unobservable and spiritual way.[97]

CONCLUSION: THE HUMAN AUTHORS' WRITINGS ARE TRULY HUMAN WORDS AND TRULY GOD'S WORDS

The Bible is not merely a compilation of human words written by people who were guided by the ordinary operations of the Holy Spirit, as are other books by believing, devout writers. These are not errant human words that merely function to lead people to Christ; they are words of conceptual truth that actually can lead people to the real Christ and faithfulness. The biblical concept of truth has two emphases—reliable information about reality and fidelity to it. One cannot substitute for the other. So also the biblical view of error has two emphases—mistaken information about what is or ought to be and unfaithfulness to this reality or morality. For an abundant Christian life a person must avoid both misinformation and unfaithfulness.

The Holy Spirit illumines the mind to objective Christianity, to know what is to be believed and why. This truth becomes the test of subjective experiences in the hearts of believers. The harmony of the objective criteria and the internal witness of the Spirit enabling us to avoid both error and infidelity is beautifully stated by Robert Clyde Johnson: "Just as the Spirit must at all times *attest* the written Word, so the written Word must at all times *test* the Spirit."[98]

How could human beings, writing merely out of their own situations, provide criteria for determining what spiritual influences were truly of God? The human authors of Scripture were equipped for their awesome task not only by all the ordinary ministries of the Spirit but also by reason of their special gifts as prophets and apostles and by the miracle of inspiration. By these means God enabled the human authors to write with a veracious authority. And through these means He has delegated His authority, which is final and ultimate, to men. These writings determine the content of distinctively Christian faith and indicate the grounds both for mental assent to its teachings and for total trust in the Christ who can save.

The objective validity of a teaching does not compel consent to it. People can withhold assent from a clear truth. A wife may not believe the guilt of her husband even though it is legally established beyond reasonable doubt. People may also withdraw from reality and rebel against moral standards. The ministry of the Spirit is not limited to establishing the objective truth of Scripture. Because sinful people, by nature, choose not to assent to its truth or to trust the Christ of whom it speaks, the witness of the Spirit must open their hearts today as He did Lydia's heart in Paul's day (Acts 16:14). But the message remains objectively true whether accepted or not and brings greater condemnation to some, while bringing eternal life to others (2 Cor. 2:15–16).

To affirm that the human words of Scripture adequately convey the divine truth does not suppose any magic or transubstantiation of the words, as Berkouwer imagines.[99] What it does mean is that the teaching of the prophetic and apostolic men conform to God's mind on the subjects of which they wrote. What they teach, limited as it is, God teaches. God has condescended to disclose His nature and changeless purposes in human language. As I have set forth elsewhere, truth is a quality of content, expressed in words. Thus it is the Bible's verbally expressed content that is inerrant—that is, wholly true.[100]

By verbally expressed content I mean the propositional content that corresponds to the mind of God. How do we know when our human ideas correspond to God's mind? God cannot deny Himself; therefore we know our ideas fail to conform to His when they involve self-contradiction. God omnisciently knows all relevant facts on any issue, and hence, for human ideas to conform to His, they must fit the facts. God's ideas are furthermore designed to guide human beings to an abundant life of sharing His fellowship and work. It follows that our ideas conform to His when they lead to authentic, fulfilling life in His fellowship and service. Hence the tests of truth involve logical noncontradiction, empirical fit, and existential viability. In affirming that the human words of the Bible are inerrant or true, I am saying that their teaching is noncontradictory, factual, and viable. One who stakes his life on their teaching will not be disappointed.

What is the chief distinguishing quality of human assertions that may be regarded as divine affirmations, as absolutes? With Augustine I suggest that one essential difference between the eternal and the temporal is the difference between the changeless and the changing. He said, "Time does not exist without some movement and transition, while in eternity there is no change."[101] In eternal wisdom God made the world and man. Hence the chief quality of wisdom (sapientia) as distinct from knowledge of the changing world (scientia) is its changelessness. Any immutable truth is God's truth wherever it may be found; it corresponds with God's changeless mind on the subject.

As we have seen, eternal wisdom, Augustine held, is not far from any of us, for in it we live and move and have our being. Man never has a complete and simultaneous vision of God's mind and so, at best, does not see as God Himself sees. While there is no equality of knowing as God knows, man's intellect is enlightened by general and special illumination "in some conformity unto that form which is equal unto Thee."[102]

All that the Bible teaches is true. It conforms to the reality of what was, is, or will be ontologically and to what ought or ought not to be ethically. We know what grace has provided for the redemption of the lost. The salvation of sinners is indeed the central concern of Scripture and should have priority. The redemptive purpose, however, is not enhanced, but hurt, by reducing the Bible to that single objective. People need to know about creation, the origin of sin, the effects of sin on history, and the purpose of the law. They need to hear of divine judgments on high and low, Jew and Gentile, great and small nations. Christians need the comfort of changeless truth regarding divine providence in the details of past history and of the eschatological triumph to come. All that Scripture affirms is inspired by God. All is true. All is profitable.

Unfortunately, Boer and Berkouwer want to have the functional values of which the Bible speaks without the consistency and factuality on which these are based. Berkouwer saw this approach to be impossible regarding the Resurrection. People are to be pitied who imagine that they have forgiveness of sins even if the resurrection of Christ is no more than a human projection of wishful thinking. What is exemplified in relation to the Resurrection holds with regard to all scriptural truth. The base of experiential values is inerrant fact. The defense of inerrancy does not displace the functional benefits of Christianity with dead orthodoxy; it preserves the only base on which the existential significance of the faith can be realized for time and eternity.

To hold the doctrine of biblical inerrancy does not solve all the problems of interpretation. It is not to affirm the inerrancy of any believer's present understanding of the Bible. It is not always easy to distinguish the teaching about once-for-all irrepeatable events from the teaching about events that can, for all practical purposes, be repeated. But in struggling to determine the meaning the Spirit intended to convey through the human authors, the same three criteria of truth operate. That interpretation is true which, without self-contradiction, fits all the relevant lines of data from the grammar, context, purpose, historical and cultural settings, and the rest of the Bible's teaching on that subject. On some difficult passages we may not be able to come to a satisfactory resolution, but the interpreter committed to inerrancy need not ask whether in fact he is handling the word of truth. His only question is whether he is interpreting the word of truth in a worthy manner (2 Tim. 2:15).

At stake here is no minor detail of Scripture but *the very essence of Christianity.* Christianity, as J. Gresham Machen argued, is not mere religious experience, as liberalism tended to say. Christianity is life or experience founded on truth—verbally stated truth, doctrinal truth.

Also at stake here is *the object of faith for salvation.* Is the object of faith in itself, as Berkouwer says, totally different from knowledge of or about the object? Is Christian faith mere trust in the person of Christ through the witness of the Holy Spirit? Or, with Paul, do we *know* whom we have believed? Are we, like Paul, convinced of the objective truth of the gospel concerning Christ, so that we may trust the *real* Christ who died and rose again (2 Tim. 1:12)?

John puts the issue beyond reasonable interpretative doubt when he writes that anyone who does not continue in the teaching of Christ (*didache*) does not have God (2 John 9). Clearly he means giving assent to the assertion that Jesus has come in the flesh—an assertion the deceivers and antichrists have denied (1 John 4:1–3; 2 John 7). He who has this Son, who became flesh and dwelt among us, has life (1 John 5:12). John wrote his Gospel not that men might trust an unknown Christ but that they might give mental assent to the assertion that Jesus is, in reality, the Christ, the Son of God, and that by believing this information they might have life in His name (John 20:31).

Just as it is indispensable to eternal life to affirm that Jesus has come in human flesh, so it is crucial to evangelicalism to affirm that the written Word has come in human words. It is not enough to say that the human words point to a Word beyond all human expression. It is not enough to say that the time-bound human words witness to the timeless Word. The confession of the early church was that Jesus is the Christ in true humanity. Analogously, the confession of the early church was that the Bible *is* God's Word in all that it teaches. Many have pointed out that what the Bible says, God says; that what the prophet says, God says; and that what the apostle says is God's commandment to the church. Just as relativism in ethics has changed "is good" to "is considered good by some in a given time or culture," so Berkouwer changes "God's Word" to "a human witness to God's Word." It sounds pious and humble

and seems to resolve many critical questions, but the implications of that subtle change are as far-reaching as the nature and
object of Christian faith, the nature of the message to be presented in missionary outreach, and the very substance of Christianity itself.

The particularism of claiming that Christ, as Redeemer, is the
only way to God and of proclaiming that the Bible is the Book
written by divine inspiration is indeed offensive to many. But I
remind you that there are many books written under the illumination of the Spirit by time-bound, godly people. Is the Bible
different from these only in degree, if in that? Or is the Bible
unique in that it is the only book ever to be supernaturally
inspired?

The tendency at large today, as in past periods of neoplatonism, Hegelianism, and pantheism, is to find God incarnate
in everything, not in just one Person, and to find God's Word in
all "sacred" books, not with unique and supreme authority in
just one Book. Surely Berkouwer and his followers do not intend
to reduce the Bible to the level of other religious literature. Yet
the view of inspiration, or I should say illumination, he presents
opens the door for those who would see the Bible as but one of
many sacred writings, pointing somehow beyond its own errancy
to a real, but unknown and unknowable, God.

THE MEANING OF INERRANCY

Paul D. Feinberg

Paul D. Feinberg is Associate Professor of Biblical and Systematic Theology at Trinity Evangelical Divinity School in Deerfield, Illinois. During 1977–78, he was Chairman of the Division of Philosophy of Religion. He is a graduate in history of the University of California, Los Angeles (B.A.); Talbot Theological Seminary (B.D. and Th.M.); and Dallas Theological Seminary (Th.D. in Systematic Theology). He is presently a candidate for the Ph.D. degree in Philosophy at the Universtiy of Chicago. Dr. Feinberg has also served on the faculty of Moody Bible Institute and has been a field evangelist for the American Board of Missions to the Jews. He has contrib-uted articles to Baker's Dictionary of Christian Ethics *and the* Wycliffe Bible Encyclopedia. *He is an ordained minister in the Evangelical Free Church of America.*

CHAPTER SUMMARY

The defense of the term and doctrine of inerrancy presupposes a clear definition. The aim of this paper is to specify the meaning of the doctrine. To this end a study of the methodology of theology is undertaken. The author concludes that the method of abduction or retroduction is most appropriate to theology as a whole and should be used in formulating a doctrine of inerrancy. Thus the phenomena of Scripture are examined, and a definition of the doctrine is formulated in terms of truth, or truthfulness. Finally, there is a discussion of qualifications, misunderstandings, and objections.

THE MEANING OF INERRANCY

It appears to me that in Ethics, as in all other philosophical studies, the difficulties and disagreements, of which its history is full, are mainly due to a very simple cause: namely to the attempt to answer questions, without first discovering precisely what question it is which you desire to answer.

G. E. *Moore*, Principia Ethica, *vii*.

W HILE MOORE undoubtedly overstates the case for discovering the precise question, he is nevertheless onto something very important. Without a proper understanding of a question, one has little hope of arriving at the right answer. Moreover, at the heart of clear and precise understanding is careful definition of the terms that make up the question. This is particularly true in theological contexts where words and dogma have a long and hoary history. The danger is always that emotions will be aroused unduly, with resultant failure to communicate the desired information adequately. All of this is to say that, without precise definition of the word *inerrancy* and of the related doctrine of inerrancy, it is difficult to answer the question as to whether or not the Bible is inerrant. That such clear and careful definition is necessary can be seen even by a superficial reading of the literature of this debate. On both sides there have been attacks on straw men and failure to engage one another on the genuine issues. Therefore, the task of this chapter is to define both the term and the doctrine of inerrancy as precisely as possible so that debate may genuinely proceed.[1]

267

Before turning to this task, however, it seems to me that some preliminary considerations are in order. First, I do not intend to defend all who have ever sought to advance a doctrine of inerrancy. Such is both impossible and unnecessary. Yet this fact needs to be emphasized, since there are some who have sought in the past, and some who are now seeking, to formulate the doctrine in an indefensible manner. Such attempts are often held up to ridicule and scorn, and all who hold to inerrancy are then tarred with the same brush. This is not to say that inerrantists have not done similar things but to emphasize a basic tenet of debate or argumentation—namely, that excessive or even false claims by some or even all defenders of a position do not prove that position to be false. To put it another way, a view may be poorly or incorrectly argued and yet be true. In order to disprove inerrancy, therefore, it must be shown that this doctrine in its most defensible formulation is false or at least that it is not as plausible as some other position.

Second, it is often claimed by those who support an inerrant Bible that they alone hold a high view of Scripture. This claim elicits the following response from Davis:

> I will criticize inerrancy, but my purpose is to strengthen—not weaken—the evangelical Christian cause by making a clear and, I hope, convincing case for an evangelical attitude toward the Bible that does not involve inerrancy. The "all or nothing" arguments of many defenders of inerrancy give the impression that there is no middle ground between inerrancy, on the one hand, and neo-orthodoxy, liberal, or even atheistic attitudes toward the Bible, on the other.[2]

Davis's quote explicitly or implicitly raises at least three distinct but related questions. (1) Are there only two possible positions on Scripture? Must one hold either to (a) inerrancy, or (b) to neoorthodox, liberal, or atheistic attitudes toward the Bible? The answer to this question is easy. There are many possible attitudes toward Scripture. (2) What is the criterion for a high view of Scripture? Specifically, is inerrancy a necessary or sufficient condition, or both, for a high view of Scripture? The answer to this question is not easy. I would guess that there is disagreement on the answer among evangelicals. It is not within the scope of this chapter to answer this question. (3) Given a satisfactory criterion for a high view of Scripture, which of the many possibilities mentioned in question 1 qualify? Obviously, the answer to this question awaits a definitive answer to question 2, which we have not attempted to give. Thus we cannot give an answer to question 3. But again this is not the issue before us.

Third, it is claimed by some who defend the inerrancy of the Bible that forfeiture of the doctrine of inerrancy leads *inevitably* to the denial of other doctrines that are central to the Christian faith. This, of course, is not necessarily true, though there are numerous examples that can be cited where this has in fact taken place. Likewise, an orthodox doctrine of Scripture is not an *absolute* hedge against heterodoxy in other theological matters. Some cults, such as Jehovah's Witnesses, have as a part of their doctrinal statement an excellent position on Scripture. On the other hand, many who have vigorously opposed belief in the inerrancy of the Bible have remained orthodox elsewhere in doctrine.

Having said this, we have not settled the matter, since it would surely seem that the *first* step toward doctrinal purity would be a correct doctrine of Scripture. Nevertheless, there are many, even among the highly educated, who hold views for which they cannot give adequate justification. Thus the question to which we are addressing ourselves is not unimportant or insignificant. It cuts to the heart and foundation of Christian theology. It is the question of theological consistency.

The aim, then, of this chapter is to discuss methodology for formulating and justifying the doctrine of inerrancy and then to define the term *inerrancy*. I will begin with a general discussion of the method by which a doctrine is constructed and justified. Then the exegetical evidence of Scripture that bears on the doctrine will be examined. This will be followed by a search for proper terminology and for a doctrine that best suits the scriptural phenomena, with special attention being given to qualifications and misunderstandings. Finally, I will reply to some important objections that might be raised against the doctrine of inerrancy but have not been treated in the course of the study.

THE PROBLEM OF METHOD

Where do theologians begin in their efforts to set forth the meaning of inerrancy? One possible answer might be a good dictionary, such as the *Oxford English Dictionary*. If we were merely trying to define the word *inerrancy*, that suggestion would not be without merit. However, we are attempting to do more than merely define a *term*; we are seeking to define or formulate a *doctrine*. This task takes us to a most fundamental inquiry, a discussion of theological method. That is, how does the theologian go about formulating or constructing a doctrine? How does the theologian theologize? Indeed, it has not been uncommon to set the whole inerrancy conflict in the context of a debate over method. Just such a case in point is Beegle's treatment in *Scripture, Tradition and Infallibility*.[3]

Beegle begins by distinguishing between deductive and inductive methodology. While every argument involves the claim that its premises provide evidence for the truth of its conclusion, deduction and induction differ in the nature of their premises and the relationship between the premises and the conclusion. In deduction the premises may be *general* assumptions or propositions from which *particular* conclusions are derived. The distinctive characteristic of deduction, however, is its demonstration of relationship between two or more propositions. Furthermore, a deductive argument involves the claim that its premises *guarantee* the truth of its conclusion. Where the premises are both the necessary and sufficient condition for the truth of the conclusion, the argument is said to be valid. Where the premises fail to provide such evidence, the argument is said to be invalid.[4]

With induction, on the other hand, the relationship between premises and conclusion is much more modest. The premises only provide *some* evidence for the conclusion. Inductive arguments are not valid or invalid. They are better or worse, depending on the degree of probability that their premises confer on their conclusions. Moreover, in induction the premises are *particulars*, and the conclusions are *generalizations*, the data being organized under the most general categories possible.[5]

Which of these methodologies is correct? Well, Beegle says that they are complementary. That is, both are needed. However, this is not the end of the matter. There is, he thinks, a priority to the inductive. To illustrate this contention he discusses the way in which an archaeologist goes about excavating a tell. The primary task is to dig down through the strata and to label each item that is found, indicating its stratum. After thoroughly excavating and labeling the items, the archaeologist examines a group of objects, such as pottery, from a single stratum. As he correlates the characteristics of a level, he finds that the pottery has certain forms and other features that distinguish it from pottery in other strata. Thus he finds that each stratum has its own type or class of pottery. This classification procedure is called stratigraphy.[6] Now when the archaeologist goes to the next tell, especially if it is nearby, he does not follow quite the same process. Having already derived from the previously discovered phenomena a classification system, he immediately assigns a piece of pottery to a period and type on the basis of its characteristics. However, even here induction has a part. If, for instance, other factors begin to call into question the original classification, there is then need for revision. Beegle therefore concludes, "The best results are obtained when induction precedes deduction."[7]

Beegle now applies this discussion to the problem of inerrancy. Those who defend inerrancy are deductivists pure and simple. They begin with certain assumptions about God and the Scriptures, namely, that God cannot lie and the Scriptures are the Word of God. From these assumptions inerrantists deduce that the Bible is without error. This approach leads to an a priori determined conclusion, to dogmatism, and to disregard for the phenomena of Scripture. Regardless of the problems of the phenomena, the inerrantist stubbornly maintains his stance on Scripture.[8]

On the other hand, the inductivist cannot accept inerrancy. He begins with the phenomena of Scripture. There he finds errors of differing kinds. He comes across historical inaccuracies. Further, there is reflected in the Bible a view of the world that is scientifically unacceptable today. And this is just the beginning. Thus, as the inductivist seeks to build a doctrine of Scripture, he must be true to the facts of the case. Therefore, try as he may, he cannot accept the idea of an inerrant Bible.[9]

Is this picture fair to the methodology of all defenders of inerrancy? I think not. There is no single methodology employed by inerrantists. In R. C. Sproul's excellent study, "The Case for Inerrancy: A Methodological Analysis," he describes at least three general approaches to the problem of method. First, he cites the confessional method, by which the Bible is confessed to be the Word of God and is so recognized by faith alone. An exponent of this method is G. C. Berkouwer. Second, there is the presuppositional method of Cornelius Van Til. In this method defending the authority and inerrancy of the Bible includes accepting the absolute authority and inerrancy of Scripture as a foundational premise. The Bible is self-attesting. Third, there is the classical method, which is both inductive and deductive, interested in external as well as internal evidence.[10]

Given that there are at least these three general approaches, Beegle is first of all wrong in lumping all defenders of inerrancy into the deductivist camp. Some, as we have seen, are more than deductivists. Moreover, even those that advocate a deductive methodology should not be so easily charged with dogmatism and closemindedness. For some, their theological a prioris are justified indirectly. Their proof is much like that used to justify the axioms of a geometric system. Since axioms are so basic, it is claimed they cannot be proven in terms of anything more primitive. Thus axioms are justified indirectly in terms of the theorems and propositions they generate and of the solutions they make possible. At any rate, while it is a priori, such methodology is concerned with the facts in some sense and, as such, should not be called dogmatic.

That is not the end of the matter, however. The question still remains as to the correct method of formulating and testing a doctrine (i.e., of giving the meaning of the doctrine). It seems that the question of methodology with respect to inerrancy cannot be divorced from the broader considerations of a general methodology for theology.[11] Unfortunately, evangelicals do not usually discuss the matter of methodology, since they are generally more interested in the *content* of theology. There are, however, two very helpful articles by evangelicals on theological methodology. They are Arthur F. Holmes's "Ordinary Language Analysis and Theological Method,"[12] and John Warwick Montgomery's "Theologian's Craft: A Discussion of Theory Formation and Theory Testing in Theology."[13] Interestingly enough, there is a good measure of agreement between the two men. Both deny that either deduction or induction alone is the method of the theologian. Holmes is quite critical of the independent use of either methodology. Deduction is the logic of mathematics. If theology were circumscribed by this logic, (1) theological thought would have to be formalized into a deductive argument; (2) the historical narratives would merely be illustrative; (3) analogy, metaphor, symbol, and poetry in the Bible would all have to be restated in logical, univocal, universal form; and (4) all events in redemptive history, as well as their application of grace, would become logically necessary.[14]

Induction, on the other hand, is formulated in three differing ways. First, there is Aristotelian induction, which sought, through intuitive abstraction of familiar categorized data, to arrive at universal principles. Such a method presupposes, and would tie theology to, an Aristotelian view of nature and man. Second, there is the induction of Francis Bacon and John Stuart Mill, which is concerned with experimental identification of causes. This approach is hardly suited to theology. There is also the induction that uses a loose approximation of Aristotle's search for general concepts, based on observation of empirical data. This approach is rejected on two grounds: complete induction is impossible, and, in practice, this is not the way the theologian proceeds.[15]

Theological method is best described by a third and more informal approach. For Montgomery this is called *abduction* or *retroduction*, after Peirce's terminology,[16] although the idea can be found as early as Aristotle.[17] On the other hand, Holmes calls his method *adduction*.[18] The difference in terminology notwithstanding, both men expound a similar methodology. While both induction and deduction are employed, no easy formula is suggested for combining the two. A paradigm, or conceptual model, is formulated through an informed and creative thinking process, generally involving the data to be explained, and is then brought back, adduced, or tested against the data for "fit," or accuracy. The method is found in theory formulation and justification in science. The theory is not created strictly by induction from data or phenomena nor by deduction from first principles. Yet both induction and deduction operate in the imagination of the scientist so that a theory is born. The same general method is true in theology. The theologian may deal with the relationship between certain propositions, leading him to make deductive inferences. At the same time, he develops doctrine from his understanding of the scriptural phenomena. But it should be noted that neither deduction nor induction operates in any formal sense.[19]

Montgomery gives a helpful example of the operation of abduction or retroduction in science. He cites the story of James Watson and Francis Crick, who discovered the molecular structure of DNA. Watson was convinced by reasons based on genetics that the structure of DNA had to be built around two spirals. The key question was the arrangement of the spirals. Watson and Crick built a model and tirelessly sought to rearrange the spirals in such a way as to get it to work. One night Crick had an intuitive revelation: the two spirals had to be symmetrical—they coiled in opposite directions, one top to bottom and the other bottom to top. This theory seemed to reflect certain laws of crystallography. It turned out to be true! The thing that is noteworthy is that both induction and deduction were at work but, as said before, in a very informal way.[20]

The one point of difference between Montgomery and Holmes is that Montgomery says nothing about a doctrine of Scripture being formulated by this method. As a matter of fact, he seems to think that such a doctrine is a part of the data, outside of or before theologizing.[21]

On the other hand, Holmes is explicit that a doctrine of inerrancy is a product of this methodology. In about one page at the end of his article he sketches his view.[22] In a reply to Holmes, Norman Geisler objects to Holmes's treatment of the doctrine of inerrancy on two grounds: (1) the inadequacy of the bases for rejecting induction and deduction and (2) a discomfort with adduction as outlined by Holmes. Geisler concludes by arguing for a methodology that proceeds *inductively* to premises about the inspiration of the Bible guaranteeing that what it teaches is true and about the fact that the Bible teaches historical, factual material. From these premises one *deduces* that the Scripture is without error in matters of history and so on.[23]

I suspect that there is greater agreement between Holmes and Geisler than a first reading of the exchange might indicate. I think that a good deal of Geisler's concern is motivated by Holmes's unfortunate use of such terms as "extrapolation to round out the doctrine of Scripture," "a model," "a word game," and the unhappy characterization of the doctrine of inerrancy as a "second-order theological construct." Theologizing is all based on the text of Scripture and is not identical with it; so in this sense, all doctrine is "second order." In my judgment there is Scripture and there is theologizing on it.[24] On the other hand, I guess that Holmes's objection to Geisler's suggestion is that in Holmes's judgment, Geisler cannot derive his conclusion without equivocation—due to the fact that the propositions from which inerrancy is deduced must be so loaded that the fallacy of equivocation is inevitable.[25] While one might be able to derive the proposition "the Bible is inerrant," this is far short of what theologians mean when they formulate the doctrine of inerrancy.

There is, however, a deep point of agreement between Geisler (and those who defend the classical method) and Holmes and Montgomery. This point of agreement is the need for the combined methods of induction and deduction, although admittedly these men would not relate the methods in the same way.

There are, in my judgment, a number of advantages in formulating the doctrine of inerrancy by abduction or retroduction.[26] (1) Retroduction retains a methodological continuity with the rest of theology. If Holmes and Montgomery are right about retroduction being the correct method for theology in general, it is difficult, without some argument, to see why the specific doctrine of inerrancy should be methodologically different. (2) It retains both induction and deduction, albeit in an informal way, so that neither logic of the classical method is lost. (3) It places justification of the doctrine of inerrancy on a broader evidential base. In the next section I will examine the exegetical evidence of Scripture that serves as evidential justification for the doctrine of inerrancy. These considerations are more numerous than an inductive argument to two premises from which inerrancy is deducted. (4) The conclusion of a retroductive argument is much more difficult to disconfirm than that of the classical argument. This point can be illustrated in the distinction made by N. R. Hanson between pattern statements (the results of abduction) and detail statements (the results of induction alone):

> Pattern statements are different from detail statements. They are not inductive summaries of detail statements. Still the statement "It is a bird" is truly empirical. Had birds been different, or had the bird-antelope been drawn differently, "It is a bird" might not have been true. In some sense it is true. If the detail statements are empirical, the pattern statements which give them sense are also empirical—though not in the same way. *To deny a detail statement is to do something within the pattern. To deny a pattern statement is to attack the conceptual framework itself, and this denial cannot function in the same way* . . . (italics mine).[27]

If Hanson is correct—and I think he is—then concern about the certainty of the conclusion in retroduction is unnecessary. It should be remembered that the first steps in the logic of the classical method are inductive, so that the conclusion that is deduced is only from *probable* premises. (5) It gives a rationale as to why a defender of inerrancy might be justified in holding and defending the doctrine of inerrancy in spite of problems with some of the phenomena. A helpful analogue can be drawn from theory justification in science. No scientific theory is without anomalies. However, these anomalies do not necessarily disconfirm the theory if that theory fits most of the data. Rather, they show that the phenomena are not fully understood or that the theory needs further amplification. The same is true with the defender of inerrancy. Because the doctrine makes intelligible so much of the phenomena, the theologian works both with phenomena and doctrine to resolve the conflict. Such a procedure removes the doctrine of inerrancy from what some have called the "Maginot-line mentality." The inerrantist can live with difficulties, knowing that one anomaly will not disconfirm or falsify his doctrine. This is as it should be, since the inerrantist claims only that when all things are known there will be no conflict between doctrine and data. (6) It retains an important distinction between the Scripture and interpretations of (hermeneutics/exegesis) and theologizing (biblical and systematic theology) on it. It is the Bible that is inerrant; neither our interpretations nor our theologizing are infallible. (7) Finally, if point 6 is correct, it leaves open the possibility that a better formulation of a doctrine may be made. This is not to deny that the phenomena and norms or models are primarly found in the Scripture. However, retroduction allows that some better way of setting forth the biblical data may be possible and can be sought. It does not mean that subjectivism and relativism are the rule of the day.

In closing the discussion of method, one final word is in order. I am not unduly optimistic that there will be agreement on methodology. This discussion too deeply touches theological and apologetical concerns where evangelicals differ widely in approach. However, it is important to notice that, while there is diversity in method, there is unity with respect to the place and importance of Scripture.

THE EXEGETICAL EVIDENCE FROM SCRIPTURE[28]

In my judgment, the doctrine of inerrancy is built on five scriptural phenomena.

1. *The Biblical Teaching on Inspiration*

The importance of the doctrine of inspiration to inerrancy cannot be overstated. As a matter of fact, until the last century one was thought to be identical with the other. To deny inerrancy was to deny inspiration. Clearly the central passage for consideration here is 2 Timothy 3:16. While all parties to the debate recognize the importance of this verse to the doctrine, it is amazing how few actually exegete it carefully.

The interpretation of this passage involves four distinct but not unrelated questions. The first has to do with the meaning of *pasa graphē* (πᾶσα γραφή). *Pasa* may be translated either by "all" or by "every." The distinction between "all Scripture" and "every Scripture" is the difference between reference to the whole body of the Old Testament (see Gal. 3:8) and particular passages of Scripture (see Acts 8:35). It is the distinction between Scripture viewed collectively and Scripture taken distributively. Some argue emphatically for "every" on the ground that the article is absent. Others point to analogous cases where *pas* is used in a technical or semitechnical phrase and where "every" cannot possibly be meant (Acts 2:36; Eph. 2:21; 3:15; Col. 4:12). It may be, however, that in these exceptions attention is being drawn to the partitive aspect of the expression. If so, then "every" would be preferable, and the phrase would indicate that each separate part of the *graphē* is in view.[29]

There are three possible meanings here for *graphē*. It could mean any writing whatsoever, since the basic word simply means "writing"; it may refer to the Old Testament, *in toto* or in part; or it may be construed to include even recent Christian literature. It is highly unlikely that the first possibility is correct. The word *graphē* is found over fifty times in the New Testament and always means one thing—the sacred writings. Some have concluded that it has become a kind of *terminus technicus* for the sacred writings. Thus, if this occurrence refers only to *some* writing, it constitutes the sole exception. It might be objected, however, that such an exception is justified, since every other use of *graphē* has the definite article (*hē graphē, hai graphai*). The answer to that objection is that the absence of the article is due to the fact that the word has attained the status of a specialized term. With only one specific meaning it (*graphē*) can be used without the article, and the absence of the article here indicates this.[30]

The second question has to do with the meaning of *theopneustos*

(θεόπνευστος). In my judgment, the importance of this word to any discussion of Scripture is decisive. *Theopneustos* is a member of a special class of adjectives called verbal adjectives. A group of these is formed by suffixing *-tos.* Further, this particular word is a compound of *theos* ("god") and *pneō* ("breathe"). The usual translation of the term is "inspired" or "inspiration." "Inspiration" may be somewhat misleading, since it could convey the idea of God's breath being infused into the Word—that is, energizing it. God does energize His Word, but that is not the point here. Adjectives of this class either (1) have the meaning of a perfect passive participle or (2) express possibility. An example of the former is *agapētos* (ἀγαπητός, "beloved"); the latter can be seen in *anektos* (ἀνεκτός , "bearable, endurable"). The passive sense is far more common.[31] Warfield, whose exhaustive and often bypassed analysis has not been matched,[32] has concluded—after a thorough examination of eighty-six words ending in *tos* and compounded with θεός —that *theopneustos* has nothing to do with *in*-spiring, but relates to the production of sacred, authoritative Scripture. The Scriptures are the spirated breath of God. For this reason, Paul can say that the Scriptures are God's speech (Gal. 3:8, 22; Rom. 9:17). God is the author of what is recorded (Acts 13:32–35), and the entirety of Scripture is the oracle of God (Rom. 3:2). Even if it could be shown that the active idea of God's breathing His breath into the Scriptures is preferable, a strong view of inspiration would not be hindered, so long as this inspiring took place once for all at the time of the writing of the text. The main thought then would be that the *graphē* is thoroughly permeated with the breath of God.

The third interpretative question has to do with the relationship between *graphē* and *theopneustos*. Our text says formally, or technically, that it is the Scriptures, not the writers, that are inspired or God-breathed. This point is important, since some who defend their belief that the Bible is not inerrant claim that it is false to assert that the writers of the sacred text never made errors of judgment. It seems quite clear that at least once one erred in what he did, for Paul tells us that he found it necessary to withstand Peter to his face (Gal. 2:11ff.). Furthermore, it is clear that at least three letters, possibly four, were written by the apostle Paul to the church at Corinth. However, only two (possibly three, depending on whether the "severe letter" was a separate letter or whether it is a part of 2 Corinthians) are preserved in our present canon. Thus, all that is required is that *Scripture* be inspired and that the extent of inspiration be identical with our present canon.

The fourth question has to do with whether *theopneustos* is to be understood as standing (1) predicatively or (2) attributively to the subject *graphē*. If the former is the case, Paul says that "every Scripture is inspired." On the other hand, if the latter is correct, then the text should read, "Every inspired Scripture" or "Every Scripture that is inspired. . . ." Both renderings are grammatically possible. It seems, however, that the predicative use of *theopneustos* is correct. These considerations are in its favor: (1) In the absence of a verb, it seems natural to construe the two adjectives (*theopneustos*, "God-breathed," and *ophelimos*, "profitable") in the same manner; (2) the construction of 2 Timothy 3:16 is identical to that of 1 Timothy 4:4, where the two adjectives are clearly predicative;[33] (3) in an attributive construction we would expect the adjective, in this case *theopneustos*, to appear before *graphē*; (4) words joined by *kai* ("and") are usually understood as linked by this conjunction; and finally, (5) the attributive interpretation seems to leave open the possibility that there might be some uninspired *graphē*.[34]

The primary argument in favor of the attributive construction is the supposed emphasis of the passage, which is said to lie not in the concept of inspiration but on the usefulness of Scripture.[35] Even if one accepts this less-likely construction, it should be noted that the attributive sense does not necessarily lead to uninspired Scriptures, as Miller so clearly demonstrates:

> At this point I should like to suggest that the implication (namely, that there are some Scriptures which are not inspired) is not necessarily in the passage at all. *Graphē* can mean only three things: If it means any writing in general (which, as we have seen, it seems never to mean in the New Testament), then it is clearly reasonable to assert that only those which are God-inspired are useful for instruction, etc. If it means the authoritative Old Testament and/or Christian literature, then it amounts to a kind of reminder that we are talking, after all, about the Scriptures, that is, the inspired writings. To speak, for example of *mortal* man is not necessarily to imply that there is any other kind (italics his).[36]

What then are the implications of this passage for our concern at hand? First, inspiration is something that has to do with the text of Scripture, surely not with the subjective interiority of the writer.[37] Such a view cannot square itself with this text. Second, the Scriptures *are* the very spirated breath of God. The view that the text becomes the Word of God when it speaks to me is, once again, outside biblical guidelines. Moreover, I think it is important to reaffirm that both the *form* and the *content* of Scripture are the very Word of God.[38] While it is true that we must resist the error of simply identifying the Word of God with an "aggregate of letters and sounds," it is nevertheless *nonsense* to think that you can separate them. The *Word* comes in *words*. Third, the doctrine of inspiration applies to *all* and to *every* Scripture. That is, the Scriptures in part and in the whole are God's Word. Note that there is no distinction between those things that are either Christological, salvific, or necessary for faith and practice and those things that are historical, scientific or incidental. Such a distinction is sometimes called limited inspiration. It is, however, not biblical. Lloyd-Jones puts the issues well:

> For the questions which immediately arise are these: Who decides what is true? Who decides what is of value? How can you discriminate between the great facts which are true and those that are false? How can you differentiate between the facts and the teaching? How can you separate this [sic] essential message of the Bible from the background in which it is presented? Not only so, but there is certainly no such division or distinction recognized in the Scripture itself. The whole Bible comes to us and offers itself to us in exactly the same way, and as a whole. There is no hint, no suspicion of a suggestion that parts of it are important and parts are not. All come to us in the same form.[39]

Although it is indeed a large and heavy burden to have to defend the Bible on all points, it is nevertheless necessary! It seems to me that those who could "relieve" us of this task overlook two quite important matters. The first is that it is simply impossible to separate the historical from the theological. They thoroughly interpenetrate one another. While the evangelical who believes the Bible is not inerrant may want to free us from the burden of defending the historical accuracy of the accounts of Pekah's reign because he cannot believe the accounts, the unbeliever cannot accept the historical nature of a resurrection. Why defend one and not the other? Certainly, the latter is much more difficult to accept than the former. The second point relates to the consequences of divorcing the historical and factual from the doctrinal and theological. Suppose for a moment that I am an unbeliever. You have just told me that the Bible has numerous inaccuracies of a historical, scientific, and possibly even ethical nature, but that it is absolutely without error in all of those wonderful, "unbelievable" things about God and heaven. Being a bit cynical, I would likely respond that you stretch the bounds of credulity in asking me to believe all these things that I have no possible way of confirming while at the same time allowing that there are numerous errors in areas that I *can* confirm. Can you blame me? It seems that our Lord sees more connection between the believability of earthly things and heavenly things (John 3:12) than do those who defend limited inspiration.

Before leaving this discussion of inspiration, let me point out that there seems to be at least one serious objection to our using this as such a strong datum in support of the doctrine of inerrancy. It has often been objected that a view such as the one I have been arguing is just too simple or one-sided. The objection is stated in a number of different ways. Sometimes it is argued that the inerrantist is guilty of an error analogous to the christological error of docetism (the denial that Christ had a human body). Others state it in terms of mechanical dictation. They argue that such a view of inspiration and inerrancy must of necessity involve not only the suspension of the abilities of the writers but also the word-by-word dictation of the *graphē*. Still others claim that this position overlooks the historical conditioning and human thought forms that must be used to convey the truth of God. Since each formulation of the objection requires a slightly different answer, I will reply to each in turn.

Does the doctrine of inerrancy lead to something like docetism? I cannot see how. Some among those who believe in inerrancy may believe that the Bible came down from heaven in a heavenly language inscribed without human hand, but they are both in the minority and wrong. The problem for those who oppose inerrancy arises because they fail to keep the biblical balance between the human and the divine. It should be remembered that it is just as wrong to overemphasize the human at the expense of the divine as it is to exalt the divine to the negation of the human. The former can be done straightforwardly by denying that the Bible is the Word of God. It may also be accomplished quite subtly, as when Bloesch suggests that the Bible is not the *immediate* Word of God but rather comes through the human medium.[40]

The problem here, at its deepest level, is a misconception about the nature of humanity. Inerrantists often use the analogy of a sinless Christ and an errorless Bible. In Christ you have both the human and the divine without sin. In the Bible you have both the human and the divine without error. Beegle's response to this is instructive. He begins by pointing out two reservations that Warfield gives in citing this analogy. Warfield says that the analogy must not be pressed too far, since (1) in Christ there is the hypostatic union, while in inscripturation there is nothing parallel to such union, and (2) in Christ the divine and the human unite to constitute a divine-human *person*, but in Scripture they only cooperate to produce a divine-human *work*. Then Beegle quotes Vawter approvingly to the effect that the analogy between sinlessness and errorlessness breaks down because sin is a disorder in man, and error is not.[41] Furthermore, in another place Beegle declares that there is nothing more consistently human than to err.

But what both Beegle and Vawter do not realize is that their claim is not strong enough. For the human element in the Scripture to necessitate errors in the text of the Bible it must be shown that errancy is essential to humanity. If so, then Adam was not human until he erred, and we will not be human in the glorified state, since we will no longer sin or err. Thus, while care must be used in pressing the analogy between Christ and the Scripture, it does show the *possibility* of an inerrant Bible, given the essential nature of humanity. Inerrancy becomes *necessary* because of the divine element.

Does the doctrine of inerrancy demand mechanical dictation? Those who oppose the doctrine often seek to push inerrantists into this mold; but this is unnecessary and unfair. I think that the proper way to express the biblical teaching on the process that produced the inspired texts is *concurrence*. That is, God and man so cooperate that the product was God's Word in human language. The author's style and personality, as well as the distinctive characteristics of the language in which he wrote, are evident in the autographs. How could this be done? The closest that one can come to an answer is the statement found in 2 Peter 2:21, but beyond that it must be admitted that what took place was a miracle, just as was the virgin birth.

Finally, do historical conditioning or context and human thought forms count against inerrancy? Not unless historical conditioning and human thought forms and language *necessarily* falsify truth. I have not seen and do not expect to see such a proof. I will say more about this below.

2. The Biblical Teaching Concerning the Accreditation of God's Message and Messenger

The second aspect of the biblical data to which the doctrine of inerrancy should appeal is the criteria set down in Scripture for the accreditation of the prophet and his message. I think this is second in importance only to the biblical teaching on inspiration and has not been used as fully as it should have been. There is a good parallel between the prophet and the Scripture. In regard to the one the communication was usually oral, although it could have been written down either at the time of reception or later; in the other the communication is written. Further, in both cases the communication has the human element as an essential part.

There are two passages in the book of Deuteronomy that bear on the subject (13:1-5 and 18:20-22). These passages contain three criteria for accreditation: (1) The prophet must not speak in the name of another god (Deut. 13:1, 2; 18:20). This criterion is obviously easy to check. The extremely serious nature of this type of false prophecy is seen in the imposition of capital punishment for the offender. Such a prophet was guilty of breaking the first commandment and was thus deserving of death. (2) The prophet must not speak a word that is not true (Deut. 13:1-5; 18:22). This and the following criterion are meant to distinguish what is God's Word from what is merely human. In 18:22, "the word does not come true (RSV)" is literally "the word is not." The point is that the word has no substance or that it is not so. "That is, the word supposedly spoken by God through the prophet was not in accord with the word of God already revealed and it was therefore automatically suspect."[42] There is harmony within the revealed will of God. (3) The prophet must not speak what does not come to pass (Deut. 18:22). This criterion refers to the judgmental or predicative word of the prophet. The truth of his words would be demonstrated in their fulfillment or failure. The prophet is accredited by the *total, absolute* truthfulness of his words.

3. The Bible's Teaching Concerning Its Own Authority

Evangelicals of all types are anxious to affirm the absolute authority of Scripture, making this an important consideration. Obviously many more passages could be cited,[43] but I will discuss only the two that, in my judgment, are most significant.

The first passage is Matthew 5:17–20. It is well known to those who have closely followed the debate over the Bible. Jesus is pointing out that a righteousness greater than that of the Pharisees is necessary for entrance into the kingdom (v. 20). In this context He talks about the authoritative and continuing nature of the law as a standard. He did not come to destroy it (v. 17). Moreover, until everything is fulfilled, heaven and earth will not pass away (v. 18). The Law's authority can be seen in the fact that every minutia will be fulfilled.

The second passage is John 10:34, 35. In a disputation with the Jews, Jesus cites Psalm 82:6, after which He says that "Scripture cannot be broken" (v. 35). Our Lord here speaks of the absolutely binding nature of the authority of Scripture.

What kind of response do those who oppose inerrancy give? Hubbard's reply is significant. With respect to Matthew 5:17–20, his answer is twofold. First, he says that the context does not support a definition of inerrancy that entails absolute accuracy down to the smallest details, namely, the "smallest letter" and the "least stroke of a pen." "The heart of the argument, then, is . . . [the] binding, persevering quality of the divine commands that Jesus did not abolish but fulfilled."[44] Second, Hubbard maintains, much of the strong language in the Sermon on the Mount—such as "until heaven and earth disappear" and "smallest letter" and "least stroke of a pen"—is hyperbole. Of some of this language Hubbard says, "A literal interpretation would not only encourage self-maiming, it would surely limit the number of times that one could discipline himself in temptation."[45] Thus the binding or authoritative nature of the law is stressed.

While one may allow that there are *some* examples of hyperbole in the Sermon on the Mount, it is simply false to claim that everything is hyperbole. Hubbard must bear the burden of proof that the passage in question is hyperbole. I see no such proof.

Hubbard gives similar treatment to John 10:34, 35. Here the issue is authority, not inerrancy. Hubbard says:

Jesus' argument seems to focus on the authority of his citation from Psalm 82:6. The statement "Scripture cannot be broken" is virtually an appeal on his part to what his Jewish opponents also believed. His aim was not to teach them new insights into the authority of Scripture, but rather to remind them of what they believed about the authority and applicability of the Scripture—an authority that made it lawful for him to be called the Son of God.[46]

I grant that these passages do not explicitly teach inerrancy and that they do not specify what a definition of inerrancy must contain. For instance, inerrancy clearly does not demand statements about "smallest letters" and "least strokes of a pen." However, Hubbard has left the ball park too early. The game is not yet over. To admit that these passages teach that the Bible is an absolute and binding authority is only to move the question one step backward. The question now before us is this: How can the Scriptures be such an authority? To what must we attribute this property? We could say that God just willed it so. However, is not a better explanation to be found in the inspiration and inerrancy of the Bible? To divorce inerrancy and authority is impossible. I have never been able to understand how one can be justified in claiming *absolute* authority for the Scriptures and at the same time deny their inerrancy. This seems to be the height of epistemological nonsense and confusion.

Let me try to illustrate the point. Suppose that I have an Amtrak railroad schedule. In describing its use to you, I tell you that it is filled with numerous errors but that it is *absolutely* authoritative and trustworthy. I think you would be extremely dubious. At least the schedule would have one thing going for it; it declares itself to be subject to change without notice. There is an objection to the point I am making, and it goes as follows: False in one thing does not make the Bible false in all it says.[47] Of course this objection is valid, but it overlooks the significant fact that if what has been said to this point is true, the Bible claims itself to be absolutely true. The Amtrak schedule makes no such claim. Beegle is aware of this reply. Thus, he says that even if his wife claims to tell the truth but is wrong, that does not mean that everything that she says is false.[48] Again, what Beegle says is true, but he has overlooked another important fact. The person speaking with respect to the Bible is not his wife but *God*. This is not some finite god but a God who has essential attributes that include omniscience, perfect goodness, and omnipotence. These make a big difference.

4. *The Way in Which Scripture Is Used by Scripture*

A fourth important phenomenon to observe is the way in which Scripture uses other Scripture in argumentation. The instances may be divided into three classes. First, there are those instances where the whole argument rests on a single word. In Matthew 22:43–45, the entire argument rests on the word *Lord*. Jesus cites Psalm 110:1 and appeals to the use of "Lord" as support for His claim to deity. In John 10:34, 35, Jesus' argument rests on the use of the single word *god* in Psalm 82:6.

Second, there is an instance where the entire argument depends on the tense of a verb. In Matthew 22:32, Jesus uses the present tense of the verb to demonstrate the truth of the resurrection. He says, "'I am the God of Abraham, the God of Isaac, and the God of Jacob.' He is not the God of the dead but of the living."

Third, in Galatians 3:16, we have an argument where the point depends on the singular number, *seed,* as opposed to the plural, *seeds.* Paul writes: "The promises were spoken to Abraham and to his seed. The Scripture does not say 'and to seeds,' meaning many people, but 'and to your seed,' meaning one person who is Christ." Now, if the text of Scripture is not inerrant, it is difficult to see the point in these arguments.[49] An easy rebuttal would be, "Well, the text may be wrong."

There is an objection that might be made against the argument just given. One might argue that there are many uses of Scripture by Scripture where the precision that I have spoken of is not demonstrated. For instance, certain uses of the Old Testament by New Testament writers seems to be very imprecise. A totally satisfactory answer to this objection would take far more space than allowed in this chapter. However, a meticulous study of these uses of the Old Testament reveals that the writers do not quote the Old Testament cavalierly but with great care.

5. *The Biblical Teaching Concerning the Character of God*

More than once in Scripture we are told that God cannot lie (Num. 23:19; 1 Sam. 15:29; Titus 1:2; Heb. 6:18). Furthermore, in Romans 3:4 Paul emphatically declares that God is true and that His trustfulness cannot be changed by the lack of faith that some have. Jesus said to God, "Your word is truth" (John 17:17). If the Scriptures are from God and His character is behind them, it seems that they cannot be in error.

Having surveyed the exegetical data of Scripture that support a doctrine of inerrancy, let us try to formulate a definition of inerrancy.

A DEFINITION OF INERRANCY

One of the factors that makes generalization about the biblical data concerning itself so difficult is the already-mentioned fact that Scripture makes no explicit statement on this matter. Although such a statement would not settle the matter decisively, as I have argued above, it would give us a running start. Lacking this, however, we must begin with a search for appropriate terminology. A number of terms have been suggested. The most common are: inspiration, indefectibility, infallibility, indeceivability, and inerrant, or without error. Let us now turn to an examination of these terms.

As has already been indicated, for at least a fair number of biblical and theological scholars of former days *inspiration* was synonymous with inerrancy. To say that the Bible is inspired was to say that it is absolutely accurate or inerrant. Two men among those who held such a view were B. B. Warfield and Charles Hodge. Today such identification tends to be more confusing than helpful. Thus I think it wise to search for another, more appropriate, term.

A second possibility, suggested by Hans Kung, is *indefectibility*.[50] Indefectibility means abiding or remaining in the truth in spite of errors that touch even on doctrine. One can hardly do better than the judgment of Bloesch on this matter: "This seems to call into question the absolute normativeness of Scripture in the church's understanding of the truth of revelation."[51] This term is clearly at odds with the data presented above. We must find a better one.

Another possibility is *infallibility*, which has a long history of theological use. Most likely the best place to begin a discussion of the term is with a definition from the *Oxford English Dictionary*. Infallibility means "the quality or fact of being infallible or exempt from liability to err" or "the quality of being unfailing or not liable to fail; unfailing certainty."[52] With the adjective *infallible* when predicated of things, this dictionary equates "not liable to fail, unfailing," "not liable to prove false, erroneous, or mistaken; that unfailingly holds good," or "not liable to fail in its action or operation."[53] Merely from the standpoint of definition, it would be difficult to maintain a *clear* distinction between this term and inerrancy, although it would always be possible to stipulate a distinction.

However, when we turn to the question of usage, the picture is more complex. Within Roman Catholic theology, *inerrant* is normally used when discussing the Bible, while *infallible* is used to designate the authority of the church, particularly with respect to the teaching function of the pope and the magisterium. Protestants, of course, do not claim infallibility for the church, and, more and more, *infallibility* has become associated with the Scriptures. More recently, it has become a term championed by many who support what has been called limited inspiration, or what today might better be called limited inerrancy. That is, those who often advance this word to the exclusion of inerrancy would, at most, defend the inerrancy of the Scriptures in areas that are "revelational," "soteriological," or are "matters of faith and doctrine." Because of the differing usages of *infallibility*, Stephen T. Davis in his recent book gives a stipulative definition reflecting this tendency. He says, "The Bible is infallible if and only if it makes no false or misleading statements on any matter of faith and practice."[54] At any rate, *infallibility* can and should properly be used of the Bible. In its lexical meaning it is not far from *inerrancy*.

Another candidate is *indeceivability*. It is questionable whether the term per se has been used to express the biblical attitude about itself. However, a long list of theologians—Briggs,[55] Berkouwer,[56] Rogers,[57] Hubbard,[58] and Bloesch[59]—like to affirm that the Bible is without error in the sense suggested by this term. These men are evangelical in their theology and have a real love and respect for the Scriptures; but they think the Bible contains inaccuracies of various kinds and thus do not like the word *inerrancy*. They would rather stick with a designation such as "without error," defined in terms of indeceivability.

Let us take a moment to examine their argument, since this position seems to be gaining wider acceptance within evangelical circles. Usually the starting place is displeasure with the word *inerrancy*, for various reasons that are discussed below. Theologians like those mentioned above prefer to speak of the Bible's authority or even its infallibility. Some can live with a statement on Scripture like that found in the Lausanne Covenant, which states that the Bible is "without error in all that it affirms."

There is a caveat. *Error* must be defined. Since it is such an important term, it is argued, we must not let just anyone specify its meaning. The place a definition must be sought is in the Scriptures themselves. The advantage, so it is claimed, is that we will not then be imposing an alien standard on the Bible. It is as though the imprecision of early historical writing is preserved in the meaning of the word *error*. For someone like Berkouwer, "without error" means free from lying and fraud.[60] For Rogers, "error" means "willful deception," and for Hubbard, "that which leads us astray from the will of God or the knowledge of his truth."[61] Thus, error becomes associated with (1) the intentionality of the writer or text and (2) the will of God, particularly as it has to do with religious or spiritual truth.[62]

What shall we say about such a proposal? There are at least two commendatory things that can be said about this attempt to reflect the attitude of the Bible toward itself. First, it recognizes that errorlessness in some sense must be attributed to the Scriptures. Second, it seeks to deal seriously with the biblical data.

There are, in my judgment, however, three reasons—methodological, biblical, and motivational—for thinking that this approach is inadequate in the final analysis. First, there is a methodological reason. As I have already stated, there is no explicit statement in Scripture to the effect that it is without error. If there were, then it would certainly be appropriate to start our definition with a study of the etymology and usage of the Hebrew and Greek terms used in this connection, but such is not possible. Error or inerrancy are theological concepts;[63] that is, they are used by the theologian to express what he thinks the biblical data demand. This fact, however, in no way counts a priori against *any* concept. For instance, *trinity* is in the same boat, since it is not to be found, *as a term*, anywhere in the Bible. As I have argued earlier, even biblical terms, when used in doctrinal or theological statements, are subject to the same constraints as are any formulations about inerrancy or error.

My second reason for rejecting the term *indeceivability* is biblical. It may be that some do not agree with the distinction between biblical and theological usage, but let us move to the level of the biblical for a moment. Let it be granted that Berkouwer, Rogers, et al., are methodologically right and I am wrong. I would still think that their conclusions are open to serious question. The reason is this: Any definition of error in terms of indeceivability as defined above appeals to too selective a sample of biblical vocabulary. To put it another way, indeceivability fails to reflect the polydimensionality of the biblical words for error. In both Hebrew and Greek the words may be classified into three groups: (1) errors where intentionality cannot possibly be involved; (2) errors where intentionality may or may not be involved; and (3) errors where intentionality must be involved. Let us take a quick look at each of these groups.

Clearly, the Bible teaches that some errors are made without intentionality.[64] Old Testament words coming from שָׁגַג (shāgag) and שָׁגָה (shāgâ) are good examples. The idea is "to stray," "to err," even "to transgress inadvertently."[65] In Job 6:24, Job says, "Teach me, and I will be quiet; show me where I have been wrong." In view of Job's contention that he was innocent he had to maintain that any error on his part was unintentional, since he was unaware of it. Again in Job 19:4 we read, "If it is true that I have gone astray, my error remains my concern alone." One cannot, without doing violence to the text, maintain that Job is referring to intentional error. It might be argued that Scripture does not hold an individual responsible for inadvertent error. But this too is simply false. From the Hebrew roots mentioned above the Old Testament has words for sins of ignorance. Leviticus 5:18 says, "He is to bring to the priest as a guilt offering a ram from the flock, one without defect and of the proper value. In this way the priest will make atonement for him for the wrong he has committed *unintentionally*, and he will be forgiven." The same is true of Greek. The word for this kind of error is ἀγνόημα (agnoēma). It means a "sin committed in ignorance."[66] In Hebrews 9:7 it is used of sins of ignorance: "But only the high priest entered the inner room, and that only once a year, and never without blood, which he offered for himself and for the sins the people had committed in ignorance."

The second class of terms has to do with errors where intentionality may or may not be involved. This seems to be the largest group. In the Old Testament a good example from this classification is שַׁל (shal). It means "a fault" or "error," and comes from the root שָׁלָה (shālâh, "to deceive" or "to be negligent").[67] It is used in 2 Samuel 6:7. Here it is difficult to tell if intentional deception or simply negligence is involved. The Greek ἀστοχέω (astocheō) means "to miss the mark."[68] The word is used three times in the New Testament (1 Tim. 1:6; 6:21;

2 Tim. 2:18). Here again, in my judgment, it is impossible to determine whether one misses the mark intentionally or unintentionally.

Finally, there is a group of words used for error that clearly includes the idea of intentionality. In the Old Testament תָּעָה (ta ʾāh) and תַּעְתֻּעִים (tā ʿʿtuʿim) are used. The first of these terms is used in the Hiphil and has as one of its meanings "to seduce,"[69] while the latter means "a fraud."[70] In the New Testament there are also two words that fall within this class, ἀποπλαγάω (apoplagaō) and πλανή (planē). The former term can mean "to seduce,"[71] the latter, "fraudulence."[72] Moreover, it is possible to cite at least two instances where lies are told with good intentions, but they are called lies nevertheless (Judg. 16:10). Authorial intention is indeed important, but its relevance is related to hermeneutics.

As should be noted from the discussion, greater emphasis has been placed on the first classification. This was done to show the inadequacy of the proposal before us. Fundamentally, the problem is that this proposal seeks to retain a good term but at too high a price—a decided weakening of meaning. For instance, if we accept Rogers's understanding of error as "willful deception," then most books ever written are inerrant.

The third reason that I find the proposal of indeceivability inadequate is motivational. In practice there is the retention of the idea of errorlessness that has a long and important history but it has been so diluted that it no longer retains its original meaning. The motivation behind this approach is not a more precise definition of *error* or *inerrancy* but ultimately the recognition of "unimportant" errors of history, science, and so forth. It is the first step in undermining the doctrine of inerrancy.

The final possibility that I have raised for an appropriate term is *inerrant,* that is "without error." *Inerrancy* itself is a relatively young word in the English language. At first it appears as though it might be a transliteration of the Latin word *inerrantia,* a participle from the verb *inerro.* However, such is not the case. *Inerrans* is used of fixed stars by Cicero and Lactantius. Boethius, who lived in the latter part of the sixth century and the early part of the seventh, used the Latin term *inerratum* in the sense of "absence of error."[73] The *Oxford English Dictionary* says that it was not until 1837 that the English *inerrant* was used in the modern sense of "exempt from error, free from mistake, infallible." Moreover, the noun *inerrancy* is said to have occurred for the first time in Thomas Hartwell Horne's formidable four-volume *Introduction to the Critical Study and Knowledge of the Holy Scriptures* (1780–1862).[74] In part 2 of volume 2 of the seventh edition (1834) he states, "Absolute inerrancy is impracticable in any printed book."[75] It is, however, possible that the word appeared as early as the first edition in 1818.

In current usage the *Oxford English Dictionary* offers this definition of *inerrancy*: "the quality or condition of being inerrant or unerring; freedom from error." For *inerrant* it gives "does not err; free from error; unerring."[76] On the other hand, *errant* is defined as follows: "the action or state of erring"; "the condition of erring in opinion; the holding of mistaken notions or beliefs"; or "something incorrectly done through ignorance or inadvertence; a mistake."[77] It is easy to see why some equate "without error" with "inerrant."

As I have noted, not all evangelicals like the designation *inerrancy*. Why is this so? Obviously, there are many reasons, stated and otherwise.

LaSor says,

> Those who defend the "inerrancy of the Bible" generally mean by that word that the Bible contains no error of any kind, whether religious, historical, geographical, geological, numerical, or of any other category. The term is not proper, for since it negates a negative idea, it does not leave room for a correct opposite.[78]

Inerrancy is unacceptable because it is essentially the negation of a negative concept. The consequence, LaSor goes on to say, is that the opposite of inerrancy is not errancy but the total infallibility of the Bible in matters of faith and practice. LaSor then points out what he thinks are scriptural problems, even inconsistencies, although he hesitates to call them outright errors.[79] One surely may wonder at this use of logic and language. Inconsistencies most certainly are errors.

Ridderbos[80] and Piepkorn[81] do not like the word *inerrancy* because it is not a biblical word. Piepkorn states the case clearly: "Lutheran clergymen and professors affirm everything that the Sacred Scriptures say about themselves and everything that the Lutheran symbols say about the Sacred Scriptures. It is significant therefore that the term 'inerrancy' does not correspond to any vocable in the Lutheran symbols."[82] Ridderbos thinks it is a theological concept.[83] On the other hand, Piepkorn classifies it as "an ecclesiastical term subject to definition by use."[84]

By far the most extensive criticism of the term *inerrancy* that I have seen comes from Pinnock. It should be noted that he has been one of the most able defenders of the doctrine of the inerrancy of the Bible and even now continues to claim that this is a good term.[85] His reasons for suggesting at least a moratorium on its use are as follows. First, he sees the word as needing major qualifications. Such words are a liability and should be avoided where possible. Second, the term does not describe any Bible that we in fact use. It refers only to the original autographs. Third, since it refers to a nonextant text, it does not assert forcibly the authority of the texts that we do have. Fourth, it misfocuses attention on the small or minor difficulties in the text rather than on the truth it intends to explain. Finally, it has become a slogan and as such is a term of "conflict and ill-feeling."[86] Thus Pinnock can conclude:

> It seems to me, in view of the serious disadvantages the term inerrancy presents, that we ought to suspend it from the list of preferred terminology for stating the evangelical doctrine of Scripture, and let it appear only in the midst of the working out of the details. It is sufficient for us in our public statements to affirm the divine inspiration and final authority of the Bible.[87]

One should not merely dismiss Pinnock's concerns without consideration. However, one may also wonder why *inerrancy* does not forcibly enough assert the authority of the Bible. Possibly there is need to express the biblical view in more than just *one* term. Nevertheless, this should not count against the use of a word if indeed it is appropriate. And the fact that it may be a slogan or may misdirect the attention of some is unfortunate, but if the concept that it seeks to convey is correct, then we must use it or a better term. All of this is just to say that I do not have an inalienable affection for the word. It is the concept of a *wholly true* Bible for which I contend. If some better word can be found, then let us use it.

But what is needed, I think, is a more clear and precise definition of inerrancy rather than a new term. People surely accept or reject the word without agreeing with or even knowing what someone else means by it.

It seems to me that the key concept both in the Scriptures and in the minds of those who use the term is truthfulness. Inerrancy has to do with *truth*. Hence, the positive side of the negative idea is that if the Bible is *inerrant*, it is *wholly true*. If this is the case, there are two ways in which the idea could be preserved. First, we could drop the term *inerrant* from the list of preferred terminology and substitute *always true and never false*. Rather than saying, "I believe the Bible is inerrant," we could say, "I believe the Bible is always or wholly true and never false." Second, we could continue using *inerrant* and clearly specify that it is always to be associated with *truth*.

Since the second is more likely to have widespread use, let me propose this definition of inerrancy. *Inerrancy means that when all facts are known, the Scriptures in their original autographs and properly interpreted will be shown to be wholly true in everything that they affirm, whether that has to do with doctrine or morality or with the social, physical, or life sciences.*

I would be willing to contend that inerrancy defined in terms of truth is a legitimate way of reflecting the biblical data. In Psalm 119, the most extended biblical statement on the Word of God, "truth" or "true" is used three times as a characterization: "Your law is true" (v. 142); "all your commands are true" (v. 151); and "all your words are true" (v. 160). Proverbs 30:5, 6 say that "every word of God has proven true" (Berkeley Version). In John 17:17 Jesus says, "Your word is truth." It is this idea that is appropriate to the English word *inerrancy*. Such a definition has the advantage of defining a negative in terms of a positive concept. Conversely, it means that the Bible is never false.

Only half the job is now done. *Truth* or *true* must be defined. Although the Bible points to truth as an essential attribute of God, it does not give us a precise theological definition. We rather see the definition in the use of the word. However, truth is an abstract and possibly ambiguous term. There is always the danger that one will only move the debate from a discussion of *error* to a debate over the meaning of *truth* or *true*.

For pristine simplicity and clarity one can hardly beat Aristotle's definitions of true and false. He said, "To say what is, is, and what is not, is not, is true. And to say what is, is not, and what is not, is, is false."[88]

More recently, the work of a Polish logician named Tarski has proved exceedingly helpful with regard to defining truth.[89] Tarski reduced the notion of truth to certain other semantic notions that were clearly—or better, widely—acceptable. The characteristics of Tarski's definition are as follows: (1) Truth is defined in terms of *language*; (2) truth is defined in terms of *sentences* (that is, truth is a property of sentences), not of individual words; and (3) truth is defined in terms of *correspondence*.[90]

OBSERVATIONS, QUALIFICATIONS, AND MISUNDERSTANDINGS

Having defined the term *inerrancy*, now let me turn to its elaboration as a doctrine. This elaboration will take the form of some observations, some qualifications, and finally some misunderstandings of the doctrine of inerrancy. The purpose of these considerations is to guide us in the application of the doctrine to the remaining phenomena of Scripture.

Observations

First, let me make two observations.

1. *No doctrine of inerrancy can determine in advance the solution to individual or specific problem passages.* The doctrine of inerrancy only gives guidelines or parameters for the handling of individual passages. It gives us the kind of phenomena over which a doctrine of inerrancy can range. It tells us that there is some sense in which what is affirmed is true. This does not guarantee universal agreement as to how a problem passage should be treated and the difficulty dissolved. Undoubtedly there will be debate as to which interpretation is best.

2. *Inerrancy is a doctrine that must be asserted, but which may not be demonstrated with respect to all the phenomena of Scripture.* There is in this definition of inerrancy the explicit recognition of both the fallibility and the finiteness of the present state of human knowledge. There are really only these two choices: either the theologian will trust the word of an omnipotent, omniscient God, who says that He controlled human agents, making it necessary for the theologian to admit his fallibility as critic, or in some sense he will declare that the aforementioned control is restricted and will affirm at least his own relative and finite omniscience as critic. Since Christ exhibited total trust in the Scriptures, can we do less? All that is claimed is that there is no final conflict with truth.

It might be objected that such a doctrine is unfalsifiable and therefore, if one were to use old positivist jargon, meaningless. There is, however, a twofold response that can and should be made against such criticism. First, such a view of inerrancy is not *in principle* unfalsifiable. There is no logical reason for our inability to gather all the facts. We can think of a world quite like ours but where we were actually in possession of all the facts. In such a world the Bible could be demonstrated as inerrant. Second, as a matter of fact, just such a world will be realized as the *eschaton*. *In practice* we will be in possession of all the facts, and then it will be shown that there is no final conflict.

Yet some might justifiably object that such a demonstration at the *eschaton* is of little help to them *now*. How is one to decide the question of the inerrancy of the Bible *now*? The answer is that there is evidence for inerrancy *now*, and that evidence is better than for any alternative view. First, there is the teaching of Scripture itself. Second, external evidence to the Bible (e.g., archaeology), while not without some problems, has confirmed the truthfulness of the Scripture over and over again.

Qualifications

There are, I think, just three qualifications that must be made to the doctrine of inerrancy. They are as follows.

1. *Inerrancy applies equally to all parts of the Scripture as originally written (autographa).* The doctrine of inerrancy applies only to the autographa, not to any copy of Scripture. This qualification is often objected to on the grounds that it serves as a neat hedge against disproving the doctrine. That is, any time there is a difficulty, one can assign the problem to the copy, claiming it does not exist in the original. Indeed, such a qualification can be a hedge, *but it need not be.* The qualification simply grows out of the recognition that *any* copy will contain some errors due to transmission.

It might be argued that, if we no longer possess the autographs, the qualification is meaningless. Such an objection is only justified on one of two grounds, neither of which applies to the Bible. The first ground is the lack of an adequate discipline of textual criticism, which is hardly the case with Scripture. The second basis is a text so corrupt that even the canons of textual criticism could not make it intelligible. Again, such is not the case in regard to Scripture.

Still one might object that such a qualification is unnecessary, since the Spirit of God uses and blesses the existent, errant copies that we possess today. The reference to autographs is another example of evangelical overbelief. Again, I think the objection is false. Those who make this objection fail to recognize the difference between an original that is inerrant but to which errors have been added through transmission and an original that has substantive errors and has been further corrupted in transmission. With respect to the former, an inerrant text can be approached through textual criticism, while in the latter case, any attempt to discover an inerrant text would be hopeless. One can formulate a parallel objection with regard to a perfectly *interpreted* Bible, and a parallel answer can be given.

2. *Inerrancy is intimately tied up with hermeneutics.* Hermeneutics is the science of biblical interpretation. Though another chapter covers this topic specifically, three short comments seem appropriate here. First, the common distinction between the Bible as given and as interpreted must be made. Though the Scriptures as given are completely true, no human interpretation of them is infallible. Second, inerrancy has as a precondition the proper application of hermeneutics. If one does not know the correct meaning of the text, he will never be justified in claiming that it is *false*. Third, a key principle in the application of hermeneutics is the analogy of faith as taught by the Reformers. This principle merely says that we should attempt to harmonize apparently contradictory statements in the Bible. That is, if there is a way of understanding a passage so that it is in harmony with the rest of Scripture and another way of understanding that conflicts with all other Scripture or parts of Scripture, the former is the correct interpretation. This often entails consideration of progress in God's revelation—not in the sense that later revelation ever falsifies, but that it often supplements, earlier revelation. Only in this way can it be affirmed that the Bible is true in the whole and in its parts.

3. *Inerrancy is related to Scripture's intention.* The point here has two aspects. First, Scripture accurately records many things that are false, for example, the falsehoods of Satan and of human beings. This point is often made in differing ways. Sometimes it is stated in terms of what the Bible *approves* as contrasted with what it merely *affirms*. Another way of putting it is to distinguish between *historical* or *descriptive* authority and *normative* authority.[91] Historical or descriptive authority applies equally to every word of an inerrant Bible. It merely means that whatever was said or done was in fact said or done. No judgment is passed as to whether it should or should not have been said or done. Norma-

tive authority, on the other hand, not only means that what was said or done was actually so but also that it should or should not have been said or done.

It should be noted again that there will not always be universal agreement as to whether a given statement falls within historical authority or normative authority. Gerstner makes the point this way:

> Suppose they [the biblical writers] did think of a three-storied universe, which was the common opinion in their day, the Bible does not err unless it teaches such as a divine revelation of truth. In fact, by showing that the writers may have personally entertained ideas now antiquated it reveals its own historical authenticity without its normative authenticity suffering.[92]

Some may be a bit surprised at such a solution. Hence Pinnock's word is in order:

> The device is certainly a neat one, and gets us around some real difficulties. However, it conceals a hazardous principle. In admitting errors into the text itself, even into the body of teaching that text affords, the point is conceded to the critics of the Bible in every age; namely, that the actual teachings of Scripture may, or may *not,* be true.[93]

The point to be made here is that we cannot preclude in advance the possibility that some of the historically or descriptively authoritative material may contain errors.[94] This does not, however, admit errors into what I have called the *teaching of Scripture.* At the same time great caution must be used in invoking this solution, since it is fraught with hazards.

Second, Scripture's intention is found in the *meanings* of the biblical sentences. I use the term *Scripture's* rather than *author's* intention to make it clear that the latter is contained in the former, or, to put it another way, the determination of intention is a hermeneutical, not psychological, task.

Misunderstandings

Finally, I think it is helpful to enumerate and discuss some misunderstandings of the doctrine of inerrancy. For some who criticize inerrancy, these would be considered qualifications. One of the grounds on which they reject the doctrine is that to be maintained it must be qualified in such a way that it becomes meaningless. I think the objection is false and specify why in the discussion below. The misunderstandings of which I speak are as follows.

1. *Inerrancy does not demand strict adherence to the rules of grammar.* One of the advantages of defining inerrancy in terms of truth and defining truth as a property of sentences is that the question of whether a grammatical error precludes an inerrant Bible is transcended. The answer is clearly no. This is as it should be. The rules of grammar are merely statements of normal usage of the language. Every day skilled writers break them in the interest of superior communication. Why should the writers of Scripture be denied this privilege?

2. *Inerrancy does not exclude the use either of figures of speech or of a given literary genre.* It is recognized by all that Scripture employs figures of speech. Some examples are meiosis (Gal. 5:14), hyperbole (Matt. 2:3), synecdoche (Gal. 1:16), personification (Gal. 3:8), and metonymy (Rom. 3:30). Figures of speech are common to ordinary communication and cannot be said to express falsehoods simply because they are not literal. While it may not always be easy to determine whether language is figurative or literal, there is nothing inherent in figurative language that prevents it from properly expressing truth and meaning.[95]

Moreover, various literary genres are employed in Scripture. There is narrative, dramatic, and apocalyptic literature. The Psalms are poetic in form. The literary style or form has nothing to do with the *truth* or *falsity* of the content conveyed in that style. Understanding of the form does, however, help in interpretation. Much more could be said here, but the issue is properly within the domain of hermeneutics.

3. *Inerrancy does not demand historical or semantic precision.* It is often stated that the doctrine of inerrancy cannot be accepted because the Bible does not reflect the canons of historical and linguistic precision recognized and required in the modern world. Like so many words used in the debate between inerrantists and errantists, *precision* is ambiguous. To some, *imprecision* has a connotation of error. This surely need not be so. As some of the divines of past ages put it, all that is necessary is that statements be adequate. I interpret this in terms of truth. Almost any statement is capable of greater precision. Any historiography, even a detailed chronicle, is still only an approximation. Let me illustrate. If we record an event as having transpired in 1978, we could obviously have said it more precisely—in the month of

May, on the 15th day, at the hour of 10 p.m., and so on. But the
original, simpler statement would still be true. The crucial point
as I see it for inerrancy is this: Is a sentence as stated *true*? If so,
there is no problem for the doctrine. Why should the modern
criterion of precision be absolutized? Should we not expect Scripture to reflect the standards of its day? Is it not arrogant to think
that our standards are right and theirs wrong?

4. *Inerrancy does not demand the technical language of modern science.*
One should not expect the writers of Scripture to use the language of modern scientific empiricism. First, it was not their
intention to provide a scientific explanation for all things. Second, popular or observational language is used even today by the
common man. As a matter of fact, the modern scientist also uses
it in certain contexts. We say, for example, that the sun "rises"
and "sets." This in no way entails a theory of solar revolution. I
am not convinced that this is not the way in which we are to
understand the so-called "three-storied" universe. Unless one
takes the statements of Scripture in crass geographic terms, I do
not see the inappropriateness of such language. I think that
much of the concern comes from a presumed similarity to certain
contemporary myths. But why should this presumption be
made? My contention is that if there is a sense in which the
"scientific" language of Scripture is true, then the doctrine of
inerrancy is not threatened. Third, it must be noted that there
are many philosophers of science who would hold that all scientific theories about the nature of reality are not descriptive but
solely instrumental or operational.[96] Thus, to absolutize the
present language of science is to be out on a limb, with someone—perhaps even a scientist—sawing away at the branch!

Let me again state the possibility that certain alleged scientific
problems may be accounted for in the distinction between descriptive or historical authority and normative authority.

5. *Inerrancy does not require verbal exactness in the citation of the Old
Testament by the New*. In some ways this issue is obscured by
discussing it in terms of the Old Testament *quotations* in the New.
For this reason I have used what I hope is a more neutral
word—*citation*. Quotation immediately gives one the picture of
our present linguistic conventions of quotation marks, ellipses,
brackets, and references. None of this was a part of the Hebrew
and Greek of biblical times. When we quote today, we quote
with verbal exactness, or we note that we have deviated from this

through one of the aforementioned conventions. However, we cite statements in many ways besides quotation. We use indirect discourse, general reference, and summary. When we recall a statement or event, we often give only the gist or general idea of what was exactly said or done. Such practice was common in the New Testament (as it has been throughout literary history), and there are no conventions to advise us which method of citation is being employed in a given passage. Furthermore, citation of any kind in the New Testament involved translation. Since the Old Testament was in Hebrew, it had to be translated into Greek, either by the New Testament writer himself or by someone else, such as a translator of the Septuagint.[97]

6. *Inerrancy does not demand that the* Logia Jesu *(the sayings of Jesus) contain the* ipsissima verba *(the exact words) of Jesus, only the* ipsissima vox *(the exact voice).* This point is closely akin to the one just made. When a New Testament writer cites the sayings of Jesus, it need not be that Jesus said those exact words. Undoubtedly the exact words of Jesus are to be found in the New Testament, but they need not be so in every instance. For one thing, many of the sayings were spoken by our Lord in Aramaic and therefore had to be translated into Greek. Moreover, as was mentioned above, the writers of the New Testament did not have available to them the linguistic conventions that we have today. Thus it is impossible for us to know which of the sayings are direct quotes, which are indirect discourse, and which are even freer renderings.[98] With regard to the sayings of Jesus what, in light of these facts, would count against inerrancy? If the sense of the words attributed to Jesus by the writers was not uttered by Jesus, or if the exact words of Jesus are so construed that they have a sense never intended by Jesus, then inerrancy would be threatened.

7. *Inerrancy does not guarantee the exhaustive comprehensiveness of any single account or of combined accounts where those are involved.* This point is somewhat related to the early statement on precision. It must be remembered that from the standpoint of any discipline, even theology, the Scriptures are partial. Often *partial* is misunderstood to mean incorrect or false. But this idea itself is false. The Bible is a complete revelation of all that man needs for faith and practice. That is, there are many things we might like to know but which God has not seen fit to reveal. It is also true that God has not seen fit to record every detail of every account.

I think that this point has implications in another direction also, namely, that of the Gospel accounts. The problems in the Gospels are well known and cannot possibly be dealt with in the limited space available here. However, a giant step forward in the quest to resolve the problems will be taken when one realizes that none of the evangelists is obligated to give an exhaustive account of any event. He has the right to record an event in light of his purposes. Moreover, it must be remembered that the accounts of all four Gospel writers together do not exhaust the details of any event mentioned. There may be some unknown bit of information that would resolve seeming conflicts. All that is required is that the sentences used by the writer be true.

8. *Inerrancy does not demand the infallibility or inerrancy of the noninspired sources used by biblical writers.* Form and redaction criticism of the biblical texts raised the question of sources as it had never been raised before. These forms of literary criticism make it necessary to face the possibility that the use of noninspired sources is much more widespread than was previously thought.[99] Thus, two comments are in order. The definition and doctrine of inerrancy here advocated does not rule out a priori the possibility, or even probability, that sources are cited with historical and descriptive authority but not normative authority. That is, the errors that these noninspired sources contain are accurately recorded, since Scripture's intention is not to approve those errors as true.[100]

SOME FINAL OBJECTIONS

Throughout the course of this chapter I have tried to deal at least with the major objections to the points made. Three additional objections are of sufficient weight to require some mention and answer. By far the most important is the first.

Has not your definition so qualified the concept of inerrancy that it is no longer meaningful? Pinnock thinks that the need for qualification is a liability and says, "This means that the discussion often has the air of unreality and even dishonesty about it."[101] Are we just avoiding the obvious fact that inerrancy is false? I do not believe so.

As a matter of fact, I seriously question whether these are qualifications at all. They are, as stated before, misunderstandings by those who reject inerrancy. If they were qualifications and they grew out of an *ad hoc* desire to prevent falsification of one's doctrine, then indeed Pinnock's and other such criticisms would be justified. However, since they are not, the picture is quite different. It must be remembered that words have more than one meaning. Thus it becomes necessary to specify which meaning is to be applied in a case in point. The more important the statement, the more precisely it needs to be specified. Notice the great care with which legal documents are prepared. What is important is the consistency of one's own treatment of a doctrine, not whether it is consistent in light of certain views imposed on it by others. Clearly it is inconsistent to hold certain views and yet claim that the Bible is inerrant, but that is not the question here. The question here is this: Is this formulation inconsistent? Or, more generally, are all formulations inconsistent?

What would really constitute a qualified view of inerrancy? In my judgment, it would be a view that retains the word and develops a doctrine, but uses the word in a sense contrary to customary usage. Such an attempt would be a case of special pleading. As I see it, our definition does not do that. It seeks to employ the term *inerrancy* in connection with *truth*, and with the usual sense of truth. I do not think these are qualifications, only attempts to specify language more precisely.

Finally, if these are indeed qualifications, they are qualifications that apply to all books, particularly those of antiquity.[102] A case of special pleading is not being advocated for the Bible. I only ask that the principle of charity, which should be used in interpreting any type of text, be applied to the Bible.

Does not the Bible itself distinguish between the authoritative Word of God and the fallible opinions of its human authors? Seeming ground for such an objection is found in 1 Corinthians 7:10 where Paul says, "To the married I give this command (not I, but the Lord)," and in verse 12 he says, "To the rest I say this (I, not the Lord)." Is this not proof positive in the text of Scripture that the Word of God must be distinguished from the fallible opinions of its human authors? Although one may interpret what Paul has to say in this way, it is neither necessary nor best. In verse 10, Paul is pointing out that what he is saying has been said before by our Lord, while in verse 12 Paul is the vehicle of new revelation. That is, what he says has not been said before. Later, in 14:37, he says that what he wrote is the command of the Lord. Thus the distinction is not between revelation and nonrevelation, infallible and fallible, but is a distinction *within* revelation (the infallible) between what is repeated by Paul and what is original with him.

Does not the apostle Paul himself contradict inerrancy in 1 Corinthians 1:16? In this passage Paul says, "Beyond that, I don't remember if I baptized anyone else." How this is supposed to bear on errancy or inerrancy is not clear. Inerrancy merely demands that the Bible is all true; it does not require total recall. Gerstner puts it well: "If Paul remembered wrongly we would have an uninspired Paul; but a Paul who does not remember is a Paul who is inspired to record that very fact for instruction (presumably, concerning the nature of Inspiration, what it does and does not include, what it does and does not exclude)."[103]

CONCLUSION

The task of this chapter has been to specify as clearly and precisely as possible what is meant by inerrancy—both the term and the doctrine. The approach used to achieve this goal was to examine the proper methodology whereby such a doctrine could be reached, then applying that method to the exegetical evidence or data. After examining a number of possible terms to express the attitude of the Bible toward itself, it was decided that among the words needed was a word to express the concept of "wholly true." It was suggested that this was the heart of the matter, whether one used *inerrancy* or not. There was, however, still a need to elaborate the way in which the doctrine functions in concrete instances. Finally, some previously unanswered objections were treated.

The conclusions of this paper concerning the doctrine of inerrancy may be summarized as follows: (1) the term *inerrancy*, like other words, is subject to misunderstanding and must be clearly defined; (2) inerrancy should be defined in terms of truth, making a number of the usual problems mute; (3) while inerrancy is not the only word that could express the concept here associated with it, it is a good word; and (4) inerrancy is not the only quality of the Bible that needs to be affirmed. After a study of the kind undertaken in this chapter, one cannot do better than to close with the words of Isaiah:

> The grass withers and the flowers fall,
>   because the breath of the LORD blows on them.
>   Surely the people are grass.
> The grass withers and the flowers fall,
>   but the word of our God stands forever.
>   (Isa. 40:7, 8)

PHILOSOPHICAL
PRESUPPOSITIONS
OF BIBLICAL ERRANCY

Norman L. Geisler

Norman L. Geisler is Professor of Systematic Theology at Dallas Theological Seminary. He is a graduate of Wheaton College, (B.A. and M.A.); Detroit Bible College, (Th.B.); and Loyola University, Chicago, (Ph.D.). He has held the positions of Christian Services Director for Northeast Suburban Youth for Christ; Pastor, Dayton Center Church, Silverwood, Michigan; Assistant Pastor, River Grove Bible Church, River Grove, Illinois; Pastor, Memorial Baptist Church, Warren, Michigan; President, Alumni of Detroit Bible College; and first president, Evangelical Philosophical Society. His teaching experience includes that of the following positions: Assistant Professor of Bible and Apologetics at Detroit Bible College, Assistant Professor of Bible and Philosophy at Trinity College, Deerfield, Illinois, Associate Professor of Philosophy at Trinity College, and Professor of Philosophy of Religion and Chairman of the Department of Philosophy of Religion, Trinity Evangelical Divinity School, Deerfield. Among his books and articles are General Introduction to the Bible; Ethics: Alternatives and Issues; Philosophy of Religion; Christ: The Key to Interpreting the Bible *(reprinted under the title of* To Understand the Bible: Look for Jesus*);* Christian Apologetics; *"Theological Method and Inerrancy: A Reply to Professor Holmes" in* Bulletin of the Evangelical Theological Society; *"Bible Manuscripts" in* Wycliffe Bible Encyclopedia; *"The Missing Premise in the Ontological Argument" in* Religious Studies; *"Analogy: The Only Answer to the Problem of Religious Language" in* Journal of the Evangelical Theological Society; *"The Christian and Social Responsibility" produced by the Development Department of Trinity Evangelical Divinity School; "A New Look at the Relevance of Thomism for Evangelical Apologetics" in* Christian Scholar's Review; *"The Extent of the Old Testament Canon" in* Current Issues in Biblical and Patristic Interpretation; *"Inerrancy of Scripture" in* The Tartan; *and "Philosophy: The Roots of Vain Deceit" in* Christianity Today. *Dr. Geisler is a member of the Evangelical Theological Society, American Philosophical Society, Evangelical Philosophical Society, and the Council of ICBI.*

CHAPTER SUMMARY

The Scriptures warn: "See to it that no one takes you captive through hollow and deceptive philosophy" (Col. 2:8). Nowhere is this danger of not heeding Paul's exhortation more apparent than in the modern neoevangelical drift from the historic biblical doctrine of inerrancy. This chapter seeks to expose some of the major philosophical presuppositions beginning with the seventeenth century that have contributed to the current crisis in biblical authority. Beginning with Francis Bacon's inductivism and proceeding through Hobbe's materialism, Spinoza's rationalism, Hume's skeptical empiricism, the authority of Scripture was progressively undermined. With Kant's agnosticism and Kierkegaard's existentialism the major philosophical presuppositions leading to a denial of the inerrancy of Scripture were firmly implanted in western theological thought. Contemporary neoevangelical denials of inerrancy borrow from one or more of these alien and unjustified philosophical presuppositions.

PHILOSOPHICAL PRESUPPOSITIONS OF BIBLICAL ERRANCY

Assuming WHAT has been well documented by others[1]—that the teaching of Jesus, the biblical writers, and virtually all of the orthodox church fathers down through the centuries have held the doctrine of the full inspiration and inerrancy of Scripture—we proceed in this chapter to ask the question: "Where and how did the modern church get off the track?" Ironically, one of the modern errantists had pinpointed the issue well. Stephen T. Davis writes:

> What leads them to liberalism, apart from cultural and personal issues, is their acceptance of certain philosophical or scientific assumptions that are inimical to evangelical theology—e.g., assumptions about what is "believable to modern people," "consistent with modern science," "acceptable by twentieth-century canons of scholarship," and the like.[2]

What is especially ironic about Davis's insight is that he himself falls prey to "certain philosophical or scientific assumptions that are inimical to evangelical theology." The reason for this is implied in the warning of the apostle: "See to it that no one takes you captive through hollow and deceptive philosophy, which depends on human tradition" (Col. 2:8). Philosophy is an exceedingly subtle discipline. Often it is that *with* which we think rather than that *about* which we think that is most important. Hence philosophical presuppositions are often imbibed uncon-

307

sciously in the study of other disciplines. It has been my experience in evangelical circles that godly scholars, unaware of the nature and implications of their scholarly research, sometimes absorb into their thinking philosophical presuppositions that are antithetical to the historical Christian position on Scripture. The results of their accepting unchristian assumptions show up only gradually in their own teaching and writing. Often these results are discovered first by students and then later by other scholars. Tragically, the person who has unwittingly bought into these presuppositions is often the last to realize it. When the fact does come to his awareness, there is the perennial temptation, not always resisted, to rewrite evangelical history to fit his new beliefs about Scripture. It would seem far more honest simply to admit, as indeed even some liberal scholars do, that the historic position was that of the full inerrancy of Scripture but that many now have come not to believe it. Since not all errantists have seen fit to be so straightforward, it is our obligation to expose the false presuppositions that undermine the full authority of Scripture and to "take captive every thought to make it obedient to Christ" (2 Cor. 10:5).

Some Ancient and Medieval Philosophical Presuppositions

The two dominant philosophies emanating from ancient Greece are Aristotelianism and Platonism. Both philosophies taught many premises that an evangelical Christian cannot accept. Aristotle taught that matter was eternal, that man was only mortal, and that God did not love the world. All are clearly contrary to Scripture. Plato taught the eternality of matter, the preexistence of the soul, and salvation by human intellectual effort. These too are opposed to Christianity.

The Alleged Aristotelian Background of Inerrancy

Jack Rogers claims that the Aristotelian exaltation of human reason and logic, adopted by certain post-Reformation theologians such as Turretin, have scholasticized orthodox Christianity and led to the doctrine of inerrancy. This doctrine, says Rogers, was later canonized by the Old Princetonians, Hodge and Warfield. In Rogers's own words,

> the Old Princeton tradition clearly has its roots in the scholasticism of Turretin and Thomas Aquinas. This tradition is a reactionary one developed to refute attacks on the Bible, especially by

the science of biblical criticism. The demand for reason prior to faith in the authority of the Bible seems wedded to a prior commitment to aristotelian philosophy.[3]

Rogers's claim, however, does not square with the facts in several ways. First, the "Aristotelian" Turretin did not originate the doctrine of inerrancy. More than a millennium before Turretin, the "Platonic" Augustine, who scarcely had an Aristotelian bone in his body, clearly held to inerrancy. Augustine wrote to Jerome, "I have learned to yield this respect and honour only to the canonical books of Scripture: of these alone do I most firmly believe that the authors were completely free from error." What did Augustine do with apparent contradictions in the Bible? To this question he replied, "I do not hesitate to suppose that either the ms. is faulty or the translator has not caught the meaning of what was said, or I myself have failed to understand it."[4] Elsewhere Augustine wrote, "It seems to me that the most disastrous consequence must follow upon our believing that anything false is found in the sacred books," for, he adds, "if you once admit into such a high sanctuary of authority one false statement, . . . there will not be left a single statement of those books which, . . . if appearing to anyone difficult in practice or hard to believe, may not by the same fatal rule be explained away."[5]

Second, Augustine, in whose broad traditions Rogers himself fits, was not the fideist Rogers would make him to be. Rogers objected to Turretin putting "reason before faith." If by this he means that one should not use the law of noncontradiction to test the consistency of an alleged revelation, the Rogers runs contrary to both Augustine and Scripture. Paul warns Timothy to avoid "contradictions," using the strong word ἀντιθέσεις (antitheseis) (1 Tim. 6:20). Indeed, if the law of noncontradiction does not apply to revelation, how can one fulfill the biblical imperative to "test the spirits" in order to find the spirit of *truth* as opposed to the spirit of *error* (1 John 4:1–3)? Likewise, it would be impossible to know a false prophet or false messiah from the true one unless the law of noncontradiction holds (cf. Matt. 24:24). If a statement can be both true and false at the same time in the same sense (which is what the law of noncontradiction forbids), there is no way to distinguish between truth and falsity.

Third, Rogers speaks as if Aristotle invented the law of noncontradiction. At best, Aristotle was but the first in the West to

discuss it in a systematic way. Ever since there has been a thinking being the law has been in operation. Indeed the law of noncontradiction reflects the very consistency of the mind of God.
Since man is made in God's image, it should not seem strange
that noncontradiction is a basic law of human thinking.

Fourth, even Rogers and other errantists use the law of noncontradiction as a pillar of their positions. The very reason they
are errantists is that they believe there are errors, or *contradictions*,
in the Bible. But how could they know there were contradictions
if they did not use the law of noncontradiction? In this sense
Rogers and the errantists must themselves place "reason prior to
faith." They do not, therefore, accept "by faith" everything affirmed in Scripture. On the contrary, they *reason* (by means of the
law of noncontradiction) that two contradictory affirmations cannot both be true and that a statement contrary to fact must be
false.

In precisely this same way Hodge, Warfield, and others used
the basic, inescapable laws of human logic in deriving the doctrine of inerrancy from Scripture. The doctrine of inerrancy is
the only valid conclusion from two clearly taught truths of Scripture: (1) the Bible is the very utterance of God; (2) whatever God
affirms is completely true and without error. Anyone familiar
with the basic laws of reasoning can readily see that one and only
one conclusion follows from these two biblical premises, namely,
whatever the Bible affirms is completely true and without error.

Finally, it was not Aquinas or Turretin who first applied logic
to God's revelation. The biblical writers themselves warn believers to "avoid . . . contradiction" and anything "contrary" to
sound doctrine (1 Tim. 6:20; 1:10 RSV). Even Tertullian, one of
the most fideistically inclined of the early fathers, said, "All the
properties of God ought to be as rational as they are natural. I
require reason in His goodness, because nothing else can be
properly accounted good than that which is rationally good;
much less can goodness itself be defected in any irrationality."[6]
Even the father of modern existentialism, Sören Kierkegaard,
affirmed that one should not believe what is absurd or contradictory[7] and went so far as to say that "the eternal essential truth
[i.e., God] is by no means in itself paradoxical."[8] If Rogers
wishes to deny that the laws of logic apply to God or to His
revelation, he is, incredible as it seems, going beyond even Tertullian and Kierkegaard into irrational fideism!

Platonic Presuppositions

A further irony in Rogers's position is his assumption of the relative harmlessness of Platonic presuppositions as they bear on the inerrancy of Scripture.[9] While Rogers consciously rejects Turretin's "Aristotelian rationalism," he unconsciously adopts a kind of Platonic "spiritualism" of his own. Plato taught that the "real" world is not the world of our senses but is the "spiritual" world of forms. Truth, for Plato, is found only in this spiritual world. The material world, the space-time world, is at best a shadow of the real world, and in certain later Gnostic forms of Platonism the bodily, material world is essentially evil.

Rogers is apparently not aware that this dualistic separation of the material and spiritual worlds is a philosophical presupposition at the root of the errancy position. Why else is it that some of those who deny the inerrancy of Scripture speak against a physical resurrection in favor of a spiritual one? We must remember how the Greek philosophers reacted when Paul spoke of the physical resurrection of Christ: they mocked (Acts 17:32). Why? Because, according to Plato and other Greek philosophers, the material is separate from and distinctly inferior to the spiritual. In short, matter doesn't really matter. Or, never mind anything except mind and the spiritual. Could this be why certain of our errancy brothers are so willing to give up some of the affirmations of the Bible about the material world and stress the "spiritual" truths as the important ones to hold as infallible?

Historically, there is little question that Platonic philosophy influenced the allegorical method of interpreting Scripture, which obscures and often denies the literal truths of Scripture. This is unmistakably a Platonic influence opposed to the position that the affirmations of the Bible should be taken with the literal and historical implications with which they were intended by God and by the human authors of Scripture. Hence, interestingly enough, the very Platonic philosophy that Rogers favors vis-a-vis Aristotle is itself the ancient forerunner of modern denials of inerrancy.

MODERN PHILOSOPHICAL PRESUPPOSITIONS
THAT UNDERMINE INERRANCY

It would take volumes to document thoroughly the various philosophies that have led to rejection of inerrancy. Space here permits mentioning only some of the more significant ones in the modern world. The seeds of this rejection were already present in the late Middle Ages and Reformation period. Roger Bacon's experimentalism and William of Ockham's skepticism are two cases in point. However, the traditional doctrine of Scripture was not seriously nor officially corrupted by such influences until after the Reformation. The most significant outbreak began in the seventeenth century, to which we turn our attention.

Francis Bacon — Inductivism

About a hundred years after the Reformation, Francis Bacon published his famous *Novum Organum* (1620), in which he set the stage for modern biblical criticism and the denial of the full authority and inerrancy of the Bible. Inerrancy is undermined in several ways in this work.

Bacon claimed all truth is discovered inductively. After tearing down the "idols" of the old deductive method of discovering truth, Bacon argued that "the best demonstration is by far experience."[10] The inductive method, said Bacon, is the true way for the interpretation of nature. One can understand how Bacon could consider his new inductive logic a valid method for scientific enquiry, but he went far beyond reasonable bounds in claiming its universal applicability. He wrote:

> It may also be asked . . . whether I speak of natural philosophy only, or whether I mean that the other sciences, logic, ethics, and politics, should be arrived on by this method. Now I certainly mean what I have said to be understood of them all; and as the common logic, governs by the syllogism, extends not only to the natural but to all science, so does mine also, which proceeds by induction, embrace everything.[11]

Science is the true model of the world. In view of this exaltation and extension of the inductive method, it is not surprising to hear Bacon say, "I am building in the human understanding a true model of the world, such as it is in fact, not such as a man's own reason would have it to be." This new and "true" model Bacon dared to claim would discover "the Creator's own stamp upon creation." He even went so far as to identify it with "the ideas of the divine."[12]

Truth is known pragmatically. Bacon saw clearly that his method implied a pragmatic test for truth, namely, if it works, it is true. "Truth and utility" he wrote, "are here the very same things."[13]

For "of all signs there is none more certain or more noble than that taken from fruits. For fruits and works are as it were sponsors and sureties for the truth of philosophies."[14] In short, all truth is tested by its results. So here we have pragmatism some three centuries before William James or John Dewey.

The separation of science and the Bible. Some have mistakenly claimed that Thomas Aquinas is responsible for separating faith and reason. This view is historically unfounded. Aquinas did make a *formal distinction* between the two realms but never an *actual separation*. For Aquinas, human reason at its best was finite and fallible and could never attain the content of the Christian faith.[15] Reason was only the servant of the theologian, a tool in the discovery and expression of one's faith.[16] But what Aquinas did not do, others such as Bacon did. Bacon, for example, completely separated the realm of reason and science from the realm of faith and religion. He wrote, "It is therefore most wise soberly to render unto faith the things that are faith's" for from the "absurd mixture of matters divine and human" proceed heresies and "fantastical philosophy." It is for this reason that "sacred theology must be drawn from the word and oracles of God, not from the light of nature, or the dictates of reason." Bacon went so far as to say, "We are obliged to believe the word of God, though our reason be shocked at it." And therefore, "the more absurd and incredible any divine mystery is, the greater honour we do to God in believing it; and so much the more noble the victory of faith."[17]

Science is excluded from Genesis and Job. In view of Bacon's complete separation of faith and science, one is not shocked to hear Bacon debunk a hermeneutics that takes the biblical affirmations in Genesis and Job as factually true. Bacon said, "Some have endeavored to build a system of natural philosophy on the first chapter of Genesis, the book of Job and other parts of Scripture; seeking thus the dead amongst the living."[18] Now certainly it is one thing to read modern scientific theory into ancient poetry[19] but it is another to exclude space-time affirmations from the book authored by the Creator of the physical universe. Surely Bacon went too far here.

It is not difficult to see how Bacon set the stage for the view that the Bible is infallible only in "spiritual matters" but does not speak to us inerrantly on historical and scientific matters. If we must render unto science what is science's (namely, *all* truth), then what is left for religion? For Bacon and even more clearly for Hobbes who followed him, the Bible serves a religious and evocative function—it leads us to honor and obey God but does not make cognitive truth claims about God nor affirmations about the physical universe.

Thomas Hobbes—Materialism

Hobbes, like Bacon, appears on the surface to be a Christian. But in view of the lack of religious toleration in those days (and the natural fear one would have to speak openly against Christianity) it may be better to understand him as a tongue-in-cheek believer. He is generally considered the father of modern materialism. There are numerous ways in which Hobbes's views directly and indirectly undermine the traditional doctrine of scriptural authority.

Materialistic sensationalism. Hobbes, the forerunner of Hume's skeptical empiricism, believed that all ideas in one's mind are reducible to sensations.[20] "There is no conception in a man's mind, which hath not at first, totally, or by parts, been begotten upon the organs of Sense. The rest are derived from that original."[21] Hobbes' materialism is very explicit. He boldly declared that

> the world (I mean not the earth only . . . , but the *universe*, that is, the whole mass of all things that are) is corporeal, that is to say, body; and hath the dimensions of magnitude, namely, length, breadth, and depth: also every part of body is likewise body, and that which is not body is no part of the universe: and because the universe is all, that which is no part of it is nothing, and consequently nowhere.[22]

God-talk is evocative but not descriptive. Hobbs argued that "there is no Idea, or conception of anything we call *Infinite*. . . . And therefore the Name *God* is used, not to make us conceive him . . . but that we may honour him."[23] Herein Hobbs is a forerunner of the logical positivists and linguistic analysts who deny the cognitivity of revelational language. As A. J. Ayer later claimed, all God-talk is literally nonsense.[24] Of course if there is no meaningfully descriptive God-talk, then none of the propositions in the Bible are meaningfully descriptive of God. Needless to say, were Hobbs right, it would work havoc with any divinely inspired propositional revelation that purports to inform us about God.

Miracles are brought into question. Hobbes discredited belief in natural religion by claiming it is based on such things as opinions about ghosts, ignorance, and fear.[25] Supernatural religion, according to Hobbes, is based on miracles. But the credibility of these miracles is seriously weakened, he says, by false miracles, contradictions, and injustice by the church that claims them to be true. Furthermore, miracles actually weaken faith because "miracles failing, faith also failed."[26] Hobbes appears to undercut the credibility of miracles by placing them in such a poor light and thus opened the door for later deists and naturalists to deny the miraculous altogether. Of course, if Hobbes's implication is right, and miracles do not occur, then obviously the Bible cannot be a supernatural revelation from God.

The Bible has absurdities we must accept by blind faith. Some have mistakenly held that Kierkegaard taught that we must make a blind leap of faith into the realm of the rationally absurd. But what Kierkegaard did not teach, Hobbes did. Claiming that our "natural reason" is the "undoubted word of God" which is "not to be folded up in the Napkin of an Implicit Faith," Hobbes claims there are "many things in God's Word above Reason; that is to say, which cannot by natural reason be either demonstrated, or confuted." These are "not comprehensible," and we must live by the "Will of obedience" to "forbear contradictions; when we so speak, as (by lawful authority) we are commanded . . . and Faith reposed in him that speaketh, though the mind be incapable of any Notion at all from the words spoken."[27] Elsewhere Hobbes speaks of the deity of Christ and of the Trinity as untranslatable "absurdities."[28] If his words are taken seriously, they represent one of the most blatant forms of blind fideism ever proposed. Of primary significance to our study is the radical separation of faith and reason and the apparent relegation of matters of faith to the unverifiable and paradoxical realm of the absurd and contradictory.

Higher criticism of the Bible. Hobbes was one of the first modern writers to engage in explicit higher criticism of Scripture. In one passage he boldly suggests that "the Scriptures by the Spirit of God in man, mean a man's spirit, inclined to Godliness."[29] After claiming that the story of Jesus healing the demon-possessed man was simply a "parable," Hobbes announces: "I see nothing at all in the Scripture, that requireth a belief, that Demoniacs were any other thing but Mad-men."[30] In brief, the miracles of the Gospels must be understood as spiritual or parabolical but not historical.

Complete separation of religion and science. In view of this kind of hermeneutical desupernaturalization of Scripture, it is little wonder that Hobbes could claim that "the Scripture was written to shew unto men the kingdom of God, and to prepare their minds to become his obedient subjects; leaving the world, and the Philosophy thereof, to the disputations of men, for the exercising of their natural reason."[31] In short, he proposed a complete separation of divine revelation and human reason, in which the latter has a monopoly of all cognitive truth and the former demands only blind obedience to its "spiritual" truths. In this respect, Hobbes not only precedes, but goes beyond, both Kierkegaard and Barth!

Benedict Spinoza—Rationalism

Higher criticism of the Bible blossoms forth in the Jewish pantheist, Spinoza. Using strict deductive rationalism, Spinoza constructed a system of higher criticism that included the following principles.

All truth is mathematically knowable. Spinoza limited truth to the self-evident or what is reducible to it.[32] He claimed that all truth —even religious truth—is mathematically knowable.[33] Anything not subject to his deductive geometric reason was rejected.

The Bible contains contradictions. It is not surprising that Spinoza concluded there are contradictions in the Bible. Samuel denies that God ever repents (1 Sam. 15:29), whereas Jeremiah declares that God does repent (Jer. 18:8–10). "Are not these two texts directly contradictory?" asked Spinoza. "Both statements are general, and each is the opposite of the other—what one flatly affirms, the other flatly denies."[34]

The Bible merely contains the Word of God. Centuries before it became the byword of modernism, Spinoza affirmed the idea that the Bible *contains*, rather than *is*, the Word of God. Speaking of Scripture, he wrote; "Insofar as it contains the word of God, it has come down to us uncorrupted." And not unlike the later liberal Christians, Spinoza claimed that one "will find nothing in what I have written repugnant either to the Word of God or to true religion and faith; . . . contrariwise, they will see that I have strengthened religion."[35] Surely with such "defenders"[35] Christianity needs no enemies!

The Bible is not propositional revelation. Centuries before Emil Brunner, Spinoza denied propositional revelation and was attacking the straw-man "paper-pope" theory. "I will show," Spinoza boldly claimed, "wherein the law of God consists, and how it cannot be contained in a certain number of books." If anyone should object that "though the law of God is written in the heart, the Bible is nonetheless the Word of God," Spinoza replied: "I fear that such objectors are too anxious to be pious, and that they are in danger of turning religion into superstition, and *worshipping paper and ink* in place of God's Word" (italics added).[36]

The Bible is authoritative only in religious matters. Like Bacon and Hobbes before him, Spinoza relegated the authority of the Bible to purely religious matters. He claimed, "I have neither said anything against the Word of God nor given any foothold to impiety." Why? Because, he continued, "a thing is called sacred and Divine when it is designated for promoting piety, and continues sacred so long as it is religiously used; if the users cease to be pious, the thing ceases to be sacred."[37] So as long as the Bible is used for religious purposes, it is a sacred book. Of course, a religious purpose was the only purpose of Scripture for Spinoza, for faith and reason were, to him, entirely separate domains. As to the question of "whether the meaning of Scripture should be made to agree with reason; or whether reason should be made to agree with Scripture," Spinoza replied, "Both parties are, as I have shown, utterly in the wrong, for either doctrine would require us to tamper with reason or with Scripture." The conclusion is clear: "Scripture does not teach philosophy, but *merely obedience,* and that all it contains has been adapted to the understanding and established opinions of the multitude" (italics added).[38] In other words, the Bible has nothing to say to reason. It is an accommodation to the false opinons of men who use their senses rather than their minds to think with. Philosophy, on the contrary, is for those who think rationally (i.e., geometrically and pantheistically). True science is the domain of the intellect; religion is for the obedient will.

Moral criteria used to determine the truth of the Bible. Commenting on the authenticity of the great love command in Matthew 22, Spinoza confidently concluded:

> This cannot be a spurious passage, nor due to a hasty and mistaken scribe, for if the Bible had ever put forth a different doctrine

it would have to change the whole of its teaching, for this is the cornerstone of religion, without which the whole fabric would fall headlong to the ground.[39]

Spinoza applied the same moral criteria for determining the authenticity of Scripture as a whole. "The only reason," he argued, "which we have for belief in Scripture or the writings of the prophets, is the doctrine we find therein and the signs by which it is confirmed," for "we see the prophets extol charity and justice above all things, and have no other object."[40] In short, if a passage teaches love and justice, it is authentic; if it does not, it is not authentic. The circularity of this procedure did not seem to occur to Spinoza's a priori mind. How do we know the biblical teachings of love and justice to begin with, unless they are derived from authenticated Scripture?

Categorical denial of the miraculous. Spinoza is one of the most strongly antisupernatural writers in the history of philosophy. The major premise of his pantheistic philosophy is that God and nature are identical.[41] The belief in miracles, he insists, is based on ignorance and is used by religious authorities to preserve faith. Spinoza reserved severe words for those who thus believed in the miraculous.

> Anyone who seeks for the true causes of miracles and strives to understand natural phenomena as an intelligent being, and not gaze upon them like a fool, is set down and denounced as an impious heretic by those, whom the masses adore as the interpreters of nature and the gods. Such a person knows that, with the removal of ignorance, the wonder which forms their only available means for proving and preserving their authority would vanish also.[42]

So dogmatic was Spinoza in his naturalism that he proudly proclaimed: "We may, then, be absolutely certain that every event which is truly described in Scripture necessarily happened, like everything else, according to natural laws."[43] Why can one make such an absolute assertion? Because, answered Spinoza, "nothing comes to pass in contravention to her [Nature's] universal laws, nay, nothing does not agree with them and follow them, for . . . she keeps a fixed and immutable order."[44] Spinoza even appealed to the Bible for proof of his incurable naturalistic presupposition. "Scripture," he declared, "makes the general assertion in several passages that nature's course is fixed and unchangeable."[45] Spinoza did not mince words when it came to miracles. He flatly declared, "A miracle, whether a contravention to, or beyond nature is a mere absurdity."[46]

Systematic higher criticism of the Bible. In light of such radical antisupernatural bias one is not surprised that Spinoza is the father of much modern biblical criticism. His *Tractatus* was one of the hottest and most controversial books in Europe in the late seventeenth century, going through numerous pseudonymous editions.[47]

Spinoza began his higher criticism with the Pentateuch. Because of certain names, geographic locations, and third-person references to Moses, he concluded that someone after Moses' time must have been the author. Hence, "as there are many passages in the Pentateuch which Moses could not have written, it follows that the belief that Moses was the author of the Pentateuch is ungrounded and irrational."[48] Who wrote it? The same person who wrote the rest of the Old Testament, namely, Ezra.[49]

Higher criticism was not reserved for the books of Moses alone. "I pass on, then, to the prophetic books," wrote Spinoza. "An examination of these assures me that the prophecies therein contained have been compiled from other books . . . but are only such as were collected here and there, so that they are fragmentary."[50] Daniel did not write the whole book of Daniel but only the section from chapter eight to the end.[51] The Old Testament canon was determined by the Pharisees.[52] The prophets did not in general speak "from revelation" and "the modes of expression and discourse adopted by the Apostles in the Epistles, show very clearly that the latter are not written by revelation and Divine command, but merely by the natural powers and judgment of the authors."[53]

As to the Gospels, "it is scarcely credible that God can have designated to narrate the life of Christ four times over, and to communicate it thus to mankind."[54] As to the crucial doctrine of the resurrection, Spinoza omitted it from the apostles' preaching, saying, "The Apostles who came after Christ, preached it to all men as the universal religion solely in virtue of Christ's passion."[55]

It is clear from this that over a century before Johann Semler,[56] and two centuries before Julius Wellhausen,[57] Spinoza[58] engaged in systematic antisupernatural criticism of the Bible. Indeed virtually all of the central emphases in modern liberalism—from the statement that "the Bible contains the Word of God" to the accommodation theory, rationalism, naturalism, the religious-only view, the moral criterion for canonicity, and even the allegorical interpretation of Scripture[59] —are found in Spinoza.

David Hume—Skeptical Empiricism

Probably the most significant philosophical figure between Spinoza and Kant with long-range and adverse affects on biblical authority was the Scottish skeptic, David Hume.[60] There are two major philosophical presuppositions emanating from Hume that undermined the doctrine of biblical inspiration and inerrancy: antisupernaturalism and radical empiricism.

Hume's empirical atomism. Like Hobbes, Hume believed that all ideas in the mind are traceable to one or more sensations derived from the five senses. There is nothing in the mind that was not first in the senses. The result of this idea was very clear to Hume: there are only two meaningful kinds of statements—definitional and factual. In the now-famous last lines of his *Inquiry Concerning Human Understanding,* Hume wrote:

> When we run over libraries, persuaded of these principles, what havoc must we make? If we take in our hands any volume—of divinity or school metaphysics, for instance—let us ask, *Does it contain any abstract reasoning concerning quantity or number?* No. *Does it contain any experimental reasoning concerning matter of fact and existence?* No. Commit it then to the flames, for it can contain nothing but sophistry and illusion.

The implications of Hume's position were captured well by A. J. Ayer in his *Language, Truth and Logic,* in which he wrote of "The Elimination of Metaphysics" (the title of his first chapter). On the basis of Hume's two kinds of premises, which Ayer called analytic and synthetic, respectively, he developed his principle of *empirical verifiability.* According to this principle, a statement, to be meaningful, must either be true by definition (such as "all triangles have three sides") or else it must be verifiable by one or more of the five senses. The principle, of course, proved to be too narrow (since it eliminated even some scientific statements) and had to be revised. But the conclusion reached by Ayer and other semantical atheists after him[61] is still with us, namely that all God-talk is meaningless. Statements such as "God loves the world" or even "God exists" are not purely definitional for the believer nor can they be empirically verified. But if the statements cannot be verified by the senses, then they are literally nonsensical. Hence, "to say that 'God exists' is to make a metaphysical utterance which cannot be either true or false."[62] Metaphysical and theological statements can be neither true nor false because they are not even meaningful. They are not really statements about reality at all but expressions of the feeling of the affirmer. As such, "moral or religious 'truths' are merely providing material for the psycho-analyst."[63] Such is the fate of biblical revelation at the hands of a logical positivism springing from the empirical philosophy of Hume.

Building on Hume's radical empiricism Paul van Buren concluded: "The empiricist in us finds the heart of the difficulty not in what is said about God, but in the very talking about God at all. We do not know 'what' God is, and we cannot understand how the word 'God' is being used."[64] Van Buren added, "Today, we cannot even understand the Nietzschian cry that 'God is dead!' for if it were so, how could we know? No, the problem now is that the *word* 'God' is dead."[65] In short, the result of Hume's empiricism is semantical atheism. The implications for propositional revelation are severe. No proposition in the Bible could be cognitively true. Likewise, no biblical declaration about God could really be informative. At best, biblical language is in this view, evocative of religious commitment; at worst, it is purely emotive expression of the religious feelings of the human writers.

Hume's antisupernaturalism. On the surface, at least, Hume's argument against miracles was not directed at the *possibility* of miracles (as was Spinoza's) but at their *credibility*. The argument may be summarized thus:

1. A law of nature is based on the highest degree of probability (because it is regular).
2. A miracle is based on the lowest degree of probability (because it is rare).
3. A wise man always bases his belief on the highest degree of probability.
4. Therefore the wise man should never believe a miracle has occurred.[66]

Despite the obvious criticism—that wise men ought not ignore the evidence for a *particular* event, say, the resurrection of Christ, in favor of the *general* evidence that all other men still remain in the grave—Hume at times went well beyond his own empirical basis in experience in arguing against miracles. Only a few pages after the above citation Hume wrote:

> A miracle is a violation of the laws of nature; and as a firm and *unalterable experience* has established these laws, the proof against a miracle, from the very nature of the fact, is as entire as any argument from experience can possibly be imagined (italics added).[67]

Hume added but a few lines later, "*Nothing is esteemed a miracle if it ever happens* in the common course of nature." It is no miracle, said Hume, that a man in good health should suddenly die. "But it is a miracle that a dead man should come to life, because that has never been observed in any age or country. There *must, therefore, be a uniform experience* against every miraculous event, otherwise the event would not merit the appelation" (italics added).[68] The emphasized phrases show how a priori and presuppositional Hume's argument really is. He begs the question in favor of antisupernaturalism by assuming from the beginning that whatever happens in the world is, ipso facto, naturally caused. Needless to say, if Hume is granted his antisupernatural presupposition, the Bible cannot be a supernatural revelation of God nor can any event, including the resurrection of Christ, be a miracle. In short, if one grants Hume's empirical atomism and naturalism, he must reject God's supernatural Word.

Immanuel Kant—Agnosticism

Immanuel Kant has been considered by many to be the crossroad thinker of modern philosophy. Before Kant the main European streams of philosophy were rationalism (Descartes, Spinoza, and Leibniz) and empiricism (Locke, Berkeley, and Hume). The rationalists stressed the *mind* and the *a priori* element of knowledge; the empiricists stressed the *senses* and the *a posteriori*. Kant began as a rationalist but was "awakened from his dogmatic slumbers" by reading David Hume. Subsequently, Kant wrote his famous *Critique of Pure Reason*, in which he synthesized rationalism and empiricism and arrived at agnosticism. Kant argued that the empiricists are right in affirming that the *content* of all knowledge comes from the senses but the rationalists are right in declaring that it is finally *formed* by the a priori categories of the mind. That is, the basic "stuff" comes via sensation but the *structure* is by intellection. The result is that knowledge is not constitutive of reality but knowledge (i.e., true propositions) is literally *constructed* by the a priori categories of the mind.

Agnosticism about knowing God by pure reason. The result of Kant's creative synthesis was agnosticism about reality. The mind knows only *after* the construction but not before. Hence, I can know the "thing-to-me" but not the "thing-in-itself." One can know what *appears* to him but not what really is. The former Kant called *phenomena* and the latter, *noumena*. Between the phenomenal and noumenal realms there is an impassable gulf fixed by the very nature of the knowing process.

There is another reason, according to Kant, why we must remain forever ignorant of reality-in-itself. It is simply this: whenever one attempts to apply the categories of his mind (such as unity or causality) to the noumenal real, he ends in hopeless contradictions and antinomies. For example, the principle of causality when so applied ends in antithesis. Thesis: everything must have a cause; hence, there must be a *first* cause to initiate the causality. Antithesis: but if everything must have a cause, then so must the "first" cause and the cause of the first cause and so on into infinity, in which case there is *no first cause* but an infinite regression of causes. Therefore, by applying the principle of causality to the noumenal realm of reality, we end in contradiction and antithesis—a proof that one ought not attempt to apply pure reason to reality.[69]

The fact/value dichotomy. One of the consequences of Kant's philosophy is the fact/value dichotomy. The "objective" world of fact is the phenomenal world of our experience. This can be known by our minds. The "subjective" world of will, however, cannot be known by "pure reason" but only by what Kant called "practical reason," by which he meant that which is morally postulated by an act of the will. In his second critique, *The Critique of Practical Reason,* Kant argued that in order to make sense of our moral duty—the categorical imperative—we must postulate both God and immorality. The argument can be summarized like this:

1. Felicity (happiness) is what all men want.
2. Morality (duty) is what all men ought to do.
3. Unity of these two, the summum bonum (greatest good), ought to be sought.
4. Now the unity of these two is not possible by finite man in this life.

5. But the moral necessity (obligation) of doing something implies the possibility of doing it; ought implies can.

6. Therefore it is morally necessary for one to postulate:
   (a) Deity to make this unity possible (i.e., the power to do it), and
   (b) Immortality to make this unity achievable (i.e., time and place to accomplish it).

"Thus God and a future life are two postulates which . . . are inseparable from the obligation which that same reason imposes upon us."[70]

Kant was very careful to point out that this is not a theoretical argument for God's existence but merely a practical postulate. Even though it is not possible to *think* (i.e., reason) that God exists, yet one must *live* as if God exists. Kant himself clearly believed that God does exist, but he was sure there were no rational proofs of God, only a moral postulate of Him. In this move by Kant one can see the big shift in modern thought from the rational to the moral.

Since Kant, Western thinkers have largely given up the quest for rational proofs of reality and have been content with something like moral presuppositions. The shift has been from the realm of mind to that of will, from the objective to the subjective, from fact to value. Kant himself said, "This moral necessity is subjective, that is, it is a want, and not *objective*, that is itself a duty, for there cannot be a duty to suppose the existence of anything."[71] Technically, then, one must not say, "*It is* morally necessary . . . " but "*I am* morally certain. . . ." The tragedy is, however, that the two domains are totally disjoined. The mind cannot *know* the realm of value; it can only *will* it. Since God is in the noumenal realm of value, it follows that reason cannot find Him; the will must choose Him. (The way is already prepared for Kierkegaard!)

This fact/value dichotomy is one of the root problems behind the denial of the full inerrancy. Many who claim the Bible is infallible only in religious or redemptive matters but not necessarily in factual areas imply this same kind of Kantian disjunction. The assumption is that inspiration and inerrancy cover only the areas of religious "value" (in which Scripture is infallible) but not those areas that may relate to tangential and nonessential "fact" (in which Scripture may be errant).

Morality is the essence of true religion. In one sense Kant's work

Religion Within the Limits of Reason Alone is a deistic classic. In it Kant used "moral reason" as the grounds for determining what is essential to true religion, a foreshadowing of Schleiermacher. Practical reason demands a moral interpretation of the Bible. "Frequently," wrote Kant, "this interpretation may, in the light of the text (of the revelation), appear forced—it may often really be forced; and yet if the text can possibly support it, it must be preferred to a literal interpretation."[72] Speaking of an ecclesiastical and biblical faith, Kant said, "We ought even now to labor industriously, by way of continuously setting free the pure religion from its present shell, which as yet cannot be spared."[73] Morality determines the Bible to be the Word of God, for the Bible's morality "cannot but convince him of its divine nature . . . and hence deserves to be regarded as a divine command."[74] Thus the essence of "this [true] religion is 'the Spirit of God, who guides into all truth' . . . which alone constitutes the element of genuine religion in each ecclesiastical faith."[75] With this inner subjective witness of the spirit alone Kant rested the case for determining not only what is true in any religion but even what is to be accepted within the Bible itself.

Following in Kant's footsteps, Rudolf Otto did his higher criticism of the Bible on the subjective basis of "the witness of the spirit." Otto wrote, "There is no harm even in the fact that the records of Christ's life are fragmentary, and that they contain manifold uncertainties, that they are intermingled with legendary and overlaid with Hellenistic elements. For the Spirit knows and recognizes what is of the Spirit."[76]

Morality eliminates the need for the miraculous. Using his moral yardstick to measure religious truth, Kant concluded that miracles are an appropriate introduction to, but not "strictly necessary" for, a moral religion such as Christianity.[77] Indeed such a religion must "in the end render superfluous the belief in miracles in general."[78] The belief that miracles can somehow aid morality Kant designates as "senseless conceit."[79] Kant did admit that the life of Christ may "all be nothing but miracles" but warns that "in the use of these historical accounts, we do not make it a tenet of religion that the knowing, believing, and professing of them are themselves means whereby we can render ourselves well-pleasing to God."[80]

As to the nature of a miracle, "we cannot know anything at all about supernatural aid."[81] One thing we can know: if an alleged

miracle "flatly contradicts morality, it cannot, despite all appearances, be of God (for example, were a father ordered to kill
his son who is, as far as he knows, perfectly innocent)."[82] It
would seem that Kant has thereby morally decided that we must
reject the story of Abraham and Isaac! This is higher criticism by
personal moral criteria not unlike modern deniers of inerrancy
who reject God's command to Israel to kill the Canaanites because they "frankly find it difficult to believe that it was God's
will."[83] Further, argued Kant, "to venture beyond these limits
[of natural effects] is rashness and immodesty, although those
who support miracles frequently pretend to exhibit a humble
and self-renouncing way of thought."[84] Indeed, the bottom line
of Kant's subtle attack on miracles is that practical reason demands that we adopt the conclusion that miracles never happen.
In a revealing passage Kant argues:

> Here we can determine nothing on the basis of knowledge of the
> object (which, by our own admission, transcends our under-
> standing) but only on the basis of the maxims which are neces-
> sary to the use of our reason. Thus, miracles must be admitted as
> [occurring] *daily* (though indeed hidden under the guise of
> natural events) or else *never*, and in the latter case they underlie
> neither our explanations by reason nor the guiding rules of our
> conduct; and since the former alternative [that they occur daily]
> is not at all compatible with reason, nothing remains but to adopt
> the latter maxim [viz, that miracles never occur], for this princi-
> ple remains ever a mere maxim for making judgments, not a
> theoretical assertion.[85]

In short, reason demands, says Kant, that we conclude that
miracles do not occur! In view of such subtle but definitive naturalism we are not surprised to see Kant reject the resurrection
account at the end of the Gospels. He wrote:

> the death of Christ with which the public record of his life ends (a
> record which, as public, might serve universally as an example for
> imitation). The more secret records, added as a sequel, of his
> *resurrection* and *ascension*, which took place before the eyes only of
> his intimates, *cannot be used in the interest of religion within the limits of
> reason alone* without doing violence to their historical valua-
> tion. . . . This is so not merely because this added sequel is an
> historical narrative (for the story which precedes it is that also)
> but because, taken literally, it involves a concept, i.e., of the
> materiality of all worldly beings, which is, indeed, very well

suited to man's mode of sensuous representation but which is most burdensome to reason in its faith regarding the future (italics added).[86]

Sören Kierkegaard—Existentialism

The existentialism of Kierkegaard, which gave rise to neoorthodoxy and much of neoevangelicalism, grew out of the soil of Kantian agnosticism. Kant had declared the noumenal to be unknowable by reason; Kierkegaard declared God to be "wholly other" and "paradoxical" to human reason (though not paradoxical in Himself). Kant made his way toward moral reality by a subjective act of the will. Kierkegaard called his similar move a "leap of faith." Kant bifurcated the realms of fact and value, and Kierkegaard, too, argued that the factual and historical have no religious significance as such.

Truth is subjectivity. Kierkegaard did not teach that truth is subjective nor that there is no objective truth. Neither did he claim that one should believe what is irrational or contradictory.[87] He did dismiss, however, objectivity as a way of knowing ultimate or religious truth because "the way of objective reflection leads to abstract thought, to mathematics, to historical knowledge of different kinds; and always it leads from the subject . . . [and] becomes infinitely indifferent."[88] Kierkegaard did, nonetheless, say that "truth is subjectivity, an objective uncertainty held fast in an appropriation process of the most passionate inwardness."[89] This is why truth is "paradoxical." "The paradoxical character of the truth is its objective uncertainty; this uncertainty is an expression for the passionate inwardness, and this passion is precisely the truth."[90] But when Kierkegaard said religious truth is "paradoxical," he did not mean it was paradoxical in itself but only to finite man. He wrote, "The eternal essential truth is by no means in itself a paradox; but it becomes paradoxical by virtue of its relationship to an existing individual."[91] Truth is a subjective encounter with God for which one has no good reason but which one must appropriate by a passionate "leap" of faith.[92]

Objective truth is not essential to Christianity. Kierkegaard himself never denied that Christianity was objectively or historically true. He wrote, "When one raises the historical question of the truth of Christianity or what is and is not Christian truth, the Scriptures at once present themselves as documents of decisive significance."[93] He personally believed in the historicity of the

Bible, of Christ, and even of the resurrection. In his *Journal*[94] he even went so far as to say, "The historicity of the redemption must be certain in the same sense as any other historical thing, but not more so, for otherwise the different spheres are confused."

Despite this admission, however, Kierkegaard wrote that the historicity of the Gospel accounts was essential to Christianity.

> If the contemporary generation had left nothing behind them but these words: "We have believed that in such and such a year God appeared among us in the humble figure of a servant, that he lived and taught in our community, and finally died," it would be more than enough.[95]

All that is really historically essential is that there was a first-century figure who died and in whom his contemporaries *believed* they found God. It is noteworthy that Kierkegaard does not even include the *belief*, to say nothing of the *fact*, of the resurrection in this skeletal historical commitment. Is it accidental that what Kierkegaard, the father of existentialism, laid down as the minimal historical necessity of Christianity is precisely what Rudolf Bultmann concluded as a result of his demythologizing method of interpretation?

Higher criticism does not affect Christianity. So far as I can determine, Kierkegaard himself never engaged in higher criticism of the biblical text. He did say, however, that even the most destructive forms of higher criticism would not be harmful to true Christianity. In a very illuminating passage he wrote:

> I assume now the opposite, that the opponents have succeeded in proving what they desire about Scripture, with a certainty transcending the most ardent wish of the most passionate hostility— what then? Have the opponents thereby abolished Christianity? By no means. Has the believer been harmed? By no means, not in the least. . . . Because the books are not written by these authors, are not authentic, are not in an integral condition, are not inspired (though this cannot be disproved, since it is an object of faith), it does not follow that these authors have not existed; and above all, it does not follow that Christ has not existed.[96]

Neither Christianity nor Christian belief is harmed, he maintained, by disproving the genuineness and authenticity of Scripture. Herein Kierkegaard left a gaping hope in the wall of the historic Christian church, through which modern higher criticism has made its destructive march.

Inspiration of Scripture is a subjective matter of faith. Again, so far as I can see, Kierkegaard did not personally deny the inspiration and authority of Scripture. Kierkegaard even attacked the idea of anyone's receiving private revelation directly from Christ. He wrote, "It is true that Christianity is built upon a revelation, but also it is limited by the definitive revelation it has received. It must not be built upon the revelations which John Doe and James Roe may get."[97] In another place he added:

> Is it not self-contradictory to accept a part of the Bible as God's Word, accept Christianity as Divine teaching—and then, when confronted with something you cannot bring into accord with your intelligence or your emotions to say God is contradicting Himself, whereas actually, it is you who are contradicting yourself, for either you must reject this Divine teaching entirely or put up with it just as it is.[98]

So it seems that Kierkegaard personally accepted the Bible as the Word of God and said, "If it is a revelation we must stand by it, *argue from it,* act in accord with it, transform our whole existence in relation to it."[99] However, his personal beliefs about the inspiration and authority of the Bible notwithstanding, in another passage Kierkegaard denied that the belief in the inspiration of the Bible had any objective basis. The basis for believing inspiration, he wrote, is purely a subjective matter of faith. "In this connection a number of topics come up for consideration: the canonicity of the individual books, their authenticity, their integrity, the trustworthiness of their authors." How do we establish all these? "A dogmatic guaranty is posited: Inspiration." So much is this doctrine sheerly a matter of faith that Kierkegaard depreciated scholarly efforts to defend the inspiration and authenticity of Scripture, adding:

> How much time, what great industry, what splendid talents, what distinguished scholarship have been requisitioned from generation to generation in order to bring this miracle [viz., "to make sure of the Scriptures historically and critically"] come to pass. And yet a little dialectical doubt touching the presuppositions may suddenly arise, sufficient for a long time to unsettle the whole, closing the subterranean way to Christianity which one has attempted to construct objectively and scientifically, *instead of letting the problem remain subjecture, as it is* (italics added).[100]

It seems clear from the foregoing discussion that Kierkegaard presents the doctrine of inspiration as unfalsifiable; it is purely and simply a matter of faith. No factual finds can either confirm it or deny it. Higher criticism cannot disprove it because it is in the realm of the subjective and not the area of the objective. In fact, we witness in Kierkegaard the continuation of the Kantian fact/value dichotomy. No fact can ever disconfirm the realm of religious value, which is forever reserved for faith alone.

Propositional is subordinate to the personal. In accord with the fact/value dichotomy, Kierkegaard makes another disjunction —that between the propositional and the personal. He never denied that the Bible is in some sense propositional revelation. Indeed, he admitted that there is an objective dimension to truth. He believed also in the basic Christian doctrines. However, Kierkegaard emphatically states, "If it is really God's view that Christianity is *only* doctrine [implying that it is *at least* doctrine], a collection of doctrinal propositions, then the New Testament is a ridiculous book."[101] What Kierkegaard was interested in, as indeed we evangelicals are deeply concerned about, is that we have more than dead, orthodox acceptance of credal statements about Christ. What is needed is wholehearted commitment to the person of Christ, known through the propositions of Scripture.

Kierkegaard, however, went far beyond the bounds of orthodoxy in the way in which he exalted the personal over the propositional. The Abraham-Isaac story in *Fear and Trembling* is a case in point.[102] The propositional revelation of God says, "Thou shall not kill." But the personal God reveals Himself to Abraham and commands, "Sacrifice your son Isaac." According to Kierkegaard, Abraham had to leave the realm of rationally understood propositions about God and, by an act of nonrational faith, accept the personal over the propositional. That is, when confronted with a conflict between the Law and the Law-Giver, one must take the person of God over propositions about God.

Kierkegaard was apparently unable to see that he made a false disjunction of the personal and propositional just as he did in regard to fact and value. He did not see that propositional revelation can also be personal. The Bible is a personal love letter from the personal God to persons He loves. We are not confronted in Scripture with the choice between God's revelation and the God of that revelation. All we know about God comes through His revelation. There are indeed times when one revelational command of God conflicts with another (as obeying God over parents [Matt. 10:37]), but there is never a time when we are asked to go beyond propositional revelation. There is no way to *know* that it is God giving the command unless we have some revelational *knowledge* about who it is that is commanding us.

God is the "Wholly Other." For Kierkegaard God is not irrational but He is suprarational to us. Human reason can neither prove Him nor know Him. God is beyond the reach of reason altogether. Of theistic proofs he wrote, "For whose sake is it that the proof is sought? Faith does not need it; aye, it must even regard proof as an enemy." It is only "when faith thus begins to lose its passion, when faith begins to cease to be faith, [that] a proof becomes necessary so as to command respect from the side of unbelief."[103] God is the "unknown something with which the Reason collides when inspired by its paradoxical passion, with the result of unsettling even man's knowledge of himself."[104] What is this "Unknown" we call God? Kierkegaard answers, "It is nothing more than a name we assign to it."[105] The very idea of proving this God exists is ridiculous. "If God does not exist it would of course be impossible to prove it; and if he does exist it would be folly to attempt it."[106]

So opposed was Kierkegaard to the idea of man's knowing God by human reason that he maintained that even in His revelation God is "wholly other." The words of the Bible are not cognitively descriptive of God. They are merely signs or pointers.[107] They are like arrows shot in the direction of God but which fall far short of their target. To treat Scripture as cognitively descriptive of God would be in effect to set it up as a paper pope.[108] "In the main," wrote Kierkegaard, " a reformation which sets the Bible aside would have as much validity now as Luther's breaking with the pope." In this regard, he continued, "the Bible societies have done irreparable damage. Christianity has long needed a religious hero who in fear and trembling had the courage to forbid people to read the Bible."[109]

AN EVANGELICAL RESPONSE

It is not our purpose here to *refute* presuppositions behind the denial of the full inspiration and inerrancy of Scripture but simply to *expose* them, as we have done above. There are, however, several important conclusions we do wish to draw from this study.

The Claim to Be Defenders of True Christianity

Almost to a man, even the most radical critics of the historic position on the authority of Scripture claimed to be true defenders of the Word of God and of essential Christianity. Bacon spoke of the Bible as "the Word of God" which is "the surest medicine against superstition and the most approved nourishment for faith . . . [which] displays the will of God." He even claimed a kind of inerrancy for the Scriptures, saying, "For he did not err who said, 'Ye err in that ye know not the Scriptures and the power of God.' "[110] Paradoxically, even Hobbes seemed to argue for the errorlessness of the Bible, saying, "For though there be many things in God's Word above Reason . . . yet there is nothing contrary to it; but when it seemeth so, the fault is either in our skillful interpretation, or erroneous Ratiocination."[111] Despite the fact that Spinoza argued that miracles were impossible and engaged in extensive higher criticism of the Bible, he claimed emphatically: "I have said nothing unworthy of Scripture or God's Word."[112] Even though Spinoza believed there were many falsehoods and contradictions in the Bible, he doggedly denied undermining confidence in Scripture:

> Perhaps I shall be told that I am overthrowing the authority of Scripture; . . . on the contrary, I have shown that my object has been to prevent the clear and uncorrupted passages being accommodated to and corrupted by the faulty ones; neither does the fact that some passages are corrupt warrant us in suspecting all. No Book ever was completely free from faults.[113]

These passages have a familiar ring. One of the modern defenders of an infallible Bible over against an inerrant one recently argued that unless we admitted minor errors in the Bible, "we could never again use the canons of criticism to support any test against the conjectural reading of liberal critics . . . and all of us agreed that the Bible is, nonetheless, totally reliable and infallible in its teachings."[114] Even Clark Pinnock, who claims to be a "defender" of inerrancy, sounds strangely reminiscent of Spinoza when he writes: "God uses fallible spokesmen all the time to deliver his word, and it does not follow that the Bible *must* be otherwise."[115]

The lesson is this: some of the men whose thinking was most destructive to inerrancy thought themselves to be doing a service to "true" Christianity. Therefore we should be wary of their modern counterparts, who think they are gaining a major triumph for Christianity by giving up "minor" truths of Scripture!

Presuppositions Are Not Proven Facts

The history of the philosophical influences leading to denial of the full authority of Scripture show unmistakably that essentially it is not new facts but old philosophies that are leading evangelicals astray. Evangelical scholars are—often unwittingly—buying into philosophical presuppositions that are inimical to the historic evangelical view of Scripture. New discoveries in science or archaeology have not prompted these recent departures from the orthodox view of Scripture. Indeed, the factual evidence is probably more supportive of the inerrancy of Scripture than ever before. The real problem is not factual but philosophical. It is the acceptance, often uncritically, of philosophical premises—such as inductivism, naturalism, rationalism, or existentialism—that are basically irreconcilable with the doctrine of the full inspiration of Scripture.

What is more, there is no compelling reason why an evangelical should accept these philosophies, which are far from proven. Non-Christian philosophers have offered more than sufficient critiques of each of them. At least no one philosophical position has proven itself to the satisfaction of its non-Christian opponents. And if non-Christians have not been compelled by the arguments to accept any one of these views, there is no reason why a Christian ought to be. Especially is this so in view of the fact that these positions are antithetical to the orthodox view of Scripture, which is at the foundation of our faith. "Beware of philosophy."

Furthermore, often the philosophical presuppositions that undermine the Christian belief in Scripture are circular or self-defeating. Antisupernaturalists, for example, presuppose the truth of naturalism in order to argue against miracles, saying in effect, "Whatever happens in the world is, ipso facto, a natural event." The semantical atheists engage in self-defeating claims such as "No language about God can be cognitively meaningful"—a statement that, to be effective, must itself be a cognitively meaningful statement about God! It is not, therefore, so much our job as Christian philosophers to refute anti-Christian arguments as it is simply to show how these are self-destructive.

A Philosophy Consistent With Biblical Revelation

Evangelicals do not all take the same philosophical approach, nor do we all come to the same philosophical conclusions. This is not all bad. What we must be careful of, however, is being sure that our philosophical approach is not inconsistent with biblical revelation or with what is presupposed by it. The Bible, for example, teaches or presupposes theism and supernaturalism. It seems to me, also, that it presupposes some kind of metaphysical realism and is opposed to complete epistemological agnosticism. Somewhere within these parameters we may carry on our intramural dialogue, but beyond this we venture only at the risk of engaging in a philosophically self-destructive and theologically erosive endeavor. What is certain is that there is no biblically or even philosophically justifiable reason why we must adopt presuppositions that are irreconcilable with the doctrine of Scripture held by the orthodox church down through the centuries. And, we might add, there are many good reasons why we should not accept them, not the least of which is that they are incompatible with the Bible's own claim about its divine authority and inerrancy.

THE INTERNAL TESTIMONY
OF THE HOLY SPIRIT

R. C. Sproul

R. C. Sproul is President, Ligonier Valley Study Center near Stahlstown in western Pennsylvania. He is a graduate of Westminster College (B.A.), Pittsburgh Theological Seminary (B.D.), and the Free University of Amsterdam (Drs.). He holds an honorary doctorate from Geneva College (Litt.D.). He has served on the faculties of Westminster College, Gordon College, and the Conwell School of Theology and was formerly Minister of Theology at the College Hill United Presbyterian Church, Cincinnati, Ohio. He is a minister in the Presbyterian Church in America. He has served as Visiting Professor at Trinity Episcopal Seminary, Sewickley, Pennsylvania, and Visiting Professor of Apologetics at Gordon-Conwell Theological Seminary, South Hamilton, Massachusetts. Dr. Sproul is the author of the following books and articles: The Symbol, The Psychology of Atheism; Discovering the Intimate Marriage; Knowing Scripture; Objections Answered; Soli Deo Gloria, *editor; and* "The Case for Inerrancy: A Methodological Analysis" *in* God's Inerrant Word, *edited by J. W. Montgomery. He is a member of the Council of ICBI.*

CHAPTER SUMMARY

The Holy Spirit is related to Scripture in many ways. Some of the most significant are those of inspiration, illumination, application, conviction, and the *testimonium*. What we are primarily concerned with in this chapter is the *testimonium*. The Spirit in the *testimonium*, or internal testimony, works to confirm the reliability of Scripture, giving us certainty that the Bible is the Word of God. The distinctive term here is *certainty*. Such is clearly the view of Augustine, Calvin, Luther, and Warfield. It is a view at variance with the existential, neoorthodox conception and with such men as Sören Kierkegaard, Martin Kahler, Emil Brunner, and Thomas Torrance. Here the truth is not the truth until or unless the personal dimension is added. In classical Christian thought, the believing individual makes a subjective response to the objective Word through the impetus of the Spirit. For the existentialist, the subjective response determines the nature of the Word through the kinetic network of the Spirit.

THE INTERNAL TESTIMONY OF THE HOLY SPIRIT

T*ESTIMONIUM SPIRITUS SANCTI internum.* This Reformation slogan, indicating the internal testimony of the Holy Spirit, has become increasingly important as the church wrestles with the question of the integrity of Holy Writ. As we face a crisis of confidence in the authority and reliability of the apostolic deposit of faith we are drawn repeatedly into deep consideration of the relationship of Word and Spirit. The *testimonium* represents but one facet, albeit a vital facet, of this complex relationship of Word and Spirit.

The Holy Spirit is related to Scripture in many ways. Some of the more significant dimensions of the Spirit's work vis-a-vis Scripture include inspiration, illumination, application (conviction), and the *testimonium.*

Inspiration concerns the role of the Spirit in initiating and superintending Word revelation. The theopneustos of 2 Timothy 3:16 points to the divine origin of Holy Scripture as God "breathes out," or *inspires,* his Word.[1] *Illumination* concerns the Spirit's work in assisting the reader to achieve clarity in understanding the content of the Word. It is the Spirit who "searches" the deep things of God and works to assist our naturally carnal minds to understand spiritual things (1 Cor. 2:10, 14). *Application* refers to the work of the Spirit in applying the content of the Scripture to the life of the believer. A special type of application is conviction, which refers to the Spirit's work of bringing an awareness of sin to the conscience of the individual and a subsequent spirit of penitence to the heart of the convicted.

In all of these activities the Spirit is linked to the Word. The Spirit is not divorced from the Word in such a way as to reduce revelation to an exercise in subjectivism. The Spirit works *with* the Word (*cum verbo*) and *through* the Word (*per verbum*), not *without* or apart from the Word (*sine verbo*).[2]

How does the *testimonium* differ from the other facets of the Word and Spirit mentioned above? The uniqueness of the *testimonium* is found in its focus on the question of *certainty*. The Spirit in His internal testimony works to confirm the reliability of Scripture, giving us certainty that the Bible is the Word of God. Thus it has been in the arena of apologetics that the *testimonium* has received much attention.

THE *TESTIMONIUM* IN CALVIN

John Calvin is usually credited with developing and giving the clearest expression to the Reformation principle of the *testimonium*. He treats this question in the early parts of the *Institutes* and in his *Letter to Sadolet*. Controversy over interpreting Calvin's view of the *testimonium* has engendered some debate, particularly with respect to issues involving apologetics and most particularly with respect to methodological questions regarding the defense of biblical infallibility.[3]

In chapter 7 of the *Institutes* Calvin sets forth his doctrine of the *testimonium*. He divides his treatment into five sections.

In section 1 Calvin deals with the foundation of certainty, whether it is from men or from God. In full view here is the issue of whether or not the authority of Scripture rests on the prior authority of the church. He writes:

> A most pernicious error has very generally prevailed—viz. that Scripture is of importance only insofar as conceded to it by the suffrage of the Church; as if that eternal and inviolable truth of God could depend on the will of men. With great insult to the Holy Spirit, it is asked, who can assure us that the Scriptures proceeded from God; who can guarantee that they have come down safe and unimpaired to our times; who can persuade us that this book is to be received with reverence, and that one expunged from the list; did not the Church regulate all these things with certainty? On the determination of the Church, therefore, it is

said, depend both the reverence which is due to Scripture and the books which are to be admitted into the canon.[4]

Here Calvin obviously had Rome in mind as he wrestled with the question of the ultimate basis for *reverence* for Scripture and with the issue of canon. Rome consistently appealed to the church's role in the formation of the canon as a basis for establishing the priority of church authority, the *testimonium ecclesiae*.

In section 2 Calvin responds to the Roman concept of *testimonium ecclesiae* with arguments drawn from the New Testament and from history.

> These ravings are admirably refuted by a single expression of an apostle. Paul testifies that the Church is "built on the foundation of the apostles and prophets" (Eph. 2:20). If the doctrine of the apostles and prophets is the foundation of the Church, the former must have had its certainty before the latter began to exist. . . . For if the Christian Church was founded at first on the writings of the prophets, and the preaching of the apostles, that doctrine, wheresoever it may be found, was certainly ascertained and sanctioned and antecedently to the Church, since, but for this, the Church herself never could have existed.[5]

Thus for Calvin the internal testimony of the Spirit is vital not only to theology in general but to ecclesiology in particular. The church is subordinate to Scripture, not the Scripture to the church.

The relationship of church to canon is critical to the conclusion of section 2. Here Calvin sets forth the classic Reformation view of church and canon:

> Nothing, therefore, can be more absurd than the fiction, that the power of judging Scripture is in the Church, and that on her nod its certainty depends. When the church receives it, and gives it the stamp of her authority, she does not make that authentic which was otherwise doubtful or controverted, but acknowledging it as the truth of God, she, as in duty bound, shows her reverence by an unhesitating assent.[6]

Here Calvin does not vitiate church authority but places it in its proper subordinate perspective. The church is indeed active in the historical process of canon formation. But the crucial point is that the church neither *creates nor validates* the canon. The canon has prior authority and validity. What the church does in the historical process of canon development is to receive it, acknowledge it to be the truth of God, show reverence to it, and give

unhesitating assent to it. Note again the proper action of the church
according to Calvin:

> 1) *receive*, 2) *acknowledge*, 3) *revere*, 4) *assent*. These terms indicate
> that the Church does not create the authority of Scripture but
> recognizes and assents to an authority which is already there.
> Characteristically Calvin chooses his words carefully, perhaps
> with a view to the terminology of the Muratorian Canon which
> was *recipere*. [7]

The role of the church in "receiving" and "acknowledging" the
Scripture is echoed in the Reformed Confessions, which follow
Calvin at this point. [8]

In section 3 Calvin responds to the Roman appeal to Augustine's famous statement in which he says that he would not
believe the gospel were he not moved by the authority of the
church. First Calvin locates the context of Augustine's remarks—the Manichaean controversy—and goes on to say:

> Augustine, therefore, does not here say that the faith of the godly
> is founded on the authority of the Church; nor does he mean that
> the certainty of the gospel depends upon it; he merely says that
> the unbelievers would have no certainty of the gospel, so as
> thereby to win Christ, were they not influenced by the consent of
> the Church. And he clearly shows this to be his meaning, by thus
> expressing himself a little before: "When I have praised my own
> creed, and ridiculed yours, who do you suppose is to judge be-
> tween us; or what more is to be done than to quit those who,
> inviting us to certainty, afterward command us to believe uncer-
> tainty, and follow those who invite us, in the first instance, to
> believe what we are not yet able to comprehend, that waxing
> stronger through faith itself, we may become able to understand
> what we believe—no longer men, but God Himself internally
> strengthening and illuminating our minds." [9]

This last citation from Augustine captures the essence of Calvin's understanding of Augustine. From that quotation we see an
incipient expression of Augustine's own doctrine of the *testimonium*. Calvin concludes that the obvious inference to be
drawn from Augustine is

> that this holy man had no intention to suspend our faith in Scrip-
> ture on the nod of decision of the Church, but only to intimate
> (what we too admit to be true) that those who are not yet en-
> lightened by the Spirit of God, become teachable by reverence for
> the Church, and thus submit to learn the faith of Christ from the

gospel. . . . But he nowhere insinuates that the authority which we give to the Scriptures depends on the definitions or devices of men. He only brings forward the universal judgment of the Church, as a point most pertinent to the cause, and one, moreover, in which he had the advantage of his opponents.[10]

In section 4 Calvin presents his view of the relationship between the *testimonium* and other evidence for the authority of Scripture. Calvin begins by asserting the superiority of the "secret testimony of the Spirit" to human conjecture. He says:

Hence, the biggest proof of Scripture is uniformly taken from the character whose word it is. . . . Our conviction of the truth of Scripture must be derived from a higher source than human conjectures, judgments, or reasons; namely, the secret testimony of the Spirit.[11]

Here Calvin makes it clear that the *testimonium* serves as the ultimate and highest ground of certainty for the believer. The *testimonium* is not placed over against reason as a form of mysticism or subjectivism. Rather, it goes beyond and transcends reason. Calvin says:

But I answer, that the testimony of the Spirit is superior to reason. For as God alone can properly bear witness to his own words, so these words will not obtain full credit on the hearts of men, until they are sealed by the inward testimony of the Spirit.[12]

Calvin's statement that "the testimony of the Spirit is superior to reason" may lead some to conclude that the reformer indulges in a flight into irrationality as a final defense for the authority of Scripture. D. F. Strausz, for example, in the nineteenth century, called this article the "Achilles Heel of Protestantism," because it moved authority out of the objectivity of revelation into the subjectivity of a secret experience that is confined to the hidden chambers of the human heart.[13]

From what follows (namely an entire chapter devoted to objective evidence for biblical authority) it is clear that Calvin is not guilty of such subjectivistic fancy. For Calvin the *testimonium* is not irrational but transrational. That is, it does not move against reason but beyond it. If this is in any way ambiguous in section 4, it becomes manifestly clear in section 5.

The introduction to section 5 gives the clearest statement of the relationship of the *testimonium* to objective evidence we can find in the *Institutes*. Calvin writes:

> Let it therefore be held as fixed, that those who are inwardly
> taught by the Holy Spirit acquiesce implicitly in Scripture; that
> Scripture, carrying its own evidence along with it, deigns not to
> submit to proofs and arguments, but owes the full conviction with
> which we ought to receive it to the testimony of the Spirit.[14]

The crucial phrases in this summary statement are (1) "acquiesce implicitly in Scripture" and (2) "Scripture, carrying its
own evidence along with it." These two phrases highlight the
balance of subjectivity and objectivity in Calvin's *testimonium*.
The effect of the internal testimony is that the believer *acquiesces*
to Scripture. The internal testimony offers no new argument or
content to the evidence found in Scripture objectively, but so
works in our hearts that we are willing to submit to what is
already there.

The concept of *acquiescence* is critical to our understanding of
Calvin and thus worthy of further consideration. Calvin here
uses the Latin verb, *acquiesce*, to which corresponds the English
meaning:

> to rest satisfied or apparently satisfied, or to rest without oppo-
> sition and discontent: usually implying previous opposition, un-
> easiness or dislike, but ultimate compliance or submission; as to
> *acquiesce* in the dispensations of Providence. Syn.—accede, agree,
> consent, submit, yield, comply, concur, conform.[15]

The implicit connotation of this *acquiescence* is agreement "without reservation or doubt."[16] We see it earlier in Augustine's
development of the concept of the *fides implicitum*.[17]

Thus Calvin describes the effect of the *testimonium* in terms of
the believer's unqualified assent to or yielding to the Scripture.
Where the believer formerly was "tossed to and fro in a sea of
doubts," he now rests peaceably in the assurance that the Bible
is indeed the Word of God.

The second crucial phrase, "that Scripture, carrying its own
evidence along with it, deigns not to submit . . ." calls attention
to the fact that, for Calvin, the *testimonium* does not function in a
vacuum. There is an inseparable relationship between *testimonium* and *objective evidence*. The *testimonium* does not function
either against the evidence or apart from the evidence but produces *acquiescence* to the evidence. The Scripture objectively gives
evidence that it is the Word of God. The Spirit does not prove
true what gives evidence of being false but rather gives us the
quiet assurance that the evidence is certain. The Spirit causes us

to submit or yield to the evidence. Our yielding is a subjective act to an objective basis of evidence.

If the relationship between *testimonium* and evidence is in any way vague in chapter 7, it becomes clear in chapter 8, in which Calvin enumerates the *indicia* or evidence the Scriptures have for their divine origin and authority. He speaks of the dignity of the matter, the heavenliness of its doctrine, the content of its parts, the majesty of its style, the antiquity of its teaching, the sincerity of its narrative, its miracles, preductive prophecies fulfilled, its use through the ages, and its witness by the blood of the martyrs. He sees this evidence not as being weak and tentative but objectively strong and compelling. He says of the Scriptures' own evidence:

> True, were I called to contend with the craftiest despisers of God, I trust, though I am not possessed of the highest ability or eloquence, I should not find it difficult to stop their obstreperous mouths; I could, without much ado, put down the boastings which they mutter in corners, were anything to be gained by refuting their cavils (VII/4).[18]

Again Calvin writes:

> There are other reasons, neither few nor feeble, by which the dignity and majesty of the Scriptures may not be only proved to the pious, but also completely vindicated against the cavils of slanderers (VIII/13).[19]

The *indicia* provide objective evidence that Calvin calls "proof." To refuse to submit to this evidence is regarded as caviling and a form of slander. Those who contend against Scripture are called obstreperous. However, in spite of the number and the power of the *indicia*, they remain incapable, in themselves, of producing a "firm faith" in Scripture unless they are accompanied by the *testimonium*. Calvin says:

> These [*indicia*], however, cannot of themselves produce a firm faith in Scripture until our heavenly Father manifest his presence in it, and thereby secure implicit reverence for it. . . . Still the human testimonies which go to confirm it will not be without effect, if they are used in subordination to that chief and highest proof as secondary helps to our weakness. But it is foolish to attempt to prove to infidels that the Scripture is the Word of God. This cannot be known to be, except by faith (VIII/13).[20]

The question Calvin leaves for us is, Why, if the *indicia* are so strong objectively, do they fail to yield certainty? Why, that is, is the *testimonium* necessary?

To answer this question we must look to Calvin's view of the depravity of man and consequently to the noetic effects of sin. We must say that man's problem with certainty here is not so much an intellectual problem as a moral, or spiritual, one. To be sure, the moral problem touches heavily on the intellect, since the prejudice of the heart against God clouds the mind and makes it "dark."

The Problem of Certainty

Since the *testimonium* is related to our certainty concerning the authority of Scripture, it is important for us to have a clear understanding of what we mean by *certainty*. The word provokes much discussion and not a little confusion, inasmuch as it is capable of different technical and common usages. Let me enumerate three distinct ways in which the word *certainty* may be used.

1. *Philosophical or Formal Certainty*

Philosophical certainty has to do with formal arguments that are so logically tight and compelling that to deny the conclusion would be to yield to manifest irrationality or absurdity. This kind of certainty can be found only within the framework of the formal relationship of propositions. The components of a syllogism serve to illustrate this. Let us examine the classical model syllogism to illustrate formal certainty:

Premise A: All men are mortal
Premise B: Socrates is a man
Conclusion: Socrates is mortal

In this syllogism the canons of logic dictate that *if* premise A is true *and* premise B is true, then the conclusion is necessarily, by resistless logic, true. Note, however, that the truth of the conclusion, though it flows irresistibly from the premises, is still ultimately dependent on the truth of the premises. Unless we can demonstrate the truth of the premises we cannot claim absolute certainty for the conclusion. Thus the certainty of the conclusion is conditioned by and dependent on the certainty of the premises. Though the conclusion follows necessarily from the premises, it could conceivably be false if one or both of the premises is false.

To state it another way, the conclusion could be formally valid but still not be materially true.

With the syllogism in view, do we know with absolute certainty that Socrates was in fact mortal? Since the conclusion rests on its premises, let us examine the certainty quotient of the premises.

Do we know with certainty that all men are mortal? If so, how do we know it? By reason? By sense perception? Could we possibly prove this statement to be true? To prove it absolutely we would have to examine every human being who has ever lived and is now alive to prove our claim. Here we run head-on into the limits of induction. To know inductively that all men are mortal we would have to observe the death of all men, including ourselves! The only way we could have absolute certainty that all men are mortal would be posthumously! It may seem ridiculous to say we do not know all men are mortal in light of the overwhelming evidence to the fact that human beings die. Millions of mortal humans have come and gone and precious few have escaped death. Even Christ died. (The notable exceptions include Enoch and Elijah. Even these two, though spared death, were never said to be *incapable* of dying.) But we are speaking here of strict, absolute certainty. Until all the data is in, we cannot make absolute universal assertions on the basis of induction. Thus an element of uncertainty, however miniscule, attends the assertion of premise A.

What about premise B? How do we know that Socrates was a man? Maybe he was an angel in disguise. Perhaps he was bionic or a figment of the creative imagination of Plato. We trust the reports of fallible men of antiquity for our information about Socrates. We have a high degree of probability that there really was a Socrates but we lack absolute certainty.

Absolute philosophical certainty is limited to relative and conditional formal relationships of propositions. We can never achieve such certainty about the real world as long as we are dependent in any way on induction. This should not lead us to undue skepticism about the possibility of knowldge but simply to a healthy awareness of the limits of our faculties of knowledge. These limits are a part of our creatureliness. As long as our capacity for knowledge is the slightest bit less than omniscient, then the problem of philosophical certainty will remain. Only a being who is omniscient can transcend the problem. In other

words, only God can have philosophical certainty. Since we are
not and cannot be gods, we are left with philosophical uncertainty.

2. *Confidence as Certainty*

In spite of the above consideration, we still answer many questions in our lives routinely by using the word *certainly*. We make
assertions to which some respond, "Are you sure?" We reply,
"Yes." But how can we be *sure* about anything if absolute certainty is beyond the scope of our ability?

Obviously when we speak of being "sure" of things or say
"certainly," we are speaking about a kind of certainty that is not
the same as a technical philosophical certainty. Here we are
using the word *certain* in a way that describes a particular feeling
state that attends a given idea or assertion. Here the word *certain*
describes a sense of confidence or assurance. Such a certainty
can manifest relative degrees of intensity, since it is more or less
subjected to a mixture of doubt.

3. *Moral Certainty*

The third variety of certainty may be termed *moral certainty* or
juridical certainty. This is the certainty of the law courts when
they use the expression "beyond reasonable doubt." Suppose we
have a case of a person who committed cold-blooded murder in
the presence of five hundred witnesses and whose ruthless act
was captured by a broadcast television camera. To compound
the evidence, the culprit was arrested while holding a smoking
gun, which fired the fatal bullet and which clearly bears his
fingerprints. The cumulative weight of this evidence is presented
by the prosecution at the trial of the accused.

Suppose now that the defense attorney for the accused seeks
exoneration on the basis of an appeal to the lack of absolute
certainty concerning the guilt of his client. He argues that (1) the
five hundred witnesses suffered a mass hallucination; (2) the
television account was a carefully contrived electronic charade;
(3) the ballistics report matching the fatal bullet with the firearm
found in the hands of his client suffers the lack of certainty found
in all inductive studies involving empirical evidence; (4) the fact
that his client's fingerprints match the prints taken from the gun
is admitted by the lawyer, but he argues that this represents the
first occasion in history where two different people are found to

have identical sets of fingerprints. Thus the defense rests its case on a philosophical appeal to the theoretical possibility that his client is a victim of strange and extraordinary circumstances. The circumstantial evidence amassed by the prosecution is presented as being less than absolutely certain so the defense asks for acquittal on the basis of "reasonable doubt."

How do we respond to such a bizarre scenario? The doubt raised by the defense may indeed be *rational*, but is it *reasonable?* The courts recognize the difference. Without a distinction between formal certainty and moral or juridical certainty, it would be impossible to convict anyone of a crime unless God Himself were both prosecutor and judge.

Thus moral certainty refers to certainty acquired from the weight of evidence that, though lacking in philosophical certainty, is weighty enough to impose moral culpability. It is precisely this kind of certainty that the *indicia* of Scripture yield.

Though Calvin does not articulate the kind of distinction outlined above, it is spelled out by his disciples. Warfield, for example, cites Quenstedt on this point:

> The exact relations of the "proofs" to the divinity of Scripture, which Calvin teaches, was sufficiently clear to be caught by his successors. It is admirably stated in the Westminster Confession of Faith. And we may add that the same conception is stated also very precisely by Quenstedt: "These motives, as well internal as external, by which we are led to the knowledge of the authority of Scripture, make the theopneusty of Sacred Scripture *probable*, and produce a *certitude which is not merely conjectural but moral* . . . they do not make the divinity of Scripture infallible and altogether indubitable. . . . That is to say, they are not of the nature of *demonstration*, but nevertheless give *moral certitude*."[21]

The bridge from moral certitude to full assurance is constructed uniquely by the *testimonium*. The testimony of the Spirit puts the heart at rest and at peace regarding the authority of Scripture.

HEART OR HEAD AS THE OBJECT OF THE *TESTIMONIUM*?

Is the *testimonium* a cognitive act of the Spirit, involving primarily the human intellect, or is the primacy of the Spirit's activity located in the heart or the will? If we examine the *Institutes* we see that in sections 4 and 5 of chapter 7 Calvin alternates between mind and heart. He refers to the heart four times and to the mind three times. This makes for some difficulty in locating the primacy of Calvin's thrust.

Perhaps the solution to this difficulty may be found in the Reformer's qualifications of the kind of faith that is affected by the *testimonium*. Calvin speaks of "full faith" (7/4), "full credit in the hearts of men" (7/4), "full conviction" (7/5), "feel perfectly assured" (7/5), "true faith" (7/5), "full conviction" (8/1), and "firm faith" (8/13).

Only the Spirit can produce the fullness of faith and conviction Calvin speaks of. The *indicia* alone do not have the power to produce that kind of faith. Warfield says of this dimension:

> This prevalent misapprehension of Calvin's meaning is due to neglect to observe the precise thing for which he affirms the *indicia* to be ineffective and the precise reason he assigns for this ineffectiveness. There is only one thing which he says they cannot do: that is to produce "sound faith." . . . And their failure to produce "sound faith" is due solely to the *subjective condition* of man, which is such that a creative operation of the Holy Spirit in the soul is requisite before he can exercise "sound faith."[22]

It is thus the sinful condition of fallen man that makes the *testimonium* necessary. Inasmuch as, outside of grace, the heart is indisposed toward God, the mind refuses to embrace the Scripture. Here we see a parallel with the Reformation tripartite notion of faith as being composed of *notitia, assensus,* and *fiducia.* The *indicia* is sufficient to produce *assensus* but not *fiducia.* Herein we may discern what Calvin means by *full* faith. It is a faith that goes beyond mere intellectual assent to an acquiescence of the heart and will to the Word of God.

Again Warfield notes: "The testimony of the Spirit is the subjective preparation of the heart to receive the objective evidence in a sympathetic embrace."[23] Again quoting Beza, Warfield writes:

> The testimony of the Spirit of adoption does not be properly in this, that we believe to be true what the Scriptures testify (for this is known also to the devils and many of the lost), but rather in this—that each applies to himself the promise of salvation in Christ of which Paul speaks in Romans VIII. 15, 16.[24]

The Lutheran Hollaz echoes the thought of Beza on this point:

> The testimony of the Holy Spirit is the supernatural act *(actus supernaturalis)* of the Holy Spirit by means of the Word of God

alternatively read or heard ... by which the heart of man is
moved, opened, illuminated, turned to the obedience of faith, so
that the illuminated man out of these internal spiritual move-
ments truly perceives the Word which is propounded to him to
have proceeded from God, and gives it therefore his unwavering
assent.[25]

Thus the *testimonium* is directed primarily at the heart of man,
with the effect on the mind being a consequence of the change of
the disposition of the heart. The *testimonium* is not a secret new
argument or separate cognitive revelation that supplements the
indicia. No new content is transmitted to the believer's mind by
the *testimonium*. The *testimonium*, as Warfield points out, "is not a
propositional revelation, but an instinctive 'sense.' "[26]

NEOORTHODOX VIEWS OF THE *TESTIMONIUM*

With the advent of dialectical, crisis, or neoorthodox views of
Scripture, a noticeable shift occurred in thinking concerning the
testimonium. In reaction against a formal, objectivized view of
Scripture, neoorthodoxy offered a more kinetic or dynamic view
of Scripture and revelation.

Over against a schema that views the Bible as the Word of
God in *esse*, the neoorthodox school located the objectivity of the
Word of God uniquely in the Person of Christ. He alone embodies or incarnates the Word. Revelation occurs as the Spirit
speaks to us through the *instrument* of Scripture. Scripture is not
itself revelation but is a *vehicle* of or witness (*Zeugnis*) to revelation. It becomes revelatory as the Spirit speaks through it. The
Scripture, then, is a vehicle of the divine-human encounter.
Without the activity of the Spirit the Scripture cannot be viewed
as objective revelation.

For Calvin the *testimonium* results in a subjective acquiescence
to an objective revelation. The Bible is the Word of God with or
without the internal testimony. For neoorthodoxy, the Bible is
not the Word of God *in essence* but only a vehicle of revelation. It
may or may not be the Word of God, depending on the testimony
of the Spirit. Objectivity is restricted to Christ and does not
extend to the biblical writings.

Following the lead of Martin Kahler,[27] Emil Brunner writes:

I believe, however, in contrast to the Apostle, in Jesus Christ *by
means of* that which He proclaims to me by the Apostle, who bears
witness to Christ. The witness of the Apostle is an *instrument* of the

divine revelation to me. But I do not give credence to the witness
of the Apostle because the Apostle is represented to me as a
trustworthy witness, and because I have already been assured
that he is "inspired"; but I believe his witness at the same moment that I believe in the Christ to whom he testifies since his
witness becomes to me the Word of God through the fact that
God, through His Spirit, permits it to dawn on me as the Word of
His truth. . . . In one act of revelation there is created within me
faith in Christ, and faith in the Scriptures which testify of
Him. . . . The Scriptures are indeed the first of the means which
God uses, but they are not the first *object* of faith, nor are they the
ground of my faith. The ground, the authority, which moves me to
faith is no other than Jesus Christ Himself, as He speaks to me
from the pages of the Scriptures through the Holy Spirit, as my
Lord and my Redeemer. This is what men of old used to call the
testimonium spiritus sancti internum. [28]

Time out! On the contrary, this is *not* what men of old used to
call the *testimonium.* As we have shown above the function of the
testimonium is not to provide us with revelatory content but to
provide us with certainty and assurance that the Bible is the
revelatory Word of God.

We quite agree with Brunner that the Scriptures are not the
object of our faith. Brunner is here guarding against any form of
bibliolatry, in which faith in the Bible supplants faith in Christ.
But it is one thing to say the Bible is not the *object* of our faith and
quite another to say the Bible does not contain *objective revelation*
of the object of my faith. Brunner and other such interpreters
throw out the baby with the bathwater and leave us ensnared in
an existential quagmire of subjectivity.

Emphasizing the "event" of revelation in terms of personal
encounter,[29] Brunner goes on to describe the dynamics of the
revelation experience:

The revelation in Jesus Christ produces the *illumination* in my
heart and mind, so that I can now see: that this man is the Christ.
Suddenly, all the barriers of time and space have faded away; I
have become "contemporary" with Christ. . . .[30] He is no more
external than my faith is external. The sense of spatial and temporal remoteness, all external objectivity, has disappeared: He
who previously spoke to me only from the outside now speaks
within me through the Holy Spirit. . . . The knowledge of the
Scriptures as the Word of God is the same as the experience of the
Holy Spirit. The truth is neither subjective nor objective, but it is
both at once; it is the truth which may be described in other

words, as the encounter of the human "I" with God's "thou" in Jesus Christ.[31]

Shades of Kierkegaard and truth as subjectivity. Brunner says that truth is not subjective. This would seem to relieve him of the charge of *subjectivism*. But then he maintains that the truth is not *objective* either. This would seem to warrant the charge. Then he says it is *both* at once. How do we understand this?

Perhaps all that Brunner means is that truth contains both objective and subjective elements. Maybe what we have here is a restatement of Calvin that the Bible is objectively the Word of God, to which the Spirit moves us to make a subjective, personal response. All truth is "personal" in the sense that for it to have subjective meaning for me I must have some kind of personal response to it, either positively or negatively. But Brunner has already made it clear that this is not what he means. Truth as such is not objective but dynamic and personal. This is a kind of *personalism* that redefines the nature of truth. Here truth is not truth until or unless the personal dimension is added. Here we see the crisis of *propositional* revelation that was triggered by the neoorthodox movement.

No one would argue that biblical truth demands personal response; that is axiomatic. The issue is, Do we have an objective revelatory truth to respond to?

Thomas Torrance develops the concept of the role of the Spirit in relationship to the Word in his essay, "The Epistemological Relevance of the Holy Spirit." He initiates this study by saying, "The epistemological relevance of the Holy Spirit lies in the dynamic and trans-formal aspects of this knowledge."[32]

Following a phenomenological pattern of thought similar to Brunner's, in which the accent is on the kinetic experimental character of revelation, Torrance says:

> On the one hand, then, the Holy Spirit through His presence brings the very Being of God to bear upon us in our experience, creating the relation to the divine Being which knowledge of God requires in order to be knowledge, but on the other hand the Spirit through His ineffable and self-effacing nature reinforces the impossibility of our conceiving in thought and expressing in speech how our thought and speech are related to God, so that our thoughts and statements by referring infinitely beyond themselves break off before Him in wonder, adoration and silence, that God may be in All in all. Through the Spirit empirical relation to

the divine Being takes place and within it we are given intuitive
knowledge of God, but the mode of our relation to Him and the
mode of our knowledge of Him must be in accordance with His
nature as *Spirit,* and therefore even though we have empirical
relation to Him and intuitive knowledge of Him, they are not
amenable to the kind of control which we exercise in relation to
creaturely objects. It is rather we who fall under the overwhelming presence of the divine Being and come under the control of
His spirit in our experience and knowledge of Him.[33]

With Torrance the accent is on kinetic, transformal, experimental, intuitive knowledge of God via the Spirit and the Word.
With this accent it is not surprising to see Torrance liken his
approach to that of Heidegger. He says, "We may want to compare it to Heidegger's leap of thought to open up the original
source of being."[34]

Thus to escape formalism or objectivism the Spirit becomes
the springboard to transpropositional knowledge of God. From
this shift in understanding of Calvin's *testimonium* we readily see
how the next critical problem of theology became the God-talk
controversy that culminated in the death-of-God movement. If
the content of revelation (not merely the internal assurance of its
veracity)becomes separated from objectivity, there is no avoiding the crisis of linguistic analysis. The "dynamic" of "kinetic
thinking" leaves us only with intuition. But what about cognitive
knowledge of God?

It is the internal dimension of the *testimonium* that makes it
vulnerable to a subjectivistic bent. If the *testimonium* has reference to the revelation itself, rather than to an inner assurance
that corroborates external objective evidence *(indicia),* there remains no authority above and beyond the private experience of
the believing individual. If the Word becomes subject to the
internal dynamics of the believing individual, it becomes no
longer the objective Word of God but the subjective word of
man. This is a grave crisis inherent in an existential approach to
revelation.

For Calvin the believing individual makes a subjective response to the objective Word through the impetus of the Spirit.
For the existentialist, the subjective response determines the
Word as it becomes the Word of God only through the kinetic
activity of the Spirit.

Though orthodoxy faces a modern intramural debate regarding the apologetic value and function of the *testimonium*, there is a

monolithic consensus among those divided over apologetics for the objective, propositional character of the Bible as the Word of God.

THE NEW TESTAMENT BASIS FOR THE TESTIMONIUM

The New Testament does not provide us with a thoroughgoing exposition of the "internal testimony" as such. This, at face value, could expose Calvin, Luther, and a host of other theologians to the charge that the doctrine has been constructed on the basis of speculative philosophy or by a "system" of theology imposed on the Scriptures arbitrarily. However, the New Testament is replete with allusions to the work of the Spirit in securing our confidence in the Word.[35] These references are scattered throughout the New Testament and include such classic texts as 2 Corinthians 4:3–6; 1 John 1:10; 2:14; 5:20; Colossians 2:2; 1 Thessalonians 1:5; Galatians 4:6; Romans 8:15–16; and others.

The work of revelation, illumination, and persuasion are carried on from a trinitarian framework, ranging from the Father's revealing Jesus' messianic identity to Peter at Caesarea Phillipi (Matt. 16:17), to Jesus' revelation of the things taught Him by the Father in secret (John 12:49–50), to the work of the Spirit in illumination. Though all members of the Trinity are active in this redemptive operation, it is the work of the Holy Spirit that is stressed by the New Testament.

Consider 1 Corinthians 2 as a classic text for the *testimonium:*

> My message and my preaching were not with wise and persuasive words, but with a demonstration of the Spirit's power, so that your faith might not rest on men's wisdom, but on God's power.
>
> We do, however, speak a message of wisdom among the mature, but not the wisdom of this age or of the rulers of this age, who are coming to nothing. No, we speak of God's secret wisdom, a wisdom that has been hidden and that God destined for our glory before time began. None of the rulers of this age understood it, for if they had, they would not have crucified the Lord of glory. However, as it is written:
>
> > "No eye has seen,
> >   no ear has heard,
> > no mind has conceived
> >   what God has prepared for those who love him"—
>
> but God has revealed it to us by his Spirit.

The Spirit searches all things, even the deep things of God. For
who among men knows the thoughts of a man except the man's
spirit within him? In the same way no one knows the thoughts of
God except the Spirit of God. (1 Cor. 2:4–11).

The theme of this passage is the supremacy of the power of
God in revelation. The Spirit searches things that go beyond
what the senses perceive. Our faith is said to "stand" in the
power of God. God reveals the secret things of Himself *through*
the *Spirit*. The Holy Spirit mediates the Word. As the apostle
notes later: This is what we speak, not in words taught us by
human wisdom but in words taught by the Spirit, expressing
spiritual truths in spiritual words (1 Cor. 2:13). Here Paul links
the apostolic words with the work of the Spirit. The Spirit is not
mentioned merely as being the *source* of the content but as being
the basis of the *persuasive power* of the words.

The same emphasis on revelation and persuasion may be seen
in 2 Corinthians 3:1–11. The writing of the Spirit on the
Christian's heart is not viewed as a gnostic esoteric experience,
but as a powerful penetration of the heart by the truth of the
content of God's revelation.[36]

The internal testimony is not an isolated work of the Spirit
ripped loose from the written Word. Rather, as the Trinity works
in harmony to effect our redemption, so the Spirit bears witness
and testifies to us inwardly of the whole content of divine revelation.

THE VIEW OF THE BIBLE HELD BY THE CHURCH: THE EARLY CHURCH THROUGH LUTHER

Robert D. Preus

Robert D. Preus is president of Concordia Theological Seminary, Ft. Wayne, Indiana. He is a graduate of Luther College (B.A.), Bethany Lutheran Seminary (B.D.), Edinburgh University (Ph.D.), and Strasbourg University, France (D. en-Theol.). He has served as pastor of several Lutheran churches and held the position of professor at Concordia Seminary, St. Louis, for seventeen years before assuming the position of president at the seminary in Ft. Wayne. His writings include The Inspiration of Scripture; The Theology of Post-Reformation Lutheranism *(two volumes);* Getting into the Theology of Concord *and other books; and articles in* Concordia Theological Monthly, The Lutheran Witness, Lutheran Layman, Scottish Journal of Theology, Affirm, *and many other periodicals. Dr. Preus is a member of the Society for Reformation Research, Concordia Historical Institute, Medieval Society of America, Archaeological Society, and the Council of ICBI.*

CHAPTER SUMMARY

The doctrine of verbal inspiration and the inerrancy and divine authority of Scripture has been the consistent teaching of the Christian church from the time of the apostles through the early church and Middle Ages to the Reformation era. A remarkable unity of belief and even terminology persists through the centuries relative to this doctrine, which appears to be taken in every case from the teachings of the New Testament itself. At the time of the Reformation a new evangelical reading of Scripture and a much stronger emphasis on the sole authority of Scripture (*sola Scriptura*), reminiscent of the New Testament itself, take definite shape.

THE VIEW OF THE BIBLE HELD BY THE CHURCH: THE EARLY CHURCH THROUGH LUTHER

THAT THE BIBLE is the Word of God, inerrant and of supreme divine authority, was a conviction held by all Christians and Christian teachers through the first 1,700 years of church history. Except in the case of certain free-thinking scholastics, such as Abelard, this fact has not really been contested by many scholars. Of course, many of the early church fathers and an even greater proportion of the medieval theologians did not directly address themselves to the subject of biblical authority. The former simply assumed the doctrine of biblical authority on the basis of an understanding of Scripture that was shared by both Tannaite Judaism and the early Christians. The latter developed a notable lack of interest in biblical studies and in seeking answers directly from Scripture for questions and concerns of the day. In any case the view of Scripture as inspired by the Spirit of God and therefore possessing divine authority and inerrancy was not a creation of early Judaism or of early Christian thought but was the inheritance of an obvious truth taught in the Scriptures. Not until the divine origin, authority, and veracity of Scripture were somehow undermined or threatened did these issues receive direct attention from Christian theologians.

But just as we can establish Scripture's teaching of its own divine origin and authority on the basis of what is assumed rather than what is explicitly articulated there, we can clearly delineate the doctrine concerning Scripture held by the Christian church and its theological leaders from postapostolic times through the Reformation era. In fact such study has been done repeatedly by eminent scholars during the past century,[1] and, except in regard to Luther, the conclusions have all been that a remarkable unity persists through this long period. On no other point do we notice such unanimity, except perhaps on the issues of dichotomy and the forbidden degrees of marriage[2]—inherited views that were never seriously questioned and therefore were simply assumed to be true.

FROM THE POSTAPOSTOLIC CHURCH THROUGH JEROME AND AUGUSTINE

It is significant that the church and the synagogue in the postapostolic age held an essentially identical view of Scripture. Normative Tannaite Judaism professed to teach nothing but what was taught explicitly or implicitly in the Old Testament Scriptures. Although their hermeneutical principles and interpretation were different from that of the New Testament writers and the early church fathers, their understanding of the nature of biblical authority seems to have been the same. Both groups believed that the contents of the Scriptures were consistent and homogeneous and that there were no contradictions in Scripture. Scripture was considered to be the Word of God in the sense of representing verbal, cognitive revelation. The idea of progressive revelation was impossible, if such a notion meant that a complete and saving revelation was not given to Moses.[3] For early Judaism there was complete correspondence and agreement between Moses and the prophetic books and the Hagiographa, which explain the Pentateuch, just as for the early Christians the New Testament explains the Old. Except for this latter difference, Christ and the New Testament writers regarded the Old Testament in much the same way as did these Jews, although interpreting it always christologically, as did the early church after the time of the apostles.

As a matter of fact, the early Christian fathers, the apostolic fathers, and the apologists always accepted the Old Testament as divinely inspired and authoritative, long before the entire New Testament canon was accepted. Like the apostles in the Book of Acts, they consistently cited the Old Testament as divinely authoritative for their proclamation of the Christian gospel. In fact the Old Testament was considered a specifically Christian book, belonging to the church even more than to the synagogue, for it witnessed to Christ and His glory (1 Peter 1:10–12).[4] The apologists were in fact brought to faith in Christ through their reading of the Old Testament Scriptures, although it is safe to assume that they were usually persuaded by the apostolic witness and understanding of the Old Testament. Ultimately Christ, the risen Lord, was the final interpreter of the Old Testament and His word was found in the apostolic tradition and the New Testament writings.[5]

Only after the time of the apologists were the New Testament writings accepted along with the Old Testament. This shift took place as a result of the gradual acceptance of the New Testament canon. The New Testament was therefore considered completely authoritative along with the Old, and the two were now seen as one unit. The New Testament was regarded as the divinely authoritative commentary on the Old.

Meanwhile another position was beginning to take shape and become articulate. Along with total commitment to the Scriptures as the norm of all doctrine, a new and clear conviction concerning the authority of oral tradition began to develop. This oral tradition, handed down from generation to generation and going back through the apostles directly to Christ, in no way conflicted with the Scriptures. But it did aid the church in interpreting the Scriptures and particularly in summarizing the Christian faith and thus protecting Christians against the aberrations of Gnostics and other heretics. To Tertullian and Irenaeus, who developed this position, such apostolic tradition, which faithfully transmitted Christ's teaching, was, like Scripture, infallible.[6] Thus, for all practical purposes we have at the turn of the third century a kind of two-source doctrine of authority in the church, with both the New Testament and the rule of faith thought to be eminently apostolic.[7] It is probably true that neither Tertullian nor Irenaeus meant to subordinate Scripture to unwritten tradition. Only Scripture could ultimately authenticate tradition. But at the same time, the ongoing tradition was necessary to counteract heretical distortions and interpretations of Scripture.

Thus the two revelatory authorities, identical in content, complemented and authenticated each other. This position was held

in a variety of forms from the third century until the time of the
Reformation, and it continued after that time in the Roman
Catholic Church. The position ultimately led to the teaching of
the Council of Trent that Scripture and unwritten tradition—
which in effect often meant the church—were coordinate authorities for doctrine.[8] We must say, however, that in practice
both the Eastern and Western fathers as a rule gave much more
deference to Scripture than to any traditional rule of faith.
Creeds were written on the basis of Scripture and in terminology
that was clearly biblical; likewise commentaries and treatises of
all sorts were based on Scripture as the source of doctrine.
Irenaeus himself, in his *Adversus Haereses*, cites Scripture no fewer
than 1,200 times. As a matter of principle he states, "We must
believe God, who has given us the right understanding, since the
Holy Scriptures are perfect, because they are spoken by the
Word of God and the Spirit of God."[9] And how else could
Irenaeus and the other Fathers have done their theology? They
could scarcely have quoted from unwritten tradition.

But whereas Irenaeus might often have alluded to a rule of
faith, the later Fathers, with the passing of the Gnostic
influence, were far less reticent to quote directly from the Scriptures. This was true of Clement of Alexandria and Origen. Although their writings are far more directly biblical, they still
regarded the so-called rule of faith as having come directly from
the apostles and as being a rule for interpreting Scripture.[10]
And both believed that such a source of doctrine was independent of the New Testament, although the content of both was
the same.[11]

After Clement and Origen the vague idea of a canon of faith
was gradually replaced by creeds and the liturgy as the form of
unwritten tradition, which, along with Scripture, served as the
basis of doctrine in the church. But we must add that liturgy and
especially the early creeds were developed and constructed on
the basis of Scripture. And if anything in the creeds or liturgy
was thought to be unscriptural, such as was the *homoousios* in the
Nicaeno-Constantinopolitan Creed, it was accepted only with
much difficulty. We must note also that, as time went on, the
great literary works of the Fathers were more and more expositions of the Scriptures; and commentaries on the creeds (such as
that of Rufinus) were often intended to offer biblical evidence for
the creedal statements. To quote J. N. D. Kelly:

Throughout the whole period Scripture and tradition ranked as complementary authorities, media different in form but coincident in content. To inquire which counted as superior or more ultimate is to pose the question in misleading and anachronistic terms. If Scripture was abundantly sufficient in principle, tradition was recognized as the surest clue to its interpretation, for in tradition the Church retained, as a legacy from the apostles which was embedded in all the organs of her institutional life, an unerring grasp of the real purport and meaning of the revelation to which Scripture and tradition alike bore witness.[12]

According to all the early church fathers, the basis for Scripture's divine authority is its divine origin and form. Scripture is the Word of God. This unanimous conviction of the early church that Scripture is God's Word was not borrowed from ancient Judaism but was derived from the New Testament, which speaks of the God-breathed nature of Scripture (2 Tim. 3:16) and of the holy writers as having been instruments of the Holy Spirit (2 Peter 1:21). The fathers assumed that Scripture was the Word of God and treated it as such, just as the New Testament writers had done in the case of the Old Testament Scriptures. The Christian fathers differed from the early Jews concerning the origin of the Torah. The Jews believed the Torah was created by God thousands of years before the creation of the world and that in time it was given by God directly to Moses without the mediation of the Spirit. Thus rabbinic theology distinguished the Torah from the rest of the Old Testament Scriptures, although all of it was believed to have been inspired. The early Christians did not share this view of the Torah. Nor did they, for the most part, engage in the kind of wooden and fanciful exegesis so common among the Jews, as seen in the Talmud. Their keen christological understanding of the Old Testament, in any event, kept them from the almost total preoccupation with the juristic exegesis so typical of the house of Shammai and the house of Hillel and also of later Tannaite Judaism.

What then precisely did the early Christians mean when they called Scripture the Word of God? Quite simply, they believed that God is the real author of the Scriptures.[13] The books of Scripture were commonly ascribed to the Holy Spirit as the author.[14] The human writers were instruments of the Holy Spirit. Both Augustine and Ambrose, against the Manichaeans, explicitly called God the author of Scripture. By the term *author* they meant one who produces or effects something. This is precisely what God did in respect to Scripture; in this sense God authored all the Scriptures.[15] And in precisely this sense the Scriptures are unique, differing from all other writings and possessing qualities and attributes (such as authority and truthfulness) which are unique by virtue of the Scripture's origin and nature.

If Scripture is really and truly, not in some metaphorical or metonymical sense, the Word of God, what then is the function of the human authors of Scripture, according to the fathers of the early church? Or, to pose the question differently, What is the relation between the Holy Spirit and the holy writers as they wrote the Scriptures? Or, to pose the identical question in still a different form, What is the notion of inspiration taught by the church fathers? Historically the term *inspiration* has been applied both to Scripture ("Scripture is inspired" [θεόπνευστος, *theo-pneustos*] the product of God's breath, 2 Tim. 3:16) and to the prophets and apostles ("the writers of Scripture were inspired" [φερόμενοι, *feromenoi*] moved by the Holy Spirit, 2 Peter 1:21). Interestingly, Jerome translated both the *theopneustos* of 2 Timothy 3:16 and the *theromenoi* of 2 Peter 1:21 with the same Latin term (*inspirata*, or *inspirati*), thus causing a certain amount of confusion unless one distinguishes between the inspiration of the Scriptures and the inspiration (something quite different) of the holy writers. The question we are considering deals with the second meaning of the term.

Usually the Greek fathers spoke of the relation of the Spirit to the writers of Scripture when they employed the term *inspired* and its synonyms.[16] The term was already in use in the Hellenistic world, along with similar terms such as θεόφορος (*theophoros*), θεοφόρητος (*theophorētos*), θεοφορούμενος (*theophoroumenos*), θεήλατος (*theēlatos*), θεοδίδακτος (*theodidaktos*), θεοκίνητος (*theokinētos*), and the like. The terms meant simply that a person entered a state in which, by divine impulse, he spoke a divine message clearly, truthfully, and profoundly. But in the Hellenistic world the idea of inspiration went further, in that such a state was ordinarily typified by a kind of *mantis* or *mania*, an ecstasy accompanied by all kinds of bizarre oddities such as foaming at the mouth, hair standing on end, and the like. Such "inspiration" was often engendered by narcotics and usually resulted in a complete loss of memory. Nor did the experiences have cognitive content. The early Christians, however, envisaged something quite different when they spoke of the inspiration of the holy writers of Scripture. Before the time of Tertullian and the Montanists, the apologists and others may have spoken in somewhat unguarded terms as they referred to the relation of the Holy Spirit to the human writers of Scripture. And they may well have uncritically borrowed phrases from Philo, who drew deeply from Hellenistic religious thought as he likened the experience of Moses and other writers of Scripture to the psychological behavior common to the mystery religions of his day. They indeed, along with the later Greek and Latin fathers, employed the idea of inspiration in a variety of contexts not suggested by biblical terms and concepts. They taught, as both the Old and New Testaments witness, that the gift of prophecy was sometimes bestowed on a person while he was in an ecstatic condition. But there is no evidence to suggest that they, and particularly those who followed the Montanist enthusiastic heresy, sought to psychologize the inspired writers of Scripture.[17] Surely among the early Christian writers there was no simple apposition or identification of philosophy and revelation, of prophecy and ecstatic enthusiasm, as we see in Philo.

In the theology of the early church, what then was the relation of the writers of Scripture to the Holy Spirit? The human writers were the *instruments*, the organs, of the Holy Spirit.[18] Augustine consistently used the ablative case when referring to the work of the Holy Spirit and the preposition *per* when referring to that of the biblical authors,[19] thus clearly bringing out the instrumental part played by the prophets and apostles in the writing of Scripture. God is the *auctor primarius* (the actual author) of Scripture, and the biblical writers were His organs through whom He spoke. This is precisely the picture presented in the New Testament (Matt. 1:22; 2:6, 17; 3:3; 4:14; Acts 2:16; 4:25). And the Nicaeno-Constantinopolitan Creed echoes the same theme when it describes the Holy Spirit as speaking through the prophets. When the Fathers use certain metaphors to illustrate the instrumentality of the biblical writers—metaphors such as flute, lyre, musical instrument, hand, and the like[20]—their imagery must not be pushed beyond the specific point of comparison. They are not suggesting that all inspiration takes place in a state of ecstasy. They are not suggesting that the human authors of Scripture are unthinking, unwilling instruments, divested of consciousness or personality or *usus scribendi*. On the contrary, they at times affirm a condescension (συγκατάβασις, *sunkatabasis*—

Chrysostom) of the Spirit whereby He condescends or accommodates Himself to the styles and personalities of the biblical writers.[21] Thus they take into account the endowments, the thought forms, the *genus loquendi* of the different writers of Scripture. Augustine, for instance, in his *De Consensu Evangelistarum* makes this fact abundantly clear, and he often notes the very human motives and selectivity that prompted the evangelists to write as they did.[22] Origen clearly repudiates any comparison between the inspiration of the biblical writers and the ecstatic oracles of paganism.[23]

And so for the fathers of the early church, with the possible exception of the pre-Montanist apologists, the total control of the Spirit over the penmen was perfectly compatible with the conscious and willing use by the holy writers of their unique endowments and styles of writing. The flute–lyre–instrument terminology was employed only to stress the instrumentality of the human authors and the monergism of divine inspiration. One might say that contributively the biblical writers were passive— the Spirit alone supplied to them *what* they were to write, the very form and content; but subjectively or psychologically (if one may use such loaded modern terms) the biblical writers were active, in full and conscious possession of their faculties. Nowhere do the Fathers try to bridge this paradox; nowhere do they seem to be troubled by it or even aware of it. They simply accept the mystery of divine inspiration.

Again, it has been averred that the practice of Augustine and others in using the verb *dictate* to describe the Holy Spirit's activity in communicating the form and content of the sacred writings to the holy writers is tantamount to teaching a mechanical theory of inspiration, reminiscent of Montanism.[24] Actually Augustine uses such terms as *inspirare, dictare, suggerere,* and *gubernare* interchangeably and in a large variety of contexts. All these verbs are used in both broader and narrower contexts. In the narrower sense the verbs could best be translated "give," "charge," "communicate," "direct," "incite."[25] The use of these various verbs was calculated to stress once again that in the writing of Scripture the initiative was God's alone, that He monergistically determined what was to be written in Scripture and that the resultant Scriptures are His Word.

And so, whether the Fathers speak of the inspiration of the writers of Scripture or of the inspiration of the Bible itself, they are affirming one fundamental truth, that Scripture is really and truly God's Word, all of it, even its minute details.[26] Scripture is therefore divinely authoritative—and infallibly true.

Correlative to Scripture's divine origin and authority is its utter truthfulness and reliability. This was the universal conviction of the early church. Never was there any doubt concerning the inerrancy of Scripture. The notion of an errant Word of God was unthinkable in those days. True, the fanciful exegesis often employed, the allegorical method, and the search for a *sensus plenior* indicate often, no doubt, the difficulty the Fathers had with the plain meaning of many biblical assertions. Augustine in his *De Consensu Evangelistarum* struggled with the seeming discrepancies among the evangelists and with the New Testament's seeming preference for the sometimes errant Septuagint over the authentic Hebrew text of the Old Testament. He was far from successful in solving these problems. But never in those days was a difficulty of Scripture solved by charging Scripture with error or untruth. Never was the unity of Scripture and Scripture's agreement with itself questioned. In fact the inerrancy of Scripture was not merely assumed[27] but was affirmed deliberately and dogmatically. We find Augustine saying that the Scriptures are unique in their inerrancy:

> Only to those books which are called canonical have I learned to give honor so that I believe most firmly that no author in these books made any error in writing. . . . I read other authors not with the thought that what they have taught and written is true just because they have manifested holiness and learning.[28]

Jerome makes many similar assertions.[29] When Augustine and Jerome speak of the truthfulness of Scripture, they include both the formal inerrancy of Scripture (Scripture does not contradict itself) and the material truthfulness of Scripture (all the assertions of Scripture correspond to what is, in fact, so).[30] According to the Fathers, Scripture is a priori true, irrefragably so. Scripture needs no verification of any kind from outside authority. We find Jerome stating with certainty:

> When you are really instructed in the Divine Scriptures, and have realized that its laws and testimonies are the bonds of truth, then you can contend with adversaries; then you will fetter them and lead them bound into captivity; then of the foes you have made captive you will make freemen of God.[31]

From Anselm to the Reformation

The decline and fall of the Roman Empire, first in the West and then in the East, was accompanied by a virtual cessation of theological output of any substance. The development of dogma was permanently frozen in the East with the classic *De Fide Orthodoxa* of John of Damascus. In the West serious and constructive theological production was arrested from the sixth century until the rise of scholastic theology. It was the rediscovery of Aristotle and the desire to coordinate theology with all human knowledge that originally incited the scholastics to engage in their monumental productions. Exegetical work was scarcely carried on. In the West neither of the biblical languages was known.

It is understandable therefore that no original contribution or advance in the area of bibliology would take place. The scholastics inherited the position of their forerunners. But if a somewhat consistent bibliology is only adumbrated in the early church, it is scarcely discernible in the scholastic era. One may range through thousands of pages of scholastic theology before finding any explicit or direct word concerning the divine origin, authority, or truthfulness of Scripture. Among the scholastics, doctrine concerning Scripture *per se* can be extracted only from their prolegomenous discussions, where they center attention primarily on questions of epistemology and discuss man's return to God, revelation, prophetic knowledge, and similar themes. Their discussion of inspiration as a supernatural charism is carried on out of epistemological and anthropological concerns.[32]

Although there is a real paucity of evidence to demonstrate a clear and explicit scholastic position concerning the *locus de scriptura*, the following summary of the greater of the medieval scholastic theologians' views on this point will reveal a definite position concerning the Scriptures and will illustrate that there is no considerable difference between the theology of the thirteenth century and that of the fifth century on this point.

Anselm

No doctrine of bibliology, or of the Word, is articulated in Anselm.[33] Although in his three best known works (*Proslogion, Monologion,* and *Cur Deus Homo?*) he is speculating as a philosopher—for he is proving rationally those things that are already accepted on faith—still behind such dialectics lies an implicit reliance on what we would call the Scripture principle. When he says at the beginning of his *Proslogion* that in believing we seek to understand (*credo ut intelligam*), his idea is simply this: It is proper for faith to seek to understand. We may never understand, Anselm grants; but if we do understand, it will be because we have started with faith. And faith, of course, depends on the divine revelation of Scripture. Here Anselm has distinguished himself as a faithful student of Augustine; and he is not consciously going beyond Augustine in any respect. The fact that he somewhat concedes to his students in working out certain doctrines dialectically may deceive us into thinking that he is a rationalist, but this is not so. He is not trying to strip revelation of its mystery but to penetrate the mysteries so far as can be done. With Anselm no clear distinction is made between theology and philosophy.

Alexander of Hales

Alexander is a little more articulate.[34] In his *Summa Theologica* he speaks somewhat of Scripture in his prolegomena. He insists that Scripture has a purpose greater than that of other histories (I,1). The history there recorded is not merely to point to individual actions of people but to assess general actions and conditions that serve to inform men and women and enable them to contemplate divine mysteries. Thus he sees in Scripture a salutary diagnostic purpose and function. The examples Alexander uses to illustrate his point are perhaps not the most fortunate: the death of Abel signifies the innocent suffering of Christ and other just people, while the wickedness of Cain represents the perversity of the unrighteous.

The mode (*modus*) of the art or science of Scripture—we might call this "theology"—is not according to the usual comprehension of the rational mind. Theology (*modus Scripturae artis*) obtains by means of the arrangement of divine wisdom that informs the soul in those things that pertain to salvation (*per dispositionem divinae sapientiae ad informationem animae in iis quae pertinent ad salutem*). If this seems to be pure intellectualism, we must remember that Alexander is speaking of theology as art or science (*scientia*), that is, as communicable. The Franciscans were not intellectualists but voluntarists (I, 1).

What he means by theology as information is made more clear when he goes on to say (I, 5) that the knowledge we gain through inspiration is more certain that what we gain through human rationalizing, and the knowledge we gain through the testimony of the Spirit is more sure than what we gain by the witness of creatures. The former certainty is the certainty of the spiritual man as opposed to the carnal man. *Modus theologiae est certior certitudine experientiae:* "The method of theology is more certain than a certitude drawn from experience." The carnal man has no knowledge but *experimento sensibilium;* the spiritual man has a certainty that is due to his possessing the spirit of contemplating divine things. The conclusion is that only knowledge given in Scripture offers absolute or, we might say, divine certainty. This emphasis of the Franciscan school that knowledge (*cognitio*) is not simply intellectual is shared by Luther and the Reformers.

Bonaventura

Little data can be gathered from Bonaventura.[35] He was in the Franciscan school and would follow Alexander. Like the earlier Franciscans, he did not differentiate closely between theology and philosophy. He simply insisted that there is no legitimate philosophy that is not oriented in God. Philosophy begins with the visible effects and argues to God, but it must always comport with revealed theology, which is drawn from Scripture. Thus there was only a methodological distinction between the two sciences. The conclusions of both were the same. The philosopher will, for instance, work out proofs for the existence of God, but only with the presupposition that he already believes in God. He does not make himself temporarily an atheist. In all of this, philosophy was the handmaid of theology, and all theology was drawn from Scripture.

Thomas Aquinas

Thomas is more explicit in his views of Scripture and its place in the theology of the church than any of the previously mentioned theologians. Again his views on Scripture are found in his prolegomena on the nature of *sacra doctrina.* He begins with a discussion of the necessity of revelation.

> It was necessary for man's salvation that there be a certain doctrine according to divine revelation, truths which exceed human reason. Even regarding those truths which human reason can investigate it was necessary that man be taught by divine revelation. For the truth about God which is learned through reason

would be known only by a few after a long time and with an admixture of errors; but the salvation of man depends upon his knowledge of this truth which is in God. Therefore, in order that salvation might the easier be brought to man and be more certain it was necessary that men be instructed concerning divine matters through divine revelation.[36]

This theology, which is learned through revelation, is different in kind (*secundum genus*) from the theology that philosophy deals with. Thomas next asks whether theology (*sacra doctrina*) is a speculative science or whether it is a practical science. It is a science that proceeds from principles that proceed from a higher science; namely, the science of God. Because this science deals with God, it is a speculative science more than a practical science. The place of Scripture in theology is made quite plain by Thomas when he asks whether sacred doctrine is argumentative. All sciences argue from principles and do not try to prove their principles. Thus it is also with theology, whose principles (*principia*) are the articles of faith. In philosophy the lower sciences cannot dispute or prove the principles of a higher science. Sacred Scripture offers the highest science, a science *sui generis*.

If a heretic or outsider admits any of the principles of Scripture, one may discuss with him with hope. In all such discussion faith in Scripture rests on infallible truth, and it is impossible to demonstrate any argument against such faith. Theology makes use of human reason, but only for the sake of clarification. "Therefore, sacred doctrine also makes use of human reason: not, however, to prove faith, for in such an event the very merit of faith would be vitiated, but to clarify (*ad manifestandum*) other things which are set forth in this doctrine." Thus theology will make use of philosophers in those matters that can be known by human reason; for example, Paul quotes Aratus (Acts 17:28). Thomas then concludes the section:

However, sacred doctrine makes use of these authorities (philosophers) only as extraneous and probable arguments. Properly theology uses the authorities of the canonical scripture as the necessary argumentation (*ex necessitate argumentando*). The authority of the doctors of the church is properly employed, but as merely probable (*probabiliter*). For our faith rests upon the revelation given to the apostles and prophets who wrote the canonical books, and not on revelation (if there be such a thing) made to other teachers. Whence Augustine says in his letter to Jerome (82): "Only to those books which are called canonical have I

learned to give honor so that I believe most firmly that no author
in these books made any error in writing. I read other authors not
with the thought that what they have thought and written is true
just because they have manifested holiness and learning!"

This surely sounds like one who believes in the divine origin of
Scripture and the *sola Scriptura* principle. Later Thomas says that
the author of sacred Scripture is God. Whatever may be his
practice later, correct principles have been set down clearly in
this prolegomena on the nature of theology. One aberration in
Thomas's position might be noted here. Rather than calling
Scripture the *principium* (source) of theology, Thomas calls the
articles of faith the *principia* (sources) of theology. From this
point later Romanist theologians go on to state that not all articles of faith are necessarily drawn from Scripture, although it is
doubtful if Thomas would have supported such an inference
from what he said. It may finally be said that if there is confusion
in Thomas between the realm of reason and the realm of tradition in theology, it is not to be found in the prolegomena but in
the way he carries out his theology; this is said in opposition to
the rather severe judgment of Harnack.[37]

In his prolegomena Thomas came closer than any other
scholastic theologian to affirming a principle of *sola Scriptura*. But
in practice he was never able to carry out anything even approximating such a principle. Yet he consciously affirmed the
inerrancy of Scripture as a fundamental assumption for the
theological enterprise. For instance, he says, "It is heretical to
say that any falsehood whatsoever is contained either in the
gospels or in any canonical Scripture."[38]

Duns Scotus

In his prolegomena Duns has much to say about revelation
and Scripture.[39] After going to great length to show the necessity
of revelation, he considers a section on the sufficiency of holy
Scripture. Against the heretics who would reject parts or the
whole of Scripture, he advanced eight arguments for the truth
(*veritas*) of Scripture. (1) Prophecy and fulfillment. (2) The
agreement of Scripture with itself. It is obvious, he says, that a
greater mind than man's created the Scriptures. (3) The authority of the writers of Scripture. Duns points out that the writers of
Scripture claim divine authority. Thus to credit their writings
with anything less than absolute authority is to charge them with

deliberate lies. (4) The diligence that was exercised in receiving the canon. The church, he says, was always careful to receive only those books that were written by prophets, who wrote by divine inspiration (*scriptura recepta sit in Canone quam auctores, non sicut homines sed sicut prophetas, divina inspiratione scripserunt*). (5) The reasonableness of the contents of Scripture. Duns claims that the things we believe from Scripture are not unreasonable, for they comport with divine perfection. (6) *De irrationalibitate errorum.* Here Duns lashes out against the insipid, asinine errors of Jews, Manichaeans, and other heretics who twist Scripture against Christ, often due to a lack of knowledge of Scripture. "Not even one passage of Scripture can be opposed." (7) The stability of the church that accepts Scripture. (One can imagine where this one proof will lead Duns.) (8) The clear proof of miracles.

After listing these eight arguments, Duns proceeds to affirm the sufficiency of Scripture for leading man on the way he ought to go. He seems to follow Origen and to approach the later Lutherans, who contended that the sufficiency of Scripture was not of such a nature that everything was in Scripture expressly, but everything (e.g., the Trinity) was there *virtualiter, sicut conclusiones in principiis.*

Concerning theology as a science, Duns begins by pointing out that science, strictly speaking, embraces four factors: (1) it is certain knowledge with no possibility of doubt or of being deceived (*cognitio certa*); (2) it is necessary knowledge and not contingent; (3) it is evident to the intellect (*sit causata a causa evidente intellectui*); and (4) it can be demonstrated by reasoning and discursive argument. According to the first three factors, theology is *in itself* a science, but not for us. In the sense that theology deals with God's external operations, it is not a science, because it is not necessary (4,1).

Theological science—Duns would prefer the word *wisdom*—does not depend on any other science. Although metaphysics deals with God, still theology does not derive any *principia* from metaphysics. The principles of theology are accepted on faith, on authority. Nor can theology be demonstrated by any *principia entis.* Here he differs from Thomas. And we see the cleavage between the two philosophers, or theologians. Duns is still basically a voluntarist. He would not give the same weight to reason and demonstration as did Thomas. More weight is given to faith and authority, which, unfortunately, ultimately becomes the au-

thority of the church. Thus we find Duns differing also with
Thomas in teaching that theology is *scientia practica,* whereas
Thomas said it was chiefly a *scientia speculativa.* Of all the scholastic theologians, Duns says more about the intrinsic authority and
inerrancy of Scripture than does any other. Some of his points
summarized above were actually taken over by Protestant theologians during the period of orthodoxy. But with all his insistence on the authority, truthfulness, and even sufficiency of Scripture, Duns was far from affirming a *sola Scriptura* principle and
even farther from putting anything approximating such a principle into action.

In Thomas and Duns we see how difficult it is to maintain *sola
Scriptura* against the encroachments of reason on the one hand
and of church authority on the other.

MARTIN LUTHER

Our brief survey of the history of the doctrine of biblical inspiration from apostolic times to the Reformation ends with Luther
(see the following chapter for his successors), although we can
offer only a cursory view of his position. He represents the end of
one era (the Middle Ages) and the beginning of another (the
Reformation). There is no need to examine the position of other,
lesser Reformers such as Melanchthon, Flacius (who did a pro-
digious amount of pioneer work in biblical studies), and others.
On no important point do they differ from Luther in his attitude
toward Scripture and in his use of it.[40]

Although Luther inherited the unanimous high view of Scripture held by the early church and throughout the Middle Ages,
he brought with him, for a number of reasons, a different approach to Scripture from that of his more immediate predecessors. Thus his convictions concerning the divine origin of Scripture and biblical authority and inerrancy—convictions held by
the Fathers and assumed, although at times submerged, by the
scholastics—were informed by a new evangelical hermeneutic
and approach to theology. The significance of this fact can
scarcely be overemphasized.

What is so different, even revolutionary, in Luther's approach
to Scripture? Certainly one factor that sets him apart from the
scholastic theology from which he had emerged was the
humanistic influence of the day, with its solid emphasis on
philology and on theology as exegesis of Scripture—a scholarly

emphasis that prompted Luther to learn the biblical languages, lecture on books of the Bible, and ultimately to translate the Bible into German. But this factor alone does not explain the dynamics of Luther's doctrine of Scripture and the great theological influence of that doctrine.

It has been conjectured that Luther's personal experience, issuing from his discovery of the gospel of justification by faith in Scripture, is the key to understanding his doctrine of the Word.[41] But such a theory puts the cart before the horse and misunderstands Luther's own view of the subsidiary place of experience in relation to the power and authority of the divine Word.

No, Luther discovered a number of things about the form and content of Scripture that, though taken for granted, had previously been unappreciated and ignored.

First, he learned that theological science or wisdom is a *habitus* or charism not merely given by the Holy Spirit, as all the medieval theologians had taught, but given by the Spirit *through the Scriptures.* To be a theologian one must first of all be scriptural. One must read and reread the Scriptures,[42] grapple with them,[43] understand their intended sense without human gloss,[44] and yield to them.[45] In short, the theologian must be a *bonus textualis* first and foremost.

> The first concern of a theologian should be to be well acquainted with the text of Scripture (a *bonus textualis,* as they call it). He should adhere to this primary principle: In sacred matters there is no arguing or philosophizing; for if one were to operate with the rational and probable arguments in this area, it would be possible for me to twist all the articles of faith just as easily as Arius, the Sacramentarians, and the Anabaptists did. But in theology we must only hear and believe and be convinced at heart that God is truthful, however absurd that which God says in His Word may appear to be to reason.[46]

Luther never tires of stressing the point that the Holy Spirit makes a person a theologian only by leading him to an understanding and acceptance of the words of Scripture.

> This is our foundation: where the Holy Scripture establishes something that must be believed, there we must not deviate from the words, as they sound, neither from the order as it stands, unless an express article of faith (based on clear Scripture passages) compels us to interpret the words otherwise, or arrange them differently. Else, what would become of the Bible?[47]

Again Luther says:

> You should meditate, that is, not in the heart alone, but also
> externally, work on and ply the oral speech and the lettered words
> in the Book, read them and reread them again and again, noting
> carefully and reflecting upon what the Holy Spirit means by these
> words. And have a care that you do not tire of it or think it
> enough if you have read, heard, said, it once or twice, and now
> profoundly understand it all; for in that manner a person will
> never become much of a theologian.[48]

It is significant that the old accepted catholic assumptions
regarding Scripture's divine origin and authority are assumed
throughout these urgent admonitions of Luther concerning the
making of a theologian.

It is Luther's utter adherence to the Scriptures as the source of
all theology that led to his discovery of the gospel of justification
in Romans 1:16. This same regard for Scripture and yielding to it
led to his insight, followed by that of Melanchthon and also the
Reformed theologians, that Scripture ought to be divided into
the themes of Law and Gospel and similar hermeneutical break-
throughs. Certainly it was also this confident, biblicistic dependence on the Scriptures that brought about his rejection of
philosophy and philosophical principles in establishing theology
(such as the principle of Aristotle and Aquinas: *finitum non est
capax infiniti*). Luther says:

> Paul takes them all together, himself, an angel from heaven,
> teachers upon the earth, and masters of all kinds, and subjects
> them to the Holy Scripture. Scripture must reign as queen, all
> must obey and be subject to her, not teachers, judges, or arbiters
> over her; but they must be simply witnesses, pupils and confes-
> sors of it, whether they be pope or Luther or Augustine or an
> angel from heaven.[49]

As he rehearses what makes a Christian a theologian, Luther has
already articulated a clear position regarding biblical authority,
but in an eminently practical, not a theoretical, context.

Second, like the church fathers, Luther saw the Scriptures as
Christocentric in their entire sweep and soteriological in their
purpose—but again in the practical context of the consistent
hermeneutical application that informs his entire theological activity. To Luther, "Christ is the sum and truth of Scripture."[50]
"The Scriptures from beginning to end do not reveal anyone
besides the Messiah, the Son of God, who should come and

through His sacrifice carry and take away the sins of the world."[51] "The entire Scripture points only to Christ."[52] "Outside the book of the Holy Spirit, namely the holy Scriptures, one does not find Christ."[53] Such statements concerning the Christocentricity of the Old and New Testaments could be multiplied.[54]

The principle of the Christocentricity of Scripture was not something Luther inherited from the early church and then imposed on the Scriptures. He derived the principle from Scripture itself; he found Christ there inductively through sound and serious exegesis, as is made abundantly clear from his commentaries on Genesis, Deuteronomy, Psalms, and Isaiah. Luther's personal theological Christocentricity, while derived from Scripture, informs his exegesis of Scripture. It is not only possible for him, but incumbent on him, to read the Old Testament in the light of the New just as he read the New in the light of the Old. Such a practice is in harmony with his belief—and the belief of the entire church catholic in the light of Luke 24:25–27; Romans 15:4; 2 Timothy 3:15, and other passages—in the unity of Scripture and in the hermeneutical principle that Scripture is its own interpreter.[55] It was just his failure to find Christ and justification by faith in certain books of the Old and New Testaments (all *antilegomena*) that prompted Luther to depreciate the value of these books and question their canonicity.[56] In fact he at times appears to depreciate the Bible itself in comparison with the pearl of great price that is found in it. For instance, he says:

> I beg and faithfully warn every pious Christian not to stumble at the simplicity of language and the stories that will often meet him there. He should not doubt that however simple they may seem, these are the very words, deeds, judgments, and history of the high majesty and wisdom of God; for this is the Scripture which makes fools of all the wise and prudent and is open only to babes and fools, as Christ says, Matthew 11:25. Away with your overweening conceit! Think of Scripture as the loftiest and noblest of holy things, as the richest lode, which will never be mined out, so that you may find the divine wisdom which God places before you in such foolish and ordinary form. He does this in order to quench all pride. Here you will find the swaddling clothes and the manger in which Christ lies, to which the angels directed the shepherds, Luke 2:12. Mean and poor are the swaddling clothes, but precious is the treasure, Christ, lying in them.[57]

Far from belittling Scripture by this statement, Luther enhances it; that is his very purpose as he speaks in such a way. To him Scripture is of supreme value (and how often does he extol the value of Scripture[58]), not merely because of its form as God's Word and revelation, but because of its content and message, which is Christ, the crucified and risen Savior of the world.

But there is another reason why Luther valued the Scriptures so highly, namely, their power; power to comfort, to save, to regenerate, to lead the child of God to eternal life. In this sense and for this purpose God speaks mightily to us in the sacred Scriptures.[59] This is the very purpose of the Holy Spirit, even as He diligently describes the most shameful, adulterous history, the most despised, filthy, and damnable things in Scripture: to teach, reprove, admonish, bless, and save us.[60] Luther never tires of extolling the practical value of Scripture for the life of a believer. It makes us happy, trustful, confident Christians and puts us at peace with God.[61] It is our defense against the temptations of the devil, the world, and our flesh.[62] It instructs us in the true worship and service of God[63] and in how to be a good theologian.[64] It sanctifies, reforms, and comforts us.[65] But most important of all, we learn about God and His grace in Scripture, and so we gain eternal life.[66] In this is the great power of the Scripture. For Scripture not only points us to Christ; it shares Christ with us and bestows Him on us. It brings us to faith, and through it the Holy Spirit comes to us with all His treasures and blessings.[67] Scripture does all this; it possesses the intrinsic power to do so because it is God's Word, because the Spirit of God is never separated from it,[68] and because its message is Christ. "All the works which Christ performed are recorded in the Word, and in the Word and through the Word He will give us everything, and without the Word He will give us nothing."[69] To be sure, the preached gospel has all the power of the written Word of Scripture; but the preached word (and all theology) is to be drawn only from the one divine foundation of Scripture.

Luther's deep and personal conviction concerning the power of the Scriptures is the *third* factor in his new approach to Scripture.

And so Luther's doctrine of the divine origin of Scripture, its authority and inerrancy, must be viewed in the light of the aforementioned three aspects of his approach to Scripture: (1) the Holy Spirit makes one a theologian through Scripture alone, (2) Christ's atonement is the burden and "chief article" of all Scripture,[70] and (3) the Scriptures are powerful to work faith and make one wise for salvation. It is not that Luther's bibliology is based on these three insights; on the contrary, his understanding concerning these issues is drawn *from* Scripture.[71] But the hermeneutical preunderstanding Luther brings with him to the study of Scripture results in a far more practical and evangelical view of biblical authority than had previously been held.

What specifically, then, does Luther teach on the three issues here under consideration: the divine origin of Scripture, the authority of Scripture, and the inerrancy of Scripture? Formally his views were identical to those of the early church and of the Middle Ages.

Divine Origin or Inspiration

Although Luther, like his predecessors and immediate followers, rarely spoke of inspiration as such, he said in literally hundreds of instances that Scripture is the Word of God, that God speaks through Scripture, and that God is the author of Scripture.[72] There is no way in which one can anachronistically interpret Luther as advancing some sort of preliberal notion that the Bible merely *contains* the Word of God or pre-Barthian notion that God in some way, where and when it pleases Him, makes the words of men (in Scripture) *His* Word.[73] Luther simply and ingenuously says, "You are so to deal with the Scriptures that you bear in mind that God Himself is saying this."[74] We fear and tremble before the very words of Scripture because they are God's words, all of them, for "whoever despises a single word of God does not regard any as important."[75] Matthew, Paul, and Peter were indeed men, but should anyone believe that their words and doctrine were only the words of men and not of God, he is a hardened and blinded blasphemer who should be avoided.[76] "It is cursed unbelief and the odious flesh which will not permit us to see and know that God speaks to us in Scripture and that it is God's Word, but tells us that it is the word merely of Isaiah, Paul, or some other mere man, who has not created heaven and earth."[77] That Scripture is the Word of God means for Luther that it is materially and formally so, word for word, His Word, verbally inspired. "The Holy Scriptures are the Word of God, written and (I might say) lettered and formed in letters, just as Christ is the eternal Word of God veiled in the human nature."[78] The very order of the words found in Scripture are intentionally arranged by the Holy Spirit.[79] Thus, not merely the phrases and expressions in Scripture are divine but the very words and their arrangement.[80] "The prophets do not set forth statements that they have spun up in their own mind. What they have heard from God Himself . . . they proclaim and set forth."[81] And if the holy evangelists arrange their Gospels differently from each other, this too has been determined by the Holy Spirit.[82]

Authority

To Luther, Scripture derives its divine authority not from its content, which is the Gospel and the Law, but from its form. It is authoritative because it is the Word of God.[83] That Scripture is authoritative means that it alone is the source and norm of doctrine. "No doctrine in the Church can come from anywhere but the Holy Scripture; it is our only source of doctrine."[84] And only Scripture is the authority, the source, and the norm of doctrine. "There is no other evidence of Christian proof on earth but the Holy Scripture."[85] Luther rejoices and revels in the certainty he has as one bound by the authority of Scripture: "One passage of Scripture has more authority than all the books of the world."[86] In commenting on Galatians 1:8, he says:

> Paul takes them all together, himself, an angel from heaven, teachers upon the earth, the masters of all kinds, and subjects them to Holy Scripture. Scripture must reign as queen, all must obey and be subject to her, not to teachers, judges, or arbiters over her. No, all these must be simply witnesses, pupils and confessors of Scripture, whether they be pope or Luther or Augustine or an angel from heaven.[87]

It is obvious that neither reason, nor philosophy, nor experience, nor pope, nor church council can be regarded as an authority beside Scripture; but all must conform to Scripture. Nor may any of these be allowed to interpret Scripture in a way that is contrary to its plain and clear meaning.[88] Otherwise, "what would become of the Bible?" Scripture would be relegated to the position of a waxen nose and lose its authority entirely. If Scripture is not the authority alone, it is not the authority at all.[89] Luther not only affirmed the *sola Scriptura* principle, he practiced it.

Inerrancy

The divine origin, authority, and inerrancy of Scripture all hang together for Luther. Each concept entails the other. In contexts where he defends the authority of Scripture, Luther

affirms or alludes to its divine origin. As he debates his case for
sola Scriptura against Romanists or enthusiasts he maintains that
the Holy Spirit caused the biblical writers to write clearly,
truthfully, and without equivocation. For Luther, the notion of
an authoritative but *errant* Word of God would have been utter
nonsense. No such idea could have been entertained prior to the
rise of subjective idealism and existentialism. When Luther or
any of the Reformers defended the authority of Scripture, which
was his chief concern, he was *eo ipso* affirming also Scripture's
divine nature and total veracity. In fact it is very doubtful if
Luther ever carefully distinguished between the three concepts.

In his usual blunt and ingenuous way, Luther affirmed the
absolute infallibility and truthfulness of Scripture. For Luther, as
for those who went before him, this meant that Scripture (1) does
not err to deceive in any way and (2) does not contradict itself.

Thus we find him saying, relative to the first aspect of inerrancy: "Natural reason produces heresy and error. Faith teaches
and adheres to the pure truth. He who adheres to the Scriptures
will find that they do not lie or deceive."[90] "Scripture cannot
err."[91] "The Scriptures have never erred."[92] If Scripture seems
to err, it is our fault for not understanding it properly or yielding
to it.

> The Holy Spirit has been blamed for not speaking correctly; He
> speaks like a drunkard or a fool, He so mixes up things, and uses
> wild, queer words and statements. But it is our fault, who have
> not understood the language nor known the matter of the proph-
> ets. For it cannot be otherwise; the Holy Ghost is wise and makes
> the prophets also wise. A wise man must be able to speak cor-
> rectly; that holds true without fail.[93]

This statement of Luther indicates also that Scripture is *infallibly*
true in all its assertions, irrefragable. We need not test it with
reason, experience, or any other authority. Its utterances can
and ought to be accepted a priori.[94] This means taking our
reason captive. For the simple words of Scripture often seem to
be in opposition to science, evidence, and experience. "As the
Word says, so it must come to pass, although all the world, mind
and understanding, and all things are against it."[95] And, of
course, it is because Scripture is the Word of God that it is
infallibly true.[96]

The second aspect of inerrancy, namely, that Scripture cannot
contradict itself, is affirmed by Luther with equal vigor: "Scrip-

ture agrees with itself everywhere."[97] In fact "it is certain that Scripture cannot disagree with itself."[98] Only a foolish, coarse, hardened hypocrite will find contradictions in Holy Writ. "It is impossible that Scripture should contradict itself; it only appears so to senseless and obstinate hypocrites."[99] Luther's doctrine of inerrancy at this point agrees with his catholic commitment to the unity of Scripture and becomes along with the analogy of Scripture, a fundamental hermeneutical rule. If Scripture should contradict itself at any point, then all exegesis, interpretation, and theologizing end in chaos.

It was "all or nothing" for Luther as he carried out his theological work and based his teaching on the inerrant word of Scripture. To claim to have found even one error in Scripture was blasphemy against God and against all of Scripture. "Whoever belies and blasphemes God in one word, or speaks as if it were a trifling thing, he blasphemes God in everything, and regards all blasphemy of God unimportant."[100] This is Luther's "domino theory" vis-a-vis the veracity of Scripture. Speaking against the fanatics, who tended often to make light of the external word of Scripture, Luther says:

> They do not believe that they [the words of Scripture] are God's words. For if they believed they were God's words they would not call them poor, miserable words but would regard such words and titles as greater than the whole world and would fear and tremble before them as before God Himself. For whoever despises a single word of God does not regard any as important.[101]

Again Luther writes:

> Whoever is so bold that he ventures to accuse God of fraud and deception in a single word and does so willfully again and again after he has been warned and instructed once or twice will likewise certainly venture to accuse God of fraud and deception in all of His words. Therefore it is true, absolutely and without exception, that everything is believed or nothing is believed. The Holy Spirit does not suffer Himself to be separated or divided so that He should teach and cause to be believed one doctrine rightly and another falsely.[102]

CONCLUSIONS

What conclusions can we draw from this very cursory sketch of the view of the Bible held by the church through the ages? We have found a remarkable, essential agreement among the leading church fathers, the Scholastics, and the first Reformer in their view toward the Bible—of its divine inspiration, authority, and veracity. Only heretics ventured to reject the universal faith of the church on these issues. We have found that through the centuries, from the apostles to the Reformation, the belief that Scripture was really and truly God's Word always entailed belief also in the divine authority and inerrancy of Scripture. Scripture is divinely authoritative and infallible just because it is God's Word. Thus biblical evidence or exegesis specifically supporting biblical authority or inerrancy is rarely explicitly offered, for these divine properties were simply assumed to obtain in the case of a divine Scripture. Throughout all these centuries the authority of Scripture in theological work and in the life of the church was the prime concern. When Scripture speaks, God speaks.

Not much speculation was advanced concerning the nature of inspiration, except to reject Platonic, Montanist, and other erroneous or exaggerated theories. It was always enough simply to affirm Scripture's divine origin and its nature as God's authoritative Word. Again, the inerrancy of Scripture as such was never given a great deal of attention or defended at length. This was unnecessary because it was simply assumed by all that for a cognitive word to be authoritative in any meaningful sense it *must* be inerrant, inerrant in the sense that it *always* speaks the truth. A simple correspondence idea of truth lies behind every assertion concerning Scripture's reliability or truthfulness. No other idea could have occurred to the theologians and church leaders of this long era. The assertions of Scripture are true in the sense that they correspond to what has happened in history or will happen in the future or to what simply obtains in regard to God and all that is revealed in Scripture about Him and His dealing with men.

Such an idea of truth also underlay the approach to Scripture by those who used the allegorical method of interpretation or sought a *sensus plenior* or a fourfold sense in Scripture; otherwise why would they resort to such a program as they attempted to find significance in verses that, on the surface, seemed trivial?

Although we find a remarkable unity concerning the divine nature of Scripture during this long period of history, we discover also that such unity is no absolute safeguard against poor exegesis, fanciful and wrong hermeneutics, false doctrine, and controversy. Although we learn from history that a high view of

Scripture is essential for good exegesis, it does not guarantee good exegesis. Not until the time of Luther was the sufficiency of Scripture clearly enunciated and practiced consistently, although the divine authority of Scripture was always held. Not until the Reformation did the idea of the Christocentricity of Scripture amount to more than a kind of shibboleth. It was rarely a working hermeneutical rule (drawn from Scripture) to get at the intended (literal) sense of Scripture. And a high view of Scripture does not necessarily lead to love of the Scriptures, a desire to search them and live in them and by them.

But if this unity we have traced concerning the nature and authority of the cognitive source of theology does not automatically lead to unity of doctrine in the church, it at least forms a basis of discussion. During the first fifteen hundred years of church history the common belief concerning the divine source of Christian doctrine was certainly the greatest single factor in making doctrinal discussion possible among Christians—and also fruitful and at times successful. There was always the conviction within Christendom that pure doctrine was based on the Scriptures, that it was a great blessing to the church, and that unity in doctrine was possible. Today this is not the case. When the divine origin, authority, and infallibility of Scripture is denied or subverted, pure doctrine in the church becomes an impossibility and the very desire for it as the highest honor of God and help for the proclamation of the gospel is considered naive or even presumptuous.

We have learned many things from our brief study of the view of the Bible held by the church through the ages, and perhaps unlearned a few things. But the most important is the lesson that the quality of theology in the church—and the church lives by its theology—although it may descend below the level of its view of Scripture, will rarely rise above it.

THE VIEW OF THE BIBLE HELD BY THE CHURCH: CALVIN AND THE WESTMINSTER DIVINES

John H. Gerstner

John H. Gerstner is Professor of Church History, Pittsburgh Theological Seminary, Pittsburgh, Pennsylvania, and Visiting Professor, Trinity Evangelical Divinity School, Deerfield, Illinois. He is a graduate of Westminster College, (B.A.), Westminster Theological Seminary, (B.Th., M.Th.), and Harvard University, (Ph.D.). He holds honorary degrees from Tarkio College, (D.D.) and Westminster College (L.H.D.). Among his many books and articles are: Calvin's Political Influence in the United States; The Epistle to the Ephesians; The Gospel According to Rome; An Inerrancy Primer; A Predestination Primer; Reasons for Faith; A Reconciliation Primer; Steps to Salvation: A Study in the Evangelistic Message of Jonathan Edwards; Survey of the Cults; Theology for Everyman; Theology of the Major Sects; *"Warfield's Case for Biblical Inerrancy"* in God's Inerrant Word, *edited by John Warwick Montgomery; and "The Message of the Word"* in The Bible: The Living Word of Revelation, *edited by Merrill C. Tenney. Dr. Gerstner has served as a contributing editor for* Christianity Today. *He is a member of the Evangelical Theological Society, the American Church History Society, the American Theological Libraries Association, and the Council of ICBI. Earlier in his career he held two pastorates in western Pennsylvania.*

CHAPTER SUMMARY

In this chapter the author shows with many proofs that John Calvin and the Calvinists at the Westminster Assembly held to the doctrine of inerrancy. The difficult matter is to explain why some knowledgeable scholars cannot accept that fact. The debate did not arise because of what Calvin and Westminster wrote, but because of what some scholars *errantly* deduce from what they wrote. For example, Calvin's being critical about a certain text's inclusion in the Bible at all is thought to indicate his being critical of the Bible itself.

THE VIEW OF THE BIBLE HELD BY THE CHURCH: CALVIN AND THE WESTMINSTER DIVINES

INTRODUCTION

The Reformation was not a revolution. The intent of the Protestant Reformation was not to create new doctrine or establish a new church. Rather, the impetus of the movement was to bring into bold relief crucial doctrines obscured by the process of sacerdotalism within the medieval Roman Catholic Church. The doctrine of *sola fide* was not new, finding its classical expression in Augustine's *De Spiritu et Littera*; neither was *sola Scriptura*, in principle, invented by Luther.

Inerrancy has been the classic view of Scripture throughout church history. To view it as the brain child of seventeenth-century Protestant scholasticism or the *de novo* creation of the "Old Princeton" school is to distort history. To be sure, this assertion has been brought into question again and again in the twentieth century. In the first quarter of this century we saw the rise of neoorthodoxy, under the leadership of Karl Barth, Emil Brunner, and Paul Althaus. While this school sought a restoration of some semblance of the Reformed faith over against the excessives of nineteenth-century liberalism, it also sought to "correct" orthodoxy at several points—most notably, the notion of inerrancy in light of modern conclusions drawn from negative higher criticism.

With the advent of neoorthodoxy came the attempt by some of

its advocates to show that neoorthodoxy was not deviating from classical views of Scripture but was merely reforming views that crept in via a reification of the dynamic view of Scripture taught by Calvin and Luther. Protestant scholasticism allegedly had ossified the vitality of the sixteenth century. The dynamic Scripture was made "static" through theories of verbal inspiration and inerrancy. The chief culprit in making the pure Reformation-century view obscure was supposedly the Old Princeton school, as embodied particularly in Benjamin B. Warfield.

Of late, many evangelical scholars have echoed the protest of earlier Barthians, maintaining that inerrancy indeed reflects a late development of, even departure from, the classical view. Some evangelical scholars not only favor a view of partial biblical inerrancy but insist that the historic Christian church believed it. I will attempt in this chapter to show that the main historic path of the Reformed tradition in particular has been that of full inerrancy.

It is significant that the current fourth edition of *The New Columbia Encyclopedia*[1] recognizes the classical character of the concept of inerrancy. While this most massive and comprehensive one-volume encyclopedia in the world possesses a great deal of religious information, it is essentially secular in viewpoint and generally quite objective. Its matter-of-fact statement is therefore all the more impressive:

> The traditional Christian view of the Bible is that it was *all* written under the guidance of God and that it is, therefore, *all true*, literally or under the veil of allegory. *In recent times*, however, the view of many Protestants has been influenced by the pronouncements of critics (see Higher Criticism). This has produced a counter-reaction in the form of fundamentalism, whose chief emphasis has been in the inerrancy of the Bible (italics added).[2]

The traditional Christian view is that the Bible is "all true." What "Fundamentalism" has reacted to is deviation from the historic norm.

If secularists, outside the internecine struggles of churchmen, recognize the obvious thrust of Christian history, why then is the matter debated so strenuously within the church? Laymen especially are puzzled and bewildered when their trusted mentors, who are regarded as experts, differ about this matter of the church's historic position on inerrancy. Why do men who have studied the subject thoroughly so often come to differing and even conflicting conclusions? How can lay people understand the matter if the scholars maintain exactly opposite interpretations of the very same data? Such confusion is quite frustrating to laymen and causes some to despair of ever being able to resolve the conflicts.

This problem is not so difficult to explain as it may appear at first glance. The trouble is rarely in the sources of information. Two chief factors are frequently at work when data are misinterpreted. One factor involves a weakness of character, namely, prejudice. The other factor involves weakness of deductive skill. The accumulation of data requires inductive skill. The analysis and interpretation of the data requires deductive skill. At times the two weakness factors just mentioned may be closely interrelated. People with normally great powers of deduction may fail if their minds are governed by prejudice.

There is a general tendency in church history for those who deviate from orthodoxy to try to prove that their deviation is, in reality, an exercise in restoration and reformation. To be sure, in some circles, radical novelty is regarded as the touchstone of progress and truth. But in other circles, most especially within the mainstream of Christendom, it is often regarded as the kiss of death. Most heretics in the history of the church have initially sought to defend their views by appeals at least to segments of Scripture. Only after their exegesis was seen to be faulty did they seek to attack the credibility of Scripture itself. Appeals to the Bible and/or tradition are a commonplace method for those who seek widespread endorsement of ideas or doctrines that in fact are contrary to the teaching of both.

In the current controversy over inerrancy let us not assume that we are dealing with sinister manipulations of the data commonly characteristic of rank heretics. I prefer to assume that the problem among evangelicals is not so much one of blind prejudice but of weaknesses and pitfalls in the area of deduction.

Some scholars of massive learning are not well skilled in drawing conclusions. Some laymen who know nothing of the subject matter, except what the experts tell them, can easily see that certain conclusions drawn by the experts do not follow from the data presented by the experts themselves. Thus they may be benefited by the scholar's learning and not much harmed by his *non sequiturs*.

There are five very common *non sequiturs* (things that do not follow) in the field we are about to survey. If the reader will master them, he will, we believe, avoid a great deal of misunderstanding.[3]

1. The phenomenal *non sequitur*
2. The accommodation *non sequitur*
3. The emphasis *non sequitur*
4. The critical *non sequitur*
5. The docetist *non sequitur*

The *phenomenal non sequitur*: The Bible's representing things as they *appear* (phenomena) has occasioned the leap of logic that concludes it contains error, because that is not the way things *are*. Obviously, this conclusion does not follow. If the Bible taught that things *appeared* one way, and they did *not appear* that way, that would be error. But for the Bible to teach that things appear one way when they actually are another way is not error. A simple illustration is assuming that the Bible is in error when it refers to a "sunrise" (a term that describes how things appear) because that is not the way things are (the sun does not "rise").[4]

The *accommodation non sequitur*: The Bible's representing God as accommodating Himself to human language has occasioned the leap of logic that concludes His Word contains error because accommodation to human language involves accommodation to human error. Obviously, this conclusion also is not right. It does not follow that, because God accommodates Himself to human language, He must accommodate Himself to human error. This would follow by logical necessity only if it were first proven that all human language could only err. This would not even be theoretically possible to prove for it would require the use of human language to prove that human language always errs. Accommodation may be coupled with the phenomenal *non sequitur* by asserting that God accommodates us by using phenomenal language. An example is the supposition that the Bible's representing God as "repenting" (which is how it looks to us) is an error because of God's unchangeableness (which is how it is).[5]

The *emphasis non sequitur*: The Bible's emphasizing certain things has occasioned the leap of logic that concludes it contains error because it must be indifferent to other unemphasized things. But it does not follow that because the Bible stresses one thing, it errs in the things it does not stress. For example, it does not follow from the Bible's stress on salvation that it may err with impunity in mere historical details.[6]

The *critical non sequitur:* The fact that theologians of the church perform the work of textual critics has occasioned the leap of logic that concludes that these critics must therefore believe the Bible contains error. But it does not follow that because a scholar examines a text to see whether or not it *belongs* to the Bible he therefore believes the *Bible* can err. For example, if Luther at one point denied that the Book of James belonged in the Bible it does not mean that Luther believed the Bible itself was errant.[7]

The *docetic non sequitur:* The Bible's representing itself as the Word of God written by men has occasioned the leap of logic that concludes it is therefore errant. Obviously this conclusion does not follow. "To err is human" may be descriptive of the fact that people do err and that error is characteristic of them rather than of God. But it does not follow that people *always* err, even apart from the matter of inspiration. Certainly it does not follow that if God *inspired* men He would be incapable of keeping them free of human error in writing. For example, it does not follow from the Bible's saying that God used Paul in the writing of the Epistles that God could not keep those Epistles free from error.[8]

Equipped with this logical geiger counter to detect hidden mines and booby traps in the field of sound reasoning, let us tread very carefully, though hastily, on the path of history since the Reformation in an attempt to ascertain the Reformed tradition concerning biblical inspiration and inerrancy.[9]

JOHN CALVIN

Though the Reformation begins properly with Luther, Dr. Preus in his excellent chapter has already adequately discussed this Reformer. I will begin, then, with the work of Calvin.

Karl Barth precisely summarized the Reformation view of Calvin on the Bible as follows:

> In the Reformation doctrine of inspiration the following points must be decisive.
> I. The Reformers took over unquestionably and unreservedly the statement on the inspiration, and indeed the verbal inspiration of the Bible, as it is explicitly and implicitly contained in those Pauline passages which we have taken as our basis, even including the formula that God is the author of the Bible, and occasionally making use of the idea of a dictation through the Biblical writers. How could it be otherwise? Not with less but with greater

and more radical seriousness they wanted to proclaim the subjection of the Church to the Bible as the Word of God and its authority as such. . . . Luther is not inconsistent when we hear him thundering polemically at the end of his life: "Therefore, we either believe roundly and wholly and utterly, or we believe nothing: the Holy Ghost doth not let Himself be severed or parted, that He should let one part be taught or believed truly and the other part falsely. . . . For it is the fashion of all heretics that they begin first with a single article, but they must then all be denied and altogether, like a ring which is of no further value when it has a break or cut, or a bell which when it is cracked in one place will not ring anymore and is quite useless." (*Kurzes Bekenntnis vom heiligen Sakrament* 1544 W.A. 54, 158, 28). Therefore Calvin is not guilty of any disloyalty to the Reformation tendency when he says of Holy Scripture that its authority is recognized only when it . . . is realized that *autorem eius esse deum.* In Calvin's sermon on 2 Timothy 3:16ff. (C.R. 54, 238ff.) God is constantly described as the *author of Holy Scripture and in his commentary on the same passage we seem to hear a perfect echo of the voice of the Early Church. . . . In spite of the use of these concepts neither a mantico-mechanical nor a docetic conception of Biblical inspiration is in the actual sphere of Calvin's thinking.*[10]

Though Barth saw a basic harmony between Luther and Calvin on Scripture, Brunner did not. Brunner did not see the inerrancy doctrine in Luther but saw it correctly at least in Calvin.

Calvin is already moving away from Luther toward the doctrine of Verbal Inspiration. His doctrine of the Bible is entirely the traditional, formally authoritative view. The writings of the Apostles *"pro dei oraculis habenda sunt* [are oracles that have been received from God]" (Institutio, iv, 8, 9). Therefore, we must accept *"quidquid in sacris scripturis traditum est sine exceptione* [whatever is delivered in the Scripture without exception]" (I., 18, 4). The belief *"auctorem eius (sc: scripturae) esse deum* [God is the author of all Scripture]" precedes all doctrine (I., 7, 4). That again is the old view.[11]

In spite of Barth's and Brunner's recognition of Calvin's view of Scripture some have persisted in asserting that inerrancy was a later intrusion into the Reformed tradition. Though the Calvin corpus has been canvassed repeatedly to demonstrate the Reformer's doctrine of Scripture, some have still balked at granting that he held to inerrancy. Nothing that modern opponents of inerrancy have presented, cited, deduced, or inferred in any way whatsoever shows that Calvin held any other view of Scripture than that of absolute inerrancy. Brunner[12] and Dowey[13] find verbal inspiration in Calvin. Bromiley even finds dictation.[14] Kenneth Kantzer's doctoral thesis may be the most thorough demonstration of Calvin's teaching of inerrancy,[15] and John Murray[16] and J. I. Packer[17] agree with him, though they find problems.

If problems exist with Calvin they are basically related to the *non sequiturs* outlined above. To be sure, Calvin wrote no major formal treatise on Scripture. That is not at all surprising inasmuch as the doctrine was not an issue of his day. His debate with Rome was not over the inspiration or inerrancy of Scripture. Both sides tacitly assumed the position. When Calvin does speak explicitly on Scripture, his view is asserted unambiguously. He refers to Scripture as:

"The sure and infallible record"[18]
"The inerring standard"[19]
"The pure Word of God"[20]
"The infallible rule of His Holy Truth"[21]
"Free from every stain or defect"[22]
"The inerring certainty"[23]
"The certain and unerring rule"[24]
"Unerring light"[25]
"Infallible Word of God"[26]
"Has nothing belonging to man mixed with it"[27]
"Inviolable"[28]
"Infallible oracles"[29]

Though Calvin does not employ the noun *inerrancy* he makes ample use of the adjectival form *inerring*. He also uses *infallible*. Thus for Calvin the Bible is an inerring, infallible book. That is what is generally understood to be meant by *inerrancy*.

Calvin's classic statement on Scripture is important:

> When it pleased God to raise up a more visible form of the Church, he willed to have His Word set down and sealed in writing. . . . He commanded also that the prophecies be committed to writing and be accounted part of His Word. To these at the same time histories were added, also the labour of the prophets, but composed under the Holy Spirit's dictation. I include the psalms with the prophecies. . . . That whole body [*corpus*], therefore, made up of law, prophecies, psalms and histories was the Lord's Word for the ancient people. . . . Let this be a firm principle; No other word is to be held as the Word of God, and given place as such in the Church, than what is contained first in the Law and the Prophets, then in the writings of the apostles, ...

[who] were to expound the ancient Scripture and to show that what is taught there has been fulfilled in Christ. Yet they were not to do this except from the Lord, that is, with Christ's Spirit going before them and in a sense dictating their words. . . . [They] were sure and genuine penmen [*certi et authentici amanuenses*] of the Holy Spirit, and their writings are therefore to be considered oracles of God: and the sole office of others is to teach what is provided and sealed in the Holy Scriptures.[30]

Again, in Calvin's comments on 2 Timothy 3:16 we read:

In order to uphold the authority of Scripture, he [Paul] declares it to be divinely inspired: for if it be so, it is beyond all controversy that men should receive it with reverence. . . . Whoever then wishes to profit in the Scriptures, let him first of all lay down as a settled point this—that the law and the prophecies are not teaching [*doctrinam*] delivered by the will of men, but dictated [*dictatum*] by the Holy Ghost. . . . Moses and the prophets did not utter at random what we have from their hand, but, since they spoke by divine impulse, they confidently and fearlessly testified, as was actually the case, that it was the mouth of the Lord that spoke [*os Domini loguutum esse*]. . . . We owe to the Scripture the same reverence which we owe to God, because it has proceeded from Him alone.[31]

When Calvin speaks of the reverence we owe to Scripture, why do not modern critics of inerrancy rise up and accuse the Reformer of bibliolatry? So strong is this theme of reverence before the Holy Word that Calvin exclaims, "The full authority which they [the Scriptures] obtain with the faithful proceeds from no other consideration than that they are persuaded that they proceeded from heaven, *as if God had been heard giving utterance to them.*[32]

With such strong explicit statements from Calvin, it may seem surprising, indeed astonishing, that anyone would ever challenge the statement that Calvin was an advocate of inerrancy. Yet the challenge has come. We see examples of the challenge in Fullerton, Doumergue, Schiverger,[33] Painer, and De Grost, to name but a few.

Why does the challenge come? We could speculate that Calvin, like so many other scholars underwent a progressive development of thought in which ideas blossomed but were later corrected or discarded. For example, we can distinguish between "early Barth" and "later Barth" and between "early Berkouwer" and "later Berkouwer." Thus, perhaps, the citations from Calvin indicate a careful process of "selection" from the massive fifty-nine volumes of the *Corpus Reformatorum*.

This speculative procedure fails miserably, as every student of Calvin knows. We cannot find explicit statements of Calvin that would indicate such a "corrective" development. On the contrary, his view of Scripture is sprinkled through a wide variety of his works over a vast number of years. He went to his grave committed to a lofty view of Scripture. His deathbed utterance of 1564 has been recorded for us:

> As for my doctrine, I have taught faithfully, and God has given me grace to write, which I have done faithfully as I could; and I have not corrupted one single passage of Scripture nor twisted it so far as I know. . . .[34]

The primary basis of the challenge to Calvin's view of inerrancy comes from an analysis of his exegetical practice. Though it is virtually universally agreed that Calvin held to a theory of inerrancy, that theory was thought by some to be belied by his practice as a critical exegete. Here the *non sequiturs* rear up and charge into the picture.

The *phenomenal non sequitur* appears with respect to Calvin's comments regarding the Bible and natural science. He maintains that the biblical writers simply wrote in popular style, and popular style does not need to be and indeed cannot be harmonized with science. Popular style is one thing; technical style is another. Attention is called to an illustration from Calvin in which Moses called the moon one of the two great lights, whereas in fact it is much smaller than Saturn, as was known even in Calvin's day. There is no problem of harmonization, however. As Calvin says, Moses is talking about things as they *appear* to the naked eye, and the astronomer about things as they *are*, as seen through the telescope (*non sequitur no. 1*). If the astronomer said that Saturn appeared to be bigger than the moon, he would be in error. If Moses had said that the moon *is* larger than Saturn, he would have been in error. But Moses is not in error, and Calvin is not implying error in Moses, though Rogers suggests that Calvin acknowledged scientific error in Moses and yet was indifferent to it.[35] Here is what Calvin says in the matter:

> Moses here addresses himself to our senses. . . . By this method (as I have before observed) the dishonesty of those men is sufficiently rebuked, who censure Moses for not speaking with greater exactness. . . . Moses wrote in popular style things which,

> without instruction, all ordinary persons, endued with common
> sense are able to understand. . . . But had he spoken on things
> generally unknown, the uneducated might have pleaded in excuse
> that such subjects were beyond their capacity. . . . Moses, there-
> fore, rather adapts his discourse to common usage. . . . There is
> therefore no reason why janglers should deride the unskillfulness
> of Moses in making the moon a secondary luminary; for he does
> not call us up into heaven, he only proposes things which lie open
> before our eyes.[36]

Closely related to phenomenal matters are questions arising
from Calvin's view of divine accommodation in revelation. Here
care is needed in interpreting Calvin lest we slip into the pitfall of
non sequitur no. 2, *accommodation.* At the heart of Calvin's theology
was his doctrine of the incomprehensibility of God. This doctrine
set the boundaries of divine-human communication. Calvin was
zealous to maintain and preserve the *difference* between man and
God as well as the points of similarity. When treating the matter
of those dimensions of God's being that are incomprehensible,
Calvin speaks of accommodation. He says:

> God cannot reveal Himself to us in any other way than by a
> comparison with things which we know; . . . in order to know God
> we must not frame a likeness of Him according to our own fancy,
> but we must take ourselves to the Word in which His lively image
> is exhibited to us.[37]

This accommodation by which God speaks to us in our language, according to our perspective, is not an accommodation to
human error but to human levels of understanding.

> If God, accommodating Himself to the limited capacity of men,
> speaks in a humble and lowly style, this manner of teaching is
> despised as too simple; but if He rises to a higher style, with the
> view of giving greater authority to His Word, men, to excuse their
> ignorance, will pretend that it is too obscure. As these two vices
> are very prevalent in the world, the Holy Spirit so tempers His
> style as that the sublimity of the truths which he teaches is not
> hidden even from those of the weakest capacity, provided they are
> of a submissive and teachable disposition, and bring with them
> an earnest desire to be instructed.[38]

Calvin saw no conflict between inerrant inspiration and accommodation. In fact, accommodation only stresses the point
that Calvin regarded the Bible to be inspired, for the accommodation is *divine* accommodating. His favorite metaphor for

accommodation is that of "stammering" or "lisping." God is said to "prattle" to us in Scripture with a kind of baby talk in order to stoop to our level of understanding. Thus, while the Scriptures provide simple levels of understanding of the incomprehensible God, it does not follow from such simplicity that it is therefore errant. An infant may lisp, stammer, and prattle and at the same time be truthful about what he is stammering. No one was ever convicted of perjury simply for lisping.

Calvin's textual criticism has also provoked charges of practice inconsistent with theory. Calvin allows for scribal errors by copyists of the original manuscripts. He allows for variations of chronological order in the Synoptics. He allows for round numbers and the proper use of hyperbole. He even acknowledges the use of intemperate language by the writer of the Psalms but quickly points out the truth of the Bible in all of this.[39] Calvin rejected the Pauline authorship of Hebrews. Yet Calvin never made the leap of logic of some of his interpreters, who conclude that the practice of various forms of textual and canonical criticism implies a denial of inspiration or inerrancy. Calvin avoided *non sequitur* no. 4 (*critical*).

POST-REFORMATION SCHOLASTICISM

A. A. Hodge has written somewhere that the seventeenth century with its Scholasticism was the golden age of Protestantism.[40] What Hodge felt to be a natural development and fruition of the Reformation, many today consider a distortion and rigidifying. They see a difference of kind rather than of degree, a degeneration rather than a shift of emphasis.[41] The difference amounts, however, simply to the Scholastics being more academic, pedantic, and methodical. In a word, the Scholastics were more scholarly.

Therefore, to say of the Lutheran Scholastic, John Gerhard, that his "doctrine of Scripture . . . was not an article of faith, but the *principium* (foundation) of other articles of faith" and that he therein differed from his mentor, Luther, is unjustified.[42] We have shown that Luther had some reason for faith in the Bible as God's Word, as also did Calvin. Once the Bible was recognized as the Word of God, it of course became the *principium* for all truth that it revealed. What else? Even those who hold to partial inspiration believe that the inspired part (if they could identify it) is the Word of God and is to be believed.

Rogers says of the great Reformed Scholastic, Francis Turretin: "Because reasonable proofs must precede faith, Turretin felt it necessary to harmonize every apparent inconsistency in the biblical text. He refused to admit that the sacred writers could slip in memory or err in the smallest matters."[43] Rogers seems to think that Turretin first harmonized every "apparent inconsistency" before he could have faith in the Bible as the Word of God. But he cites no evidence of this, and we are certain that he can find none. Why, then, does he think this?—apparently because Turretin really did refuse to admit any biblical errors "in the smallest matters." If this is Roger's line of reasoning, it is an example of further *non sequiturs*:

1. Turretin admitted no errors in the Bible.
2. Inconsistencies would involve error.
3. Therefore, Turretin:
   a. would admit no inconsistency in the Bible,
   b. would harmonize all apparent inconsistencies, and
   c. would not believe the Bible as the Word of God until he had completed the harmonizations.

It is 3b and 3c that are the *non sequiturs* Rogers apparently does not notice. It does not follow (and it did not follow for Turretin) that because a person believes there are no errors or inconsistencies in the Bible he can harmonize all apparent ones. It is enough that he can show that apparent inconsistencies are not incapable of harmonization. Obviously, if a person does not have to harmonize every apparent inconsistency even *after* believing the Bible to be the Word of God, he does not have to do so *before* believing it.

The jibe of Dill Allison that although Turretin "claimed to be expounding Reformed theology, he never quoted Calvin"[44] is mind-boggling to anyone who knows Turretin's constant allusion to, and saturation with, John Calvin, whom he admired almost to the point of idolatry.

THE WESTMINSTER CONFESSION OF FAITH

The Westminster Confession of Faith is Presbyterianism's most influential creed. Chapter 1, "Of the Holy Scripture," is its most influential and noble chapter. Inerrancy is its indubitable teaching, although the word *inerrancy* itself is not used but only equivalents.[45]

The most extensive and scholarly study ever made of this

confession is undoubtedly Jack Rogers's massive, erudite, able, and influential study, *Scripture and the Westminster Confession*.[46] Only his persistent misunderstanding of the faith/reason and total/partial inspiration themes vitiates its value. Because of that volume's significance, Rogers's comments on Westminster in *Biblical Authority* are especially important.

Rogers begins with the fideistic interpretation of the Confession characteristic of his major work:

> Philosophically, the Westminster divines remained in the Augustinian tradition of faith leading to understanding. Samuel Rutherford stated the position: "The believer is the most reasonable man in the world, he who doth all by faith, doth all by the light of sound reason."[47]

Here Rogers cites one of the Westminster divines least disposed to his own thesis, quoting a statement from Rutherford that refutes rather than supports it. If the reader ponders the above quotation, he can see that it boomerangs against the one who cited it. It is meant to show that the Scots divine, Rutherford, operated on the faith-before-reason principle, but it reveals the opposite. Rutherford calls the believer "reasonable." In other words, there are reasons for faith, for to act by faith is to act by reasoning: "He who doth all by faith, doth all by the light of sound reason." Gillespie, another of the "eleven" primary drafters of the Westminster Confession, could not have said it better. This is a utilization, not a crucifixion, of reason. There are reasons for faith. It is no crucifixion of the intellect to extol reasonable faith.

Yet Rogers continues:

> The "works of creation and providence" reinforce in persons that knowledge which has been suppressed and because of which a person is inexcusable for his sin. Thus there is no "natural theology" in the Thomistic fashion, asserting that persons can know God by reason based on sense experience prior to God's revelation.[48]

Here the point of "reinforce" is missed, just as "confirmation" was in the Calvin discussion. How can creation and providence "reinforce" innate knowledge of God unless they too reveal God? And what is this but "natural theology," whether exactly the same as that of Aquinas or not?

Leaving natural theology and turning to biblical revelation, we read: "The authority of Scripture in section iv was not made dependent on the testimony of any person or church, but on God, the author of Scripture."[49] True, but what Protestant or Roman Catholic Scholastic ever said that the authority of Scripture was "dependent on the testimony of any person or church?" Everyone recognizes that the authority of the Bible rests only on its being God's Word. The testimony of the church or any other proofs are cited only to try to prove that the Bible is the Word of God. If it is the Word of God, its authority is intrinsic. The debate is finished. No "Aristotelian Scholasticism" would try to demonstrate by external evidence the "Bible's authority." All it would try to demonstrate is the Bible's inspiration; and if it succeeded in that, the authority of the Bible would be established *ipso facto.*

Of course Reynolds, whom Rogers cites, would say that a person's faith—be he Platonist, Aristotelian, Protestant, Roman Catholic, or Jew—is assent "grounded upon the authority of authenticalness of a Narrator, . . ." if that Narrator is believed to be God. Men recognize this in their natural state. The point is only that they do not "see" it spiritually. Reynolds explained this very well in his essay "The Sinfulness of Sin": "A man, in divine truths, [may] be spiritually ignorant, even where in some respect he may be said to know. For the Scriptures pronounce men ignorant of those things which they see and know."[50] Reynolds is here arguing with the Socinians who deny "spiritual" knowledge altogether in biblical matters. He would now have to argue with Rogers, who denies "natural" knowledge altogether in the same matters. We continue:

> Section v climaxed the development of the first half of the chapter with the statement that, while many arguments for the truth and authority of Holy Scripture can be adduced, only the witness of the Holy Spirit in a person's heart can persuade that person that Scripture is the Word of God.[51]

This is the statement by which Rogers refutes Rogers on his most fundamental thesis, namely, that faith precedes reason in the historic doctrine of the church and in that of Westminster. True to Westminster, he writes, "While many arguments for the truth and authority of Holy Scripture can be adduced, only the witness of the Holy Spirit in a person's heart can persuade."

That is, there are arguments of reason that precede faith, though they do not "persuade." This is the view of Origen, Augustine, Aquinas, Luther, Calvin, Turretin, Edwards, and Princeton, but it is not Rogers's faith-before-rationality. The rational is *first;* then, *if the Spirit wills,* comes saving knowledge.

Rogers notes that the last five sections of the Confession delineate the "saving content of Scripture," "the whole counsel of God concerning all things necessary for His own glory, man's salvation, faith and life." Then follows this *non sequitur* (no. 3): "Scripture was not an encyclopedia of answers to every sort of question for the divines."[52] The *non sequitur* (because the Bible is concerned primarily with salvation it is not concerned with other details) is meant to avoid the inevitable inerrancy doctrine. The "saving *content*" is supposed to be one thing, the saving *context* another thing. But they are inseparably woven together in Scripture! No Westminster divine questioned this truth, and Jack Rogers does not logically deny it. So it does not follow from the fact that the Bible reveals the counsel of God for our faith and life that it does not include reliable answers to incidental questions.

Rogers returns to Rutherford, saying that according to Rutherford, Scripture was not to "communicate information on science. He listed areas in which Scripture is *not* our rule, e.g., 'not in things of Art and Science, as to speak Latin, to demonstrate conclusions of Astronomy.' "[53] It is true that for Rutherford (as for all other inerrantists) the Bible is not a textbook of Latin grammar or astronomy, but Rutherford never granted any error of the Bible in matters of science or said that any textbook on science could correctly maintain that Scripture ever erred. Rogers continues with a statement from Rutherford that illustrates *our* point excellently:

Samuel Rutherford, in a tract against the Roman Catholics, asked: "How do we know that Scripture is the Word of God?" If ever there was a place one might expect a divine to use the Roman Catholic's own style of rational arguments as later Scholastic Protestants did, it was here. Rutherford instead appealed to the Spirit of Christ speaking in Scripture: "Sheep are docile creatures, Ioh. 10.27. *My sheep heare my voyce, I know them and they follow me* . . . so the instinct of Grace knoweth the voyce of the Beloved amongst many voyces, Cant. 2.8, and this discerning power is in the Subject."[54]

When the question is raised, How do we know that Scripture is the Word of God? the word *know* is clearly used in the sense of "savingly know." This is evident from Rutherford's answer, which shows that the believer knows Christ's voice savingly by an "instinct of Grace." No *mere* rational knowledge is meant, and therefore no mere rational arguments that Rutherford shared with the Roman Catholics are given. He is not speaking of a knowledge that is "abundantly evidenced" by the many arguments but of a persuasion that comes only from the Holy Spirit. Contrary to Rogers, if ever there was a place where one might expect a Protestant divine to use the Roman Catholic's style of mere rational arguments, it was *not* here.

In conclusion, we read, "For the Westminster divines the final judge in controversies of religions was not just the bare word of Scripture, interpreted by human logic, but the Spirit of Christ leading us in Scripture to its central saving witness to him.[55]

For the Westminster divines the final judge in controversies was the bare Word of God interpreted by human logic, but the Holy Spirit surely assisted the devout interpreter and spoke in the Word He had inspired. Nevertheless, the divines never appealed to something the Spirit was supposedly saying apart from the sound exegesis of His Word. They never attacked an exegesis as not coming from the Spirit but as not coming from the text. As Rogers has noted, these men were not mystics. They did not appeal to any mystical Word but only to the written Word. And they applied their exegesis to *all* questions of religion, such as church government, and not merely to "its central saving witness" to Christ.

In a word, Westminster is saying, What God has joined together—Word and Spirit—let no man put asunder. It is the Spirit who enables the saint savingly to understand the Word, and it is the Word that enables him to understand that it is the Spirit who is enabling him.

AMERICAN THEOLOGY

Before coming to the inerrancy position of old Princeton, we may note that Princeton had no monopoly on this view. Inerrancy was essentially the American position before, as well as after, old Princeton. We will take but one example prior to the Princeton development—that of America's most distinguished theologian, Jonathan Edwards (d. 1758).

Jonathan Edwards

Surprise is sometimes expressed that the Westminster Confession of Faith, chapter 1, "Of the Holy Scripture," does not mention directly the argument for inspiration from miracles. We say "directly" because the phrase "incomparable excellencies that do abundantly evidence the Bible to be the Word of God" amounts to an argument from miracles, for how do these things show the Bible to be the Word of *God* except that they affirm God as the miraculous author behind the men He inspired? Nevertheless, miracles are not mentioned explicitly, and that surprises some.[56] It is interesting, therefore, to find that Edwards, who expressly makes much of the argument from miraculous attestation,[57] subordinates it nonetheless to the "internal" evidence.

In his unpublished sermon on Exodus 9:12–16,[58] Edwards preached that "God gives men good evidence of the truth of his word." This evidence is internal ("evident stamp") especially, but external also. In fact, "there is as much in the gospel to show that it is no work of men, as there is in the sun in the firmament."[59]

This internal evidence appears to include many matters. Edwards approaches the Bible in the context of human need, arguing as follows: First, it is evident that all men have offended God; second, they are sure from providence that God is friendly and placable; third, God is not willing to be reconciled without being willing to reveal terms; fourth, if willing, He must have revealed terms; and, fifth, if the Bible does not have this revelation, the revelation does not exist.[60] After all, there are only three groups of mankind: (1) those who receive the Bible, (2) the Muslims, who derive from it; and (3) the heathen, whose gods are idols and who are judged by the light of nature and philosophy.[61] What insights the heathen do have come from tradition.[62]

Perhaps nowhere has Edwards stated his view of the internal perfections of Scripture better than in the early *Miscellany* 338:

> The Scriptures are evidence of their own divine authority as a human being is evident by the motions, behaviour and speech of a body of a human form and contexture, or that the body is animated by a rational mind. For we know no otherwise than by the consistency, harmony and concurrence of the train of actions and sounds, and their agreement to all that we can suppose to be a

rational mind. . . . So there is that wondrous universal harmony
and consent and concurrence in the aim and drift, such as universal appearance of a wonderful, florious design, such stamps
everywhere of exalted and divine wisdom, majesty, and holiness
in matter, manner, contexture and aim, that the evidence is the
same that the Scriptures are the word and work of a divine mind;
to one that is thoroughly acquainted with them, as 'tis that the
words and actions of an understanding man are from a rational
mind, to one that is of a long time been his familiar acquaintance.

An infant, he continues, does not understand that this "rational
mind" is behind a man because it does not understand the
symptoms. "So 'tis with men that are so little acquainted with
the Scripture, as infants with the actions of human bodies.
[They] cannot see any evidence of a divine mind as the origin of
it, because they have not comprehension enough to apprehend
the harmony, wisdom, etc."[63] Putting the whole matter suc-
cinctly, Edwards says that the Bible "shines bright with the
amiable simplicity of truth."

As for his argument from miracles as attestation of the biblical
revelation, we will confine ourselves to just one miracle: the
Jews. "The Jewish nation have, from their very beginning, been
a remarkable standing evidence of the truth of revealed religion."[64] An earlier *Miscellany* had shown proof that the Jewish
religion was divine because of Jewish pride, which could never
have accounted for their exalted religion but would rather have
worked against it.[65]

That Jonathan Edwards believed in and taught the verbal
inerrancy of the Bible we shall attempt to show by some miscel-
laneous citations from various works, though it is fully evident in
almost everything that he ever wrote or spoke.

First, *Notes on the Bible* (hereafter cited as *NB*) 215:[66] The
"seeming difference" in the account of the numbers of Israel
when David numbered his people (2 Sam. 24:9) and the Chronicles account needs to be explained. Edwards will not admit that
inspiration does not extend to such external, nonreligious data.
He first refers to a standard contemporary author, Bedford, and
then offers his own conjectures. These do not concern us here,
where we are interested only in showing what his view was and
not how he defended it.

Second, *NB* 220:[67] deals with "the accounts of the four
evangelists, concerning the resurrection of Christ, reconciled."
Edwards then proceeds to deal with this thorny historical prob-

lem harmonistically, at the time when Herman Reimarus was using the problem to attack the traditional position and destructive modern criticism was beginning in earnest.

Third, NB 222:[68] Here Edwards takes several pages to explain why 2 Chronicles 22:12 seems to make Ahaziah, the son of Jehoram, two years older than his father.

Fourth, NB 233:[69] The "seeming inconsistency" in the blind Bartimaeus episode is "thus to be solved. . . ."

Fifth, NB 328:[70] I will quote this note in full for two reasons. First, it gives a characteristic example of some texts as going beyond the understanding of the human writer. Second, at least three times Edwards explicitly refers the text to the Holy Spirit's inspiration, at the same time that the human authorship of the "Psalmist" is treated with absolute seriousness:

> Psalm xix. 4, 5, 6. It appears to me very likely that the Holy Ghost in these expressions, which he most immediately uses about the rising of the sun, has an eye to the rising of the Sun of righteousness from the grave, and that the expressions that the Holy Ghost here uses are conformed to such a view. The times of the Old Testament are times of night in comparison to the gospel day, and are so represented in Scripture, and therefore the approach of the day of the New Testament dispensation in the birth of Christ, is called the day-spring from on high visiting the earth. Luke i. 78. "Through the tender mercy of our God, whereby the day-spring from on high hath visited us;" and the commencing of the gospel dispensation as it was introduced by Christ, is called the Sun of righteousness rising. Mal. iv. 2. But this gospel-dispensation commences with the resurrection of Christ. Therein the Sun of righteousness rises from under the earth, as the sun appears to do in the morning, and comes forth as a bridegroom. He rose as the joyful, glorious bridegroom of his church; for Christ, especially as risen again, is the proper bridegroom, or husband of his church, as the apostle teaches. Rom. vii. 7. "Wherefore, my brethren, ye also are become dead to the law by the body of Christ, that ye should be married to another, even to him who is raised from the dead, that we should bring forth fruit to God."
>
> He that was covered with contempt, and overwhelmed in a deluge of sorrow, hath purchased and won his spouse; (for he loved the church and gave himself for it, that he might present it to himself;) now he comes forth as a bridegroom to bring home his purchased spouse to him in spiritual marriage, as he soon after did in the conversion of such multitudes, making his people

willing in the day of his power and hath also done many times since, and will do in a yet more glorious degree. And as the sun when it rises comes forth like a bridegroom gloriously adorned, so Christ in his resurrection entered on his state of glory. After his state of sufferings, he rose to shine forth in ineffable glory as the King of heaven and earth, that he might be a glorious bridegroom in whom his church might be unspeakably happy. Here the psalmist says that God has placed a tabernacle for the sun in the heavens; so God the Father had prepared an abode in heaven for Jesus Christ; he had set a throne for him there, to which he ascended after he rose. The sun after it is risen ascends up to the midst of heaven, and then at that end of its race descends again to the earth; so Christ when he rose from the grave ascended up to the height of heaven, and far above all heavens, but at the end of the gospel-day will descend again to the earth.

It is here said that the risen sun rejoiceth as a strong man to run his race. So Christ, when he rose, rose as a man of war, as the Lord strong and mighty, the Lord mighty in battle; he rose to conquer his enemies, and to show forth his glorious power in subduing all things to himself, during that race which he had to run, which is from his resurrection to the end of the world, when he will return to the earth again.

Here the going forth of the sun is from the end of heaven and his circuit to the end of it and nothing is hid from the heat thereof; so Christ rose from the grave to send forth his light and truth to the utmost ends of the earth, that had hitherto been confined to one nation, and to rule over all nations in the kingdom of his grace. Thus his line goes out through all the earth, and his words to the end of the world, so that there is no speech or language where his voice is not heard, as is here said of the line and voice of the sun and heavenly bodies in the two foregoing verses, which are by the apostle interpreted of the gospel of Jesus Christ. Rom. x. 16, 17, 18. "But they have not all obeyed the gospel; for Esaias saith, Lord, who hath believed our report? so then faith cometh by hearing, and hearing by the word of God. But I say, Have they not heard? Yes, verily, their sound went into all the earth, and their words until the ends of the world."

That the Holy Ghost here has a mystical meaning, and has respect to the light of the Sun of righteousness, and not merely the light of the natural sun, is confirmed by the verses that follow, in which the psalmist himself seems to apply them to the word of God, which is the light of that sun, even of Jesus Christ, who himself revealed the word of God: see the very next words, "The law of the Lord is perfect, converting the soul; the testimony of the Lord is sure, making wise the simple."

Sixth, *NB* 434:[71] Edwards here sees the "penman of the Psalms" as writing "by the inspiration of the Spirit of God as much as the prophets when they wrote their prophecies, the following things do confirm." Five arguments in support of this observation are offered.

Seventh, *Miscellany* (hereafter designated as M) 229:[72]

> God had a design and meaning which the penman never thought of, which he makes appear these ways: by his own interpretation, and by his directing the penman to such a phrase and manner of speaking, that has a much more exact agreement and consonancy with the thing remotely pointed to, than with the thing meant by the penman.

Thus the words of Scripture are not only the words of the Holy Spirit but their transcendent meaning is not even understood by the human writers in some instances.

Eighth, M352:

> Moses, then, was so intimately conversant with God and so continually under the divine conduct, it can't be thought that when he wrote the history of the creation and fall of man, and the history of the church from the creation, that he should not be under the divine direction in such an affair. Doubtless he wrote by God's direction, as we are informed that he wrote the law and the history of the Israelitish church.

We remember that Moses wrote many tedious genealogical and historical details as well as the grand passages concerning God and redemption.

Ninth, M358:

> God took this care with respect to the books of the Old Testament, that no books should be received by the Jewish church and delivered down in the canon of the Old Testament, but what was his word and owned by Christ. We may therefore conclude that he would still take the same care of his church with respect to the New Testament.

Tenth, M426: After discussing principles of interpretation, Edwards comes to this conclusion about the Bible as the Word of God: "God may reveal things in Scripture, which way he pleases, if by what he there reveals the thing is any way clearly discovered to the understanding or eye of the mind, 'tis our duty to receive it as his revelation." This is Edwards's equivalent of the classic expression that "what the Bible says, God says."

Eleventh, M1144: "That the prophets after they had once had intercourse with God by immediate revelation from God gain'd acquaintance with (him) so as afterward to know him, as it were to know his voice or know what was indeed a revelation from God is confirmed by 1. Sam. 3. 7." In this text referred to, God is represented as speaking in human words to Samuel. For Edwards the revelation came in words. The prophets' "Thus saith the Lord" therefore is to be construed literally.

Twelfth, M303, an unpublished sermon on 1 Corinthians 2:11–13: Here, in referring to the Scripture, Edwards uses the term *dictated*, but that he does not conceive of the Bible writers as passive is very clear in all his writings, as in this discussion of the penning of *The Song of Songs:*

> I imagine that Solomon when he wrote this song being a very philosophical, musing man, and a pious man, and of a very loving temper, set himself in his own musings to imagine and to point forth to himself a pure, virtuous, pious and entire love; and represented the musings and feelings of his mind, that in a philosophical and religious frame was carried away in a sort of transport: and in that his musings and the train of his imaginations were guided and led on by the Spirit of God. Solomon, in his wisdom and great experience, had learned the vanity of all other love than of such a sort of one. God's Spirit made use of his loving inclination, joined with his musing philosophical disposition, and so directed and conducted it in this train of imagination, as to represent the love that there is between Christ and his spouse. God saw it very needful and exceeding useful, that there should be some such representation of it. The relation that there is between Christ and the church, we know, is very often compared to that that there is between a man and his wife; yea this similitude is abundantly insisted on almost everywhere in the Scripture; and a virtuous and pious and pure love between a man and his spouse, is very much of an image of the love between Christ and the church. So that it is not at all strange that the Spirit of God, which is love, should direct a holy amorous disposition after such a manner, as to make such a representation; and 'tis very agreeable to other the like representations.

Although for Edwards all of Scripture is given by divine inspiration, God accomplishes this in at least two different ways—by "immediate inspiration" and by divine "direction": "We ought to distinguish between those things which were written in the sacred books by the immediate inspiration of the Holy Spirit, and those which were only committed to writing by the direction of the Holy Spirit."[73]

Finally, and in a word, for Jonathan Edwards "All Scripture says to us is certainly true. There you hear Christ speaking."[74] That is the very definition of inerrancy.

Liberals find this baffling in Edwards but they find it indisputably his opinion:

> George Gordon has written, "It is not edifying to see Edwards, in the full movement of speculation, suddenly pause, begin a new section of his essay, and lug into his argument proof texts from every corner of the Bible to cover the incompleteness of his rational procedure." Peter Gay has very recently written that Edwards was in a biblical "cage." . . . Perry Miller, more than any other student of the Enlightenment, has admired the intellectuality of Jonathan Edwards. Miller senses that in many ways Edwards was not only abreast of our times but ahead of them; nevertheless, he felt Edwards was reactionary in some respects even to his own age.[75]

Still more recently John E. Smith, the General Editor of *The Works of Jonathan Edwards* (New Haven, Conn.: Yale University Press, 1959), has written:

> The central problem is this: Edwards, on the one hand, accepted totally the tradition established by the Reformers with respect to the absolute primacy and authority of the Bible, and he could approach the biblical writings with that conviction of their inerrancy and literal truth which one usually associates with Protestant fundamentalism.[76]

Princeton Theology

After an interesting survey of the development of Princeton theology from Archibald Alexander to B. B. Warfield—in which Rogers sees it as interpreting Westminster in terms of Turretin, incorporating the Aristotelian common sense philosophy, and increasingly rigidifying its own position to the point of the inerrancy of the autographs (all of this highly debatable, and worthy of debate here if we had space)—Rogers observes, "Since the original texts were not available, Warfield seemed to have an unassailable apologetic stance."[77]

First of all, since no evangelical scholar ever defended an infallible translation, where can the written Word of God be located but in the original texts, or autographs? This was always assumed. Warfield was no innovator. It is true that some believed the text was transmitted "pure," but in that case we would *have* the autographa. There is no question in any case but that the autographs alone were the written Word of God. Warfield would be amused to be given credit for discovering the obvious.

Second, Warfield believed that we virtually did have the autographa in the form of a highly reliable text.[78] He did not consider himself, therefore, "unassailable." One modern teacher refers to the appeal to the autographa as "weasel words," an accusation that surely is as unfair as it is scurrilous. Did the Westminster divines suppose that the Word of God was located anywhere other than in the autographs? Where is the "rigidifying?"

But to continue:

> Influenced by this principle [the reliability of sense perception], Hodge showed no trace of the theory of accommodation held by Origen, Chrysostom, Augustine, and Calvin, to explain that we do not know God as he is but only his saving mercy adapted to our understanding. For Hodge: "We are certain, therefore, that our ideas of God, founded on the testimony of his Word, correspond to what He really is, and constitute true knowledge."[79]

We have already shown that Rogers's interpretation of accommodation in the above-named fathers is misleading and erroneous (*non sequitur* no. 2). Hodge is not really differing from the fathers. After enumerating a dozen Bible verses teaching the immutability of God, Hodge remarks about the phenomenological character of God's repentance: "Those passages of Scripture in which God is said to repent, are to be interpreted on the same principle as those in which He is said to ride upon the wings of the wind, or walk through the earth."[80] God is accommodating Himself by using phenomenological language. Hodge also taught the incomprehensibility of God as clearly as did Calvin or any father of the church.[81]

A CONTINUING REFORMED TRADITION

Mention is often made of James Orr, Abraham Kuyper, Herman Bavinck, and G. C. Berkouwer as respected evangelicals who either did not postulate inerrancy or made a fideistic approach to the Bible in the nineteenth and twentieth centuries. We will not challenge this point. Many other names could be added, and from other centuries as well. But the names of Origen, Augustine, Aquinas, Luther, Calvin, the Westminster divines, Edwards, and the Princetonians, along with the general tradition of the church from the beginning, must be enrolled under the banner of inerrancy.

Inerrancy has almost always been maintained along with biblical criticism. Criticism was never rejected by Hodge, Warfield, Lindsell, or any other scholarly inerrancy advocate of whom we have ever heard. These men and others have tried many claims of many biblical critics and found them wanting, but that they rejected biblical criticism as such is unsupported by evidence. Warfield was noted as a New Testament critic, as was his famous successor, J. G. Machen. A. T. Robertson was champion extraordinary of the historico-grammatical method. When charges are made to the contrary, it is usually because the *science* of biblical criticism is being confused with the *negativism* of some biblical critics.

Turning now to Berkouwer's concept of biblical errancy for passing notice (since a thorough critique can be found elsewhere in this volume), we read:

> Berkouwer commented that when error in the sense of incorrectness is used on the same level as error in the biblical sense of sin and deception we are quite far removed from the serious manner in which error is dealt with in Scripture.[82]

Here Berkouwer seems to allow that the Bible may contain errors in the sense of "incorrectness," since these errors are not on a "level" with such errors as "sin and deception." This can only mean that if the Bible is the Word of God, then—though He cannot deceive—God can yet be incorrect, can err, can make mistakes. This view does more than "damage reverence for Scripture." It damages reverence for God Himself and illustrates a subtle form of *non sequitur* no. 3.

We realize that these are serious charges—but they are not unwarranted. They do not imply, however, that those who are guilty are deliberately so. We believe they are not. We believe that if they ever see validity in our charge, they will, as earnest Christians, eschew their error in charging God, in His Word, with error.

Loretz, in *Das Ende der Inspirations Theologie,* entitles chapter 20, "Die Wahrheit der Bibel—das theologische Pseudoproblem der absoluten Irrtumslosigheit der Heilige Schrift" (The Truth of the Bible—The Theological Pseudo Problem of the Absolute Inerrancy of the Holy Scriptures). He calls inerrancy a pseudo-problem and thus disposes of it as a nonissue. Why is it a false problem or nonproblem? Because the Bible is Semitic, and the concept of inerrancy is Greek: the Bible is affectional, inerrancy is rational; the Bible is nonlogical, inerrancy is logical. It is a case of apples and oranges, according to Loretz. Those who hold to inerrancy simply ask the wrong questions and get irrelevant answers. This is Rogers's theme with different names: *Semitic* for Platonic-Augustinian-Reformation-Berkouwer; *Greek* for Aristotelian-Thomistic-Scholastic-Warfield. But in fact, of course, the Jews could think and the Greeks could feel, and the only thing "pseudo" in this whole matter is calling inerrancy a "pseudoproblem."

B. B. WARFIELD
VERSUS G. C. BERKOUWER
ON SCRIPTURE

Henry Krabbendam

Henry Krabbendam is Associate Professor in Biblical Studies and Missions, Covenant College, Lookout Mountain, Tennessee. He is a graduate of Theologische Hoogeschool, Kampen, The Netherlands (B.A. and B.D. equivalent), and Westminster Theological Seminary (Th.M. and Th.D.). He has served as a pastor in Ottawa, Canada, in the Canadian Reformed Church, and in Sunnyvale, California, in the Orthodox Presbyterian Church. Dr. Krabbendam is an ordained minister in the Orthodox Presbyterian Church and is a member of the Advisory Board for ICBI.

CHAPTER SUMMARY

This study contrasts the views of Warfield and Berkouwer on Scripture. It is shown that their views of Scripture, both as the Word of God and as the word of men, are totally and radically divergent. Their difference with regard to the inerrancy of the Bible exposes two antagonistic traditions of long standing.

B. B. WARFIELD
VS. G. C. BERKOUWER
ON SCRIPTURE

INTRODUCTION

It may seem somewhat surprising, at first, to see Warfield pitted against Berkouwer. After all, Warfield died before Berkouwer appeared on the theological scene. Yet, although a direct confrontation between the two never took place, there are at least two good reasons for squaring off Warfield's position against that of Berkouwer.

First, Warfield and Berkouwer, men of acknowledged stature and pervasive influence, are increasingly recognized as the two most noted exponents of two divergent views of Scripture.[1] Warfield, undoubtedly the most distinguished representative of the Old Princeton position on Scripture, never grew weary in his extensive writings on the subject to defend the plenary, verbal inspiration, and therefore the inerrancy, of the Bible. His repeated and thorough preoccupation with the inspiration of Scripture has not only placed a stamp on American Reformed and Presbyterian thought but has even gained him the accolade of being the greatest contributor ever to this theme.[2] Berkouwer, on the other hand, an equally prolific writer, has the distinction— dubious in the eyes of many—of having become the fountainhead of a new type of thinking in the Reformed and evangelical world that, also in the area of Scripture, has left the old and traditional paths. His view of, and emphasis on, the humanity of

413

Scripture led him and his followers to the denial of its inerrancy.

Second, Warfield and Berkouwer appear to emerge today as the two most-noted exponents of two divergent views and as representatives of those who hold to one or the other of these antagonistic traditions of long standing. Berkouwer claims to have discovered Aristotelian influences in Warfield's approach to Scripture. His followers are even more explicit in their criticism. They charge that the Old Princeton school of Alexander, the Hodges, and Warfield fell victim to a scholastic methodology since it patterned its theology after Turretin, who allegedly was strongly influenced by Thomas Aquinas and the Aristotelian tradition and thus had deviated from the methodology of the Reformers. John Owen is said to be Turretin's counterpart in the British Isles. Thus the battle lines are drawn. On the one hand, there is the line of Aristotle, Thomas, Turretin, Owen, and Old Princeton, culminating in Warfield. On the other hand, still according to Warfield's critics, there is the line of Scripture, Augustine, the Reformers, the Westminster divines, Kuyper, Bavinck and, finally, Berkouwer.[3]

It must be added that one can easily reconstruct an equally telling battle array from Warfield's works. Warfield would place the line of Scripture, Augustine, the Reformers, the Westminster divines, and Old Princeton over against what he calls rationalistic and mystical thinkers. Among the rationalistic thinkers he places humanists such as Erasmus, Socinians, early Arminians, scholastic thinkers (his own term), and critical German scholars. These all hold that the Bible is at best only in part inspired and therefore only in part authoritative. Some are of the opinion that only the mysteries of faith are inspired and not things that are discoverable by human reason. Others believe that Scripture is inspired only in matters of faith and practice and not in matters of history and science. Again, others hold that the Bible is inspired in its thoughts and its concepts but not in its words. Among the mystical thinkers Warfield specifically names Schleiermacher and his followers. They generally subordinate all external authority to internal authority as they "define inspiration not as an activity of God rendering the Scriptural writings as such infallible and authoritative, but as they correlate to revelation in the process of the attainment of truth by the prophet himself—the subjective factor in the conception of divine truth by this chosen instrument of God."[4]

Quite possibly Warfield may be regarded as too general in describing those who object to the plenary inspiration of Scripture as being either rationalistic or mystical and in characterizing Schleiermacher's position as mystical. It seems, indeed, questionable to identify Schleiermacher's sophisticated theological approach as mystical without any further explanation and to lump him together with earlier mystics without differentiation. But Warfield cannot be faulted for holding that the view of Scripture as errant has either rationalistic or "irrationalistic" (designated as mystical) roots. In fact, as will be demonstrated later, with this observation he points to, if not comes to grip with, the fundamental issue.

Given Warfield's general description and characterization of the battle lines, there is little doubt that he and Berkouwer would find themselves in opposite camps. In fact, there is every reason to believe that, according to Warfield, Berkouwer's emphasis on, and usage of, the concept of "correlation" would betray a strand of thinking that would place him in the climate of Schleiermacher's theology—and of neoorthodoxy.[5]

All this is not to say that a comparison of Warfield and Berkouwer is without complications. On the contrary, it must be recognized that Warfield never had the opportunity to update and sharpen his arguments to face this new challenge. Further, it ought to be noted that there are two phases to be distinguished in Berkouwer's thinking. In the first one his views are practically identical to those of Warfield. In fact in several instances Berkouwer adds new, incisive, and helpful insights. In the second phase there is an unmistakable and decisive shift. Berkouwer becomes critical of Warfield and the position he espoused. He also explains in what way he believes he has moved beyond his first phase.[6]

These complications, however, should not be unduly pressed. After all, it may be said that Warfield's statement and defense of the inspiration and inerrancy of Scripture is so thorough and perceptive that, to a great extent, the challenge posed by Berkouwer and his followers seems to have been anticipated and countered, implicitly and principially. Also, Berkouwer's shift brings his own new position into even sharper focus and, if anything, enhances the fruitfulness of an encounter between the two "pointmen" in the present debate about Scripture.

In the main body of this chapter I will analyze two major

issues, under the headings *Scripture as God's Word* and *Scripture as Man's Word*. Each section will compare the views of Warfield, the early Berkouwer, and the later Berkouwer, in that order. A final appraisal will be presented in the Conclusion.

Warfield has expressed his views on Scripture in the form of addresses and articles, most of which have been collected in the two volumes already referred to, *The Inspiration and Authority of the Bible* and *Selected Shorter Writings of Benjamin B. Warfield*, vol. 2. Berkouwer published his original position in his *Problem of Biblical Criticism*.[7] His later thought is reflected in numerous articles as well as in three larger works, *The Second Vatican Council and the New Catholicism*, *Holy Scripture*, and *A Half Century of Theology*.[8] These six volumes form the basis for the comparison.

SCRIPTURE AS GOD'S WORD

Warfield

Fundamental to Warfield's position on Scripture is his view of inspiration. He develops this view from the two classical passages, 2 Timothy 3:16 and 2 Peter 1:21. The former states that "all Scripture" is *theopneustos* and therefore profitable for a variety of purposes. The latter predicates of every "prophecy of Scripture" that "men spoke [the prophecies] from God as they were carried along by the Holy Spirit."

In conjunction with 2 Timothy 3:16, Warfield points out that the term *inspiration*, which is not a specific biblical term, leaves a lot to be desired. Only because it was too firmly fixed in the common ecclesiastical and theological parlance was he willing to maintain it as the technical designation of the action of God in giving the Scriptures. Under no circumstances, however, should it receive its meaning from etymological implications or historical considerations. It was introduced in the church by the Latin translation (Vulgate) of 2 Timothy 3:16 and eventually adopted by the King James Version as well as by most subsequent translations.[9] Warfield emphasizes that the Greek term *theopneustos* does not denote "*in*spiring" or "*in*spiration," but rather "spiring" or "spiration." This implies that the Scripture is not a human product of what was "breathed into" the human writers by God but rather a divine product "breathed out" by God through the instrumentality of human authors. Warfield writes:

What it says of Scripture is, not that it is "breathed into by God" or is the product of Divine "inbreathing" into its human authors, but that it is breathed out by God, "God-breathed," the product of the creative breath of God. In a word, what is declared by this fundamental passage is simply that the Scriptures are a Divine product, without any indication of how God has operated in producing them. No term could have been chosen, however, which would have more emphatically asserted the Divine production of Scripture than that which is here employed. The "breath of God" is in Scripture just the symbol of His almighty power, the bearer of his creative Word. . . . When Paul declares, then, that "every scripture," or "all scripture" is the product of the Divine breath, "is God-breathed," he asserts with as much energy as he could employ that Scripture is the product of a specifically Divine operation.[10]

Thus 2 Timothy 3:16 conveys that Scripture is of divine origination and precisely for that reason is of such value for so many purposes.

In 2 Peter 1:21, Peter complements the teaching of Paul in 2 Timothy 3:16. He states as well that the "prophecy of Scripture," most likely encompassing the totality of Scripture and thus comparable to Paul's "every scripture," is of divine origin. Men spoke from God! In addition to this, however, he emphasizes the agency of the Spirit. Thus the Scripture as a divine product came about because the Holy Spirit brought the human instruments to the goal set for them by God.

Warfield observes that in this context

the proximate stress is laid . . . not on the spiritual value of Scripture . . . but on the Divine trustworthiness of Scripture. Because this is the way every prophecy of Scripture "has been brought," it affords a more sure basis of confidence than even the testimony of human witnesses.[11]

In his article entitled "God-inspired Scripture," Warfield returns once more to the subject matter. The major point he wishes to get across is that the term *theopneustos* has a passive rather than an active or quasi-active meaning, underscoring the fact that Scripture originates in God and not in man. The conclusion of his article will function as an appropriate summary of his views on inspiration.

What is *theopneustos* is "God-breathed," produced by the creative breath of the Almighty. And Scripture is called *theopneustos* in order to designate it as "God-breathed," the product of Divine spiration, the creation of that Spirit who is in all the spheres of the Divine activity the executive of the Godhead. . . . What it affirms is that the Scriptures owe their origin to an activity of God the Holy Ghost and are in the highest and truest sense His creation. It is on this foundation of Divine origin that all the high attributes of Scripture are built.[12]

Warfield not only shows that the God-breathed character of Scripture secures once and for all that it is the Word of God, fit for its purposes and reliable in its contents, but he also adduces corroborating evidence to that effect in a variety of articles.

First, Warfield researches the terms *Scripture* and *Scriptures*, the phrase "the oracles of God," and the formula "It is written."

As to the terms *Scripture* and *Scriptures*, he demonstrates that, whether the singular or the plural is used,

> the application of the term to the Old Testament writings by the writers of the New Testament is based on the conception of these Old Testament writings as a unitary whole, and designates this body of writings in their entirety as the one well-known authoritative documentation of the Divine word . . . as a single document set over against all other documents by reason of its unique Divinity and indefectible authority, by which it is constituted in every passage and declaration the final arbiter of belief and practice.[13]

With regard to the phrase, "the oracles of God" (occurring in Acts 7:38; Rom. 3:12; Heb. 5:12; 1 Peter 4:11), Warfield concludes a study of it as follows:

> The designation of the Scriptures as *ta logia tou theou* fairly shouts to us out of the pages of the New Testament that to its writers the Scriptures of the Old Testament were the very Word of God in the highest and strictest sense that term can bear—the express utterance, in all their parts and each and every of their words, of the Most High—the "oracles of God."[14]

He comes to a similar conclusion following his examination of the rather common formula "It is written."

> When a New Testament writer says, "It is written," there can arise no doubt where what he thus adduces as possessing absolute authority over the thought and consciences of men is to be found written. The simple adduction in this solemn and decisive manner of a written authority, carries with it the implication that the appeal is made to the indefectible authority of the Scriptures of God, which in all their parts and in every one of their declarations are clothed with the authority of God Himself.[15]

Second, Warfield brings out a variety of ways in which the New Testament writers simply take their point of departure in the absolute identification of Scripture as the Word of God. The following list will serve to show this.

(1) Scripture passages of the Old Testament that are quoted, referred to, or alluded to in the New Testament are introduced as spoken by God either explicitly or implicitly (see Matt. 19:4ff.; Mark 10:5ff.; Acts 13:34ff.; Rom. 15:9ff.; 1 Cor. 6:16; 2 Cor. 6:2; Gal. 3:16; Eph. 4:8; 5:14; Heb. 1:5ff.; 8:8). At times the human instrumentality is mentioned (see Matt. 1:22; 2:15).

(2) Vice versa, words that are spoken in the Old Testament by God are introduced as spoken by Scripture (see Rom. 9:17 and Gal. 3:18).

(3) Scripture passages of the Old Testament that are quoted in the New Testament are introduced as spoken by the Holy Spirit (see Heb. 3:7 and 9:8). For the additional mention of human instrumentality, see Acts 1:16.

(4) Formulas such as "God says," and "The Spirit says," are stated in the present tense, indicating that the Bible is the living Word of God here and now (see Acts 13:35; Rom. 15:10; Heb. 1:7–10; 3:7).

(5) An Old Testament quotation is on one occasion characterized by the Lord Jesus as both the Word of God and as Scripture that "cannot be broken" (John 10:34–35).

(6) On occasions a verb in the present tense and a noun in the singular, which occur in an Old Testament passage quoted in the New Testament as spoken by God, are shown to be fundamental for essential doctrines. Even the minutest parts of Scripture as the Word of God contain a message (see Matt. 22:32 and Gal. 3:16).

This list impressively shows the close identification of God and Scripture in the minds of the New Testament writers.[16]

Third, Warfield pays special attention to the nature and authority of the New Testament. He recognizes that the evidence presented in the previous section technically pertains only to the Old Testament. But he proceeds to demonstrate that the New Testament writings are in the same category as those of the Old Testament. The authors of the New Testament regarded the books of the New Testament as Scripture and on a par with the Scripture of the Old Testament (2 Peter 3:16). They quote the Old Testament and the New Testament in the same context and as having the same authority (1 Tim. 5:18). They write with authority (2 Thess. 3:6, 12; 2 Cor. 10:8). They attest that their authority comes from God (1 Cor. 14:37; 1 Thess. 4:2, 15). They impose their writings on the church as the touchstone for fellowship (2 Thess. 3:14). They insist that the church listen to them rather than even to angels (Gal. 1:7, 8). All this is possible because they were instruments of the Spirit of God (1 Cor. 2:13; 1 Peter 1:13).[17]

From all this evidence only one conclusion can be drawn: Scripture in its totality, comprising both Old and New Testaments, is a divine product, although given through human meditation. It is the Word of God and is thus fully authoritative and fully functional for its purposes.

The Early Berkouwer

The early Berkouwer uses both the term *theopneustic* and the term *inspired* in conjunction with Scripture. However, he does not examine or define either one of them. His major interest is the exploration of the meaning and implications of "organic inspiration," in contradistinction to "mechanical inspiration." But in discussing the designation "organic inspiration," he provides sufficient ground to conclude that at this stage his view of inspiration is parallel to that of Warfield. He states that the theopneusty of Scripture, taught in 2 Timothy 3:16, points to an organic inspiration, in which there is "a *taking into service* of the total man with his own personality and his activity" (organic), and the "divine, sovereign act . . . the effect of which came to us in the trustworthy and infallible Scripture" (inspiration).[18] While Berkouwer mentions both aspects, it must be added that, at this stage of his thinking, the primacy belongs to the latter. In light of 2 Peter 1:20–21, he emphasizes that private interpretation is not permitted, precisely because the human writers were "carried along" by the Spirit. There are human authors. There is human mediation. But the word of prophecy is not a human matter, nor does it breathe a human atmosphere, for the simple reason that it did not proceed from man but from the Spirit. The human element always must be viewed in the light of the divine origin. This gives to the prophetic word its depth, fullness, and authority, and demands from its interpreters respect both for that word and for the purpose of the Spirit with that word.[19]

Against this backdrop Berkouwer's usage of the word *mystery* must be understood. When he speaks about the "mystery of the Spirit" and the "mystery of the written *Word of God*," he wishes to indicate that the way in which God, through the agency of the Spirit and the instrumentality of sinful men, produced a trustworthy and infallible document is beyond human comprehension. This point is important to remember inasmuch as in his later thinking the word *mystery* is given a different connotation.[20]

The attempt that Berkouwer makes to corroborate his position that Scripture is the Word of God without any qualification and reservation is minimal compared to that made by Warfield. But it is no less telling. He points to the formula "It is written." Biblical criticism, in his opinion, has never seriously considered the unalterable opposition, contained in these words, to any and every attempt to drive a wedge between Scripture and the Word of God.[21] The reason why Berkouwer does not turn to further evidence seems to be twofold. First, his early work on biblical criticism is apologetic in nature, rather than exegetical. Second, his view of Scripture as the trustworthy and infallible Word of God is so settled that he takes it as the absolute and unassailable point of departure.

The Later Berkouwer

In his later phase, Berkouwer filled the vacuum that was present in his earlier work. He now deals extensively with the notion of the *theopneusty* of Scripture in connection with 2 Timothy 3:16. Lexicographically, he is in full accord with Warfield. With Warfield he rejects "inspiration" as an acceptable translation. With Warfield he stresses the passive meaning of the term. Berkouwer's final conclusion, however, is subtly different:

> Thus, *theopneustos* points to an essential relationship between the breath of the Spirit and the *graphē*. This is the mystery of Scripture which the church desired to express in its confession. This mystery is the uniqueness through which Holy Scripture in all its humanity was distinguished from all other human writings. . . . One hears in this passage that the written Scripture cannot be understood in a correct way without the breath of the Spirit.[22]

This statement is fallacious on three counts. First, the emphasis is upon Scripture in all its *humanity*. This is not the emphasis of Scripture. Neither is it the emphasis of Warfield. The latter correctly observes that 2 Timothy 3:16 brings Scripture as a divine

product into focus. Second, the context of the statement makes
clear that the humanity of Scripture should not be distinguished
from the humanity of other human writings. Thus the "mystery
of the Scriptures" has a connotation that is vastly different from
that in Berkouwer's early work. *Then* Berkouwer wished to convey that Scripture is word for word identical with the infallible
Word of God, in spite of its human mediation. *Now* he intends to
say that Scripture is used by God in spite of its fallible humanity that it shares with other writings.[23] Third, the focus of
2 Timothy 3:16 is on the *fact* of the written Scripture as produced
by the breath of God. This is one of the grounds on which
Warfield concluded to the inerrancy of Scripture. The focus of
Berkouwer is on the *understanding* of the written Scripture as
produced by the breath of the Spirit. This allows him to make
room for Scripture as a human and errant document. Berkouwer's focus is clearly unacceptable.

The same subtle, but fundamental, difference is noticeable in
Berkouwer's discussion of 2 Peter 1:21. He writes:

> The . . . "from God" gives a unique quality of trustworthiness to
> these human words, which is essential to the God-breathed Scrip-
> ture. . . . The firmness of these human words is the mystery of the
> Spirit.[24]

This quotation is objectionable for two reasons. First, the stress
is on the humanity of the words. The text, however, states that
what the prophets spoke is the firm Word of God. The human
mediation is brought into view, but the emphasis is on the divine
origin and the divine characteristics of the prophetic word. This
is also Warfield's conclusion. Second, the subtlety of this quotation cannot really be grasped until, once again, we understand
what "humanity" implies for Berkouwer. What he is saying can
be paraphrased as follows. The human words of Scripture, that
are no different from all other human words and therefore cannot
lay claim to trustworthiness and firmness, receive the quality of
trustworthiness and firmness from God. That is the "mystery of
the Spirit." Once again, the mystery is not that the prophetic
word is firm, though it is produced through human mediation,
but rather that the prophetic word is firm in spite of its fallibility.[25]

The difference between Warfield and Berkouwer, which at
first may be somewhat difficult to spot, is indeed fundamental.
Warfield (and the early Berkouwer) place the emphasis on the

divine element in Scripture. Scripture has a divine origin and is a divine product. As such it is truthworthy to the reader and fit for its purpose. The later Berkouwer gives center stage to the humanity of Scripture, its human origin, its human composition, its human understanding, and its human relativity. The emphasis on the human element in connection with 2 Timothy 3:16 and 2 Peter 1:21 does not reflect the contents and scope of these passages, but is certainly in line with Berkouwer's general approach.

All this is not to say that Berkouwer refuses to speak about Scripture as the Word of God. Quite the contrary! He maintains that *Sacra Scriptura est Verbum Dei*. But what does he mean by this phrase?

In stating his view of Scripture as the Word of God he does not build up his case exegetically. Instead, he takes his point of departure in an undeniable and, in his opinion, legitimate fact of the history of biblical studies. This fact is the rise of the critical-historical method. Historical criticism focused attention on the Scriptures as human writings, was based on the irrefutable fact that its authors were human, and was fueled by the conviction that one should not continue to speak about the divine side of Scripture only. This precipitated a crisis with regard to Scripture as the Word of God. To Berkouwer this crisis was unavoidable:

> An honest approach to Scripture through historical examination simply had to result in questioning the church's traditional confession that *Sacra Scriptura est Verbum Dei*. For various reasons students of Scripture began to wonder more and more whether Holy Scripture as God's Word was truly beyond all criticism as the indubitable *vox Dei*, as a book—however human—of indisputably divine signature.[26]

Berkouwer declares himself not at all unhappy with this development. In fact, he sees a distinct possibility that the critical-historical examination of Scripture will improve the understanding and proclamation of its message. Hence he does not mind that the church once again must face the "question concerning the meaning of *est* in the confession: *Sacra Scriptura est Verbum Dei*."[27]

To react to the critical-historical method in a manner that extols the divine aspect of Scripture and renders the human element insignificant or irrelevant is unacceptable to Berkouwer. He characterizes that as a docetic approach. Docetism in

Christology emphasizes the divinity of Christ at the expense of his humanity. Berkouwer warns that the church should never follow this pattern in its approach to Scripture and thus minimize or obscure the human aspect.[28]

In this context Berkouwer is critical of post-Reformation theology, with its stress on the "unique, supernatural, divine quality of Holy Scripture." In his opinion, the view of Scripture that this theology espouses, however influential it may have become, is Aristotelian and faulty. Berkouwer writes:

> This faulty view has occurred as theologians in immediate relation to . . . certainty, began to interpret the word *est* in the expression *Sacra Scriptura est Verbum Dei* in such a manner that Scripture's divinity was thought to be found in its inner substantial form and had become an essential predicate of Holy Scripture as an inspired book that was elevated to the level of a source of supernatural truths.[29]

Berkouwer's objection to post-Reformation theology is threefold. An analysis of this threefold objection will also make clear how he himself intends to handle the crisis of the "controversial Bible" and in which way he understands and subscribes to the phrase *Sacra Scriptura est Verbum Dei*.

First, Berkouwer protests against the notion that Scripture is to be regarded as a "stupendous, supernatural miracle," in which the "human words are transubstantiated into something divine." Over against that he does not tire of stressing that Scripture is a prophetic-apostolic and consequently human testimony, witness, or attestation. He writes:

> The way of the Word did not exclude the ministry of man. Throughout Scripture we see that man comes to the fore in his ministry and witness. The fact that Scripture and the prophets are *from God* . . . does not rule out the human witness in divine monergism, but includes this witness in a unique manner. God's Word has not come to us as a stupendous supernatural miracle that shies away from every link with the human in order thus to be truly divine. Rather, when God speaks, human voices ring in our ears.[30]

The nature of the phrase *Sacra Scriptura est Verbum Dei* must be understood against this backdrop. Berkouwer holds that God reaches out to man in the form of the human words of Scripture. When man is confronted with Scripture, however, he hears, first of all, "human voices." When he is taught by the Spirit, he will recognize in these voices the Word of God and will acknowledge it as such. The phrase *Sacra Scriptura est Verbum Dei* is such an acknowledgment on the part of the church. It is a response to human words. It is a confessional response to human words. It is a confessional response that these human words are the Word of God. Berkouwer writes, "Of the humanly written (*Scriptura*) it is confessed: *est Verbum Dei*," and "The 'is' of the confession . . . relates the mystery of God's Word to the wholly human witness."[31]

Second, Berkouwer objects strenuously to a formalized conception of Scripture and its attributes as well as to a formalized submission to Scripture. A formalized approach to both the conception of and the submission to Scripture, according to Berkouwer, will isolate the Scripture in its written form from the contents of Scripture, the message of the gospel. Berkouwer states that the relationship between God's speaking and the human word can, without exaggeration, be described as identity. In this connection he refers to many of the passages and phrases that Warfield discussed. He pays specific attention to the formula "It is written." In fact, he reminisces how in his earlier work he was powerfully gripped by it and how, on the strength of adherence to this formula, in his estimation, the Reformed view of Scripture was driven into isolation. He still expresses his commitment to this formula as well as other phrases and passages that identify Scripture as the Word of God. But he now declares himself an unalterable foe of any *formalized* identity. Disclosing a second aspect of the nature of the phrase *Sacra Scriptura est Verbum Dei*, he writes:

> The confession concerning Scripture—with its emphatic "is"—does not imply the worship of a book. At issue is whether and in what way faith is related to the "*gospel* promised *in* Holy Scripture." Scripture is central because of its nature and intent. For this Scripture is only referred to because its sense and intent is the divine message of salvation . . . the written Word of God can never be formally isolated, because precisely that written Scripture testifies of salvation and is directed toward salvation. And in that context words can become living words . . . full of authority. In "It is written" lies the perspective of God's speaking and the power and blessings of the written Word.[32]

The phrase, in short, is a confessional statement on the part of the church that the human voices of Scripture constitute the

Word of God, but only by virtue of the gospel contained in them.

Third, Berkouwer opposes strongly the idea that the identification of Scripture as the Word of God is an a priori postulate, an epistemological issue, or a transcendental presupposition. He insists that reflection on, and confession with regard to, Scripture, its nature, its attributes, and its function, must originate in and proceed from a Spirit-taught heart, a walk of faith, and a life of submission to the message of Scripture.[33] Thus the third aspect of *Sacra Scriptura est Verbum Dei* emerges. It is a confessional statement that is uttered in faith, which is in turn accompanied by subjection to the contents of Scripture.

In summary, the Scriptures can be called the Word of God. In fact they can be identified as such. But this can have meaning only when it is done by way of a confession that has in view the contents of Scripture and is rooted in genuine faith.

The gap between Warfield and Berkouwer now appears to be immense. Warfield holds that Scripture is the Word of God and that the phrase *Sacra Scriptura est Verbum Dei* is true and meaningful, whether confessed or not, both in contents and in form, whether believed or not. So did the early Berkouwer. The later Berkouwer, however, calls this an Aristotelian position. The biblical evidence that Warfield so carefully adduced to substantiate his position apparently did not make an impact on Berkouwer. Even Berkouwer's own early work proved unsatisfactory to him. The question must eventually be faced as to why the later Berkouwer made the shift—in the face of the biblical evidence and against his own earlier convictions. Before this can be determined, however, a comparison of these two men will be made in regard to their views of the humanity of Scripture.

SCRIPTURE AS MAN'S WORD

Warfield

Since Warfield characterized Scripture as being not so much a human product breathed *into* by the Spirit as a divine product breathed *out* by God through the instrumentality of the human authors,[34] the question becomes pressing as to how he envisioned the relationship of the divine and the human with regard to Scripture. Did he emphasize the divine element to the point that Scripture is deified and its humanity is relegated to obscurity, or even excluded? The answer to this question must be decidedly in the negative. Warfield rejects the so-called mechanical theory of Scripture production, in which inspiration is conceived as dictation and the human writers regarded as implements rather than instruments and as pens rather than pensmen.[35] He marshalls several arguments against the mechanical theory by showing that Scripture is fully man's word. First, he points to the numerous times the New Testament refers to Scripture in terms of its human authors (e.g., Matt. 22:24; Mark 12:19; John 12:39; Rom. 11:9). Second, he points out that passages of the Old Testament are quoted in the New Testament as being spoken by men, even if these men were "in the Spirit" (see Mark 12:36). Third, he emphasizes the obvious marks of human authorship, such as peculiarities and differences in vocabulary and style.[36]

Although Warfield rejects the dictation theory, he is just as critical of the opposite extreme, which in his opinion is the more common error, namely the exclusion of the divine factor from the origin and nature of Scripture. While Scripture is fully man's word, it is not a purely human book.[37]

In rejecting both extremes—Scripture as a purely divine or as a purely human book—Warfield does not opt for the solution of its being partly divine and partly human. The Bible is not divided between two factors that are mutually exclusive, so that the one limits the other and the entrance of the one spells the exit of the other.[38] No, the evidence that shows the Scripture both as the Word of God and the word of man leads to the conclusion that the Bible is simultaneously the divine utterance of God and the product of man's effort. Warfield writes:

> The human and divine factors in inspiration are conceived of as flowing confluently and harmoniously to the production of a common product. Of every word of Scripture is it to be affirmed, in turn, that it is God's word and that it is man's word. All the qualities of divinity and humanity are to be sought and found in every portion and element of the Scripture. While, on the other hand, no quality inconsistent with either divinity or humanity can be found in any portion or element of Scripture.[39]

The concept, in which the Bible is regarded as both a human product in every part and every word and a divine product to the smallest detail, Warfield calls *concursus*. Both the divine and the human elements form the inseparable constituents of one simple uncompounded product in which the human coloration and variety, as well as the divine perfection and infallibility, are acknowledged.[40] Thus Warfield holds that, according to the Word of God and the doctrine of the church,

> by a special, supranatural, extraordinary influence of the Holy Ghost, the sacred writers have been guided in their writing in such a way, as while their humanity was not superseded, it was yet so dominated that their words became at the same time the words of God, and thus, in every case and all alike, absolutely infallible.[41]

Warfield emphasizes that the concept of *concursus* is not unique to the relationship of the divine and the human factors with regard to the origin and nature of Scripture. He points out that the same relationship obtains with regard to the act of faith as both a work of God and an activity of man.[42]

It must be evident by now that Warfield holds to the plenary, verbal inspiration of the Scriptures as the Word of God,[43] and that by virtue of that inspiration they are fully true, fully authoritative, fully infallible,[44] and fully inerrant.[45] Because of the present controversy regarding the inerrancy of Scripture, Warfield's view on that issue will now be explored further. The following quotation will both serve as a summary of Warfield's position stated thus far and set the stage for the discussion of his view of inerrancy.

> The Church, then, has held from the beginning that the Bible is the Word of God in such a sense that its words, though written by men and bearing indelibly impressed upon them the marks of their human origin, were written, nevertheless, under such an influence of the Holy Ghost as to be also the words of God, the adequate expression of His mind and will. It has always recognized that this concept of co-authorship implies that the Spirit's superintendence extends to the choice of the words by the human authors (verbal inspiration), and preserves its product from everything inconsistent with a divine authorship—thus securing, among other things, that entire truthfulness which is everywhere presupposed in and asserted for Scripture by the Biblical writers (inerrancy).[46]

It must be noted in connection with this statement that Warfield did not construe a difference between infallibility and inerrancy. The substance of the one term is the substance of the other.[47] It is this common substance that is in view when he writes:

The Bible is inspired not *in part* but *fully* in all its elements alike
. . . matters of history and science as well as of faith and practice,
words as well as thoughts.[48] The whole of Scripture in all its parts
and in all its elements, down to the least minutiae, in form of
expression as well as in substance of teaching, is from God . . .
[and has] a quality which is truly superhuman.[49] [There is] the
ineradicable inability of the whole negative school to distinguish
between *difficulties* and *proven errors.* If then we ask what we are to
do with the numerous phenomena of Scripture inconsistent with
verbal inspiration, which, so it is alleged, "criticism" has brought
to light, we must reply: Challenge them in the name of the New
Testament doctrine and ask for their credentials. They have no
credentials that can stand before that challenge. No single error
has as yet been demonstrated to occur in the Scriptures as given
by God to His church. And every critical student knows . . . that
the progress of investigation has been a continuous process of
removing difficulties, until scarcely a shred of the old list of "Biblical Errors" remains to hide the nakedness of this moribund
contention.[50]

In the final analysis, Warfield holds to his views on
Scripture—its plenary, verbal, inspiration; its truth; its authority; its infallibility/inerrancy—because it is based on the
"exegetical fact," "the common place of exegetical science," of
the witness of Scripture, of the Lord Jesus Christ, and of the
apostles.[51] Furthermore, he sees this witness reflected in the
views of the apostolic church, of Augustine, of the Reformers, of
the Westminster divines, and of the later British theologians.[52]
He even sees this witness recognized by scholars who personally
reject the high view of Scripture.[53]

Obedient to the witness of Scripture, of Christ, and of the
apostles, buoyed by the heartfelt acknowledgment of this witness
on the part of the church and even assisted by the grudging
admission of the fact of that witness by critical scholars, Warfield
went time and again about the wearisome business of refuting
those who, in his own words, were "ever bringing forth 'novel-
ties' from the waste paper basket of the past."[54]

Thus he resists "attempts to make the use of the Septuagint by
the New Testament writers, in their quotations from the Old
Testament, into an argument against plenary inspiration."[55]

Thus he responds to the objections against inerrancy arising
from the fact that the original autographs are no longer extant,
the subsequent copies are not without blemish, and the translations are not perfect.[56]

Thus he criticized the assertion of accommodation on the part of the biblical authors, as if they presented mistaken views, adopted from their contemporaries, as truths.[57]

Thus he points out that "not a single case of error can be proved," whether "historical," "doctrinal," or "scientific."[58]

It is fitting to quote at this point the closing statements of one of Warfield's addresses. It summarizes his stand and the goal of this stand.

> But how can I close without expression of thanks to him who has loved us so as to give us so pure a record of His will—God-given in all its parts, even though cast in the forms of human speech—infallible in all its statements—divine even to the smallest particle! . . . Let us bless God . . . for His inspired Word! And may He grant that we may always cherish, love, venerate it, and conform all out life and thinking to it! So may we find safety for our feet, and peaceful security for our souls.[59]

The Early Berkouwer

As to the humanity of Scripture, the early Berkouwer is in complete agreement with Warfield. Over against the theory of mechanical inspiration, he opts for so-called organic inspiration. With this terminology he wishes to convey that inspiration is an act of God's Spirit in which He takes the total man with his personality, his cultural milieu, and his historical setting into His service. This guarantees that the Scripture is a fully human book. Berkouwer is quite aware that this view evokes new problems and dangers. The temptation is there to construe, under the cover of "organic inspiration," a human factor that is independent of, competitive with, or even inimical to the divine factor. Thus one may regard certain words, thoughts, and concepts in Scripture sections (as Gen. 1–3) simply as human input. This input, then, would reflect antiquated science, differing views of history, or outdated culture and may, therefore, under no circumstances be identified with, or qualify as, universally valid, divine communication. Use of the term *organic*, in Berkouwer's opinion, endangers divine inspiration. It is hardly surprising that he proceeds to condemn this approach in no uncertain terms as an unacceptable and unwarranted dualism of the divine and human factor. He charges that this dualism is born out of the desire to compromise with certain results of science that are allegedly unassailable and, apart from this dualism, could not be assimilated in the thinking of the Christian. He argues that it constitutes a capitulation to a type of accommodation of the divine revelation that destroys the trustworthiness of Holy Scripture. He concludes that it violates the mystery of Scripture as both Word of God and word of man and is on a par with several theories that claim to have found the key that opens the door to discovery of the real Word of God in the Scriptures.

Berkouwer's own view is that the doctrine of the organic inspiration of Scripture serves its purpose only when it produces an ever-increasing understanding of the Scripture as the Word of God. The reason is simple. This doctrine was designed to convey the fact that the divine act of inspiration takes the human factor into its service in such a way that it produces the one infallible Word of God. It points, therefore, to the mystery and miracle of Scripture. Through imperfect human instruments and in an incomprehensible manner, God the Holy Spirit saw fit to give to mankind the utterly and completely trustworthy Word of God.[60]

It is remarkable how the views of the early Berkouwer run parallel to those of Warfield. Both hold that in the inspiration of Scripture the Spirit of God displays His omnipotence in the utilization of human instruments in such a fashion that to be human is no longer identical with being fallible and errant. A fully trustworthy and infallible Bible is the result.[61]

Also with regard to the inerrancy of Scripture one finds the early Berkouwer in complete agreement with Warfield.

First, with him he holds to Scripture as the written Word of God by virtue of its inspiration and, therefore, to its complete trustworthiness, its absolute authority, and its full infallibility.[62]

Second, there is no evidence that he distinguishes between infallibility and inerrancy. In fact, at one point he uses these terms interchangeably.[63]

Third, he demonstrates that the Reformed tradition—the extent to which he introduces historical arguments for the doctrine of inspiration—consistently has defended the inspiration and infallibility/inerrancy of Scripture.[64]

Fourth, he speaks out against the theory that the Bible authors as well as the Lord Jesus Christ, knowingly or unknowingly, accommodated their teachings to false or errant views peculiar to their times. This, of course, would at least partially jeopardize the truth and trustworthiness of these teachings. An example of such accommodation would be the presentation of an outdated and unacceptable cosmology. Berkouwer's solution to this and

similar problems is twofold. (1) At times the Bible adapts itself to
the level of the hearers or readers. This may prevent the total
truth from being told. But it certainly does not imply that falsehoods are conveyed. Adaptation, therefore, must be sharply distinguished from accommodation. (2) At other times, Scripture
uses the language of observation, which is common to all people
of all ages. It is a language that does not aim at scientific precision. Therefore, it may not be accused of conveying scientific
falsehoods. Again, observation language must be sharply distinguished from accommodation. The aforementioned example falls
in the category of observation language.[65]

Fifth, he emphasizes that the Reformed concept of Scripture as
the inspired, trustworthy, authoritative, infallible, inerrant
Word of God forces it into a unique, but isolated and lonely
position. In commenting on this position, however, he directs
this important warning to his readers:

> If the isolation of the Reformed view of Scripture is truly of
> significance, then it may not consist of an utterance of a formal-
> theoretical persuasion as to the quality of the Bible, but must be
> indissolubly connected with the actual listening and submission
> to the authority of Holy Scripture as the Word of the living God.
> The confession of the authority and infallibility of Scripture is not
> an *empty a priori*, which later can be "filled" with a variety of
> contents, but a confession which has significance for *all of life* and
> in the submission of life in everyday reality to the authority of
> Scripture it will prove to what extent the isolation is, indeed,
> seriously meant.

> He who accepts the Reformed confession with regard to Scripture
> in the full sense of the words is deeply convinced that it is not a
> matter of a purely theoretical persuasion as to the "quality" of
> Holy Scripture, but a confession that only then is truly a confes-
> sion of faith when it is accepted and verbalized *in* faithful submis-
> sion to the authority of the Word of the Lord. It is a confession
> that does not stand "by itself," but a confession of faith in Jesus
> Christ who comes to us in the Word.[66]

Berkouwer's message is clear. A truly biblical view of Scripture and all its attributes meets at least three requirements. It is
not so much a matter of the mind (formal-theoretical, purely
theoretical) as it is a matter of the heart (confession of faith). It is
not so much a verbal pronouncement (confession) as it is an
expression of an obedient life (submission to authority). It is not
so much an abstract entity ("by itself") as it is the embrace of an

"object" (the contents of Scripture, personified in Christ). This is not to say that Berkouwer would despise a "correct view" of Scripture but simply that this is never an end in itself but in a very real way only a beginning.

The Later Berkouwer

In the later phase of his thinking, there is a fundamental change not only in his view of Scripture as God's Word but also in his position with regard to Scripture as man's word. In his attempt to arrive at the proper outlook on the humanity of Scripture he intends to avoid both what he calls a supernatural and an antisupernatural approach. The first one, in his estimation, calls the Word of God a "miraculous phenomenon" and sees the mystery of Scripture in the light of supernaturalism. "It presupposed and stressed the supernatural origin of Scripture, and thus little attention was given to the actual historical origin of Scripture, or to the fact that men had written it."[67] The second one would hold Scripture to be a natural phenomenon and forms a threat to the divine aspect by its exclusive emphasis on the humanity of Scripture. The former is typified by the mechanical theory of inspiration, the latter by an unrestricted criticism. Berkouwer appears well aware of the fact that the church resorted to the phrase *organic inspiration* in order to escape both extremes. It meant to honor both God as the principal author of Scripture and the Bible writers as instrumental authors. The term *instrumental,* however, is not acceptable to Berkouwer any more, without at least some important qualifications. After all, the words *organ* or *instrument* can serve the purposes of both supernaturalism and antisupernaturalism. An instrument can be quite mechanical and an organ can be quite independent. Neither term, therefore, guarantees *per se* that the divine and human elements will not be competitive of, limit, or threaten one another.

The only way to transcend this competition is to abandon all theoretical, formalized efforts to settle the relationship between the divine and the human. Undoubtedly Berkouwer would now classify Warfield's as well as his own earlier solution to the problem of the relationship of the divine and the human under the heading of such efforts. After all, whether the concept of *concursus* is used or not, Warfield and the early Berkouwer regard the Bible as being both and simultaneously, divine and human.

They characterize that fact as an incomprehensible mystery and a praiseworthy wonder. The later Berkouwer simply sees in such approach the supernatural extreme exemplified, even if mechanical inspiration is rejected and organic inspiration is championed. For what is left of the importance of the human element? It is programed by the divine factor, which blocks the human authors from making any significant contributions in the origin and composition of Scripture other than their own style and effectively prevents the critical-historical method from pointing these out.

But what, then, is the later Berkouwer's alternative that will supposedly transcend the competition of the divine and human elements? He formulates this alternative in terms of Scripture as being the God-breathed, prophetic-apostolic, human witness or testimony to Christ. The pivotal word is witness or testimony. Scripture is and remains a human word. The human will never dissolve into the divine. But further, it is not simply and solely a human word. It is also God's Word, inasmuch as it is God-breathed and Spirit-related. Finally, it is not formally the Word of God but it is the Word of God only as and by virtue of the witness concerning Christ. Berkouwer writes:

> The mystery of the God-breathed Scripture is not meant to place us before a theoretical problem of how Scripture could possibly and conceivably be both God's Word and man's word, and how they could be "united." It rather places us before the mystery of Christ. . . . Every word about the God-breathed character of Scripture is meaningless if Holy Scripture is not understood as the witness concerning Christ. . . . The Word of God did not come to us as a great and isolated miracle but as a miracle and secret of Scripture, of the human witness empowered by the Spirit. . . . God's Word . . . does not return to him void but . . . is heard, understood, and proclaimed in the form of the word of human witnesses. It comes to us in the midst of an overwhelming multiformity of human witnesses, of human questions and answers of skepticism and trust, of faith and unbelief.[68]

Berkouwer's view of Scripture stands or falls with the word *witness*. This word safeguards Scripture from being identified as the Word of God in a "supernatural" fashion. Such identification would dehumanize the authors in spite of a possible protest against the mechanical theory of inspiration. It also safeguards Scripture from being demoted to a fable in an "antisupernatural" fashion. Such demotion would destroy the message of the authors. On the one hand, it is the only perspective from which the theopneusty of Scripture and the "taking into service" of the human authors can be understood. On the other hand, it is the only perspective from which the message remains in view. It seems that Berkouwer has achieved what he set out to do. Scripture as witness is fully man's word and fully God's Word, although not God's Word formally. This would destroy the humanity of Scripture (and we would have only supernaturalism). At the same time, Scripture as witness is fully God's Word and man's word, although God's Word only because of its *scopus*. Without this, the divinity of Scripture would be eliminated (the view of antisupernaturalism). Allegedly, the term *witness*, in the way it functions in Berkouwer's later thinking, has enabled him to overcome the competition between the divine and the human elements. Where the concept of *concursus* in the final analysis fails, there the term *witness* succeeds.[69] Eventually the question must be asked as to whether this claim has a basis in fact.

Berkouwer's position with regard to the inerrancy of Scripture is an outflow of his view of the "witness character" of Scripture as to its human side.

Berkouwer apparently wishes to go beyond both the liberal accommodation theory and the post-Reformation inerrancy position. The first one he calls dualistic and rationalistic. Its aim is to separate the kernel from the husk by means of the scientific method. The second one he calls formalistic and monergistic. Its goal is to demonstrate the exactness and correctness of all data of Scripture on the basis of its divinity.

In Berkouwer's opinion neither one of these two approaches has really understood the witness character of Scripture. This is his deepest objection, both to the liberal accommodation theory and to the post-Reformation inerrancy position.

This witness character implies, on the one hand, that Scripture is intensely human. As such it is time-bound and time-related. This means that the authors shared the views and conceptions of the period in which they lived, did not know anything more than did their contemporaries about the sciences, and held to the social structures, cultural patterns, and specific customs peculiar to their age. Not only do the scientific method and biblical research show this, but also the historical nature of Scripture alerts us to this. To characterize previous levels of knowledge as error is objectionable to Berkouwer. It would be tantamount to losing sight of this historical nature.

On the other hand, this witness character does not exclude the truth that Scripture is genuinely divine. Its divinity is bound up with its goal, its purpose, it message, and its scope. Scripture is the witness to Christ, crucified and risen. This scope is centralizing and unifying. The many authors, with their many backgrounds and many approaches, all give witness to the one Christ. Berkouwer does not tire of stressing that Scripture can be read and understood only in the light of its central scope. Any other approach is formalized and sterile. For examples of such formalized approach, Berkouwer points to the effects undertaken to establish that Scripture is either errant and unreliable or inerrant and reliable. In the first case inaccuracies and contradictions are emphasized. In the second, only the presence of difficulties with regard to facts or of a need for the harmonization of details is granted. Berkouwer's reaction is simply this: Both approaches formalize the notion of error when they define it in terms of correctness and exactness, and, therefore, both become irrelevant. The Scriptures are intensely human, with all that this entails. So what else can one expect but to come across facts that are inaccurate and details that cannot be harmonized? This is not a big thing, either to be stressed or denied. At the same time the Scriptures are genuinely divine because of their message and scope. By virtue of its witness to that scope, which is Christ crucified and risen, Scripture is totally reliable and absolutely infallible. Scripture could only be errant in the biblical sense of the word if its scope, its truth, would lack reality. Further, man can only err in that same sense of the word if he swerves from that scope, apostatizes from the truth as it is in Christ. It is highly ironical that both opponents and proponents of a formalized inerrancy may never have been confronted with the biblical message and, therefore, in the final analysis may hold to the practical errancy of Scripture and may have fallen victim to what really constitutes error—rejection of its central message of Christ crucified and risen.[70]

In summary, Berkouwer sees in Scripture the God-breathed, human witness to Christ. As such it is both human and divine. Its divinity does not impinge on its humanity. Biblical research is unrestricted. It may freely utilize the scientific approach, including the critical-historical and form-historical methods. By the same token, its humanity does not impinge on its divinity. It will joyfully focus its attention on the message of Scripture and become captive to it.

It may be wise to insert at this point an example of how Berkouwer wishes to honor both the human and the divine sides. In his early thinking he defended the traditional Reformed view of Genesis 1–3, in which the historicity of these chapters was fully maintained. He held that Adam and Eve were created and fell into sin exactly as described in the text. In his later thinking there is a fundamentally different approach. He speaks sympathetically about the new Roman Catholic theology that wishes to take into account the literary, scientific, and historico-cultural background of these chapters on the one hand and to focus attention on their religious intent on the other. Thus both the humanity of the author would be honored and the inviolability of the divine message secured. The upshot of this approach, in which supposedly respect is shown to Scripture by giving the original sense of the material its due, is among other things that monogenism is denied. The critical, literary, scientific, and historico-cultural method dictated this conclusion. But how can this be squared with Paul's teaching in Romans 5? The answer to this question is said to be simple. Paul's teaching has to be read and understood in the light of the aforementioned conclusion. Paul apparently accommodated himself to an Old Testament image in order to suit his own purposes! The early Berkouwer registers a strong and eloquent protest against such approach. The later Berkouwer takes its critics to task for failing to see that the method, exemplified by the new Roman Catholic theology, serves to clarify its message and bring it into a sharp focus. But what, then, is the message of Genesis 1–3? To confine ourselves to Genesis 1, Berkouwer holds that it is representative of Israel's polemical stance against mythical theogonies and aims to open a perspective to the incomparable nature of Yahweh. In spite of many protests to the contrary, the religious message seems to evaporate in generalities under the onslaught of the critical-historical method.[71]

In conclusion, the battle lines appear to be drawn. Warfield and Berkouwer prove, indeed, to be "point men" in the debate that rages about the nature of Scripture.

Conclusion

The positions have now been laid out. Warfield and the early Berkouwer hold that Scripture is the Word of God in the sense that the human words as God-breathed are a divine product. As such they are true, trustworthy, infallible, inerrant, and authoritative in every pronouncement they make, in every subject matter they address, and in every area in which they speak—as well as being fit to be the means of regeneration, justification, and sanctification. The later Berkouwer holds that Scripture is the word of man in the same sense in which every other human document is the word of man. At the same time, it is nevertheless in the act of faith proclaimed by the apostles and confessed by the church as the God-breathed Word of God by virtue of its witness to Christ.

As has been indicated already, both positions recognize a mystery. Warfield and the early Berkouwer find the mystery in the *way* in which God produces an infallible book through the mediation of fallible writers. They recognized this as a mystery because God has not seen fit to disclose the way from the origin (God) to the product (Scripture). The later Berkouwer finds the mystery in the *fact* that God uses a fallible book to convey a divine message. Berkouwer is forced to refer to this as a mystery because the realm of revelation and faith is not continuous with that of the written or spoken word. The former mystery is epistemological, the latter metaphysical, in nature. As will be shown, Berkouwer's later approach is dialectical.

The fundamental difference of the two positions emerges specifically in their implications. Warfield and the early Berkouwer are armed with an infallible book as a divine gift that enables them to address all men, at all times, in all places, in all circumstances, and in all areas of their lives, and to give them specific directives. Much more than certainty is at stake. When the later Berkouwer states that the objection to a "controversial Bible" is rooted in the fear that the ground for certainty will be lost,[72] at worst he masks the real issue and at best he is only partially right. First—and at worst—he masks the real issue. It is no coincidence that Berkouwer begins his book on Scripture with a chapter entitled, "Holy Scripture and Certainty." When he changed his view of Scripture, the matter of certainty immediately became a problem. His own shift forced the issue on him. Indeed, it could not but become the fundamental problem.

If Scripture suffers from the same human relativity as do all other human writings, is there any ground left for religious as well as epistemological certainty? This issue does not originate in the fear of people, but in the fact of Berkouwer's shift.

Second, at best Berkouwer is only partially right. When God's people object to a "controversial Bible," it is not simply because of loss of certainty. They recognize that Scripture is a tool for a task, an instrument for a purpose, and a means to an end. It is given for salvation, which consists of regeneration, justification, and sanctification. Hence, as soldiers in the army of Christ, they will resist at all cost, the blunting of the sword of the Spirit of God. They know that the loss of the tool will jeopardize the task, that the loss of the instrument will cloud the purpose, and that the loss of the means will endanger the end. They recognize, in the terms of the early Berkouwer, that biblical criticism will inevitably lead to "de-Christianization" and secularization.[73] For that reason they wage the battle *for* the Bible. Salvation in all its component elements is at stake. Of course, they also recognize, along with the early Berkouwer, that merely a formally correct view of Scripture is not sufficient.

The implications of Berkouwer's position are saddening. The question is inescapable. What precisely *is* the content, the message, the scope of the Scriptures? This is known supposedly through the words of Scripture as witness. But at this point a serious problem emerges. As a human document Scripture is within the range of the critical-historical method. The claim is indeed made that the result of critical-historical study will be a better understanding of Scripture. But what guarantee is there that its content will not be reduced to an intolerable minimum? Berkouwer insists that the content itself guarantees this. But then the original question returns with even greater force. What precisely is the content of Scripture that controls the critical-historical method, which applies its "acids" to the words of Scripture, which in turn witness to the content of Scripture? Without further discussion of the vicious circle that is quite apparent in this question, we find that the answer of Berkouwer is finally this: The content of Scripture is divine, namely, Jesus Christ, crucified and risen. But this will not do. The *words* "Jesus Christ, crucified and risen" are not themselves divine and cannot constitute the content of Scripture. They are at best a witness to the content of Scripture. As such they are open to the onslaught of the critical-historical method. Hence the question, What precisely *is* the content of Scripture? has not really been answered. Can it be answered at all? It appears not, because the content itself is not human, though every *word* of Scripture is human and subject to all the liabilities connected with its humanness. The fundamental problem is that the realm of the divine and the realm of the human are not continuous. They indeed presuppose one another; the content of Scripture is in need of the witness of Scripture. But they also exclude one another; the content of Scripture may not be identified with Scripture. They do not coincide at a single point. Both the correlation of revelation and faith and the charge of docetism are indicative of this essentially dialectic approach. As to the correlation, revelation is said to be open only to faith and must never be identified with Scripture. As to the charge of docetism, the human is said to vanish when the divine enters. Both the correlation and the charge are rooted in the bedrock conviction of the mutual exclusiveness of the divine and the human and are not understandable apart from it.

In conclusion, upon this dialectic approach, the content of Scripture is subject to an ever-increasing reductionism by virtue of the nature of the human element and is in principle unnamable by virtue of the nature of the divine element. The history of the approach demonstrates this. Barth writes an extensive systematic theology in reflecting on the Word of God as it is echoed in the words of Scripture. Bultmann criticizes Barth on two counts. He holds that Barth does not take either the nature of the human aspect or the nature of the divine aspect sufficiently seriously. The former would require a much more radical application of the critical-historical method. The latter would demand the recognition that one cannot really reflect on the Word of God. In other words, Barth is supposed to be too timid regarding the human aspect and too bold regarding the divine. Bultmann intends to remedy this situation. Since the Word of God itself is by definition beyond the reach of man, he reflects on man as he responds to the Word of God. This appears to make him less bold. Further, by authority of the critical-historical method he declares that the content of Scripture is the act of God in Jesus Christ who graces man with authentic existence. He is indeed much less timid than Barth! His reduction of the content of Scripture is staggering. It is interesting to note that Bultmann's pupil Braun reduces the content even further. He questions the propriety of speaking about God. Finally he defines the word *God* as "a kind of co-humanity."[74] As a result of this type of thinking, Barth criticized Bultmann's school for its "flat-tire theology."[75] It is equally interesting to note that Barth's pupil Ott inquires into the transcendental conditions for the usage of any language and any words whatsoever. Does any language and do any words, human as they are, have any naming power at all with regard to the divine? In these two pupils of Barth and Bultmann the dialectic approach has run its course. The content of Scripture is reduced to an intolerable minimum and appears to be in principle unnamable. A critic called both the schools of Barth and Bultmann, in spite of their seeming differences, "bloodless."[76] This point is well made.

It must be seriously considered whether Berkouwer's failure to devote a separate chapter in his book *Holy Scripture* to the content of Scripture is not rooted in an impotence that is bound up with the dialectic approach. After all, the concept of the content is so central in the structure of his thinking that one might have expected a careful discussion of it. At any rate, Berkouwer's followers had better be warned that the course they have taken will lead, in principle, to the inevitable loss of the content of the gospel.

This brings us to a final question. Why did Berkouwer move from his earlier to his later position? Several observations are needed before an attempt is made to answer this question.

First, Warfield's writings did not succeed in preventing Berkouwer from changing his position. Space does not allow an evaluation of Warfield's apologetic method at this point. But it is commonly agreed that Warfield used basically an inductive methodology. It is apparent that in Berkouwer's case this methodology was not effective. In fact, it is ironic that induction had a decidedly negative influence on Berkouwer. After all, it was mainly the results of the critical-historical method that made him waver in his original stand. It should be noted at this juncture that the inductive method is never neutral;[77] it is always the tool of a deeper-lying conviction. Berkouwer failed to recognize this, since he was captivated by the alleged objectivity of the scientific approach.

Second, Berkouwer's own early writings did not prevent the shift in his views either. Again, space does not allow for the evaluation of the apologetic methods of the early and the later

Berkouwer. But it may be stated that in his early thought he was thoroughly presuppositional, as is quite apparent in his *Problem of Biblical Criticism.*[78] His central thesis is that the critical-historical method in principle has no boundaries. Once it is unleashed, it can no longer be curtailed. Against this backdrop he characterizes the solution of neoorthodoxy as a "way out."[79] Neoorthodoxy distinguishes between the realm of ordinary history (*Historie*) and a realm that transcends ordinary history (*Geschichte*). The former is within reach of the acids of the critical-historical method. The latter is not. It is the contention of the early Berkouwer that the intolerable reductionism of the critical-historical method compelled neoorthodoxy to posit a "storm-free," "invulnerable" area as a "way out" of the difficulties produced by this method. This is indeed a plausible explanation of the historical development, but only from his own perspective. His major, presuppositional premise, to which he held without wavering in his early phase, was that the Bible is a divine product and therefore an infallible book. His minor premise was that the critical-historical method is destructive for that book. His conclusion was that those who espouse the critical-historical method must seek a "way out" of the predicament in which they find themselves. In his later writings Berkouwer sees more sharply, and more correctly, that neoorthodoxy does not view itself as seeking a "way out" of a predicament but rather as presenting "*the* way" to the certainty of faith.[80] What is more important, however, is that there can be no doubt that the later Berkouwer endorses and adopts the neoorthodox position. A comparison of his *Holy Scripture* and Barth's *Church Dogmatics* I, 2, which sets forth his view of Scripture, shows that there is basic agreement between the two men on Scripture as witness, on the mystery of Scripture, on the meaning of "*est*" in the formula *Sacra Scriptura est Verbum Dei*, and on the notion of kerygma.[81] As to the last, both are of the opinion that certainty of faith does not rest on an allegedly inerrant Bible, which would be unassailable to the reductionism of the critical-historical method, but on the kerygma that is beyond the reach of this method. In his early writings Berkouwer is adamant that the kerygma cannot be regarded as a proven "storm-free" area.[82] In his later thinking the shift is dramatic. The Bible has become "controversial." That leaves the kerygma as the only *apologia* to show that the way of faith is and remains accessible.[83]

What was described by the early Berkouwer as "a way out" appears to be not only *the* way of neoorthodoxy but also *the* way of the later Berkouwer. What Berkouwer has failed to recognize, both in his earlier and later writings, is that the way of neoorthodoxy is the way of apostate thinking and possibly even of an apostate heart. This will now further be substantiated.

When man apostatizes from God and declares the throne of the universe vacant, the world in which he lives becomes immediately contingent and without order. Since man, however, cannot live in such a world, he introduces his own principle of necessity or order. Greek philosophy is a case in point. Heraclitus saw in this world an irrational flux without any real semblance of order, although he introduced a principle of order in terms of the logos. Parmenides gave the world the imprint of rationalistic necessity and set out to disprove the possibility of any movement whatsoever. Plato's goal was to effect a synthesis between the two types of philosophizing in which both the particulars and the universals would be accounted for. He distinguished to that end between a lower realm of matter (flux, particulars) and a higher realm of form (order, universals). Aristotle's philosophy was a variation on a theme. He charged that there was no continuity between the two realms and introduced his theory of the immanent forms, in which the lower form functions as matter for the higher form and higher matter functions as form for lower matter in the chain of being. It is commonly agreed, however, that Aristotle also was not able to bring about the synthesis between the two poles. The reason is that he and his predecessors were trapped in their dialectic in which both poles mutually presuppose and preclude one another. Both disorder and order are constituent elements of an apostate view of the world. But they can never be reconciled. They are discontinuous at every single point. It ought to be noted that in ancient thought the disorder pole was regarded as the greatest threat. Hence primacy was assigned to the form, or order, pole. The ancients were fearful of the threat of the contingent—the lack of order and predictability. This is also visible in the Babylonian religions, where chaos (the world of the contingent) was supposedly offset by the cult (the principle of order). The tragedy of this thought is that the real problem, namely of sin, is replaced by a pseudo-problem, namely of contingency and chance. The way of the "form" is proclaimed as *the* way. Not only, however, will it be unable to solve the pseudo-problem, but also, as the way of an apostate methodology, it will prove to be the way of death.

In modern thought a similar pattern emerges. Leibniz saw the world as a rationalistic totality. Hume emphasized the contingent element. Kant attempted to synthesize both views in proposing a realm of nature (theoretical thought, necessity) and a realm of freedom (faith, contingency). Hegel rearranged the relationship between the two principles but stayed faithful to the basic theme. Kierkegaard reacted violently against the rationalism of Hegel and emphasized the realm of freedom in terms of the primacy of the momentary act of existential faith. Again, the basic dialectic becomes visible. At this juncture, however, the regimenting rationalism of the order pole (nature) is viewed as the greatest threat. The deep suspicion of the technocratic society is illustrative of this shift. The dialectic of modern thought is not different from that of ancient thought, but the field is reversed. The ancients emphasized the primacy of the order pole (form) as the answer to disconcerting discontinuity. The moderns assign the primacy to the contingency pole (freedom) to save from a stifling rationalism. The way of the freedom pole now becomes *the* way. The nature pole, to be sure, has a definite autonomy, but the freedom pole transcends it, controls it, and limits it. In the meantime, the tragedy remains. The one pseudo-problem is substituted for another one. The "demonic" is now found in the abundance of regimentation. Once again the problem of sin is suppressed. And because of this the new way of the old apostate methodology can be nothing else but the way of death.

Against this background the structure and danger of modern theology came into focus. They are the structure and danger of modern thought. Modern theology grants the critical-historical method a definite but limited autonomy. At the same time, the content of the gospel transcends the realm of nature. As such it is inviolable. It is not simply to be viewed as a way out. It is the way of a so-called gospel that reflects a reality in which the realm of nature does not have the final word.

What a difference there is between the way of modern theology and the way of the biblical gospel. Modern theology is caught in the dialectic of continuity and discontinuity, whatever terminology is used. The language may resemble the Bible more (Barth) or less (Bultmann). But this is a peripheral matter. The biblical gospel takes sin and the divine solution to sin seriously. The implications of both ways have already been mentioned.

By now several things must have become clear.

First, it must have become clear why Warfield was commended for joining the fundamental issue when he stated that opposition to Scripture had either a rationalistic or an irrationalistic root. Scripture becomes the target either of the one or of the other pole of the dialectic. In modern theology it became the target of both. The critical-historical method (rationalistic) reduced the content of the gospel. The revelation pole (irrationalistic) determined that the content is in principle unnamable. On either count, Scripture may not be identified as a divine product that is infallible in its human form.

Second, it must have become clear why Berkouwer and his followers bring in the charge of Aristotelianism against those who in the footsteps of post-Reformation theologians hold to the verbal inspiration and inerrancy of Scripture as a human document. This view must appear as a rationalistic threat from the perspective of a dialectic approach that assigns primacy to the "freedom" pole. This is not to say that post-Reformation theology is without any scholastic blemishes. But it *is* to say that identification of Scripture and the Word of God, as Warfield states and defends it, is not rationalistic Aristotelianism.

This brings us back to the question, Why did Berkouwer shift his position so radically? The answer is not easy. Generally speaking, the adoption of a methodology that has the indelible imprint of apostasy and that is basically a dead-end street may have one of two roots.

First, it is possible that an apostate methodology arises from an apostate heart. In this connection it must be maintained that the idea that the rejection of biblical inerrancy is not a matter of "evangelical commitment, but of evangelical comprehension"[84] is untenable. The rejection of biblical inerrancy may very well imply lack of heart commitment to God.

Second, it is possible that an apostate methodology to a greater or lesser extent has slipped into the thinking of a man who is otherwise committed to Christ. In that case, however, it is not likely, to say the least, that he is conscious of the origin and nature of his conviction. It also must be questioned whether such a person is guided by a competent leadership into, and has a sufficiently strong interest in, a holy life. Scripture teaches that God's people under right leadership and with a goal of holy living will not be swayed by every wind of doctrine (Eph. 4:11–14), including an erroneous wind in the concept of Scripture. Indeed, how can a person be swayed to blunt the sword of the Spirit when he sees it effectively used as an instrument of sanctification by the leadership of the church and experiences it as such in his own life? Finally, it ought to be recognized that such a person, if he is in a teaching position in the church of Christ, may have every intention to make a contribution to the kingdom of God. But what guarantee does he, or the church, have that he will escape building with wood, hay, and stubble? The consequences are serious (see 1 Cor. 3:12–15).

In short, one's rejection of biblical inerrancy appears to indicate the rebellion of his heart or to be bound up with a deficiency in his life. To call the matter of biblical inerrancy, therefore, an epistemological problem does not deal with the fundamental issue. Berkouwer and his followers are in the grip of a dialectic that arises from apostasy and can arise *only* from apostasy. This is the transcendental root of the structure of modern theology, the thought of the later Berkouwer, and the wholesale rejection of biblical inerrancy. Whether in any given case this root is in the form of an apostate heart or only of an apostate methodology cannot be determined in a book. What can be determined, however, is that the grip of the dialectic, precisely because it is rooted in apostasy of one kind or another, can be broken only by repentance. Hence it is fitting that at the conclusion of this chapter, *and arising from its contents,* an appeal is made for just that (2 Tim. 2:24–26).

NOTES

Notes on Chapter 1

[1]This notion is, I believe, quite foundationless. There seems to be no evidence that the early church knew of a supposed intention by the evangelists not to write history, and the early Christians were in the best position to know. We know that they strongly rejected the peculiar tenets of gnosticism as being untrue to apostolic teaching.

[2]On radical criticism of the Gospels, see "Additional Note" pp. 32ff.; on higher criticism in general, see chapter 4.

[3]I resist the temptation to develop this point beyond a footnote. My own undogmatic view is that Matthew was written in Hebrew or Aramaic, between A.D. 33 and 42; Mark in about 44, followed shortly after by a Greek translation of Matthew; Luke in the early 50s; and John in the early 60s.

[4]Much of what follows is taken from chapter 1 of the author's *Christ and the Bible* (Downers Grove: InterVarsity, 1973).

[5]This sentence echoes B. B. Warfield in *Biblical Foundations* (Grand Rapids: Eerdmans, 1958), p. 58, which echoes an earlier sentence of Augustine (*Confessions*, xiii. 29).

[6]These accounts are discussed in the author's *Our Lord's View of the Old Testament* (London: Inter-Varsity, 1964), pp. 11–14.

[7]T. T. Perowne, *Obadiah and Jonah* (Cambridge, 1894), p. 51. The book of Jonah is further discussed in *Christ and the Bible*, pp. 74-75.

[8]"The Law" or "the Law and the Prophets" often seems to be shorthand for "the Law, the Prophets, and the Writings," the three sections of the Old Testament Scriptures. The Psalms, which occupy a great place in the thought of Jesus, belong to the Writings. Yet in quoting Psalm 82:6 He says, "Is it not written in your *Law?*" (John 10:34). "The Writings" did not become the universally accepted title of the third section of the Old Testament canon until much later. See further, *Christ and the Bible*, p. 158, n. 3.

[9]G. Vos, *The Teaching of Jesus Concerning the Kingdom of God and the Church* (Philadelphia: Presbyterian & Reformed, 1951), pp. 61ff.

[10]H. R. Boer, *Above the Battle? The Bible and Its Critics* (Grand Rapids: Eerdmans, 1975), p. 95, says, "Jesus again and again accommodated himself to existing beliefs which we no longer accept."

[11]C. H. Dood, *According to the Scriptures* (London: Fontana, 1952), pp. 109ff.

[12]J. Barr, *Fundamentalism* (London: SCM, 1977), pp. 73ff.

[13]See *Christ and the Bible* pp. 100ff. For a full treatment see R. T. France, *Jesus and the Old Testament: His Application of the Old Testament Passages to Himself and His Mission* (London: Tyndale, 1971).

[14]Metonymy is a common figure of speech. The name of one thing is used for that of another with which it is associated. Here the names of the Author and of the Work authored are used interchangeably.

[15]S. T. Davis, *The Debate About the Bible: Inerrancy Versus Infallibility* (Philadelphia: Westminster, 1977), p. 118.

[16]J. K. S. Reid, *The Authority of Scripture* (London: Harper, 1957), pp. 260ff.

[17]B. H. Branscomb, *Jesus and the Law of Moses* (London: Harper, 1930), p. 155.

[18]See D. Daube, *New Testament and Rabbinic Judaism* (London: Athlone, 1956), pp. 60ff.

[19]We do not know much about the operation of the *lex talionis* in Old Testament times. It seems unlikely that it was intended, except in the case of murder, to be taken literally. Exodus 21:18–36 suggests that payment of damages was the customary retribution. In most forms of Islamic law, regulations regarding retribution limit its severity. The "heirs of blood" must exact *not more than* equivalent damage or injury. Physical injury is normally ruled out since there is no way of ensuring exact equivalence. A tariff of payments is generally stipulated. The folly of tribal revenge is seen most clearly when one tribe considers itself superior to another (which it usually does). It will then demand two or three deaths in return for one.

[20]B. B. Warfield, *The Inspiration and Authority of the Bible* (London: Presbyterian & Reformed, 1959), p. 119.

[21]This point is made by R. T. France in *Jesus and the Old Testament* (London: Tyndale, 1971), which deals with the subject carefully and in detail, and to which I am greatly indebted in regard to the "Additional Note" at the end of this chapter.

[22]H. E. W. Turner, *Historicity and the Gospels* (London: Mowbray, 1963).

[23]R. H. Fuller, *Interpreting the Miracles* (London: Westminster, 1963), pp. 26ff.

[24]R. T. France, *The Use of the Old Testament by Jesus according to the Synoptic Gospels* (Bristol University Ph.D. thesis, 1966), p. 326.

Notes on Chapter 2

[1]It should be noted that "apostle" and "writer of New Testament Scripture" are interchanged in this paper. It is not assumed that all New Testament writers were apostles in the strict sense, but that they all had Spirit-endowed power in writing. It seems quite proper, therefore, to call their books "apostolic writings." See N. H. Ridderbos, *The Authority of the New Testament Scriptures* (Philadelphia: Presbyterian & Reformed, 1963), pp. 13–33.

[2]For a highly instructive treatment of Jesus' "pesher" interpretations and the distinctive approach of His disciples, see Richard Longenecker, *Biblical Exegesis in the Apostolic Period* (Grand Rapids: Eerdmans, 1975), pp. 70–75, 98–103, 140–57, 210–11.

[3]Matthew, in particular, gives extensive development to Jesus as the Teacher (cf. his use of διδάσκω, διδάσκαλος. n.b. *TDNT*, 2.138-65). Matthew also gives the greatest emphasis to quotation of biblical materials using the pesher method. Cf. F. C. Grant, "Matthew, Gospel of," *IDB*, 3.302–13. Grant gives a list with brief comments on 61 Old Testament quotations in Matthew. Longenecker (*Biblical Exegesis*, pp. 140–57), discusses eleven Matthean quotations which he views as pesher.

[4]For detailed treatment of these and other Gospel texts, see John F. Wenham's "Christ's View of Scripture" (chapter 1) or his *Christ and the Bible* (Downers Grove: InterVarsity, 1973).

[5]It is, of course, common in modern theology to argue the contrary position—that is, that the reported views of Jesus are *not* the views of Jesus but the views of the writers set forth as the views of Jesus; cf. N. Perrin, *Rediscovering the Teaching of Jesus* (New York: Harper and Row, 1967), pp. 15–20. If this view is adopted, the discernment of Jesus' *own* views would obviously be virtually impossible.

[6]Roger Nicole, "New Testament Use of the Old," *Revelation and the Bible*, ed. Carl. F. H. Henry (Grand Rapids: Baker, 1958), pp. 137–38. Nicole's essay contains a number of helpful points that may aid anyone who wants a good survey of the phenomena. Many of the implications for the doctrine of inspiration are developed. Cf. also Longenecker on the phenomena of quotations in *Biblical Exegesis*, pp. 164–70.

[7]D. Hay, "New Testament Interpretation of the Old Testament," "Interpretation, History of," *IDB* Sup., p. 443.

[8]It is well known that the Scripture writers cite various readings of the Hebrew and Greek (LXX) texts. They often appear to handle the text quite freely, which is a problem for defenders of inerrancy. Yet the Old Testament textual criticism is by no means complete, and the phenomena of variant readings may simply witness to the existence of numerous translations and textual traditions in biblical times. See. R. Longenecker, *Biblical Exegesis*, pp. 113–14.

[9]For interesting material reflecting the out-of-balance character of many modern exegetes who, using the historical-critical method, focus on the human author to the neglect of the divine author, see K. Barth, *The Epistle to the Romans*, trans. E. Hoskyns (London: Oxford University, 1933) p. 1; B. S. Childs, *Biblical Theology in Crisis* (Philadelphia:

Westminster, 1970), chapter 8, "Recovering an Exegetical Tradition," pp. 139–47; and B. S. Childs, *The Book of Exodus: A Critical, Theological Commentary* (Philadelphia: Westminster, 1974), p. ix.
   [10]Gottlob Schrenk, " γράφω," TDNT, 1. 747.
   [11]B. B. Warfield," 'It Says:' "Scripture Says:' 'God Says,' " *The Presbyterian and Reformed Review* 10 (1899), pp. 472–510, reprinted in *The Inspiration and Authority of the Bible*, ed. by Samuel G. Craig (Philadelphia: Presbyterian and Reformed, 1951), pp. 299–348.
   [12]E. Earle Ellis, *Paul's Use of the Old Testament* (Grand Rapids: Eerdmans, 1957). See pp. 22–25 on introductory formulas.
   [13]See C. E. B. Cranfield, *The Epistle to the Romans*, ICC (Edinburgh: T. & T. Clark, 1975) 1.178–79. On λόγιον see G. Kittel, TDNT, 4.140–43 and the long, classic article by B. B. Warfield, "The Oracles of God," originally in *The Presbyterian and Reformed Review*, 11 (1900), pp. 217–60, reprinted in *The Inspiration and Authority of the Bible*, pp. 351–407.
   [14]BAG, p. 165.
   [15]B. B. Warfield, "The Terms 'Scripture' and 'Scriptures' as Employed in the New Testament," reprinted in *The Inspiration and Authority of the Bible*, pp. 229–41.
   [16]G. Schrenk, TDNT, 1.755. Cf. also Richard N. Longenecker, *Biblical Exegesis*, pp. 19, 48, 49.
   [17]C. F. D. Moule, *An Idiom Book of New Testament Greek* (Cambridge: At the University, 1953), p. 95. Niger Turner, *A Grammar of New Testament Greek*, ed. James H. Moulton (Edinburgh: T. & T. Clark, 1963). Vol. III, Syntax, says the following on *pas* ("all, every"): "In the interests of exegesis it is important to ask how much is involved in the Hellenistic deviation from classical standards as to the def. art. with πᾶς . First of all, πᾶς before an anarthrous noun means *every* in the sense of *any*; not every individual, like ἕκαστος , but any you please." His translation of πασα γραφή in the text under consideration (2 Tim. 3:16) is, "*whatever is* Scripture," p. 199. But he goes on to say, "On the other hand, this anarthrous πᾶς also means *all, the whole of,* just as it does when it has the article. It may be that is due to Hebraic influence; for כָּל־בָּשָׂר becomes πᾶσα σάρξ *all flesh . . . ,* " pp. 199–200. He cites thirteen examples of this usage in the New Testament. 2 Tim. 3:16 could just as well be cited under this category.
   [18]BDF, p. 70.
   [19]J. N. D. Kelly, *A Commentary on the Pastoral Epistles* (New York: Harper & Row, 1963), p. 203. For a contrary opinion, see Martin Dibelious and Hans Conzelman, *The Pastoral Epistles*, trans. by P. Buttolph and A. Yarbro (Philadelphia: Fortress, 1962), p. 120.
   [20]Kelly, *Pastoral Epistles*, p. 203.
   [21]BAG s.v., Bauer⁵ "Von Gott Eingegeben, Inspiriert."
   [22]B. B. Warfield, reprinted in *The Inspiration and Authority of the Bible*, pp. 245–96, from *The Presbyterian and Reformed Review* 11 (1900), pp. 89-130, "God-Inspired Scripture."
   [23]For example, cf. TDNT, s.v.; BAG, s.v.; Kelly, *Pastoral Epistles*.
   [24]Hermann L. Strack and Paul Billerbeck, *Kommentar zum Neuen Testament aus Talmud und Midrasch* (Munich: C. H. Beck, reprint 1969), IV/I.435–51.
   [25]E. Schweizer, TDNT, 6.454.
   [26]H. Kleinknecht, TDNT, 6.345–46.
   [27]Ibid., pp. 358–59.
   [28]The Petrine authorship of 2 Peter is strongly disputed in some circles. The evangelical case is stoutly maintained by Donald Guthrie, *New Testament Introduction* (London: Tyndale, 1970), and Michael Green, *2 Peter and Jude: An Introduction and Commentary* (London: Tyndale, 1968).
   [29]Cf. the discussion in K. H. Schelkle, *Die Petrusbriefe Der Judasbrief* (Freiburg: Herder, 1976), p. 201. J. N. D. Kelly, *The Epistles of Peter and of Jude* (New York: Harper and Row, 1969), pp. 323-25.
   [30]Michael Green, *The Second Epistle General of Peter and the General Epistle of Jude: An Introduction and Commentary* (London: Tyndale, 1968), pp. 89–90.
   [31]Ibid., p. 91.

[32]Loeb Edition, trans. H. St. J. Thackeray, 1:179.

[33]Herman Ridderbos, *Studies in Scripture and Its Authority* (Grand Rapids: Eerdmans, 1978), p. 28.

[34]Ibid., p. 29.

[35]Ibid., p. 21.

[36]C. K. Barrett writes, "Paul distinguishes sharply his own judgment from a pronouncement traceable to Jesus, but this does not mean that he regards his charge here as having no authority, or even significantly less authority than that of verse 10." *A Commentary on the First Epistle to the Corinthians* (New York: Harper and Row, 1968), p. 163.

[37]On the concepts of the truth and witness, see James M. Boice, *Witness and Revelation in the Gospel of John* (Grand Rapids: Zondervan, 1970).

Notes on Chapter 3

[1]William LaSor, "Life Under Tension—Fuller Theological Seminary and The Battle for the Bible," in *The Authority of Scripture at Fuller* (Pasadena, Calif.: Fuller Theological Seminary Alumni, *Theology, News and Notes*, Special Issue, 1976), pp. 5–10, 23–28).

[2]Ibid., p. 25, claiming that these are "ten times that given in the parallel account in Samuel or Kings." In point of fact, there are only three such cases: 1 Chronicles 19:18, 21–25, and 2 Chronicles 2:10 (in the latter two of which the items being counted seem to differ); cf. J. B. Payne, "The Validity of Numbers in Chronicles," *Near East Archaeological Society Bulletin*, New Series, 11 (1978).

[3]2 Chronicles is higher; in seven instances the parallel is higher; cf. Payne, "Validity of Numbers."

[4]An interpretation going back to the fifth Christian century, if not earlier, IDB, 2:366.

[5]G. L. Archer, "An Eighteenth Dynasty Rameses," JETS 17 (1974), pp. 49–50.

[6]Ibid., *A Survey of OT Introduction*, rev. ed. (Chicago: Moody, 1974), pp. 223–34.

[7]According to his more extended comments, "Life Under Tension," p. 27.

[8]*The Battle for the Bible* (Grand Rapids: Zondervan, 1976), pp. 174–76.

[9]Ibid., pp. 37–38.

[10]Dewey M. Beegle, *Scripture, Tradition and Infallibility* (Grand Rapids: Eerdmans, 1973), pp. 175–97.

[11]Ibid., p. 178.

[12]Edwin Thiele, *A Chronology of the Hebrew Kings* (Grand Rapids: Zondervan, 1977), pp. 46–51, 58–60.

[13]Beegle, *Scripture, Tradition, and Infallibility*, p. 183.

[14]For details see my SOTI, rev. ed., p. 289, footnote.

[15]Beegle, *Scripture Tradition and Infallibility*, pp. 186–88.

[16]Ibid., p. 192.

[17]Ibid., p. 194.

[18]Ibid., pp. 194–95.

Notes on Chapter 4

[1]This is recognized even by those who are currently seeking to combine this negative criticism with some form of biblical authority; cf. Peter Stuhlmacher, *Historical Criticism and Theological Interpretation of Scripture* (Philadelphia: Fortress, 1977), p. 65, who concedes, "Historical criticism is the agent of a repeated and growing rupture of vital contact between biblical tradition and our own time." More bluntly, S. T. Davis in *The Debate About the Bible* (Philadelphia: Westminster, 1977) says, on p. 91, "The rise of biblical

criticism has been an important factor in the erosion of the strength of orthodoxy in the Christian church in the past century."

[2]R. N. Soulen, *Handbook of Biblical Criticism* (Atlanta: John Knox, 1976), p. 27; cf. pp. 101–2, where he concludes that "lower criticism is an unhappy term . . . because of its pejorative sound." It seems to sound unimportant or simple in comparison with higher criticism. The very fact, however, that fewer students engage in lower criticism than in higher witnesses to the more advanced linguistic and technical skills that textual criticism requires.

[3]Harry Boer, *Above the Battle? The Bible and Its Critics* (Grand Rapids: Eerdmans, 1977), p. 18.

[4]William LaSor, "Life Under Tension—Fuller Theological Seminary and the Battle for the Bible," in *The Authority of Scripture at Fuller* (Pasadena, Calif., Fuller Theological Seminary Alumni: *Theology, News and Notes,* Special Issue, 1976), p. 26.

[5]Boer, *Above the Battle?* p. 16.

[6]Hermeneutics (plural) refers to clarification of an author's originally intended meaning in contrast to the "new hermeneutic" (singular), which seeks rather to constitute meaning. Cf. Krister Stendahl's distinction between "what it meant" and liberalism's modern search for "what it means" in his article "Biblical Theology, Contemporary," IDB 1.419.

[7]James M. Robinson, *The New Hermeneutic* (New York: Harper and Row, 1964), p. 15.

[8]George Eldon Ladd, "Year of Study in Germany Sharpens Perspectives," *Fuller Seminary* (January 1959), pp. 4–5.

[9]Kasemann, *Das Neue Testament als Kanon* (Gottingen: 1970), pp. 371, 407–8, in Gerhard Maier, *The End of the Historical-Critical Method* (St. Louis: Concordia, 1977), p. 20.

[10]H. H. Rowley, *The Old Testament and Modern Study* (Oxford University: 1951), XV.

[11]*St. Louis Globe–Democrat* (January 29, 1974), p. 6A.

[12]Norman Gottwald, *A Light to the Nations* (New York: Harper, 1959), pp., 9, 13.

[13]E. J. Young, *Introduction,* rev. ed. (Grand Rapids: Eerdmans, 1960), p. 6.

[14]Samuel J. Schultz, "Today's Critic—Presuppositions, Tools, and Methods," BETS 3 (1960), pp. 37–88.

[15]Ibid.

[16]Maier, *End of the Method,* p. 11, in which he assigns the origin of this approach to Johann Semler.

[17]Ladd, "Year of Study," p. 5.

[18]Stuhlmacher, *Historical Criticism,* pp. 39–40.

[19]Cf. W. P. Walters, "Joseph Smith Among the Egyptians," JETS 16 (1973), pp. 25–45.

[20]Cf. chapter 1 above, "Christ's View of Scripture."

[21]One of six parade examples of phenomenological difficulties that are raised against biblical inerrancy by S. T. Davis, *The Debate,* pp. 102–4.

[22]Negative critics may assert otherwise, saying that, "actually they [the biblical narratives] abound in errors, including many contradictory statements" (so M. Burrows, *An Outline of Biblical Theology* [Philadelphia: Westminster, 1946], p. 44), but cf. chapter 3 of this volume. While evangelicals, however, can and do receive encouragement from the relatively few discrepancies that remain unanswered by today's increased knowledge, it is still important to caution that Christian commitment to Scripture does not depend on their infrequency. It is not as though the discovery of additional problems would thereby alter the basis for the evangelical's belief, namely Christ's authentication of Scripture.

[23]Stuhlmacher, *Historical Criticism,* p. 62.

[24]Soulen, *Handbook,* p. 78; cf. N. H. Ridderbos, "Reversals of Old Testament Criticism," C. F. H. Henry, ed., *Revelation and the Bible* (Grand Rapids: Baker, 1958), p. 348, where he objects: "Scholars seem to think they can go to work with an objective, scientific method; in other words, in these respects it seems the Old Testament must be handled as any other book."

454 NOTES

²⁵Maier, *End of the Method*, p. 16.

²⁶Young, *Introduction*, pp. 6–7; cf. Soulen, *Handbook*, p. 78, "If the Historical Critical Method by definition rules out the Divine as a causative factor in history, of what help can it be to the Church in understanding the Bible, which views God and history in precisely that way?" Maier (*End of the Method*, p. 39) concludes: "Divine intervention . . . and a Scripture brought into being by God's Spirit cannot predeterminately be captured in a law of analogy to a this-worldly event."

²⁷Ibid., p. 25; cf. p. 49.

²⁸Ridderbos, "Reversals of Criticism," p. 348.

²⁹Soulen, *Handbook*, p. 78.

³⁰Maier (*End of the Method*, p. 70) defends Scripture even in such matters of alleged scientific error as the sun standing still over Gibeon or the rabbit chewing its cud. The inaccuracy of Stuhlmacher's recent review of his book, which claimed that "his suggested way of . . . exegesis does not seem to differ greatly from that suggested by his former mentor" (W. W. Gasque and C. E. Armerding, "Both Testaments," *Christianity Today* 22 [1978] 700), becomes apparent when one observes Stuhlmacher's own repudiation of Maier's "pietistic . . . half-hearted criticism," *Historical Criticism*, pp. 69–71. Yet Maier still concedes the possibility of contradictions within Scripture, that "God would have to put up with them," and specifically rejects inerrancy in favor of "infallibility" (*End of the Method*, pp. 55, 70, 71).

³¹Stuhlmacher, *Historical Criticism*, pp. 54–55, 61–62.

³²Davis's primary difficulty with biblical inerrancy (*The Debate*, pp. 97, 126). Yet in almost the same breath he insists, "There are philosophical assumptions that some biblical critics make about the Bible—e.g., that supernatural events such as resurrections and other miracles are just not the sort of things that happen—that lead them to . . . unacceptable conclusions," ibid., p. 117.

³³Stuhlmacher, *Historical Criticism*, pp. 83–85.

³⁴Maier, *End of the Method*, p. 35.

³⁵In a sense, Warfield's approach was also initially inductive (see chapter 14), for he sought to gather all the data in Scripture and from it to induce the Bible's own revealed doctrine of inspiration. But once he had thus formulated the doctrine, he operated deductively from it. Further data, i.e., men's evaluations derived from their observations of difficulties in the content of Scripture, did not constitute legitimate input for determining the definition of inspiration, that had to be, by its nature, a revealed truth.

³⁶J. B. Payne, "*Apeitheō*: Current Resistance to Biblical Inerrancy," *BETS* 10 (1967), pp. 5–6.

³⁷Negative critics have been quick to fault evangelicals for imprecision in this area; cf. Boer (*Above the Battle?* p. 42): "There is an undefined point on the higher critical scale—varying from one evangelical community to another—beyond which, by virtue of some mystical consensus, critical inquiry may not go"; or Stuhlmacher's charge that Maier has inadequately solved the hermeneutical problem of Scripture exposition in the church, because his concept "of a spiritual, self-evident Bible exposition within the circle of the reborn . . . came to grief a hundred times in church history" (*Historical Criticism*, pp. 69–70).

³⁸Ibid., p. 70; though in Maier's defense it should be noted that what he approved was the examining of "certain literary forms, *such as* hymns, prayers . . . parables . . . *and the like*" (*End of the Method*, p. 84).

³⁹K. A. Kitchen, *Ancient Orient and Old Testament* (Chicago: InterVarsity, 1966), pp. 91–96.

⁴⁰G. A. Archer, *Survey of OT Introduction*, rev. ed. (Chicago: Moody, 1975), pp. 459–60).

⁴¹Maier, *End of the Method*, p. 80.

⁴²Emil Brunner, *Revelation and Reason* (Philadelphia: Westminster, 1946), p. 274. When Brunner, however, went on to accuse those who hold the orthodox Hodge-Warfield position of "apologetic artifice"—saying that they claimed "The Bible 'at present' was not free from errors, but the 'original' text was perfect . . . [and] was still the same Bible

. . . although it was very different from the present one"—he was being unfair in two ways. On the one hand, evangelicals do not claim great textual differences, but usually make quite a point of how very few (and insignificant) the passages are whose wording now remains in doubt. On the other hand, they do not claim a need today for the same perfect Bible originally given by God. Evangelicals refuse to base their commitment to the inerrancy of the Scriptural autographs on needs of any sort, whether of God (as if he *had* to ordain inspiration along with revelation) or of man (as if we *have* to have anything more than a reasonably adequate guide to salvation)—except for that general need of maintaining the truthfulness of Jesus Christ. Cf. Payne, *"Apeitheō,"* p. 8.

[43]Boer, *Above the Battle?* pp. 18, 29.

[44]G. R. Osborne, "Redaction Criticism and the Great Commission," JETS 19 (1976), pp. 80, 84.

[45]Points raised at the Chicago Congress on Biblical Inerrancy by Stanley N. Gundry, to whom the author acknowledges his indebtedness.

[46]George Adam Smith, *The Book of Isaiah* (*The Expositors' Bible;* New York: Hodder & Stoughton: n.d.), p. 2.6. Thus, for example, in a listing of the differences that caused the split at Concordia Seminary, St. Louis, when the more liberal faculty maintained that "the Book of Isaiah may have two authors," the denominational president laid down this statement as the historic position of Missouri Synod Lutheranism: "Whatever the Bible says about the authorship of certain books in the Bible is to be accepted without question" (*St. Louis Globe–Democrat* [January 26, 1974], p. 1A).

[47]Samuel Sandmel, *The Hebrew Scriptures* (New York: Knopf, 1963), pp. 55–56. As a further illustration, not simply of disregard for the biblical statements about its own authenticity, but even of perverting them, consider R. H. Pfeiffer's denial of Jeremiah 46–52: "Since the editor of the book compiled his collection with the intention of including it in Jeremiah's book, as shown by his titles in 46:1, 13; 47:1; 49:34; 50:1 . . . it is obvious that the edition of Jeremiah's book circulating at that time did not contain a series of [such] foreign oracles" (*Introduction to the OT,* rev. ed. [New York: Harper, 1948], p. 506).

[48]Gene Tucker, *Form Criticism of the OT* (Philadelphia: Fortress, 1971), p. 30.

[49]Ibid., pp. 20, 31.

[50]Walter Rast, *Tradition History and the OT* (Philadelphia: Fortress, 1972), pp. 47, 49–50.

[51]S. R. Driver, *An Introduction to the Literature of the OT,* 8th ed. (Edinburgh. T. & T. Clark, 1909), pp. 17–18.

[52]Francis Patton, The Inspiration of the Scriptures (Philadelphia: Presbyterian Board of Publication, 1869), pp. 99–104.

[53]J. B. Payne, *An Outline of Hebrew History* (Grand Rapids: Baker, 1954), pp. 66–67.

[54]J. B. Payne, "The Unity of Isaiah: Evidence From Chapters 36–39," BETS 6 (1963), pp. 50–56; and "Eighth Century Israelite Background of Isaiah 40–66," WTJ 29–30 (1967–1968), pp. 179–90, 50–58, 185–203.

[55]Clark Pinnock, "The Inerrancy Debate Among the Evangelicals," *Authority at Fuller,* p. 13.

[56]Cf. the "Summary of the NT Evidence," in E. J. Young, *Who Wrote Isaiah?* (Grand Rapids: Eerdmans, 1912), p. 12.

[57]J. B. Payne, "Ethical Issues in the Responses to *The Battle for the Bible,*" *Presbyterian* 3 (1977), p. 102.

[58]Young, Introduction, pp. 755, 764.

[59]As is recognized also by negative critics; e.g., "The early Christian exegesis followed by Jewish interpretation in finding the desecration of the sanctuary, end of ch 9, in the Roman destruction of Jerusalem, an interpretation followed by Jesus himself in expecting the future setting up of the 'Abomination of Desolation,' " ICC, *Daniel,* p. 62.

[60]Boer, *Above the Battle?* pp. 95–96.

[61]Such possibilities are outlined, e.g., in E. F. Harrison, *Introduction to the NT,* rev. ed. (Grand Rapids: Eerdmans, 1971), pp. 331–32.

[62]Cf. IDB 2.108–12; so also Harrison, *Introduction*, pp. 332–39.

[63]B. M. Metzger, *The NT: Its Background, Growth, and Content* (Nashville: Abingdon, 1965), p. 258.

[64]Maier, *End of the Method*, p. 35.

[65]Stuhlmacher, *Historical Criticism*, pp. 38, 20; cf. p. 59, where he insists, "The decision is irrevocable."

[66]Cf. N. R. Ridderbos's previously cited article (note 23) with this title.

[67]E. Yamauchi, *Composition and Corroboration in Classical and Biblical Studies* (Philadelphia: Presbyterian and Reformed, 1966).

[68]Concerning Daniel, see Joyce G. Baldwin, "Is There Pseudonymity in the OT?" *Themelious*, 4:1 (1978), pp. 6–11. These are points raised at the Chicago Congress on Biblical Inerrancy by Prof. Edwin Yamauchi, to whom the writer acknowledges his indebtednesses.

[69]Rev. edition (Grand Rapids: Eerdmans 1977), I:v.

[70]He describes this as "maximal conservatism," *Fundamentalism* (London: SCM Press, 1977). He asserts, for example, "If the Word of God expressly and inerrantly teaches us that Psalm 110 was written or composed by David, then it is of no use to argue that, far from being a work of Maccabean origin, it was very old, going back perhaps to the year 900 B.C., written therefore quite soon after David. . . . This does not satisfy the dogmatic argument at all; on the contrary . . . this would show the Bible to be utterly unreliable and prove Jesus himself to have been untrustworthy," p. 87.

[71]Cf. Payne, "The Uneasy Conscience of Modern Liberal Exegesis," BETS 1:1 (1958), pp. 14–18.

[72]R. K. Harrison, "British OT Study," *Christianity Today* 5 (1961): 392.

[73]See footnote 4.

[74]Boer, *Above the Battle?* pp. 80–81.

[75]James Barr, *Old and New in Interpretation* (New York: Harper and Row, 1966), p. 202; cf. Walter Wink, *The Bible in Human Transformation* (Philadelphia: Fortress, 1973), pp. 12, 15, on the Wellhausian hypothesis and its effect on conservative students.

[76]Cf, Payne, "Faith and History in the OT," BETS 11 (1968) p. 116; and, "Biblical Inspiration: Current Issues," *The* [Cincinnati Bible] *Seminary Review*, 17 (1972), p. 61.

[77]Soulen, *Handbook*, p. 26.

[78]Davis, *The Debate*, pp. 71, 75.

[79]Otto Baab, "OT Theology: Its Possibility and Methodology," W. R. Willoughby, *The Study of the Bible Today and Tomorrow* (University of Chicago, 1947), pp. 401, 403. Cf. T. C. Vriezen's later claim, "For the theologian . . . who wants to read the OT in a scholarly fashion . . . it is his critical research which will help him to sift the spiritual true from the false, the original elements from the secondary ideas." Yet he too acknowledges the inevitable results: "That the judgments arrived at will often be subjective is unavoidable, it will therefore take a long time before agreement can be reached in the Christian Church even on matters of detail. But [as he adds, with what suggests a whistling-in-the-dark indomitability] this does not release us from the obligation of striving after this agreement with patience and faith," *An Outline of OT Theology* (Newton, Mass.: Branford, 1960), pp. 9–10.

[80]Davis, *The Debate*, pp. 58–59. Cf. F. C. Grant's oft-quoted admission that in the New Testament "it is everywhere taken for granted that Scripture is trustworthy, infallible, and inerrant," *Introduction to NT Thought* (Nashville: Abingdon-Cokesbury, 1950), p. 75.

[81]Boer, *Above the Battle?*, p. 91.

[82]Abraham Kuyper, *Revelation and Inspiration* (New York: Scribner's, 1910), p. 429.

[83]Boer, *Above the Battle?* pp. 95–96.

[84]Davis, *The Debate*, pp. 123–24.

[85]Sigmund Mowinckel, *The OT as Word of God* (New York: Abingdon, 1959), p. 74.

[86]J. I. Packer, *"Fundamentalism" and the Word of God* (London: Inter-Varsity, 1958), p. 21; cf. Payne, *"Apeitheō"* 12–13, and, in the present study, chapter 1, "Christ's View of Scripture."

[87]R. K. Harrison, *Introduction to the OT* (Grand Rapids: Eerdmans, 1969), p. 82.

[88]Ridderbos, "Reversals," p. 350.

[89]Boer, *Above the Battle?* p. 101. He further observes, "When critical or secular scholarship discovers data that supports the biblical record, these are widely and gladly used. When discovered data call the biblical record into question at any point, there is no comparable concern to enter into dialogue."

[90]Ibid., p. 81.

Notes on Chapter 5

[1]The phrase is from Bernard Ramm, *Protestant Biblical Interpretation*, 3rd rev. ed. (Grand Rapids: Baker, 1970), p. vii.

[2]Especially in Kornelis Miskotte, *Zur Biblischen Hermeneutik* (Zollikon: Evangelischer Verlag, 1959), pp. 42–46, as reviewed by Peter Rhea Jones, *"Biblical Hermeneutics,"* Rev. Exp. 72 (1975), pp. 139–42; J. M. Robinson, "Hermeneutic Since Barth," *New Frontiers in Theology*, eds. J. M. Robinson and J. B. Cobb, (New York: Harper and Row, 1964), pp. 1–77.

[3]See E. F. Scott, "The Limitations of the Historical Method," *Studies in Early Christianity*, ed. Shirley Jackson Case, (New York: Century, 1928), p. 5; O. C. Edwards, Jr., "Historical-Critical Method's Failure of Nerve and a Prescription for a Tonic: A Review of Some Recent Literature," ATR 59 (1977), pp. 116–17; W. C. Kaiser, Jr., "The Current Crisis in Exegesis and the Apostolic Use of Deuteronomy 25:4 in 1 Corinthians 9:8–10," JETS 21 (1978), esp. pp. 3–11.

[4]Major exponents of the school of new criticism are R. S. Crane, Northrup Frye, I.A. Richards, Oscar Walzel, W. K. Wimsatt. For a definition and criticism, see E. D. Hirsch, *The Aims of Interpretation* (Chicago: University Press, 1976), pp. 124–30.

[5]Brevard S. Childs, *Biblical Theology in Crisis* (Philadelphia: Westminster, 1970), pp. 97–114; Gerald T. Sheppard, "Canon Criticism: The Proposal of Brevard Childs and an Assessment for Evangelical Hermeneutics," *Studia Biblica et Theologica* 6 (1976), pp. 3–17.

[6]A fairly recent review article is Robert Lapointe, "Hermeneutics Today," BTB 2 (1972), pp. 107–54.

[7]E. D. Hirsch, *Validity in Interpretation* (New Haven: Yale University Press, 1967); idem, *Aims*.

[8]Hirsch, *Aims*, p. 4.

[9]Ibid., pp. 4, 36, 49.

[10]Hirsch, *Validity*, p. 8. Unfortunately, even Hirsch undermined his own judgments in his later work, *Aims*. See our critique and references in "the Current Crisis," pp. 3–4, and nn. 6–7.

[11]Sheppard, "Canon Criticism," p. 17.

[12]I am indebted for many of my ideas in these rules to Moses Stuart, "Remarks on Hahn's Definition of Interpretation and Some Topics Connected With It," *The Biblical Repository* 1 (1831), pp. 139–159; idem, "Are the Same Principles of Interpretation to be Applied to the Scriptures as to Other Books?" *The Biblical Repository* 2 (1832), pp. 124–37.

[13]Walter C. Kaiser, Jr., "The Eschatological Hermeneutics of Epangelicalism: Promise Theology," JETS 13 (1970), pp. 94–96; idem, "The Single Intent of Scripture," in *Evangelical Roots: A Tribute to Wilbur Smith*, ed. Kenneth Kantzer (Nashville: Nelson, 1978), pp. 125–26.

[14]Kaiser, "Single Intent," pp. 126–28.

[15]Ibid., pp. 128–31.

[16]Ibid., pp. 131–33.

[17]Ibid., pp. 133–34.

[18]That brings us the infamous interpretation of the dichotomy between the "letter"

and the "spirit" of Scripture attributed to 2 Corinthians 3:6; Romans 2:29; 7:6. We reject this interpretation, however, as failing to understand at all what Paul meant in these passages. See ibid., pp. 134–36 and W. C. Kaiser, Jr., "The Weightier and Lighter Matters of the Law," in *Current Issues in Biblical and Patristic Interpretation,* ed. Gerald Hawthorne (Grand Rapids: Eerdmans, 1975), pp. 187–88.

[19]E.g., Richard Longenecker, *Biblical Exegesis in the Apostolic Period* (Grand Rapids: Eerdmans, 1975), p. 126. In fairness to Longenecker, I should say, however, that he explicitly wants to limit such allegorical privileges to the apostles due to their "revelatory stance." Whether he can convince others to do so is another problem.

[20]For a good discussion of this text, see Robert J. Kepple, "An Analysis of Antiochene Exegesis of Galatians 4:24–26," WTJ 39 (1977), pp. 239–49.

[21]Walter C. Kaiser, Jr., "Current Crisis," pp. 11–18.

[22]This phrase is generally translated "and to change my voice tone." Yet Augustus Hahn, "On the Grammatico-Historical Interpretation of the Scripures," *The Biblical Repository* 1 (1831), p. 133, argued that the change was from argument to accommodating the Galatians in their own allegories so they could see Paul's preceding point. This suggestion should not be dismissed, as is almost universally done by commentators. "My little children," urges Paul, "I could wish indeed that I were present now with you, but to change my tone (let me put it to you this way) . . . all these classes of things can be allegorized (as follows)." In other words, his tone may well indicate his substance as well as his manner. Hahn's full quote is: "*Gladly were I now with you, my children, and would speak with each of you in particular, according to his special wants, consequently, with each one differently,* in order to convince each of you after his own opinions and prejudices, that his union of Judaism with Christianity is to be rejected. . . . For I am hesitating in respect to you; i.e., doubtful how I shall rightly address you. But ye now, who would gladly retain the yoke of Judaism (and how the Judaizing teachers and their Rabbins allegorized is well known), tell me, do you understand the law? I will explain it then to you—*allaxai ten phonen*—in your own way; in order thus to convince you. . . ."

[23]Not only Ellicott but also John Eadie (*Epistle to the Galatians* [Edinburgh: T. & T. Clark, 1884], p. 359) make the point that this text does not say "which things have been allegorized" already, but that the whole class of these things in Genesis may be grouped and allegorized now (present participle) for the present purposes.

[24]J. Stafford Wright, "The Perspicuity of Scripture," *Theological Students Fellowship Letter* (Summer, 1959), p. 6.

[25]Bishop Herbert Marsh [*A Course of Lectures . . . in Theological Learning* [Boston: Cummings and Hilliard, 1815], p. 18) explains: "When [the Reformers] argued for the perspicuity of the Bible, they intended not to argue against the application of *learning,* but against the application of *tradition* to the exposition of Scripture. . . . In rejecting *tradition* as necessary to make the Bible perspicuous, they never meant to declare that the Bible was alike perspicuous [in its total message] to the *learned* and unlearned (italics his)."

[26]C. H. Dodd, *The Authority of the Bible* (London: Fontana, 1960). It was published originally in 1928, revised in 1938, 1960. In those days it was "a current phrase," ibid., p. 248; see pp. 248–63 for his whole discussion.

[27]Ibid., p. 263.

[28]This analysis is dependent on James Barr, *The Bible in the Modern World* (New York: Harper and Row, 1973), pp. 144–46. I am also indebted to J. I. Packer for almost the same analysis in "An Evangelical View of Progressive Revelation," in *Evangelical Roots: A Tribute to Wilbur Smith,* ed. Kenneth Kantzer (Nashville: Nelson, 1978), pp. 143–58, especially pp. 146–48.

[29]Those who believe there was direct or implied permission for polygamy in the Old Testament usually point to three passages: Exodus 21:7–11; Deuteronomy 21:15–17; and 2 Samuel 12:7–8. The first passage is cleared up in modern versions that follow the Hebrew text with its "not" in verse 8 instead of following the LXX as some earlier English versions did; by omitting "wife" in verse 10, since there is no Hebrew word for it there; and by properly rendering the Hebrew of the rest of verse 10 as "her food, clothing,

and lodging," *not* "her food, clothing and marital rights." In Deuteronomy 21:16–17 the problem is again a translation problem as can be seen from the identical translation of the various versions of the Polyglott and the identical tense in the Hebrew in the compound clause "If a man *has* had two wives . . . and they *have* borne him sons. . . ." Thus Moses rules not on a man who currently has two wives, but on one who has had two. Finally, 2 Samuel 12:7–8: Saul's wives Ahinoam (mother of David's wife Michal) and Rizpah are never listed as David's wives. In fact, had God authorized David to marry Ahinoam, it would have violated the prohibition against incest specifically stated in Levital law and backed with a threat of burning for its violation; thus the phrase in 2 Samuel means nothing more than the fact that God delivered everything Saul had into David's hands, yet he stole from Uriah! See the very perceptive work by S. E. Dwight, *The Hebrew Wife: Or the Law of Marriage Examined in Relation to the Lawfulness of Polygamy and to the Extent of the Law of Incest* (New York: Leavitt, 1836), pp. 14–24.

[30]The list is a modification of James Orr's list in his chapter, "The Progressiveness of Revelation: Moral Difficulties," *The Problem of the Old Testament* (London: Nisbet, 1909), p. 466. Also see H. S. Curr, "Progressive Revelation," *Journal of the Transactions of the Victorian Institute* 83 (1951), pp. 1–23, especially p. 7.

[31]William Brenton Greene, Jr., "The Ethics of the OT," PTR 27 (1929), pp. 153–92; 313–66. Most of this essay may now be conveniently located in *Classical Evangelical Essays in OT Interpretation*, ed. Walter C. Kaiser, Jr. (Grand Rapids: Baker, 1972), pp. 207–35.

[32]George E. Mendenhall, "The 'Vengeance' of Yahweh," *The Tenth Generation* (Baltimore: Johns Hopkins University Press, 1973), p. 70.

[33]Abraham Heschel, *The Prophets* (New York: Harper and Row, 1962), pp. 279–306.

[34]See the exceptionally fine article by Chalmers Martin, "Imprecations in the Psalms," PTR 1 (1903), pp. 537–53—now available in *Classical Evangelical Essays*, pp. 113–32. Also see the best article on the most offensive of all Psalms (137): Howard Osgood, "Dashing the Little Ones Against the Rock," PTR 1 (1903), pp. 23–37.

[35]Orr, *Problem of Old Testament*, p. 473.

[36]Richard N. Longenecker, *Biblical Exegesis in the Apostolic Period* (Grand Rapids: Eerdmans, 1975), p. 218. Also see the similar but less cautious approach of Donald A. Hagner, "The Old Testament in the New Testament," *Interpreting the Word of God*, eds. Samuel Schultz and Morris Inch (Chicago: Moody, 1976), pp. 78–104. As an example of one who takes his cue from this principle and asserts, "The necessity of recognizing the mystical sense is quite evident from the way in which the New Testament interprets the old," see L. Berkhof, *Principles of Biblical Interpretation* (Grand Rapids: Baker, 1952), pp. 140ff.

[37]Longenecker, *Biblical Exegesis*, p. 203.

[38]Hagner, "The Old Testament," p. 103.

[39]Frederic Gardiner, "The New Testament Use of the Old," in *The Old and New Testaments in Their Mutual Relations* (New York: James Pott, 1885), pp. 317–18.

[40]W. C. Kaiser, Jr., "The Davidic Promise and the Inclusion of the Gentiles (Amos 9:9–15 and Acts 15:13–18): A Test Passage for Theological Systems," JETS 20 (1977), pp. 97–111.

[41]Milton S. Terry, *Biblical Hermeneutics* (New York: Easton and Mains, 1883), p. 383. He there cites Owen and Ryle as supporting his view to the effect that "if Scripture has more than one meaning, it has no meaning at all." He says, "I hold that the words of Scripture were intended to have one definite sense and that our first objective should be to discover that sense, and adhere rigidly to it."

[42]E.g., Thomas Hartwell Horne, *Introduction to the Critical Study and Knowledge of the Holy Scriptures* (New York: Robert Carter, 1859), 1:643.

[43]Willis J. Beecher, *The Prophets and the Promise* (Grand Rapids: Baker, 1975), p. 130.

[44]Ibid., p. 361. Also see W. C. Kaiser, Jr., "Messianic Prophecies in the Old Testament," *Dreams, Visions, and Oracles*, Eds. Carl E. Armerding and Ward Gasque (Grand Rapids: Baker, 1977), pp. 75–88.

[45]Patrick Fairbairn, "The Historical Element in God's Revelation," *Revelation of the*

Law (Edinburgh: T. & T. Clark, 1869), now available in *Classical Evangelical Essays*, ed. W. C. Kaiser, Jr. (Grand Rapids: Baker, 1972), pp. 74–75.

[46]For additional examples, see Matthew 15:7; 22:31; Mark 7:6; Acts 4:11; Romans 4:23ff.; 15:4; 1 Corinthians 10:11; Hebrews 10:15; 12:15–17.

[47]Kaiser, "Current Crisis," pp. 11–18.

[48]For additional background, see Robert C. Sproul, "Controversy at Culture Gap," *Eternity* 27 (1976); 12–13; Alan Johnson, "History and Culture in New Testament Interpretation," *Interpreting the Word of God*, eds. Samuel Schultz and Morris Inch (Chicago: Moody, 1976), pp. 128–61; Edwin M. Yamauchi, "Christianity and Cultural Differences," *Christianity Today* 16 (1971): 901–4.

[49]W. C. Kaiser, Jr., "Paul, Women and the Church," *Worldwide Challenge* 3 (1976): 9–12.

[50]J. Oliver Buswell, *A Systematic Theology of the Christian Religion* (Grand Rapids: Zondervan, 1962), 1:368–73.

[51]See Bruce Waltke, *Creation and Chaos* (Portland: Western Conservative Baptist Seminary, 1974), pp. 1–17. Also see John N. Oswalt, "The Myth of the Dragon and Old Testament Faith," *Evangelical Quarterly* 49 (1977): 163–72. He concludes that Isaiah 51, Job 40, and Psalm 72 used the myth material of the Near East for nonmythical purposes and never once shared its mythical outlook, contrary to various assurances of B. S. Childs and Mary Wakeman.

[52]John McKenzie, S. J., "A Note on Psalm 73 (74): 13–15," Th St 2 (1950), p. 281.

[53]See our case and references in W. C. Kaiser, Jr., "The Literary Form of Genesis 1–11," *New Perspectives on the Old Testament,* ed. J. Barton Payne (Waco: Word, 1970), pp. 52–54, nn. 16–20.

[54]Kaiser, "Literary Form," pp. 57–58, nn. 42–45.

[55]E. W. Bullinger, *Figures of Speech* (Grand Rapids: Baker, 1968, r.p. 1898), pp. 1032–33.

Notes on Chapter 6

[1]E. J. Young, *Thy Word Is Truth* (Grand Rapids: Eerdmans, 1957), pp. 88–89.

[2]Archibald Alexander, *Evidences of the Authenticity, Inspiration, and Canonical Authority of the Holy Scriptures* (Philadelphia: Presbyterian Board of Publication, 1836), p. 229.

[3]Charles Hodge, *Systematic Theology*, vol. 1 (1872–73; reprinted., Grand Rapids: Eerdmans, 1960), pp. 152, 163.

[4]Archibald A. Hodge and Benjamin B. Warfield, "Inspiration," *The Presbyterian Review* 7 (April 1881), pp. 227, 236, 238.

[5]B. B. Warfield, "The Inerrancy of the Original Autographs," reprinted in *Selected Shorter Writings of Benjamin B. Warfield,* vol. 2, ed. John E. Meeter (Nutley, N.J.: Presbyterian and Reformed, 1973), pp. 581–82.

[6]Cornelius Van Til, *A Christian Theory of Knowledge* (Nutley, N.J.: Presbyterian and Reformed, 1969), p. 27.

[7]Bernard Ramm, *Special Revelation and the Word of God* (Grand Rapids: Eerdmans, 1961), pp. 134–35.

[8]Abraham Kuyper, *Principles of Sacred Theology* (Grand Rapids: Eerdmans, 1954), pp. 405ff.

[9]Henry Preserved Smith, *Inspiration and Inerrancy* (Cincinnati: Robert Clark, 1893), pp. 97–98, 107–12; R. Laird Harris, *Inspiration and Canonicity of the Bible,* rev. ed. (Grand Rapids: Zondervan, 1969), p. 87; Jack Rogers, "The Church Doctrine of Biblical Authority," in *Biblical Authority,* ed. Jack Rogers (Waco: Word, 1977), pp. 30, 31, 36; Clark Pinnock, "Three Views of the Bible in Contemporary Theology," in *Biblical Authority,* ed. Rogers, p. 62; Clark Pinnock, *Biblical Revelation* (Chicago: Moody 1971), p. 156; Dewey

M. Beegle, *Scripture, Tradition, and Infallibility* (Grand Rapids: Eerdmans, 1973), pp. 163–64.

[10]Cf. John Murray, *Calvin on Scripture and Divine Sovereignty* (Philadelphia: Presbyterian and Reformed, 1960), pp. 27–28.

[11]Cf. M. Reu, *Luther and the Scriptures* (Columbus, Ohio: Wartburg, 1944), pp. 57–59.

[12]Warfield, "Inerrancy of the Original Autographs," pp. 586–87.

[13]B. B. Warfield, "The Westminster Confession and the Original Autographs," in *Selected Shorter Writings*, vol. 2, pp. 591–92; Beegle, *Scripture, Tradition, and Infallibility*, p. 144.

[14]Warfield, "The Inerrancy of the Original Autographs," pp. 580–82, 586–87; "The Westminster Confession and the Original Autographs," pp. 588–94.

[15]Hodge and Warfield, "Inspiration," pp. 238, 245.

[16]Edwin H. Palmer, Response to Editor, *The Banner*, vol. 112, no. 43 (Nov. 11, 1977): 25.

[17]J. Gresham Machen, *The Christian Faith and the Modern World* (Grand Rapids: Eerdmans, 1936), pp. 38–39; W. H. Griffith Thomas, "Inspiration," *Bibliotheca Sacra*, vol. 118, no. 469 (Jan.–Mar., 1961), p. 43; James M. Gray, "The Inspiration of the Bible," in *The Fundamentals*, vol. 2 (Bible Institute of Los Angeles, 1917), p. 12; Lewis Sperry Chafer, *Systematic Theology*, vol. 1 (Dallas Seminary Press, 1947), p. 71; Loraine Boettner, *Studies in Theology* (Grand Rapids: Eerdmans, 1957), p. 14; E. J. Young, *Thy Word is Truth*, p. 55; R. Surburg, *How Dependable is the Bible* (Philadelphia and New York: Lippincott, 1972), p. 68; J. I. Packer, *"Fundamentalism" and the Word of God* (Grand Rapids: Eerdmans, 1958), p. 90; John R. Stott, *Understanding the Bible* (Glendale: Gospel Light, 1972), p. 187; Carl F. H. Henry, *God, Revelation, and Authority*, vol. 2 (Waco: Word, 1976), p. 14.

[18]Smith, *Inspiration and Inerrancy*, p. 145; C. A. Briggs, *The Bible, the Church, and the Reason* (New York: Scribner, 1892), p. 97.

[19]Warfield, "Inerrancy of the Original Autographs," p. 585.

[20]Smith, *Inspiration and Inerrancy*, p. 144.

[21]David Hubbard, "The Current Tensions: Is There a Way Out?" in *Biblical Authority*, ed. Rogers, p. 156.

[22]C. A. Briggs, "Critical Theories of the Sacred Scriptures in Relation to Their Inspiration," *The Presbyterian Review*, vol. 2 (1881): 573–74.

[23]Emil Brunner, *Revelation and Reason: The Christian Doctrine of Faith and Knowledge*, trans. Olive Wyon (Philadelphia: Westminster, 1946), p. 274.

[24]Cf. Young, *Thy Word Is Truth*, pp. 85–86; Pinnock, *Biblical Revelation*, p. 81.

[25]Warfield, "The Westminster Confession and the Original Autographs," p. 588.

[26]Lester DeKoster, editorials in *The Banner* for August 19, 26, and September 2, 1977.

[27]I am dependent for some of these examples on J. Barton Payne, "The Plank Bridge: Inerrancy and the Biblical Autographs," *United Evangelical Action* 24 (December 1965): 16–18.

[28]G. C. Berkouwer, *Holy Scripture*, trans. and ed. Jack Rogers (Grand Rapids: Eerdmans, 1975), p. 217.

[29]F. F. Bruce, "Foreword" to Beegle's *Scripture, Tradition, and Infallibility*, p. 8.

[30]Beegle, *Scripture, Tradition, and Infallibility*, p. 156.

[31]Cf. Berkeley Mickelsen, "The Bible's Own Approach to Authority," in *Biblical Authority*, ed. Rogers, pp. 83, 95.

[32]Beegle, *Scripture, Tradition, and Infallibility*, Chapter 7.

[33]John Wenham, *Christ and the Bible* (Downers Grove, Ill.: InterVarsity, 1972), p. 164; Carl F. H. Henry, *God, Revelation and Authority*, vol. 2, p. 14.

[34]As suggested by Pinnock in "Three Views of the Bible in Contemporary Theology," p. 63.

[35]Ibid., p. 63; Sidney Chapman, "Bahnsen on Inspiration," *Evangelical Quarterly*, vol. XLVII, no. 3 (July–September 1975): 167.

[36]Beegle, *Scripture, Tradition, and Infallibility*, pp. 154–55, 164–66.

[37]Payne, "Plank Bridge," p. 17.

[38]C. F. Keil, *Biblical Commentary on the Old Testament: The Book of the Kings*, trans. James Martin (Grand Rapids: Eerdmans, 1970), p. 478.

[39]Such is the view of many expositors; cf. Lange's Commentary, vol. 6; Karl Chr. W. F. Bähr, with Edwin Harwood and W. G. Sumner, *The Books of the Kings* (New York: Scribner, Armstrong and Co., 1872), book 2, p. 258; Payne, "Plank Bridge," p. 17.

[40]Cf. Richard N. Longenecker, "Ancient Amanuenses and the Pauline Epistles," in *New Dimensions in New Testament Study*, ed. R. N. Longenecker and M. C. Tenney (Grand Rapids: Zondervan, 1976), pp. 288–92.

[41]Cf. Payne, "Plank Bridge," p. 18.

[42]Beegle, *Scripture, Tradition, and Infallibility*, pp. 170–71, cf. p. 173.

[43]Cf. Payne, "Plank Bridge," p. 17.

[44]See Pinnock, *Biblical Revelation*, p. 83.

[45]See Berkouwer, *Holy Scripture*, pp. 223, 225.

[46]See L. I. Evans, "Biblical Scholarship and Inspiration," in Smith, *Inspiration and Inerrancy*, pp. 47, 66–67; Mickelsen, "The Bible's Approach to Authority," pp. 85ff.

[47]J. A. Fitzmyer, "The Use of Explicit Old Testament Quotations in Qumran Literature and in the New Testament," *New Testament Studies*, (1961), p. 332.

[48]DeKoster, editorial in *The Banner* (September 2, 1977), p. 4.

[49]See Smith, *Inspiration and Inerrancy*, pp. 135–36, cf. pp. 62–63; Pinnock, "Three Views of the Bible in Contemporary Theology," p. 65; Stephen T. Davis, *The Debate About the Bible* (Philadelphia: Westminster, 1977), pp. 79–81; Paul Rhees, Foreword to *Biblical Authority*, ed. Rogers, p. 12.

[50]See the discussion of word groups over against parchment and ink in Greg L. Bahnsen, "Autographs, Amanuenses, and Restricted Inspiration," *Evangelical Quarterly*, vol. 45, no. 2 (April–June 1973): 101–3.

[51]Cf. John Warwick Montgomery, "Biblical Inerrancy: What Is at Stake?" in *God's Inerrant Word*, ed. J. W. Montgomery (Minneapolis: Bethany Fellowship, 1974), pp. 36–37.

[52]B. B. Warfield, *An Introduction to the Textual Criticism of the New Testament* (New York: Thomas Whittaker, 1887), p. 3.

[53]Francis L. Patton, *The Inspiration of the Scriptures* (Philadelphia: Presbyterian Board of Publication, 1869), p. 113.

[54]Pinnock, *Biblical Revelation*, p. 86.

[55]Clark H. Pinnock, *A Defense of Biblical Infallibility* (Philadelphia: Presbyterian and Reformed, 1967), p. 15.

[56]Henry, *God, Revelation, and Authority* 2, p. 14.

[57]Palmer, reply to editor, *The Banner* (November 11, 1977), p. 24. Norman Geisler and William Nix express this point of view in terms of a contrast between actual inspiration (reserved for the autographs) and virtual inspiration (applied to good copies or translations) in *A General Introduction to the Bible* (Chicago: Moody, 1968), p. 33.

[58]E.g., Smith (and Evans), *Inspiration and Inerrancy*, pp. 63, 144; Harry R. Boer, *Above the Battle? The Bible and Its Critics* (Grand Rapids: Eerdmans, 1977), p. 84; Beegle, *Scripture, Tradition, and Infallibility*, pp. 148–149; Gerstner also cites Briggs, Loetscher, and Sandeen in "Warfield's Case for Biblical Inerrancy," in *God's Inerrant Word*, ed. Montgomery, pp. 136–37.

[59]Rogers, "The Church Doctrine of Biblical Authority," p. 39; Pinnock, "Three Views of the Bible," p. 65.

[60]Montgomery, "Biblical Inerrancy: What Is at Stake?" p. 36.

[61]Davis, *The Debate About the Bible*, p. 25.

[62]Warfield, *Introduction to Textual Criticism*, p. 15.

[63]Warfield, "Inerrancy of Original Autographs," p. 584.

[64]Beegle, *Scripture, Tradition, and Infallibility*, pp. 163, 165.

[65]Pinnock, *Defense of Biblical Infallibility*, p. 15.

[66]Beegle, *Scripture, Tradition, and Infallibility*, pp. 154, 155.

67Young, *Thy Word Is Truth*, pp. 56–57.
68Gerstner, "Warfield's Case for Biblical Inerrancy," p. 137.
69Montgomery, "Biblical Inerrancy: What Is at Stake?" p. 35.
70Patton, *Inspiration of the Scriptures*, p. 112; Gray, "Inspiration of the Bible," pp. 12–13.
71Pinnock, *Biblical Revelation*, p. 82.
72Warfield, "Inerrancy of Original Autographs," p. 582.
73Cf. Bahnsen, "Autographs, Amanuenses, and Restricted Inspiration," pp. 104–5.
74Fredson Bowers, *Textual and Literary Criticism* (Cambridge: University Press, 1966), p. 8.
75Fredson Bowers, "Hamlet's 'Sullied' or 'Solid' Flesh," *Shakespeare Survey* IX (1956): 44–48. The embarrassment that can come to a literary critic who assimilates copyist errors is illustrated by the case of Matthiesseni John Nichol's "Melville's 'Soiled' Fish of the Sea," *American Literature* XXI (1949): 338–39.
76Warfield, "Inerrancy of Original Autographs," p. 582.
77Bahnsen, "Autographs, Amanuenses, and Restricted Inspiration," pp. 102–3.
78Ibid., p. 103.
79Henry, *God, Revelation, and Authority* 2, p. 13.
80Orr, *Revelation and Inspiration*, p. 200.
81Ramm, *Special Revelation and the Word of God*, p. 207.
82Davis, *Debate About the Bible*, p. 116.
83A. C. Piepkorn, "What Does 'Inerrancy' Mean?" *Concordia Theological Monthly* XXXVI (1965): 590.
84Evans, "Biblical Scholarship and Inspiration," p. 62.
85Gray, "Inspiration of the Bible," p. 13.
86Young, *Thy Word Is Truth*, pp. 89–90.
87Ibid., pp. 86, 89; cf. Rene Pache, *The Inspiration and Authority of Scripture* (Chicago: Moody, 1969), p. 135.
88Gray, "Inspiration of the Bible," p. 13.
89Young, *Thy Word Is Truth*, p. 87.
90Van Til, *Introduction to Systematic Theology* (syllabus, Westminster Theological Seminary, reprinted 1966, now published by the den Dulk Christian Foundation as part of the series "In Defense of the Faith"), p. 153.
91Harris, *Inspiration and Canonicity of the Bible*, pp. 88–89.
92Cf. Beegle, *Scripture, Tradition, and Infallibility*, p. 158; Young, *They Word Is Truth*, p. 89.
93Davis, *Debate About the Bible*, pp. 78–79.
94E.g., Pinnock, "Three Views of the Bible," p. 66.
95E.g., Kuyper, *Encyclopedia of Sacred Theology* III, p. 67; Pache, *Inspiration and Authority of Scripture*, pp. 138–39; Wenham, *Christ and the Bible*, p. 186; Geisler and Nix, *General Introduction to Bible*, pp. 32–33; E. Sauer, *From Eternity to Eternity* (London: Paternoster, 1954), p. 110; Pinnock, *Biblical Revelation*, p. 83; Harold Lindsell, *The Battle for the Bible* (Grand Rapids: Zondervan, 1976), p. 36.
96Cf. Beegle, *Scripture, Tradition, and Infallibility*, p. 159; Davis, *Debate About the Bible*, pp. 79–80.
97E.g., Wenham, *Christ and the Bible*, p. 186.
98Young, *Thy Word Is Truth*, p. 61.
99Cf. ibid., p. 88; Pache, *Inspiration and Authority of Scripture*, pp. 135–36; L. Gaussen, *The Divine Inspiration of the Bible* (Grand Rapids: Kregel, 1841; reprint edition, 1971), pp. 159–60.
100Wenham, *Christ and the Bible*, p. 186.
101Pinnock, *Biblical Revelation*, p. 74.
102Cornelius Van Til, "Introduction" to B. B. Warfield, *Inspiration and Authority of the Bible* (Philadelphia: Presbyterian and Reformed, 1948), p. 46; Van Til, *The Doctrine of Scripture* (den Dulk Christian Foundation, 1967), p. 39; Van Til, *Christian Theory of Knowledge* (Nutley, N.J.: Presbyterian and Reformed, 1969), pp. 34–36.

[103]Henry, *God, Revelation, and Authority* 2, p. 14; cf. Van Til, "Introduction" to *Inspiration and Authority of Bible*, p. 4.

[104]Robert Reymond, "Preface" to Pinnock, *Defense of Biblical Infallibility*.

[105]Orr, *Revelation and Inspiration*, pp. 155–56.

[106]Cf. Kuyper, *Encyclopedia of Sacred Theology* III, pp. 68–69; Pinnock, *Biblical Revelation*, p. 83.

[107]John Skilton, "The Transmission of the Scriptures," in *The Infallible Word*, rev. ed., ed. N. B. Stonehouse and P. Woolley (Philadelphia: Presbyterian and Reformed, 1946), p. 143.

[108]Packer, *"Fundamentalism" and the Word of God*, pp. 90–91.

[109]Van Til, *Christian Theory of Knowledge*, p. 28. The critical implications of not presupposing God's sovereign control of all things are pressed in this regard by Van Til against those who would question original inerrancy: for instance, Beegle (cf. *Doctrine of Scripture*, pp. 72–91) and Brunner ("Introduction" to *Inspiration and Authority of Bible*, pp. 46ff.).

[110]Young, *Thy Word Is Truth*, p. 87.

[111]Geisler and Nix, *General Introduction to the Bible*, p. 32.

[112]Pinnock, *Biblical Revelation*, p. 85; cf. Skilton, "Transmission of the Scriptures," p. 167.

[113]Ibid., p. 82.

[114]Cf. Young, *Thy Word Is Truth*, p. 87; Ramm, *Special Revelation and the Word of God*, p. 191; F. F. Bruce, "Foreword," p. 9, and Beegle, *Scripture, Tradition, and Infallibility*, p. 157.

[115]Harris, *Inspiration and Canonicity of the Bible*, p. 96.

[116]See Skilton, "Transmission of the Scriptures;" Wenham, *Christ and the Bible*, chapter 7; Geisler and Nix, *General Introduction to the Bible*, part III, for competent surveys.

[117]Frederic Kenyon, *Our Bible and the Ancient Manuscripts*, rev. (New York: Harper, 1940), p. 23.

[118]Johannes G. Vos, "Bible," *The Encyclopedia of Christianity*, vol. 1, ed. Edwin Palmer (Delaware: National Foundation of Christian Education, 1964), p. 659.

[119]Warfield, *Introduction to Textual Criticism*, pp. 12–13, 14–15.

[120]Warfield, "Inerrancy of Original Autographs," pp. 583–84.

[121]Warfield, "Westminster Confession and the Original Autographs," pp. 589, 590.

[122]Young, *Thy Word Is Truth*, pp. 56–57.

[123]Harris, *Inspiration and Canonicity of the Bible*, p. 94.

[124]Pinnock, *Biblical Revelation*, p. 82; Pinnock, *Defense of Biblical Infallibility*, p. 15; Geisler and Nix, *General Introduction to the Bible*, p. 32; Lindsell, *Battle for the Bible*, p. 27; Lindsell, *God's Incomparable Word* (Wheaton: Victor, 1977), p. 25.

[125]George Mavrodes, "The Inspiration of Autographs," *Evangelical Quarterly*, vol. 61, no. 1 (1969):19–29.

[126]Cf. Beegle, *Scripture, Tradition, and Infallibility*, pp. 152, 160; Smith, *Inspiration and Inerrancy*, p. 122.

[127]Cf. Bruce, "Foreword" to *Scripture, Tradition, and Infallibility*, pp. 8–9.

[128]Bahnsen, "Autographs, Amanuenses, and Restricted Inspiration," pp. 100–110.

[129]Cf. Pinnock, *Biblical Revelation*, p. 83; Longenecker, "Ancient Amanuenses and the Pauline Epistles," p. 296; Warfield, *Limited Inspiration* (Philadelphia: Presbyterian and Reformed, n.d.), pp. 18–19.

[130]Sidney Chapman, "Bahnsen on Inspiration," pp. 162–67.

[131]Cf. Davis, *Debate About the Bible*, pp. 64–65. Beegle uses a similar argument from linguistic labels to conclude that the Septuagint copies in the NT age were inspired; see Payne, "Plank Bridge," p. 17.

[132]I argue this on pp. 102–3 of my article "Autographs" but Chapman confuses the argument about the original *text* with another one about the original *manuscripts*. A rebuttal to Chapman's critique of elements of my own argument is not relevant here, although significant misunderstandings of that argument and fallacious attempts to undermine it would be noteworthy.

Notes on Chapter 7

[1]See Acts 28:25; Heb. 3:7; 10:15.

[2]See John 7:16ff.; 8:26–28, 38–47; 12:48–50.

[3]See Matt. 7:28ff.; 24:35.

[4]Karl Barth, *Church Dogmatics*, 2 vols. (Edinburgh: T. & T. Clark, 1956), 1:504. Barth glosses *theopneustos* as meaning "given and filled and ruled by the Spirit of God, and actively outbreathing and spreading abroad and making known the Spirit of God." This combination of passive and active meanings may well be expressing truth, but the word *theopneustos* signifies only the former, not the latter.

[5]B. B. Warfield, "God-inspired Scripture," in *The Inspiration and Authority of the Bible* (Philadelphia: Presbyterian and Reformed, 1948), pp. 245ff.

[6]If, as is grammatically possible, though somewhat more harsh linguistically and less appropriate contextually, the first words of the verse are rendered, "All Scripture inspired by God is also profitable," the point remains unaffected. It is inspiration (= inspiredness) as such that constitutes the ground of canonicity. On the translation, see the judicious remarks of Donald Guthrie, *The Pastoral Epistles* (London: Tyndale, and Grand Rapids: Eerdmans, 1957), pp. 163ff.

[7]On prophecy and the passion, see Mark 8:31–33; 9:31; 10:33; 12:10ff.; 14:21; Matt. 26:52–54; Luke 9:31; 18:31–33; 22:37; etc.

[8]See Rom. 16:25ff.; 1 Cor. 2:1–36; 14:37 (cf. 7:40, where "I think" expresses not doubt but ironical challenge—"I, too, think I have God's Spirit—don't you agree that I have?"); 1 Thess. 1:5; 2:13; 4:1ff., 15; 2 Thess. 3:4, 6, 10–14; 1 John 1:1–5; 4:1–6, et al.

[9]It is fashionable today to stress the linguistic diversity of the New Testament documents rather than the substantial oneness of their teaching (see, e.g., James D. G. Dunn, *Unity and Diversity in the New Testament*, London: SCM, 1977); however, their oneness has often been established (see e.g., A. M. Hunter, *The Unity of the New Testament*, London: SCM, 1944).

[10]Ludwig Wittgenstein, *Tractatus Logico-Philosophicus*, trans., C. K. Ogden (London: Kegan Paul, 1922), pp. 27, 186–89. A current counterpart of Wittgenstein's philosophically based denial that life-problems are expressible and thus communicable is Dennis Nineham's denial, based on his personal and amateur reading of the sociology of knowledge, that we can ever get into the minds of persons shaped by bygone cultures so as to grasp with certainty the thoughts behind their words when they spoke of ultimate realities. See Nineham, *The Use and Abuse of the Bible* (London: Macmillan, 1976); and for criticism, Ronald H. Preston, "Need Dr. Nineham Be So Negative?" *Expository Times*, June 1979, pp. 275ff.

[11]John Macquarrie, *God–Talk* (London: SCM; New York: Harper and Row, 1967), pp. 23ff.

[12]For more on this, see A. C. Thiselton, "Understanding God's Word Today" in *Obeying Christ in a Changing World, I: The Lord Christ*, ed. John Stott (London: Collins, 1977), pp. 90–122; idem, "Semantics and New Testament Interpretation" in *New Testament Interpretation*, ed. I. Howard Marshall (Exeter: Paternoster; and Grand Rapids: Eerdmans, 1977), pp. 75–104; James Barr, *The Semantics of Biblical Language* (London: Oxford University Press, 1961).

[13]Ian T. Ramsey, *Religious Language* (London: SCM, 1957); *Models and Mystery* (London: Oxford University Press, 1964); *Christian Discourse* (London: Oxford University Press, 1965).

[14]Macquarrie, *God–Talk*.

[15]Austin Farrer, *The Glass of Vision* (London: Dacre, 1948).

[16]Eric L. Mascall, *Existence and Analogy* (London: Longmans, 1949); idem, *Words and Images* (London: Longmans, 1957).

[17]See their contributions to *Faith and Logic*, ed. Basil Mitchell (London: Allen and Unwin, 1957).

[18]Frederick Ferré, *Language, Logic and God* (London: Collins, 1970), pp. 231ff.

[19]John Frame, "God and Biblical Language," in *God's Inerrant Word*, ed. J. W. Montgomery (Minneapolis: Bethany Fellowship, 1973), pp. 173ff. It is worth underlining the point implicit in Frame's equation of transcendence with lordship. Lordship, comprising the relation of upholding, directing, and controlling all created things in both their motion and their rest, is the only concept of transcendence that Scripture yields; the Kantian–Barthian ideas of metaphysical remoteness from us, obscurity to us, and evasion of all the categories of human (though God-given!) language, are simply not there.

[20]C. S. Lewis, "Introduction" to J. B. Phillips, *Letters to Young Churches* (London: Bles, 1947).

[21]Calvin, *Institutes* I.viii.1, referring to the New Testament preaching of the Kingdom.

[22]Calvin, *Commentary on John*, on John 3:12.

[23]See R. B. Braithwaite, *An Empiricist's View of the Nature of Religious Belief* (CUP, 1955, reprinted in *The Philosophy of Religion*, ed. Basil Mitchell, CUP, 1971), pp. 72ff. "A religious assertion, for me, is the assertion of an intention to carry out a certain behavior policy, subsumable under a sufficiently general principle to be a moral one, together with the implicit or explicit statement, but not the assertion, of certain stories," p. 89.

[24]See, for expositions of this line of thought, A. J. Ayer, *Language, Truth and Logic*, 2nd ed., (London: Gollancz, 1946); A. Flew, in "Theology and Falsification," *The Philosophy of Religion*, pp. 13ff.; Kai Nielsen, *Contemporary Critiques of Religion* (London: Macmillan, 1971).

[25]This critique is well developed by Ferrè, *Language, Logic, and God*, chap. 6; see also E. J. Carnell, *An Introduction to Christian Apologetics*, 4th ed. (Grand Rapids: Eerdmans, 1952), pp. 140–51.

[26]Mitchell, *The Justification of Religious Belief* (London: Macmillan, 1973), p. 19.

[27]See on this C. F. H. Henry, *God, Revelation and Authority*, vol. 1 (Waco: Word, 1976), chap. 5.

Notes on Chapter 8

[1]Clark Pinnock, "Three Views of the Bible in Contemporary Theology," in *Biblical Authority*, ed. Jack Rogers (Waco: Word, 1977), p. 71.

[2]Ibid., pp. 60–61.

[3]Clark Pinnock, *Biblical Revelation* (Chicago: Moody, 1971), p. 176.

[4]Harry R. Boer, *Above the Bible? The Bible and Its Critics* (Grand Rapids: Eerdmans, 1975), p. 45.

[5]Ibid., p. 42.

[6]Ibid., pp. 75–76.

[7]Ibid., p. 42.

[8]Ibid., pp. 44, 82.

[9]Charles Davis, *A Question of Conscience* (New York: Harper and Row, 1967), p. 234.

[10]Ibid., p. 235.

[11]Ibid., p. 237.

[12]Ibid.

[13]Ibid., pp. 237–38.

[14]Ibid., p. 239.

[15]Leslie Dewart, *The Future of Belief* (New York: Herder and Herder, 1966), p. 95.

[16]Ibid., p. 113.

[17]Ibid., p. 110.

[18]Ibid., p. 121.

[19]Hans Kung, *On Being a Christian* (Garden City, N.Y.: Doubleday, 1976).

[20]Ibid., p. 465.

[21]Ibid., p. 466.

22Ibid., pp. 466–67.

23Ibid., p. 467.

24Ibid.

25G. C. Berkouwer, *Holy Scripture* (Grand Rapids: Eerdmans, 1975), p. 18.

26Ibid., p. 19.

27Ibid., p. 31.

28Ibid., p. 22.

29Ibid., p. 23.

30Ibid., p. 34.

31Ibid., p. 18.

32Ibid., p. 19.

33Ibid.

34Ibid., p. 32.

35Ibid., p. 60.

36Ibid.

37Ibid., p. 85.

38Ibid., p. 201.

39Ibid., p. 215.

40Ibid., pp. 145, 151, 152, 154.

41Ibid., p. 162.

42Ibid., p. 166.

43Ibid., p. 168.

44Ibid., p. 140.

45Ibid., p. 142.

46Ibid., p. 145.

47Ibid., p. 146.

48Ibid., p. 185.

49Ibid., p. 187.

50Ibid., p. 190.

51Ibid., p. 194.

52Ibid., p. 207.

53Ibid., p. 272.

54Ibid., p. 20.

55Ibid., p. 264.

56Gordon R. Lewis, *Testing Christianity's Truth–Claims: Approaches to Christian Apologetics* (Chicago: Moody, 1976).

57Berkouwer, *Holy Scripture*, p. 266.

58Ibid., p. 252.

59Ibid.

60Ibid., p. 253.

61Ibid.

62Ibid.

63Ibid., p. 256.

64Ibid., p. 258.

65Ibid., p. 259.

66Richard J. Coleman, *Issues of Theological Warfare: Evangelicals and Liberals* (Grand Rapids: Eerdmans, 1972), p. 101.

67Ibid.

68Gordon R. Lewis, *Decide for Yourself* (Downers Grive: InterVarsity, 1970), pp. 41–45.

69Gordon R. Lewis, "Revelational Basis of Trinitarianism," *Christianity Today* (January 4, 1963): 20–22 [328–30].

70Gustave F. Oehler, *Theology of the Old Testament* (1883; reprint ed., Grand Rapids: Zondervan, m.d.), p. 482.

71Augustine, *Confessions* XI, 28, *Great Books of The Western World*, pp. 18, 98.

72In his "Review of *Holy Scripture*," *Christianity Today*, Nov. 21, 1975, p. 44.

[73]Carl Henry, *God, Revelation and Authority* (Waco: Word, 1976), 2:126–27.

[74]Ibid., p. 127.

[75]Eugene Nida, *Message and Mission* (New York: Harper and Row, 1960), p. 90.

[76]G. C. Berkouwer, *Man: The Image of God* (Grand Rapids: Eerdmans, 1962), pp. 45, 88, 98.

[77]Karl Barth, *The Humanity of God* (Richmond, Virginia: John Knox, 1960), p. 41.

[78]Ibid., p. 45.

[79]Karl Barth, *Church Dogmatics I*, (Edinburgh: T. & T. Clark, 1936), 1:127.

[80]G. C. Berkouwer, *General Revelation* (Grand Rapids: Eerdmans, 1955).

[81]Gordon R. Lewis, *Testing Christianity's Truth Claims*, pp. 176–284.

[82]B. B. Warfield, *The Inspiration and Authority of the Bible* (Philadelphia: Presbyterian and Reformed, 1948), pp. 155–56.

[83]G. C. Berkouwer, *Holy Scripture*, p. 177.

[84]J. Spykman, "Accommodation," ed. Edwin A. Palmer, *The Encyclopedia of Christianity*, (Wilmington, Delaware: The National Foundation for Christian Education, 1964), 1:43.

[85]Bernard Ramm, *Special Revelation and the Word of God* (Grand Rapids: Eerdmans, 1961), p. 36.

[86]Ibid., p. 156.

[87]Ibid., p. 159.

[88]Hans Kung, *On Being a Christian*, p. 465.

[89]Ibid.

[90]Ibid., p. 467.

[91]Berkouwer, *Holy Scripture*, p. 145.

[92]Ibid., p. 150.

[93]Ibid., p. 151.

[94]Gordon R. Lewis, *Judge for Yourself* (Downers Grove: InterVarsity, 1974), pp. 46–60.

[95]Charles Hodge, *Systematic Theology*, 3 vols. (Grand Rapids: Eerdmans, 1960), 1:169.

[96]Ramm, *Special Revelation*, p. 59.

[97]Augustine, *Gospel of John*, 55:4; *Nicene and Post-Nicene Fathers*, 7:300.

[98]Robert Clyde Johnson, *Authority in Protestant Theology* (Philadelphia: Westminster, 1959), p. 56.

[99]Berkouwer, *Holy Scripture*, p. 146.

[100]Gordon R. Lewis, "What Does Infallibility Mean?" *Journal of the Evangelical Theological Society*. 6 (Winter 1963): 18–27.

[101]Augustine, *City of God*, 11:6; *Nicene and Post Nicene Fathers*, 2:208.

[102]Augustine, *Trinity* IX, II, 16; NPNF, 3:132.

Notes on Chapter 9

[1]In dealing with the question of inerrancy, there are a number of closely related but distinct issues. In my judgment, failure to note the complexity of the problem has kept debate from being as precise as possible. Thus it is helpful to distinguish between the theological doctrine of inerrancy and the definition of the term *inerrancy*. In connection with the doctrine, there are the questions of how a doctrine is *constructed* and how it is *justified*. At the heart of these matters is the exegetical data from which the doctrine grows and against which it is tested. If indeed the Scripture teaches such a doctrine, there is then the matter of defining or establishing the precise meaning of the term *inerrancy*. It should be noted that a definition of *inerrant* can be given in a question-begging way. It would be question-begging and therefore wrong, to assert that if the Bible does teach its own inerrancy, a satisfactory definition of the term is impossible of attainment or else to state the definition so broadly that it is meaningless. The procedure that this discussion follows is intended to be consistent with the principles and objectives just mentioned.

[2]Stephen T. Davis, *The Debate About the Bible* (Philadelphia: Westminster, 1977), pp. 20–21.

[3]Dewey M. Beegle, *Scripture, Tradition and Infallibility* (Grand Rapids: Eerdmans, 1973).

[4]Irving M. Copi, *Introduction to Logic*, 3rd ed. (New York: Macmillan, 1968), pp. 20–21.

[5]Ibid.

[6]Beegle, *Scripture, Tradition and Infallibility*, p. 16.

[7]Ibid., p. 17.

[8]Ibid., pp. 175–224. "Phenomena," as used by Beegle and others, refers to Scripture simply as it *appears*.

[9]Ibid.

[10]R. C. Sproul, "The Case for Inerrancy: A Methodological Analysis," in *God's Inerrant Word: An International Symposium on the Trustworthiness of Scripture*, ed. John Warwick Montgomery (Minneapolis: Bethany Fellowship, 1973), pp. 242–61.

[11]One might with some justification argue that the doctrine of Scripture is foundational. From this foundation, which is "theory neutral," one has reasons for higher-order beliefs. One can see a recent exposition of this view, called foundationalism, in the work of John L. Pollock, *Knowledge and Justification* (Princeton, N.J.: Princeton University Press, 1974). More recently, the picture that philosophers (particularly philosophers of science) have painted is quite different. At the heart of the change is the recognition that there is no such thing as theory-neutral experience; theory is operative at all levels. The importance of the point for the theologian is that theoretical considerations are at work in all levels of his task, even at the level of hermeneutics and exegesis. Much more could be said, but a good source for studying this issue is *The Structure of Scientific Theories*, ed. Frederick Suppe, 2nd ed. (Urbana: University of Illinois Press, 1977).

[12]Arthur F. Holmes, "Ordinary Language Analysis and Theological Method," *Bulletin of the Evangelical Theological Society* 11 (Summer 1968): 131–38.

[13]John Warwick Montgomery, "The Theologian's Craft: A Discussion of Theory Formation and Theory Testing in Theology," *The Suicide of Christian Theology* (Minneapolis: Bethany Fellowship, 1970), pp. 267–313.

[14]Holmes, "Ordinary Language Analysis," p. 133.

[15]Ibid., p. 134.

[16]C. S. Peirce, *Collected Papers*, Harvard ed., 5.146; 5.171; 5.189; and 5.274, cf. 5.276.

[17]Aristotle, *Prior Analytics*, ii.25; cf. *Posterior Analytics*, ii. 19.

[18]Holmes, "Ordinary Language Analysis," p. 135ff.

[19]Ibid., Montgomery, "The Theologian's Craft," pp. 276–79. For further references to the method see the following: Suppe, *Structure of Scientific Theories;* Mary Hesses, *Models and Analogics in Science* (South Bend: University of Notre Dame Press, 1961); Stephen Toulmin, *Foresight and Understanding* (Hutchinson University Library, 1961); Norwood Hanson, *Patterns of Discovery* (Cambridge: Cambridge University Press, 1958); Ian Ramsey, *Models and Mystery* (Oxford: Oxford University Press, 1964) and *Religion and Science*; Frederick Ferré, "Mapping the Logic of Models in Science and Theology," *The Christian Scholar* 46 (1963): 9ff. It is important to note that I am not claiming that theology is science or vice versa, only that they employ a similar method.

[20]Montgomery, "The Theologian's Craft," pp. 272–73.

[21]Ibid., pp. 283–88.

[22]Holmes, "Ordinary Language Analysis," pp. 137–38.

[23]Norman L. Geisler, "Theological Method and Inerrancy: A Reply to Professor Holmes," *Bulletin of the Evangelical Theological Society* 11 (Summer 1968): 139–46. See also A. F. Holmes, "Reply to N. L. Geisler," *Bulletin of the Evangelical Society*, 11 (Fall 1968): 194–95.

[24]See references in footnote 19 for arguments to this effect.

[25]Holmes, "Ordinary Language Analyisis," p. 137. In a letter dated October 31, 1978, Holmes adds, "However much progress we make *inductively*, the resultant generalization still amounts to less than total inerrancy: at best probability will result. Further, I think that no set of biblical statements supplies sufficient premises to *deduce* total inerrancy as defined and qualified by careful theologians."

[26]In advocating abduction as the method of formulating and justifying inerrancy, I am suggesting a modification of what has been called the classical method (see Sproul, "Case for Inerrancy"). Rather than following an ordered procedure of steps, all matters become a part of the data from which the doctrine is formulated and against which it is tested. Moreover, it should be quite clear that the charge of circularity against the doctrine of inerrancy is no more justified than the claim that our scientific theories are all circular. The evidential base contains both external and internal data. Beyond that, the doctrine is tested against the data for accuracy.

[27]Hanson, *Patterns of Discovery*, pp. 87–90.

[28]At first I thought of entitling this section "The Phenomena of Scripture." However, although I still believe the material presented to be part of the phenomena of Scripture, I think such a heading would be misleading. "Phenomena of Scripture" has a very specific meaning in the history of the debate over inerrancy. It has been taken to mean a neutral or presuppositionless approach to the Bible simply as it appears. It is important to see that the biblical teaching about itself is a part of these phenomena and, as John Warwick Montgomery points out, it is exceedingly important to see which phenomena are primarily in the formulation of a doctrine. "To know how to treat biblical passages containing apparent errors or contradictions, we must determine what kind of book the Bible is. A doctrine of limited biblical authority derived from passages manifesting difficulties is as false as induction and as flagrant a denial of the analogy of Scripture as is a morally imperfect Christology derived from questionable acts on Jesus' part. In both cases, proper induction requires that we go to the express biblical teaching on the subject (Jesus' deity; Scripture's authority) and allow this to create the pattern for treating particular problems." (John W. Montgomery, "Inductive Inerrancy," *Christianity Today* [March 3, 1967], p. 48.)

Second, the evidence presented here for inerrancy is by no means exhaustive. Even the biblical evidence is not exhuastive. Moreover, one may cite historical and epistemological arguments, as well as others, in support of the doctrine.

[29]Donald Guthrie, *The Pastoral Epistles* (Grand Rapids: Eerdmans, 1957), 1963.

[30]Ed. L. Miller, "Plenary Inspiration and 2 Timothy 3:16," *Lutheran Quarterly*, XVII (February 1965), pp. 57, 58.

[31]Bruce M. Metzger, *Lexical Aids for Students of New Testament Greek*, New Edition (Princeton, NJ: Theological Book Agency, 1970), p. 44. See also F. Blass and A. Debrunner, *A Greek Grammar of the New Testament and Other Early Christian Literature*, trans. and revised by Robert W. Funk (Chicago: University of Chicago Press, 1961), pp. 61–63 and Nigel Turner, *A Grammar of New Testament Greek* (Edinburgh: T & T Clark, 1963), 3:150–65.

[32]B. B. Warfield, *The Inspiration and Authority of the Bible* (Philadelphia: Presbyterian and Reformed, 1948), pp. 281–83.

[33]Miller, "Plenary Inspiration," p. 59.

[34]Ibid.

[35]Martin Dibelius and Hans Conzelmann, *The Pastoral Epistles*, trans. Philip Bultolph and Adela Yarbro (Philadelphia: Fortress, 1972), p. 120.

[36]Miller, "Plenary Inspiration," p. 59.

[37]Bernard L. Ramm, "Scripture as a Theological Concept," *Review and Expositor* 71 (February 1974): 157–58.

[38]Cf. this view with that of Charles A. Briggs, *The Bible, the Church and Reason* (New York: Scribner, 1893), p. 91.

[39]D. M. Lloyd-Jones, *Authority* (Chicago: Inter-Varsity, 1958), p. 35.

[40]Donald G. Bloesch, *Essentials of Evangelical Theology: God, Authority, and Salvation* (San Francisco: Harper and Row, 1978), pp. 74–78.

[41]Beegle, *Scripture, Tradition and Infallibility*, pp. 289–90.

[42]P. C. Craige, "The Book of Deuteronomy" in *The New International Commentary on the Old Testament* (Grand Rapids: Eerdmans, 1976), pp. 262–64.

[43]E.g., Acts 1:16, 3:24, 25; Rom. 9:17; 2 Cor. 6:16; Gal. 3:8.

[44]David Hubbard, "The Current Tensions: Is There a Way Out?" in *Biblical Authority*, ed. Jack Rogers (Waco: Word, 1977), p. 172.
[45]Ibid., p. 173.
[46]Ibid.
[47]Beegle, *Scripture, Tradition and Infallibility*, pp. 280ff.
[48]Ibid.
[49]Roger Nicole, "New Testament Use of the Old Testament," in *Revelation and the Bible*, ed. Carl F. H. Henry (Grand Rapids: Baker, 1958), p. 139, gives twenty-four examples of the way in which New Testament arguments are based on one Old Testament word.
[50]Hans Kung, *Infallible? An Inquiry*, trans. Edward Quinn (Garden City, N.Y.: Doubleday, 1971), pp. 139ff., 181ff.
[51]Bloesch, *Essentials of Evangelical Theology*, p. 68.
[52]*Oxford English Dictionary*, p. 1426.
[53]Ibid.
[54]Davis, *Debate About the Bible*, p. 23.
[55]Briggs, *Bible, Church and Reason*, pp. 91–95.
[56]G. C. Berkouwer, *Holy Scripture*, trans. and ed. Jack Rogers (Grand Rapids: Eerdmans, 1975).
[57]Jack Rogers, "The Church Doctrine of Authority," in *Biblical Authority*, ed. Jack Rogers (Waco: Word, 1977).
[58]Hubbard, "Current Tensions."
[59]Bloesch, *Essentials of Evangelical Theology*, pp. 67–70.
[60]Berkouwer, *Holy Scripture*, pp. 184–94.
[61]Rogers, "Church Doctrine of Authority," p. 46.
[62]Hubbard, "Current Tensions," p. 168.
[63]Herman Ridderbos, "An Attempt at the Theological Definition of Inerrancy, Infallibility, and Authority," *International Reformed Bulletin*, 32 and 33, 11th year (January-April, 1968), pp. 27–41.
[64]In Jeremiah 37:14, where there is an unintentional lie that is called a lie nevertheless.
[65]Francis Brown, S. R. Driver, and Charles A. Briggs, *A Hebrew and English Lexicon of the Old Testament*, trans. Edward Robinson (Oxford: Clarendon, 1907), pp. 992–93.
[66]W. Bauer, W. F. Arndt, and F. W. Gingrich, *A Greek–English Lexicon of the New Testament*, 2nd ed. (Chicago: University of Chicago Press, 1957), p. 11.
[67]Brown et al., *Hebrew and English Lexicon*.
[68]Bauer, Arndt, and Gingrich, *Greek–English Lexicon*, p. 117.
[69]Brown et al., *Hebrew and English Lexicon*, p. 1073.
[70]Ibid., p. 1074.
[71]Bauer, Arndt, and Gengrich, *Greek-English Lexicon*, p. 96.
[72]Ibid., p. 671.
[73]*Oxford English Dictionary*, p. 1424.
[74]Ibid.
[75]Ibid.
[76]Ibid.
[77]Ibid., p. 892.
[78]William Sanford LaSor, "Life Under Tension—Fuller Theological Seminary and 'The Battle for the Bible,'" *Theology, News and Notes*, Special Issue, Fuller Theological Seminary (1976), p. 23.
[79]Ibid., pp. 23–25.
[80]Ridderbos, "Attempt at the Theological Definition."
[81]Arthur Carl Piepkorn, "What Does 'Inerrancy' Mean?" *Concordia Theological Monthly* 36 (1963): 577–93.
[82]Ibid., p. 577.
[83]Ridderbos, "Attempt at Theological Definition," pp. 33ff.
[84]Piepkorn, "What Does 'Inerrancy' Mean?"
[85]Clark Pinnock's *Biblical Revelation: The Foundation of Christian Theology* (Chicago:

Moody, 1971) is the able defense of inerrancy to which I refer. In his more recent works, Pinnock has been increasingly critical of the doctrine and its defenders, although he has claimed that he still holds the doctrine. One can trace this change in attitude, if not in substance, in the following articles: "Inspiration and Authority: A Truce Proposal," *The Other Side* (May-June, 1976), pp. 61-65 (This article was sent to Theological Student Fellowship, and all references are to this latter publication); "The Inerrancy Debate Among the Evangelicals," *Theology, News and Notes*, Special Edition, Fuller Theological Seminary, 1976, pp. 11-13; and "Three Views of the Bible in Contemporary Theology," in *Biblical Authority*, ed. Jack Rogers (Waco: Word, 1977), pp. 47-73.

[86]Pinnock, "Truce Proposal," p. 4.

[87]Ibid.

[88]Aristotle, *Metaphysics*, 1011b, 26ff.

[89]Alfred Tarski, "The Concept of Truth in Formalized Languages," in *Logic, Semantics, Metamathematics* trans. J. H. Woodger (New York: Oxford, 1956).

[90]The introduction of Tarski was suggested in an earlier draft of the chapter. Such a project seems to me to have some merit, but its full-blown explication and defense awaits further work. Some have suggested reservations since Tarski's work is formulated for formalized or ideal languages not natural languages. Some philosophers, however, have defended its applicability to natural languages as well. Cf. Donald Davidson, "Truth and Meaning," *Synthese* 17 (September 1967): 304-23, and Hartry Field, "Tarski's Theory of Truth," *The Journal of Philosophy* 69 (July 13, 1972): 347-75.

[91]John Gerstner, *Biblical Inerrancy Primer* (Grand Rapids: Baker, 1965), p. 49.

[92]Ibid.

[93]Pinnock, *Biblical Revelation*, pp. 77-78.

[94]I wish to emphasize that before such a case could be claimed two things must be shown. First, we must show that something is simply affirmed and, second, that it is false. I do not assert that any such cases do in fact exist, only that such a possibility *could* be compatible with a doctrine of inerrancy. Given what the Bible teaches about itself, *if* such an error *were found*, then such an explanation would be necessary. I seriously doubt that this kind of solution is necessary.

[95]William R. Eichhorst, "The Issue of Biblical Inerrancy in Definition and Defense," *Grace Journal* 10 (Winter 1969): 8.

[96]Suppe, *Structure of Scientific Theories*.

[97]Eichhorst, "Issue of Biblical Inerrancy," p. 7. Cf. Roger Nicole, "New Testament Use of the Old Testament," in *Revelation and the Bible*, ed. Carl F. H. Henry (Grand Rapids: Baker, 1958), p. 144.

[98]Grant R. Osborne, "Redaction Criticism and the Great Commission: A Case Study Toward a Biblical Understanding of Inerrancy," *Journal of the Evangelical Theological Society* 19 (Spring 1976): 83-85. I think Osborne is right in claiming that we do not need the exact words of Jesus in every instance. I have tried to explain why and under what conditions the voice of Jesus is sufficient. It might be helpful to say that when we lack the exact words of Jesus, we still have the *identical meaning*, which can be achieved in various ways. Thus, it should be clear that I disagree with the way Osborne applies the point in Matthew 28:18.

[99]Joseph A. Hill, "The Bible and Non-Inspired Sources," *Bulletin of the Evangelical Theological Society* 3 (Fall 1960): 78-100.

[100]Again, it should be noted that I am only talking about possibility. I have serious doubts that such a solution to biblical problems is needed, but this whole issue is a hermeneutical matter (e.g., the laying down of principles to decide which is descriptive and which is normative authority).

[101]Pinnock, "Truce Proposal," p. 4.

[102]This can be substantiated by examining principles for the interpretation of literature. All that I am arguing is that the Bible is not a special case and thus does not involve special pleading.

[103]Gerstner, *Biblical Inerrancy Primer*, p. 44.

Notes on Chapter 10

[1]See chapters 12 and 13.
[2]Stephen T. Davis, *The Debate About the Bible* (Philadelphia: Westminster, 1977), p. 139.
[3]Jack Rogers, *Biblical Authority* (Waco: Word, 1977), p. 45.
[4]Augustine, *Letters*, LXXXII, 3.
[5]Ibid., XXVIII, 3.
[6]Tertullian, *Against Marcion*, I, 23.
[7]Sören Kierkegaard, *Concluding Unscientific Postscript* (Princeton: Princeton University Press, 1941), p. 504.
[8]Ibid., p. 183.
[9]Rogers, *Biblical Authority*, pp. 18–23.
[10]Francis Bacon, *The New Organon* (New York: Bobbs-Merrill, 1960), Book I, 70.
[11]Ibid., CXXVII.
[12]Ibid., CXXIV.
[13]Ibid.
[14]Ibid., LXXIII.
[15]Thomas Aquinas, *Summa Contra Gentiles*, I, 4, 3–5.
[16]Thomas Aquinas, *Summa Theologica*, II-II, 2, 10.
[17]Francis Bacon, *New Organon*, Book I, 45, and Book IX.
[18]Ibid., Book I, 65.
[19]Harry Rimmer read the modern wave theory of light into Job 38:7, which speaks of stars "singing." *The Harmony of Science and Scripture* (Grand Rapids: Eerdmans, 1952), p. 127.
[20]Thomas Hobbes, *Leviathan* (New York: Washington Square, 1964), I.
[21]Ibid., p. 1.
[22]Thomas Hobbes, *Leviathan*, from *Great Books of the Western World* (Encyclopedia Britannica, 1952), vol. 23.
[23]Hobbes, *Leviathan*, (Washington Square Press), III, p. 13.
[24]See A. J. Ayer, *Language, Truth and Logic* (New York: Dover Publications, n.d.), chap. 1.
[25]Hobbes, *Leviathan* (Washington Square Press), XII, pp. 73–74.
[26]Hobbes, *Leviathan* (*Great Books*), chap. 12, p. 83.
[27]Hobbes, *Leviathan* (Washington Square Press), pp. 267, 268.
[28]Ibid., p. 52.
[29]Ibid., p. 50.
[30]Ibid., p. 51.
[31]Ibid.
[32]Benedict De Spinoza. *The Rationalists*, hereafter referred to as *Ethics* (Garden City, New York: Doubleday, 1960), p. 247. Benedict De Spinoza, *The Chief Works of Benedict De Spinoza*, translated from the Latin, with an introduction by R. H. M. Elwes, vol. I, *Introduction, Tractatus Theologico-Politicus, Tractatus Politicus*, hereafter referred to as *Tractatus* (London: George Bell, 1883), p. 81.
[33]Spinoza, *Ethics*, p. 210.
[34]Spinoza, *Tractatus*, p. 194.
[35]Ibid., p. 165.
[36]Ibid., p. 166.
[37]Ibid., p. 167.
[38]Ibid., p. 190.
[39]Ibid., p. 172.
[40]Ibid., pp. 196, 197.
[41]Spinoza, *Ethics*, pp. 322, 327.
[42]Ibid., p. 212.
[43]Spinoza, *Tractatus*, p. 92.

[44]Ibid., p. 83.
[45]Ibid., p. 96.
[46]Ibid., p. 87.
[47]For the documentation of this point (which is a correction of the mistaken statement in the *Encyclopedia of Philosophy*, "Spinoza," Vol. 7, p. 531, that it "was not discovered for publication until the late eighteenth century") I am indebted to Dr. John Woodbridge.
[48]Spinoza, *Tractatus*, p. 126.
[49]Ibid., p. 128.
[50]Ibid., p. 147.
[51]Ibid., p. 150.
[52]Ibid., p. 155.
[53]Ibid., p. 159.
[54]Ibid., p. 171.
[55]Ibid., p. 170.
[56]Died A.D. 1791.
[57]Died A.D. 1918.
[58]Died A.D. 1677.
[59]Spinoza, *Ethics*, p. 24; *Tractatus*, p. 93.
[60]Died A.D. 1776.
[61]Such as Paul van Buren, *The Secular Meaning of the Gospel* (New York: Macmillan, 1963).
[62]Ayer, *Language, Truth and Logic*, p. 115.
[63]Ibid., p. 120.
[64]van Buren, *The Secular Meaning*, p. 84.
[65]Ibid., p. 103.
[66]David Hume, *An Inquiry Concerning Human Understanding* (New York: Bobbs-Merrill, 1955), Sect. X, pp. 117ff.
[67]Ibid., p. 122.
[68]Ibid., pp. 122, 123.
[69]Kant here confused the principle of sufficient reason, which holds that *everything* has a reason or cause, and the principle of causality (from Aquinas), which holds that only *finite* changing things need a cause. The former leads to contradictions; the latter does not.
[70]Immanuel Kant, *Critique of Pure Reason* (New York: St Martin's, 1965), p. 639.
[71]Immanuel Kant, *The Existence of God*, edited by John Hick (New York: Macmillan, 1964), p. 139.
[72]Immanuel Kant, *Religion Within the Limits of Reason Alone* (New York: Harper and Row, 1960), pp. 101–2.
[73]Ibid., note on p. 126.
[74]Ibid., p. 104.
[75]Ibid., p. 103.
[76]R. Otto, *The Idea of the Holy*, trans. John Harvey (Oxford University Press, 1967), p. 162.
[77]Kant, *Religion Within the Limits of Reason Alone*, p. 79.
[78]Ibid.
[79]Ibid., p. 83.
[80]Ibid., pp. 79, 80.
[81]Ibid., p. 179.
[82]Ibid., pp. 81–82.
[83]Davis, *Debate About the Bible*, p. 97.
[84]Kant, *Religion Within Limits*, p. 84.
[85]Ibid.
[86]Ibid., footnote on p. 119.
[87]Kierkegaard, *Concluding Unscientific Postscript*, p. 504.
[88]Ibid., p. 173.
[89]Ibid., p. 182.

[90]Ibid., p. 183.

[91]Ibid.

[92]Sören Kierkegaard, *Philosophical Fragments* (Princeton: Princeton University Press, 1936), p. 53.

[93]Kierkegaard, *Concluding Unscientific Postscript*, p. 25.

[94]Quoted in *A Kierkegaardian Critique*, ed. Howard Johnson (New York: Harper and Bros., 1962), p. 213.

[95]Kierkegaard, *Philosophical Fragments*, p. 130.

[96]Kierkegaard, *Concluding Unscientific Postscript*, p. 31.

[97]Sören Kierkegaard, *On Revelation and Authority*, trans. Walter Lowrie (Princeton: Princeton University Press, 1955), p. 92.

[98]G. M. Andersen, ed. and trans., *The Diary of S. Kierkegaard* (London: Peter Owen, 1960), p. 166.

[99]Kierkegaard, *On Revelation and Authority*, pp. 100–101.

[100]Kierkegaard, *Concluding Unscientific Postscript*, p. 26.

[101]R. G. Smith, ed. and trans., *The Last Years: Journals of S. Kierkegaard 1853–55* (New York: Harper and Row, 1965), p. 275 (hereafter referred to as *Journals*).

[102]Sören Kierkegaard, *Fear and Trembling* (Garden City, New York: Doubleday, 1954).

[103]Kierkegaard, *Concluding Unscientific Postscript*, p. 32.

[104]Kierkegaard, *Philosophical Fragments*, p. 49.

[105]Ibid., p. 49.

[106]Ibid.

[107]Kierkegaard, *Journals*, p. 208.

[108]A good analysis of Kierkegaard's view of religious language, especially as it comes out in Barth, may be found in Bapttista Mondin's excellent book, *The Principle of Analogy in Protestant and Catholic Theology* (The Hague: Nijhoff, 1963), chap. 5–7.

[109]Kierkegaard, *Journals*, p. 209.

[110]Bacon, *New Organon*, Book I, 89.

[111]Hobbes, *Leviathan* (Washington Square Press), pp. 267–68.

[112]Spinoza, *Tractatus*, p. 166.

[113]Ibid., p. 154.

[114]William LaSor, *Theological News and Notes* (Fuller Theological Seminary, 1976), p. 7.

[115]Clark Pinnock, *Biblical Authority*, ed. Jack Rogers (Waco: Word, 1977), p. 64.

Notes on Chapter 11

[1]B. B. Warfield, *The Inspiration and Authority of the Bible* (Philadelphia: Presbyterian and Reformed, 1948), p. 133.

[2]G. C. Berkouwer, *De Heilige Schrift*, 2 vols. (Kampen: Kok, 1966), 1:74.

[3]For a survey of modern theological controversy surrounding the *testimonium* see Bernard Ramm, *The Witness of the Spirit* (Grand Rapids: Eerdmans, 1959).

[4]John Calvin, *Institutes of the Christian Religion*, trans. Henry Beveridge, I (Grand Rapids: Eerdmans, 1964), pp. 68–69.

[5]Ibid., p. 69.

[6]Ibid.,

[7]Berkouwer, *De Heilige Schrift*, 1:89.

[8]See II Helvetic Confession, Chapter 1; Belgic Confession, Article V; and Westminster Confession, I: 4, 5.

[9]Calvin, *Institutes*, p. 70.

[10]Ibid., pp. 70–71.

[11]Ibid., p. 71.

[12]Ibid.

[13]Berkouwer, *De Heilige Schrift*, 1:42.
[14]Calvin, *Institutes*, p. 72.
[15]Webster's New Twentieth Century Dictionary (unabridged) General Editor, Jim L. McKechnie (New York: Collins-World, 1975)
[16]Ibid.
[17]See Harnack's treatment of the development of the *fides impliciticm* in Roman Catholic thought in his *History of Dogma*, vols, IV and V.
[18]Calvin, *Institutes*, pp. 71-72.
[19]Ibid., pp. 82-83.
[20]Ibid., p. 83.
[21]B. B. Warfield, *Calvin and Augustine* (Philadelphia: Presbyterian and Reformed, 1956), p. 74.
[22]Ibid., p. 87.
[23]Ibid., p. 86.
[24]Ibid., p. 77
[25]Ibid.
[26]Ibid., p. 80.
[27]See Martin Kahler, *The So-Called Historical Jesus and the Historic Biblical Christ*, trans. Carl E. Bracten (Philadelphia: Fortress, 1964).
[28]Emil Brunner, *Revelation and Reason*, trans. Olive Wyon (Philadelphia: Westminster, 1946), pp. 168ff.
[29]See Brunner's more comprehensive treatment of this in *The Divine Human Encounter*, trans. Amandus W. Loos (Philadelphia: Westminster, 1943).
[30]Compare this concept of "contemporary" with Kierkegaard's concept of the "moment" and Bultmann's theology of timelessness with the emphasis on *hic et nunc* encounter.
[31]Brunner, *Revelation and Reason*, pp. 170-71.
[32]Thomas F. Torrance, "The Epistemological Relevance of the Holy Spirit," in *Ex Auditu Verbi*, ed. R. Schippers, G. E. Meuleman, J. T. Balcher, and H. M. Kuitert (Kampen: Kok, 1965), p. 273.
[33]Ibid., p. 282.
[34]Ibid., p. 283.
[35]For an excellent comprehensive survey of the biblical texts relevant to the discussion see Bernard Ramm's, *The Witness of the Spirit*, pp. 42-61
[36]See Philip Edgcumbe Hughes's *Paul's Second Epistle to the Corinthians* in the N.I.C. series for an exposition of this section.

Notes on Chapter 12

[1]The entire history of the development of the doctrine concerning Scripture was treated by two nineteenth-century theologians, W. Rohnert, *Die Inspiration der heiligen Schrift und ihre Bestreiter* (Leipzig: Verlag von Georg Böhme, 1889), and Wilhelm Koelling, *Die Lehre von der Theopneustie* (Breslau: Verlag von Carl Dülfer, 1891). Similar studies have been carried out by Roman Catholic theologians who write more briefly on the subject but offer massive evidence. I refer to Sebastianus Tromp, *De Sacrae Scripturae Inspiratione* (Rome: Apud Aedes Universitatis Gregorianae, 1953) and Cardinal Autustinus Bea, *De Inspiratione et Inerrantia Sacrae Scripturae* (Rome: Pontificum Institutum Biblicum, 1954); *De Scripturae Inspiratione. Quaestiones Historicae et Dogmaticae* (Rome: Pontificum Institutum Biblicum, 1935). None of these studies is particularly penetrating, and each is meant only to be an overview of the doctrine through the history of the church; nevertheless each offers vast data to support a unity of belief concerning biblical inspiration and authority extending from apostolic times through the sixteenth and seventeenth centuries. Excel-

lent monographs have also been written on the bibliology of specific church fathers and theologians. On Augustine, A. D. R. Polman's *The Word of God according to St. Augustine*, trans. A. J. Pomerans(Grand Rapids: Eerdmans, 1961) is perhaps the best study, clearing up many previous misunderstandings. See also Charles Joseph Costello, *St. Augustine's Doctrine on the Inspiration and Canonicity of Scripture* (Washington: Catholic University of America, 1930). The bibliology of the Patristic period is touched on by several good patrologies: Bertold Altaner, *Patrology*, trans. Hilda C. Graef (New York: Herder and Herder, 1959); Adolf Harnack, *History of Dogma*, trans. Niel Buchanan (London: Williams and Norgate, 1896); Johanes Quasten, *Patrology* (Utrecht: Spectrum, n.d.); F. Cayré, *Manuel of Patrology* (Paris: Descleé, 1940). For the Medieval period see Martin Grabmann, *Mitelalterliches Geistesleben* (Munich: M. Hueber, 1926); Frederik Copelston, *A History of Philosophy* (Westminster, Md.: Newman, 1953). The two best books on Luther are the German study by Wilhelm Walther, *Das Erbe der Reformation* (Leipzig: A. Duchert, 1918), and the English work by Michael Reu, *Luther and the Scriptures* (Columbus: Wartburg, 1944). Reu borrows heavily from Walther. A recent work on Luther's hermeneutics is also most valuable, and, like Reu and Walther, a corrective of many nineteenth- and early-twentieth century caricatures of Luther's position: E. Thestrup Pedersen, *Luther som Skriftfortolker* (Copenhagen: Nyt Nordisk Forlag Arnold Busck, 1959). Copious bibliographies and references to further secondary sources are found in many of the above works.

²See John Gerhard, *Loci Theologici* (Tübingen, 1787, Cotta Ed.), 17:80ff.; 15:253ff.

³For a thorough treatment of early normative Judaism's doctrine of Scripture and revelation see George Foot Moore, *Judaism* (Cambridge: Harvard University Press, 1917), 1:235–262, still considered the most complete and scholarly treatment of the subject. Moore also points out how early Judaism and early Christian thought differ in their interpretation of Scripture. Cf. H. Strack and B. Billerbeck, *Kommentar zum Neuen Testament aus Talmud und Midrasch* (Muenchen: Beck, 1928), 4:415–451: "Excurs: Der Kanon des Alten Testaments und seine Inspiration."

⁴Justin, I *Apol.* 32, 2: *Dial.* 29, 2.

⁵Justin, I *Apol.* 42, 4; 67, 7; *Dial.* 53, 1.

⁶Tertullian, *De Praescript.* 21; Irenaeus, *Haer.* 4, 26, 2. Cf. J. N. D. Kelly, *Early Christian Doctrines* (London: Adam & Charles Black, 1958), pp. 35–41 passim.

⁷Harry Wolfson in *The Philosophy of the Church Fathers* (Cambridge: Harvard University Press, 1956) distinguishes between a "single faith theory" of Tertullian and Origen and a "double faith theory" taught by Clement of Alexandria and others. The latter theory places philosophy and theology on a kind of par as the basis of faith.

⁸See Henrici Denzinger, *Enchiridion Symbolorum*, ed. 31 (Rome: Herder, 1957), pp. 783–86. The extent to which this position can distort a true understanding of Scripture according to the authority and norms of ecclesiastical exegesis (thought to be unwritten divinely revealed tradition) is seen in recent times in *Vigilantiae*, the apostolic letter of Leo XIII in 1903 in which he states, "As we were saying, the nature of the divine books is such that in order to dissipate the religious obscurity with which they are shrouded we must never count on the laws of hermeneutics, but must address ourselves to the Church, which has been given by God to mankind as a guide and teacher." See *Rome and the Study of Scripture*, ed. Conrad Lewis, OSB (St. Meinrad, Ind.: Grail, 1958), p. 32.

⁹*Haer.* 2, 47. Cf. 3, 1.

¹⁰Clement, *Strom.* 7, 16, 93.

¹¹Origen, *De princ.* 3, 1, 1.

¹²Kelly, *Early Christian Doctrines*, pp. 47–48.

¹³Denzinger, *Enchiridion Biblicum*, 23, 26, 27, 28, 32, 42, 62, 66, 110, 116. Ambrose, *Ep.* 8, 10 (PL 16, 953); Augustine, *Cont. Faus.* 15, 1 (PL 11, 295): *Cont. Adimantum*, 16, 3 (PL 42, 157).

¹⁴Jerome, *Ep.* 70, 7; *Is.* 29, 9ff. Origen, *Cont. Cels.* 59ff.; Tertullian, *Apol.* 18; Augustine, *Adv. Marc.* 4, 22. Cf. Rohnert, *Die Inspiration*, 95.

[15]Cf. Bea, *De Inspiratione*, pp. 11–12. Cf. Bea, "Deus auctor Sacrae Scripturae: Herkunft und Bedeutung der Formel," *Angelicum* 20 (1943), pp. 16–31

[16]Bea, *De Inspiratione*, pp. 3ff. Cf. G. W. H. Lampe, *A Patristic Greek Lexicon* (Oxford: Clarendon, 1961) under θεόπνευστος and related terms.

[17]One must take issue with Hermann Sasse at this point. See "Sacra Scriptura, Bemerkungen zur Inspirationslehre Augustins" in *Festschrift Franz Dornseiff*, ed. Horst Kusch (Leipzig: VEB Bibliographisches Institut, 1953), pp. 262–73. Sasse contends that not only Athenagoras (*Legatio pro Christianis* 9) and Pseudo-Justin (*Cohortatio ad Graecos* 8, 37), with their unfortunate comparison of biblical inspiration with the description of the Sibyl of Cumae in the sixth book of the Aeneid, but also Augustine copied Philo's doctrine of inspiration. Polman and Kelly deny this, and with more than ample evidence. The fact that Augustine, for apologetic reasons, compares (*De consen. evang.* 1, pp. 19ff.) the inspiration of Sibyl with that of the prophets and apostles affects neither his doctrine of inspiration nor his exegesis of Scripture. Actually, Augustine's apologetics is formally quite like that of Elijah on Mt. Carmel (1 Kings 18).

[18]Athenagoras, *Leg. pro Christ.*, 7 (PG 6, 386); Theophilus of Antioch, *autolyc.* 2, 9. 10 (PG 6, 1063); Jerome, *Ep.* 65, 7 (PL 22, 627); Gregory the Great, *in Job, praef.* 1 (PL 75, 515). Cf. Heb. 3:7; 10:15.

[19]Polman, *The Word of God*, p. 51.

[20]Athenagoras, *Leg. pro Christ.*, 9; Pseudo-Justin, *Cohortatio ad Graecos*, 8; Chrysostom, *in Joh. hom.* 1, 1; Hippolytus *De Antichristo* 2 (PG 6, 386). Jerome, *Ep.* 65, 7(PL 22, 627); *De Ps.* 88.

[21]In Genesis 2:21 (PG 53, 121; 24, 135).

[22]See Polman, *The Word of God*, pp. 47–51.

[23]Origen, *Cont. Cels.* 7, 3.

[24]Sasse, "Sacra Scriptura," p. 267. Sasse says that the term *dictare* reduces the inspired writer to a mere tool of the Holy Spirit like a typewriter, whereas *suggerere* includes human cooperation (of some kind). Hence there is an ambivalence in Augustine's doctrine.

[25]Polman, *The Word of God*, pp. 44–46, proves this point conclusively. Cf. my book, *The Inspiration of Scripture* (Edinburgh: Oliver & Boyd, 1957), pp. 71–73, where exactly the same conclusion is drawn on the basis of the Latin works of Lutheran orthodoxy as the post-Reformation Lutherans employed the same terminology as Augustine and the Western church fathers.

[26]For the doctrine of plenary inspiration in the Fathers see Kelly, *Early Christian Doctrines*, p. 61.

[27]Clement of Rome, 1 *Cor.* 45, 2 (PG 1, 30); Chrysostom, *in Ps.* 4, 11 (PG 55, 57); see Tromp, *De Sacrae*, pp. 125–26.

[28]Augustine, *Epist.* 82, 1, 3; Cf. *Epist.* 8 (ad Hieronymum), 3, 3.

[29]For a listing and discussion of these statements see the encyclical letter of Pope Benedict XV commemorating the fifteenth centenary of the death of St. Jerome, entitled, "Spiritus Paraclitus" and found in Lewis, *Rome*, pp. 43ff.

[30]Tromp, *De Sacrae*, pp. 125ff.

[31]Jerome, *Ep. ad Fabiolam* 78, 30, cited in Lewis, *Rome*, p. 48. Cf. *Ep. ad Theophilum*, 82, 7, 2, cited in Lewis, *Rome*, p. 49: "The apostles are one thing, other writers another; the former always tell the truth, the latter—as being mere men—sometimes err." The fact that church fathers such as Chrysostom and Jerome clearly taught that the Holy Spirit accommodated Himself to the *usus loquendi* and to the natural endowments and concerns of the human authors of Scripture (as well as to the concerns and needs of the readers of Scripture) never implies that in their opinion God ever accommodated Himself to error as He inspired men to write His Word.

[32]The best discussion of Thomas Aquinas's doctrine of inspiration is by Pierre Benoit in Paul Synave and Pierre Benoit, *Prophecy and Inspiration* (New York: Desclee, 1961). Benoit's main thesis is to demonstrate against J. B. Franzelin, *Tractatus de divina traditione et Scriptura* (Rome, 1870) that Thomas in fact taught a doctrine of verbal inspiration.

Others who write about the Scholastic doctrine concerning Scripture have very little to say (e.g., Bea, Rohnert, Koelling, et al.).

[33]Anselm of Canterbury. *Opera Omnia* (London: Thomas Nelson, 1946), vols. 1 and 2.

[34]Alexander of Hales. *Summa Theologica* (Rome: ad claras aquas, 1924–48).

[35]Bonaventura. *Opera Theologica Selecta* (Florence: Luaracchi, 1934).

[36]Thomas Aquinas. *Summa Theologica* (Rome: Marietti, 1948).

[37]Harnack, *History of Dogma*, 6.169.

[38]*In Iob*. 13, lect. 1.

[39]Duns Scotus. *Opera omnia* (Vatican City: typus polyglotis Vaticanis, 1901–1946).

[40]One need only compare the discussions of Melanchthon's doctrine of Scripture by Hans Engeland, *Glauben und Handeln* (Munich: C. Kaiser, 1931) and the discussions of Flacius's view of Scripture by Gunter Moldaenke, *Schriftverständnis und Schriftdeuätung im Zeitalter der Reformation. I. Matthias Flacius Illyricus* (Stuttgart: W. Kohlhammer, 1936) with E. Thestrup Pedersen's discussion of Luther's doctrine of the Word, his hermeneutics and exegesis in *Luther som Skriftfortolker* (Copenhagen: Nyt Nordisk Forlag Arnold Busck, 1959) to learn that there is no essential difference between the position of Luther and that of the other conservative Reformers on the doctrine of Scripture. Older historians such as Isaac Dorner, *History of Protestant Theology*, trans. George Robson and Sophia Taylor (Edinburgh: T. & T. Clark, 1871) and more significantly Otto Ritschl, *Dogmengeschichte des Protestamtismus* (Leipzig: J. C. Hinrichs'sche Buchhandlung, 1908–27) and their followers find only superficial differences, of which they sometimes make too much and which have been corrected by the exhaustive studies of Wilhelm Walther and Michael Reu. I base much of the following discussion on their evidence and conclusions.

[41]This view is advanced, for instance, by Rupert Davies, *The Problem of Authority in the Continental Reformers* (London: Epworth, 1946). He says, "The almost immediate result of his [Luther's] experience of justification by faith was the conviction that the Scriptures provide the whole and authoritative source of truth."

[42]See W² 18, 732; 18, 332.

Note the following keys to abbreviations used in this and following notes.

Er. Lat.=Martin Luther, *Opera Latina* (Frankfort and Erlangen: Heyder and Simmer, 1865–73).

WA=D. *Martin Luthers Werke,* Kirtische Gesamtausgabe (Weimar: Böhlau, 1883).

W²=Martin Luther, *Sämmtliche Schriften*, herausgegeben von Dr. Joh. Georg Walch, 2. Auflage (St. Louis: Concordia, 1881–1930).

[43]W² 6, 96. This implies using the analogy of Scripture, W² 15, 1271; WA46, 726.

[44]WA 10, 1, 1, 417: "Our faith must above all things be based on clear Scriptures, which are to be understood simply according to the sound and meaning of words"; cf. W² 3, 21; 22, 577. And the intended sense is only one, W² 18, 1447; 11, 313; 1, 950-52.

[45]W² 13, 1898; WA 24, 19.

[46]W² 5, 456.

[47]WA 18, 147.

[48]W² 14, 435.

[49]WA 40, 1, 120; cf. WA 10, 2, 256; WA 10, 1, 80: "There is no other evidence of Christian proof on earth but the Holy Scriptures"; cf. W² 9, 1238; 19, 19ff.; 9, 650; 16, 2212; 8, 1110.

[50]WA 3, 620.

[51]W² 17, 1070.

[52]WA 2, 73.

[53]W² 9. 1775.

[54]W² 8, 191; 11, 526; 3, 1958–59; 1964; 8, 111; 9, 855, 1818; 9, 1774; WA 17, 2, 234; 52, 509. See Petersen, *Luther*, pp. 251–70, for a thorough discussion of Luther's exegesis on this point and many more similar citations from Luther.

[55]See Petersen, *Luther*, pp. 93–106.

[56]His principle seems to be summarized in the following overstatement: "Whatever does not teach Christ is not apostolic, even though St. Peter or Paul taught it; again, what

preaches Christ would be apostolic, even though Judas, Anas, Pilate and Herod taught it." W² 14, 129. For a definitive discussion of Luther's views on canonicity see Reu, *Luther and the Scriptures*, pp. 38–48. Reu demonstrates beyond question that Luther's views on canonicity affect in no way his doctrine of biblical inspiration and authority.

[57]At times Luther opposes Christ to Scripture. "If our adversaries urge Scripture, we urge Christ against Scripture." Again: "One must not understand Scripture contrary to Christ, but in favor of him; therefore Scripture must be brought into relation to Christ or must not be regarded as Scripture." W² 19, 1441. But here Luther is simply applying his hermeneutical principle of Christocentricity: Scripture simply cannot teach anything against the vicarious atonement of Christ (cf. WA 24, 549, 18; 42, 368, 35; 42, 277, 20) and the doctrine of justification. This is his intention also as he calls Christ the *dominus et rex scripturae* (WA 40, 1, 419ff.). He means simply that the law passages must not be allowed to mitigate against those Christological statements in Scripture that teach justification by faith.

[58]W² 19, 1734: "A saying of Holy Scripture is worth more than all the books in the world." W² 9, 831: "When the devil takes the word which brings eternal life, he has taken away everything." W² 9, 654: "If the Word is falsified and God is denied and blasphemed then there can be no hope for salvation." (cf. W² 9, 111, 655, 885, 1788, 1792, 1802). W² 9, 1819: "God gave us Holy Scripture that we should not only read it, but also search, meditate, and ponder on it. In this way one will find eternal life in it." We note the soteriological purpose of Scripture implied in these and similar statements of Luther.

[59]W² 9, 1800.

[60]W² 2, 1200ff.; cf. 1, 1344; WA 17, 11, 39.

[61]W² 4, 2098.

[62]W² 6, 439, 3, 18; 2, 1385; 5, 274.

[63]W² 4, 1424; 13, 573; 13, 2215–16.

[64]W² 14, 435.

[65]W² 23, 2085; 4, 1559.

[66]W² 9, 1819; cf. 1788.

[67]W² 5, 271; 3, 760; 5, 415; WA 11, 33.

[68]W² 18, 1811; Erl. (German) 4, 307; 8, 288, 18, 215; 51, 377–88.

[69]W² 13, 1556.

[70]See *Smalcald Articles* 1, 11, 1ff.

[71]And there is no reason to conclude with Otto Ritschl (*Dogmengeschiehte*, 4. 167–70) that the Lutheran teaching concerning the power of Scripture was derived from a peculiar doctrine of inspiration. After all, Reformed theologians shared Luther's view of the divine origin of Scripture, but never went as far as he in extolling the power of the Word.

[72]W² 7, 2090; 9, 1811; 9, 1808: "In Scripture one reads not human, but the most high Word of God. God wants students who diligently regard Scripture and heed its words." 9, 1818: "Because we hold that the Holy Scriptures are God's Word which can save us, therefore we should read and study them so that we find Christ revealed and witnessed to in them." Here one discerns that the power of Scripture is dependent on its divine origin. 1, 531; 22, 39, 25; 3, 1890: "So, then the entire Scriptures are assigned to the Holy Ghost." Cf. 9, 1821, 1852; 7, 113; 3, 21; 3, 1895; 16, 2182; 14, 21, 3, 785; WA 401, 57; 17, 11, 39.

[73]Karl Barth, *Church Dogmatics*, trans. G. T. Thomson, G. W. Bromily, et al. (Edinburgh: T. & T. Clark, 1936–39), 1, 1, 123.

[74]W² 3, 21.

[75]WA 26, 449.

[76]Er. (German), 28, 342; cf. ibid. 28, 343.

[77]W² 9, 1800.

[78]W² 9, 1770; WA 3, 347; 262.

[79]W² 19, 1104. Cf. WA 47, 193.

[80]W² 4, 1960 (WA 40, 111, 254): "Not only the words [*vocabula*], but also the mode of expression [*phrasis*], which the Holy Ghost and Scripture use, are divine."

[81]W[2] 4, 1492. Cf. W[2] 3, 785; WA 17, 11, 39.

[82]WA 8, 508.

[83]W[2] 8, 38, 9, 839; 3, 325; 13, 1559; 5, 933; 22, 1661; 9, 1238; 9, 87.

[84]W[2] 9, 87. Cf. W[2] 3, 503; 9, 86, 915; 1, 1290; 8, 1110; 13, 1911; 20, 213; 19, 1071; 20, 213; 19, 1071; 3, 325; 15, 1295; 22, 1661; 9, 87; 19, 19ff. 1238; 16, 2212; 8, 1110. WA 18, 147; 10, 1, 1, 417.

[85]WA 10, 1, 80.

[86]W[2] 19, 1734.

[87]WA 40, 1, 120.

[88]WA 23, 119, 11ff.; 147, 23ff.

[89]WA 40, 111, 254; 37, 40. Cf. Reu, p. 61 passim.

[90]W[2] 11, 162.

[91]W[2] 14, 1073.

[92]W[2] 15, 1481; 9, 356.

[93]W[2] 14, 1418.

[94]W[2]2, 1893; 19, 1309, 1442; 22, 1852; 3, 478; 13, 241; 9, 1839.

[95]W[2] 8, 1105. Cf. 13, 241: "We should not be offended by the Word of God, even though it really sounds amazing, incredible and impossible, but we should firmly take our stand on it. If God has spoken it, then it must surely be so."

[96]W[2] 17, 1339; 20, 775; 13, 2478.

[97]W[2] 3, 18.

[98]W[2] 20, 798.

[99]W[2] 9, 356. Cf. WA 40, 1, 420.

[100]W[2] 20, 775.

[101]WA 26, 49.

[102]WA 54, 158. Cf. 56, 249; 32, 59; 50, 269. Michael Reu, *Luther and the Scriptures*, p. 56 et passim, has assembled these and many other passages from Luther to show that his position on this point was well thought out and consistent. To Luther, theology and Scripture, according to Reu, were one unbroken golden chain. If one link is broken, the whole chain is broken and pulls apart. See Reu's notes on p. 150.

Reu, following Wilhelm Walther, also shows with vast evidence that Luther believed in the inerrancy of Scripture also when it spoke of matters seemingly not directly pertaining to doctrine. The very few derogatory remarks Luther made concerning certain passages (either out of frustration because they seemed to conflict with other biblical statements [cf. WA 28, 269; 32, 642] or because of his propensity for hyperbole) are easily explained by Reu and are more than offset by the hundreds of statements of Luther showing his utter commitment to the divine authority and inerrancy of Scripture.

Many theologians and scholars have pointed to Luther's several derogatory remarks against the Epistle of James and some of the other antilegomena to argue that he had a very free, if not low, attitude toward at least some of the Scriptures as touching their authority (inerrancy). This argument is entirely fallacious. We must recall that, unlike the Roman Catholics and the Reformed, Luther and later Lutherans never taught that the New Testament canon was closed; therefore the antilegomena must remain antilegomena. These books simply were doubted in the early church, and one cannot deny history. Thus, when Luther found that (in his opinion) the theology of James and other antilegomena of the New Testament was different or inferior to that of Paul or John or other New Testament books, he concluded that James was not part of the canon. It was his very high regard for the Bible formally and in terms of its message that forced him (mistakenly) to exclude James from the canon rather than to leave it in the canon as a book containing theology inferior to the rest of Scripture. One may well fault Luther for acting in such a way, and most Lutherans of his day and after his day have done so, but the fact that he would take such a radical position against James as to exclude it from the canon shows Luther's high view of all the canonical Scriptures.

Notes on Chapter 13

[1] *The New Columbia Encyclopedia*, ed. William H. Harris and Judith S. Levey, (New York and London: Columbia University Press, 1975).

[2] Ibid., p. 291.

[3] I will refer to these *non sequiturs* throughout the article. The reader may wish to consult the list below. Incidentally, I wish to express my deep gratitude to R. C. Sproul for his critique of this chapter, without holding him in any way responsible for any of its defects.

[4] A. H. Strong asks, "Would it be preferable, in the Old Testament if we should read: 'When the revolution of the earth upon its axis caused the rays of the solar luminary to impinge horizontally upon the retina, Isaac went out to meditate' (Gen. 24:36)?" *Systematic Theology* (Philadelphia: Griffith and Rowland, 1907), 1:223. The great inerrantist Martin Luther was himself committing this *non sequitur* when he condemned Copernicus's heliocentrism.

[5] Arthur Lindsley, "The Principle of Accommodation," an unpublished Pittsburgh Theological Seminary paper (1975), gives a sound current discussion and critique of this *non sequitur*.

[6] George MacDonald carried this *non sequitur* to its logical conclusion when he wrote, "It is Jesus who is the revelation of God, not the Bible." Cited by William A. Glover in *Evangelical Nonconformists and Higher Criticism in the Nineteenth Century* (London: Independent, 1954), p. 82.

[7] Emil Brunner illustrates this *non sequitur* when discussing John Calvin in *Revelation and Reason: The Christian Doctrine of Faith and Knowledge*, trans. Olive Wyon (Philadelphia: Westminster, 1946), p. 275.

[8] This has been a persistent *non sequitur* in neoorthodoxy generally, and Karl Barth has specialized in it; cf. *Church Dogmatics*, vol. 1, *The Doctrine of the Word of God*, second half-volume, ed. G. W. Bromiley and T. F. Torrance (Edinburgh: T. & T. Clark, 1956), pp. 523ff. Klaas Runia has astutely criticized Barth in *Karl Barth's Doctrine of Holy Scripture* (Grand Rapids: Eerdmans, 1962) in an *ad hominem* manner by observing that Barth himself believed that Jesus Christ was true man, without his humanity preventing his sinlessness. See also R. C. Sproul's critique of this *non sequitur* on Barth in "The Case for Inerrancy: A Methodological Analysis" in *God's Inerrant Word*, ed. J. W. Montgomery (Minneapolis: Bethany Fellowship, 1974), pp. 255–57.

[9] The history of the doctrine of inspiration has been repeatedly and thoroughly researched. In addition to extensive studies in encyclopedias and histories of doctrine, innumerable monographs have appeared on the subject in general as well as on details such as "alleged discrepancies," as in John Haley, *An Examination of the Alleged Discrepancies of the Bible* (Nashville: Goodpasture, 1951) and on individual theologians, as in A. D. R. Pohlman, *The Word of God According to St. Augustine* (Grand Rapids: Eerdmans, 1961). It is sufficient here to note a few of the more important general historical works. Classical nineteenth-century studies included: William Lee, *The Inspiration of Holy Scripture* (New York: Robert Carter and Brothers, 1858); George T. Ladd, *The Doctrine of Sacred Scripture: A Critical, Historical and Dogmatic Inquiry*, 2 vols. (New York: Scribner, 1883). More recent works are William Sanday, *Inspiration: Eight Lectures on the Early History and Origin of the Doctrine of Biblical Inspiration* (London: Longmans, 1903); G. D. Barry, *The Inspiration and Authority of the Holy Scripture: A Study of the Literature of the First Five Centuries* (New York: Macmillan, 1919); Daniel J. Theron, *Evidence of Tradition* (Grand Rapids: Baker, 1958); Johannes Beumer, *Die Inspiration der Heiligen Schrift* (Freiberg, Basel, and Vienna: Herder, 1968); Bruce Vawter, *Biblical Inspiration* (Philadelphia: Westminster; London: Hutchinson, 1972); Robert M. Grant, *A Short History of the Interpretation of the Bible*, rev. ed. (New York, London: Macmillan, 1972); Daniel Loretz, *Das Ende der Inspirations Theologie: Chancencines Neubeginns*, 2 vols. (Stuttgart: Katholisches Bibelwerk, 1974).

Just before this volume went to the printer a copy of Stephen T. Davis, *The Debate About the Bible* (Philadelphia: Westminster, 1977) came into my hands. Though not a historical study, it is a most acute analysis of the contemporary debate. While attacking inerrancy and defending a so-called infallibilist position, it is one of the most judicious, balanced, fair critiques I have ever read. Davis avoids virtually all *non sequiturs*, argues to the point, honors motives, recognizes differences, all the while unambiguously affirming orthodox doctrines himself. He admirably embodies the concept of a "worthy opponent." Nevertheless, I believe his argument against inerrancy and for "infallibilism" fails utterly. His attack is unsuccessful because he admits that he cannot prove that "errors" actually do exist in the Bible (cf. chap. 5, p. 141), and this leaves him with only one feeble argument, namely, that the Bible does not explicitly use the word *inerrant* in its self-description. But if it calls itself God's Word many times, thus indicating the inspiration not only of the writers but of the writings as well, what can a divine Word be but an inerrant Word? The mountain is laboring and not even bringing forth a mouse. Davis's own infallibilist position self-destructs, for he admits that his Bible may even err on any crucial doctrine (though he hopes not and thinks it will not), and he admits that ultimate reliance for truth is on his own mind, Scripture notwithstanding (p. 70). Over two hundred years ago, Jonathan Edwards demolished this very argument found in deist Matthew Tindal as presented in his *Christianity As Old As Creation*, Miscellany 1340 in H. G. Townsend, *The Philosophy of Jonathan Edwards* (Eugene: University of Oregon Press, 1955) so thoroughly that I doubt that, if Davis had read that critique, his *Debate About the Bible* would ever have been written.

[10]Barth, *Doctrine of the Word of God*, part 2, p. 520.

[11]Emil Brunner, *The Christian Doctrine of God*, trans. Olive Wyon (Philadelphia: Westminster, 1959), p. 111. Brunner also admits that Calvin, like Luther, thought that scholars could compute on the basis of biblical genealogies (*Revelation and Reason*, p. 278, note 13).

[12]This kind of thinking leads Grant to remark that "by his acceptance of the primacy of faith in exegesis Calvin opened the way for subjectivism even while he tried to exclude it" (*Short History of Interpretation*, p. 134) and even Brunner thought Calvin was too subjective (*Revelation and Reason*, p. 269). Admittedly, Calvin's phraseology at times suggests subjectivity.

[13]Edward Dowey, *The Knowledge of God in Calvin's Theology* (New York: Columbia University Press, 1952), p. 100.

[14]Bromiley, *Church Doctrine of Inspiration*, p. 210.

[15]This makes Kantzer's assertion of Calvin's inerrancy position in *Inspiration and Interpretation*, ed. John F. Walvoord (Grand Rapids: Eerdmans, 1957), p. 137, all the more impressive.

[16]John Murray, *Calvin on Scripture and Divine Sovereignty* (Grand Rapids: Baker, 1960).

[17]James I. Packer, "Calvin's View of Scripture" in *God's Inerrant Word*, ed. J. W. Montgomery (Minneapolis: Bethany Fellowship, 1974), pp. 95–114.

[18]*Job*, p. 744, as cited by Kantzer in *Inspiration and Interpretation*. The following quotes are likewise cited by Kantzer. Kantzer cites Calvin's *Institutes*, the Beveridge translation, 3 vols. (Edinburgh: The Calvin Translation Society, 1845).

[19]*Institutes*, I, 149.

[20]*Institutes*, III, 166; *Minor Prophets*, II, 177.

[21]*Hebrews*, p. xxi.

[22]*Minor Prophets*, I, 506.

[23]*Psalms*, II, 429.

[24]*Psalms*, v, ii.

[25]*Psalms*, iv. 480.

[26]*Institutes*, II, 58, and III, 309.

[27]*II Timothy*, p. 249.

[28]*Minor Prophets*, III, 200, and *John*, I, 420.

[29]*Catholic Epistles*, p. 131.

[30]*Institutes*, IV. viii. 8ff.; cf. I. vi, 2, as cited by Packer in *God's Inerrant Word*.

[31]Packer, "Calvin's View," p. 102.

[32]*Institutes*, vii, I.

[33]As cited by Kantzer in *Inspiration and Interpretation*, pp. 142–44.
[34]*CR*, 9, 893b.
[35]Rogers, "Church Doctrine of Biblical Inspiration," pp. 28–29. Cf. Charles W. Shields, *The Trial of Servetus by the Senate of Geneva: A Review of the Official Records and Contemporary Writings* (Philadelphia: MacCalla, 1893), p. 17; C. T. Ohner, *Michael Servetus: His Life and Teachings* (Philadelphia: Lippincott, 1810), p. 49; C. Manzoni, *Umanesimo ad Eresia: M. Serveto* (Napoli: Guida Editori, 1974), p. 30.
[36]*Genesis*, as cited by Lindsley, "Principle of Accommodation," p. 33.
[37]*Isaiah* (40:18).
[38]*Psalms* (78:3).
[39]See Kanzter, *Inspiration and Interpretation*, pp. 144–46.
[40]To see the thoroughness of Reformed Scholasticism's development of the inerrancy doctrine, cf. Heinrick Heppe, *Reformed Dogmatics*, trans. G. T. Thomson (London: Allen and Unwin, 1950), pp. 12–47. Robert Preus's *Inspiration of Scripture: A Study of the Theology of the 17th-Century Lutheran Dogmaticians* (Edinburgh and London: Oliver and Boyd, 1955) does the same for Lutheran scholasticism. Seventeenth-century Roman Catholic scholasticism was also active in this area (cf. Vawter, *Biblical Inspiration*, p. 66, citing Suarez).
[41]This is a common evaluation by neoorthodox theologians such as Barth and Brunner, who see themselves as truer to the Reformation than its immediate successors. But R. M. Grant also unfortunately remarks that "the later Reformation did not follow Luther, however, and it came to insist on tradition principles of Verbal Inspiration and Infallibility which has been alien to him" (*Short History*, p. 135). As we have seen, Luther also contended that the words of canonical Scripture were the inerrant words of God, as his successors confirmed. Bromiley, revealing his fideism, takes a middle path, recognizing that the Scholastics represented only a shift of emphasis but feeling that, with them, "non-biblical rationalism threatens" ("Church Doctrine of Inspiration," p. 213).
[42]Rogers, "Church Doctrine of Biblical Inspiration," p. 30.
[43]Ibid.
[44]Ibid., p. 31. When I read the Allison statement I leafed through a few pages in the middle of an English translation of Turretin's systematic theology I used with students and found at casual glancing a half dozen citations of Calvin, more than half of which were quotations. Furthermore, the statement that the *Helvetic Consensus* of Heidegger and Turretin "announced that textual criticism of the Old Testament would 'bring the foundation of our faith and its inviolable authority into perilous hazard' " (ibid.) is distressing. Any reader unfamiliar with the *Consensus* would suppose from this statement that it was opposed to biblical criticism as such. If anyone will read the two relevant paragraphs in *Creeds of the Churches*, ed. John Leith (New York: Doubleday, 1963), pp. 310–11, he will see that the concern of the *Consensus* was with mere conjectural emendation of the "Hebrew original" by the critics, "sometimes from their own reason alone." One does not have to agree with the critical opinion of the *Consensus* to recognize that its genuine concern was that the word of man might be substituted for the Word of God. I believe in textual criticism myself, but I know textual critics who emend the text at the drop of their critical hats, including sometimes the text of the New Testament, which has no vowel point problem. I oppose such subjective textual criticism and am therefore (like the *Consensus*) sometimes thought, unfairly, to be opposed to valid textual criticism.
[45]Cf. also chap. 14: "By this faith a Christian believeth to be true *whatsoever* is revealed in the Word, for the authority of God Himself speaketh therein."
[46]Jack B. Rogers, *Scripture and the Westminster Confession* (Grand Rapids: Eerdmans, 1967).
[47]Rogers, "Church Doctrine of Biblical Inspiration," p. 33.
[48]Ibid.
[49]Ibid.
[50]B. Riveley, ed., *The Whole Works of the Right Rev. Edward Reynolds*, 6 vols. (London: Holdsworth, 1826), I; 103.
[51]Rogers, "Church Doctrine of Biblical Inspiration," pp. 33–34.

[52]Ibid., p. 34. Note the caricature of the inerrantists' position by making it represent the Bible as an "encyclopedia of answers to every sort of question." Caricature of another view usually reveals the threadbare character of one's own in that it requires a distortion of the opposition in order to survive.

[53]Ibid., p. 34.

[54]Ibid., p. 35.

[55]Ibid.

[56]Cf. E. D. Morris, *Theology of the Westminster Symbols* (Columbus: Champlin, 1900).

[57]Dozens of his *Miscellanies* refer to this subject directly and indirectly.

[58]Cited with the kind permission of the Beinecke Library and Rare Book Room, Yale University.

[59]Sermon on Ephesians 3:10 in *The Works of President Edwards* (New York: Carvill, 1930), 7:66ff.

[60]Unpublished sermon outline on 2 Timothy 3:16, points 6 and 7.

[61]Unpublished sermon on Luke, 1:77–79.

[62]Jonathan Edwards, *Miscellany* 1337. Cf. 1338.

[63]Ibid.

[64]Edwards, *Miscellany* 1290–91.

[65]Edwards, *Miscellany* 811.

[66]*Works of Jonathan Edwards, A.M.*, Revised and corrected by Edward Hickman, 2 vols. (London: William Ball, 1837), 2:739.

[67]Ibid., p. 786.

[68]Ibid., p. 742.

[69]Ibid., p. 789.

[70]Ibid., p. 747.

[71]Ibid., p. 745.

[72]Many of Edwards's *Miscellanies* have been published, but my citations are from the manuscripts, which were used with the kind permission of Beinecke Rare Book Room, Yale University.

[73]*Works*, II, p. 498.

[74]Outline sermon on 2 Timothy 3:16 in *Selections from the Unpublished Writings of Jonathan Edwards*, ed. Alexander B. Grosart (Edinburgh: Ballantyne, 1865).

[75]John H. Gerstner, "An Outline of the Apologetics of Jonathan Edwards," *Bibliotheca Sacra* 133 (July-September 1976): 195.

[76]*Review of Metaphysics* 30 (December 1976): 306.

[77]Rogers, "Church Doctrine and Biblical Inspiration," p. 39.

[78]Cf. John H. Gerstner, "Warfield's Case for Biblical Inerrancy," in *God's Inerrant Word*, pp. 136–37.

[79]Ibid., p. 40.

[80]Charles Hodge, *Systematic Theology* (New York: Scribner, 1873), 1:391.

[81]Ibid., pp. 337–38.

[82]*Biblical Authority*, p. 44.

Notes on Chapter 14

[1]*Biblical Authority*, ed. Jack Rogers (Waco: Word, 1977), pp. 9–10.

[2]*God's Inerrant Word*, ed. J. W. Montgomery (Minneapolis: Bethany Fellowship, 1974), p. 115.

[3]G. C. Berkouwer, *De Heilige Schrift* (Kampen: Kok, 1966), vol. I, p. 34; cf. *Holy Scripture* (Grand Rapids: Eerdmans, 1975), p. 32; *Biblical Authority*, pp. 17–46, 152ff.

[4]*Selected Shorter Writings of Benjamin B. Warfield*, ed. John E. Meeter, vol. 2 (Nutley: Presbyterian and Reformed, 1973), pp. 619–20; B. B. Warfield, *The Inspiration and Authority of the Bible* (Philadelphia: Presbyterian and Reformed, 1964), pp. 112–14.

[5]It has been generally acknowledged that the concept of the correlation between faith and revelation is the essential element in Berkouwer's dogmatic methodology. Cf. G. E. Meuleman, "De correlatie van geloof en Openbaring bij G. C. Berkouwer," in *Gereformeerd Theologisch Tijdschrift*, November 1965; A. D. R. Polman, "Berkouwer als Dogmaticus," in *Gereformeerd Weekblad*, October 8, 1965; and R. C. Sproul, "The Case for Inerrancy: A Methodological Analysis," in *God's Inerrant Word*, p. 243. Cf. also G. W. de Jong, *De theologie van Dr. G. C. Berkouwer* (Kampen: Kok, 1971), passim.

[6]H. Berkhof, "De methode van Berkouwer's theologie" in *Ex Auditu Verbi*, ed. R. Schippers, G. E. Meuleman, J. T. Bakker, and H. M. Kuitert (Kampen: Kok, 1965), pp. 44–48, is of the opinion that in Berkouwer's thinking, in spite of its continuity, three phases can be distinguished. In the first phase he maintains the "absolute authority of Scripture," in the second phase he emphasizes the "redemptive contents of Scripture," and in the third phase the focus shifts to the "existential scope of Scripture." This was reported to the American public by R. C. Sproul in *God's Inerrant Word*, pp. 243–44. What has not been reported, however, is that Berkouwer, in his response to Berkhof's analysis, objects to the construct of a third phase, but does not contest the transition from the first to the second phase. Cf. F. W. Buytendach, *Aspekete van die vorm/inhoud-problematiek met betrekking tot die organiese skirifinspirasie in die nuwere Gereformeerde theologie in Nederland* (Amsterdam: Ton Bolland, 1972), pp. 330–31. Berkhof's distinction between a second and third phase indeed leaves something to be desired. It cannot be denied that Berkouwer's emphasis shifts from the formal authority of the Scriptures as the Word of God to the contents of the Scriptures as witness. But Berkhof's description of the third phase creates the impression that eventually a Bultmannian type of existentialist theology came to place its stamp on Berkouwer's thinking. This idea is not defensible. His theologizing, following the shift away from his original position, bears throughout the mark of the influence of Karl Barth. This has been correctly observed by A. D. R. Polman; cf. Buytendach, *Aspekte*, p. 333. Hence it is preferable to speak of two phases, the second of which increasingly shows, and would not have been possible without, the influence of the Barthian type of neoorthodoxy. Cf. de Jong, *De theologie van Dr. G. C. Berkouwer*, pp. 32–47, for Berkouwer's change of attitude toward the theology of Karl Barth. It is difficult to determine precisely when the shift in Berkouwer's thinking took place. Some scholars question the advisability of construing a shift of phases in Berkouwer's theology. They prefer to speak of an evolution in which he increasingly listens both to Scripture and to the new theology that wishes to understand Scripture in the modern setting; cf. de Jong, *De theologie*, pp. 11–12. That Berkouwer's theology gradually evolves is readily admitted. In fact this explains why it is not easy to pinpoint the shift in his thinking. But that there *is* a shift cannot be denied. In his earlier phase he severely criticized the new theology in the light of Scripture. In his later phase he listens to Scripture in the light of the new theology; cf. F. W. Buytendach, *Aspekte*, pp. 329–447. The shift in Berkouwer's thinking can be narrowed down to the years 1945 to 1950. First, Meuleman speaks about a difference between Berkouwer's writings from before and after 1945. Second, in 1947 Berkouwer published his *Karl Barth en de kinderdoop* (Kampen: Kok). In this work he begins to dissociate himself from his negative judgment of Barth's theology pronounced in 1937 in *Karl Barth* (Kampen: Kok), without yet giving the positive evaluation that would characterize his *Triumph of Grace in the Theology of Karl Barth* (Kampen: Kok), published in 1954; cf. de Jong, *De theologie*, pp. 11, 42–43.

[7]G. C. Berkouwer, *Het probleem der Schriftkritiek* (Kampen: Kok, n.d.). Regrettably this book has never been translated into the English language.

[8]G. C. Berkouwer, *The Second Vatican Council and the New Catholicism* (Grand Rapids: Eerdmans, 1965); *Holy Scripture* (Grand Rapids: Eerdmans, 1975); and *A Half Century of Theology* (Grand Rapids: Eerdmans, 1977).

[9]Warfield, *Inspiration and Authority*, pp. 153–54.

[10]Ibid., p. 133.

[11]Ibid., p. 137.

[12]Ibid., p. 296.

[13]Ibid., pp. 234–35, 238–39.
[14]Ibid., p. 407.
[15]Ibid., p. 240.
[16]Ibid., pp. 138–49, 229–40, 299–349. 351–407; note esp. p. 426 and *Selected Shorter Writings*, p. 635.
[17]Warfield, *Inspiration and Authority*, pp. 163–64, 426–27; cf. *Selected Shorter Writings*, pp. 539–40.
[18]Berkouwer, *Het probleem*, pp. 315–18.
[19]Berkouwer, "De mening des Geestes," in *Gereformeerd Weekblad*, January 6, 13, 20, 1961.
[20]Berkouwer, *Het Probleem*, p. 293.
[21]Ibid., pp. 387–90.
[22]Berkouwer, *Holy Scripture*, p. 140.
[23]Cf. Berkouwer, "Vragen rondom de Belijdenis," in *Gereformeerd Theologisch Tijdschrift* (February 1961), pp. 1–41, esp. 36–37. In this article Berkouwer asks the suggestive question as to whether the Word of God, which transcends every confession of the church, does not imply that also Scripture, fully human as it is, shares in the relativity of every human testimony. He does not see any difference between the humanity of Scripture and the humanity of other writings. To insist on such a difference would amount to an unwarranted "supranaturalization" of Scripture. Cf. Buytendach, *Aspekte*, pp. 340–41.
[24]Berkouwer, *Holy Scripture*, p. 142.
[25]For this analysis of Berkouwer's views of 2 Tim. 3:16 and 2 Peter 1:21, see the perceptive and helpful remarks of Buytendach, *Aspekte*, pp. 415–19.
[26]Cf. Berkouwer, *Holy Scripture*, pp. 14–15; see also pp. 67, 111.
[27]Ibid., pp. 16–17.
[28]Ibid., pp. 17–18. For the charge of docetism see the analysis and rebuttal by Sproul in *God's Inerrant Word*, pp. 255–56.
[29]Ibid., p. 32.
[30]Ibid., p. 145; see also pp. 22, 37, 50, 73, 104, 148, 150–52, 167.
[31]Ibid., pp. 143, 145, 148, 164.
[32]Ibid., pp. 147, 149; see also Berkouwer, *Half Century of Theology*, pp. 139–41.
[33]Berkouwer, *Holy Scripture*, pp. 49, 142, 149, 308.
[34]Warfield, *Inspiration and Authority*, p. 143.
[35]Ibid., p. 437; cf. *Selected Shorter Writings*, p. 545.
[36]Warfield, *Inspiration and Authority*, pp. 151–52, 421–22, 437–38; cf. *Selected Shorter Writings*, pp. 542–44, 628.
[37]*Selected Shorter Writings*, p. 544.
[38]Ibid., pp. 546, 630–31.
[39]Ibid., p. 547; see also pp. 629, 631; *Inspiration and Authority*, p. 158.
[40]Warfield, *Inspiration and Authority*, p. 422; cf. *Selected Shorter Writings*, pp. 624, 631.
[41]Warfield, *Inspiration and Authority;* see esp. p. 160.
[42]Ibid., p. 160.
[43]Ibid., pp. 108, 116–19, 127, 171; cf. *Selected Shorter Writings*, pp. 588, 593, 627.
[44]Warfield, *Inspiration and Authority*, p. 420 for fully true; pp. 140, 144–45, 158, 161, 316, for fully authoritative; and pp. 112, 420 for fully infallible; cf. *Selected Shorter Writings*, pp. 537ff.
[45]For references see notes 46ff.
[46]Warfield, *Inspiration and Authority*, p. 173.
[47]See ibid., pp. 173, 420, where Warfield makes virtually identical statements about the nature of Scripture and uses *infallible* in the one context and *inerrant* in the other. The terms are clearly interchangeable.
[48]Ibid., p. 113.
[49]Ibid., pp. 150, 158.
[50]Ibid., p. 225; cf. *Selected Shorter Writings*, p. 633.

[51]Warfield, *Inspiration and Authority*, pp. 116–19, 128, 175ff., 180, 218–19, 427–28; cf. *Selected Shorter Writings*, p. 635.

[52]Warfield, *Inspiration and Authority*, pp. 107–9; cf. *Selected Shorter Writings*, pp. 572ff. Note the several quotations given on these pages. They show that inerrancy was a doctrine that was universally accepted by the church. For further supporting evidence, see *Inspiration and Interpretation*, ed. John F. Walvoord (Grand Rapids: Eerdmans, 1957); Clark H. Pinnock, *Biblical Revelation* (Chicago: Moody, 1971), pp. 147–174; and *God's Inerrant Word*.

[53]Warfield *Inspiration and Authority*, pp. 175, 196, 200. Warfield refers to Farrar's admission that Paul regarded Scripture as "absolutely infallible even in accidental details and passing allusions." Cf. *Selected Shorter Writings*, p. 634.

[54]*Selected Shorter Writings*, p. 550.

[55]Ibid., pp. 549–59, esp. 558–59

[56]Ibid., pp. 580–94.

[57]Ibid., pp. 189–95.

[58]Warfield, *Inspiration and Authority*, p. 440.

[59]Ibid., pp. 441–42.

[60]Berkouwer, *Het probleem*, pp. 314–53, especially pp. 314–19, 322–23, 326–27, 352–53.

[61]The wording of this conclusion resembles closely a statement by the early Berkouwer, quoted in Buytendach, *Aspekte*, p. 332. It is interesting to note that also with regard to the parallel between incarnation and inscripturation the views of the early Berkouwer and Warfield are practically identical. Like Warfield, Berkouwer refuses to press the analogy too heavily. At the same time, also like Warfield, he speaks about the wonder of a pure and trustworthy revelation that came about in spite of the weakness of human instrumentality and the inadequacy of human language and because of the powerful influence of the Spirit. Berkouwer, *Het probleem*, pp. 353–83, esp. pp. 381–82.

[62]Cf. Berkouwer, *Het probleem*, pp. 323, 353, 389 for the trustworthiness of Scripture; pp. 256, 265, 316, 384, 387, 388 for its authority; and pp. 326, 355 for its infallibility; see p. 250 for all three.

[63]Ibid., pp. 203, 205–6.

[64]Ibid., pp. 252ff.

[65]Ibid., pp. 322ff.

[66]Ibid., pp. 297, 384; see also p. 277.

[67]Berkouwer, *Holy Scripture*, p. 151; see also pp. 152ff.

[68]Ibid., pp. 162–63, 167.

[69]Berkouwer, *De Heilige Schrift*, 2:48–49, discounts the idea that the *concursus* concept sheds any helpful light on the relationship between the divine and the human element. Only the perspective of the human witness can further our understanding. He talks about "totaal andere perspectieven, van waaruit de theopneustie alleen valt te verstaan. Het is het perspectief van het menselijk *getuigenis.*" Regrettably this section is not found in *Holy Scripture,* which is only a partial translation of the two original volumes on Scripture. The fundamental importance Berkouwer attaches to the term *witness* is accentuated by his polemical stance against E. P. Clowney's criticism of this term and its use in modern thought. The usually mild-mannered Berkouwer condemns this criticism in rather forceful terms. For Berkouwer everything is at stake at this point. See *Holy Scripture*, pp. 163ff. His attempt to back up his understanding of *witness* with Scripture references is not convincing.

[70]Berkouwer, *Holy Scripture*, pp. 181–84, 189, 202–3, 242ff., 264–65.

[71]Berkouwer, *Het probleem*, pp. 265ff.; *The Second Vatican Council*, pp. 119ff.; *De Heilige Schrift*, 2:294–327; *Holy Scripture*, pp. 292ff.

[72]Berkouwer, *Holy Scripture*, pp. 9ff.

[73]Berkouwer, *Het probleem*, pp. 383–89.

[74]H. Braun, *Gesammelte Studien zum Neuen Testament und seiner Umwelt* (Tübingen: Mohr, 1962), pp. 337, 341.

[75]K. Barth, *How I Changed My Mind* (Richmond: John Knox, 1966), p. 83.

[76]H. Bock, in *Post Bultmann Locutum*, ed. H. Symanowski (Hamburg-Bergstedt: Herbert Reich, 1965), 2:57–58.

[77]See chapter 10 where the philosophical presuppositions of inductivism are examined.

[78]Berkouwer, *Het probleem*, pp. 219, 226, 248, 255, 257, 261, 275–78.

[79]Ibid., pp. 60–61, 67, 83, 92.

[80]Berkouwer, *Half Century of Theology*, p. 132.

[81]K. Barth, *Church Dogmatics*, I, 2, pp. 505ff. Cf. also the unpublished Master's Thesis of W. A. Macaulay, Jr., *Karl Barth's View of the Inspiration of Scripture*, submitted to the Faculty of Westminster Theological Seminary in 1974. A perusal of this thesis brought to my attention the striking parallel between Berkouwer and Barth in their doctrine of Scripture. They approach the material from the same perspective. Because of this they encounter the same problems and treat them in a similar manner. They come basically to the same conclusions.

[82]Berkouwer, *Het probleem*, pp. 96–109.

[83]Berkouwer, *Holy Scripture*, pp. 37, 61, 138, 210, 214, 246–53, 327–45, 366; *Second Vatican Council*, pp. 124–34.

[84]*Biblical Authority*, p. 10.

APPENDIX

THE CHICAGO STATEMENT
ON BIBLICAL INERRANCY

The authority of Scripture is a key issue for the Christian Church in this and every age. Those who profess faith in Jesus Christ as Lord and Savior are called to show the reality of their discipleship by humbly and faithfully obeying God's written Word. To stray from Scripture in faith or conduct is disloyalty to our Master. Recognition of the total truth and trustworthiness of Holy Scripture is essential to a full grasp and adequate confession of its authority.

The following Statement affirms this inerrancy of Scripture afresh, making clear our understanding of it and warning against its denial. We are persuaded that to deny it is to set aside the witness of Jesus Christ and of the Holy Spirit and to refuse that submission to the claims of God's own Word which marks true Christian faith. We see it as our timely duty to make this affirmation in the face of current lapses from the truth of inerrancy among our fellow Christians and misunderstanding of this doctrine in the world at large.

This Statement consists of three parts: a Summary Statement, Articles of Affirmation and Denial, and an accompanying Exposition. It has been prepared in the course of a three-day consultation in Chicago. Those who have signed the Summary Statement and the Articles wish to affirm their own conviction as to the inerrancy of Scripture and to encourage and challenge one another and all Christians to growing appreciation and understanding of this doctrine. We acknowledge the limitations of a document prepared in a brief, intensive conference and do not propose that this Statement be given creedal weight. Yet we rejoice in the deepening of our own convictions through our discussions together, and we pray that the Statement we have signed may be used to the glory of our God toward a new reformation of the Church in its faith, life, and mission.

We offer this Statement in a spirit, not of contention, but of humility and love, which we purpose by God's grace to maintain in any future dialogue arising out of what we have said. We gladly acknowledge that many who deny the inerrancy of Scripture do not display the consequences of this denial in the rest of their belief and behavior, and we are conscious that we who confess this doctrine often deny it in life by failing to bring our thoughts and deeds, our traditions and habits, into true subjection to the divine Word.

We invite response to this statement from any who see reason to amend its affirmations about Scripture by the light of Scripture itself, under whose infallible authority we stand as we speak. We claim no personal infallibility for the witness we bear, and for any help which enables us to strengthen this testimony to God's Word we shall be grateful.

A SHORT STATEMENT

1. God, who is Himself Truth and speaks truth only, has inspired Holy Scripture in order thereby to reveal Himself to lost mankind through Jesus Christ as Creator and Lord, Redeemer and Judge. Holy Scripture is God's witness to Himself.

2. Holy Scripture, being God's own Word, written by men prepared and superintended by His Spirit, is of infallible divine authority in all matters upon which it touches: it is to be believed, as God's instruction, in all that it affirms; obeyed, as God's command, in all that it requires; embraced, as God's pledge, in all that it promises.

3. The Holy Spirit, Scripture's divine Author, both authenticates it to us by His inward witness and opens our minds to understand its meaning.

4. Being wholly and verbally God-given, Scripture is without error or fault in all its teaching, no less in what it states about God's acts in creation, about the events of world history, and about its own literary origins under God, than in its witness to God's saving grace in individual lives.

5. The authority of Scripture is inescapably impaired if this total divine inerrancy is in any way limited or disregarded, or made relative to a view of truth contrary to the Bible's own; and such lapses bring serious loss to both the individual and the Church.

ARTICLES OF AFFIRMATION AND DENIAL

Article I

We affirm that the Holy Scriptures are to be received as the authoritative Word of God.

We deny that the Scriptures receive their authority from the Church, tradition, or any other human source.

Article II

We affirm that the Scriptures are the supreme written norm by which God binds the conscience, and that the authority of the Church is subordinate to that of Scripture.

We deny that Church creeds, councils, or declarations have authority greater than or equal to the authority of the Bible.

Article III

We affirm that the written Word in its entirety is revelation given by God.

We deny that the Bible is merely a witness to revelation, or only becomes revelation in encounter, or depends on the responses of men for its validity.

Article IV

We affirm that God who made mankind in His image has used language as a means of revelation.

We deny that human language is so limited by our creatureliness that it is rendered inadequate as a vehicle for divine revelation. We further deny that the corruption of human culture and language through sin has thwarted God's work of inspiration.

Article V

We affirm that God's revelation in the Holy Scriptures was progressive.

We deny that later revelation, which may fulfill earlier revelation, ever corrects or contradicts it. We further deny that any normative revelation has been given since the completion of the New Testament writings.

Article VI

We affirm that the whole of Scripture and all its parts, down to the very words of the original, were given by divine inspiration.

We deny that the inspiration of Scripture can rightly be affirmed of the whole without the parts, or of some parts but not the whole.

Article VII

We affirm that inspiration was the work in which God by His Spirit, through human writers, gave us His Word. The origin of Scripture is divine. The mode of divine inspiration remains largely a mystery to us.

We deny that inspiration can be reduced to human insight, or to heightened states of consciousness of any kind.

Article VIII

We affirm that God in His Work of inspiration utilized the distinctive personalities and literary styles of the writers whom He had chosen and prepared.

We deny that God, in causing these writers to use the very words that He chose, overrode their personalities.

Article IX

We affirm that inspiration, though not conferring omniscience, guaranteed true and trustworthy utterance on all matters of which the Biblical authors were moved to speak and write.

We deny that the finitude or fallenness of these writers, by necessity or otherwise, introduced distortion or falsehood into God's Word.

Article X

We affirm that inspiration, strictly speaking, applies only to the autographic text of Scripture, which in the providence of God can be ascertained from available manuscripts with great accuracy. We further affirm that copies and translations of Scripture are the Word of God to the extent that they faithfully represent the original.

We deny that any essential element of the Christian faith is affected by the absence of the autographs. We further deny that this absence renders the assertion of Biblical inerrancy invalid or irrelevant.

Article XI

We affirm that Scripture, having been given by divine inspiration, is infallible, so that, far from misleading us, it is true and reliable in all the matters it addresses.

We deny that it is possible for the Bible to be at the same time infallible and errant in its assertions. Infallibility and inerrancy may be distinguished, but not separated.

Article XII

We affirm that Scripture in its entirety is inerrant, being free from all falsehood, fraud, or deceit.

We deny that Biblical infallibility and inerrancy are limited to spiritual, religious, or redemptive themes, exclusive of assertions in the fields of history and science. We further deny that scientific hypotheses about earth history may properly be used to overturn the teaching of Scripture on creation and the flood.

Article XIII

We affirm the propriety of using inerrancy as a theological term with reference to the complete truthfulness of Scripture.

We deny that it is proper to evaluate Scripture according to standards of truth and error that are alien to its usage or purpose. We further deny that inerrancy is negated by Biblical phenomena such as a lack of modern technical precision, irregularities of grammar or spelling, observational descriptions of nature, the reporting of falsehoods, the use of hyperbole and round numbers, the topical arrangement of material, variant selections of material in parallel accounts, or the use of free citations.

Article XIV

We affirm the unity and internal consistency of Scripture.

We deny that alleged errors and discrepancies that have not yet been resolved vitiate the truth claims of the Bible.

Article XV

We affirm that the doctrine of inerrancy is grounded in the teaching of the Bible about inspiration.

We deny that Jesus' teaching about Scripture may be dismissed by appeals to accommodation or to any natural limitation of His humanity.

Article XVI

We affirm that the doctrine of inerrancy has been integral to the Church's faith throughout its history.

We deny that inerrancy is a doctrine invented by Scholastic Protestantism, or is a reactionary position postulated in response to negative higher criticism.

Article XVII

We affirm that the Holy Spirit bears witness to the Scriptures, assuring believers of the truthfulness of God's written Word.

We deny that this witness of the Holy Spirit operates in isolation from or against Scripture.

Article XVIII

We affirm that the text of Scripture is to be interpreted by grammatico-historical exegesis, taking account of its literary forms and devices, and that Scripture is to interpret Scripture.

We deny the legitimacy of any treatment of the text or quest for sources lying behind it that leads to relativizing, dehistoricizing, or discounting its teaching, or rejecting its claims to authorship.

Article XIX

We affirm that a confession of the full authority, infallibility, and inerrancy of Scripture is vital to a sound understanding of the whole of the Christian faith. We further affirm that such confession should lead to increasing conformity to the image of Christ.

We deny that such confession is necessary for salvation. However, we further deny that inerrancy can be rejected without grave consequences, both to the individual and to the Church.

EXPOSITION

Our understanding of the doctrine of inerrancy must be set in the
context of the broader teachings of the Scripture concerning itself. This
exposition gives an account of the outline of doctrine from which our
summary statement and articles are drawn.

Creation, Revelation, and Inspiration

The Triune God, who formed all things by his creative utterances
and governs all things by His Word of decree, made mankind in His
own image for a life of communion with Himself, on the model of the
eternal fellowship of loving communication within the Godhead. As
God's image-bearer, man was to hear God's Word addressed to him
and to respond in the joy of adoring obedience. Over and above God's
self-disclosure in the created order and the sequence of events within it,
human beings from Adam on have received verbal messages from Him,
either directly, as stated in Scripture, or indirectly in the form of part or
all of Scripture itself.

When Adam fell, the Creator did not abandon mankind to final
judgment but promised salvation and began to reveal Himself as Redeemer in a sequence of historical events centering on Abraham's family and culminating in the life, death, resurrection, present heavenly
ministry, and promised return of Jesus Christ. Within this frame God
has from time to time spoken specific words of judgment and mercy,
promise and command, to sinful human beings so drawing them into a
covenant relation of mutual commitment between Him and them in
which He blesses them with gifts of grace and they bless Him in responsive adoration. Moses, whom God used as mediator to carry His words
to His people at the time of the Exodus, stands at the head of a long line
of prophets in whose mouths and writings God put His words for
delivery to Israel. God's purpose in this succession of messages was to
maintain His covenant by causing His people to know His Name—that
is, His nature—and His will both of precept and purpose in the present
and for the future. This line of prophetic spokesmen from God came to
completion in Jesus Christ, God's incarnate Word, who was Himself a
prophet—more than a prophet, but not less—and in the apostles and
prophets of the first Christian generation. When God's final and
climactic message, His word to the world concerning Jesus Christ, had
been spoken and elucidated by those in the apostolic circle, the sequence of revealed messages ceased. Henceforth the Church was to live
and know God by what He had already said, and said for all time.

At Sinai God wrote the terms of His covenant on tables of stone, as
His enduring witness and for lasting accessibility, and throughout the
period of prophetic and apostolic revelation He prompted men to write
the messages given to and through them, along with celebratory rec-

ords of His dealings with His people, plus moral reflections on covenant life and forms of praise and prayer for covenant mercy. The theological reality of inspiration in the producing of Biblical documents corresponds to that of spoken prophecies: although the human writers' personalities were expressed in what they wrote, the words were divinely constituted. Thus, what Scripture says, God says; its authority is His authority, for He is its ultimate Author, having given it through the minds and words of chosen and prepared men who in freedom and faithfulness "spoke from God as they were carried along by the Holy Spirit" (1 Peter 1:21). Holy Scripture must be acknowledged as the Word of God by virtue of its divine origin.

Authority: Christ and the Bible

Jesus Christ, the Son of God who is the Word made flesh, our Prophet, Priest, and King, is the ultimate Mediator of God's communication to man, as He is of all God's gifts of grace. The revelation He gave was more than verbal; He revealed the Father by His presence and His deeds as well. Yet His words were crucially important; for He was God, He spoke from the Father, and His words will judge all men at the last day.

As the prophesied Messiah, Jesus Christ is the central theme of Scripture. The Old Testament looked ahead to Him; the New Testament looks back to His first coming and on to His second. Canonical Scripture is the divinely inspired and therefore normative witness to Christ. No hermeneutic, therefore, of which the historical Christ is not the focal point is acceptable. Holy Scripture must be treated as what it essentially is—the witness of the Father to the incarnate Son.

It appears that the Old Testament canon had been fixed by the time of Jesus. The New Testament canon is likewise now closed inasmuch as no new apostolic witness to the historical Christ can now be borne. No new revelation (as distinct from Spirit-given understanding of existing revelation) will be given until Christ comes again. The canon was created in principle by divine inspiration. The Church's part was to discern the canon which God had created, not to devise one of its own.

The word *canon*, signifying a rule or standard, is a pointer to authority, which means the right to rule and control. Authority in Christianity belongs to God in His revelation, which means, on the one hand, Jesus Christ, the living Word, and, on the other hand, Holy Scripture, the written Word. But the authority of Christ and that of Scripture are one. As our Prophet, Christ testified that Scripture cannot be broken. As our Priest and King, He devoted His earthly life to fulfilling the law and the prophets, even dying in obedience to the words of Messianic prophecy. Thus, as He saw Scripture attesting Him and His authority, so by His own submission to Scripture He attested its authority. As He bowed to His Father's instruction given in His Bible (our Old Testament), so He requires His disciples to do—not, however, in isolation but in conjunction with the apostolic witness to Himself which He undertook to inspire by His gift of the Holy Spirit. So Christians show themselves faithful servants of their Lord by bowing to the divine instruction given in the prophetic and apostolic writings which together make up our Bible.

By authenticating each other's authority, Christ and Scripture coalesce into a single fount of authority. The Biblically-interpreted Christ and the Christ-centered, Christ-proclaiming Bible are from this standpoint one. As from the fact of inspiration we infer that what Scripture says, God says, so from the revealed relation between Jesus Christ and Scripture we may equally declare that what Scripture says, Christ says.

Infallibility, Inerrancy, Interpretation

Holy Scripture, as the inspired Word of God witnessing authoritatively to Jesus Christ, may properly be called *infallible* and *inerrant*. These negative terms have a special value, for they explicitly safeguard crucial positive truths.

Infallible signifies the quality of neither misleading nor being misled and so safeguards in categorical terms the truth that Holy Scripture is a sure, safe, and reliable rule and guide in all matters.

Similarly, *inerrant* signifies the quality of being free from all falsehood or mistake and so safeguards the truth that Holy Scripture is entirely true and trustworthy in all its assertions.

We affirm that canonical Scripture should always be interpreted on the basis that it is infallible and inerrant. However, in determining what the God-taught writer is asserting in each passage, we must pay the most careful attention to its claims and character as a human production. In inspiration, God utilized the culture and conventions of his penman's milieu, a milieu that God controls in His sovereign providence; it is misinterpretation to imagine otherwise.

So history must be treated as history, poetry as poetry, hyperbole and metaphor as hyperbole and metaphor, generalization and approximation as what they are, and so forth. Differences between literary conventions in Bible times and in ours must also be observed: since, for instance, non-chronological narration and imprecise citation were conventional and acceptable and violated no expectations in those days, we must not regard these things as faults when we find them in Bible writers. When total precision of a particular kind was not expected nor aimed at, it is no error not to have achieved it. Scripture is inerrant, not

in the sense of being absolutely precise by modern standards, but in the
sense of making good its claims and achieving that measure of focused
truth at which its authors aimed.

The truthfulness of Scripture is not negated by the appearance in it of
irregularities of grammar or spelling, phenomenal descriptions of nature, reports of false statements (*e.g.*, the lies of Satan), or seeming
discrepancies between one passage and another. It is not right to set the
so-called "phenomena" of Scripture against the teaching of Scripture
about itself. Apparent inconsistencies should not be ignored. Solution
of them, where this can be convincingly achieved, will encourage our
faith, and where for the present no convincing solution is at hand we
shall significantly honor God by trusting His assurance that His Word
is true, despite these appearances, and by maintaining our confidence
that one day they will be seen to have been illusions.

Inasmuch as all Scripture is the product of a single divine mind,
interpretation must stay within the bounds of the analogy of Scripture
and eschew hypotheses that would correct one Biblical passage by
another, whether in the name of progressive revelation or of the imperfect enlightenment of the inspired writer's mind.

Although Holy Scripture is nowhere culture-bound in the sense that
its teaching lacks universal validity, it is sometimes culturally conditioned by the customs and conventional view of a particular period,
so that the application of its principles today calls for a different sort of
action.

Skepticism and Criticism

Since the Renaissance, and more particularly since the Enlightenment, world-views have been developed which involve skepticism
about basic Christian tenets. Such are the agnosticism which denies
that God is knowable, the rationalism which denies that He is incomprehensible, the idealism which denies that He is transcendent, and the
existentialism which denies rationality in His relationships with us.
When these un- and anti-biblical principles seep into men's theologies
at presuppositional level, as today they frequently do, faithful interpretation of Holy Scripture becomes impossible.

Transmission and Translation

Since God has nowhere promised an inerrant transmission of Scripture, it is necessary to affirm that only the autographic text of the
original documents was inspired and to maintain the need of textual
criticism as a means of detecting any slips that may have crept into the
text in the course of its transmission. The verdict of this science, however, is that the Hebrew and Greek text appear to be amazingly well

preserved, so that we are amply justified in affirming, with the Westminster Confession, a singular providence of God in this matter and in declaring that the authority of Scripture is in no way jeopardized by the fact that the copies we possess are not entirely error-free.

Similarly, no translation is or can be perfect, and all translations are an additional step away from the *autographa*. Yet the verdict of linguistic science is that English-speaking Christians, at least, are exceedingly well served in these days with a host of excellent translations and have no cause for hesitating to conclude that the true Word of God is within their reach. Indeed, in view of the frequent repetition in Scripture of the main matters with which it deals and also of the Holy Spirit's constant witness to and through the Word, no serious translation of Holy Scripture will so destroy its meaning as to render it unable to make its reader "wise for salvation through faith in Christ Jesus" (2 Tim. 3:15).

Inerrancy and Authority

In our affirmation of the authority of Scripture as involving its total truth, we are consciously standing with Christ and His apostles, indeed with the whole Bible and with the main stream of church history from the first days until very recently. We are concerned at the casual, inadvertent, and seemingly thoughtless way in which a belief of such far-reaching importance has been given up by so many in our day.

We are conscious too that great and grave confusion results from ceasing to maintain the total truth of the Bible whose authority one professes to acknowledge. The result of taking this step is that the Bible which God gave loses its authority, and what has authority instead is a Bible reduced in content according to the demands of one's critical reasonings and in principle reducible still further once one has started. This means that at bottom independent reason now has authority, as opposed to Scriptural teaching. If this is not seen and if for the time being basic evangelical doctrines are still held, persons denying the full truth of Scripture may claim an evangelical identity while methodologically they have moved away from the evangelical principle of knowledge to an unstable subjectivism, and will find it hard not to move further.

We affirm that what Scripture says, God says. May He be glorified. Amen and Amen.

INDEXES

INDEXES

BIOGRAPHICAL INDEX

SUBJECT INDEX

Abductive theological method, 273
Above the Battle? (Boer), 231
Accommodation, 14, 141-44, 251, 282, 388
Accreditation of biblical authors, 283
Acquiescence, 342
Adduction, 273
Against Apion (Josephus), 49
Agnosticism, advocated by Kant, 322
Allegory
  in Christ's teachings, 7
  hermeneutics of, 125
Amos, authorship of, 99
Analogy, principle of, 93
Angels, number of, at Jesus' tomb, 62
Apostolic authority, as viewed by the apostles, 51
Apostolic fathers, bibliology of, 39-53, 358
Apostolic theology, concept of God, 241-44
Application, role of the Holy Spirit in, 337
Authority
  of God, 207
  of Scripture, 502
Authority of the Bible, The (Dodd), 130
Authorship of Scripture
  in Augustine's writings, 363ff.
  in Berkouwer's early writings, 430
  in Berkouwer's later writings, 433
  in Chrysostom's writings, 364
  divine superintendence of, 241, 249, 254
  and inspiration, 251
  and man's theomorphism, 245
  in the Nicaeno-Constantinopolitan Creed, 363
  in Origen's writings, 364
  in Warfield's writings, 426

Autographa
  biblical attitude toward, 159-68
  equivalent to modern text, 161ff.
  inerrancy of, 151-93
  inscripturation of, 154-59
  no longer in existence, 189
  problems in defining, 190
  scholastic attitudes toward, 159-68
  why inerrancy is restricted to, 171-84

Bible
  authority of, 497
  canon of, 499
  Christocentricity of, 499
Bibliology
  of Alexander of Hales, 367
  of Ambrose, 361
  of American theology, 400
  of Anselm, 366
  of the apostolic fathers, 358-61
  of Augustine, 361
  of Berkouwer, 420-26, 430-46
  of Bonaventura, 368
  of Calvin, 389-95
  of Clement of Alexandria, 360
  of Duns Scotus, 320
  of Edwards, Jonathan, 401
  of Gerhard, John, 395
  of Irenaeus, 359
  of Luther, Martin, 372
  of the medieval scholars, 366-72
  of Origen, 360
  of post-Reformation scholasticism, 395
  of the pre-Reformation church, 357-82
  of Princeton theologians, 407
  of Rutherford, Samuel, 399
  of Tannaite Judaism, 358
  of Tertullian, 359
  of Thomas Aquinas, 368
  of Turretin, Francis, 396
  of Warfield, B. B., 407-20, 426-30, 438-46

511

SCRIPTURE INDEX